De Gruyter Handbook of Business Families

De Gruyter Handbooks in Business, Economics and Finance

De Gruyter Handbook of Personal Finance
Edited by: John E. Grable and Swarn Chatterjee

De Gruyter Handbook of Entrepreneurial Finance
Edited by: David Lingelbach

De Gruyter Handbook of Organizational Conflict Management
Edited by: LaVena Wilkin and Yashwant Pathak

De Gruyter Handbook of Sustainable Development and Finance
Edited by: Timothy Cadman and Tapan Sarker

De Gruyter Handbook of Responsible Project Management
Edited by: Beverly L. Pasian and Nigel Williams

For more information, scan QR code below or visit https://www.degruyter.com/serial/dghbef-b/html

De Gruyter Handbook of Business Families

Edited by
Michael Carney and Marleen Dieleman

DE GRUYTER

ISBN 978-3-11-162035-0
e-ISBN (PDF) 978-3-11-072796-8
e-ISBN (EPUB) 978-3-11-072805-7
ISSN 2748-016X
e-ISSN 2748-0178

Library of Congress Control Number: 2022945191

Bibliographic information published by the Deutsche Nationalbibliothek
The Deutsche Nationalbibliothek lists this publication in the Deutsche Nationalbibliografie;
detailed bibliographic data are available on the internet at http://dnb.dnb.de.

www.degruyter.com

Contents

Part III: Governing the Business Family

List of Contributors

Sophie Bacq is the Larry and Barbara Sharpf Associate Professor of Entrepreneurship at Indiana University Kelley School of Business. Her research program centres on entrepreneurial action aiming to solve intractable social and environmental problems. More specifically, Sophie examines and theorizes about social entrepreneurship and societal impact at the individual, organizational, and civic levels of analysis.

Rodrigo Basco is a Professor at American University of Sharjah and holds the Sheikh Saoud bin Khalid bin Al-Qassimi Chair in Family Business. He is the Board Chairman of STEP Project Global Consortium and Associate Editor of the *Journal of Family Business Strategy*. His research focuses on entrepreneurship, management, and regional development with special interest in family firms.

Navneet Bhatnagar is Assistant Professor of Strategic Management at the Indian Institute of Management Raipur, India. Earlier, he was Associate Director at the Thomas Schmidheiny Centre for Family Enterprise, Indian School of Business, Hyderabad, India. He has authored several research articles on family business, published in top journals including the Journal of Business Ethics, among others. He has also authored several monographs and case studies on family businesses. Navneet holds a PhD from IIT Madras and the Advanced Certificate in Family Business Advising awarded by the Family Firm Institute, Boston.

Alexandra Bertschi-Michel, PhD, is a post-doctoral researcher at the University of Bern, Switzerland. She received her PhD in philosophy of management at the Centre for family business, University of St. Gallen, Switzerland. Her research interests focus on advisors in family firms, family firm succession, private equity in family firms, and turnaround management in family firms and her articles have been published, amongst others, in *Entrepreneurship Theory & Practice, Family Business Review, Long Range Planning,* and *Small Business Economics.* Besides her academic career, Alexandra Bertschi-Michel is also active as a family firm advisor in succession related matters.

Zografia Bika is a Professor of Entrepreneurship at the University of East Anglia (UEA), Norwich Business School, UK. Her research focuses on rural, family, and institutional entrepreneurship issues using a sociological lens, and has been published in journals such as *Family Business Review, Regional Studies, Entrepreneurship and Regional Development, European Management Review, Sociological Review, Environment and Planning A,* and *Human Relations.* Her family business research was funded by the UK Economic and Social Research Council and won the "Best Family Business Paper" Award at the 2018 US Academy of Management Annual Meeting and the 2020 US Family Firm Institute "Best Unpublished Research Paper" Award.

Mara Brumana is an Assistant Professor at the Department of Management, Information, and Production Engineering, University of Bergamo, Italy, and Affiliated Researcher at the Institute of Change Management and Management Development at WU Vienna University of Economics and Business. She is also a research member of the Research Centre for Young and Family Enterprise (CYFE) at the University of Bergamo. Mara's research interests revolve around the understanding of how and why the embeddedness of firms, and of family firms in particular, in a social and institutional context shapes their decision-making process and behaviour.

Giovanna Campopiano is Associate Professor of Strategic Management and Entrepreneurship, in the Department of Management, Information, and Production Engineering at the University of Bergamo. She is board member of the CYFE, university-based Centre for Young and Family Enterprise. Giovanna's research mainly focuses on the strategic and behavioural aspects of family

https://doi.org/10.1515/9783110727968-203

business governance and management, and their effect on succession, growth, and corporate entrepreneurship, as well as gender and corporate social responsibility.

Michael Carney is the Concordia University Research Chair in Strategy and Entrepreneurship at the John Molson School of Business, Montréal. His research interests are comparative institutional analysis, emerging market business groups, and family firms. He is the former editor-in-chief of the *Asia Pacific Journal of Management.*

Leonardo Centeno-Caffarena, PhD, is the Executive Director (ai) of CEPRODEF (Centre for the Development of the Family Business) and an Associate Professor from Keiser University. His research focuses on institutions, family firms, and entrepreneurship.

Ravee Chittoor is Associate Professor of Strategy and International Business at the Peter B. Gustavson School of Business, University of Victoria. His research focuses on understanding the various ways by which institutions shape firm strategies.

Andrea Colli is Professor at Bocconi University. He holds a PhD in Economic and Social History. His research focuses on family capitalism in the long run and on the relationship between the governance structures, the strategies, and organization of family business groups.

Marleen Dieleman is an Associate Professor at the National University of Singapore. She holds a PhD from Leiden University in the Netherlands. Her research focuses on family business groups from Asia. She has published in numerous academic journals and her work has been covered in international media.

Allan Discua Cruz, PhD, is the Director of the Centre for Family Business at Lancaster University Management School, UK. His research focus relates to stewardship, paradox, and relational lenses. His work has appeared in *Entrepreneurship Theory and Practice, Journal of Business Ethics, Journal of Business Research, Business History, Journal of Family Business Strategy, International Journal of Entrepreneurship and Behaviour Research, Entrepreneurship and Regional Development,* and the *International Small Business Journal.*

Ramzi Fathallah is an Assistant Professor of Entrepreneurship and Family Business at Telfer School of Management, University of Ottawa. He holds a master's degree in management from LSE and a PhD in Entrepreneurship from Ivey Business School. His research lies at the intersections of entrepreneurship, family business, and international business. He is also a fourth-generation member of a 100-year-old family business.

Neus Feliu, PhD, is a partner at Lansberg Gersick & Advisors. An economist and organizational psychologist by training, Neus holds a PhD from ESADE Business School. Her research and consultative work focus on the ownership dimension of family enterprises, which encompasses ownership strategies and its governance.

Yasaman Gorji is an associate Professor in Strategic Management, International Business and Entrepreneurship at ESSCA School of Management, France. Her areas of research include network theory, business families, entrepreneurship, and gender studies.

Toshio Goto is a Research Professor at Japan University of Economics in Tokyo. He holds an MBA from Harvard Business School, and a bachelor's degree from The University of Tokyo (Economics). His research is focused on the sustainable growth of the family business.

Carole Howorth is Emeritus Professor at the University of York. She was previously Chair of Sustainable and Ethical Entrepreneurship at York and has also held Chairs at the University of Bradford and Lancaster University Management School. Carole researches contexts and topics where social values and business imperatives intersect, particularly family businesses and social enterprises.

Trevor Israelsen is a PhD candidate at the Gustavson School of Business at the University of Victoria. His research focuses on the historical processes through which entrepreneurial projects emerge, evolve, and are institutionalized across generations in business and society.

Peter Jaskiewicz is the University Research Chair in Enduring Entrepreneurship and the Academic Director of the Family Enterprise Legacy Institute (www.familyenterpriseinstitute.ca) at the Telfer School of Management, University of Ottawa. His research focuses on how families can effectively govern their enterprises, and how their enterprises can be successfully rejuvenated and transitioned for generations to come.

Nadine Kammerlander is a chaired professor at WHU – Otto Beisheim School of Management where she is also director of the Institute of Family Business and Mittelstand. Her research interests focus on leadership, governance, and innovation in family firms and family offices. Her research has been published in numerous academic journals and books.

Martin R. Kemp is Head of Research at the IFB Research Foundation in the UK. He holds a PhD from the University of Bristol, and master's degrees from Manchester University and the University of Surrey. His research interests are in sustainable development, health, and social policy; the role of business in society and the social impact of business.

Heiko Kleve, Sociologist and Social Scientist, is professor of the endowed chair of the "Witten Institute for Family Business" (WIFU) for Organization and Development of Business Families, Faculty of Management, Economics, and Society, Witten/Herdecke University, Germany. Since 2020 he is also the Academic Director of the WIFU. His research areas are systems theory of the business family, socialization in business families, family strategy, systemic and post-modern theories, and methods in applied social sciences.

Juliette Koning is Professor of Business in Society at the School of Business and Economics at Maastricht University, the Netherlands. Trained as an anthropologist she investigates religion, ethnicity, kinship, identity, and ethics in organizational leadership and entrepreneurship. Juliette is Associate Editor of Human Relations.

Hanna Kuusela is an Academy Research Fellow and a Senior Researcher at Tampere University. She holds a PhD from Goldsmiths College. She works in the intersection of culture and economy, focusing her research on economic elites and on the role of culture in understanding economic phenomena.

Rania Labaki, PhD, is Associate Professor of finance and family business at EDHEC Business School, Director of EDHEC Family Business Research Centre, and Family Business Fellow at Cornell University. She is also Board Member of IFERA, Editor of *Entrepreneurship Research Journal,* and Affiliate Advisor at LGA. Her main interests revolve around the interplay between family dynamics, decision-making, and governance design in the family business.

Jian Bai Li is an Assistant Professor at National University of Singapore Business School. He holds a PhD from Stanford University. His research focuses on social networks and organizations, with a particular emphasis on family businesses in emerging economies.

Nava Michael-Tsabari is the Founder and Director of the Raya Strauss Centre for Family Firm Research at Coller School of Management, Tel Aviv University. She holds the first PhD on family firms in Israel, from the Technion. Her research focuses on emotions, organizational behaviour, and how the owning family influences the business.

Tommaso Minola is Associate Professor at the Department of Management, Information and Production Engineering (DIGIP), and Co-founder and Director of the Centre for Young and Family Enterprise (CYFE) at the University of Bergamo. In his research, he is interested in studying how different dimensions of the enterprising individual (e.g., motivation, cognition, behaviour) and of the entrepreneurial firm (e.g., goals and resource allocation) are affected by embeddedness in social contexts. In particular, he looks at the family and the university as contexts particularly relevant for venture creation, development, and performance.

Lina Nagel is a PhD candidate and scientific associate at the WIFU chair for Organization and Development of Business Families (Witten/Herdecke University). Her research is focused on conflict dynamics and communication patterns of business families, cybernetic theory, systemic thinking, conflict prevention and resolution. She is a conflict trainer and mediator.

Robert Nason is Associate Professor of Strategy and Organization and William Dawson Scholar in the Desautels Faculty of Management at McGill University. Rob's research explores the role of entrepreneurship in society and is currently focused on entrepreneurship and economic inequality – examining entrepreneurial activity in contexts of poverty and wealth.

Timothy J. Nichol is a Pro Vice Chancellor at Liverpool John Moores University in the UK. He holds a PhD from the University of York and a master's degree from Oxford University. His research is focused on the relationship between governance and power in multi-generation family-owned businesses.

Henning Piezunka is an Associate Professor at INSEAD. He holds a PhD from Stanford University, a master's degree from the London School for Economics, as well as from the University of Mannheim. His research is focused on how organizations and people can collaborate and compete more effectively.

Kavil Ramachandran is Professor of Entrepreneurship and Senior Advisor of the Thomas Schmidheiny Centre for Family Enterprise at the Indian School of Business. He earned his PhD from the Cranfield University, UK, and has specialized in family business, strategy, and entrepreneurship.

Sabine B. Rau works with enterprising families around the world supporting them to design their tailored governance structures and processes, moderating succession, and developing and delivering tailored Next Generation development programs. She holds a PhD from the University of Bayreuth, Germany, and is Visiting Professor at Telfer Business School, University of Ottawa, Canada, as well as at ESMT Berlin, Germany.

Elena Rivo-López, PhD in Economics and Business Management, MBA from ICADE, is an Associate Professor at the University of Vigo. Her research is focused on family businesses from multiple perspectives: value creation, corporate governance, corporate social responsibility, entrepreneurship, and family office.

Peter Rosa is the George David Emeritus Professor of Entrepreneurship and Family Business at the University of Edinburgh Business School UEBS, and is a Visiting Professor at the Makerere University Business School in Uganda. He was the Head of the Entrepreneurship and Innovation Group and Directed their Centre for Entrepreneurship and Innovation at UEBS from 2004–2015. He has a special interest in processes of portfolio entrepreneurship and the dynamics of family business groups.

Tom A. Rüsen is the Managing Director and Honorary Professor of the WIFU (Witten/Herdecke University). His teaching, research, and consulting activities focus on the installation of family management systems and family strategy processes as well as succession and conflict counseling. The main areas of his research include the examination of conflict and crisis dynamics, structural risks in family businesses, mental models in business families, and family strategies.

Georges Samara is the winner of the Extraordinary Doctorate Award (2018), the Academy of Management Best Family Business Paper Award (2019), and the Best Published Paper Award by the International Association of Business and Society (2020), in addition to more than 10 international best research paper nominations and awards. Georges is currently an Assistant Professor at the University of Sharjah. He also acts as a family business consultant and has participated in setting up programs and delivering many executive education courses for family businesses.

Arist von Schlippe, psychologist and systemic counselor, is Chair of Leadership and Dynamics in Family Business at the WIFU (Witten/Herdecke University). He graduated with a PhD in psychology specializing in family therapy and family psychology. His research topics are family strategy and family governance, succession, role of stories, and value transmission in business families, transgenerational entrepreneurship, negotiation, and conflict resolution, as well as parental coaching in non-violent resistance.

Nastaran Simarasl is an Associate Professor of Strategic Management and Entrepreneurship at California State Polytechnic University, Pomona. She holds a PhD in Entrepreneurship and Strategic Management from the University of Tennessee, Knoxville, and a PhD in Organizational Behaviour from the University of Isfahan. Her research focuses on the intersection of institutions, entrepreneurship, and gender. Her papers have been published in academic journals, including *Family Business Review* and *Strategic Entrepreneurship Journal*.

Myung-Seon Song is a PhD candidate in National University of Singapore Business School. Her research interests focus on family office, entrepreneurial finance, and merger and acquisition. She earned her BA and MS from Ewha Women University and received her MA in Business Strategy from Rice University.

Dinah Spitzley is a post-doctoral student at the Friedrichshafen Institute for Family Entrepreneurship (FIF) at Zeppelin University, Germany, as well as affiliated Researcher at the EQUA-Foundation in Munich, Germany. Furthermore, she has founded her own start-up at the intersection of research and practice, which is a digital exchange and information platform for the next generation in enterprising families. Her research interests focus on the next generation within enterprising families especially looking at the family aspect. In particular, she looks at strategic decisions of the next generation within the family business as well as looking at venturing activities of the next generation.

Roy Suddaby is the Winspear Professor of Management at the Peter B. Gustavson School of Business, University of Victoria, and Professor of Entrepreneurship at the Carson College of Business, Washington State University. His research focuses on processes of organizational, institutional, and societal change.

Michiel Verver is an Assistant Professor at the Department of Organization Sciences, VU Amsterdam. His academic interest lies in employing anthropological concepts – kinship, ethnicity, patronage, culture, and context – to study entrepreneurship. Michiel focuses on entrepreneurship among business families, migrants, and ethnic minorities, and social entrepreneurship in Cambodia, Thailand and the Netherlands.

Mónica Villanueva-Villar, PhD in Economics and Business Management, is an Associate Professor at the University of Vigo. Her research is focused on family businesses from a financial perspective.

Arpita Vyas is a Research Assistant at the Sheikh Saoud bin Khalid bin Khalid Al-Qassimi Chair in Family Business and the Project Manager at STEP Project Global Consortium. She has recently graduated from the American University of Sharjah with a BS in Business Administration, specializing in Accounting.

Michael Carney and Marleen Dieleman

1 Business Families: An Introduction

Abstract: Family business is a growing scholarly field that has recently seen calls to investigate different types of family businesses and connect more clearly with adjacent disciplines. We take up these challenges in this *De Gruyter Handbook of Business Families* by expanding our reach beyond the single-family with a single business. We investigate business families who may engage in joint entrepreneurial, investment, or philanthropic activities, identifying four overlapping research streams. The first is the family behind the firm, which explores the relatively neglected dynamics between individuals with family ties that shape the interaction between family and business. The second is business families with multiple businesses, which looks at a portfolio of activities jointly run by a family in space and time. We describe the third stream of research as governing the business family, which refers to how business families adopt formal rules and processes around their joint activities. Finally, we address the institutionalization of wealth and business families in society. This section explores the multi-generational business family as influenced by and influencing its broader socio-economic context. This handbook positions business families as a vibrant new research field with contributions straddling different disciplines and geographies.

Keywords: business families, kinship, business group, family firm governance, wealth

Introduction

A growing community recognizes that family businesses play a significant role in most economies. In line with this, family business is a rapidly developing research area worldwide, situated within the broader management field. *Family Business Review* and the *Journal of Family Business Strategy* are recognized scholarly journals that serve this community, with both having seen their prestige and impact factor increase over the years (Rovelli, Ferasso, De Massis, & Kraus, 2022). Several books and handbooks provide an overview of the state of research on family business (e.g., Calabrò, 2020; Kellermanns & Hoy, 2016; Memili & Dibrell, 2019). Moreover, leading journals in management, such as *Strategic Management Journal*, *Journal of International Business*, or *Administrative Science Quarterly* regularly publish family business research, thereby raising interest among mainstream academics in strategy, organizational behaviour, and international business. This *De Gruyter Handbook of Business*

Michael Carney, Concordia University
Marleen Dieleman, National University of Singapore

https://doi.org/10.1515/9783110727968-001

Families focuses on a relatively new construct within the family business field that has the potential for original theorizing and connections to other disciplines: business families.

The Origins of the Family Business Field

From the outset, family business scholars have recognized that management theories, often based on agency theory (Jensen & Meckling, 1976), treat the firm as an entity with multiple dispersed and distant owners. Conversely, family firms are characterized by long-lasting family influence, producing a union of emotions and economic objectives. The complex interaction of economic goals and emotions produced new theories, such as socio-emotional wealth (Gómez-Mejía, Cruz, Berrone, & De Castro, 2011), generating a torrent of studies about the differences between family and nonfamily firms (Dawson & Mussolino, 2014). With the evolution of family business research, scholars have paid more attention to differences among family firms (Daspit, Chrisman, Ashton, & Evangelopoulos, 2021). Scholars now recognize the considerable variety among family firms in their features and goals.

Thus, recent literature reviewers have called on family business scholars to reorient the field by incorporating insights from other disciplines to capture this variety (Rovelli et al., 2022). Others suggest family business research should gravitate away from the limits of "reified theory" (Schulze & Kellermans, 2015) by drawing parallels with other social phenomena. Indeed, promising work has already appeared that offers insights by employing theory from adjacent fields, such as family science (Combs et al., 2020), kinship (Stewart, 2003), network theory (Li & Piezunka, 2020), and entrepreneurship (Zellweger, Nason, & Nordqvist, 2012).

Opportunities for Original Theorizing through the Lens of Business Families

This handbook aims to expand on these emerging directions. To do so, we enlarge the field's boundaries by interrogating the implicit assumption of "single firm-single family", characterizing much of the early research on family business (Steier, Chrisman, & Chua, 2015). Indeed, researchers now accept that many families own or control multiple businesses and possess substantial wealth beyond firm ownership in the form of financial and non-financial assets. Diversified family wealth is especially apparent in emerging markets, where business families practice wealth diversification through separate legal entities. This also occurs in developed markets where multi-generational entrepreneurial families establish ventures or use accumulated wealth to develop non-business activities such as philanthropy. We propose that extended families involved in multiple activities beyond a single firm are important phenomena that merit detailed investigation.

Business Families: Surveying a Multi-Thematic Landscape

Early family business research insisted that family businesses were unique and that existing management theories had little relevance for such firms (Gersick, Davis, Hampton, & Lansberg, 1997). The claim for uniqueness marginalized the field for a while and prompted a search for broader recognition. The subsequent quest to establish the field's scientific status engendered a search for a precise definition of the family firm, with scholars searching for its "essential" characteristics (Chua, Chrisman, & Sharma, 1999; Dawson & Mussolino, 2014). However, "essentializing" the family firm produced a "definitional logjam" (Litz, 2008, p. 218) with scores of incompatible definitions applied to empirical studies. The pursuit of precision was perhaps unsuitable for a fuzzy and elastic phenomenon encompassing a range of businesses from the family farm to large multi-national enterprises. Nevertheless, the concern with definitions created a helpful vocabulary that advanced family businesses and raised the field's status by attracting the attention of mainstream organization scholars.

In Search of Definitions

Today the definition of family firms is most often captured in terms of the influence a family has over a firm, resulting from a combination of family ownership and family members' involvement in the business (e.g., Konig, Kammerlander, & Enders, 2013). What counts as a managerial influence and family ownership is operationalized differently across studies and legal jurisdictions, complicating definitional issues (e.g., O'Boyle, Pollack, & Rutherford, 2012). More fundamentally, though, defining family business in terms of ownership stakes and influence is problematic in two seemingly contradictory ways: the resulting definitions are too broad and overly narrow.

First, it is too broad because a very large proportion of both small and large firms would qualify as family firms. Arregle et al. (2021), for instance, suggest that half of the world's GDP is generated by family firms, most of them small or medium-sized. La Porta and colleagues (1999) studied large corporations in 27 wealthy economies and found concentrated ownership, often by a family, to be significant in most while suggesting that this would be even more prominent in emerging markets. Such a broad definition that captures most of the world's small and large firms makes it hard to make meaningful claims regarding the commonalities between them as compared to other types of firms.

On the other hand, this definition is also overly narrow as it takes a single business as the unit of analysis. This definition excludes families who control multiple business units and one or more businesses in combination with other activities such as portfolio investing or philanthropy. Also excluded are extended entrepreneurial families where several family members independently control other businesses, which may be connected through resource or information sharing.

Consistent with emerging research about the heterogeneity of family firms, we acknowledge that not all family businesses are single legal entities and that families themselves are composed of multiple actors with diverse interests. We reason that the current definitions of family firms exclude important types of business families, providing scholars with an opportunity to extend the field's conceptual boundaries to accommodate the potential complexity of more loosely connected collectives of kinship ties and entrepreneurial activities. The generic term that has appeared in the family business literature is business families to capture this diverse phenomenon.

The Emergence of Business Families' Research

A common view is that business families emerge late in the life cycle of a single business, when the legacy business no longer dictates family members' interests. Over time, the single business focus is displaced by a broader view on what it means for an extended family to engage in shared or separate entrepreneurial activities (Steier, Chrisman, & Chua, 2015). Zellweger (2012) observes that when a family firm is successful, the family often changes the way it perceives itself from a family business to a business family. In the latter case, family members shed their identities as nurturers and protectors of a single business. Instead, business family members derive their identity as developing multiple businesses.

Several streams of scholarship interested in the heterogeneous structures of family businesses now employ the term business families. Despite increasing recognition of the phenomenon of business families that transcend the single-business-single-family perspective, a standard business family definition has yet to emerge. Rather than striving for a universal definition, we argue it may be productive to survey the research themes scholars employ to study business families. To do so, we outline the contours of the business family landscape by classifying streams of research into four broad and sometimes overlapping themes.

First, some scholars argue that family business research has neglected the "families behind the business". These scholars draw on adjacent disciplines such as family science (e.g., Combs et al., 2020), anthropology (e.g., Stewart, 2003), and network theory (e.g., Li & Piezunka, 2020). While most work in family business explores families based upon hereditary principles focusing on those family members performing roles in the business, recent work shows that family members outside the business perform variegated functions in a multiplex organizational system (Li & Piezunka, 2020). Others explore the establishment of family boundaries, questioning the narrow focus on blood ties and marriages and exploring the notion of kinship (e.g., Verver & Koning, 2018). Indeed, some business families may be ruthless in limiting claims on family wealth by distant relatives while others are more inclusive, being perceived more fruitfully as clans or ethnic communities. Advocates of this approach argue that a "business family's" lens provides a better account of a business family's organizational governance practices.

In a second research theme, scholars see business families primarily as families owning multiple businesses, such as diversified business groups, families with a portfolio of firms, or families who use their wealth to become investors or philanthropists. Much of this research sees business families as owning several enterprises while planning to involve family members in the future (Le Breton-Miller & Miller, 2018), leading to a focus on the process of business creation. Business families can be entrepreneurial, experiencing growth through internationalization and diversifications (Bjornberg, Elstrodt, & Pandit, 2015). These scholars enumerate differences between family firms and business families in terms of the numbers of enterprises under their control. Family firms are focused and conservative while business families engage in innovation and diversify capital over multiple operating businesses or passive investments. An early overview of the distinction between family business and business families echoes this view, suggesting that a portfolio approach to doing business, in turn, stimulates new paths to growth, innovation and cross-generational sustainability (Steier, Chrisman, & Chua, 2015), and family identity (Brinkerink et al., 2020). Similarly, others focus upon business families' entrepreneurial vigour, resulting in the broader set of business activities (e.g., Le Breton-Miller & Miller, 2018; Zellweger, Nason, & Nordqvist, 2012). Yet others move beyond the single business focus by revealing family office diversification strategies (Rosplock & Hauser, 2014; Wessel, Decker, Lange, & Hack, 2014) or family philanthropy (Feliu & Botero, 2016).

The third theme concerns how families govern and organize diversified assets. The objective of these business families is to generate and manage long-term family wealth (Brinkerink et al., 2020; Michael-Tsabari, Labaki, & Zachary, 2014). Typical single-family firms employ simple, functional structures. In contrast, business families, which are usually more complex, create formal and informal governance mechanisms like family offices and legal instruments, such as holding companies, trusts, and foundations, which can hybridize to reflect shifting cultural and institutional norms (Arregle, Hitt, Sirmon, & Very, 2007; Burt, Opper, & Zou, 2021; Boers & Nordqvist, 2020). Research on business family governance implies that business families must be actively managed to retain cohesion. Business families expect future generations to continue expanding the family's wealth and reputation so that successful succession may depend on future generations' willingness to engage in appropriate socialization processes leading to governance and management roles. Governing the business family entails the cultivation of "most trusted" advisors and the engagement of advisors in specialized professions (Harrington, 2012; Strike, Bertschi-Michel, & Kammerlander, 2018). These governance roles provide rationalizing elements into what is understood as an emotional and often conflicting atmosphere comprising of multiple generations and family members with different levels of involvement in the family's portfolio of activities.

Fourth, sociological and critical theories of the institutionalization of business families consider the social implications of business family persistence. Institutionalizing the business family as a wealth accumulation mechanism in a family unit (Nason, Mazzelli, & Carney, 2019) has social and economic implications for wealth and equality (e.g., Carney & Nason, 2018). However, it is unclear whether the enhanced governance mechanisms lead to sustained wealth concentration since societies may institute countervailing means to appropriate and redistribute family wealth. In any case, the emphasis on the perpetuation of family wealth has recently grown along with the growing social concern with increasing economic inequality. Indeed, economists interested in family business groups similarly voiced concerns about the concentration of wealth and power in the hands of business families and the implications for economic development, especially in emerging markets (Morck & Yeung, 2003; Fogel, 2006). Another scholarly line of research of the institutionalized business family is concerned with their status in society, which is observed to be variable. Some business families enjoy a totemic status; part of an elevated social class, whose members gain access to prominent roles in politics, philanthropy, and prestigious professions. In contrast, others possess only a precarious position in society, such as migrant families (Portes & Martinez, 2020; Portes & Sensenbrenner, 1993) and a diaspora of ethnic families (Landa, 2016). These business families may occupy a leading position in a society's capitalist class yet remain subject to discrimination and social hostility. This stream encompasses the political, sociological, and institutional determinants of business families' strategies, organizational structures, practices, and processes. Much of this research adopts a critical approach concerned with the extent to which business families contribute to society or the extent to which they evade such responsibilities (e.g., Harrington, 2016a; 2016b).

Business Families: A Thematic Framework

In summary, with our thematic approach, we identify four overlapping research streams concerned with specific aspects of the business family (see Figure 1.1). The first is the family behind the firm, which explores the relatively neglected dynamics of individuals with kinship ties that shape the interaction between family and business. The second is business families with multiple businesses, which examines a portfolio of commercial and non-commercial activities jointly run by a family. We describe the third stream of research as governing the business family, which refers to how business families adopt formal rules and processes, including family offices, family constitutions, and advisors. We describe the last theme as the institutionalization of wealth and business families in society, which offers opportunities to situate the business family within a broader socio-economic context.

While we recognize that these thematic dimensions are distinctive research streams, we argue that a more coherent understanding of business families could advance the literature. Thus, we refer to business families in this handbook broadly as *"extended families connected by kinship who jointly manage commonly held assets and activities, institutionalized through family governance strategies, and whose collective wealth exerts a significant impact on society"*.

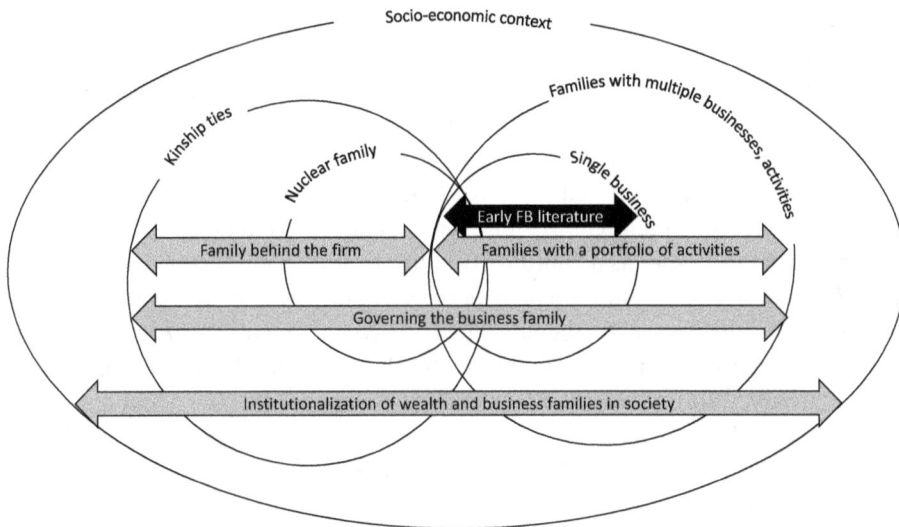

Figure 1.1: Business families – The thematic landscape.

We expect each of the four themes to represent the preliminary phase of business family research with ample opportunities for new theorization. In what follows, we select a subset of prior literature on these four themes while also introducing the papers in this handbook. We conclude with the contributions of the *De Gruyter Handbook* towards developing the field of business families.

Business Families as the Family Behind the Firm

Prior Research

In this first perspective on the family behind the firm, scholars assert the primacy of families in business and the family characteristics and processes that influence the management of the family-owned firm (Combs et al., 2020; Brinkerink et al., 2020; Kleve et al., 2020a, 2020b; Li & Piezunka, 2020; Stewart, 2003). A common argument in this perspective is that the family element is underplayed within the field of family business, although scholars draw from separate research traditions in making this argument. We classify contributions in this stream according to the type of family that is the focus of the research: nuclear families, extended transgenerational families, and kinship groupings.

The first stream of research focuses on family dynamics in nuclear families. For instance, Moores (2009) draws upon the well-known three-circle model of the family firm and that the focus on the family should be the defining feature of the family business paradigm. Combs (2020) offers comprehensive coverage of this perspective by drawing upon the substantial literature of family science and a diverse range of other views that focus on the different types of family structure and their potential to shed light on questions of family business management. These factors include the structure of family relationships, family member roles, family transitions and important family events. Li and Piezunka (2020) pursue a similar goal by drawing on network theory to highlight the influence of multiplex relationships, in particular the role of the mother as a "third party" during father-son successions.

A second stream offers a broader perspective on families by looking at older families with many members, thereby moving beyond the realm of the nuclear family. Some scholars have referred to this as the cluster theory (Michael-Tsabari, Labaki, & Zachary, 2014). Similarly, Kleve and his colleagues (2020a) adopt a systems perspective on dynastic business families based on a study of seven German dynastic families. They find that business family membership, defined by ownership, is likely to rise exponentially through the generations. This study calls for a better understanding of how business families with more than a hundred members organize and communicate. Larger groupings of family members have also caught the attention of scholars using identity as a lens. For instance, Brinkerink and colleagues (2020) show that business families may develop identities that are only loosely related to the business's operations. Faced with disruptive innovation, according to this study, business families have relatively elastic identities, allowing them to respond faster to challenges to the business. Similarly, Dieleman and Koning (2020) argue that family values and aspirations may change across generations, affecting the business. Thus, these studies underline Combs's suggestion that there are benefits of linking the two constructs of family and business.

Third, there is notable work by scholars drawing on anthropology to critically examine the construct of the family, pushing it further beyond the extended, transgenerational family and redefining it through the lens of the actors in terms of their perceptions and lived experiences of who constitutes a family member. For instance, Stewart (2003) introduced a kinship perspective to clarify the dynamics between family and business. Being bound by shared extended kinship values amplifies entrepreneurial activities and attitudes towards family business. Developing this idea, Verver and Koning (2018) argue that the family's boundaries extend beyond close-family ties and may incorporate communal and ethnic relations.

Overview of the Chapters in this Section

This handbook continues the renewed interest in the family behind the firm with new scholarly contributions. First, Li and Piezunka's chapter, entitled "Family Businesses as Multiplex Relationships", provides a framework rooted in network theory that enables a more detailed examination of the extent to which the family members view their connection to the business. The underlying construct used is multiplexity, which recognizes that individuals may be connected simultaneously in multiple domains. If relationships transpose, such as when family members who are previously connected in the family domain and subsequently enter the business, the presence of connections in prior domains affects the interactions in the new domain. Thus, by summing the network of multiplex relationships of family members and studying the effects of transpositions, one can explain family dynamics in a more structured manner. This is consequential in families characterized by cliques and cleavages compared with closed, cohesive family networks. Li and Piezunka conclude that the multiplexity framework has a particular resonance in large business families, such as business groups, which have received considerable attention. However, few scholars have examined the effects of multiplex family dynamics that affect group behaviour and outcomes. Moreover, Li and Piezunka propose that a multiplex framework could illuminate the effects of "submerged" family members, who do not hold business roles but still impact family business decisions through their network ties. The multiplex ties of family members can further shed light on the coupling and segregation between family and business and how it is managed through transpositions of personal networks. Overall, their contribution offers a detailed and systematic method for investigating family members' network ties.

The next chapter, by Kleve, Nagel, Köllner, Rüsen, and von Schlippe, is entitled "Family, Organization, and Networks – A New Approach to a Systems Theory of the Business Family". Drawing on their prior work in taking a systems theory approach, they distinguish between three types of business families: nuclear, formally organized business families, and extensive business families comprising hundreds of shareholders. Kleve and his colleagues describe the third type, as business families 3.0, suggesting these face additional challenges in developing formal and informal networks among often distantly related shareholders who are only weakly connected. Kleve and colleagues argue that leading members of such families could create more cohesive family relations by initiating and maintaining extended family social networks. However, understanding such strategies requires new theoretical perspectives on family business progression. Thus, while the previous chapter by Li and Piezunka focused on mapping these family networks, this chapter recognizes that networks can be functionally created and maintained to support the evolution of business families.

Recognizing that business families need enterprising family members to sustain themselves, Rau, in her chapter entitled "Resilient Enterprising Families", asks why some entrepreneurial families are more resilient than others. Drawing on insights from parenting psychology, she proposes that the differences between authoritarian and permissive parenting styles matter for developing entrepreneurial capabilities in subsequent generations. Parenting styles, in turn, depend on the parent's own needs, motives and the context. Family characteristics and capabilities, viewed in this context, shape the talent available in business families while individual behaviours in the family domain, including parenting styles, can explain the long-term viability of business families.

The theme of entrepreneurial families continues in the next chapter by Minola, Spitzley, Campopiano, and Brumana entitled: "Enterprising Families: An Embeddedness Perspective on Offspring's Entrepreneurial Career Preferences, Cognitions, and Actions". This study examines the factors that stimulate entrepreneurship among the upcoming business family generation. Using a multi-country dataset of university students, they consider interface factors between individuals, the family, and the family business that encourage next generations to join an existing business or start a new venture. Relevant factors in the decision include the encouragement and business experience received from their parents, the university context, and their intentions to start a business. Overall, they identify the powerful imprinting effect of an entrepreneurial legacy and argue that family business owners should not automatically expect their children to succeed in running the family business, but rather stimulate them to become entrepreneurial.

The next chapter, by Koning and Verver, entitled "Kinship and Family Businesses on the Move: A Review and a Research Agenda", considers the business family at a broader level through a systematic review of the kinship construct, which considers interpersonal ties based on relatedness. They see promise in critically examining the core concept of family by studying the sociocultural dynamics, meanings and manifestations of relatedness while pointing out that the process of creating and articulating relatedness is context-specific and not necessarily limited to blood ties or marriage. The kinship logic, they point out by building on Carsten (2000) and Stewart (2003), is a moral one, which contrasts with the amoral logic of markets, focusing more on the lived experiences of relatedness, which can vary across cultural contexts. In this manner, a kinship lens can overcome some of the fixtures in family business research assumptions about the nuclear family, western-centric contexts, and the relative focus on the business rather than the moral dynamics of lived experiences of relatedness. The chapter presents novel research directions that dissects promising threads of family firm heterogeneity.

Business Families with Multiple Businesses

Prior Research

While some families limit themselves to a single business, there is substantial evidence that many business families create multiple businesses, especially those that have experienced more than one generation (Steier et al., 2015). These business families cultivate resources that enable their participation in multi-business, multi-market activities (Le Breton–Miller & Miller, 2018). In these settings, scholars transfer attention from the business to entrepreneurial processes and how they are sustained across generations (e.g., Zellweger, Nason, & Nordqvist, 2012). We classify three types of multi-business families – family business groups, families as portfolio entrepreneurs, and dynastic families who sustain their wealth and social status across the generations. We briefly review the sometimes-overlapping literature that addresses their features.

First, there is significant literature, primarily in economics and finance, on the phenomenon of family business groups. As scholars enlarged their horizons beyond the North American and European contexts to emerging markets, they documented a range of family business groups, initially in Latin America (Strachan, 1976) and later in South and East Asia. Recent research documents the incidence of family business groups in many parts of the world (Masulis et al., 2011), including Europe (Colpan & Hikino, 2017). While the primary focus of family business group research is on the structure and functioning of constituent businesses, other scholars have focused on the family processes that generate their entry into multiple, diversified businesses (e.g., Bertrand et al., 2008; Redding, 1990). Some business group research identifies deep-lying cultural and historical factors that shape elite families' behaviours in Japanese (Shiba, 1997), Korean (Biggart, 1998), and Indian (Tripathi, 2007) business groups. Other research focuses on family involvement in politics (Dieleman & Sachs, 2008), their responses to shifting institutional environments (Carney & Gedajlovic, 2002), and the often-precarious position of ethnic minority business families (Chirot & Reid, 1997). Overall, this literature seeks to understand the evolution of business groups due to contextual factors.

Second, there is a growing literature stream on families as portfolio entrepreneurs. While the family business group literature primarily adopts a contextual perspective to explain the diversification and structural forms, the portfolio entrepreneurship literature views diversification primarily as the result of available resources (e.g., Sieger, Zellweger, Nason, & Clinton, 2011; Jaskiewicz, Combs, & Rau, 2014). Portfolio scholars are primarily family business specialists who consider the business family's motivations and resources as a departure point in understanding entrepreneurial processes (e.g., Jaskiewicz et al., 2014; Sieger et al., 2011). These family-specific characteristics may result in sustained intergenerational venturing (Rosa, Howorth, & Cruz, 2013). These outcomes can alter a business family's perception of their identity as an "entrepreneurial family" rather than identifying as a single-family business to be preserved and transferred to the coming generation (Nordqvist & Melin, 2010). In doing so, the scholarship connects family business studies to entrepreneurship.

Beyond the issue of entrepreneurship and business creation, there is an emerging stream of business family activities, including their passive investments channelled through family offices and other wealth management mechanisms. In some cases, business families shed their ownership of operating businesses, becoming financial business family entities or rentier families (Carney & Nason, 2018), generating income from diversified financial and non-financial assets. For example, Dunn (1980) describes the US Weyerhauser, founded in 1860, initially as a logging, pulp, and paper business. But, by the 1970s, the family exited ownership of these businesses, becoming a private equity investor in California's Silicon Valley. Thus, exiting from ownership and operational control, a business family's activities can comprise of passive, arms-length investing (Schickinger, Leitterstorf, & Kammerlander, 2018).

A third research stream focuses on multi-generational business families and their transitions across time. Research on multi-generational dynastic families suggests that the family enterprise will evolve through strategic renewal, innovation, unrelated diversification, and internationalization. Much of this literature adopts a historical perspective on durable business families, such as the Rockefellers and the Rothschilds (Landes, 2006), and eminent European business families whose histories coincided with national industrial development (James, 2009). Scholars using this perspective often combine an inside out and outside in approach, recognizing both external factors influencing family firm trajectories across generations while leaving space for the role of internal factors such as family conflict or strategic intent. Much of the work in this stream attempts to explain the family processes of responding and adapting to social and political contingencies. Relatedly, there is a promising body of research adopting a rhetorical history perspective to consider how business families interpret their history to renew the business often by striking out in new directions (Labaki, Bernhard, & Cailluet, 2018; Sasaki et al., 2020; Sasaki et al., 2019; Sinha et al., 2020).

Overview of the Chapters in this Section

This handbook focuses on multi-business families' combination of internal and external drivers for change, with several chapters moving the business families' literature in new directions. The first chapter in this section fits into the portfolio stream that investigates the family dynamics behind multiple venture creation, drawing on entrepreneurship theory and family dynamics. Moving beyond explaining why business families create multiple firms, Bhatnagar and Ramachandran's chapter entitled "Influence of Next-Generation Family Champions on New Venture Creation by Business Families: An Indian Perspective" explores two new dimensions: generational differences in venture creation and the selection of new ventures. Utilizing four Indian business family cases, they distinguish two broad types of business families: conservatives and pathfinders. The former stay closer to an original family business legacy, whereas the latter depart along an adventurous path, proceeding beyond the family's original focus. They suggest new ventures can be of a business or social nature and can be embedded in or extending the initial focus, yielding four types of activities, reflecting on the role of senior and next generations in the choice of the venture. Overall, the chapter illuminates entrepreneurial processes in business families by providing a fine-grained classification of new venture selection, with intergenerational dynamics as the primary driver of portfolio outcomes.

The following chapter is Michael-Tsabari's "All My Firms? Managing SEW Affective Endowments in Business Family Portfolios". She questions whether portfolio business families have the same level of affection for each firm. Comparable to the previous chapter, the author observes how internal family dynamics explain portfolio decisions. Using the theory of socio-emotional wealth (SEW), Michael-Tsabari considers why some families value the emotional component of their firms differently. Because scholars have primarily developed SEW for single business families, she theorizes that socio-emotional wealth attributed to a firm is based on the stocks and flows, which may vary among family firms within the portfolio and individuals in a family. When business families add or divest firms from the portfolio, decisions will reflect perceived SEW stock and flows. Family perceptions reflect multiple factors, including the firm's centrality in the portfolio, length of ownership, family control and financial performance, social desirability, and owners' characteristics. With her chapter, Michael-Tsabari shows significant scope to advance the SEW literature through a business family perspective.

The third chapter in this section, entitled "Business Family Reputation, Internal Markets, and Holdup Agency Costs", by Bacq and Nason, similarly draws on the business family to advance a management theory, in this case, agency theory. Like the literature on family business groups, it uses agency logic to explain business family behaviour, suggesting that business families have unique advantages in specific contexts. They focus on the hold-up problem, where employees have limited incentives to invest in firm-specific skills. The hold-up problem is particularly pressing in family firms, which tend to promote based on nepotism rather than skillset. The authors argue that business families with multiple businesses do not suffer to the same extent. Unlike single business firms, concerned with control of a particular business entity, business families with multiple firms are more likely to pursue wealth and business survival by investing in reputation as a credible ex-ante signal to attract high-quality employees. The authors reason that business families' internal labour markets can compensate for underdeveloped labour markets by investing in training and development and allocating skilled employees to appropriate subsidiaries, providing a sustainable source of advantage over single-business firms.

The next chapter discusses the theme of weak institutional environments and the internationalization of family business groups, combining external and internal factors. Fathallah and Samara, in their chapter entitled "The Transformative Function of Weak Institutional Environments: The case of Business Families in the Arab Middle East" challenge predominant SEW perspectives that business families are reluctant overseas investors. Based on case studies of Middle Eastern family-owned business groups, they argue that contrasting motivations determine internationalization. First, skills in cultivating social ties and a reputation for trustworthiness as a means of navigating around weak institutional structures provide the basis of competitive advantage in entering markets in countries with comparable institutional conditions. Secondly, business families seek to expand their operations into a mature institutional context as a means of learning new skills while preserving family wealth and physical security. In this perspective, internationalization is driven by the complementarity between economic gain and SEW preservation.

Rosa and Bika, in the next chapter entitled "Evolutionary Long-term Entrepreneurial Processes in Business Families" take an even more extensive longitudinal perspective to the study of entrepreneurship while exploring the factors affecting the transgenerational continuity of business families. Drawing on socio-economic evolutionary theories of organizational change and using two contrasting cases from Scotland and Uganda, they argue that the interaction between historical processes and strategic planning can best explain such transgenerational processes within business families. Long term strategizing, an advantage of family firms, is seen by these authors as an intention, punctuated by frequent unpredictable events in the course of a business family's history. While families continuously adapt and innovate, significant and unpredictable events, such as military conflict or dramatic shifts in government policy, force families to adjust their routines, thereby instituting change rapidly. These changes, the authors argue, are best studied at the business family level rather than at the business level. While the business level may show more volatility, the business families studied were able to weather storms through shifting to other lines of business, thereby maintaining continuity. The authors conclude that evolutionary theory has advantages for family business scholars and has much in common with the emergent strategy proposed by Mintzberg (1994).

A similar approach combining strategic intent by families placed within a specific historical institutional context is taken by Colli, in his chapter entitled "Entrepreneurial Multi-business Families – Evidence from Continental Europe". Distinguishing between mono-business, investment-oriented, and entrepreneurial multi-business families, Colli argues that the latter are exceptionally skilled in the active management of multiple ventures across generations. Although business families' developmental trajectories differ, he suggests that, in the European context, most surviving entrepreneurial families began as single business entities and progressed from related diversification to non-related diversification across multiple generations. Generational shifts, firm, and family resources, and historical changes shaping economic opportunities and constraints are all influential in determining the shape of the trajectory. As the entrepreneurial family moves towards unrelated diversification, managing multiple ventures becomes crucial, including the reliance on professionals as family members recede from active management but still make a difference through their interventions, long-term orientation, and values. It is these skills, Colli argues, that underpin the longevity of entrepreneurial multi-business families.

Governing the Business Family

Prior Research

There is a growing stream of family governance research (Suess, 2014), including many practitioner-oriented articles advocating the use of governance mechanisms such as family assemblies, constitutions, and councils (Aronoff & Ward, 2016). Scholars have begun to examine whether these mechanisms are related to better business performance (e.g., Artega & Menendez-Requejo, 2017), but hitherto this literature mainly concerns single-business families. The multi-faceted, multi-generational relationships in business families and the complexity of owning a diverse assets business portfolio have encouraged scholars to pay more attention to the problems of family governance in large business families (Nordqvist & Melin, 2010; Suess, 2014). This research also calls attention to the role of intergenerational wealth transfer mechanisms such as estates and trusts (Harrington, 2012). Genealogical kinship links may travel well beyond the business families' desired boundaries as kinship norms in some societies can be expansive, radiating out in concentric circles and fuelling exponential growth in family members. If business families generously accept distant relatives' claims on family wealth, they may dilute enterprise resources (Portes, 1998). Thus, active engagement with business family consultants and advisors may help delineate the boundaries of the family and rationalize the allocation of wealth through the establishment of formal governance mechanisms, such as a family office.

Expertise around these complex psychological, legal, and financial governance issues is often beyond the scope of even the most sophisticated business family, thus calling for professional advisors. In response, a range of new professions is emerging and multiplying to provide advice to business families (Gersick, 2015; Reay, Pearson, & Gibb Dyer, 2013). Attention has turned to the role of advisors in business family governance comprised of the most trusted advisors, trust and estate planners, executive search firms, and a plethora of other family business consultants, although scholarly work has yet to examine this proliferation of advisory services and their effectiveness (Harrington, 2017; Zellweger & Kammerlander, 2015).

Overview of the Chapters in this Section

The chapters in this section survey the development of several strands of business family governance. Reflecting their complexity, business families are prone to progressively elaborating governance entities, such as advisory boards, family councils, and family offices. Labaki and Feliu originate the concept of Ownership Top Governance Teams (O-TGT), in their chapter entitled: "Introducing "Top Governance Teams": Towards an Extension of the Family Business Cluster Model". The O-TGT is an organic but hierarchical entity intended to respond to increased agency costs when families expand. The team is at the interface of several oversights and decision-making entities coordinating family members' divergent socio-emotional and financial needs. Based upon two case vignettes, Labaki and Feliu develop a series of normative propositions about this hybridized governance instrument's structure and cohesive functioning.

Howorth, Kemp, and Nichol, in their chapter entitled "Codes of Governance for Family Businesses" provide a description and critical analysis of national codes of "good governance and guidance" recently established in a range of European and Middle Eastern countries. The authors lament that most governance codes assume ownership of a single firm, are similar across countries and appear to reflect an Anglo-Saxon corporate governance model while adhering to the OECD's definition of corporate governance. Without exception, the codes assume the role of governance is wealth maximization with little recognition of broader social responsibility. The codes typically omit consideration of business families' multi-business ownership businesses. The authors conclude that the academic community could articulate a more nuanced conceptualization of business family heterogeneity and needs to ensure that their research feeds into policy and practitioner communities.

Tackling another popular family governance feature employed by large business families, Song examines the family office in her chapter entitled "Family Office

Research: A Primer". The chapter outlines the definition, types, and functions of family offices and provides a comprehensive review of the literature, suggesting multiple areas for further study. This agenda for future research includes seeking a better understanding of the family's logic when investing or administering wealth and a better understanding of the influence of the family on the strategy of operating or investee companies. Whereas family offices have captured the attention of business families and their advisors and bankers, she argues that there is still scant understanding among scholars of the logic that entrepreneurial families apply to administer family assets and investments.

In their chapter, "Family Wealth Governance and the Role of Advisors", Kammerlander and Bertschi-Michel distinguish between the Most Trusted Business Advisor (MTBA) and Most Trusted Wealth Advisor (MTWA). The important role of the former in shaping business families' strategic decision-making (Strike & Rerup, 2016) and succession processes (Bertschi-Michel & Kammerlander, 2015) is now well established in the literature. By shifting the focus of analysis to the governance of the business family, Kammerlander and Bertschi-Michel draw attention to the brokerage role of wealth advisors within the family, mitigating potential conflict by accommodating individual family members' risk preferences for wealth management. The chapter also identifies important differences in trusted wealth advisors' soft skills and financial expertise, and their role in enforcing agreed rules of family member participation and education.

In his chapter entitled "How Can a Family Control its Business Without Ownership Influence? A Case Study of Suzuki Corp", Goto offers an alternative viewpoint on business families, with a case study on the lingering influence that founding business families have on firms founded by ancestors. While most business families own multiple firms, this chapter considers a case where business families hold no ownership stake in the firms their ancestors founded, yet continue to exert influence on them. Japanese society reveres business families and affords institutional protection that supports multi-century firms (Sasaki, Ravasi, & Micellota, 2019). Indeed, dynastic family control of firms with no family ownership is common in Japan (Bennedsen et al., 2021). In this cultural context, Goto examines the example of the present-day Suzuki Motor Corporation, which had several family CEOs despite having no family ownership since 1949. Goto describes how family members orchestrated social institutions to retain a tenuous hold on control by applying a resource-based view. He also explores the gradual erosion of family influence. Attributing the lingering family influence on the sticky presence of human and social capital and trust in the family among stakeholders, he argues that these resources outlive the more fleeting contribution of financial capital.

Human and social capital is also the focus of the last chapter in this section by Gorji and Simarasl, entitled "How Business Families Advance Their Members' Careers: The Case of Show Business Families". The authors also depart from the firm-based emphasis, documenting the career management strategies of business families who do not own a firm. Instead, these families penetrate professions and project-based industries and assist their members in entering and succeeding in these careers. These business families work on projects and use human, social, and reputational capital during their professional careers as a source of income while sharing this with kin through their business connections in a process they refer to as a spillover approach. Often dismissed as nepotism, these business family practices in promoting kinship can be generalized beyond Hollywood to other areas of endeavours such as politics, athletics, and the professions. Bellow describes these business family networks as fictive corporations, which are "highly disciplined organizations built of relatives, friends, and associates knit together by nepotism and quasi-nepotistic ties" (2004, p. 425). This chapter and Goto's chapter provide ample reason to rethink the nature of business families as tied to a firm. These business families benefit from kinship ties to sustain positive career outcomes while elevating the collective status of the family in a manner that is similar to business-owning families.

Institutionalization of Wealth and Business Families in Society

Prior Research

A stream of research now gaining recognition relies on institutional theory to explain how structural elements beyond the firm shape family firm behaviour and performance (Soleimanof, Rutherford, & Webb, 2018). Consistent with institutional perspectives, we argue that business families are deeply rooted in society and exercise agency to perpetuate their wealth and status. Conversely, elements in the socio-economic context, such as the quality of the legal system, the structure of family property rights, the political regime, and social stratification, determine the structure of their social links. In this final section of the handbook, we present chapters focused on the impact of society on particular types of business families and how institutionalized business families, in turn, impact society.

Earlier sections have established that business families often own substantial wealth beyond the firm (or firms) while engaging in non-commercial activities such as philanthropy. Much wealth management is outsourced to family offices and other professions. A recently articulated and intriguing question concerns whether such governance mechanisms increase longevity for business families. Much of the early family business literature predicted high mortality rates for family-owned firms, with few surviving the first generation (Ward, 1988). An influential strand of the succession literature finds that adequately qualified family managers are rare (Pérez-González, 2006) due to the non-heritability of business acumen (Becker &

Tomes, 1994). Some attribute failure to habitual intra-family conflict and family feuds (Gordon & Nicholson, 2010). Others identify institutional and cultural drivers of mortality such as cultural norms of equal inheritance among males that fracture family firms into autonomous entities (Bertrand et al., 2008; Carney, Gedajlovic, & Strike, 2014), a recurring pattern of "potential dynasties constantly dissolving" (Redding, 1990: 134). Generational dissolution of family wealth occurs in aggressive tax and inheritance regimes (Beckert, 2018; Ellul, Pagano, & Panunzi, 2010). Thus, many family business scholars treat long-lived wealth as the exception rather than the norm.

However, opposing literature points to the perpetuation of family wealth and status, which proposes business families develop various strategies to maintain their positions in society. This work is resurgent in the wake of Thomas Picketty's (2014) *"Capital in the twenty-first century"* that isolated economic mechanisms driving wealth inequality. Scholarly research by family business academics is mostly silent on the role of family business in economic inequality (Carney & Nason, 2018). Research in critical sociology points to the strategies business families use to institutionalize their position in the upper reaches of the class structure (Kuusela, 2018; Gilding, 2005). These strategies include philanthropy to legitimize an altruistic depiction of business family wealth (Sklair & Glucksberg, 2021). Other emerging research shows business families adapt to shifting social norms about the role of elites in society (Bika & Frazer, 2020).

Overview of the Chapters in this Section

This handbook advances business family research with several chapters on the institutionalization of dynastic family elites. In her sociological study of business family's "class making", Kuusela detects several business family practices that increase cross-generational family wealth while elevating their status as an elite social class. The basic premise of her chapter entitled "Institutionalizing Family Legacy, Reproducing Dynasties" is that business families in meritocratic societies must provide legitimate justifications for dynastic wealth. To do so, business families manage the family by teaching "responsible ownership" and instilling the soft skills associated with legitimating narratives. A growing number of "next gen" training programs offered by universities and global financial wealth management professionals cater to these needs. The global diffusion of legitimating narratives is complemented by professional advisors' activities and lobbying networks such as the Family Firm Institute and Family Business Network. The close ties between these networking organizations and the academic community have produced many academic publications such as the *Family Business Review* and the *Journal of Wealth Management*. In explicating the animating agency behind such projects, Kuusela brings a critical perspective on the globalizing "family-related organizational eco-system" (De Massis, Kotlar, & Manelli, 2021).

In a social class analysis of business families, Carney and Nason's "The Varieties of Business Families: A Capitalist Class Perspective on Business Family Diversity" de-scribes centrifugal social pressures that produce autonomy for family members as they pursue their interests. These pressures are contrasted with centripetal forces that enhance family cohesion. Drawing upon theories of family identity, social net-work preferences, and intergenerational family solidarity, they identify three stable archetypal business families, described as rentiers or financial families, cohesive fo-cused business families, and diversified family business groups. These archetypes in-habit specific social and economic positions in a segmented capitalist class. While each business family archetype seeks to perpetuate its wealth and status, Carney and Nason discuss the socio-economic challenges that threaten to erode class status. Their chapter urges family business scholars to go beyond firm-based definitions to examine business family behaviour in the context of social class segments.

Business families can influence society and establish a favourable public image through charity. Building on the concept of philanthrocapitalism (e.g., Sklair & Glucksberg, 2021), Rivo-López and Villanueva-Villar's "Philanthropy Through Family Offices" investigates the growing professionalization of business family philanthropy. They narrate three case studies of extreme wealth, including the Ortega (Inditex group), Kristiansen (Lego), and Walton (Wal-Mart) business families and their philan-thropic endeavours. Initially perceived as charity and giving back to society, philan-thropy shifted from a pure altruistic concern to a desire for return on investment by projecting family identity, or cultivating reputational capital, and engaging and edu-cating family members about their social obligations. Contemporary philanthropy is now depicted as returning wealth to society, but growing economic inequality chal-lenges the credibility of such redistributive activity. Because exculpatory narratives justifying extreme wealth can create skepticism among public audiences, the messag-ing behind philanthropy requires skillful crafting. Hence, business families outsource the management of family philanthropy to highly schooled professionals in founda-tions and family offices. Their chapter illustrates that the face of business family phi-lanthropy continues to evolve. In its contemporary guise, business families channel financial resources into foundations and family offices to support social entre-preneurship or "impact investing". The authors conclude that the cost-benefit cal-culus of this most recent shift in the rationalization of extreme wealth remains to be determined.

Suddaby, Jaskiewicz, Israelsen, and Chittoor's "Traditional Authority in Social Context: Explaining the Relation Between Types of Family and Types of Family-Controlled Business Groups" integrates several of the principal themes in this hand-book. Their argument suggests prevailing forms of authority in national and re-gional social contexts explain the heterogeneity and ubiquity of family-controlled business groups in a wide range of societies. Focusing on the family behind the firms and business families with multiple firms, they link a prior organizational typology of business groups and discuss how culture and society legitimate forms of traditional and rational-legal authority as depicted by Max Weber. Using two dimensions of cross-cultural variation – the traditional versus secular dimensional survival versus self-expression dimension – they offer a configurational model describing the relationship between cultural context type of legitimate authority and prevalent organizational form of the business group. While family business groups research rarely depicts the existence of business groups in advanced Anglo-Saxon economies, such the UK and Canada, they find specific communities grounded in traditional authority underpinning family business groups. For example, religious communities may abide by traditional modes of authority, consistent with the emergence of extended family business groups.

While much of the business family contributions in this handbook concentrated on their entrepreneurial dynamism, elite status, and robust capacity for governing complex family dynamics, Discua Cruz and Centeno-Caffarana identify migrant business families' precarity. The chapter "Migrant Business Families in Central America" contrasts the diverging experience of Arab Palestinian migrant families in Honduras and German Protestant migrant business families in Nicaragua in the late 19th century. Initially, the Arab Palestinian community was prohibited from high-status land ownership for agricultural production and confined to the low-status role as a "middlemen minority" (for a classic treatment of the subject see Bonacich, 1973). Despite community animosity, Arab Palestinian business families prospered in establishing major businesses and expanded their operations across the Central American community. In contrast, the Protestant German migrant business families initially received a warm reception in Nicaragua and society. They celebrated their German identity while entering many lines of business, including agricultural landholding. However, in the 20th century the German identity arrested the development of these business families since the Nicaraguan government sided with the US in two world wars. In both wars, German families suffered asset confiscation at the hands of the state. The communist Sandinista regime continued this attrition of the German community throughout the 1980s. In recent years, the residual German community has revived to some degree. However, both cases demonstrate the resilience of these firms and their capacity to overcome the challenges presented by shifting circumstances, the reliance on a family and ethnic identity.

While the succession process is a staple of the family business literature, Basco and Vyas bring a novel twist to this well-established literature by describing the ambiguity created for business families in managing the process in a deeply traditional society that is modernizing rapidly. Based on a case study of the third-generation business family in the Gulf state of United Arab Emirates, whose population has expanded exponentially from 100,000 to 10 million over the firm's life, they narrate a clash between tradition and modernity. Their chapter entitled "Succession Process and the Model of Change in a Transgenerational Family Business", illustrates that family members are burdened with structural and psychological pressures that impact their core values pertaining to both business and family. The trauma of modernity undermines and disrupts existing schema for evaluating business and family decisions. The authors conclude with a model of change in transgenerational family businesses that incorporates revolution and inertia in business and family change.

Conclusion

Business families are often expansive groups of people related by kinship who have a joint interest in commonly held wealth or common activities, such as entrepreneurial or wealth preservation, or non-commercial, such as philanthropy. This handbook responds to calls to probe into the heterogeneity of family firms by exploring a unique phenomenon that defies the prevalent definition of family firms as single families influencing a single firm. The family dynamics, the development of different joint activities, their governance, and the institutionalization of such business families in society are four areas where advances have been made, but further scholarly work is warranted. We organized the chapters in this volume along these four dimensions, complemented with a concluding chapter that outlines promising lines for future research on business families. Altogether, the academic work brought together in this handbook shows that reaching across disciplinary boundaries and considering the heterogeneity of family firms through a focus on business families is a worthwhile project. We expect that the *De Gruyter Handbook of Business Families*, with its wide variety of scholarly contributions, will provide valuable insights and a useful departure point for the analysis of the thriving form of business organization that we call business families.

References

Aronoff, C., & Ward, J. (2016). *Family Business Governance: Maximizing Family and Business Potential*. London, UK: Palgrave Macmillan.

Arregle, J. L., Hitt, M. A., Sirmon, D. G., & Very, P. (2007). The development of organizational social capital: Attributes of family firms. *Journal of Management Studies*, 44(1), 73–95. https://doi.org/10.1111/j.1467-6486.2007.00665.x.

Arregle, J. L., Chirico, F., Kano, L., Kundu, S. K., Majocchi, A., & Schulze, W. S. (2021). Family firm internationalization: Past research and an agenda for the future. *Journal of International Business Studies*. https://doi.org/10.1057/s41267-021-00425-2.

Artega, R., & Menendez-Requejo, S. (2017). Family constitution and business performance: Moderating factors. *Family Business Review*, 30(4), 320–338. https://doi.org/10.1177%2F0894486517732438.

Becker, G. S., & Tomes, N. (1994). Human capital and the rise and fall of families. In *Human Capital: A Theoretical and Empirical Analysis with Special Reference to Education* (3, pp. 257–298). National Bureau of Economic Research, Inc.

Beckert, J. (2018). *Inherited Wealth*. Princeton: Princeton University Press.

Bellow, A. (2004). *In Praise of Nepotism: A History of Family Enterprise from King David to George W. Bush*. New York: Anchor Publishing.

Bennedsen, M., Mehrotra, V., Shim, J., & Wiwattanakantang, Y. (2021). Dynastic control without ownership: Evidence from post-war Japan. *Journal of Financial Economics*, 142(2), 831–843. https://doi.org/10.1016/j.jfineco.2021.06.018.

Bertrand, M., Johnson, S., Samphantharak, K., & Schoar, A. (2008). Mixing family with business: A study of Thai business groups and the families behind them. *Journal of financial Economics*, 88(3), 466–498.

Bertschi-Michel, A., & Kammerlander, N. (2015). Trusted advisors in a family business's succession-planning process – An agency perspective. *Journal of Family Business Strategy*, 6(1), 45–57. http://dx.doi.org/10.1016/j.jfbs.2014.10.005.

Biggart, N. (1998). Deep finance: The organizational bases of South Korea's financial collapse. *Journal of Management Inquiry*, 7(4), 311–320. http://dx.doi.org/10.1177/105649269874007.

Bika, Z. & Frazer, M. (2021). The affective extension of 'family' in the context of changing elite business networks. *Human Relations*, 74(12): 1951–1993.

Bjornberg, A., Elstrodt, H., & Pandit, V. (2015). Joining the family business: An emerging opportunity for investors. McKinsey & Company. Retrieved February 14, 2022, from https://www.mckinsey.com/industries/financial-services/our-insights/joining-the-family-business-an-emerging-opportunity-for-investors.

Boers, B., & Nordqvist, M. (2020). Family businesses as hybrid organizations. In *Handbook on Hybrid Organizations* (pp. 507–521). Cheltenham, UK: Edward Elgar Publishing.

Bonacich, E. (1973). A theory of middleman minorities. *American Sociological Review*, 583–594. https://doi.org/10.2307/2094409.

Brinkerink, J., Rondi, E., Benedetti, C., & Arzubiaga, U. (2020). Family business or business family? Organizational identity elasticity and strategic responses to disruptive innovation. *Journal of Family Business Strategy*, 11(4). https://doi.org/10.1016/j.jfbs.2020.100360.

Burt, R. S., Opper, S., & Zou, N. (2021). Social network and family business: Uncovering hybrid family firms. *Social Networks*, 65, 141–156. https://doi.org/10.1016/j.socnet.2020.12.005.

Calabrò, A. (Eds.). (2020). *A Research Agenda for Family Business*. Cheltenham, UK: Edward Elgar Publishing. https://doi.org/10.4337/9781788974073.

Carney, M., & Gedajlovic, E. (2002). The co-evolution of institutional environments and organizational strategies: The rise of family business groups in the ASEAN region. *Organization Studies*, 23(1), 1–29. http://dx.doi.org/10.1177/017084060202300101.

Carney, M., Gedajlovic, E., & Strike, V. M. (2014). Dead money: Inheritance law and the longevity of family firms. *Entrepreneurship Theory and Practice*, 38(6), 1261–1283. https://doi.org/10.1111%2Fetap.12123.

Carney, M., & Nason, R. S. (2018). Family business and the 1%. *Business & Society*, 57(6), 1191–1215. https://doi.org/10.1177%2F0007650316661165.

Carsten, J. (2000). Introduction: Cultures of relatedness. In J. Carsten (Ed.), *Cultures of Relatedness: New Approaches to the Study of Kinship* (pp. 1–36). Cambridge: Cambridge University Press.

Chirot, D., & Reid, A. (1997). *Essential Outsiders: Chinese and Jews in the Modern Transformation of Southeast Asia and Central Europe*. University of Washington Press.

Chua, J. H., Chrisman, J. J., & Sharma, P. (1999). Defining the family business by behavior. *Entrepreneurship Theory and Practice*, 23(4), 19–39. https://doi.org/10.1177%2F104225879902300402.

Colpan, A.M. & Hikino, T. (2017). (eds.). *Business Groups in the West: Origins*, Evolution *and* Resilience. Oxford: Oxford University Press.

Combs, J. G., Shanine, K. K., Burrows, S., Allen, J. S., & Pounds, T. W. (2020). What do we know about business families? Setting the stage for leveraging family science theories. *Family Business Review*, 33(1), 38–63. https://doi.org/10.1177/0894486519863508.

Daspit, J. J., Chrisman, J. J., Ashton, T., & Evangelopoulos, N. (2021). Family firm heterogeneity: A definition, common themes, scholarly progress, and directions forward. *Family Business Review*, 34(3), 296–322. https://doi.org/10.1177%2F08944865211008350.

Dawson, A., & Mussolino, D. (2014). Exploring what makes family firms different: Discrete or overlapping constructs in the literature? *Journal of Family Business Strategy*, 5, 169–183. http://dx.doi.org/10.1016/j.jfbs.2013.11.004.

De Massis, A., Kotlar, J., & Manelli, L. (2021). Family firms, family boundary organizations, and the family-related organizational ecosystem. *Family Business Review*, 34(4), 350–364. https://doi.org/10.1177%2F08944865211052195.

Dieleman, M., & Koning, J. (2020). Articulating values through identity work: Advancing family business ethics research. *Journal of Business Ethics*, 163, 675–687. https://doi.org/10.1007/s10551-019-04380-9.

Dieleman, M., & Sachs, W. M. (2008). Coevolution of institutions and corporations in emerging economies: How the Salim group morphed into an institution of Suharto's crony regime. *Journal of Management Studies*, 45(7), 1274–1300. https://doi.org/10.1111/j.1467-6486.2008.00793.x.

Dunn, M. G. (1980). The family office as a coordinating mechanism within the ruling class. *Insurgent Sociologist*, 9(2–3), 8–23. https://doi.org/10.1177%2F089692058000900202.

Ellul, A., Pagano, M., & Panunzi, F. (2010). Inheritance law and investment in family firms. *American Economic Review*, 100(5), 2414–2450. https://doi.org/10.1257/aer.100.5.2414.

Feliu, N., & Botero, I. C. (2016). Philanthropy in family enterprises: A review of literature. *Family Business Review*, 29(1), 121–141. https://doi.org/10.1177%2F0894486515610962.

Fogel, K. (2006). Oligarchic family control, social economic outcomes, and the quality of government. *Journal of International Business Studies*, 37(5), 603–622. http://www.jstor.org/stable/4540371.

Gersick, K. E. (2015). Essay on Practice: Advising family enterprise in the fourth decade. *Entrepreneurship Theory and Practice*, 39(6), 1433–1450. https://doi.org/10.1111%2Fetap.12176.

Gersick, K. E., Davis, J. A., Hampton, M. M., & Lansberg, I. (1997) *Generation to Generation, Life Cycles of the Family Business*. Harvard Business School Press.

Gilding, M. (2005). Families and fortunes: Accumulation, management succession and inheritance in wealthy families. *Journal of Sociology*, 41(1), 29–45. http://dx.doi.org/10.1177/1440783305050962.

Gómez-Mejía, L., Cruz, C., Berrone, P., & De Castro, J. (2011). The bind that ties: Socioemotional wealth preservation in family firms. *Academy of Management Annals*, 5, 653–707. http://dx.doi.org/10.1080/19416520.2011.593320.

Gordon, G., & Nicholson, N. (2010). *Family Wars: Stories and Insights from Famous Family Business Feuds*. Kogan Page Publishers.

Harrington, B. (2012). Trust and estate planning: The emergence of a profession and its contribution to socioeconomic inequality. *Sociological Forum*, 27(4), 825–846. https://doi.org/10.1111/j.1573-7861.2012.01358.x.

Harrington, B. (2016a). *Capital Without Borders: Wealth Managers and the One Percent*. Harvard University Press.

Harrington, B. (2016b). Panama Papers: The real scandal is what's legal. *The Atlantic*. Retrieved February 14, 2022, from https://www.theatlantic.com/business/archive/2016/04/panama-papers-crimes/477156/

Harrington, B. (2017). Trusts and financialization. *Socio-Economic Review*, 15(1), 31–63. https://doi.org/10.1093/ser/mww014.

James, H. (2009). Family Capitalism: Wendels, Haniels, Falcks, and the Continental European Model. Harvard University Press.

Jaskiewicz, P., Combs, J. G., & Rau, S. B. (2014). Entrepreneurial legacy: Toward a theory of how some family firms nurture transgenerational entrepreneurship. *Journal of Business Venturing*, 30(1), 29–49. https://doi.org/10.1016/j.jbusvent.2014.07.001.

Jensen, M. C., & Meckling, W. H. (1976). Theory of the firm: Managerial agency costs and ownership structure. *Journal of Financial Economics*, 3, 305–360. https://doi.org/10.1016/0304-405X(76)90026-X.

Kellermanns, F., & Hoy, F. (Eds.). (2016). *The Routledge Companion to Family Business (1st ed.)*. Routledge. https://doi.org/10.4324/9781315688053.

Kleve, H., Köllner, T., von Schlippe, A., & Rüsen, T. A. (2020a). The business family 3.0: Dynastic business families as families, organizations and networks – Outline of a theory extension. *Systems Research and Behavioral Science*, 37(3), 516–526. https://doi.org/10.1002/sres.2684.

Kleve, H., Roth, S., Köllner, T., & Wetzel, R. (2020b). The tetralemma of the business family. *Journal of Organizational Change Management*, 33(2), 433–446. http://dx.doi.org/10.1108/JOCM-08-2019-0254.

Konig, A., Kammerlander, N., & Enders, A. (2013). The family innovator's dilemma: How family influence affects the adoption of discontinuous technologies by incumbent firms. *Academy of Management Review*, 38, 418–441. http://dx.doi.org/10.5465/amr.2011.0162.

Kuusela, H. (2018). Learning to own: Cross-generational meanings of wealth and class-making in wealthy Finnish families. *Sociological Review*. http://dx.doi.org/10.1177/0038026118777698.

Labaki, R., Bernard, F., & Cailluet, L. (2018). The strategic use of historical narratives in the family business. In D. Clay & E. Memili (Eds.). *Family Firms Heterogeneity*. Palgrave Macmillan.

Landa, J. T. (2016). Economic success of Chinese merchants in Southeast Asia: Identity, ethnic cooperation and conflict. *Springer-Verlag*. http://dx.doi.org/10.1007/s10818-018-9274-2.

Landes, D. (2006). *Dynasties: Fortunes and Misfortunes of the World's Great Family Businesses*. Viking.

La Porta, R., Lopez-de-Silanes, F., & Shleifer, A. (1999). Corporate ownership around the world. *Journal of Finance*, 54(2), 471–517. https://doi.org/10.1111/0022-1082.00115.

Le Breton-Miller, I., & Miller, D. (2018). Beyond the firm: Business families as entrepreneurs. *Entrepreneurship Theory and Practice*, 42(4), 527–536. https://doi.org/10.1177%2F1042258717739004.

Li, J.B., & Piezunka, H. (2020). The uniplex third: Enabling single-domain role transitions in multiplex relationships. *Administrative Science Quarterly*, 65(2), 314–358. https://doi.org/10.1177%2F0001839219845875.

Litz, R. A. (2008). Two sides of a one-sided phenomenon: conceptualizing the family business and business family as a möbius strip. *Family Business Review*, 21(3), 217–236. https://doi.org/10.1177%2F08944865080210030104.

Masulis, R. W., Pham, P. K., & Zein, J. (2011). Family business groups around the world: Financing advantages, control motivations, and organizational choices. *The Review of Financial Studies*, 24(11), 3556–3600. http://dx.doi.org/10.2139/ssrn.1363878.

Memili, E., & Dibrell, C. (Eds.). (2019). *The Palgrave Handbook of Heterogeneity among Family Firms*. Palgrave Macmillan.

Michael-Tsabari, N., Labaki, R., & Zachary, R. K. (2014). Toward the cluster model: The family firm's entrepreneurial behavior over generations. *Family Business Review*, 27(2), 161–185. https://doi.org/10.1177%2F0894486514525803.

Mintzberg, H. (1994). The fall and rise of strategic planning. *Harvard Business Review*, 107–114. Retrieved February 14, 2022, from https://www.theisrm.org/public-library/Mintzberg%20 (1994)%20Fall%20and%20Rise%20of%20Strategic%20Planning.pdf.

Moores, K. (2009). Paradigms and theory building in the domain of business families. *Family Business Review*, 22(2), 167–180. https://doi.org/10.1177%2F0894486509333372.

Morck, R., & Yeung, B. (2003). Agency problems in large family business groups. *Entrepreneurship theory and practice*, 27(4), 367–382. https://doi.org/10.1111%2F1540-8520.t01-1-00015.

Nason, R., Mazzelli, A., & Carney, M. (2019). The ties that unbind: Socialization and business-owning family reference point shift. *Academy of Management Review*, 44(4), 846–870. https://doi.org/10.5465/amr.2017.0289.

Nordqvist, M., & Melin, L. (2010). Entrepreneurial families and family firms. *Entrepreneurship & Regional Development*, 22(3–4), 211–239. http://dx.doi.org/10.1080/08985621003726119.

O'Boyle, E. H. Jr., Pollack, J. M., & Rutherford, M. W. (2012). Exploring the relation between family involvement and firms' financial performance: A meta-analysis of main and moderator effects. *Journal of Business Venturing*, 27, 1–18.

Pérez-González, F. (2006). Inherited control and firm performance. *American Economic Review*, 96(5), 1559–1588. https://doi.org/10.1257/aer.96.5.1559.

Piketty, T. (2014). *Capital in the twenty-first century* (A. Goldhammer, Trans.). France: Éditions du Seuil.

Portes, A. (1998). Social capital: Its origins and applications in modern sociology. *Annual Review of Sociology*, 24(1), 1–24. https://doi.org/10.1146/annurev.soc.24.1.1.

Portes, A., & Martinez, B. P. (2020). They are not all the same: Immigrant enterprises, transnationalism, and development. *Journal of Ethnic and Migration Studies*, 46(10), 1991–2007. https://doi.org/10.1080/1369183X.2018.1559995.

Portes, A., & Sensenbrenner, J. (1993). Embeddedness and immigration: Notes on the social determinants of economic action. *American Journal of Sociology*, 98(6), 1320–1350. http://www.jstor.org/stable/2781823.

Reay, T., Pearson, A. W., & Gibb Dyer, W. (2013). Advising family enterprise: Examining the role of family firm advisors. *Family Business Review*, 26(3), 209–214. http://doi.org/http://doi.org/10.1177/0894486513494277.

Redding, G. (1990). *The Spirit of Chinese Capitalism*. De Gruyter. https://doi.org/10.1515/9783110887709.

Rosa, P., Howorth, C., & Cruz, A. D. (2013). Habitual and portfolio entrepreneurship and the family in business. In *The Sage Handbook of Family Business* (pp. 364–382). SAGE Publications Inc. https://doi.org/10.4135/9781446247556.n18.

Rosplock, K., & Hauser, B. R. (2014). The family office landscape: Today's trends and five predictions for the family office of tomorrow. *The Journal of Wealth Management*, 17(3), 9–19.

Rovelli, P., Ferasso, M., De Massis, A., & Kraus, S. (2022). Thirty years of research in family business journals: Status quo and future directions. *Journal of Family Business Strategy*. https://doi.org/10.1016/j.jfbs.2021.100422.

Sasaki, I., Kotlar, J., Ravasi, D., & Vaara, E. (2020). Dealing with revered past: Historical identity statements and strategic change in Japanese family firms. *Strategic Management Journal*, 41 (3), 590–623. https://doi.org/10.1002/smj.3065.

Sasaki, I., Ravasi, D., & Micelotta, E. (2019). Family firms as institutions: Cultural reproduction and status maintenance among multi-centenary Shinise in Kyoto. *Organization Studies*, 40(6), 793–831. https://doi.org/10.1177%2F0170840618818596.

Schickinger, A., Leitterstorf, M. P., & Kammerlander, N. (2018). Private equity and family firms: A systematic review and categorization of the field. *Journal of Family Business Strategy*, 9(4), 268–292. https://doi.org/10.1016/j.jfbs.2018.09.002.

Schulze, W. S., & Kellermanns, F. W. (2015). Reifying Socioemotional Wealth. Entrepreneurship Theory and Practice, 39(3), 447–459. https://doi.org/10.1111/etap.12159.

Shiba, S., & Shimotani, M. (1997). *Beyond the Firm: Business Groups in International and Historical Perspective (2nd ed.).* Oxford University Press on Demand.

Sieger, P., Zellweger, T., Nason, R. S., & Clinton, E. (2011). Portfolio entrepreneurship in family firms: A resource-based perspective. *Strategic Entrepreneurship Journal*, 5(4), 327–351. https://doi.org/10.1002/sej.120.

Sinha, P. N., Jaskiewicz, P., Gibb, J., & Combs, J. G. (2020). Managing history: How New Zealand's Gallagher Group used rhetorical narratives to reprioritize and modify imprinted strategic guideposts. *Strategic Management Journal*, 41(3), 557–589. https://doi.org/10.1002/smj.3037.

Sklair, J., & Glucksberg, L. (2021). Philanthrocapitalism as wealth management strategy: Philanthropy, inheritance and succession planning among the global elite. *The Sociological Review*, 69(2), 314–329. https://doi.org/10.1177%2F0038026120963479.

Soleimanof, S., Rutherford, M., & Webb, J. W. (2018). The intersection of family firms and institutional contexts: A review and agenda for future research. *Family Business Review*, 3(1), 32–53. https://doi.org/10.1177%2F0894486517736446.

Steier, L. P., Chrisman, J. J., & Chua, J. H. (2015). Governance challenges in family businesses and business families. *Entrepreneurship Theory and Practice*, 39(6), 1265–1280. https://doi.org/10.1111/etap.12180.

Stewart, A. (2003). Help one another, use one another: Toward an anthropology of family business. *Entrepreneurship Theory and Practice*, 27(4), 383–396. https://doi.org/10.1111%2F1540-8520.00016.

Strachan, H. W. (1976). *Family and other business groups in economic development: The case of Nicaragua.* Praeger Publishers.

Strike, V. M., Bertschi-Michel, A., & Kammerlander, N. (2018). Unpacking the black box of family business advising: Insights from psychology. *Family Business Review*, 31(1), 80–124. https://doi.org/10.1177%2F0894486517735169.

Strike, V. M., & Rerup, C. (2016). Mediated sensemaking. *Academy of Management Journal*, 59(3), 880–905. https://doi.org/10.5465/amj.2012.0665.

Suess, J. (2014). Family governance – Literature review and the development of a conceptual model. *Journal of Family Business Strategy*, 5, 138–155. https://doi.org/10.1016/j.jfbs.2014.02.001.

Tripathi, D., & Jumani, J. (2007). *The Concise Oxford History of Indian Business.* Oxford University Press.

Verver, M., & Koning, J. (2018). Toward a kinship perspective on entrepreneurship. *Entrepreneurship Theory and Practice*, 42(4), 631–666. http://dx.doi.org/10.1111/etap.12274.

Ward, J. L. (1988). The special role of strategic planning for family businesses. *Family Business Review*, 1(2), 105–117. https://doi.org/10.1111/j.1741-6248.1988.00105.x.

Wessel, S., Decker, C., Lange, K. S., & Hack, A. (2014). One size does not fit all: Entrepreneurial families' reliance on family offices. *European Management Journal*, 32(1), 37–45. https://doi.org/10.1016/j.emj.2013.08.003.

Zellweger, T., & Kammerlander, N. (2015). Article commentary: Family, wealth, and governance: An agency account. *Entrepreneurship Theory and Practice*, 39(6), 1281–1303. https://doi.org/10.1111%2Fetap.12182.

Zellweger, T., Nason, R., & Nordqvist, M. (2012). From longevity of firms to transgenerational entrepreneurship of families: Introducing family entrepreneurial orientation. *Family Business Review*, 25(2), 136–155. http://dx.doi.org/10.1177/0894486511423531.

Part I: **Business Families as the Family Behind the Firm**

Jian Bai Li and Henning Piezunka

2 Family Businesses as Multiplex Relationships

Abstract: The name "family business" suggests an obvious but defining feature of such organizations: what happens in the family affects the business – and vice versa. Despite this linkage, the research on family business is surprisingly deficient of a theoretical framework with which scholars can use to study and understand how relationships and networks in the family and the business impact each other. Drawing from social network theory, we suggest that the framework on *multiplexity* can enable scholars of family businesses to effectively examine relationship dynamics and network structure in both the business and the family. We illustrate how deploying the multiplexity framework enables scholars (a) to strengthen their contribution to research on family business as it helps to explain behaviour, relational dynamics, and performance in family businesses; and (b) to make the research on family business more broadly relevant for the fields of social networks and organization theory.

Keywords: multiplexity, network structure, coupling, segregation, transposition, submerged actors

Introduction

This chapter proposes network multiplexity as a theoretical framework with which scholars can study family businesses – specifically, how relationships and networks in the family impact the business, and vice versa. We argue the multiplexity framework to be helpful for the study of family businesses for two reasons. First, the multiplexity framework enables a closer, more detailed examination of the degree to which the family is coupled to versus segregated from the business – and the consequences of this coupling/segregation. Second, the multiplexity framework allows scholars to study how the structure of networks in the family impacts organizational processes and dynamics in the business.

Jian Bai Li, National University of Singapore
Henning Piezunka, INSEAD

https://doi.org/10.1515/9783110727968-002

Properties of Multiplex Relationships and Networks

Multiplex relationships are dyadic, interpersonal relationships in which actors interact across multiple social and economic domains (Granovetter, 1985; Ingram & Roberts, 2000; Kuwabara, Luo, & Sheldon, 2010). Relationships between family members who co-own and co-manage businesses, in general, tend to be multiplex relationships, since such relationships involve interactions in two clear domains: the family and the business (Chua et al., 1999; Miller et al., 2007; Gomez-Mejia et al., 2007; Sharma et al., 2012).

The key mechanism underlying multiplex relationships is *transposition*. That is, when actors who already share relationships in one domain begin interacting with each other in a second domain, they often bring elements of their relationship from the first domain into the second (Uzzi, 1996; Hardin, 2002; Zelizer, 2005). As the research on family businesses have found, family members who co-own and co-manage a business often bring the trust and mutual dedication characteristic to family relationships into their interactions in the business (Landes, 2006; Miller & Le Breton-Miller, 2005; Ward, 2004). Yet trust and dedication are not the only elements that can be transposed: multiplex relationships in family businesses can also transpose family hierarchies (Luo & Chung, 2005), family roles (Handler, 1990), and internal divisions in the family (Li & Piezunka, 2020) into the business. In this sense, then, the mechanism of transposition characteristic to multiplexity may serve as a more general framework for conceptualizing how the family affects the business: whereas much of the family business research has tended to focus on how the psychological or emotional motivations stemming from the family affects the management and performance of the business (Gomez-Mejia et al., 2007; James, 2006; Miller et al., 2008; Berrone et al., 2010), the mechanism of transposition enables scholars to also think about how relational characteristics in the family impacts interactions and outcomes in the business.

We may extend from the dyadic multiplex relationship to conceptualize the *multiplex network*, which we define as a network where a significant proportion of constituent relationships exist across multiple social and economic domains, like the family and business domains for family businesses. An example would be the following hypothetical network composed mostly of executives of a family business.

Figure 2.1 presents a hypothetical multiplex network involving four members of a family business. Note that, here, actors A, B, C, and D, are involved in both the business and the family domains – they share relationships both as executives in the same.

This network exemplifies two key features of multiplex networks in general. First, not every actor in the network is involved in all domains the network exists across. Here, actors A, B, C, and D are involved in both family and business domains – they would be the family member who are also executives in the business. But actor E is involved in only the business domain this actor would be a non-

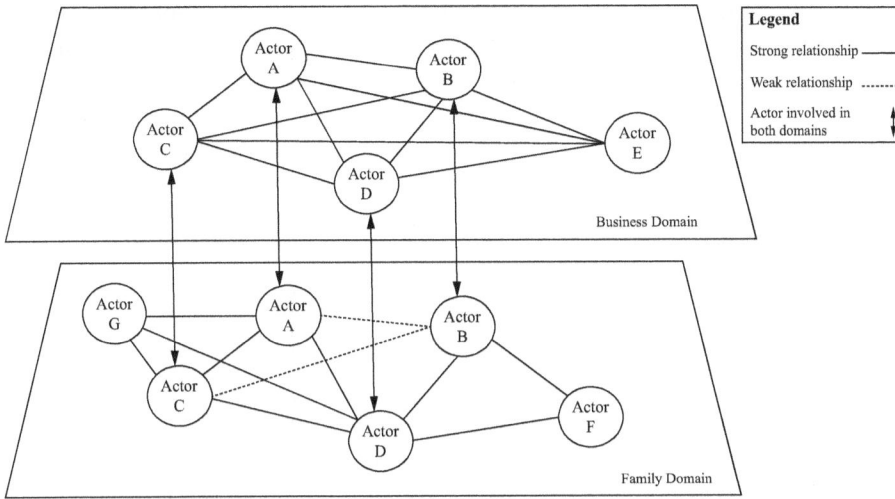

Figure 2.1: Hypothetical Multiplex Network of Family Business Executives.

family executive. And actors F and G are involved in only the family domain they would be members of the controlling family who aren't directly involved in the business. And these features, we argue, is reflective of the multiplex networks that typically make up the top echelons of family businesses: while most members of such networks are involved in both family and business, some are nevertheless involved in only the business (Martinez & Aldrich, 2011; Stewart & Hitt, 2012), and some are involved in only the family (Moores, 2009). In other words, a multiplex network is typically comprised of both *multiplex actors* who are involved across multiple domains as well as *uniplex actors* who are involved in only one domain (i.e., family members not active in the businesses, and business executives who are not part of the family).

Second, notice how, even amongst the multiplex actors in the hypothetical network displayed in Figure 2.1, the *structures* of their relationships in the business versus family domains are not identical. The network amongst actors A, B, C, and D in the business domain manifest as a highly closed network – that is, a network where all actors are connected to all others (Coleman, 1988; 1990). But the network amongst these same four actors in the family domain exhibits much less closure (Simmel, 1950) – that is, that actors A, B, C, and D are far less interconnected in the family than they are in the business. This is because, in the family domain, actors A, C, and D form a strong, interconnected triad, while actor B is the more isolated individual who only shares a strong relationship to actor D. One can readily imagine how such a multiplex network with dissimilar structures across domains may manifest in real-world family businesses. For instance, in a business run by three brothers and a distant cousin, these four individuals would all be embedded within a single closed network in the business domain, but the cousin would likely be the more isolated individual vis-à-vis the brothers within the family domain. The larger point is that the structure of the network within which multiplex actors are embedded need not be identical in every domain that they are involved in the same group of actors can be embedded in a closed network in one domain but a far more open one in another.

Network Closure in the Family and Dynamics in the Business

We believe that the multiplexity framework would enable several fruitful avenues of research into family businesses. One such avenue would to be study how the degree of network closure in the family affects relational dynamics in the business. This is an under-examined issue in the research on family businesses.

Indeed, much of the research on family businesses has implicitly assumed that the family underlying the business consisted of a single, cohesive closed network. Consider many of the characteristics that research has associated with family businesses – both positive characteristics such as trust and long-term dedication (Miller & Le Breton-Miller, 2005; Lansberg, 1999; Pierce et al., 2001; Wasserman, 2006; Arregle et al., 2007) as well as negative ones such as reduced capacity for capitalizing on the knowledge of non-family managers and innovation (Sirmon & Hitt, 2003; Chrisman et al., 2005; Sequeira & Rasheed, 2006; Van Geenhuizen & Soetanto, 2012; Martinez & Aldrich, 2014). These are also characteristics that the social networks literature identify as properties of strong, cohesive closed networks, that is, closed networks tend to engender strong trust and mutual dedication (Coleman, 1988; Portes & Sensenbrenner, 1993; Burt, 2001) but also limit the abilities of established network members to access novel information, make use of knowledge from network outsiders, and innovate (Reagans & McEvily, 2003; Aral & Van Alstyne, 2011; Ter Wal et al., 2016). And so, the aforementioned characteristics of family businesses that research has identified can actually be explained if one assumes the network that executives in such businesses share in the *family domain* to be closed networks characterized by high levels of interconnectedness and internal cohesion. In other words, implicit to what research has identified as characteristics of family businesses is an assumption that the structure of the family network underlying such businesses are closed.

Yet, the family networks underlying family businesses, in terms of their structure, are not always closed. This is so because divisions, factions, and cliques can exist in the family – just as they do in any other network. Indeed, research has noted how family networks can be characterized by cleavages between separate branches, between blood relatives versus in-laws, and between members of different genders (Bertrand et al., 2008). Structurally speaking, when family networks are comprised of distinct cliques separated by cleavages, then would then be much less interconnected – and therefore much less closed – compared to their counterparts with no such cleavages, since family members in such networks would tend to form strong relationships within their own respective cliques and refrain from interacting, across cleavages, with members of other cliques. And so, despite research generally portraying the family networks underlying family businesses to be structurally closed and cohesive, such networks can, in fact, manifest as more open networks – that is, networks where significant numbers of members are *not* strongly connected to all other members and where significant gaps and cleavages exist (Burt, 2001).

We surmise that the degree to which the family networks underlying family businesses are open versus closed bear important implications for how family business executives work, interact, and cooperate in the business. To see how this is so, consider the networks underlying two hypothetical family businesses, with each network comprising five actors that are involved in both family and business domains. The first network is illustrated in Figure 2.2, and the second network is illustrated in Figure 2.3.

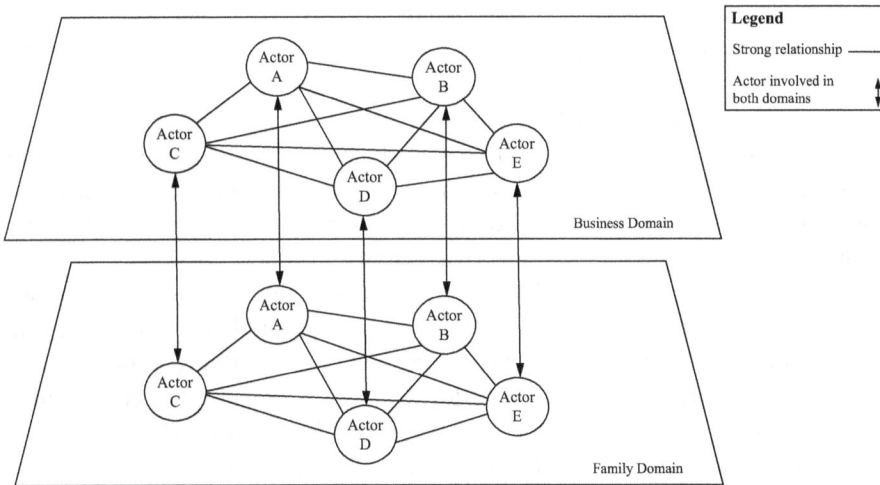

Figure 2.2: Hypothetical Multiplex Network with Closed Structure in the Family Domain.

In both networks, the network structure *in the business domain* remains identical: the business domain network shared by the five actors illustrated manifests as completely closed in both networks #1 and #2. This is not an unreasonable supposition: if actors in both networks #1 and #2 work as top managers in family businesses, then both sets of actors would likely interact frequently in the business domain, such that the network of their interactions for both would likely manifest

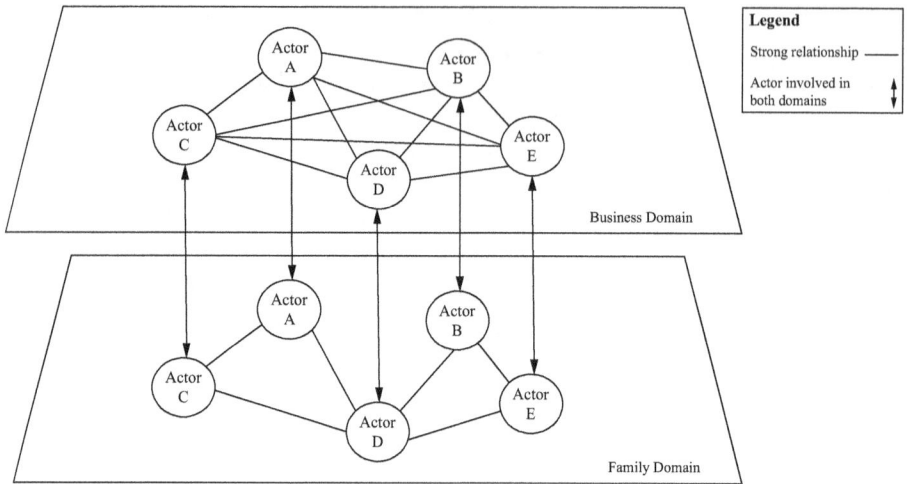

Figure 2.3: Hypothetical Multiplex Network with Open Structure in the Family Domain.

as completely closed in the manner illustrated. The difference between networks #1 and #2 is *in the family domain*. Here, network #1 manifests as a completely closed network in the family. This would correspond to the scenario where a single, cohesive kinship group co-owns and co-manages a business – such as, for example, when five brothers run a business together. But network #2 manifests as two distinctive triadic factions: actors A, C, and D belong to one family faction, actors D, B, and E belong to a separate faction, and the two factors are welded together by actor D. This would correspond to the scenario where two separate kinship factions within a larger, extended family co-owns and co-manages a business – such as, for example, when two groups of in-laws run a business together.

Both network #1 and network #2 may comprise family members that co-own and co-manage businesses, but their internal dynamics would likely exhibit significant differences. For network #1, the high degree of closure in the family would likely engender strong levels of trust, loyalty, and dedication (Coleman, 1988; Portes & Sensenbrenner, 1993; Burt, 2001) amongst the five actors involved. Such trust, loyalty, and mutual support would then be transposed into the business domain, thereby giving rise to the long-term dedication and far-sighted stewardship that research has often associated with family businesses (Arregle et al., 2007; Miller et al., 2008; Le Breton-Miller et al., 2011). In contrast, for network #2, the structural division between the two factions may create distance, suspicions, and even conflicts of interest between members of these two factions – that is, between actors A and C on one side and actors B and E on the other side.

There is an additional dynamic that could develop in network #2 but not in network #1. Notice how actor D is the only actor in the family domain that is tied to both actors A and C and to actors B and E. That is, structurally speaking, actor D is the "one in the middle" between the clique comprised of actors A and C and the clique comprised of actors B and E. As Krackhardt (1999) noted, this type of structure often results in the "one in the middle" – actors D here – becoming subjected to conflicting pressures from the two cliques that he or she is connected to. Specifically, actors A and C here could demand that actor D lend them partisan support against actors B and E, while actors B and E could make similar types of demands on actor D against actors A and C. This would effectively tear actor D in two directions and further exacerbate conflicts within the network. Now recall also that network #2 is also a multiplex network – and that multiplex networks transpose not only trust and dedication but also divisions and feuds. So, when the divisions, suspicions, and feuds originating from the structure of network #2 in the family domain is transposed into interactions in the business domain, we would likely not witness loyalty and dedication but rather conflicts, bickering, and self-serving behaviour in the family business – indeed, Li and Piezunk (2020) observed precisely this sort of conflicts and bickering in family businesses emerging from structural cleavages in the network within the family domain.

The bigger point we wish to emphasize here is that the multiplexity framework would enable family businesses researchers to examine, in greater detail, the structure of relationships and interactions between family business executives in the *family domain* (indeed, please see Arregle, Hitt, and Mari [2019] for a study that has already begun to examine this relational aspect of family businesses). This is crucial because, quite often, two family businesses may look identical if one only looks at the pattern of relationships and interactions between key executives within the business domain. Notice, indeed, how networks #1 and #2 look structurally identical in the business domain – and that any differences in how family business executives within these two networks work, interact, and cooperate (or not cooperate) would be unexplainable unless one also examined the structure of these two networks in the family domain.

In this regard, the multiplexity framework may present researchers with a path forward for resolving the ongoing debate in the family business literature regarding how family involvement affects business performance. Indeed, while one stream of research within the literature on family businesses asserts that family involvement should improve business performance due to the family owners and managers' far-sighted stewardship and long-term dedication to the business (Arregle et al., 2007; Miller & Le Breton-Miller, 2005; Landes, 2006), another stream of research from the same literature argues that family involvement would actually harm business performance due to the risk-aversion, nepotism, and other self-serving behaviour of these family owners and family managers (Morck et al., 2000; Morck & Yeung, 2003; Claessens et al., 2002; Lubatkin et al., 2007; Miller et al., 2010). And while some studies have attempted to reconcile the debate between these two streams of research, they have focused predominantly on characteristics of the *business* – such as multi-generational involvement in the business or the influence of family CEOs – as the explanatory variables that determine whether family involvement positively or negatively affects business performance (Le Breton-Miller et al., 2011; Ashforth & Johnson, 2002; Perez-Gonzalez, 2006; Bennedsen et al., 2007; Le Breton-Miller & Miller, 2009; Zellweger, 2014). What we add here is that, in addition to examining characteristics of the business, scholars could also make fruitful progress on resolving this debate by looking more closely at the family domain – specifically, at the *structure of networks* that executives share in the family. A group of executives that are all embedded within a single strong, closed network in the family are much more likely to trust, support, and cooperate with each other – and therefore more likely to exhibit far-sighted stewardship in the business. In contrast, a group of executives embedded in a family network characterized by disparate cliques and clear cleavages are more likely to mistrust each other and feud in the family – and therefore more likely to engage in self-serving behaviour in the business. Thus, by allowing the explicit examination of network structures across family and business domains, the multiplexity framework may further enrich our understandings of how the family affects the business.

The multiplexity framework may also prove useful for examining the dynamics within businesses owned and run by large, extended families – such as, for example, family-owned business groups (Lincoln, Gerlach, & Takahashi, 1992; Granovetter, 1995; Keister, 2001). Here, research has looked at how the family relationships underlying business groups may help these organizations compensate for underdeveloped market institutions (Khanna & Palepu, 1997; 1999), encourage cooperation (Khanna & Palepu, 2000), and improve firm performance (Luo & Chung, 2005). But surprisingly, few studies in this line of research have directly examined the structure of relationships within the family and how these structures impact relational dynamics and performance of the business group. The multiplexity framework would allow future studies to address this gap by enabling scholars to directly study the relational dynamics engendered by a complex of different types of relationships (Li, 2021) and different clusters of networks (Li & Piezunka, 2020) within a large, extended family or a family with multiple generations. This, in turn, would enable scholars to further advance our understanding of how relationships and networks in a large, extended family impacts cooperation, information transfer, and organizational dynamics within the business group that such a family would own and run.

Overall, the multiplexity framework presents new opportunities for research on family businesses by enabling a closer examination of how the structure of family networks affects relationship dynamics and interactions in the business domain – and, by extension, business innovation and performance. In doing so, this framework would enable scholars to make further inroads into our understandings of how networks in the family are structured I relationships and interactions in the business – and how both family-specific and cross-domain network structures affect the management and performance of the business. As such, the multiplexity framework may constitute one fruitful avenue for scholars to better understand the network structural characteristics of the families that own and run businesses

(Renzulli, Aldrich, and Moody, 2000; Moores, 2009; Jennings, Breitkreuz, & James, 2014; Zamudio, Anokhin, and Kellermans, 2014).

The Influence of "Submerged" Family Members

The multiplexity framework may also enable scholars to more closely study the influence of the "submerged" family members on relational dynamics and interactions in the business domain. We define these "submerged" family members, for a family business, as the *members of the controlling family who themselves do not hold formal positions in the business and are not directly involved in either business ownership or management.*

By and large, the research on family businesses has been silent on the influence of these submerged family members. Indeed, in examining family involvement in the business, research has focused almost exclusively on members of the controlling family who are directly involved and hold formal positions in the business – such as, for example, family owners (Sirmon et al., 2008; Achmad et al., 2009; Handler, 1989; Gersick et al., 1997; Anderson & Reeb, 2003), family managers (Chua et al., 2009; Songini & Gnan, 2009), and family business successors (Sharma, Chrisman, & Chua, 1996; Bennedsen et al., 2007; Handler, 1990; Cabrera-Suarez, 2005; Pyromalis & Vozikis, 2009). The submerged family members are implicitly acknowledged as members of the larger family network underlying family businesses (Anderson, Jack, & Dodd, 2005), yet how these submerged family members exert influences in both the family and business domains remains largely under-addressed – and, more importantly, under-theorized – within the family business literature (Stewart & Hitt, 2012).

The multiplexity framework would present a way for family business scholars to examine and theorize on the influence of submerged family members on relational dynamics and interactions in both the family and the business. Specifically, if family businesses are conceptualized as multiplex networks, then the submerged family members would be conceptualized as *uniplex actors* – that is, as actors who are involved in these multiplex networks in only one (the family) domain – who exert their influence by altering the structure and dynamics of these networks within the family domain.

To see how this is so, consider the multiplex networks that characterize two hypothetical family businesses, with network #1 (which characterize the first family business) illustrated in Figure 2.4 and network #2 (which characterize the second family business) illustrated in Figure 2.5. For illustrative purposes, we assume here that both family businesses are co-owned and co-managed by two siblings, which means that both networks #1 and #2 would manifest as a relational dyad in the business domain. The difference between these two networks lies in the family domain. For network #1, the mother of the two siblings that co-own and co-manage the business is alive and well. Although she isn't directly involved in the business, she works actively in the family domain to mediate between the two siblings (i.e., her two sons) and resolve any disagreements that may arise between them. But for network #2, both parents of the two siblings that co-own and co-manage the business are deceased, and there is no third party in the family to mediate between these two siblings. This means that, while both networks look identical in the business domain, they would be structurally different in the family domain: here, network #1 would manifest as a triad, while network #2 would manifest as a dyad. We illustrate these two networks in Figures 2.4 and 2.5.

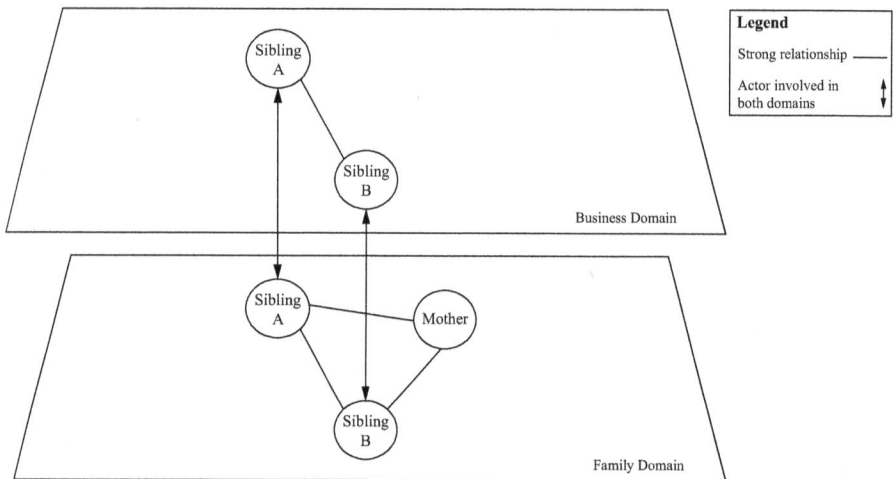

Figure 2.4: Hypothetical Dyad with Uniplex Third in the Family Domain.

In network #1, even though the mother is not directly involved in the business domain, her presence and activity in the family domain would likely influence the two siblings to become more cooperative in family and business. This is so for two reasons. First, the presence of the mother in the family itself changes the structure of network #1 in the family domain from a dyad to a triad. Since the structural properties of network triads tend to encourage cooperation and discourage self-serving behaviour (Simmel, 1950; Tortoriello & Krackhardt, 2010), the presence of the mother in the family – by altering the structure of the family network from a dyad to a triad – in and of itself would suppress conflicts between the two siblings and encourage them to behave more cooperatively. Second, the mother's position as the third party to the two siblings in the family domain would also enable her to play the role of the mediator between them (Obstfeld, 2005), thereby allowing her to resolve disagreements and adjudicate disputes between her two sons (Fernandez & Gould, 1994; Samila et al., 2016). So, in addition to the structural implications of

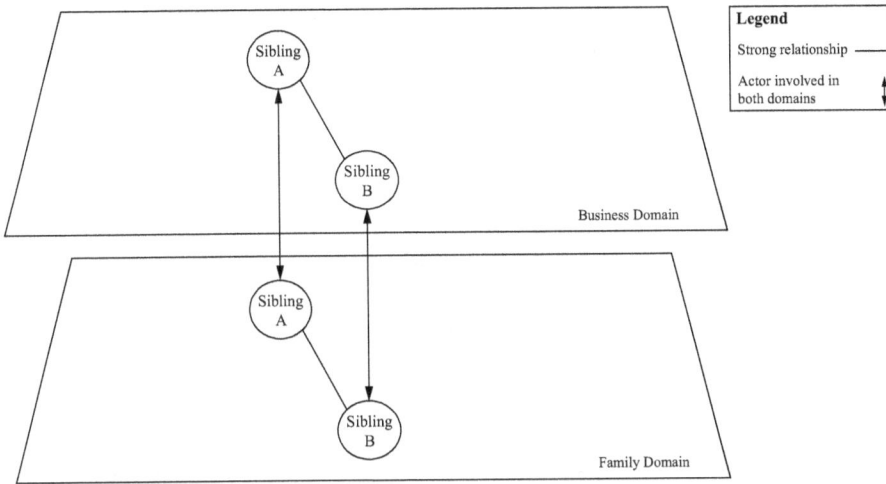

Figure 2.5: Hypothetical Dyad without Uniplex Third in the Family Domain.

her presence, the mother's activities in the family domain would also reduce the likelihood for conflicts to arise between the two siblings. And such increased cooperativity and reduced conflicts in the family, when transposed into the business, likely results in more effective professional collaborations – and reduced likelihood for self-serving behaviour – in interactions between the two siblings, thereby enabling more effective management of the business and, by extension, better long-run business performance.

In contrast, in network #2, the absence of a third party in the family would likely render the two siblings more conflict-prone in their relational interactions in both family and business domains. Lacking a third party to act as both a judge and tiebreaker (Simmel, 1950) in the family, the two siblings in network #2 would not be able to easily resolve the disagreements that would inevitably arise in their interactions. Such unresolved disagreements would then linger and fester, engendering larger conflicts that may erupt in these two siblings' professional collaborations and derail business performance. In this manner, the absence of a third submerged family member in network #2 makes siblings conflicts much more likely in network #2 than in network #1.

Our example of how submerged family members may critically affect relational dynamics, interactions, and professional collaborations between family business executives is but one. There are others – indeed, Li and Piezunka (2020) presents an example of how the mother, despite being uninvolved in the business domain, may nevertheless exert a positive influence on the succession process involving the father (i.e., her husband, who is also the company CEO) and the son (who is the company successor). The bigger point here is that submerged family members, by altering the structure and dynamics of family networks, may exert significant influences on how family business executives interact and collaborate despite being uninvolved in the business themselves. As such, examining such submerged family members more closely – and theorizing on the mechanisms by which they exert their influence – may be another fruitful avenue of research for scholars of family businesses.

The Determinants of Segregation versus Coupling between Family and Business Domains

Lastly, the multiplexity framework enables a more detailed examination of is the *degree* to which the family and the business are coupled versus segregated – and how decision-makers in family businesses can manage this degree of domain segregation.

Thus far, the research on family businesses has treated the family and the business domains as coupled. Indeed, research defines family businesses as organizations as economic organizations with significant family involvement (Lansberg et al., 1988; Chua et al., 1999; Sharma et al., 2012). Some scholars emphasize the involvement of family in terms of family actors' possession ownership of the business (Handler, 1989; Gersick et al., 1997; Yu et al., 2012) or involvement in management of the business (Davis, 1982; Zahra & Sharma, 2004). Others focus on family involvement in terms of the influence of family values, family aspirations, family interests, family perspectives, and family stories on the business (Wiseman & Gomez-Mejia, 1998; Klein et al., 2005; Bertrand & Schoar, 2006; Gomez-Mejia et al., 2007; Holt, Rutherford, & Kuratko, 2010; Kammerlander et al., 2015). The common strand here is a consistent acknowledgement that, in family businesses, what happens in the family domain significantly affects what happens in the business domain – that is, that the family and business domains are strongly coupled. After all, if these two domains are segregated, then elements of the family domain would not exert much influence on professional interactions and organizational processes in the business domain.

This, in turn, means that research implicitly assumes the *transposition* of elements from the family domain into the business domain to be a rather indiscriminate process. Indeed, a perusal of the family business literature seems to suggest that family businesses tend to transpose both the positive and the negative from family into business in a seemingly wholesale manner. Family businesses transpose mutual support (Sequeira et al., 2007), far-sighted stewardship (Davis et al., 1997; Arthurs & Busenitz, 2003; Arregle et al., 2007), and altruistic values (Lubatkin, Schulze, & Ling, 2005; Lubatkin et al., 2007) from the family domain into the business domain, and they can also transpose self-serving motivations (Morck et al., 2000), risk aversion (Wiseman & Gomez-Mejia, 1998; Bertrand & Schoar, 2006; Miller et al., 2010), and nepotism (Claessens et al., 2002; Volpin, 2002). This recognition that family businesses transpose both positive and negative elements from the family into the business has led to an ongoing debate regarding whether family involvement improves or harms business performance (Le Breton-Miller et al., 2011; Miller and Le Breton-Miller, 2021). We do not seek to settle this debate here, but we do wish to point out that this debate wouldbe easier to settle if research accounted for the possibility that decision-makers in family businesses are actually *selective* about what they transpose from the family into the business. After all, if family businesses could somehow transpose *only the positive elements* from family into business, then they would have a much easier time ensuring that family involvement is net positive for business management and performance. Thus, the fact that research remains inconclusive regarding what family businesses transpose – and whether such cross-domain transposition is positive for the business reveals an implicit assumption regarding the indiscriminate nature of the family-to-business transposition process.

The multiplexity framework allows future research to examine more closely the mechanisms by which decision-makers in family businesses manage this family-to-business transposition process. Indeed, by conceptualizing the family and the business as separate domains, the multiplexity framework allows for the possibility of decision-makers in family businesses to selectively adjust the degree to which these two domains are coupled versus segregated. Specifically, they could ensure that the family and business domains are coupled with regards to family trust, family values, and family stewardship, thereby allowing these positive elements to be transposed from family to business. At the same time, they could enforce boundaries between the family domain and the business domain to prevent the transposition of nepotism and self-serving behaviour, such that the two domains remain segregated with regards to these negative elements. The bigger point here is that the degree to which the family and business domains are coupled versus segregated need not be – and probably are not – uniform with regards to all elements. Family business decision-makers can ensure that these two domains are coupled with regards to certain elements and segregated with regards to others, thereby ensuring that only the positive elements – such as trust, stewardship, and mutual support – are selectively transposed from the family domain into the business domain (Kammerlander et al., 2022).

More recent work has already begun to examine how family businesses manage the degree of segregation between family and business domains – and how they ensure that only positive elements are selectively transposed from family into business. For example, in a study of family business successions, Li and Piezunka (2020) theorize that the uniplex third – which they define as an actor who is connected to a dyadic multiplex relationship in only one domain – may act as a "domain manager" who legislates, for the multiplex relationship he or she is connected to, when the family and business domains should be coupled, when the two domains should be segregated, and what can or cannot be transposed across domains. We can hypothesize another: a family business may formalize a strict set of "family laws" or "family edicts" that stipulate how much the business domain should be coupled to the family domain and what can or cannot be transposed across domains.

Overall, the multiplexity framework enables scholars of family businesses to conceptualize family and business as separate domains whose degree of segregation can be selectively managed. Future research may thus fruitfully utilize this framework to gain more understanding of *how* family businesses manage the family-to-business transposition process and what they do to ensure that only positive elements from the family are brought into business interactions and management.

Conclusion

The purpose of this chapter is to present network multiplexity as a useful framework for future research on family businesses. Prior research has conceptualized family businesses as stewards (Arregle et al., 2007; Miller & Le Breton-Miller, 2005), as bundles of principal and agents (Morck et al., 2000; Bertrand & Schoar, 2006), and as organizational instantiations of socio-emotional wealth (Gomez-Mejia et al., 2007; Berrone et al., 2010; Rousseau et al., 2018). These perspectives have usefully and significant expanded our understandings of family businesses, yet they do not enable a theoretical conceptualization of how the structure of relationships and networks in the family domain impact the relational dynamics, interactions, and the performance of the business.

By conceptualizing family businesses as multiplex networks, scholars may fruitfully expand our understandings of how actors, relationships, and networks in the family – many of which are not visible if one looks at only the business domain – may yet affect innovation, relational conflict, and long-term performance in the business. This would enrich our understanding of the *family* domain underlying family businesses, thereby complementing findings from prior research regarding the business domain. We thus hope that this chapter would inspire future research to examine phenomena at the intersection of family businesses and social networks using the multiplexity framework.

References

Achmad, T., Rusmin, J. Neilson, & Tower, G. (2009). The iniquitous influence of family ownership structures on corporate governance. *Journal of Global Business Issues*, 3, 41–49.

Anderson, A. R., Jack, S. L., & Dodd, S. D. (2005). The role of family members in entrepreneurial networks: Beyond the boundaries of the family firm. *Family Business Review*, 18, 135–154.

Anderson, R. C., & Reeb, D. M. (2003). Founding-family ownership and firm performance: Evidence from S&P 500. *Journal of Finance*, 58, 1801–1328.

Aral, S., & Van Alstyne, M. (2011). The diversity-bandwidth trade-off. *American Journal of Sociology*, 117(1),90–171.

Arregle, J.L., Hitt., M.A., & Mari I. (2019). A missing link in family firms' internationalization research: Family structures. *Journal of International Business Studies*, 50, 809–825.

Arregle, J. L., Hitt, M. A., Sirmon, D. G., & Very, P. (2007). The development of organizational capital: Attributes of family firms. *Journal of Management Studies*, 44(1),73–95.

Arthurs, J. D., & Busenitz, L. (2003). The boundaries and limitations of agency theory and stewardship theory in the venture capitalist/entrepreneur relationship. *Entrepreneurship Theory and Practice*, 28(2),145–162.

Ashforth, B. E., & Johnson, S. A. (2002). Which hat to wear? The relative salience of multiple identities in organizational contexts. In M. A. Hogg & D. J. Terry (Eds.), *Social Identity Processes in Organizational Contexts*, 31–48. New York: Psychological Press.

Bennedsen, M., Nielson, K., Perez-Gonzalez, F., & Wolfenzon, D. (2007). Inside the family firm: The role of families in succession decisions and performance. *Quarterly Journal of Economics*, 122(2),647–691.

Berrone, P., Cruz, C., Gomez-Mejia, L. R., & Larraza-Kintana, M. (2010). Socioemotional wealth and corporate responses to institutional pressures: Do family-controlled firms pollute less? *Administrative Science Quarterly*, 55, 82–113.

Bertrand, M., & Schoar, A. (2006). The role of family in family firms. *Journal of Economic Perspectives*, 20(2),73–96.

Bertrand, M., Johnson, S., Samphantharak, K., & Schoar, A. (2008). Mixing family with business: A study of Thai business groups and the families behind them. *Journal of Financial Economics*, 88, 466–498.

Burt, R. (2001). Structural holes versus network closure as social capital. In N. Lin, K. S. Cook, & R. S. Burt (Eds.), *Social Capital: Theory and Research*, 31–56. New York: Aldine de Gruyter.

Cabrera-Suarez, K. (2005). Leadership transfer and the successor's development in the family firm. *Leadership Quarterly*, 16, 71–96.

Chrisman, J. J., Chua, J. H., & Sharma, P. (2005). Trends and directions in the development of strategic management theory of the family firm. *Entrepreneurship Theory and Practice*, 29, 555–575.

Chua, J. H., Chrisman, J. J., & Sharma, P. (1999). Defining the family business by behavior. *Entrepreneurship Theory and Practice*, 23(4),19–39.

Chua, J. H., Chrisman, J. J., & Bergiel, E. B. (2009). An agency theoretic analysis of the professionalized family firm. *Entrepreneurship Theory and Practice*, 33, 355–372.

Claessens, S., Djankov, S., Fan, J., & Lang, L. (2002). Disentangling the incentive and entrenchment effects of large shareholdings. *Journal of Finance*, 57(6),2741–2771.

Coleman, J. S. (1988). Social capital in the creation of human capital. *American Journal of Sociology*, 94, 95–120.

Coleman, J. S. (1990). *Foundations of Social Theory*. Cambridge, MA: Harvard University Press.

Davis, J. A. (1982). *The Influence of Life-stage on Father-son Work Relationships in Family Companies* (Doctoral dissertation). Cambridge: MA: Harvard University.

Davis. J. H., Schoorman, R., & Donaldson, L. (1997). Toward a stewardship theory of management. *Academy of Management Review*, 22(1),20–47.

Fernandez, R. M., & Gould, R. V. (1994). A dilemma of state power: Brokerage and influence in the national health policy domain. *American Journal of Sociology*, 99, 1455–1491.

Gersick, K. E., Davis, J. A., Hampton, M. M., & Lansberg, I. (1997). *Generation to Generation: Life Cycles of Family Business*. Boston: Harvard Business School Press.

Gomez-Mejia, L. R., Haynes, K., Nunez-Nickel, M., Jacobson, J. L., & Moyano-Fuentes, J. (2007). Socioemotional wealth and business risks in family-controlled firms: Evidence from Spanish olive oil mills. *Administrative Science Quarterly*, 52, 106–137.

Granovetter, M. (1985). Economic action and social structure: The problem of embeddedness. *American Journal of Sociology*, 91, 481–510.

Granovetter, M. (1995). Coase revisited: Business groups in the modern economy. *Industrial and Corporate Change*, 4, 93–140.

Handler, W. C. (1989). Methodological issues and considerations in studying family businesses. *Family Business Review*, 2, 257–276.

Handler, W. C. (1990). Succession in family firms: A mutual role adjustment between entrepreneur and next-generation family members. *Entrepreneurship Theory and Practice*, 15(1),37–51

Hardin, R. 2002. *Trust and Trustworthiness*. New York: Russell Sage.

Holt, D. T., Rutherford, M. W., & Kuratko, D. F. (2010). Advancing the field of family business research: Further testing the measurement properties of the F-PEC. *Family Business Review*, 23, 76–88.

Ingram, P., & Roberts, P. W. (2000). Friendships among competitors in the Sydney hotel industry. *American Journal of Sociology*, 106, 387–423.

James, H. S. (2006). *Family Capitalism*. Cambridge, MA: Belknap Press of Harvard University Press.

Jennings, J. E., Breitkreuz, R. S., & James, A. E. (2014). Theories from family science: A review and roadmap for family business research. In L. Melin, M. Nordqvist, & P. Sharma (Eds.), *The SAGE Handbook of Family Business*, 47–60. Thousand Oaks, CA: Sage.

Kammerlander, N., Dessi, C., Bird, M., Floris, M., & Murru, A. (2015). The impact of shared stories on family firm innovation: A multicase study. *Family Business Review*, 28(4),332–354.

Keister, L. A. (2001). Exchange structures in transition: Lending and trade relations in Chinese business groups. *American Sociological Review*, 66, 336–360.

Khanna, T., & Palepu, K. (1997). Why focused strategies may be wrong for emerging markets. *Harvard Business Review*, 75(4),41–51.

Khanna, T., & Palepu, K. (1999). Policy shocks, market intermediaries, and corporate strategy: The evolution of business groups in Chile and India. *Journal of Economics and Management Strategy*, 8, 271–310.

Khanna, T., & Palepu, K. (2000). The future of business groups in emerging markets: Long-run evidence from Chile. *Academy of Management Journal*, 43, 268–285.

Klein, S. B., Astrachan, J. H., & Smyrnios, K. X. (2005). The F-PEC scale of family influence: Construction, validation, and further implications for theory. *Entrepreneurship Theory and Practice*, 29, 321–339.

Krackhardt, D. (1999). The ties that torture: Simmelian tie analysis in organizations. *Research in the Sociology of Organizations*, 16, 183–210.

Kuwabara, K., Luo, J. & Sheldon, O. (2010). Multiplex exchange relations. *Advances in Group Processes*, 27, 239–268.

Landes, D. S. (2006). *Dynasties: Fortunes and Misfortunes of the World's Great Family Businesses*. New York: Viking.

Lansberg, I. (1999). *Succeeding Generations: Realizing the Dream of Families in Business*. Boston: Harvard Business School Press.

Lansberg, I., Perrow, E. L., &. Rogolsky, S. (1988). Family business as an emerging field. *Family Business Review*, 1, 1–8.

Le Breton-Miller, I., & Miller, D. (2009). Agency vs. stewardship in public family firms: A social embeddedness reconciliation. *Entrepreneurship Theory and Practice*, 33(6),1169–1191.

Le Breton-Miller, I., Miller, D., & Lester, R. H. (2011). Stewardship or agency? A social embeddedness reconciliation of conduct and performance in public family businesses. *Organization Science*, 22(3),704–721.

Li, J. B. (2021). On the problem of obligatory relationships. Working paper.

Li, J. B., & Piezunka, H. (2020). The uniplex third: Enabling single-domain role transitions in multiplex relationships. *Administrative Science Quarterly*, 65(2),314–358.

Lincoln, J. R., Gerlach, M. L., & Takahashi, P. (1992). Keiretsu networks in the Japanese economy. *American Sociological Review*, 57, 561–585.

Lubatkin, M. H., Schulze, W. S., & Ling, Y. (2005). The effects of parental altruism on the governance of family-managed firms. *Journal of Organizational Behavior*, 26, 313–330.

Lubatkin, M. H., Ling, Y., & Schulze, W. (2007). An organizational justice-based view of self-control and agency costs in family firms. *Journal of Management Studies*, 44(6),955–971.

Luo, X., & Chung, S. (2005). Keeping it all in the family: The role of particularistic relationships in business group performance during institutional transition. *Administrative Science Quarterly*, 50, 404–439.

Martinez, M. A., & Aldrich, H. (2011). Networking strategies for entrepreneurs: Balancing cohesion and diversity. *International Journal of Entrepreneurial Behaviour and Research*, 17(1),7–38.

Martinez, M. A., & Aldrich, H. (2014). Sociological theories applied to family businesses. In L. Melin, M. Nordqvist, & P. Sharma (Eds.), *The SAGE Handbook of Family Business*, 85–95. Thousand Oaks, CA: Sage.

Miller, D., & Le Breton-Miller, I. (2005). *Managing the Long Run: Lessons in Competitive Advantage from Great Family Businesses*. Boston: Harvard Business School Press.

Miller, D., & Le Breton-Miller, I. (2021). Family firms: A breed of extremes? *Entrepreneurship Theory and Practice*, 45(4), 663–681.

Miller, D., Le Breton-Miller, I., & Scholnick, B. (2008). Stewardship vs. stagnation in small family vs. non-family firms. *Journal of Management Studies*, 45(1),51–78.

Miller, D., Le Breton-Miller, I., & Lester, R. (2010). Family ownership and acquisition behavior in publicly traded companies. *Strategic Management Journal*, 31(1),201–223.

Miller, D., Le Breton-Miller, I., Lester, R. H., & Cannella, A. (2007). Are family firms really superior performers? *Journal of Corporate Finance*, 13, 829–858.

Moores, K. (2009). Paradigms and theory building in the domain of business families. *Family Business Review*, 22(2),167–180.

Morck, R. K., & Yeung, B. (2003). Agency problems in large family business groups. *Entrepreneurship Theory and Practice*, 27(4),367–382.

Morck, R. K., Stangeland, D., & Yeung, B. (2000). Inherited wealth, corporate control and economic growth. In R. K. Morck (Eds.), *Concentrated Corporate Ownership*, 319–369. Chicago: University of Chicago Press.

Obstfeld, D. (2005). Social networks, the *tertius iungens* orientation, and involvement in innovation. *Administrative Science Quarterly*, 50, 100–130.

Perez-Gonzalez, F. (2006). Inherited control and firm performance. *American Economic Review*, 96(5),1559–1588.

Pierce, J., Kostova, T., & Dirks, K. (2001). Toward a theory of psychological ownership in organizations. *Academy of Management Review*, 26(2),298–310.

Portes, A., & Sensenbrenner, J. (1993). Embeddedness and immigration: Notes on the social determinants of economic action. *American Journal of Sociology*, 98, 1320–1350.

Pyromalis, V. D., &. Vozikis, G. S. (2009). Mapping the successful succession process in family firms: Evidence from Greece. *International Entrepreneurship and Management Journal*, 5, 439–460.

Reagans, R., & McEvily, B. (2003). Network structure and knowledge transfer: The effects of cohesion and range. *Administrative Science Quarterly*, 48, 240–267.

Renzulli, L.A., Aldrich, H., & Moody, J. (2000). Family matters: Gender, networks, and entrepreneurial outcomes. *Social Forces*, 79(2), 523–546.

Rousseau, M. B., Kellermans, F., Zellweger, T, & Beck, T. E. (2018). Relationship conflict, family name congruence, and socioemotional wealth in family firms. *Family Business Review*, 31, 397–416.

Samila, S., Oettl, A., & Hasan, S. (2016). Helpful thirds and the durability of collaborative ties. *SSRN Electronic Journal*. Retrieved from < https://papers.ssrn.com/sol3/papers.cfm?abstract_id=2601338>.

Sequeira, J., Mueller, S. L. & McGee, J. E. (2007). The influence of social ties and self-efficacy in forming entrepreneurial intentions and motivating nascent behavior. *Journal of Developmental Entrepreneurship*, 12(3),275–293.

Sequeira, J.M., & Rasheed, A. A. (2006). Start-up and growth of immigrant small businesses: The impact of social and human capital. *Journal of Developmental Entrepreneurship*, 11(4),357–375.

Sharma, P., Chrisman, J. J., & Chua, J. H. (1996). *A Review and Annotated Bibliography of Family Business Studies*. London: Kluwer Academic.

Sharma, P., Chrisman, J. J., & Gersick, K. E. (2012). 25 years of *Family Business Review*: Reflections on the past and perspective for the future. *Family Business Review*, 25(1),5–15.

Simmel, G. (1950). *The Sociology of Georg Simmel*. New York: Free Press.

Sirmon, D. G., & Hitt, M. A. (2003). Managing resources: Linking unique resources, management, and wealth creation in family firms. *Entrepreneurship Theory and Practice*, 27, 339–358.

Sirmon, D. G., Arregle, J. L., Hitt, M. A., & Webb, J. W. (2008). The role of family influence in firms' strategic responses to threat of imitation. *Entrepreneurship Theory and Practice*, 32, 979–998.

Songini, L., & Gnan, L. (2009). Women, glass ceiling, and professionalization in family SMEs: A missed link. *Journal of Enterprising Culture*, 17, 497–525.

Stewart, A., & Hitt, M. A. (2012). Why can't a family business be more like a nonfamily business? Modes of professionalization in family firms. *Family Business Review*, 25(1),58–86.

Ter Wal, A. L. J., Alexy, O., Block, J., & Sandner, P. G. (2016). The best of both worlds: The benefits of open-specialized and closed-diverse syndication networks for new ventures' success. *Administrative Science Quarterly*, 61, 393–432.

Tortoriello, M., & Krackhardt, D. (2010). Activating cross-boundary knowledge: The role of Simmelian ties in the generation of innovations. *Academy of Management Journal*, 53, 167–181.

Uzzi, B. (1996). The sources and consequences of embeddedness for the economic performance of organizations: The network effect. *American Sociological Review*, 61, 674–698.

Van Geenhuizen, M., & Soetanto, D. P. (2012). Open innovation among university spin-off firms: What is in it for them, and what can cities do? *Innovation: The European Journal of Social Science Research*, 25(2),191–207.

Volpin, P. F. (2002). Governance with poor investor protection: Evidence from top executive turnover in Italy. *Journal of Financial Economics*, 64(1),61–90.

Ward, J. L. (2004). *Perpetuating the Family Business: 50 Lessons Learned from Long Lasting, Successful Families in Business*. Marietta, GA: Family Enterprise Publishers.

Wasserman, N. (2006). Stewards, agents, and the founder discount. *Academy of Management Journal*, 49(5),960–976.

Wiseman, R., & Gomez-Mejia, L. R. (1998). A behavioral model of managerial risk taking. *Academy of Management Review*, 23(1),133–153.

Yu, A., Lumpkin, G. T., Sorenson, R. L., & Brigham, K. H. (2012). The landscape of family business outcomes: A summary and numerical taxonomy of dependent variables. *Family Business Review*, 25(1): 33–57.

Zahra, S., & Sharma, P. (2004). Family business research: A strategic reflection. *Family Business Review*, 17, 331–346.

Zamudio, C., Anokhin, S., & Kellermanns, F.W. (2014). Network analysis: A concise review and suggestions for family business research. *Journal of Family Business Strategy*, 5, 63–71.

Zelizer, V. A. R. (2005). *The Purchase of Intimacy*. Princeton, NJ: Princeton University Press.

Zellweger, T. (2014). Toward a paradox perspective of family firms: The moderating role of collective mindfulness in controlling families. In L. Melin, M. Mordqvist, & P. Sharma (Eds.), *The SAGE Handbook of Family Business*: 461–466. Thousand Oaks, CA: Sage.

Heiko Kleve, Lina Nagel, Tom Rüsen, and Arist von Schlippe

3 Family, Organization, and Network: A New Approach to a Systems Theory of the Business Family

Abstract: The purpose of this chapter is to provide a systemic view of large business families. In particular, we offer a useful perspective on the specific challenges confronting this type of family business (business family 3.0). We distinguish between three types of business family, including nuclear business families (business family 1.0) and more formally organized business families (business family 2.0). Both these business family types must manage the contradicting logics of the family and the organization. Because business family 3.0 often comprises several hundred shareholders who own multiple business entities, it must address additional challenges. Our findings suggest that for such families to perform effectively they must establish both formal and informal networks among often distantly related shareholders who share only weak links. The leaders of business families 3.0 must initiate, shape, and maintain such social networks; accordingly, families of this type require additional and extended theoretical perspectives regarding family businesses. Drawing on prior work in sociology, we introduce a systems theory of large-scale business families to highlight the characteristics, particularities, and challenges in this type of extended business family.[1]

Keywords: business family, social networks, weak links, systems theory, extended business family

Introduction

Until the 1990s, it was widely understood in the social and economic sciences that the prevalence of family businesses in the economy is a transitional stage in the process of modernization (Chandler, 1990; Simmel, 1989 [1890]; Sombart, 2019 [1927]; Weber, 1993 [1920]). A new generation of researchers is much more reluctant to accept this definitive prediction. Family ownership and management persist

---

[1] The elaboration of this chapter is based on several papers in which we have already worked out the theory of the entrepreneurial family 3.0: in particular Kleve et al. (2020), Koellner et al. (2021), and Rüsen, Kleve & v. Schlippe (2021).

Heiko Kleve, Lina Nagel, Tom Rüsen, Arist von Schlippe, Witten/Herdecke University

https://doi.org/10.1515/9783110727968-003

under capitalism and in some of the most advanced capitalist economies. In Germany, for example, between 60% and 95% of all companies are family-owned and controlled.[2] These data demonstrate the enduring relevance of the business family and urge us to gain a better understanding of the business family and its internal processes (Kleve & Koellner, 2019).

Theoretical and empirical research abounds on an extensive range of subjects in the field of family sociology. Surprisingly, however, research on large business families is scarce. While earlier studies into family businesses recognized an integrated family and business system, later research has focused primarily on business and business-related theories (Combs et al., 2020). More recent research, therefore, has contributed substantially to understanding the impact of small nuclear business families by generating more knowledge about how business families shape the family business (Combs et al., 2020) and considering the impact of families' heterogeneity (Jaskiewicz & Dyer, 2017) and the reciprocal interplay of family and business (Jaskiewicz et al., 2017). It has furthermore contributed to an understanding of how family and business shape particular strategy processes in the business, such as digitalization strategies (Bretschneider et al., 2020), through the existence of the family and their role in the management of the family business.

Families in general, and business families in particular, have undergone significant changes in recent decades. Forms of communication and socialization have altered considerably and left an imprint on the organization of the family (Caspary, 2018). In addition, inheritance patterns have also evolved: traditionally, it was common for the family firm to pass to the eldest son, neglecting daughters completely. Recently, the distribution of shares to all possible inheritors – including daughters and adopted children – has become more common. This has dramatically increased the number of shareholders in family firms: as a result, large business families have emerged much faster than in former times, with several dozens – or even hundreds – of individual family shareholders. In these so-called dynasties, mutual interaction and cooperation cannot be assumed but must be created.

Moreover, we would like to deepen the analysis of temporal dimensions in the family business literature, with relevance beyond the development of the family firm and the business family over time, as analyzed by Gersick et al. (1997, 1999). We suggest an interpretation of the business family as a unique entity that bridges short-term individual – often acquisitive – activities with the kinds of long-term exchanges that are perceived as legitimate and even laudable (this idea is taken from Parry and Bloch [1989] who developed this perspective in another setting). In this way, we draw attention to the fact that business families tend to keep the business under family control over generations (Tucker, 2011).

---

2 For figures for Germany see, for example, v. Schlippe, Rüsen & Groth (2021).

Accordingly, the concept of the "duplicated family"[3] as the core of a systems theory of the business family was put forward by the Witten Institute for Family Business (WIFU) at the University of Witten/Herdecke (v. Schlippe et al., 2021; v. Schlippe & Frank, 2013). It emerged from a project in which 12 of the biggest German family businesses participated. The scholars met with the research partners from the business families to engage in a joint learning and development process based on a qualitative research design derived from the concept of systemic action research (Burns, 2007). The aim of the project was, firstly, to generate research results and, secondly, to look for feasible solutions to the problems facing the various business families. This was achieved by having members of these families – in particular representatives of the family committees – present their ideas and practices regarding family strategy to one another.

Based on a critical review of the Three Circles Model (Tagiuri & Davis, 1996) frequently cited in the literature on family business, the analysis led to an initial attempt to formulate a systems theory of the business family (v. Schlippe et al., 2021; v. Schlippe & Frank, 2013). The focus was shifted from a barely definable notion of the "overlapping" of family, business, and ownership (what precisely does "overlap" here?) to the concept of the "duplicated" family. It is not the case that three systems conflict with one another here; rather, the business family is constantly forced to oscillate between the logic of the "family" and that of the "business family", thereby having to cope with the paradoxes that accompany this process. Rather than a logic of overlapping, or the idea that either one domain or the other applies at any given time, this approach creates a perspective of simultaneity and "polycontexturality" (Knudsen & Vogd, 2014), in which both domains apply at the same time. In terms of family communication, the problem of differentiating between the logic of communication in the two domains of family and business consistently arises, together with managing the expectation structures that these two logics involve. In this connection, the family strategy must define clear "context markers" (Bateson, 1972, p. 289) that offer family members orientation. Any theory of family business, therefore, according to v. Schlippe et al. (2021), must primarily be a theory of the business family and address the challenges that confront this type of family. A further investigation of already existing implicit "context markers" in business families, and the ways of defining them through family strategy processes, is pending and would be of great scientific interest.

---

3 The concept of the "duplicated family" will be described in "II. Business Family 2.0 – The organization level and formally organized business families".

Methodological Background

The background to this chapter is the "Big Family Management" research project (Rüsen, Kleve, & v. Schlippe, 2021). Initiated in 2017, it is a collaboration between the authors and representatives of seven well-known large German business families, each comprising 80 to 650 family shareholders. The oldest family business was founded at the end of the 17th century, the youngest at the end of the 19th century. The seven companies operate in the chemical and pharmaceutical, consumer goods and plastics-processing industries. The research meetings took place over a whole day, twice a year, with two business family representatives and five researchers. On these days, preselected topics and concrete predetermined questions were addressed by the representatives together with the researchers. Over 50 hours' of interview data were collected including recordings from conversations, discussions, and workshops. Similarities and differences were discussed and observed, partly using the "reflecting team" systemic consultation tool (Andersen, 1991). The researchers made second-order observations (Luhmann, 2012) about distinctions concerning the family strategy operating in the business families. The business families were then confronted with these observations, enabling the researchers not just to reproduce the self-descriptions produced by the business families but, rather, to mark those aspects that the participants noticed and considered needed explanation from an observer's perspective. The goal of this process was for family representatives to realise that unconscious family strategies that are taken for granted are in fact contingent: they differ depending on the decisions made (Koellner et al., 2020).

Following the surveys, the researchers analyzed the content, framed it theoretically and made the results available to the participants. Thus, any initial observation was critically discussed with the business family representatives. The procedure follows an iterative research process, common in qualitative and ethnographic research (Spradley, 2005). More analyses are planned to gain further detailed knowledge.

In the dynastic families observed, consisting of up to a couple of hundred members and with extensive shareholder groups, at least three problems arise:
- First: The members barely know each other personally
- Second: Even shareholder meetings and family days have long been unable to include all those potentially involved
- Third: There is highly elaborate management of the complexity and diversity of individuals and opinions is required in providing relevant information to shareholders and in coordinating the latter's opinion-forming process and communication

We draw on the logic of action research and reconstructive social research, in which both practitioners and researchers are involved in a joint learning process: the research subject itself undergoes change during the research process, and learning experiences – consistently re-applied in practice – become the focus of reflection (Bohnsack, 2000; Burns, 2007). The research questions were selected jointly and were thus important for both the researchers and the family members. The following issues were specifically addressed:

- How do numerically large business families organize their family management?
- How do they organize their communication to ensure both formal and informal interaction?
- What problems arise in terms of organization and communication in these families and what solution strategies are feasible?

Development and Complexity Stages Beyond Small Nuclear Families

Even in the initial phases of the new project, it has become clear that the concept of the duplicated family only partially describes large business families, which may consist of several hundred members. Of course, they also must permanently balance the logic of a "classic" family with that of an organized business family, but they are called upon to do more than this. They must provide a third function: aside from being a family and a formally organized business family they also become a dynastic family network (see also Jaffe & Lane, 2004, p. 82; Bergfeld & Weber, 2011). A business family can only reach this dynastic stage of development with an advanced degree of organization and structure (Jaffe & Lane, 2004). This type of family thus differs considerably from smaller business families.

Small or nuclear families regard themselves as the primary socialization context for individuals, integrating their members holistically and, consequently, focused on satisfying the fundamental biopsychosocial needs of their members. In addition, they are called upon as business families to gradually organize themselves formally in order to cope with the growing complexity of the business and family – setting up committees, implementing family strategy processes and structuring their decisions relating to both the family and the business based on family governance concepts.

However, neither the classic family concept nor the model of the formally organized business family is capable of addressing the problem of informal cohesion and internal family cooperation in large, dynastic family corporations. For this purpose, an additional social mechanism is required that becomes established beyond bond-oriented family relations and beyond the professional relations found in organized business families. This mechanism, or form of social relationship, is referred to here as a network of unspecific give-and-take (Axelrod, 1984). We define this type of family network as being based on the values shared by the members of the owner families and an underlying motivation of wanting to belong to a transgenerational community in which responsibility is shared and in which rules limiting individual freedom are observed.

Our research aims to contribute to business family research by developing a systems theory of the business family that can understand the different development and complexity stages of the business family beyond the level of small nuclear families (Kushins, E. R. & Behounek, E., 2020). These three development and complexity stages – also called the business family types – are the business family as a small and nuclear family (business family 1.0), the business family as a formal organization (business family 2.0) and the business family as a network (business family 3.0). The three different stages require the business families in question to position themselves differently in relation to the business – working out this positioning towards the business is something that Frank et al. consider necessary in order to avoid the risk of being a burden rather than a success factor in the business (2019, p. 264f).

In the following, we will reflect on the three types from the perspective of systems theory, showing that all three social forms in question might be described as solutions to specific inter-relationship proms.

Business Family 1.0 – The Family Level and Nuclear Families as Business Families

Small and nuclear families have two to three generations. They are characterized by an atypical tendency in our functionally differentiated modern society to bind their members holistically and integrate them biopsychosocially (e.g., Fuchs, 1999; Luhmann, 1990; Simon, 2000). As a result, families are capable of solving a social problem that can be defined as an anthropological constant of human existence: the fact that the socialization of a human being (especially in the early years) requires social bonds which ideally satisfy all of their biological, mental, and social needs (cf., e.g., Grossmann & Grossmann, 1995; v. Sydow, 2002). The desire to belong to a group of people and have social bonds is among the most fundamental human needs (Baumeister & Leary, 1995). The family guarantees, or at least ought to guarantee, the satisfaction of these needs in accordance with social expectations, as demonstrated by public outrage over child welfare reports. This relational context is what we call business family 1.0.

Systems theory describes the communication medium of this social form as love (Luhmann, 1998). From a sociological perspective, we do not look at the physical and psychological inner world but rather at the relationship. Therefore, we do not understand love as a feeling but, rather, as a particular way in which people relate to each other and shape their interactions. The communication medium of love is what characterises family communication. It goes hand-in-hand with the fact that the respective world perceptions of family members are closely linked, their lifestyles aligned with one another. Other family members become a crucial contextual factor of one's own life. Love, furthermore, requires positive reciprocity, which is the reason why family relationships develop and manifest themselves holistically, based on declarations of love. This holistic aspect is shown in family members seeing each other in their entirety, not just in their role as an employee, for example, as would be the case in the organizational context of a non-family business. Facts and relationship aspects tend to be closely linked and, therefore, almost all communication topics can easily be emotionally or affectively charged and liable to escalate. In this context, Luhmann talks of "full inclusion" – the tendency of a family to exaggerate communication and expand it to "everything". He writes, "Walking, for example . . . when it happens in the home, is almost inevitably observed as communication and therefore becomes – within the network of the observation of observations – communication"[4] (Luhmann, 1990, p. 205). We can say that families are characterized by a particular kind of reciprocity, a give-and-take that binds the ones to whom life is given (the children) to those by whom life is given (the parents, grandparents, etc.). As a result, and since infants and children depend on their parents to provide and care for them, the human conscience develops as a kind of family conscience that rewards any actions that confirm the membership of the primary family group with positive feelings, while actions which could damage this membership are associated with negative and/or guilty feelings (Hondrich, 2004).

While all these aspects apply to any family type, an additional key factor in business families increases the complexity of their lives: the co-evolution and structural coupling (Wimmer et al., 2018, p. 18f; Simon et al., 2015, p. 7f) of the family and the business. The family business property is, firstly, tied into the family members' socialization and identity-building in everyday life. Secondly, there is a transgenerational component, connected to the history and the future of the family. This co-evolution of the family and business is what distinguishes the family business from other types of businesses and families. Business families become more business-like, and family businesses become more family-like – both are significantly shaped by this mutual influence (Simon, 1999, 2012; Wimmer et al., 2018). Regarding communication, business families are constantly confronted with the intermingling of bond-oriented and decision-making communication (cf. v. Schlippe et al., 2021).

When the business family 1.0 (Figure 3.1) becomes larger, due to the transgenerational handover of the business over time, tasks and succession-planning often start to require more regulation (Rüsen, Groth, & v. Schlippe, 2021; Groth et al., 2020) and slowly lead to the establishment of, first, governance structures and, ideally, family strategy (Rüsen & Löhde, 2021). When family businesses are in the third or fourth generation, if not before, and consist of several nuclear families who own the company, it

---

4 Translated from German by the authors.

BF 1.0 Family/ Business Family	Business Family 1.0 • Usually 1st to 3rd generation • Nuclear families with a manageable number of family members from one family or a few nuclear families • Reciprocal attachment-related give-and-take • Prone to conflicts due to contradicting communication logics • Learn to be a business family, differentiate between, and deal with the two logics • Communication medium: love (Luhmann, 1998)

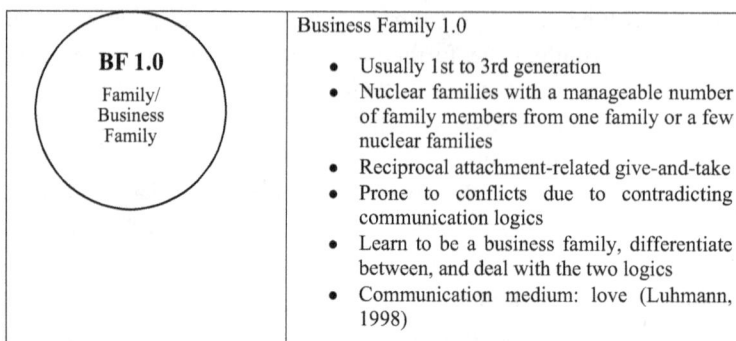

Figure 3.1: Business family 1.0.

becomes necessary for business-related communication and family cohesion to be managed explicitly (Koeberle-Schmid et al., 2018; Kormann, 2018; v. Schlippe et al., 2021).

Business Family 2.0 – The Organizational Level and Formally Organized Business Families

While business families 1.0 must learn to differentiate between the family and the business logic, business families 2.0 (Figure 3.2) have already reached this level of professionalism. They are able to adopt the qualities of formal organizations to become a specific form of family organization (cf., e.g., v. Schlippe et al., 2021; Simon, Wimmer, & Groth, 2005; Wimmer et al., 2018). They develop what Frank et al. (2019; 2010) term the "enterpriseness" of business families, in which they develop structures "based on the structural coupling with the business (or businesses) and the family" and "accept business-related rules and expectations as parts of their family life or even acknowledging their identity-generating value" (2019, p. 264).

From a systemic perspective, formal organizations solve problems differently from families: instead of operating in a bond-oriented way, they depend on factual decisions and only refer to individuals regarding their role in the business context (partial inclusion). Therefore, they include people in their communication based on factual elements, competence, performance, position, and division of labour (Luhmann, 2018). In order to become formally organized, business families, therefore, have to be able to follow what the business family 1.0 had to establish: a decision-making logic. They must be able to handle family relationships as functional and factual and address only the job-related parts and roles of a person. This can be a huge challenge for the business family because their actions (e.g., the allocation or exclusion of positions) are often understood in the family logic. As von Schlippe, Rüsen, and Groth (2021) explain:

In business families [. . .] it is not possible to separate work and family in the same way as in other families: their members are required to perform additional functions. As such, there is some competition between the family and the business family: the expectations that the family as a family has towards its members and the expectations the business family has may differ widely. It is as if the presence of the business forces the family to duplicate itself, being a private, emotionally attached family on the one hand, yet also being a well-structured business family – in both cases it is family, but both represent very different social systems. The family and the business family are one and the same, yet distinct – a paradoxical answer to the paradoxical requirements of the family business.

Business families, furthermore, (at least from a legal point of view) only include family members who have ownership interests in the business. The business family, therefore, must put in place committees, functions, and positions. In this process, they often develop a family strategy and governance which structures the business family strategically, oriented to the future (Rüsen & Löhde, 2021).

In the long-term, this kind of professionalization and decision-making process can lead to an increasing number of less active or even completely distinterested family shareholders. The latter may still observe the development of the business, have expectations regarding information and participation, contribute to elections and participate in meetings of the business family or shareholders; besides this, they remain passive. As the number of owners expands, the way in which these numerous shareholders engage with the business becomes more crucial, in other words, how this specific form of social capital is secured as a central aspect of the resource of familiness (Frank, Lueger, Nosé, & Suchy, 2010; Weismeier-Sammer, Frank, & v. Schlippe, 2013). This is a crucial point since it makes a difference whether the business owners solely maintain their profit orientation or whether there is a significant focus on passing the business to the next generation. In family businesses this can lead to conflicts.

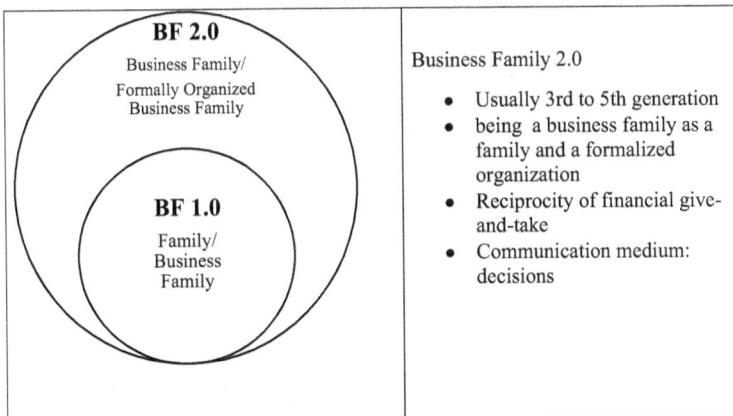

Figure 3.2: Business family 2.0.

With the growth of the business, family management becomes more complex and the demands on those in charge increase (Astrachan & Pieper, 2011; Horváth, Kirchdörfer, & v. Schlippe, 2015; Rüsen, 2020). As a result, it becomes increasingly difficult to encourage and maintain active involvement in family matters, cooperation within the family and secure it in the long run. This leads to the main challenge often facing large business families with several hundred family shareholders: internal, especially informal, relations and collaborations cannot be taken for granted and must be actively encouraged and established. This is where a third social form emerges as a solution for the problems just described: the family network.

Business Family 3.0 – The Network Level and Large Dynastic Business Families

When the business family 2.0 reaches a fifth, sixth or seventh generation, if it is shaped by egalitarian inheritance relationships, the number of family shareholders and of nuclear families within the business family often rises. The family shareholder group of fifty or more consists of a number of nuclear families that, as a whole, make up the business family (Figure 3.3). With the number of members, the complexity grows.[5] Jaffe describes the characteristics of the development of the first to fourth generations. He observes that "[g]enerative families evolve into complex extended families, moving from a single wealth-creator couple to successors often loosely connected to each other, their legacy, and their shared business and financial interests" (2020, p. 61) and that the transition to an extended family goes hand-in-hand with the arrival of new complexities (Jaffe, 2020, p. 69). The main challenge for these business families is to retain the interest of the family members in the business affairs and possibly strengthen it. Operating with the organizational principles just described is not sufficient for the network family. They must – in addition – deal with the challenges that go along with being organized as a network. The network level business family is the most differentiated type; it includes all the challenges and specifics of the other business family types (see Jaffe, 2020, p. 81) and make these visible. Through family governance, it is possible to stimulate, create and maintain community-oriented network relationships and, thus, establish a lived culture of a social community.

The main challenge facing the business family 3.0 is less about developing formal structures but rather about establishing a "shared extended family identity" (see Jaffe, 2020, p. 69) and a culture that ensures the emotional attachment between the members and towards the business (Koellner, 2022). Without this attachment,

---

5 For a practical guide about dynamics in growing business families, see Kleve (2020).

the focus on handing the business over to future generations cannot usually be maintained:

> If they succeed, the extended family becomes a dynastic family with a shared heritage but increasingly loose connection and identification as a family. The inheritors may take steps to build shared identity, connection, and partnership capability. When they do, they become more than just wealthy dynasties; they become generative families. (Jaffe, 2020, p. 61f)

The network structures are based on the reciprocity of a financial and functional "give-and-take". This basic principle develops rather informally: it can be stimulated and initiated through formal organization but, to be ensured in the long-term, informality needs to be increased. This may be achieved by increasing the chances for contact and personal exchange. Many very large family firms support these networks by planning family-based activities or regional meetings between business family members who live far away from one another, including young family members from an early age.

With this network approach, we draw attention to the wider context and the embeddedness of entrepreneurship and the business family, as several authors have suggested (Basco, 2017; Granovetter, 1985; Hann & Hart, 2009; Koellner, 2011; Polanyi, 2001; Welter, 2011; Wright et al., 2014). Based on our findings, we suggest the inclusion of three dimensions of embeddedness in relation to the business family:

1. A setting composed of smaller nuclear families that are not completely part of the business family
2. Wider social relationships with friends, colleagues, and acquaintances
3. Society at large

In the following sections, we will summarize the main characteristics of large dynastic business families (Figure 3.3).

The Threefold Task of the Business Family 3.0

Summarizing our arguments so far, the business family 1.0 faces the challenge of becoming a business family and managing the often-contradictory logics of the business (decision logic) and the family (attachment logic). The business family 2.0 faces the challenge of establishing formal structures while managing the challenges of the "duplicated family" at the same time. The task of the business family 3.0 goes beyond that: they, in a way, have to triple themselves by remaining a family, and also becoming a formally organized business family and a dynastic family network (see Bergfeld & Weber, 2011; Jaffe & Lane, 2004). At the same time, they must establish a culture that keeps the family members identified with the business.

The network logic brings a whole new element to the business family that needs to be handled: "On the one hand there is the nuclear family, which is not organized very differently from most other families, and on the other hand there is the network of cousins (sometimes with very distant relationships), parents, grandparents, uncles, great aunts etc. that derives from joint ownership and is likewise known as "family"[6] (Simon, 2012, p. 72). Jaffe and Lane (2004, p. 82) use similar words when they talk about 'dynastic families': "We feel it is an appropriate term for a network of families who are joined as an economic unit". They particularly point out that this type of network does not (or at least not only) involve individuals organizing themselves; it also includes a number of independent business families that are often barely connected to the business beyond their name.

Such networks can be understood as a relationship context that is realized beyond the relationship of the nuclear family and its integration into the organization (Kleve, 2017a, 2017b). Network relationships solve the problem of social integration where interpersonal social relationships can be regulated neither through close kinship ties nor through formal organizational contexts. Friendships, acquaintances, and neighbourhood relationships fall into this category. Therefore, we suggest describing the social relations between remotely related members of very large business families (from approx. 80 to 100 members upwards, often many more) as social network relationships. We make this the starting point for a systems theory of large dynastic business families and propose the following thesis: The better these families can stimulate and permanently stabilise the network, the more sustainable the family cohesion and intra-family cooperation will be.

Compensation Logics in Social Systems

One elementary quality of social behaviour is balancing feelings of obligation (Homans, 1961; Stegbauer, 2011). According to Gouldner, social structures are more likely to be stable where they reciprocate as functional exchange relationships (Gouldner, 1959; Gouldner 1960; Uehara, 1995). This reciprocity (Boszormenyi-Nagy & Spark, 1973; Chrisman, Chua, & Sharma, 2005, p. 569) is closely linked to the need for justice. Montada questions when we are even with someone and how there can ever be compensation given what our ancestors have sacrificed and achieved (2003). A closer look at the difference between types of compensation logic swiftly reveals that these differ considerably between family, organization, and network.

– In a family, it is likely that compensatory acts are long-term and, often, out of proportion to the original effort. For example, take a single mother who has gone to great lengths to enable her daughter to study at university: the mother

---

6 This quote is translated from German by the authors.

will experience a sense of just compensation when the daughter dedicates her master's thesis to her, thanking her with a symbolic gift or a personal speech. Years of hard work may be compensated by just a "thank you" (Stierlin, 2005). Feeling compensated may not always be the case though. Differences between "internal balance sheets" within the family can result in severe conflict and dispute, because ideas about compensatory acts and the expectations of compensation that accompany them can vary considerably, even within families (Stierlin, 1997; Boszormenyi-Nagy & Spark, 1973). They may be connected to specific "psychological contracts", and the expectations they involve can be interpreted very differently (v. Schlippe & Hülsbeck, 2016).

– The expectations of compensation in organizations are entirely different. The give-and-take balance here is embedded in contractual law, usually expressed in financial terms – on a shorter-term basis through remuneration, payment, or salary and in the medium-term through career opportunities. In both families and businesses, the expectation of compensation derives from the membership of a system. In networks, a different situation applies: here membership only comes about through the dynamic of give-and-take.

– Network relations occur when reciprocity of unspecific give-and-take develops between at least two individuals. The attribute "unspecific" clearly indicates that this is not a formalized relationship in which the form of the give-and-take balance is to be legally codified. The only thing clear in network relations is that those who have received something are faced with the expectation – and have the expectation themselves, according to the concept of the so-called "expectation of expectations" (Luhmann, 1995, p. 304f) – that they are to give something back in due course: "The anticipation of expectations induces all participants to take up orientations that reciprocally overlap in time and are, in this sense structural" (Luhmann, 1995, p. 305). The equilibrium between "give-and-take" is subject to the views of the other people involved: in dynastic families, this may even involve transgenerational expectations. At a certain point in time, and also from an objective point of view, the giving back must be regarded as appropriate so that it can be offset as part of the give-and-take within the network context as a whole. Thus, in networks in particular, social, and interpersonal actions can simultaneously be regarded as having an economic value (Stierlin, 1997). As such, action is a give-and-take exchange – a giving and a giving back, a process of reciprocity (Hondrich, 2001, 2004; Simon & C/O/N/E/C/T/A, 1998; Stegbauer, 2011). In dynastic families, the transfer of often valuable shares to the next generation implicitly involves a promise to preserve these company assets, increase their value and pass them on, in turn, to the subsequent generation. As long as this chain of expectation is reproduced and the offspring of the benefitting family behave according to expectations, the network can be said to retain its equilibrium.

Such reciprocal processes create obligations and loyalties that go beyond close family relations and beyond the positions, functions and expectations associated with an organization. However, these obligations and loyalties can only apply permanently and be implemented on a long-term basis if the balance between give-and-take is not complete from the perspective of those involved: it is the difference between give-and-take that secures the bond. If a person receives something, they give slightly more back than they received; in this way, new expectations of giving back develop: "If someone does us a favor, we feel obliged to return it. Generally speaking, the return favor is greater than the original favor" (Werth & Mayer, 2008, p. 319, the so-called "tit for tat plus one"). However, unlike in economically or legally regulated formal relationships within organizations, the reciprocity in network relations does not underlie any objective criteria. The give-and-take of the individuals involved will be defined by, and depend on, the subjective balance sheet systems and the set of values that applies within the family network (see Simon et al., 1998; Stierlin, 1997).

Finally, another distinction is important in understanding network relations, namely the difference between direct and generalized reciprocity (Stegbauer, 2011). Direct reciprocity is about the give-and-take between two people, while generalized reciprocity refers to a give-and-take that can be attributed to the group or system to which the individuals involved belong. In the context of the latter, a party who receives something from the business family will be obliged to give back to the business family as a network system.

The Family Network as a Stable Structure Over Time

The family network includes many nuclear families and their members; their membership is not formalized, however, but rather stimulated and realized by an ongoing process of give-and-take. Such family networks are, therefore, characterized by a structure of reciprocity based on unspecific, informal give-and-take. This form of give-and-take can be found in the economic system as well but there it concerns the exchange of goods or services for money, while in the business family 3.0 – and in social network systems in general – it is rather about unspecific communication. Something is taken from the participants without any rules about when and how they will receive anything back. The only certainty is that something must be given back – whenever and whatever that might be. Furthermore, what is given back must be judged as appropriate by the recipient.

As such, social networks generate a structure that follows the expectation that taking goes alongside giving at a given time. This expectation applies to all the network participants. Luhmann (1997, p. 651) describes such reciprocal give-and-take phenomena in the context of pre-modern tribal societies:

Every gift creates a temporarily imbalanced situation. [. . .] And since society has no beginning and no end but is communicated in a recursive network of memories and expectations,
there is strictly speaking no such thing as a 'voluntary' service that is not in itself a service in
return, itself creating an obligation to provide a return service[7] (Luhmann, 1997, p. 651f).

Finally, it is interesting to look at the question of how much time can elapse between the giving and taking before the expectation of reciprocity becomes overdue.
In his analysis of human cooperation, Axelrod (1984) explains the phenomenon of
the so-called "robustness of reciprocity": network relations are more robust in
terms of their reciprocity when the "shadow of the future" is substantial, that is,
when the likelihood of the individuals meeting again is high enough that they are
interested in future interaction (Axelrod, 1984). Precisely this requirement applies
in business families, as membership is based on kinship and shared ownership.
Time provides a particular context in business families: the network preserves past
traditions, committing its members to what has been given by their ancestors, and
is also an innovating force, focused towards future family shareholders by defining
current corporate ownership as a loan on trust that is also to be made available to
future generations.

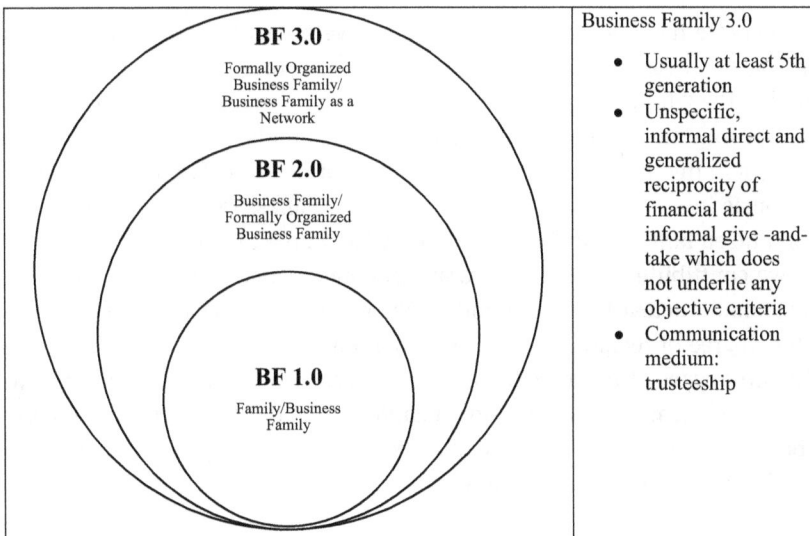

BF 3.0

Formally Organized
Business Family/
Business Family as a
Network

BF 2.0

Business Family/
Formally Organized
Business Family

BF 1.0

Family/Business
Family

Business Family 3.0

- Usually at least 5th
  generation
- Unspecific,
  informal direct and
  generalized
  reciprocity of
  financial and
  informal give -and-
  take which does
  not underlie any
  objective criteria
- Communication
  medium:
  trusteeship

Figure 3.3: Business family 3.0.

---

7 This quote is translated from German by the authors. For the English version see Luhmann, 2012.

While the primary contribution of this paper is a framework to guide future research on business families on a network level, the specifics, requirements, and challenges that apply here may be generalized to other family types. They apply whenever large families stay in touch over generations due to kinship and a joint venture. This joint venture is not necessarily business-related as in business families. For example, Scottish and Irish clans with their – mostly – distantly related family members are connected through common surnames, ancestry, and heritage (Nicholls, 2003; Way, 1995). Their joint venture can be maintained by preserving their identity, culture, and history by formal representations of identity and informal referential networks in business, politics, and other areas of elite society. Another example is found in noble families, in which the family members may no longer have any political power but still stay connected through common values, surnames, identity, or property. The decisive factor is that a unifying, exclusive joint venture exists that outsiders cannot join as they do not have kinship.

Conclusion

In this chapter, we have demonstrated that the development of theory relating to large, dynastic business families is still developing. Our insights show that the existing model of the "duplicated business family" can be extended in the case of dynastic families to a model of the triplicated business family. By introducing three different stages in the development and complexity of business families – business family 1.0 consisting of small and nuclear families, business family 2.0 comprising formally organized families, and business family 3.0 where the family operates as a network – we contribute to a business family systems theory that goes beyond understanding small nuclear business families. We set out the typical number of generations, the degree of reciprocity, and the communication medium that constitute each of the three types of business family. By observing the network perspective to supplement the systemic family and organizational theory of the business family, we have been able to explain and describe observations and dynamics specific to each of the three types of business family.

References

Andersen, T. (Ed.). (1991). *The Reflecting Team: Dialogues and Dialogues about the Dialogues.* New York: Norton.

Astrachan, J. H., & Pieper, T. M. (2011). Developing responsible owners in family business. In EQUA-Stiftung (Ed.), *Gesellschafterkompetenz – Die Verantwortung der Eigentümer von Familienunternehmen* (pp. 102–110). Bonn: Unternehmer Medien.

Axelrod, R. (1984). *The Evolution of Cooperation*. New York: Basic Books.

Basco, R. (2017). Epilogue: Multiple embeddedness contexts for entrepreneurship. In M. Ramirez-Pasillas, E. Brundin, & M. Markowska (Eds.) *Contextualizing Entrepreneurship in Developing and Emerging Economies* (pp. 329–336). London: Edward Edgar.

Bateson, G. (1972). *Steps to an Ecology of Mind*. Chicago: University of Chicago Press.

Baumeister, R. F., & Leary, M. R. (1995). The need to belong: Desire for interpersonal attachments as a fundamental human motivation. *Psychological Bulletin*, 117(3), 497–529.

Bergfeld, M. M. H., & Weber, F. M. (2011). Dynasties of innovation: Highly performing German family firms and the owners' role for innovation. *International Journal of Entrepreneurship and Innovation Management*, 13(1), 80–94.

Bohnsack, R. (2000). *Rekonstruktive Sozialforschung. Einführung in Methodologie und Praxis qualitativer Forschung (4th ed.)*. Opladen: Leske & Budrich.

Boszormenyi-Nagy, J., & Spark, G. (1973). *Invisible Loyalties: Reciprocity in Intergenerational Family Therapy*. New York: Harper & Row.

Bretschneider, U., Heider, A. K., Rüsen, T. A., & Hülsbeck, M. (2020). *Digitalisation Strategies in Family Business: On Specific Digitalisation Approaches for Business Families and Family Businesses*. WIFU Practical Guide.

Burns, D. (2007). *Systemic Action Research: A Strategy for Whole System Change*. Bristol: Policy Press.

Caspary, S. (2018). Das Familienunternehmen als Sozialisationskontext für Unternehmerkinder. Wiesbaden: Springer.

Chandler, A. D. (1990). Scale and Scope: The Dynamics of Industrial Capitalism. Cambridge, MA: Harvard University Press.

Chrisman, J. J., Chua, J. H., & Sharma, P. (2005). Trends and Directions in the Development of a Strategic Management Theory of the Family Firm. Entrepreneurship Theory and Practice, 29(5), 555–575.

Combs, J. G., Shanine, K. K., Burrows, S., Allen, J. S., & Pounds, T. W. (2020). What do we know about business families? Setting the stage for leveraging family science theories. *Family Business Review*, 33(1), 38–63.

Frank, H., Lueger, M., Nosé, L., & Suchy, D. (2010). The concept of 'familiness': Literature review and systems theory-based reflections. *Journal of Family Business Strategy*, 1(3), 119–130.

Frank, H., Suess-reyes, J., Fuetsch, E., & Kessler, A. (2019). Introducing the enterpriseness of business families: A research agenda. In E. Memili & C. Dibrell (Eds.), *The Palgrave Handbook of Heterogeneity among Family Firms* (pp. 263–296). Cham: Palgrave Macmillan.

Fuchs, P. (1999). *Liebe, Sex und Solche Sachen. Zur Konstruktion moderner Intimsysteme.* Konstanz: UVK.

Gersick, K., Davis, J., McCollom Hampton, M., & Lansberg, I. (1997). *Generation to Generation: Life Cycles of the Family Business*. Boston, MA: Harvard University Press.

Gersick, K., Lansberg, I., Desjardins, M., & Dunn, B. (1999). Stages and transitions: Managing change in the family business. *Family Business Review*, 12(4), 287–297.

Gimeno, A., Baulenas, G., & Coma-Cross, J. (2010). *Family business models – Practical solutions for the family business*. London, New York: Palgrave MacMillan.

Gouldner, A. W. (1959). Reciprocity and Autonomy in Functional Theory. Symposium on Sociological Theory.

Gouldner, A. W. (1960). The norm of reciprocity: A preliminary statement. *American Sociological Review*, 25(2), 161–178.

Granovetter, M. (1985). Economic action and social structures: The problem of embeddedness. *American Journal of Sociology*, 91, 481–510.

Grossmann, K. E., & Grossmann, K. (1995). Frühkindliche Bindung und Entwicklung individueller Psychodynamik über den Lebenslauf. *Familiendynamik*, 20(2), 171–192.

Groth, T., Rüsen, T. A., & Schlippe, A. v. (2020). *Securing Succession in a Family Business Across Generations. How succession May be Organised in Businesses and among Shareholders (2nd rev.)*. WIFU Practical Guide.

Hann, C. M., & Hart, K. (Eds). (2009). *Market and Society: The Great Transformation Today*. Cambridge: Cambridge University Press.

Homans, G. C. (1961). *Its* Elementary Forms. Harcourt: Brace & World.

Hondrich, K.-O. (2001). *Der Neue Mensch*. Frankfurt: Suhrkamp.

Hondrich, K.-O. (2004). *Liebe in Zeiten der Weltgesellschaft*. Frankfurt: Suhrkamp.

Horváth, P., Kirchdörfer, R., & Schlippe, A. v. (2015). Gesellschafterkompetenz – der gut informierte Gesellschafter. *Familienunternehmen und Stiftungen*, 4(1), 3–6.

Jaffe, D. T. (2020). The first four generations. In D. T. Jaffe (Ed.). *Borrowed from Your Grandchildren* (pp. 61–85). New Jersey: Wiley & Sons.

Jaffe, D. T., & Lane, S. H. (2004). Sustaining a family dynasty: Key issues facing complex multigenerational business- and investment-owning families. *Family Business Review*, 17(1), 81–98.

Jaskiewicz, P., Combs, J. G., Shanine, K. K., & Kacmar, K. M. (2017). Introducing the family: A review of family science with implicatImanagment research. *Academy of Management Annals*, 11(1), 309–341.

Jaskiewicz, P., & Dyer, W. G. (2017). Addressing the elephant in the room: disentangling family heterogeneity to advance family business research. *Family Business Review*, 30(2), 111–118.

Kleve, H. (2017a). Die Wechselseitigkeit von Geben und Nehmen. Netzwerke als soziale Systeme. *Systhema*, 31(2), 110–121.

Kleve, H. (2017b). Reziprozität ermöglichen. Vernetzung aus systemtheoretischer Perspektive. *Kontext*, 48(4), 353–367.

Kleve, H. (2020). The dynamics in growing business families. The power of elementary system rules for cohesion and communication. WIFU Practical Guide.

Kleve, H., & Koellner, T. (Eds.). (2019). *Die Soziologie der Unternehmerfamilie: Grundlagen, Entwicklungslinien, Perspektiven*. Wiesbaden: Springer VS.

Kleve, H., Koellner, T., von Schlippe, A., & Rüsen, T. (2020). The business family 3.0: Dynastic business families as families, organizations and networks – Outline of a theory extension. *Sysetems Research and Behavioral Science*, 1–11.

Knudsen, M., & Vogd, W. (2014). Introduction: Health care, systems theory and polycontexturality. In Knudsen, M., & Vogd, W. (Eds.), *Systems Theory and the Sociology of Health and Illness* (pp. 1–22). London: Routledge.

Koeberle-Schmid, A., Fahrion, H.-J., & Witt, P. (2018). Family Business Governance als Erfolgsfaktor von Familienunternehmen. In A. Koeberle-Schmid, H.-J. Fahrion, & P. Witt (Eds.), *Family Business Governance – Erfolgreiche Führung von Familienunternehmen*, 3rd ed. (pp. 23–42). Berlin: Erich Schmidt.

Koellner, T. (2011). Built with Gold or Tears? Moral Discourses on Church Construction and the Role of Entrepreneurial Donations. In J. Zigon (ed.), *Multiple Moralities and Religions in Post-Soviet Russia*, 191–213. New York: Berghahn Books.

Koellner, T. 2022 (forthcoming). *Family Firms and Business Families in Cross-Cultural Perspective: Bringing Anthropology Back In*. New York: Palgrave Macmillan.

Koellner, T., Simons, F., Kleve, H., von Schlippe, A., & Rüsen, T. A. (2020). Vermögensmanagement in großen Unternehmerfamilien: Zwischen individuellem Anspruch und kollektiver Verantwortung. *ZfKE – Zeitschrift Für KMU Und Entrepreneurship*, 68(3–4), 191–217.

Kormann, H. (2018). *Zusammenhalt der Unternehmerfamilie: Verträge, Vermögensmanagement, Kommunikation (2nd revision)*. Berlin: Springer.

Kushins, E. R. & Behounek, E. (2020). Using Sociological Theory to Problematize Family Business Research. *Journal of Family Business Strategy*, 11 (1).

Luhmann, N. (1990). *Sozialsystem Familie. In Soziologische Aufklärung 5. Konstruktivistische Perspektiven*. Opladen: Westdeutscher Verlag.

Luhmann, N. (1995). *Social Systems*. Stanford: Stanford University Press.

Luhmann, N. (1997): *Die Gesellschaft der Gesellschaft*. 2 Volumes. Frankfurt: Suhrkamp.

Luhmann, N. (1998). *Love as Passion. The Codification of Intimacy*. Stanford: Stanford University Press.

Luhmann, N. (2012): *Theory of Society*. 2 Volumes. Stanford: Stanford University Press.

Luhmann, N. (2018). *Organization and Decision*. Cambridge: Cambridge University Press.

Montada, L. (2003). Justice, equity, and fairness in human relations. In Millon, T. J., & Lerner, M. (Eds.), *Handbook of Psychology, Vol. 5* (pp. 537–568). Hoboken, NJ: Wiley-Blackwell.

Nicholls, K. (2003). *Gaelic and Gaelicized Ireland in the Middle Ages (2nd edition)*. Dublin: The Lilliput Press.

Parry, J., & M. Bloch. (1989). Introduction: Money and the morality of exchange. In Parry, J., & Bloch, M. (Eds.), *Money and the morality of exchange* (pp. 1–32). Cambridge: Cambridge University Press.

Polanyi, K. (2001 [1944]). *The Great Transformation*. Boston: Beacon Press.

Rüsen, T. A. (2020). *Professional Ownership in Business* Families. *The Success Factor for Long-Lasting Family Businesses*. WIFU Practical Guide.

Rüsen, T. A., Groth, T., & von Schlippe, A. (2021). 10 Golden Principles to Guide Your Succession Planning. Entrepreneur and Innovation Exchange. Published online at FamilyBusiness.org.

Rüsen, T. A., Kleve, H., & Schlippe, A. v. (2021). *Managing Family Business Dynasties – Networks, Organization, and Planning in Germany*. Cham: Springer Nature.

Rüsen, T. A., & Löhde, A. S. (2021). *The Business Family and its Family Strategy*. WIFU Study.

Rüsen, T. A., Schlippe, A., Groth, T., & Gimeno, A. (2020). *Mental Models of Family Businesses. How Business Families See Themselves and Their Connection to the family business*. WIFU Practical Guide.

Schlippe, A. v., & Frank, H. (2013). The theory of social systems as a framework for understanding family businesses. *Family Relations*, 62(3), 384–398.

Schlippe, A. v., & Hülsbeck, M. (2016). Psychologische Kontrakte in Familienunternehmen. *Familienunternehmen und Strategie*, 6(4), 122–127.

Schlippe, A. v., Rüsen, T. A., & Groth, T. (2021). *The Two Sides of the Business Family. Governance and Strategy Across Generations*. Berlin/New York: Springer.

Simmel, G. (1989 [1890]). *Gesamtausgabe in 24 Bänden: Band 2: Über soziale Differenzierung. Die Probleme der Geschichtsphilosophie*. Berlin: Suhrkamp Taschenbuchverlag.

Simon, F. B. (1999). Organisationen und Familien als soziale Systeme unterschiedlichen Typs. *Soziale Systeme*, 5, 181–200.

Simon, F. B. (2000). Grenzfunktionen der Familie. *System Familie*, 13, 140–148.

Simon, F. B. (2012). *Einführung in die Theorie des Familienunternehmens*. Heidelberg: Carl-Auer.

Simon, F. B., & C/O/N/E/C/T/A-Autorengruppe. (1998). Radikale Marktwirtschaft. *Grundlagen des systemischen Managements*. Heidelberg: Carl Auer Systeme.

Simon, F. B., Wimmer, R., & Groth, T. (2005). *Mehr-Generationen-Familienunternehmen*. Heidelberg: Carl Auer Systeme.

Sombart, W. (2019 [1927]). *Modern Capitalism – Volume 1: The Pre-Capitalist Economy: a Systematic Historical Depiction of Pan-European Economic Life from its Origins to the Present Day*. Wellington: K A Nitz.

Spradley, J. (2005): *Participant Observation*. South Melbourne: Wadsworth, Thomson Learning.

Stegbauer, C. (2011). *Reziprozität. Einführung in Soziale Formen der Gegenseitigkeit*. Wiesbaden: Verlag für Sozialwissenschaften.

Stierlin, H. (1997). Verrechnungsnotstände: Über Gerechtigkeit in sich wandelnden Beziehungen. *Familiendynamik*, 22(2), 136–155.

Stierlin, H. (2005). *Gerechtigkeit in nahen Beziehungen*. Heidelberg: Carl Auer Systeme.

Stiftung Familienunternehmen (Ed.). (2014). *Die volkswirtschaftliche Bedeutung von Familienunternehmen*. München: Stiftung Familienunternehmen.

Sydow, K. von (2002). Systemic Attachment Theory and therapeutic practice: A proposal. *Clinical Psychology & Psychotherapy*, 9(2), 77–90.

Tagiuri, R., & Davis, J. A. (1996). Bivalent attributes of the family firm. *Family Business Review*, 9(2), 199–208.

Tucker, J. (2011). Keeping the business in the family and the family in business – "What is the legacy?" *Journal of Family Business Management* 5(2), 182–191.

Uehara, E. S. (1995). Reciprocity reconsidered: Gouldner's "moral norm of reciprocity" and social support. *Journal of Social and Personal Relationships*, 12, 483–502.

Way, G. (1995). *Scottish Clan & Family Encyclopedia*. Glasgow: Harper Collins.

Weber, M. (1993 [1920]). *The Sociology of Religion*. Boston: Beacon Press.

Weismeier-Sammer, D., Frank, H., & Schlippe, A. v. (2013). Untangling "familiness": A literature review and directions for future research. *The International Journal of Entrepreneurship and Innovation*, 14(3), 165–177.

Welter, F. (2011). Contextualizing Entrepreneurship: Conceptual challenges and ways forward. *Entrepreneurship Theory and Practice*, 35(1), 165–184.

Werth, L., & Mayer, J. (2008). *Sozialpsychologie*. Berlin: Spektrum Akademischer Verlag.

Wimmer, R., Domayer, E., Oswald, M., Vater, G. (2018). *Fa–milienunternehmen – Auslaufmodell oder Erfolgstyp? (3rd edition)*. Wiesbaden: Springer/Gabler.

Wright, M., Chrisman, J. J., Chua, J. H., & Steier, L. P. (2014). Family enterprise and context. *Entrepreneurship Theory and Practice*, 38(6), 1247–1260.

Sabine B. Rau

4 Resilient Enterprising Families

Abstract: Resilient enterprising families rely on the next generation members to continue their businesses. In this chapter, I discuss how parental styles enable or disenable next generation members to act entrepreneurial in the sense that they act persistent, show creative problem solving, and get absorbed with what they are doing. While authoritarian parental style hinders creative problem solving, reduces persistence and absorption, as well as permissive parental style reduces creative problem solving, hinders persistence and absorption, authoritative style supports all three dimensions.

Keywords: enterprising families, resilience, parental style, entrepreneurial behaviour

Introduction

Enterprising families, families whose members are active in either their focal family business, in the business group of their family, in their own start-up or family business, or in their family office, contribute to their respective economy by employing people, paying taxes, and providing new products and/or services. Growth in an economy is mainly driven by innovation (Ahlstrom, 2010; Garud, Tuertscher & van de Veen, 2013) and enterprising families are – among others – drivers of innovation (Jaskiewicz, Combs, & Rau, 2015). While entrepreneurs have been studied intensively, scholars only recently started to focus on the families behind them.

Resilient enterprising families, that is, families with the ability to overcome adversities and bounce back in the face of disruptive events (Masten, Best, & Garmezy, 1990; Ong et al., 2006; Williams et al., 2017) rely on next generation members who are prepared to continue to support their family and their enterprise. These next generation members growing up in the family, are prone to parental behaviour, and will, after completing their education and gaining experience inside or outside their family's business or businesses, take over responsibility at least as owners of the enterprises, or, in some cases, as stewards of their family's wealth after the sale of the business. Some of them will as well take over as leaders of the family enterprise.

While most enterprising families tend to lose their innovative drive latest by the third generation (Block, 2012; Cruz & Nordqvist, 2012), some are more resilient and stay entrepreneurial throughout the generations (Rau, Werner, & Schell, 2019). Why are some enterprising families more resilient than others? Why do members of some enterprising families have more resources and capabilities at hand to pursue

Sabine B. Rau, University of Ottawa and ESMT Berlin

https://doi.org/10.1515/9783110727968-004

an entrepreneurial path than others? Research has shown that while entrepreneurial intention is due to personality (Rauch & Frese 2007; Zhao & Seibert 2006), upbringing and respective role models (Chlosta, Patzelt, Klein, & Dormann, 2012; Schmitt-Rodermund, 2004), the entrepreneurial activity is due to the interaction within the family, to cohesion, childhood involvement, strategic education, entrepreneurial bridging, and strategic succession (Jaskiewicz et al., 2015). So far, we know that cohesion of, and interaction within the family play a pivotal role. What is still missing is how a specific type of interaction supports or hinders the next generation to build up resources and capabilities needed for being entrepreneurial and resilient.

In combining the perspectives of different types of upbringing (Schmitt-Rodermund, 2004) and capabilities needed to be more entrepreneurial (Cardon, Wincent, Singh, & Drnovsek, 2009), I developed a theoretical concept under which circumstances next generation members of enterprising families will turn out to be more or less entrepreneurial and, thus, contribute to their family's resilience. In a nutshell, families in which next generation members are rather belittled than enabled lack entrepreneurial spirit in the next generation. I will show that the tendency for parents to belittle their children is grounded in a rather transactional approach, in the sense that their children must satisfy the parents' need for reputation as parents, for cohesion, or for any other emotional status compared to a rather transformational approach, in which children are supported to develop their own profile with related strengths and weaknesses.

Children's Entrepreneurial Behaviour and Parenting Style

Entrepreneurial behaviour of children from business families results in corporate entrepreneurship, activities that lead to strategic renewal, innovation, or the creation of new ventures out of the focal family firm, also called corporate venturing (Jaskiewicz, Combs, & Rau, in press; Sharma and Chrisman, 1999). With entrepreneurially behaving offspring, family firms become more resilient, for example, they adapt to changing environments, overcome adversities, and are prepared to bounce back in the face of disruptive events (Masten et al., 1990; Ong et al., 2006; Williams et al., 2017). Entrepreneurial behaviour encompasses creative problem solving, for example, the production of novel and useful ideas or actions (Woodman, Sawyer, & Griffin, 1993), persistence, meant as the continuation of effortful action despite failures, impediments, or threats, either imagined or real (Gimeno, Folta, Cooper, & Woo, 1997; Howard & Crayne, 2018), and absorption in the sense of being fully concentrated and deeply engrossed in one's work (Schindelhutte, Morris, & Allen, 2006).

Entrepreneurial behaviour is, based on the child's personality, which is largely learned behaviour with a strong influence not only of rational economic arguments, but as well of identity-based, emotional roots (Gruber & McMillan, 2017). Prior research showed that entrepreneurial young adults show a specific profile with respect to the big five personality traits (for a meta-review on the big five personality traits and entrepreneurship see Zhao & Seibert, 2006), namely a low level of agreeableness and neuroticism, and a high level on extraversion, conscientiousness, and openness (Schmitt-Rodermund, 2004). These results are in line with prior research on personality types (De Fruyt, & Mervielde, 1997; Holland, 1985), which highlightened that not all entrepreneurial types become entrepreneurs, but most entrepreneurial individuals show the specific interests, abilities, and behaviours.

Displayed entrepreneurial behaviour like creative problem solving, persistence, and absorption develops within the family context where the pivotal role of parents is two-fold; on the one hand they provide – or do not provide – role models of being entrepreneurial (Chlosta et al., 2012; Scherer, Adams, Carley, & Wiebe, 1989), on the other hand, they groom certain behaviours as they expect, remunerate, punish, and tell and re-tell stories from the past of the family, so-called entrepreneurial legacies (Jaskiewicz et al., 2015; Kammerlander et al., 2015). In the following, I posit the question how different parenting styles (Baumrind, 1971; Schmitt-Rodermund, 2004) might or might not support the development of creative problem solving, persistence, and absorption.

Parenting styles go back to Baumrind (1971) who stated that different ways of bringing up their children will result in different behaviour as an adult. The three main parenting styles distinguished are authoritarian, permissive, and authoritative. While authoritarian parents are highly demanding, but not responsive, authoritative parents balance demandingness and responsiveness. Permissive parents can either display a lack of control, thus low demandingness, combined with high responsiveness, called indulgent permissive, while those who do display low demandingness and low responsiveness constitute the group of negligent permissive (Maccoby & Martin, 1983). Research has shown that children raised in an authoritarian manner have lower self-esteem, lesser autonomous decision-making skills, as well as a lost sense of identity combined with anxiety (Baumrind, 1971; Schmitt-Rodermund, 2004). Children raised with a permissive parental style, that is, with a lack of control, either with or without responsiveness, are less achievement-oriented and less mature. At the same time, they over-estimate their own achievements, which is in line with their lower sense of identity. Finally, when raised in an authoritative manner, children are mentally healthier, more independent, have a higher self-esteem, and are achievement-oriented (Baumrind, 1971; Schmitt-Rodermund, 2004). Children from authoritative parents had better grades at school (Steinberg, Elmen, & Mounts, 1989). We can conclude that authoritative parenting enables children to take their own, informed decisions within set boundaries, to learn from their failures, and to more adequately attribute their failure and successes.

Entrepreneurial next generation members engage in creative problem solving, which requires them doing something for the first time and creating new knowledge

(Woodman et al., 1993). Next generation members experience situations as that they either facilitate or hinder creative problem solving, despite their own personality tendency to be creative. Woodward and colleagues (1993, p. 294f) summarized that

> individual creativity is a function of antecedent conditions (e.g., past reinforcement history, biographical variables), cognitive style and ability (e.g., divergent thinking, ideational fluency), personality factors (e.g., self-esteem, locus of control), relevant knowledge, motivation, social influences (e.g., social facilitation, social rewards), and contextual influences (e.g., physical environment, task and time constraint).

Furthermore, creative problem solution is supported by families where open sharing of information, thus high responsiveness among other factors, is prevalent. As creative solutions involve an element of newness, they come with some risks and are consequently more likely in families which support risk-taking behaviours and less likely in those families that display a high level of control by the parents.

Max, the 14-year-old next generation member of an enterprising family, calls his mother as he has excess baggage weight, but no money left when trying to check in for his flight home from boarding school. Here is what his mother answers: "Look, I am in a meeting so is dad. You yourself created this problem and therefore you have to solve it. Either you take something not so valuable out of your suitcase and leave it at the airport. Or you look for a young stewardess and flirt your way in or you start crying and try to convince an older stewardess." Max comes home with all his luggage. "Mum, you have no clue about females. I looked for an older stewardess and flirted with her", he proudly states.

By offering different potential solutions while at the same time not solving Max's problem, his mother showed an authoritative approach.

Proposition 1a: *Authoritative parental style enhances children's creative problem-solving behaviours.*

Proposition 1b: *Authoritarian parental style hinders children's creative problem-solving behaviours.*

Proposition 1c: *Permissive parental style reduces children's creative problem-solving behaviours.*

Persistence for some next generation members is habitual and they apply it broadly in whatever they are active in. For others, it is only in place in very specific situations, while again others nearly never show persistence. As persistence is important for young generation members to contribute and achieve their goals, as well as it is crucial for being entrepreneurial, the question about influence of parental style on the development of persistence comes up. Persistence nowadays is seen as a multidimensional construct (Howard & Crayne, 2018), and is in its essence the maintenance of effort towards a goal over an extended period of time (Duckworth & Quinn, 2009). It includes persistence despite difficulties, persistence despite fear, and inappropriate persistence (Howard & Crayne, 2018). The first two are relevant for entrepreneurial behaviour. Parenting style influences persistence in a two-fold way; firstly, when demandingness is high for results, whether academic results, achievement in sports, performing arts, or community engagement, persistence is fostered, while when demandingness is low, the opposite is the case. Secondly, a heightened level of anxiety diminishes persistence in most cases while in only some, it supports it. Overall, high levels of responsiveness combined with demandingness supports the development of persistence.

Proposition 2a: *Authoritative parental style enhances children's persistence.*
Proposition 2b: *Authoritarian parental style reduces most children's persistence while it supports it in rare cases.*
Proposition 2c: *Permissive parental style hinders children's persistence.*

Absorption, introduced by Kanter in 1977, and defined as "being fully concentrated and happily engrossed in one's work, whereby time passes quickly and one has difficulties with detaching oneself from work" (Schaufeli & Bakker, 2004, p. 295) is the third entrepreneurial behaviour relevant for next generation members enhancing the resilience of their family and their business. While dedication, namely being strongly involved in one's work and experiencing a sense of significance, in its essence is cognitive, absorption is behavioural (Schaufeli et al., 2002) and persists during the transition from school to work-life (Hartung, Porfeli, & Vondracek, 2005). To develop the behaviour of absorption, early childhood behaviour must be regulated by consistent, transparent, and reliable rules through the parents as part of absorption is rooted in controlling one's own immediate wishes. To forgo immediate wishes to finally be remunerated for reaching an even higher goal fosters behaviour, which later supports the behaviour of absorption. Permissive parents' failure to regulate their children's behaviour results in children who fail to learn appropriate forms of self-regulation (DeHart, Pelham, & Tennen, 2006). In a different way, authoritarian parents do not support self-regulation as they exert high parental control over their children.

Proposition 3a: *Authoritative parental style enhances absorption.*
Proposition 3b: *Authoritarian parental style reduces absorption.*
Proposition 3c: *Permissive parental style hinders children's absorption.*

Summing up, entrepreneurial behaviour of creative problem-solving, persistence, and absorption is largely supported by authoritative parenting style while authoritarian parenting style reduces these behaviours, all other factors assumed similar. Permissive parenting style, whether indulgent or negligent, hinders children to develop entrepreneurial behaviour. The questions here is why some parents from enterprising families opt for other than the authoritative parenting style.

Parents' Motivation and Reference Point for Opting for a Specific Parenting Style

Parenting style is influenced not only by the parents' motives and their reference point, but as well by their personality (for meta-analysis see Prinzie et al., 2009), the child's temperament (Rothbart, Ahadi, & Evans, 2000; Rothbart & Bates, 2006), and the parents' effort in upbringing and parenting (Schoppe-Sullivan, McBride, & Ho, 2004). However, in this paper, I solely concentrate on motives and reference points of parents as there are differences for motives and reference points concerning enterprising families and families without their own business. In some enterprising families' entrepreneurial legacies, stories about prior successes, and on how they overcame adversaries, are told (Jaskiewicz et al., 2015; Kammerlander et al., 2015), reference points can be found in older generations, and in-group/out-group definitions differ largely from non-business-related families.

Motivation of any individual is manifold. While the three big motives for what people do have been described as power, achievement, and affiliation (McClelland, 1985), Kehr (2004) differentiates between explicit and implicit motives. Building on the dual system approach of motivation (Allport, 1937; Freud, 1967; Lewin, 1926), he summarizes explicit motives as the reasons people self-attribute for their actions (McClelland, Atkinson, Clark, & Lowell, 1953). Theses motives are consciously accessible and strongly influenced by social demands and normative pressures (Kehr, 2004). Implicit motives are associative networks connecting situational cues with basic affective reactions and implicit behavioural tendencies (McClelland, et al., 1953). They are related to unconscious needs (Maslow, 1943) as well as to basic and organistic needs (Deci & Ryan, 2000). While explicit motives are consciously accessible, implicit motives are subconsciously aroused and lead to affective preferences and implicit behavioural impulses (McClelland, 1985; McClelland et al., 1989).

Explicit motives for parents to choose a specific parental style can be found due to their related social class, ethnic, and cultural background (Kagitcibasi, 1996) as well as social demands such as Zeitgeist-related discussions on how to raise children, for example, never to let a newborn cry, feeding them whenever they demand for it, or not to punish wrong-doing physically (Jungert et al., 2015). Time and context provide parents with these types of social demands, and as discussions change, so do the "how-to-rules" for parenting. While in western industrialized societies prior to World War II authoritarian parenting style was prevalent, after the war a more permissive style was promoted. And following the Zeitgeist of upbringing, the self-attribution of parents for the parenting style oftentimes refers to the actual style accepted by societal groups. To deliberately choose an upbringing style that goes against the actual model of upbringing requires the parents to justify their behaviour constantly.

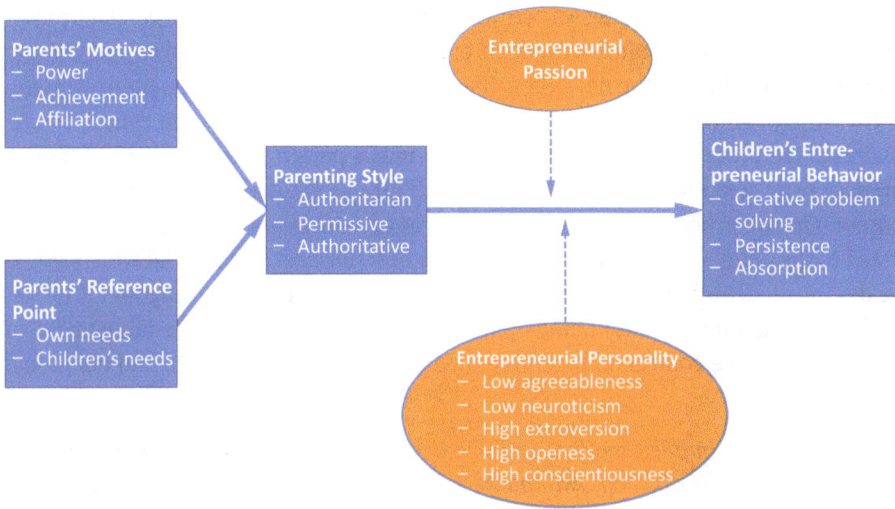

Figure 4.1: Parents' motives, reference point, and related parenting style and children's entrepreneurial behaviour.
Source: own.

Furthermore, the reference point for parental behaviour differs from enterprising family to enterprising family as does their temporal orientation (Ancona, Okhuysen, & Perlow, 2001; Sharma, Salvato, & Reay, 2014). While for some, the reference point is their peers from kindergarten to school to playgroup, thus, within their own generation, for others it is their family network including their parents and grandparents, their temporal orientation is a rather longitudinal. The more the parents' reference point for parental behaviour is presence-oriented on the one hand and related to peers outside of the group of enterprising families, the more likely they will follow the Zeitgeist.

Proposition 4a: *The actual model of upbringing in a certain context and time influences parents' style of parenting and serves as justification.*

Proposition 4b: *Parenting style in an enterprising family is influenced by the acceptance or rejection of the parental behaviour by their peers.*

Proposition 4c: *The reference point for parental behaviour moderates the acceptance or rejection of a certain Zeitgeist.*

Implicit motives for parental behaviour are harder to grasp as they relate to unconscious needs (Maslow, 1943; Kehr, 2004). The following two factors are interesting, namely for whom do parents act and, secondly, what is their primary driving motivation, is it, power, achievement, or affiliation. Parents can groom their children to satisfy their own immediate needs for power, achievement, or affiliation which is called controlled parenting motivation (Jungert et al., 2015). Especially in enterprising families, the motivation to raise a "crown prince" can be rooted in the need for power over the business even after retirement or for acceptance by their own parents and parents-in-law, thus, in the need for achievement expressed by grandparents. Observing a parent-child-relationship where the parent closely monitors the child's behaviour and overprotects the child can be rooted in the parent's need for control (power motive) or in need to have a "friend-at-hand", thus, in an affiliation motive of the parent. On the other hand, the motivation for certain behaviour can be solely oriented at the child's well-being or its chance to best develop its potential which would be described as autonomous parenting motivation. Jungert and colleagues (2015) describe the outcome of autonomous parenting motivation as positive adjustment of the children while controlled parenting motivation led to behavioural and emotional problems.

Proposition 5a: *Implicit motivation for a certain parental style can be oriented towards their own (parents') needs or towards the child's needs.*

Proposition 5b: *Parenting style depends upon the primary driver of implicit needs of the parents, power, achievement, or affiliation.*

Discussion

Parenting style largely influences the entrepreneurial behaviour of the next generation of enterprising families. Figure 4.1 summarizes the arguments made in this chapter. I have discussed which parenting style supports entrepreneurial behaviour and the related antecedents such as creating problem solving, persistence and absorption. The result is rather straight forward, while permissive and authoritarian parenting styles hinder the development of entrepreneurial behaviour, an authoritative parenting style fosters it. As entrepreneurial behaviour is needed for ongoing innovation, which in itself is a prerequisite of longevity, the question remains why parents from enterprising families do not unequivocally opt for an authoritative parenting style. Reasons could be lack of knowledge, interest, time, or effort.

Looking deeper into the motives, both, explicit and implicit motives, I discussed that the point of reference can differ in terms of the child's well-being and development versus the parent's well-being and acceptance in their respective reference group. Parents who focus on fulfilling the societal norms, whether of their peer group or of their enterprising family network, behave different from those who primarily have the future of the child in their mind when deciding how to raise the child. In other words, parents who exert power and control over their child in order to satisfy their own needs will rather hinder the development of entrepreneurial behaviour.

I hope that this paper will serve as a starting point to look deeper into the relation of parents' motivation, children's well-being, and development of entrepreneurial behaviour and the interaction of both with personality traits, context variables such as societal norms and support. It is the family of the family business that is – still – the most under researched, yet the most important variable for the longevity of family businesses around the world.

References

Ahlstrom, D. (2010). Innovation and growth: How business contributes to society. *Academy of Management Perspectives*, 24(3),11–24.

Allport, G. W. 1937. *Personality: A Psychological Interpretation*. New York: Holt.

Ancona, D. G., Okhuysen, G.A., & Perlow, L.A. (2001). Taking time to integrate temporal research. *Academy of Management Review*, 26(4),512–529.

Baumrind, D. (1971). Current pattern of parental authority. *Developmental Psychology*, 44, 1–103.

Block, J. (2012). R&D investments in family and founder firms: An agency perspective. *Journal of Business Venturing*, 27(2),248–265.

Cardon, M. S., Wincent, J., Singh, J., & Drnovsek, M. (2009). The nature and experience of entrepreneurial passion. *Academy of Management Review*, 34(3),511–532.

Chlosta, S., Patzelt, H., Klein, S. B., & Dormann, C. (2012). Parental role models and the decision to become self-employed: The moderating effect of personality. *Small Business Economics*, 38, 121–138.

Cruz, C., & Nordqvist, M. (2012). Entrepreneurial orientation in family firms: A generational perspective. *Small Business Economics*, 38(1),33–49.

De Fruyt, F., & Mervielde, I. (1997). The five-factor model of personality and Hollands RIASEC interest types. *Personality and Individual Differences*, 23, 87–103.

Deci, E.L., Ryan, R. M. (2000). The "what" and "why" of goal pursuits: Human needs and the self-determination of behavior. *Psychological Inquiry* 11 (4): 227–268.

DeHart, T., Pelham, B. W., & Tennen, H. (2006). What lies beneath: Parenting style and implicit self-esteem. *Journal of Experimental Social Psychology*, 42, 1–17.

Duckworth, A. L., & Quinn, P. D. (2009). Development and validation of the Short Grit Scale (GRIT-S). *Journal of Personality Assessment*, 91, 166–174.

Freud, S. (1967; first published in 1905) Die Verdrängung [the repression]. In A. Freud (Ed.), *Gesammelte Werke aus den Jahren 1913–1917* (pp. 247–261). Frankfurt am Main. Fischer.

Garud, R., Tuertscher, P., & van de Veen, A. H. (2013). Perspectives on innovation processes. *Academy of Management Annals*, 7(1),775–819.

Gimeno, J., Folta, T. B., Cooper, A. C., & Woo, C. Y. (1997). Survival of the fittest? Entrepreneurial human capital and the persistence of underperforming firms. *Administrative Science Quarterly*, 42, 750–783.

Gruber, M., & MacMillan, I.C. (2017). Entrepreneurial behavior: A reconceptualization and extension based on identity theory. *Strategic Entrepreneurship Journal*, 11(3),271–286.

Hartung, P., Porfeli, E., & Vondracek, F. (2005). Child vocational development: A review and reconsideration. *Journal of Vocational Behavior*, 66, 385–419.

Holland, J. L. (1985). *Making Vocational Choices. A Theory on Vocational Personalities and Work Environments*. Englewood Cliffs, NJ: Prentice-Hall.

Howard, M. C., & Crayne, M. P. (2018). Persistence: Defining the multidimensional construct and creating a measure. *Personality and Individual Differences*, 139, 77–89.

Jaskiewicz, P., Combs, J. G., & Rau, S. B. (in press). Coming home versus striking out: Entrepreneurship among business family non-successors. *Journal of Small Business Management*.

Jaskiewicz, P., Combs, J. G., & Rau, S. B. (2015). Entrepreneurial legacy: Toward a theory of how some family firms nurture transgenerational entrepreneurship. *Journal of Business Venturing*, 30(1),29–49.

Jungert, T., Landry, R., Joussemet, M., Mageau, G., Gingras, I., & Koestner, R. (2015). Autonomous and controlled motivation for parenting: Associations with parent and child outcomes. *Journal of Child and Family Studies*, 24, 1932–1942.

Kammerlander, N., Dessi, C., Bird, M., Floris, M., & Murru, A. (2015). The impact of shared stories on family firm innovation: A multicase study, *Family Business Review*, 28(4),332–354.

Kanter, R. N. (1977). *Work and Family in the United States: A Critical Review and Agenda for Research and Public Policy*. New York: Russell Sage.

Kehr, H. M. (2004). Integrating implicit motives, explicit motives, and perceived abilities: The compensation model of work motivation and volition. *Academy of Management Journal*, 29(3),479–499.

Kagitcibasi, C. 1996. *Family and human development across cultures*. Mahwah, NJ. Lawrence Erdbaum.

Lewin, K. (1926). Untersuchungen zur Handlungs- und Affektpsychologie, I: Vorbemerkungen über die psychischen Kräfte und Energien und über die Struktur der Seele. *Psychologische Forschung*, 7, 294–329.

Maccoby E, Martin J. (1983). Socialization in the context of the family: Parent-child interaction. In: Mussen P.H. (ed), *Handbook of Child Psychology*. Wiley: New York, 1–101.

Maslow, A. H. (1943). A theory of human motivation. *Psychological Review*, 50(4),370–396.

Masten, A. S., Best, K. M., & Garmezy, N. (1990). Resilience and development: Contributions from the study of children who overcome adversity. *Development and Psychopathology*, 2(4),425–444.

McClelland, D. C., Koestner, R., & Weinberger, J. 1989. How do self-attributed and implicit motives differ? *Psychological Review*, 96: 690–702.

McClelland, D. C. (1985). How motives, skills, and values determine what people do. *American Psyhologist*, 40, 812–825.

McClelland, D. C., Atkinson, J. W., Clark, R. A., & Lowell, E. L. (1953). *The achievement motive*. New York: Appleton Century-Crofts.

Ong, A. D., Bergeman, C., Bisconti, T. L., & Wallace, K. A. (2006). Psychological resilience, positive emotions, and successful adaptation to stress in later life. *Journal of Personality and Social Psychology*, 91(4),730–751.

Prinzie, P., Stams, G. J. J. M., Dekovic, M., Reijntjes, A. H. A., & Belsky, J. (2009). The relations between parents' big five personality factors and parenting: A meta-analytic review. *Journal of Personality and Social Psychology*, 97, 351–362.

Rau, S.B., Werner, A., & Schell, S. (2019). Psychological ownership as a driving factor of innovation in older family firms. *Journal of Family Business Strategy*, 10(4), 100246.

Rauch, A., & Frese, M. (2007). Let's put the person back into entrepreneurship research: A meta-analysis on the relationship between business owners' personality and business creation and success. *European Journal of Work and Organizational Psychology*, 16(4),353–385.

Rothbart, M. K., Ahadi, S. A., & Evans, D. E. (2000). Investigations of temperament at three to seven years: The Children's Behavior Questionnaire. *Child Development*, 72, 1394–1408.

Rothbart, M. K., & Bates, J. E. (2006). Temperament. In Eisenberg, N., Damon, W., & Lerner, R.M. (Eds.), *Handbook of Child Psychology. Vol.3: Social, emotional, and personality development, 6th edition* (pp. 99–166). Hoboken, NJ: Wiley.

Schaufeli, W. B., & Bakker, A. B. (2004). Job demands, job resources, and their relationship with burnout and engagement: a multi-sample study. *Journal of Organizational Behavior*, 25, 293–315.

Schaufeli, W. B., Martinez, I., Pinto, A. M., Salanova, M., & Bakker, A. (2002). Burnout and engagement in university students: A cross-national study. *Journal of Cross-Cultural Psychology*, 33, 464–481.

Scherer, R. F., Adams, J. S., Carley, S. S., & Wiebe, F. A. (1989). Role model performance effects on development of entrepreneurial career preference. *Entrepreneurship Theory and Practice*, 13, 53–71.

Schindehutte, M., Morris, M., & Allen, J. (2006). Beyond achievement: Entrepreneurship as extreme experience. *Small Business Economics*, 27, 349–368.

Schmitt-Rodermund, E. (2004). Pathways to successful entrepreneurship: Parenting, personality, early entrepreneurial competence, and interests. *Journal of Vocational Behavior*, 65(3),498–518.

Schoppe-Sullivan, S. J., McBride, B. A., & Ho, M. R. (2004). Unidimensional versus multidimensional perspectives on father involvement. *Fathering*, 2(2),147–163.

Sharma, P., & Chrisman, J. (1999). Toward a reconciliation of the definitional issues in the field of corporate entrepreneurship. *Entrepreneurship Theory and Practice*, 23, 11–28.

Sharma, P., Salvato, C., & Reay, T. (2014). Temporal dimension of family enterprise research. *Family Business Review*, 27(1),10–19.

Steinberg, L., Elmen, J. D., & Mounts, N. S. (1989). Authoritative parenting, psychosocial maturity, and academic success among adolescents. *Child Development*, 60(6),1424–1436.

Williams, R. O. (1992). Successful ownership in business families. *Family Business Review*, 5(2),161–172.

Williams, T. A., Gruber, D. A., Sutcliffe, K. M., Shepherd, D. A., & Zhao, E.Y. (2017). Organizational response to adversity: Fusing crisis management and resilience research streams. *Academy of Management Annals*, 11, (2), 733–769.

Woodman, R. W., Sawyer, J. E., & Griffin, R. W. (1993). Towards a theory of organizational creativity. *Academy of Management Review*, 18, 293–321.

Zhao, H., & Seibert, S. E. (2006). The big five personality dimensions and entrepreneurial status: A meta-analytical review. *Journal of Applied Psychology*, 91(2),259–271.

Tommaso Minola, Dinah Spitzley, Giovanna Campopiano,
and Mara Brumana

5 Enterprising Families: An Embeddedness Perspective on Offspring's Entrepreneurial Career Preferences, Cognitions, and Actions

Abstract: We present an "enterprising family embeddedness" perspective and its association with offspring's entrepreneurial outcomes (i.e., career preferences, cognitions, and actions). Cognizant of the lack of empirical evidence on the embeddedness of entrepreneurship in a family where at least one individual is an entrepreneur, that is, the enterprising family, we exploit a rich dataset of university students in multiple countries from the GUESS project. We offer an overview of how different combinations of factors at the interface of the individual, family, and family business domains relate to entrepreneurial intentions, cognitions, and founding experience of individuals. This perspective provides the opportunity to illustrate high degrees of heterogeneity in the association between the enterprising family and offspring's entrepreneurial outcomes and to open several new research directions.

Keywords: enterprising family, family embeddedness, entrepreneurship, GUESS, career

Introduction

The entrepreneurial process does not occur in a vacuum and is instead affected by the social context in which the entrepreneurial agent is embedded (Welter & Gartner, 2016). Values, habits, and beliefs, together with other situational factors, influence entrepreneurial outcomes (McMullen et al., 2021).

Stemming from the family embeddedness perspective on entrepreneurship (Aldrich & Cliff, 2003), the role of the *family* as a social institution has been explored by entrepreneurship and family business scholars as a crucial antecedent of new venture creation (Rogoff & Heck, 2003). Moreover, research has supported the need to integrate family science theories in the current debate on business families to better understand the nuances of the family context (Olson, 2000), as well as the consequences of

---

Tommaso Minola, Giovanna Campopiano, Mara Brumana, University of Bergamo and Center for Young and Family Enterprise (CYFE)
Dinah Spitzley, Zeppelin University

https://doi.org/10.1515/9783110727968-005

embeddedness in the family on entrepreneurial outcomes (Combs et al., 2020; Jaskie-wicz et al., 2017). In particular, there is an increasing interest in exploring the role of the *enterprising family*, namely a "family that runs one or more businesses, and that has an intent to grow these businesses with the family as the foundation" (Habbershon & Pis-trui, 2002; Nordqvist & Melin, 2010, p. 221), as a driver of entrepreneurship (Aldrich et al., 2021; Le Breton-Miller & Miller, 2018; Minola et al., 2016). Intergenerational transmis-sion of entrepreneurship (Criaco et al., 2017; Pittino et al., 2018), or entrepreneurial leg-acy (Combs et al., 2021; Jaskiewicz et al., 2015) are some of the labels used to describe the process through which the exposure to the family and the family business shapes the entrepreneurial career preferences, cognitions, and actions of individuals. The en-trepreneurial intentions of offspring can manifest in their preference for two alternative entrepreneurial career paths, either taking over the family business or founding a new venture (Block et al., 2013; Zellweger, Sieger, & Halter, 2011). On the one hand, the exist-ing literature suggests that the availability of resources, learning opportunities, and role models by the enterprising family can motivate or discourage offspring to create a new firm (Criaco et al., 2017; Le Breton-Miller & Miller, 2018). On the other hand, scholars argue that the emotional and normative attachment to the family business can push offspring towards succession as the preferred career path or refrain them from making such a choice (Hamilton, 2011; Sharma & Irving, 2005). However, empirical evidence on the "enterprising family embeddedness" of new venture creation is scant.

By taking advantage of an explorative albeit comprehensive descriptive data elabo-ration on a large cross-country sample of 49,457 students with an enterprising family background, we aim to cover this empirical gap and offer an overview of how different combinations of factors at the interface of the *individual, family*, and *family business* do-mains relate to offspring's entrepreneurial career preferences, cognitions, and founding experiences. Our empirical evidence is in line with previous research pointing to the en-terprising family background as a trigger of entrepreneurial career intentions and activi-ties by offspring (Chang et al., 2009; Laspita et al., 2012; Schoon & Duckworth, 2012; Sieger & Minola, 2017; Sørensen, 2007; Steier, 2007). In particular, the tendency of the next generation, under certain conditions, to venture out of the family business rather that succeeding, poses a challenge to family business scholars and suggests a shift from a focus on a "single-family-with-a-single-business" to an enterprising family comprised of individual members with loosely connected activities (Aldrich et al., 2021; Combs et al., 2021). Moreover, the richness of our dataset allows us to detect specific configurations of individual, family, and family business characteristics leading to diverse entrepreneur-ial outcomes. Our results also highlight that the embeddedness of the individuals in the university environment, besides the enterprising family, also plays a role. This suggests the need to further explore the interplay of the different social contexts (such as family and university) in which the individual is embedded, to understand entrepreneurial ca-reer choices. Overall, we suggest the enterprising family embeddedness perspective on offspring's entrepreneurial outcome as a promising research avenue for both entre-preneurship and family business scholars.

The remainder of the chapter is structured as follows. In the next section, we illustrate the empirical setting and methodological approach. In the following section, we report our results with particular attention to the interplay of individual, family, and family business domains. Results are discussed in the last section of the chapter, where we also list the contributions of this study and future lines of research.

Method

Sample and Procedure

We explored the "enterprising family embeddedness" of offspring's entrepreneurial career preferences, cognitions, and actions, by taking advantage of an international sample of university students (Zellweger et al., 2011, 2016). The initial sample included students *with* an enterprising family background (parents were majority owners of at least one firm) as well as students *without* an enterprising family background; then, for the main analysis, we only focused on the former. A sample of university students was particularly suitable for our research objective to understand the entrepreneurial cognition and founding experience of individuals, considering whether and how they were embedded in enterprising families. First, the participants were in positions where they were making decisions about their career paths including the option of taking an entrepreneurial career path (Hahn et al., 2020; Meoli et al., 2020). Second, they were socially embedded in the university environment, which offered knowledge and opportunities for both business creation (Colombo & Piva, 2020) and succession (Zellweger et al., 2011). Third, our sample was also rich in information on the depiction of students' family and family business, where existent.

Specifically, the empirical analysis of this chapter was based on survey-data from the 2018 wave of the Global University Entrepreneurial Spirit Students' Survey (GUESSS), which included the answers of university students from 54 countries. The total sample included offspring with an enterprising family background (49,457 individuals with at least one parent who owned the majority of at least one firm) as well as students without an enterprising family background (159,179 individuals who did not report any firm in the hands of either parent), which led to a total sample of 208,636 students.[1]

---

[1] We could not explicitly test for potential non-response bias because the GUESSS data collection procedure involved different starting and closing dates per countries and universities, thereby precluding the possibility of identifying and comparing early and late respondents in a reliable way (Oppenheim, 1966). However, we formed two groups of respondents (early and late) in different countries, and we did not detect any significant differences between the two groups; this mitigates the concern for non-response bias (Sieger & Minola, 2017; Zellweger et al., 2011).

However, to account for the heterogeneity of enterprising families and under-stand how family and business factors influence offspring's entrepreneurial cogni-tions and founding experience both in contrast to individuals without an enterprising family background and among individuals with an enterprising family background, we created 27 subsamples (see Tables 5.1 and 5.2) based on *individual, family,*and *family business* factors. Sample splitting allowed observation of the univariate statis-tics and differences across relevant dimensions of analysis, which was an approach we deemed suitable for this exploratory empirical contribution. In a first step, we split the total sample of university students considering whether they were individu-als with an enterprising family background (i.e., next-gen sample) or not. Having an enterprising family background was indeed considered as a relevant factor to explain the entrepreneurial career choice of individuals (Criaco et al., 2017; Pittino et al., 2018; Sieger & Minola, 2017; Zellweger et al., 2011). We then continued the analysis using the next-gen sample (49,457 individuals) only and split it along 11 variables at the interface of individual, family, and business domains.

The first set of subsamples was obtained by splitting the next-gen sample along dimensions describing the interface between *family* and *family business* domains: first, whether the mother, the father, or both parents were majority owners of a business and second, whether either parent was operationally leading the business or not (Block et al., 2013; Campopiano et al., 2020; Gimenez-Jimenez et al., 2018).

The second set of subsamples was obtained by splitting the sample of individu-als with an enterprising family background along dimensions describing the inter-face between *individual* and *family* domains, in particular by the number of siblings of these students (three groups: no siblings, meaning the next-gen was an only child; one or two siblings; three or more siblings) (Calabrò et al., 2018) and verbal encouragement, namely parents' encouragement associated with their children's educational development which made them confident in their human and entre-preneurship capital (Turner et al., 2003) (two groups: high, i.e., above the sample median, or low, i.e., below the sample median).

The third set of subsamples was obtained by splitting the next-gen sample along dimensions describing the interface between *individual* and *family business* domains. In particular, we considered a number of factors as antecedent of entrepreneurial cognition and founding decisions by individuals with an enterprising family back-ground. First, we looked at whether the next-gen had personal ownership in the busi-ness (three groups: less than 50%, between 50% and 99%, and 100%) (see, e.g., studies on multi-generational involvement in ownership, Eddleston et al., 2008; Ward & Dolan, 1998) and, second, at whether the next-gen viewed the parent(s)-owned business as a "family business" (Chua et al., 1999; Uhlaner et al., 2012). Third, similar to what Pittino and colleagues (2018) did with their dichotomous variable "family business experience", we considered whether the individuals with an enter-prising family background were working in the family business or not. Finally, their perception of the performance of the family business was considered a relevant factor to explain the entrepreneurial outcome of individuals with an enterprising business background (Criaco et al., 2017; two groups: above or below the median perceived performance).

The fourth and last set of subsamples was obtained by splitting the next-gen sample along dimensions describing the interface between *individual, family,* and *family business* domains. Instrumental assistance, career-related modeling, and emotional support (Turner et al., 2003) were used in this respect. In particular, we created six subsamples on those variables based on the median split. A more precise description of the scale-based variables from Turner et al. (2003) is reported in the section entitled *Enterprising Family Background Variables* below.

For each of the described (sub)samples, we observed a number of entrepreneurial outcomes regarding entrepreneurial career preferences, cognitions, and actions. As suggested by extant literature and existing theorizing about the family embeddedness perspective on entrepreneurship (Aldrich & Cliff, 2003), entrepreneurial outcomes may be associated with offspring's embeddedness in an enterprising family. Embeddedness in an enterprising family can manifest with variables at individual, family, and business levels. Figure 5.1 depicts and summarizes the framework underpinning our empirical strategy.

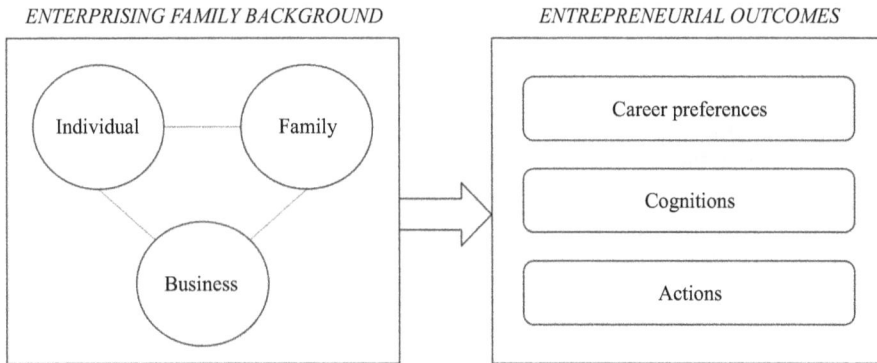

ENTERPRISING FAMILY BACKGROUND   *ENTREPRENEURIAL OUTCOMES*

Figure 5.1: The "enterprising family embeddedness" framework underpinning the empirical strategy.

For each of the 27 subsamples, we calculated the descriptive statistics (means, median, or counts depending on the type of variable, whether scale, dummy, or count variables). We then compared these statistics to draw conclusions from them. The size and description of the whole sample and the 27 subsamples can be found in Tables 5.1 and 5.2.

Measures

Table 5.1: Entrepreneurial Outcomes for the Whole Sample and Across Subsamples Along the Interfaces of Family (F)-Family Business (FB) and Family (F)-Individual (I) Domains.

		Overall			F-FB Variables		
		Full sample	Enterprising family background (EFB)		EFB & parents' ownership in the business		
			Y	N	Father	Mother	Both
	Sample #	0	0a	0b	1a	1b	1c
	Sample Size	208,636	49,457	159,179	22,983	6,038	29,420
Immediately after studies	% of respondents with *founding* as career intention	9.05	11.19	8.38	10.16	11.21	13.37
	% of respondents with *succeeding* (in the family business) as career intention	1.81	5.83	N/A	5.15	3.88	8.10
	% of respondents with *succeeding* (in another business) as career intention	0.71	0.94	0.64	0.89	0.93	0.96
5 years after studies	% of respondents with *founding* as career intention	34.66	37.17	33.88	35.78	37.88	41.51
	% of respondents with *succeeding* (in the family business) as career intention	2.09	6.09	0.84	5.68	3.86	8.18
	% of respondents with *succeeding* (in another business) as career intention	2.16	2.62	2.02	2.48	2.42	2.91

F-I Variables						
EFB & parents' operational involvement in the business		EFB & number of siblings			EFB & verbal encouragement	
Y	N	0	1–2	3+	High	Low
2a	2b	3a	3b	3c	4a	4b
20,037	17,374	23,478	13,182	5,453	29,420	20,037
7.99	17.09	14.35	7.19	10.51	13.40	7.95
5.19	7.00	6.65	4.57	5.46	6.42	4.96
0.70	1.39	1.15	0.61	1.05	1.02	0.82
37.68	36.24	36.55	34.83	42.31	38.26	35.58
5.96	6.33	6.43	5.52	5.70	6.05	6.15
2.39	3.04	2.78	2.19	3.04	2.69	2.53

Table 5.1 (continued)

		Overall			F-FB Variables		
		Full sample	Enterprising family background (EFB)		EFB & parents' ownership in the business		
			Y	N	Father	Mother	Both
Entrepreneurial cognition	University environment	4.43	4.59 (1.68)	4.38 (1.66)	4.57 (1.67)	4.49 (1.67)	4.65 (1.70)
	Program learning	4.37	4.56 (1.63)	4.31 (1.64)	4.54 (1.62)	4.46 (1.63)	4.61 (1.66)
	Entrepreneurship intention	4.50	4.76 (1.66)	4.43 (1.72)	4.76 (1.64)	4.60 (1.66)	4.84 (1.69)
	Entrepreneurship attitude	3.98	4.32 (1.86)	3.89 (1.91)	4.28 (1.86)	4.16 (1.85)	4.43 (1.88)
	Entrepreneurial self-efficacy	4.48	4.72 (1.38)	4.42 (1.46)	4.71 (1.37)	4.61 (1.38)	4.80 (1.38)
	Locus of control	5.13	5.24 (1.18)	5.10 (1.24)	5.23 (1.17)	5.23 (1.15)	5.31 (1.19)
	Subjective norms (family)	5.62	5.89 (1.38)	5.53 (1.54)	5.38 (1.38)	5.85 (1.39)	6.06 (1.32)
	Subjective norms (friends)	5.67	5.82 (1.29)	5.62 (1.37)	5.79 (1.28)	5.77 (1.32)	5.92 (1.27)
	Subjective norms (students)	5.40	5.54 (1.42)	5.36 (1.46)	5.52 (1.40)	5.47 (1.44)	5.62 (1.26)
Gestation activities	% of respondents that have not completed any of the gestation activities	8.72	0.2	12.72	0.23	0	0.26
	Number of gestation activities	3.68	2.43	2.15	2.12	2.47	2.77

		F-I Variables				
EFB & parents' operational involvement in the business		EFB & number of siblings			EFB & verbal encouragement	
Y	N	0	1–2	3+	High	Low
4.48	4.80	4.65	4.44	5.64	4.76	4.35
(1.65)	(1.70)	(1.71)	(1.64)	(1.68)	(1.72)	(1.59)
4.40	4.85	4.68	4.35	4.58	4.74	4.29
(1.61)	(1.63)	(1.64)	(1.61)	(1.63)	(1.67)	(1.53)
4.75	4.80	4.67	4.68	5.05	4.89	4.63
(1.66)	(1.63)	(1.68)	(1.64)	(1.63)	(1.72)	(1.58)
4.29	4.41	4.20	4.20	4.69	4.44	4.20
(1.86)	(1.82)	(1.86)	(1.84)	(1.84)	(1.93)	(1.78)
4.71	4.78	4.66	4.69	4.88	4.89	4.56
(1.37)	(1.39)	(1.38)	(1.36)	(1.38)	(1.41)	(1.33)
5.25	5.22	5.25	5.20	5.33	5.45	5.05
(1.17)	(1.21)	(1.17)	(1.17)	(1.22)	(1.15)	(1.17)
5.90	5.87	5.89	5.83	5.98	6.06	5.64
(1.36)	(1.41)	(1.38)	(1.38)	(1.37)	(1.33)	(1.41)
5.84	5.77	5.81	5.80	5.89	5.96	5.61
(1.26)	(1.35)	(1.31)	(1.27)	(1.29)	(1.27)	(1.29)
5.54	5.53	5.53	5.51	5.61	5.67	5.34
(1.40)	(1.46)	(1.44)	(1.40)	(1.43)	(1.43)	(1.39)
0.40	0.26	0.59	0.28	0.32	0.34	0.38
2.51	1.94	2.52	2.16	2.54	2.78	2.27

Table 5.1 (continued)

		Overall			F-FB Variables		
		Full sample	Enterprising family background (EFB)		EFB & parents' ownership in the business		
			Y	N	Father	Mother	Both
New firm ownership (nascent)	% respondents with ownership =0	2.85	0.60	2.87	0	0	1.89
	% respondents with ownership =100	26.93	27.71	26.92	27.16	15.79	33.96
	% respondents with co-owners =0	31.52	30.49	31.52	35.80	15.79	31.37
	% respondents with female co-owners =0	35.13	42.50	35.08	50.00	16.67	44.00
	% respondents with relative co-owners =0	58.73	70.00	58.65	73.68	66.67	72.00
	% respondents with peer co-owners =0	44.46	48.75	44.63	50.00	33.33	48.00
New firm ownership (actual)	% respondents with ownership =0	6.63	4.73	8.04	4.14	3.61	5.49
	% respondents with ownership =100	34.23	27.84	38.97	23.95	32.19	35.40
	% respondents with female ownership =0	27.10	20.75	32.49	22.12	17.99	22.18
	% respondents with female ownership =100	3.50	12.14	15.61	9.47	18.94	15.06

| EFB & parents' operational involvement in the business | | F-I Variables | | | | |
| | | EFB & number of siblings | | | EFB & verbal encouragement | |
Y	N	0	1–2	3+	High	Low
0.69	0	1.45	0	0	1.72	0
30.56	9.09	31.88	23.40	15.63	25.86	28.70
32.39	18.18	39.71	21.28	12.90	33.93	28.70
40.00	93.34	41.93	42.31	52.94	35.72	46.15
72.31	60.00	70.96	84.61	52.94	71.43	69.23
47.69	53.34	45.16	46.16	52.95	50.01	48.07
0	0	0	0	0	0	0
0	0	0	0	0	0	0
0	0	0	0	0	0	0
0	0	0	0	0	0	0

Table 5.2: Entrepreneurial Outcomes Across Subsamples Along the Interfaces of Family Business (FB)-Individual (I) and Family (F)-Individual (I)-Family Business (FB) Domains.

		FB-I variables						
		EFB & personal ownership in the family business			EFB & business regarded as "family business" by the respondent		EFB & respondent has been working for the family business	
		<50%	50–99%	100%	Yes	No	Yes	No
	Sample #	5a	5b	5c	6a	6b	7a	7b
	Sample Size	44,569	46,648	2,809	22,324	27,133	17,147	32,310
Immediately after studies	% of respondents with *founding* as career intention	7.50	11.59	10.50	8.45	13.44	8.95	12.83
	% of respondents with *succeeding* (in the family business) as career intention	4.70	6.93	6.12	6.86	4.98	7.63	4.87
	% of respondents with *succeeding* (in another business) as career intention	0.70	1.30	0.82	0.75	1.10	0.75	1.04
5 years after studies	% of respondents with *founding* as career intention	36.90	37.09	39.77	37.46	36.94	38.94	36.24
	% of respondents with *succeeding* (in the family business) as career intention	5.70	6.93	5.84	7.61	4.84	8.39	4.87
	% of respondents with *succeeding* (in another business) as career intention	2.40	2.84	2.81	2.45	2.76	2.54	2.66

	F-I-FB variables						
EFB & FB performance		**EFB & IA**		**EFB & CRM**		**EFB & ES**	
High	**Low**	**High**	**Low**	**High**	**Low**	**High**	**Low**
8a	8b	9a	9b	10a	10b	11a	11b
32,478	16,979	33,911	15,546	31,014	18,443	31,508	17,949
13.75	6.29	13.71	5.69	13.46	7.36	14.29	5.74
7.41	2.79	7.71	1.72	7.37	3.23	7.91	2.16
1.13	0.58	1.13	0.53	1.07	0.73	1.19	0.50
38.73	34.20	38.96	33.27	39.08	33.97	38.72	34.46
7.51	3.37	7.73	2.50	7.27	4.10	7.93	2.86
2.90	2.09	2.78	2.27	2.76	2.39	2.88	2.17

Table 5.2 (continued)

		EFB & personal ownership in the family business			EFB & business regarded as "family business" by the respondent		EFB & respondent has been working for the family business	
		<50%	50–99%	100%	Yes	No	Yes	No
Entrepreneurial cognition	University environment	4.42 (1.64)	4.94 (1.60)	4.65 (1.72)	4.56 (1.64)	4.62 (1.71)	5.64 (1.62)	4.57 (1.71)
	Program learning	4.35 (1.60)	4.91 (1.55)	4.62 (1.68)	4.51 (1.60)	4.60 (1.65)	4.58 (1.59)	4.55 (1.65)
	Entrepreneurship intention	4.69 (1.66)	5.21 (1.52)	4.92 (1.69)	4.84 (1.64)	4.65 (1.68)	4.93 (1.61)	4.63 (1.68)
	Entrepreneurship attitude	4.22 (1.85)	5.01 (1.68)	4.54 (1.89)	4.42 (1.84)	4.18 (1.87)	4.55 (1.83)	4.14 (1.86)
	Entrepreneurial self-efficacy	4.56 (1.40)	5.23 (1.30)	4.95 (1.42)	4.81 (1.86)	4.62 (1.39)	4.90 (1.33)	4.60 (1.39)
	Locus of control	5.21 (1.18)	5.49 (1.15)	5.37 (1.22)	5.29 (1.17)	5.19 (1.19)	5.33 (1.15)	5.18 (1.20)
	Subjective norms (family)	5.85 (1.38)	6.00 (1.32)	5.96 (1.41)	5.95 (1.34)	5.84 (1.40)	5.96 (1.33)	5.85 (1.40)
	Subjective norms (friends)	5.81 (1.27)	5.84 (1.30)	5.92 (1.29)	5.86 (1.25)	5.79 (1.32)	5.86 (1.25)	5.80 (1.31)
	Subjective norms (students)	5.50 (1.40)	5.62 (1.41)	5.63 (1.44)	5.57 (1.39)	5.51 (1.44)	5.57 (1.38)	5.52 (1.44)
Gestation activities	% of respondents that have not completed any of the gestation activities	0.40	0.13	0.22	0.26	0.60	0.38	0.30
	Number of gestation activities	2.44	1.29	1.43	2.53	2.31	2.30	2.56

			F-I-FB variables				
EFB & FB performance		EFB & IA		EFB & CRM		EFB & ES	
High	Low	High	Low	High	Low	High	Low
4.85	4.10	4.85	4.02	4.80	4.24	4.88	4.08
(1.66)	(1.60)	(1.64)	(1.63)	(1.70)	(1.58)	(1.63)	(1.63)
4.86	3.99	4.88	3.87	4.78	4.19	4.93	3.90
(1.59)	(1.55)	(1.56)	(1.56)	(1.65)	(1.53)	(1.55)	(1.57)
5.13	4.30	4.83	4.19	5.03	4.47	5.22	4.25
(1.56)	(1.66)	(1.70)	(1.70)	(1.65)	(1.61)	(1.47)	(1.70)
4.77	3.73	4.83	3.59	4.62	3.99	4.93	3.64
(1.77)	(1.80)	(1.70)	(1.82)	(1.88)	(1.77)	(1.66)	(1.83)
5.08	4.27	5.10	4.20	4.99	4.44	5.14	4.27
(1.30)	(1.34)	(1.25)	(1.37)	(1.37)	(1.33)	(1.26)	(1.35)
5.49	4.93	5.43	4.99	5.47	5.00	5.45	5.02
(1.09)	(1.22)	(1.11)	(1.22)	(1.13)	(1.18)	(1.13)	(1.19)
6.05	5.58	6.01	5.61	6.06	5.60	6.01	5.67
(1.28)	(1.50)	(1.30)	(1.49)	(1.31)	(1.44)	(1.31)	(1.47)
5.93	5.62	5.89	5.66	5.95	5.59	5.88	5.72
(1.25)	(1.34)	(1.26)	(1.33)	(1.25)	(1.32)	(1.28)	(1.30)
5.66	5.31	5.63	5.33	5.67	5.31	5.63	5.37
(1.39)	(1.44)	(1.40)	(1.45)	(1.41)	(1.41)	(1.40)	(1.44)
0.26	0.55	0.24	0.59	0.26	0.47	0.25	0.57
2.39	2.48	2.51	2.33	2.54	2.32	2.48	2.37

Table 5.2 (continued)

		FB-I variables						
		EFB & personal ownership in the family business			EFB & business regarded as "family business" by the respondent		EFB & respondent has been working for the family business	
		<50%	50–99%	100%	Yes	No	Yes	No
New firm ownership (nascent)	% respondents with ownership =0	0.68	0	0	0	1.33	0	1.61
	% respondents with ownership =100	25.68	33.33	55.56	29.67	25.33	33.65	17.74
	% respondents with co-owners =0	27.40	55.56	55.56	33.33	27.03	37.86	18.03
Female co-founders (nascent)	% respondents with female co-owners =0	41.33	33.30	100	43.60	40.60	51.16	32.43
Relative co-founders (nascent)	% respondents with relative co-owners =0	73.34	0	50.00	64.10	81.10	69.76	70.26
Peer co-founders (nascent)	% respondents with peer co-owners =0	49.33	33.40	50.00	51.29	46.00	53.48	43.24
New firm ownership (actual)	% respondents with ownership =0	0	0	0	0	0	0	0
	% respondents with ownership =100	0	0	0	0	0	0	0
Female co-ownership (actual)	% respondents with female ownership =0	0	0	0	0	0	0	0
	% respondents with female ownership =100	0	0	0	0	0	0	0

	F-I-FB variables						
EFB & FB performance		EFB & IA		EFB & CRM		EFB & ES	
High	Low	High	Low	High	Low	High	Low
1.18	0	1.02	0	1.15	0	1.06	0
24.71	30.86	27.55	27.94	31.03	24.05	24.47	31.94
28.92	32.10	30.21	30.88	35.29	25.32	29.35	31.94
41.85	43.24	41.67	43.74	47.62	36.84	40.90	44.43
69.77	70.28	70.83	68.74	69.05	71.06	61.37	80.55
57.10	45.40	45.84	53.12	50.01	47.36	43.18	55.54
0	0	0	0	0	0	0	0
0	0	0	0	0	0	0	0
0	0	0	0	0	0	0	0
0	0	0	0	0	0	0	0

Entrepreneurial Outcomes

We used a number of variables to capture offspring's entrepreneurial outcomes. The first set of variables included understanding the next-gen's *career preferences*. We measured the preferred career choice immediately after studies and five years after finishing studies (count variables) (Zellweger et al., 2011). Respondents could choose one among the following options: 1) founding one's own firm, 2) succession in family business, and 3) succession in another business.

The second set of variables involved measuring the next-gen's *entrepreneurial cognitions* based on the following constructs: university environment, program learning, founding intention, entrepreneurship attitude, entrepreneurial self-efficacy, locus of control, and subjective norms. University environment was determined as the average of the following items evaluated on a seven-point Likert scale (Franke & Lüthje, 2004): (1) The atmosphere at my university inspires me to develop ideas for new businesses; (2) There is a favourable climate for becoming an entrepreneur at my university; and (3) At my university, students are encouraged to engage in entrepreneurial activities. The Cronbach alpha of this measure was 0.95 (next generation sample) (0.90 for the full sample). Program learning was measured by asking students to evaluate the following items on a seven-point Likert scale (Souitaris et al., 2007): The courses and offerings I attended (1) . . . increased my understanding of the attitudes, values, and motivations of entrepreneurs; (2) . . . increased my understanding of the actions someone has to take to start a business; (3) . . . enhanced my practical management skills to start a business; (4) . . . enhanced my ability to develop networks; and (5) . . . enhanced my ability to identify an opportunity. Program learning corresponded to the average of items 1 to 5, with a Cronbach alpha of 0.93 (0.93).

Building upon the Theory of Planned Behaviour (TPB) (Ajzen, 1991) we also considered founding intention and its antecedents, namely entrepreneurship attitude, entrepreneurial self-efficacy, locus of control, and subjective norms. Founding intention was measured as the average of the following items based on a seven-point Likert scale (Liñán & Chen, 2009): (1) I am ready to do anything to be an entrepreneur, (2) My professional goal is to become an entrepreneur, (3) I will make every effort to start and run my own business, (4) I am determined to create a business in the future, (5) I have very seriously thought of starting a business, and (6) I have a strong intention to start a business someday (Cronbach's alpha = 0.96 (0.96)). Entrepreneurship attitude was obtained from answers to the following items based on a seven-point Likert scale (Liñán & Chen, 2009): (1) Being an entrepreneur implies more advantages than disadvantages to me; (2) A career as an entrepreneur is attractive to me; (3) If I had the opportunity and resources, I would become an entrepreneur; (4) Being an entrepreneur would entail great satisfaction for me; and (5) Among various options, I would rather become an entrepreneur. The Cronbach's alpha equaled 0.94 (0.94). Entrepreneurial self-efficacy was also measured as the average of the following items on a seven-point Likert scale (Chen et al., 1998; George & Zhou, 2001; Zhao et al., 2005): Please indicate your level of competence in performing the following tasks: (1) Identifying new business opportunities, (2) Creating new products and services, (3) Managing innovation within a business, (4) Being a leader and communicator, (5) Building up a professional network, (6) Commercializing a new idea or development, (7) Successfully managing a business (Cronbach's alpha: 0.93 (0.93)). Locus of control was measured using the average of the following items based on a seven-point Likert scale (Levenson, 1973): (1) I am usually able to protect my personal interests; (2) When I make plans, I am almost certain to make them work; (3) I can pretty much determine what will happen in my life (Cronbach's alpha: 0.75 (0.77)). Subjective norms were measured as single items on a seven-point Likert scale (very negatively or very positively) as an answer to the following question (Liñán & Chen, 2009): If you pursued a career as an entrepreneur, how would people in your environment react? (1) Your close family, (2) Your friends, and (3) Your fellow students.

Third, in terms of *actions/behaviour*, to capture the development of the gestation process by nascent entrepreneurial offspring, gestation activities of a planned business were also measured, as a count variable. The respondents had the opportunity to select one or more from a set of 11 activities in response to the following question that was asked only of nascent entrepreneurial offspring, that is, those who had not yet founded the new venture, but had deliberately chosen to do so in the future: "Which of the following activities have you (or somebody else from the founding team) already carried out in order to start your own business?" The answers were: (1) Discussed product or business idea with potential customers; (2) Collected information about markets or competitors; (3) Written a business plan; (4) Started product/service development; (5) Started marketing or promotion efforts; (6) Purchased material, equipment, or machinery for the business; (7) Attempted to obtain external funding; (8) Applied for a patent, copyright, or trademark; (9) Registered the business; (10) Sold a product or service; or (11) Nothing of the above done so far. We counted the number of chosen activities per respondent and presented them in percentages, per each subsample, as an average of all students belonging to such a subsample. We also indicated, per each subsample, the percentage of respondents with no gestation activities at all.

Another set of variables included (always in terms of *actions/behaviour*) aims at understanding the new firm ownership, for nascent entrepreneurs only, hence referred to as the planned venture: ownership share in the hands of the respondent; number of co-owners; number of female co-owners; number of co-owners from relatives; number of co-owners from peers (friends or fellow students). The last set of variables included aims at understanding the new firm ownership, for actual entrepreneurs only, hence referred to as the already existing new venture: ownership share in the hands of the respondent and share of females among all persons working for the business, including the respondent.

Enterprising Family Background Variables

Most sample-split variables were based on simple survey items and were mostly binary (e.g., whether parents were majority owners of at least one firm, with responses being "Yes" or "No"). A set of variables was scale-based and was made up of the four factors from "The Career-Related Parent Support Scale": instrumental assistance (IA, median being 4.00 on a seven-point Likert scale), career-related modeling (CRM, median being 5.67 on a seven-point Likert scale), verbal encouragement (VE, median being 6.67 on a seven-point Likert scale), and emotional support (ES, median being 3.67 on a seven-point Likert scale) (Turner et al., 2003). They were obtained from answers to the following question: "The following items pertain to how your parents behaved toward you while you were growing up. Please indicate your level of agreement with the following statements." IA (Cronbach's alpha = 0.90) was measured as the average of the following items: (1) My parents talked to me about how what I am learning will someday be able to help me in their business, (2) My parents taught me things that I will someday be able to use in their business, and (3) My parents gave me chores that taught me skills I can use in my future career in their business. CRM (Cronbach's alpha = 0.91) was measured as the average of the following items: (1) My parents told me about the kind of work they do at their business, (2) My parents told me about things that happen to them at their business, and (3) My parents have taken me to their business. VE (Cronbach's alpha = 0.88) was measured as the average of the following items: (1) My parents encouraged me to learn as much as I could at school, (2) My parents encouraged me to get good grades, and (3) My parents told me they were proud of me when I did well in school. ES (Cronbach's alpha = 0.93) was measured as the average of the following items: (1) My parents talked to me about what fun my future job in their business could be, (2) My parents said things that made me happy when I learned something I might use in their business, and (3) I get excited when we talk about what a great job I might have someday in their business. While IA, CRM, and ES made a connection among the individual, the family, and the family business, VE only referred to the individual in relation to his/her family.

Findings

Tables 5.1 and 5.2 report descriptive statistics across relevant dimensions of analysis for the whole sample and the subsamples identified by the abovementioned variables at the interface of individual, family, and family business domains.

From the whole sample (first column, Table 5.1), it should be noted that, among entrepreneurial career intentions, founding intention was substantially higher than succession ones (be it in the family business or in another business); also, the fact that entrepreneurial career intentions were higher when referring to five years after studies is aligned with previous studies, mirroring a generalized tendency to procrastinate founding processes after graduation (Sieger et al., 2019). Lastly, among the founding intention and its TPB antecedents, social norms were the dimensions with the higher scores, likely reflecting the high degree of social embeddedness that students have, both in their university and in their family environment (Hahn et al., 2020). Apart from the subsample 0b, all the remaining analyses were obtained by focusing only on students *with* an enterprising family background.

Enterprising Family Background

Subsamples 0a and 0b refer, respectively, to students who had an enterprising family background, and those who had not. We refer both to a short time horizon, that is, immediately after studies, and to five years after, reported in brackets hereafter. Students with an enterprising family background showed higher entrepreneurial career intentions considering both founding, 11.19% (37.17%) versus 8.38% (33.88%), and succession in another business, 0.94% (2.62%) versus 0.64% (2.02%); succession in the family business accounted for 5.83% (6.09%) in subsample 0a (while it had no meaning, and hence cannot be calculated, in subsample 0b made by individuals without an enterprising family background). Interestingly, students with an enterprising family background not only reported generalized higher scores in founding intention and all its TPB antecedents, but also in the perception of favourability of the university environment towards entrepreneurship and of learning from entrepreneurship education, possibly confirming an interaction of students' embeddedness in the enterprising family and the university when it comes to entrepreneurship education and learning (Hahn et al., 2019). In terms of nascent entrepreneurship, students with an enterprising family background had a higher engagement in gestation activities (2.43 vs. 2.15 average number of activities performed and 0.2% vs. 12.72% the fraction of students who had *not* performed any gestation activity). A slight difference between students with and without an enterprising family background was also visible in terms of ownership of the planned venture, the latter being more likely (2.87% vs. 0.60%) to possess 0% ownership, and slightly less likely (26.92% vs. 27.71%) to have 100% of the shares. Students without an enterprising family background were also more likely to involve women (about 65% vs. 58%), peers (about 56% vs. 52%), and relatives (about 42% vs. 30%) in the planned venture ownership. The results concerning relatives were particularly interesting, especially if combined with the high fraction of enterprising family offspring intending to set up their own venture, as they indicated a strong tendency to do so separately from the family. When the actual new venture created by an active founder was observed, instead of the planned one by the nascent ones, only 4.73% of active founders with an enterprising family background had no ownership in such a venture, compared to 8.04% of those without an enterprising family background.

In the following sections, we consider dimensions at the interfaces of family (F), family business (FB), and individual (I) domains.

Gender of Parent Entrepreneurs (F-FB)

Subsamples 1a, 1b, and 1c refer, respectively, to students whose father (only), mother (only), or both parents were majority owners of the family firm. A two-sided pattern was particularly evident: on the one hand, father-only students had the lowest likelihood to report founding intention (10.16% after studies and 35.78% 5 years after) while students with both parents as entrepreneurs had the highest (13.37% and 41.51%). On the other hand, mother-only students had the lowest likelihood to report succession intention (3.88% after studies and 3.86% 5 years after) while both-parent students had the highest (8.10% and 8.18%). Taken together, these results suggest that having both-parent entrepreneurs is associated more strongly with entrepreneurship career preferences. Reinforcing this pattern, all entrepreneurial university (environment and learning) and intention-related variables were higher for students in this category. They also had the highest fraction of nascent entrepreneurs who will entirely own the firm (33.96%, compared to 27.16% and 15.79% for father- and mother-only, respectively) and the highest number of gestation activities performed (2.77, compared to 2.47 and 2.12). The mother-only students had the highest likelihood to involve women (about 84%) and relatives (about 33%) in the nascent venture and in the active new venture (about 82%; this case also reported the highest likelihood of having a women-only new venture, about 19%).

Parental Involvement in the Family Business (F-FB)

Subsamples 2a and 2b refer, respectively, to students whose parents were operationally involved in the family firm, and those who were not. The former reported substantially and systematically lower values of entrepreneurial career preferences, in both time horizons (except for founding intention 5 years after studies). Since such a pattern pertains to both founding and succession intention, it might be argued that parents' operational involvement in the family business acts as an overall discouragement factor for entrepreneurial careers. To dig deeper into this evidence, further insight came from entrepreneurial university, overall founding intention, and most TPB variables, which were higher when parents were not operationally involved in the family firm. Students in the opposite case, instead, reported a slightly lower level of subjective norms and locus of control, resonating with a lower likelihood to be a solo-founder, 9.09% versus 30.56%, and not to have a co-founder, 18.18% versus 32.39%; they also planned to involve their relatives more (40% vs. 28%) compared to students with parents who were operationally involved. Collectively, these findings seem to suggest a "negative" view of parental operational involvement, associated with lower desirability and feasibility, but higher normative constraints towards new venture creation. Finally, when parents were operationally involved, students reported a higher likelihood not to have engaged in any gestation activity (40% vs. 26%), but also a higher number of gestation activities performed (2.51 vs. 1.94).

Number of Siblings (F-I)

Subsamples 3a, 3b, and 3c refer, respectively, to students with an enterprising family background who had 0, 1–2, and 3+ siblings. Students who had grown up as an only child had higher entrepreneurial career preferences, with the only exception for founding intention at 5 years, where those with 3+ siblings had the highest likelihood to show such a preference. This category also had the highest scores in entrepreneurial university perception, overall founding intention as a career preference, and most TPB antecedents. A pattern also emerged according to which a growing number of siblings was associated with a lower likelihood of being solo-founders among nascent entrepreneurs (31.88%, 23.40%, and 15.63% likelihood to fully own the planned venture for the three siblings-based categories respectively, together with 39.71%, 21.28%, and 12.90% likelihood not to have any co-owner). Children without siblings were also more likely not to have engaged in any gestation activity in the nascent entrepreneurship process (59% vs. 28% and 32%), while those with 1–2 siblings had the lowest number of gestation activities performed (2.16 vs. 2.52 and 2.54 for 0 and 3+ siblings, respectively). These results confirm that the number of siblings, as a measure of the complexity and distinctiveness of an enterprising family, represents a source of heterogeneity in (transgenerational) entrepreneurship processes.

Verbal Encouragement (VE) (F-I)

Subsamples 4a and 4b refer, respectively, to students who reported having received a high and low level of VE, as a type of family support. At a high level of VE, students with an enterprising family background reported the same pattern as subsample 3c (with 3+ siblings) in terms of entrepreneurial career preferences, cognition (i.e., entrepreneurial university, overall founding intention, and TPB antecedents), and solo-founders' nascent entrepreneurship. In terms of gestation activities in the nascent entrepreneurship process, at a high level of VE, students had a somewhat lower likelihood to be inactive (34% vs. 38%) and showed a higher number of gestation activities performed (2.78 vs. 2.27).

Offspring's Personal Ownership in the Family Business (FB-I)

Subsamples 5a, 5b, and 5c refer, respectively, to students (with enterprising family background) who possessed less than 50%, between 50% and 99%, and 100% shares of their family business. At a low level of family business ownership, students manifested the highest likelihood to express entrepreneurial career preferences. Students in the second category (50%–99%) instead showed the highest entrepreneurial cognition variables. Students in the third category (100%) showed the highest likelihood to engage in solo-founder nascent entrepreneurship (highest likelihood to fully own the venture and not have co-owners, both at 55.56%). In terms of gestation activities in the nascent entrepreneurship process, students possessing 50%–99% of the parents' business had less likelihood to be inactive (13% vs. 40% and 22% for <50% and 100% ownership, respectively) and a markedly lower number of gestation activities performed (1.29 vs. 2.44 and 1.43).

Parents' Firm Considered as a "Family Business" (FB-I)

Subsamples 6a and 6b refer, respectively, to students with an enterprising family background who reported the perception of their parents' firm as a "family business" and those who did not. The former showed higher entrepreneurial career preferences (except founding intention, immediately after studies), but lower entrepreneurial cognition. They were also more likely to engage in solo-founders' nascent entrepreneurship, to be considerably less inactive (26% vs. 60%) and perform a somewhat higher number of gestation activities (2.53 vs. 2.31).

Work Experience in the Family Business (FB-I)

Subsamples 7a and 7b refer, respectively, to students with an enterprising family background who reported having worked for their family business and those who did not. The former showed a response pattern substantially equivalent to those who perceived their parents' firm as a family business (6a), except for gestation

activities in the nascent entrepreneurship process; in fact, students with work experience in their family business were more likely to be inactive (38% vs. 30%) and to
have performed less activities (2.30 vs. 2.56).

Family Business Perceived Performance (FB-I)

Subsamples 8a and 8b refer, respectively, to students with an enterprising family
background who perceived their parents' firm as having performed better and
worse than its competitors over the last three years (median performance being 4.4
on a seven-point Likert scale of five-items accounting for sales growth). The former
showed a response pattern substantially equivalent to those who perceived their
parents' firm as a family business (6a), except for gestation activities in the nascent
entrepreneurship process; in fact, students with a better parents' family business
performance were less likely to be inactive (26% vs. 55%) but have little less activities performed (2.39 vs. 2.48).

Instrumental Assistance (IA), Career-Related Modeling (CRM), and Emotional Support (ES) (F-I-FB)

Subsamples 9a (10a/11a) and 9b (10b/11b) refer, respectively, to students who reported having received a high and low level of IA (CR/ES) as a proxy of family support. In all three cases, high levels of family support were associated with higher
entrepreneurial career preferences, entrepreneurial cognition and – only in the
cases of CRM and ES – a higher likelihood of engaging in solo-founders' nascent
entrepreneurship. In terms of gestation activities in the nascent entrepreneurship
process, students in the "high support" subsamples (9a, 10a, and 11a) showed a response pattern substantially equivalent to those who perceived their parents' firm
as a family business (6a).

Discussion

We discussed the notion of "enterprising family embeddedness" by modeling how
exposure to an enterprising family relates to the offspring's entrepreneurial career
preferences, cognitions, and actions.

The results emerging from our explorative analysis of the GUESS data highlight that having an enterprising family background spurs individuals to potentially
pursue an entrepreneurial career by founding a new venture rather than taking
over the family business, with founding intentions becoming even bolder when

considering a five-year time horizon. This suggests a significant *imprinting* effect of belonging to an enterprising family in the crucial moment when young adults develop intentions concerning their career (Zellweger et al., 2011). This effect might be due to the role of identification of individuals with their close relatives, whose salience is high (Signori & Fassin, 2021); it also proves the relevance of nurturing an *entrepreneurial legacy* in the enterprising family, as an antecedent of transgenerational entrepreneurship (Jaskiewicz et al., 2015). However, the preference for founding a new venture rather than taking the lead in the existing family enterprise suggests that the entrepreneurial legacy nurtured and developed within the enterprising family often translates into entrepreneurial actions beyond the boundaries of the existing business. Hence, we claim entrepreneurial legacy is an attribute not just characterizing family businesses, but enterprising families more broadly, where entrepreneurial legacy plays along with family dimensions, such as cohesiveness and flexibility (Combs et al., 2021). These results have crucial implications for the family business research field. Particularly, they call for a shift from a focus on the "single-family-with-a-single-business" to the enterprising family, that is, family members with loosely connected activities and income sources, as a unit of analysis.

Individuals with an enterprising family background are less likely to want to start a new venture with relatives, peers, and women, thus making the potential entrepreneurial team less rich (Matthews & Moser, 1996). Having an enterprising family background makes individuals intend to pursue their own venture, as in a sense they would be instilled with an entrepreneurial spirit (Au et al., 2013).

Whether both parents are entrepreneurs results in a higher likelihood to develop the intention to both start a new venture and take over the parents' business. Having both parents as entrepreneurs seems to offer a cognitive advantage that can spur an entrepreneurial career. Opportunity identification as well as access to resources could be more easily achievable by individuals who have been groomed in an enterprising family, where both parents had a stake in the business (Aldrich & Kim, 2007; Laspita et al., 2012). However, if parents are operationally involved in the existing business, the next generation seems discouraged to opt for an entrepreneurial career. This might suggest that negative feedback might be installed if the next-gen grow in an enterprising family where both parents might be completely absorbed by the business daily routines, also at times overlooking their next-gen's needs and interests (Ainsworth & Cox, 2003).

It is interesting to observe that individuals with an enterprising family background are more likely to start a business with no ownership commitment than individuals with no enterprising family background; however, the opposite is true if we consider individuals who are active founders and have already launched their new venture. This difference between intentional and actual entrepreneurs could be explained by considering the different types of commitment in place when considering the opportunity to start their own venture with respect to actually launching it (Fayolle et al., 2011; Huang et al., 2019).

Being a member of a numerous family rather than an only child seems to be associated with entrepreneurial career preferences, cognitions, and actions. Our results add to recent studies considering kinship relationships to explain pro-organizational behaviours in family businesses (Madison et al., 2021) and succession outcomes due to birth order (Calabrò et al., 2018). Moreover, they complement the discussion put forward by Aldrich et al. (2021) on the importance of considering household dimensions to explain family business outcomes. With our findings, we show that those dimensions are also fundamental to explaining the next generation members' entrepreneurial career preferences, cognitions, and actions.

Additionally, it is relevant that these entrepreneurial outcomes are dependent on whether the next generation members of an enterprising family actually own shares in the parents' business, which adds to the discussion about generational ownership dispersion (Eddleston et al., 2008). Similarly, considering the parents' business as a "family" business, working experience in it, and the level of perceived performance of the parents' business with respect to competitors might relate to individuals' engagement with an entrepreneurial career.

We also find that embeddedness in the family is complementary to and interacts with embeddedness in the university (Hahn et al., 2020). On the one hand, this gives room for reflections on the role of entrepreneurial education in shaping the entrepreneurial career preferences, cognitions, and actions of next generation members of an enterprising family. On the other, it highlights that the literature on entrepreneurship education, which steadily seeks to understand the role of the context to assess the impact of courses and programs, especially when investigating university students and youths, should not overlook the family and the enterprising family environment as relevant contexts from a cognitive point of view.

Contributions and Future Research Directions

Our findings contribute to different lines of research at the interface of entrepreneurship and family business (Rogoff & Heck, 2003; Uhlaner et al., 2012). Our study suggests an enterprising family embeddedness of entrepreneurship and offers novel and more fine-grained evidence on the effect of having an enterprising family background on individuals' entrepreneurial outcomes (Combs et al., 2021). Family-level antecedents of venture creation (e.g., number of siblings or gender of the household members) (Aldrich & Cliff, 2003) can be enriched by looking at the interdependence of individual, family, and business dimensions. We argue that these three domains play in concert to determine individuals' entrepreneurial outcomes and thus, offer a more comprehensive view on the simultaneous role of dimensions at different levels of analysis (Le Breton-Miller & Miller, 2018).

Moreover, the effect on next generation members, which we ascribe to the enterprising family embeddedness, is more complex than simply deciding to take over the family business (e.g., Aldrich et al., 2021) or looking for a career outside of it (e.g., Block et al., 2013). Our findings show the nuanced impact of enterprising family embeddedness on entrepreneurial outcomes, thus considering the diverse steps determining the decision to embrace an entrepreneurial career (Combs et al., 2021).

Stemming from these contributions, our study calls for future research to further investigate enterprising family embeddedness. First, we prompt scholars to develop theoretical models to explain the interaction of different levels of analysis (e.g., Short et al., 2016). For example, the micro-foundational perspective can help theorize the phenomenon of enterprising family embeddedness. Looking at the micro–macro relations (De Massis & Foss, 2018; Mazzelli et al., 2020), there is an opportunity to extend our understanding of the dual and triple interactions of individual, family, and family business dimensions on entrepreneurial outcomes (Ruzzene et al., 2020; Soleimanof et al., 2019). This would require methodological approaches that allow the study of these interactions, such as experimental design (Jiang & Munyon, 2016; Lude & Prügl, 2021), multi-level analysis, or hierarchical Bayes models (Block et al., 2014).

Second, future research might consider how the assumptions of family theories (Combs et al., 2020; James et al., 2012; Jaskiewicz et al., 2017) can inform the family enterprising embeddedness perspective (Figure 5.1). For instance, systemic views of family firms (Olson et al., 2003; Tagiuri & Davis, 1996; Von Schlippe & Frank, 2013) focus on the roles or communication schema of family members belonging to different systems (Minola et al., 2016; Prügl & Spitzley, 2021); however, little is known about how they interact with each other and with individual-level dimensions making the enterprising family function.

Third, whereas our focus was on the entrepreneurial career choices available to individuals, namely founding or taking over an existing business, we know that only a fraction of students intend to, or will actually, become entrepreneurs (UNDESA, 2020); the majority of young adults, instead, aim at wage-paid jobs (Sieger et al., 2019). Future research can explore the effect of enterprising family embeddedness on a broader array of career intentions including, for example, employment in large or small and medium enterprises.

Fourth, our findings show that being embedded in an enterprising family and university is a twofold embeddedness, where both influence individuals' entrepreneurial career preferences, cognitions, and actions. Future research can consider how enterprising family and university embeddedness affect entrepreneurial outcomes in different contexts, considering the interaction with other types of embeddedness (e.g., community and associations, industry, co-working environments, etc.).

Finally, though no less important, scholars might also challenge the notion of embeddedness as having a positive meaning and influence, considering whether it can be deleterious. For example, there are studies showing how family resources might be detrimental to spurring on entrepreneurial initiatives (Sieger & Minola,

2017). Similarly, family science scholars suggest that high degrees of family cohesion might lead to poor business outcomes, such as innovation, when coupled with low adaptability of the controlling family and conformity in its communication style (Combs et al., 2020; Olson, 2000). As an extreme case, an unexplored area relates to the idea of disembeddedness, as in the case of refugees who have fled countries, communities, and families in some cases, which might trigger novel entrepreneurial endeavours (Alkhaled & Berglund, 2018).

Conclusion

This chapter investigates individual, family, and family business domains and how they relate to individuals' entrepreneurial career preferences, cognitions, and actions. Using a large sample of university students with and without an enterprising family background, we propose an "enterprising family embeddedness" perspective to unfold the complexity of antecedents of individuals' entrepreneurial outcomes. Distinguishing among individuals who express the intention to start their own ventures rather than take the lead of the family business (if at least one of their parents owns a firm) or of another business, and considering any individuals who are nascent or active entrepreneurs, this work moves a first step towards a framework that encompasses these multi-level antecedents and accounts for their interactions that relate to individuals' career preferences, cognitions, and actions.

We humbly believe that this chapter contributes to the debate on the role of enterprising families, scratching the surface of the complex and relevant domains that characterize the social embeddedness of entrepreneurship, not only in the family, but also at other contextual levels, such as the university environment.

References

Ainsworth, S., & Cox, J. W. (2003). Families divided: Culture and control in small family business. *Organization Studies*, 24(9), 1463–1485.

Ajzen, I. (1991). The theory of planned behavior. *Organizational Behavior and Human Decision Processes*, 50(2), 179–211.

Aldrich, H. E., Brumana, M., Campopiano, G., & Minola, T. (2021). Embedded but not asleep: Entrepreneurship and family business research in the 21st century. *Journal of Family Business Strategy*, 12(1).

Aldrich, H. E., & Cliff, J. E. (2003). The pervasive effects of family on entrepreneurship: Toward a family embeddedness perspective. *Journal of Business Venturing*, 18(5), 573–596.

Aldrich, H. E., & Kim, P. H. (2007). A life course perspective on occupational inheritance: Self-employed parents and their children. In M. Ruef & M. Lounsbury (Eds.), *Research in the Sociology of Organizations* (pp. 33–82). Bingley: Emerald Group Publishing.

Alkhaled, S., & Berglund, K. (2018). 'And now I'm free': Women's empowerment and emancipation through entrepreneurship in Saudi Arabia and Sweden. *Entrepreneurship & Regional Development*, 30(7–8), 877–900.

Au, K., Chiang, F. F., Birtch, T. A., & Ding, Z. (2013). Incubating the next generation to venture: The case of a family business in Hong Kong. *Asia Pacific Journal of Management*, 30(3), 749–767.

Block, J. H., Miller, D., & Wagner, D. (2014). Bayesian methods in family business research. *Journal of Family Business Strategy*, 5(1), 97–104.

Block, J., Thurik, R., Van der Zwan, P., & Walter, S. (2013). Business takeover or new venture? Individual and environmental determinants from a cross-country study. *Entrepreneurship Theory and Practice*, 37(5), 1099–1121.

Calabrò, A., Minichilli, A., Amore, M. D., & Brogi, M. (2018). The courage to choose! Primogeniture and leadership succession in family firms. *Strategic Management Journal*, 39(7), 2014–2035.

Campopiano, G., Brumana, M., Minola, T., & Cassia, L. (2020). Does growth represent chimera or Bellerophon for a family business? The role of entrepreneurial orientation and family influence nuances. *European Management Review*, 17(3), 765–783.

Chang, E. P. C., Memili, E., Chrisman, J. J., Kellermanns, F. W., & Chua, J. H. (2009). Family social capital, venture preparedness, and start-up decisions: A study of Hispanic entrepreneurs in New England. *Family Business Review*, 22(3), 1–15.

Chen, C. C., Greene, P. G., & Crick, A. (1998). Does entrepreneurial self-efficacy distinguish entrepreneurs from managers? *Journal of Business Venturing*, 13(4), 295–316.

Chua, J. H., Chrisman, J. J., & Sharma, P. (1999). Defining the family business by behavior. *Entrepreneurship Theory and Practice*, 23(4), 19–39.

Colombo, M. G., & Piva, E. (2020). Start-ups launched by recent STEM university graduates: The impact of university education on entrepreneurial entry. *Research Policy*, 49(6).

Combs, J. G., Jaskiewicz, P., Rau, S. B., & Agrawal, R. (2021). Inheriting the legacy but not the business: When and where do family nonsuccessors become entrepreneurial? *Journal of Small Business Management*, 1–30.

Combs, J. G., Shanine, K. K., Burrows, S., Allen, J. S., & Pounds, T. W. (2020). What do we know about business families? Setting the stage for leveraging family science theories. *Family Business Review*, 33(1), 38–63.

Criaco, G., Sieger, P., Wennberg, K., Chirico, F., & Minola, T. (2017). Parents' performance in entrepreneurship as a "double-edged sword" for the intergenerational transmission of entrepreneurship. *Small Business Economics*, 49(4), 841–864.

De Massis, A., & Foss, N. J. (2018). Advancing family business research: The promise of microfoundations. *Family Business Review*, 31(4), 386–396.

Eddleston, K. A., Otondo, R. F., & Kellermanns, F. W. (2008). Conflict, participative decision-making, and generational ownership dispersion: A multilevel analysis. *Journal of Small Business Management*, 46(3), 456–484.

Fayolle, A., Basso, O., & Tornikoski, E. T. (2011). Entrepreneurial commitment and new venture creation: A conceptual exploration. In Hindle, K. & Klyver, K. (Eds.), *Handbook of Research on New Venture Creation*. Cheltenham, UK: Edward Elgar Publishing.

Franke, N., & Lüthje, C. (2004). Entrepreneurial intentions of business students—A benchmarking study. *International Journal of Innovation and Technology Management*, 1(03), 269–288.

George, J. M., & Zhou, J. (2001). When openness to experience and conscientiousness are related to creative behavior: An interactional approach. *Journal of Applied Psychology*, 86(3), 513.

Gimenez Jimenez, D. A., Calabrò, A., Edelman, L. F., Minola, T., & Cassia, L. (2018, July). The impact of affective commitment and in-group-collectivism on daughters' succession intentions. *Academy of Management Proceedings*, 1, 17353. Briarcliff Manor, NY: Academy of Management.

Habbershon, T. G., & Pistrui, J. (2002). Enterprising families domain: Family-influenced ownership groups in pursuit of transgenerational wealth. *Family Business Review*, 15(3), 223–237.

Hahn, D., Minola, T., Bosio, G., & Cassia, L. (2020). The impact of entrepreneurship education on university students' entrepreneurial skills: A family embeddedness perspective. *Small Business Economics*, 55, 257–282.

Hamilton, E. (2011). Entrepreneurial learning in family business: A situated learning perspective. *Journal of Small Business and Enterprise Development*, 18(1), 8–26.

Huang, T. Y., Souitaris, V., & Barsade, S. G. (2019). Which matters more? Group fear versus hope in entrepreneurial escalation of commitment. *Strategic Management Journal*, 40(11), 1852–1881.

James, A. E., Jennings, J. E., & Breitkreuz, R. S. (2012). Worlds apart? Rebridging the distance between family science and family business research. *Family Business Review*, 25(1), 87–108.

Jaskiewicz, P., Combs, J. G., & Rau, S. B. (2015). Entrepreneurial legacy: Toward a theory of how some family firms nurture transgenerational entrepreneurship. *Journal of Business Venturing*, 30(1), 29–49.

Jaskiewicz, P., Combs, J. G., Shanine, K. K., & Kacmar, K. M. (2017). Introducing the family: A review of family science with implications for management research. *Academy of Management Annals*, 11(1), 309–341.

Jiang, D. S., & Munyon, T. P. (2016). More than a feeling: The promise of experimental approaches for building affective and cognitive microfoundations of family firm behavior. *The Routledge Companion to Family Business*, 385–400.

Laspita, S., Breugst, N., Heblich, S., & Patzelt, H. (2012). Intergenerational transmission of entrepreneurial intentions. *Journal of Business Venturing*, 27(4), 414–435.

Le Breton-Miller, I., & Miller, D. (2018). Beyond the firm: Business families as entrepreneurs. *Entrepreneurship Theory and Practice*, 42(4), 527–536

Levenson, H. (1973). Multidimensional locus of control in psychiatric patients. *Journal of Consulting and Clinical Psychology*, 41(3), 397–404.

Liñán, F., & Chen, Y. W. (2009). Development and cross-cultural application of a specific instrument to measure entrepreneurial intentions. *Entrepreneurship Theory and Practice*, 33(3), 593–617.

Lude, M., & Prügl, R. (2021). Experimental studies in family business research. *Journal of Family Business Strategy*, 12(1).

Madison, K., Eddleston, K. A., Kellermanns, F. W., & Powell, G. N. (2021). Kinship and gender in family firms: New insights into employees' organizational citizenship behavior. *Family Business Review*, 34(3), 270–295.

Matthews, C. H., & Moser, S. B. (1996). A longitudinal investigation of the impact of family background. *Journal of Small Business Management*, 34(2), 29–43.

Mazzelli, A., De Massis, A., Petruzzelli, A. M., Del Giudice, M., & Khan, Z. (2020). Behind ambidextrous search: The microfoundations of search in family and non-family firms. *Long Range Planning*, 53(6).

McMullen, J. S., Ingram, K. M., & Adams, J. (2021). What makes an entrepreneurship study entrepreneurial? Toward a unified theory of entrepreneurial agency. *Entrepreneurship Theory and Practice*, 45(5), 1197–1238.

Meoli, A., Fini, R., Sobrero, M., & Wiklund, J. (2020). How entrepreneurial intentions influence entrepreneurial career choices: The moderating influence of social context. *Journal of Business Venturing*, 35(3).

Minola, T., Brumana, M., Campopiano, G., Garrett, R. P., & Cassia, L. (2016). Corporate venturing in family business: A developmental approach of the enterprising family. *Strategic Entrepreneurship Journal*, 10(4), 395–412.

Nordqvist, M., & Melin, L. (2010). Entrepreneurial families and family firms. *Entrepreneurship and Regional Development*, 22(3/4), 211–239.

Olson, D. H. (2000). Circumplex model of marital and family systems. *Journal of Family Therapy*, 22(2), 144–167.

Olson, P. D., Zuiker, V. S., Danes, S. M., Stafford, K., Heck, R. K., & Duncan, K. A. (2003). The impact of the family and the business on family business sustainability. *Journal of Business Venturing*, 18(5), 639–666.

Oppenheim, A. N. (1966). *Questionnaire Design and Attitude Measurement*. New York: Free Press.

Pittino, D., Visintin, F., & Lauto, G. (2018). Fly away from the nest? A configurational analysis of family embeddedness and individual attributes in the entrepreneurial entry decision by next-generation members. *Family Business Review*, 31(3), 271–294.

Prügl, R., & Spitzley, D. I. (2021). Responding to digital transformation by external corporate venturing: An enterprising family identity and communication patterns perspective. *Journal of Management Studies*, 58(1), 135–164.

Rogoff, E. G., & Heck, R. K. Z. (2003). Evolving research in entrepreneurship and family business: Recognizing family as the oxygen that feeds the fire of entrepreneurship. *Journal of Business Venturing*, 18(5), 559–566.

Ruzzene, A., Brumana, M., & Minola, T. (2020). A causal mechanistic perspective on micro-foundations in family business: The case of CE. In *Academy of Management Proceedings*, 1, 20513. Briarcliff Manor, NY: Academy of Management.

Schoon, I., & Duckworth, K. (2012). Who becomes an entrepreneur? Early life experiences as predictors of entrepreneurship. *Developmental Psychology*, 48(6), 1719–1726.

Sharma, P., & Irving, P. G. (2005). Four bases of family business successor commitment: Antecedents and consequences. *Entrepreneurship Theory and Practice*, 29(1), 13–33.

Short, J. C., Sharma, P., Lumpkin, G. T., & Pearson, A. W. (2016). Oh, the places we'll Go! Reviewing past, present, and future possibilities in family business research. *Family Business Review*, 29(1), 11–16.

Sieger, P., Fueglistaller, U., Zellweger, T., & Braun, I. (2019). *Global student entrepreneurship 2018: Insights from 54 countries*. St. Gallen/Bern: KMU-HSG/IMU.

Sieger, P., & Minola, T. (2017). The family's financial support as a "poisoned gift": A family embeddedness perspective on entrepreneurial intentions. *Journal of Small Business Management*, 55, 179–204.

Signori, S., & Fassin, Y. (2021). Family Members' Salience in Family Business: An Identity-Based Stakeholder Approach. *Journal of Business Ethics*, 1–21.

Soleimanof, S., Singh, K., & Holt, D. T. (2019). Micro-foundations of corporate entrepreneurship in family firms: An institution-based perspective. *Entrepreneurship Theory and Practice*, 43(2), 274–281.

Sørensen, J. B. (2007). Closure and exposure: Mechanisms in the intergenerational transmission of self-employment. *The Sociology of Entrepreneurship*, 25, 83–124.

Souitaris, V., Zerbinati, S., & Al-Laham, A. (2007). Do entrepreneurship programmes raise entrepreneurial intention of science and engineering students? The effect of learning, inspiration and resources. *Journal of Business Venturing*, 22(4), 566–591.

Steier, L. (2007). New venture creation and organization: A familial sub-narrative. *Journal of Business Research*, 60(10), 1099–1107.

Tagiuri, R., & Davis, J. (1996). Bivalent attributes of the family firm. *Family Business Review*, 9(2), 199–208.

Turner, S. L., Alliman-Brissett, A., Lapan, R. T., Udipi, S., & Ergun, D. (2003). The career-related parent support scale. *Measurement and Evaluation in Counseling and Development*, 36(2), 83–94.

Uhlaner, L. M., Kellermanns, F. W., Eddleston, K. A., & Hoy, F. (2012). The entrepreneuring family: A new paradigm for family business research. *Small Business Economics*, 38, 1–11

UNDESA. (2020). *Exploring Youth Entrepreneurship*. New York: United Nations.

Von Schlippe, A., & Frank, H. (2013). The theory of social systems as a framework for understanding family businesses. *Family Relations*, 62(3), 384–398.

Ward, J., & Dolan, C. (1998). Defining and describing family business ownership configurations. *Family Business Review*, 11(4), 305–310.

Welter, F., & Gartner, W. B. (Eds.). (2016). *A Research Agenda for Entrepreneurship and Context*. Cheltenham, UK: Edward Elgar Publishing.

Zellweger, T., Richards, M., Sieger, P., & Patel, P. C. (2016). How much am I expected to pay for my parents' firm? An institutional logics perspective on family discounts. *Entrepreneurship Theory and Practice*, 40(5), 1041–1069.

Zellweger, T., Sieger, P., & Halter, F. (2011). Should I stay or should I go? Career choice intentions of students with family business background. *Journal of Business Venturing*, 26(5), 521–536.

Zhao, H., Seibert, S. E., & Hills, G. E. (2005). The mediating role of self-efficacy in the development of entrepreneurial intentions. *Journal of Applied Psychology*, 90(6), 1265–1272.

Juliette Koning and Michiel Verver

6 Kinship and Family Businesses on the Move: A Review and a Research Agenda

Abstract: What has the anthropological concept kinship to offer to research on family business and business families? This is the question we will address in this chapter. Building on the idea of kinship as interpersonal ties grounded in relatedness the chapter will discuss the merits of employing kinship vis-à-vis the more conventional concept of family. We argue that, while focusing on the sociocultural dynamics, meanings, and manifestations of relatedness in context, a kinship lens is particularly suitable to effectuate an analytic shift from "family business" to "business families". We subsequently show how the use of kinship as core concept and lens can break through some fixtures in the field of family business research, namely: the overarching idea of the nuclear family, the dominance of research based on western family firms, the core focus on the business (and in extension the use of business and management theories), and finally the use of the business or firm as the main unit of analysis. In doing so, we engage with recent discussion in family business and business family research. Throughout the chapter we will suggest new research directions.

Keywords: kinship, anthropology, relatedness, lived experiences, non-Western contexts

Introduction

What has the anthropological concept kinship to offer to research on family business and business families? This is the question we will address in this chapter. As far back as 2003, Alex Stewart posed that the "greatest unutilized resource for advancing the field of family business studies is the large anthropological literature on kinship and marriage" (2003, p. 383). He made the point that kinship is uniquely connected to a culture's normative order and as such a rich source for better understanding family businesses. Despite the fact that anthropological insights are seldom employed in business and management scholarship (Rosa & Caulkins, 2013) and although research that adopts a kinship perspective remains scarce, since Stewart's plea several studies have used kinship to explore the family-related dynamics in family firms and entrepreneurship (Alsos, Carter, & Ljunggren, 2014;

Juliette Koning, Maastricht University
Michiel Verver, VU Amsterdam

https://doi.org/10.1515/9783110727968-006

Karra, Tracey, & Phillips, 2006; Khayesi, George, & Antonakis, 2014; Peng, 2004; Verver & Koning, 2018).

Building on the idea of kinship as interpersonal ties grounded in relatedness (Carsten, 2000; Verver, & Koning, 2018), the chapter will show how kinship holds the promise to direct us towards the context-specific meanings of, and social processes within, the family domain, thus avoiding ethnocentric understandings of family. Following the main line of inquiry of this edited volume, we contend that using a kinship perspective for researching family businesses opens up the exploration of going beyond the one-family and/or one-firm idea that has taken root in this field of study.

This is a timely exploration, as recent reviews acknowledge the need for family business research to advance from business-related theories and explanations towards more family-related ones (see Combs et al., 2020; Jaskiewicz et al., 2020), focusing on for instance family relationships (including conflict), roles (parents, siblings), and transitions (marriage, divorce) and how these impact on family firm actions or outcomes. This reaching out to family science, or family sociology, is an interesting step and much can be gained from it, however it does not solve the rather unproblematic use of the "family" concept and the western connotation of many of the family science theories. As suggested by Yu et al. (2020, p. 134) there is also a need for more research that captures the "diversity of business-owning families" and a need to move away from the "nuclear family" in family business research.

We agree with Yu et al. (2020), but we will argue that there is also a need to look critically at the concept of kinship and to explore new directions in this field from which research into family businesses can benefit. Such new directions in kinship studies are about "the lived experiences of relatedness in local contexts" (Carsten, 2000, p. 1; see also Carsten, 2004; Sahlins, 2011). Carsten argues that kinship should include connections between people that "carry particular weight – socially, materially, affectively" (Carsten, 2000, p. 1) while Stewart (2020, p. 2) suggests an exploration of the "affective qualities of kinship to the allocation of benefits" in family firms. If we see kinship as surpassing genealogy it opens an exploration of "family" beyond blood and marriage and present a more comprehensive understanding of actions and behaviours of family businesses and business families across the globe.

In this chapter, we first discuss the merits of employing kinship vis-à-vis the more conventional concept of family. We argue that, while focusing on the sociocultural dynamics, meanings, and manifestations of relatedness in context, a kinship lens is particularly suitable to effectuate an analytic shift from "family business" to "business families". We will include examples of kinship and business research. Second, we discuss how the use of kinship as core concept and lens can break through some fixtures in the field of family business research, namely: the overarching idea of the nuclear family, the dominance of research based on western family firms, the core focus on the business (and in extension the use of business and management theories), and finally the use of the business or firm as the main unit of analysis. In doing so, we engage with recent discussion in family business and business family research. Throughout we will suggest new research directions.

Kinship as Relatedness: From Anthropology to Family Business Studies

Kinship is at the heart of anthropology. Fox, for example, argues that "kinship is to anthropology what logic is to philosophy and the nude is to art; it is the basic discipline of the subject" (1983, p. 10). Similarly, according to Eriksen kinship is "the single most important social institution" as it "takes care of one's livelihood, one's career, one's marriage, one's protection and one's social identity" (2015, p. 117). While the importance of kinship has been uncontested among anthropologists, thinking about kinship has changed considerably over the years. We consider these changes before moving to the uses of kinship in family business studies.

Early anthropological studies portrayed kinship primarily as emotional and moral relationships among spouses and siblings that result from biological parenthood. For example, Freeman (1973) argued that the centrality of kinship in societies across the globe derives from the psychobiological mechanisms of bonding that occurs in childhood, while Fortes (1972) suggests that the bilateral relationship of "each individual with and through parents" epitomizes in an "axiom of amity" that prescribes reciprocity, "regardless of whether kinsfolk actually love one another" (pp. 288–289). Building on such understanding, until the mid-20th century anthropologists such as Claude Lévi-Strauss and Lewis Henry Morgan were preoccupied with the comparative study of kinship classifications, terminology, and norms across cultures (Carsten, 2004; Peletz, 1995). This comparative project must be seen in the context of structuralist, functionalist, and evolutionary traditions in anthropology, which respectively sought to uncover the structural features of kinship systems, the functions of kinship systems in relation to other domains such as religion or politics, and the evolution of kinship systems as societies move through stages of "civilization" (Strathern, 2014). Aside from the idea that kinship is about biology and blood ties, what early studies have in common is the presumption of bounded and coherent kinship systems within individual societies.

With the waning of these paradigms since the 1970s and 1980s, anthropologists departed from the more rigid and formal approaches of their predecessors (Miller, 2007; Peletz, 2001). To begin with, scholars started challenging the widespread assumption that "blood is thicker than water". Schneider (1984) was among the first to argue against the biological determinism implied in this dictum and showed that – implicitly or explicitly – such determinism had been the fundamental assumption in kinship studies before him. Since Schneider's fundamental critique, scholars have sought to balance the biological and sociocultural dimensions of kinship. Keesing, for example, noted that kinship ties are "at once natural and created", arguing that the "special qualities" attributed to kinship ties may seem inherent to these ties themselves, but in fact "their full expression requires social development and continuous articulation" (1990, p. 160; cf. Franklin & McKinnon, 2000).

Drawing on such reconceptualizations, the field has moved from a focus on "kinship-as-being" to "kinship-as-doing", investigating the social, cultural, and political processes of creating, defining, and articulating kinship and emphasizing the choices, intentions and agency of people in doing so (McKinnon, 2016). Inspired by the interpretivist anthropology of Clifford Geertz (1973), the reconstituted field of kinship studies has moved towards "understanding concrete social actors along with the specific context in which they organize themselves and their resources as well as create meaning and order in their lives" (Peletz, 2001, p. 423). New conceptualizations emerged as a result, such as Sahlins's (2011, p. 1) notion of "mutuality of being", which he uses to denote "people who are intrinsic to one another's existence". One particularly influential conceptualization – and the one that we build on here – is Janet Carsten's (2000) notion of kinship as "relatedness". Carsten (2000) argues that we should not take the content of kinship for granted or as fixed but that kinship as relatedness needs to be investigated and explored on the ground and taken to create meaning in local contexts. Such an understanding of relatedness thus denotes a more open-ended approach, acknowledging that while kinship connections always carry specific meaning, either in social, material, or affective terms, they can also be described in other than genealogical ways.

This ontological and epistemological shift opened a host of new research avenues focusing on what being related actually means and does "for particular people living in specific localities" (Carsten, 2000, p. 1). New directions in kinship studies account for kinship's flexible and fluid character and go beyond the nuclear family (McKinnon, 2016), paving the way for the earnest consideration of ties that were earlier dismissed as "fictive" or "putative" kinship (Schneider, 1984, p. 172). These include kinship ties such as those stemming from same-sex marriages, adoption, surrogate motherhood or other aspects of new reproductive technologies, and forms of "voluntary kinship" that may be situational or ritualized (Furstenberg et al., 2020; Peletz, 1995). In addition, ethnic ties have been gauged in kinship terms as a form of "metaphoric kinship" (Eriksen, 2004, p. 59). After all, next to notions of shared territory, language, and culture, the claim of shared kinship and descent is a cornerstone of ethnic identification – as terms like "fatherland" and "mother tongue" indicate (Eriksen, 2004, p. 59) – and ethnic affiliation may similarly conjure up a sense of "enduring solidarity" and "unending moral obligation" (Bentley, 1987, p. 42). Lastly, the elasticity and dynamism of kinship relations feature prominently in recent studies on migration and mobility, which go beyond the traditional focus on kinship systems in particular localities to show how relatedness is performed across geographical distance (Andrikopoulos & Duyvendak, 2020; Carsten, 2020).

Carsten's (2000, 2004) view of kinship as a process of creating and enacting relatedness has not been without its critics. Miller, for example, takes issue with the tendency to think of kinship as an "arena of flexibility, negotiation and experience", arguing that it risks glossing over the normative and formal aspects of kinship ties, which may not always be negotiable (2007, p. 536). Similarly, Kuper (2018, p. 10) regrets that most anthropologists have come to interpret kinship as "nothing more than the symbolic representation of 'relationships'", which in his view has distracted from fundamental issues such as household organization, marriage choices and feuds over inheritance. Such critiques, however, are a reminder to always take heed of the agentic as well as material aspects of kinship (McKinnon, 2016), to acknowledge that kinship terms have moral and tactical meaning (Bloch, 1973), and to examine the enabling as well as constraining role of kinship (Ram & Holliday, 1993). In coining the term relatedness, Carsten never meant to argue that kinship is entirely fluid and flexible. Rather, she intended to "suspend a particular set of assumptions about what is entailed by the terms social and biological" (2000, p. 4).

Moving from anthropology to family business studies brings us to the work of Alex Stewart, who has long pioneered the study of kinship in family business and entrepreneurship, and more broadly propagates the value of anthropology and in-depth field research (1991, 2003, 2010a, 2010b, 2014, 2020; Stewart & Hitt, 2010, 2012; Stewart & Miner, 2011). In his seminal paper (2003, p. 385), Stewart set apart the "moral order of kinship" and the "amoral logic of markets". While the former prescribes altruism and loyalty, the latter revolves around principles of impersonal and direct exchange. The quintessence of family businesses in Stewart's interpretation is that actors need to reconcile these conflicting logics, which led him to consider business and kinship as *yin* and *yang* (Stewart & Hitt, 2010) – as forces that may complement or contradict each other, but that are always mutually dependent in the family business context. More concretely, the involvement of kinship in business has profits (e.g., extensive weak ties and strategic strong ties that provide access to resources including labour and capital) as well as costs (e.g., nepotism, ill-informed decision-making or conspicuous generosity at the expense of the business) (Stewart, 2003; Stewart & Hitt, 2010).

Interestingly, these developments in anthropology are also reflected in the business disciplines. Stewart initially adopts a narrower definition of kinship that is restricted to relationships by blood and marriage (2003), but he later acknowledges "entrepreneurial discretion" in the creation of "kin-like ties" on the basis of, for example, territory or age (2010a, pp. 294–295). He notes that "quite possibly anthropologists have overstated the importance of formally recognized kinship to the neglect of more informal forms of 'relatedness'" (2010a, p. 295). In attributing kinship to interpersonal ties outside the family, Stewart seems to acknowledge the argument of Peredo (2003) who – in a commentary on Stewart's seminal 2003 article – holds that spirituality- or community-based enterprises are kin-based businesses just like blood- and marriage-based enterprises because all operate under the kinship and market logics. This more flexible understanding of kinship also opens up more space for an examination of businesspeople's agency in enacting kinship. Stewart thus asks previously neglected questions such as: how do kinship systems affect people's choices of whom to in- or exclude from the business, how do people "bend their ties" to the benefit of the business (2010a, p. 291), and how does the employment of kinship as a resource require attention to timing and sensitivity to situational aspects (Stewart & Hitt, 2010)? Kinship dynamics, we learn from Stewart, operate at the interface of the biological (blood ties), the social (human interactions) and the cultural (symbols, norms, and values) spheres (Akhter, 2015).

Stewart proposed to re-label family business into "kinship-based business" (2003, p. 390) – although he also realizes that we are stuck with the term "family business" in popular and academic use (Stewart & Miner, 2011) – and has described the many conceptual advantages of the term kinship over family. A kinship lens is sensitive to the fact that family means different things in different cultures (Stewart & Miner, 2011), and whereas family business studies are skewed to the business side, kinship allows a refocus to family relations and dynamics, and especially to the interplay between the business and family domains (Stewart, 2010a, 2014). Also, rather than looking for the "essence" of family business, which in Stewart's view is to no avail, kinship redirects us to the "the lived experiences of people" balancing business and family life (2010b, pp. 233–237). In the remainder of this chapter, we will revisit these and related merits of kinship. We will build on Stewart's work, recent development in family business studies, and the small body of literature that employs the concept of kinship in addition or as an alternative to the more conventional concept of family (e.g., Alsos, Carter, & Ljunggren, 2014; Karra, Tracey, & Phillips, 2006; Khayesi, George, & Antonakis, 2014; Peng, 2004; Verver & Koning, 2018). In doing so, we will attempt to show that a move away from pre-given conceptualizations of family business towards an examination of the role and meaning of relatedness in context holds great potential for family business studies.

Moving Beyond *the* Family, *the* West, and *the* Business

As highlighted in the previous section on kinship as relatedness, we suggest that kinship in this wider conceptualization allows to address in meaningful ways some core questions currently posed in the wider family business literature: what do we know about the diversity and heterogeneity of families behind family businesses (Combs et al., 2020; Daspit et al., 2021; Yu et al., 2020), how can we move beyond the one-family-one-firm idea (Steier, Chrisman, & Chua, 2015), how to develop theories for family firms that are not purely based on comparisons with nonfamily firms (O'Brien et al., 2018) or go beyond theorising based on examples from western economies (Le Breton-Miller & Miller, 2018; Murithi, Vershinina, & Rodgers, 2020)? We hold that answers to these questions might be found in moving away from a fixed idea of family towards employing the more flexible and context-sensitive term kinship. A kinship lens in our view, allows breaking through some rather persistent boundaries that hamper family business studies; (1) the boundary of the nuclear family – to include a wider variety of kinship ties; (2) the boundary of "the West" – to include the non-western contexts; (3) the boundary of the business – to consider broader networks and family business groups and their sociocultural dynamics; and (4) the boundary of the business as unit of analysis – to consider the lived experiences of kin-based business. We explore each of these in the subsequent paragraphs.

In the majority of the family business literature, the family is by and large the western equivalent of the *nuclear family* with a few extensions that might include for instance siblings, aunts and uncles (extended family). Even if the terms kin or kinship are used, it is typically still rather restrictive and does not yet move beyond more classical interpretations of kinship. In their research on the role of kinship and gender in family firms, Madison et al. (2021, p. 2) for instance introduce kinship as a "demographic characteristic", including "kinship similarity" (family employees) and "kinship tie" (relationships between spouses, siblings, children, aunts/uncles, cousins) with the aim to measure organizational citizenship behaviour (OCB) in family firms. Whereas this research shows some really interesting intersections between gender and kinship, the extent of the kinship ties was predefined and restricted.

In another recent paper, Yu et al. (2020, p. 135) argue explicitly for the need to go "beyond the assumption of a family as a 'nuclear' family" and to include kinship ties in order to better understand how these ties impact firm behaviour and can help explain the priority put on socioemotional wealth (SEW) as compared to financial gain. The authors make a distinction between close and distant kin, with close kin being the nuclear family (parents, siblings, children) and distant kin including other relations such as "grandparents, aunts/uncles, nephews/nieces, cousins, and in-laws" (Yu et al., 2020, p. 135). Using an evolutionary psychology approach, the paper argues that close and distant kin impact differently on SEW, with distant kin being less focused on SEW compared to close kin. Anderson et al. (2005) and Harrington and Strike (2018) similarly argue that family members outside the nuclear family-run business are vital in that they provide professional as well as affective resources. These studies highlight the benefits of using kinship; the inclusion of wider circles of kin-relationships provide a richer understanding of family firm dynamics. There is, however, scope (and a need) to move beyond the blood and marriage type relationships that are addressed in these studies. As examples in the subsequent paragraphs will show, there are kin-relations that are overlooked in family business research while they do matter for the success of family businesses. One of the recommendations put forward by Yu et al. (2020, p. 152) is to examine definitions of "family" across geographical boundaries as interpretations of close and distant kin will vary across cultures. Echoing this, Stewart and Miner (2011, p. 8) warn against the "possibly ethnocentric connotations" of the term "family" and "family business", and indeed argue that kinship studies may help us become aware of the nuances. This is where new avenues open in our view.

These new avenues can be found in research that investigates family firms and entrepreneurship in *non-western contexts* and set forth a more inclusive approach to kinship. Hence, we see "kinship-networked villages" (Peng, 2004, p. 1069) in China that successfully protect property rights needed for the establishment of private enterprises, or kin networks based on shared communal identity in Africa that allow an increase in resources (Khayesi, George, & Antonakis, 2014), and the building of a sense of family on the basis of ethnic background in Turkey that can become a strategic tool in business development (Karra, Tracey, & Phillips, 2006). These studies demonstrate that "extra-family relationships also mimic the ties and transactions within the family" (Iyer, 2004, p. 247) and as such present a "more fluid" (Karra, Tracey, & Phillips, 2006, p. 862) understanding of family as socially negotiated rather than merely attributed by virtue of blood and marriage. In more recent work, Murithi, Vershinina, and Rodgers (2020) clearly articulate the shortcomings of a narrow view of family in family business research in the context of sub-Sahara Africa, where the notion of business family extends beyond family to include wider extended family members as well as members of the community. These businesses employ "culturally embedded social relations inside and outside the contours of the business family" to navigate the voids of the formal institutional setting (Murithi, Vershinina, & Rodgers, 2020, p. 169). It follows the point made by Carney (2005, p. 251) that "family firms may display different forms and tendencies in different institutional environments".

The complementarity of the family logic and the business logic as found in a non-western context (Murithi, Vershinina, & Rodgers, 2020) expresses the idea of kinship as articulated by us and aligns with the conclusion by Karra, Tracey, and Phillips (2006, p. 873) in their research on altruism in a Turkish family firm, in which they state that "the logic of the family [. . .] can be transferred beyond family and near kin in order to build a quasi-family based on distant kinship and ethnic ties". In our own research among ethnic Chinese business owners in Southeast Asia, we identified a variety of kinship relations, such as those based on dialect group and decent and language relatedness, offering unique linkages in support of the family businesses, such as credit arrangements, access to new sectors, supply of raw materials and goods (Verver & Koning, 2018). Like Karra, Tracey, and Phillips's (2006), our research reveals concentric circles, which move outward from nuclear and extended family to forms of ethnic affiliation, each of which is employed differently in the business, thus providing a more fine-grained analysis of how kinship and business intersect. In other words, an understanding of kinship as relatedness allows a framing of both family and ethnic ties in terms of kinship (see also Danes et al., 2008). This is timely because, whereas ethnicity is acknowledged as a prominent feature in today's societies, it is largely neglected in family firm research (Benavides-Velasco, Quintana-García, & Guzmán-Parra, 2013; Harris, 2009).

In short, non-western contexts do bring alternative views to what is and is not considered as family and that family in fact incorporates people and relationships that we might not think of in a western context, so beyond the nuclear and extended family. Research that moves beyond the West provides the family business field an opportunity to critically reflect on and assess existing concepts and theories (Murithi, Vershinina, & Rodgers, 2020). Finally, as argued by Daspit et al. (2021, p. 15; see also Andersson et al., 2018), there are opportunities to align with and further inspire research on family firm heterogeneity, "given that families differ, and even the definition of families differs, within and across geographic and cultural boundaries, studying differences in and among families holds substantial promise for advancing the study of family firm heterogeneity".

A third barrier that kinship might help "break" through is the boundary of *the business*. For long, the family firm was regarded as comprising one family and one firm. Recently this is being questioned and the field is discussing the use of the concept business family as opposed to family business where applicable. Although this development resembles the plea for more attention to investigating family firm heterogeneity, the issue at hand here is the recognition that quite a few families "own more than one business", which has implications for knowledge on family firm management, wealth distribution, succession, governance and so on (Steier, Chrisman, & Chua, 2015, p. 1266). These business families are not only involved in multiple businesses, but their "family" make-up is also often different (family groups for instance). Various terms have been employed to capture this. Carney and Gedajlovic (2002) use the term "family business groups" to refer to the highly diversified conglomerates owned and managed by ethnic Chinese families in Southeast Asia. Alternatively, Carter and Ram (2003) label the simultaneous ownership of multiple businesses as "portfolio entrepreneurship" and assess its rationale. They note that the portfolio approach is especially prominent among business families because it smoothens the division of the business(es) once there is a need to accommodate the succession of multiple siblings. This is where we see further opportunities.

Aside from going beyond the one-family-one-firm idea, breaking through the boundary of the business also takes the form of refocusing the inquiry more firmly towards the family side of the equation. As Morris and Kellermanns (2013) observe, in most research the focus is on the business (e.g., strategic planning, competitive advantage, leadership) more than on the family (well-being, family structure, value systems, etc.) of the family-business interface. In their assessment, presumptions of bounded and internally coherent family businesses hamper insight into the relational dynamics that affect business endeavours (cf. Stewart & Hitt, 2010). Stewart laments that especially in performance research little attention has been given to family dynamics such as marriage norms or inheritance structures, nor to the societal and historical factors that affect the composition of or practices within families (Stewart & Hitt, 2012). While Stewart and Hitt argue that this effectively leaves the family a "black box" (2012, p. 66), Jaskiewicz and Dyer have described the ways in which "differences among families shape family business goals, behaviours, and outcomes" as the "elephant in the room" (2017, p. 111). There are exceptions, of course, such as a study by Dyer, Nenque, and Hill (2014) investigating how family trends (e.g., marriage and fertility rates, divorce, and out-of-wedlock births) affect family human, social and financial capital, and, in turn, family business entrepreneurship among different ethnic groups in the US. Zellweger, Nason and Nordqvist (2012) shift from the firm to the family level of analysis to gain deeper understanding of value creation across generations. Another notable exception, also concerned with entrepreneurial activity in family firms, examines the ways in which household strategies and dynamics influence the development of business portfolios in rural Norway and Scotland (Alsos, Carter, & Ljunggren, 2014).

A kinship perspective would focus explicitly on such familial relations and dynamics and is therefore a promising conceptual tool to work towards a more balanced investigation of both the business and the family. Moreover, a kinship-based inquiry engages with the sociocultural dynamics and normative or moral order that underpin ties of relatedness and thereby impact on the business in multiple ways. For example, Stewart (2003) refers to Bloch's (1973) "sharing without reckoning" as comprising kinship's moral order while Peng (2004) explains that "enforceable trust" and "bounded solidarity" among kin were crucial for the reduction of transaction costs during China's early stages of market reform. Furthermore, Verver and Koning (2018) draw on Sahlins's (1972) distinction between generalized, balanced, and negative reciprocity and various forms of trust to theorize different dynamics among people that are socially and spatially more close or distant. Yet other studies draw on frameworks more commonly used in family business studies, for example, arguing that SEW represents an "affective endowment" intrinsic to kinship ties, which "spurs a strong identification between the family employee and the firm" and discourages "to trade off stockholders' welfare for their own" (Cruz, Justo, & De Castro, 2012, p. 65).

Attempts to break through the boundaries mentioned in this chapter– of the nuclear family, the West, and the business – are especially salient in existing and emerging research on business families in emerging markets (specifically so those in Asia) from which insights can be gained (Carney, 2005). As argued by Le Breton-Miller and Miller (2018, p. 527) business families (in emerging markets) are "one of the most important sources of entrepreneurial initiative and expansion as we go forward in the twenty-first century". However, research in Asia has already hinted at the extra-family relationships that make some of these business families successful with family ties and political ties coalescing to create powerful business groups

(Dieleman & Sachs, 2008; Dieleman & Boddewyn, 2012); in these cases, family ties often stretch far beyond the western idea of family and reach into communities and overseas diaspora (Ge, Carney, & Kellermanns, 2019; Redding, 1990). A kinship approach would add theorizing that includes such ties, not seeing them as externally networked but as part and parcel of relatedness or connections that carry a particular weight, as Carsten (2000) suggests. Next to proving important details on the role and meaning of various forms of capital and expertise these ties bring as an advantage to the business (see Le Breton-Miller & Miller, 2018), such broader scope allows to unpack the underlying mechanisms of these connections and what might make them work in the first place (and in extension might make the business family or family business function the way it does). As argued by Verver and Koning (2018), it is precisely these underlying sociocultural dynamics (such as varieties of trust and reciprocity) that allow specific exchanges of goods, knowledge, and information needed for the business to get started and/or grow. Hence, a kinship approach can unveil "the role of ties outside the nuclear family and the ways in which kinship's moral order affects the entrepreneurial process" (Verver & Koning, 2018, p. 653).

Finally, the fourth and last boundary to discuss is that of the *business as unit of analysis*. Earlier we looked into the shortcomings of a focus on the business at the expense of a focus on the family in family business research. This has implications for how research is conducted, and approaches chosen to do family business and business family research. So, the remaining question is, how do we shift this core focus and better capture kinship dynamics? We contend that there is merit in moving towards a more emic approach that pays attention to the lived experiences of being engaged in and part of a family firm or business family. We concur with Stewart and Miner (2011, p. 8), who suggest that "when we use the term 'family business' we think of 'business with significant kinship involvements' and leave as an empirical matter just exactly what these are". Rather than attempting to set apart family and non-family firms from the outset, a kinship lens thus appreciates the fuzzy and context-dependent nature of "family", what it means to people and how it affects business life. Put differently, recognizing that the search for a universal definition of "family business" – or "kinship-based business" for that matter – is pointless, we may instead think of these terms as working definitions, which represent "clarifications of how the scope of the research is being limited, rather than a statement of what a concept should be" (Rosa & Caulkins, 2013, p. 117).

This dovetails with developments in family business research interested in narratives (Hamilton, Cruz, & Jack, 2017), history, and traditions (Suddaby & Jaskiewicz, 2020), households as unit of analysis (Carter et al., 2017), context (Welter, 2019; Wright et al., 2014), and the various calls for qualitative research in family business scholarship (Fletcher, de Massis, & Nordqvist, 2016; Nordqvist, Hall, & Melin, 2009). These approaches place the family and their lived experiences at the heart of the inquiry and can reveal that the actors are "inextricably intertwined with the strategies behind the businesses they create and manage" (Hamilton et al., 2017, p. 3). In our own research among ethnic Chinese family business in Southeast Asia we have often used life-business history storytelling; stories that interweave the history of the business with the history of the family. This approach can untangle the wider spectrum of persons or networks of interest in the setting up and running of a family business, specifically those encapsulating family-like endowments (see Koning, 2013; Verver, 2015). An interest in kinship and thus in forms of relatedness is well served with a qualitative research approach. As argued by Fletcher, de Massis and Nordqvist (2016, p. 21), a qualitative approach in family business research "can focus on explicating actions, understandings, meanings and contradictions from the viewpoint of either significant individual people or groups of people in the family business". That these explorations are to be understood in context might be stating the obvious, although as argued by Wright et al. (2014, p. 1257) "explicit consideration of context seems likely to provide considerable opportunities for future research and theory building in the field of family business studies".

Conclusion

In this chapter, we have argued and shown that family business research will benefit from a more critical assessment of the core concept "family" on the one hand and a move away from a dominant focus on "the business" on the other. One way to do so, we argue, is to incorporate kinship as lens, concept, and theory. In the words of Eriksen (2015, p. 152), kinship is "a human universal" and this makes it quite suitable to be used in a wide variety of societal, cultural, and geographical settings. The opportunities to investigate family businesses and business families across the globe and collect a wider set of empirical findings (based on an exploration of the lived experiences of kinship interactions) can be used to add to and critically assess existing family business theorizing. The current debates in the field, as we have highlighted in this chapter, seem to be quite well-placed to embrace kinship as a core concept. We can think of the call for attuning to family firm heterogeneity, the need to look into business families where relationships are far more complex due to the multi-family and/or multi-firm dimensions, and the implication this might have for firm governance, and the call to include more research in emerging markets and non-western settings where informal institutions, exchanges and spaces dominate and co-determine a more inclusive understanding of family (including, e.g., communities, overseas diasporas and political power holders).

For a successful incorporation, one that actually will move the field forward, however, an approach to kinship is needed that goes beyond an understanding of kinship as purely based on blood and marriage. We have shown that there is a very good alternative interpretation of kinship, namely understanding kinship as relatedness that carries specific social, material, and affective significance. From such a vantage point, kinship can uncover unique relationships that bear on the family firm and can unpack the underlying sociocultural dynamics of why (and how) these relationships matter in or for the family firm. With that in mind it is reassuring that family science and family sociology research is acknowledging that there is still a narrow, biological, understanding of kinship that severely limits "understanding of the conditions that foster and sustain kinship in nonstandard family forms", and that a debate is evolving on kinship relatedness based on adoption, alternative reproduction processes, stepfamilies, transgender relationships and so on (Furstenberg et al., 2020, p. 1424). But as Carsten reminds us, kinship should not itself become a fixed entity. Research should investigate the accumulation or evaporation of kinship over time – or, in Carsten's words, "processes of 'thickening' or 'thinning' of relatedness" (Carsten, 2013, p. 247) – in congruence with processes of economic and institutional development.

References

Akhter, N. (2015). Kinship and the family business. In M. Nordqvist, L. Melin, M. Waldkirch, & G. Kumeto (Eds.), *Theoretical Perspectives on Family Businesses* (pp. 175–190). Cheltenham: Edward Elgar.

Alsos, G.A., Carter, S., & Ljunggren, E. (2014). Kinship and business: How entrepreneurial households facilitate business growth. *Entrepreneurship & Regional Development*, 26(1–2), 97–122.

Anderson, A. R., Jack, S. L., & Drakopoulou Dodd, S. (2005). The role of family members in entrepreneurial networks: Beyond the boundaries of the family firm. *Family Business Review*, 18(2),135–154.

Andersson, F.W., Johansson, D., Karlsson, J., Lodefalk, M., & Poldahl, A. (2018). The characteristics of family firms: Exploiting information on ownership, kinship, and governance using total population data. *Small Business Economics*, 51(3),539–556.

Andrikopoulos, A., & Duyvendak, J.W. (2020). Migration, mobility and the dynamics of kinship: New barriers, new assemblages. *Ethnography*, 21(3),299–318.

Benavides-Velasco, C. A., Quintana-García, C., & Guzmán-Parra, V. F. (2013). Trends in family business research. *Small Business Economics*, 40(1),41–57.

Bentley, G. C. (1987). Ethnicity and practice. *Comparative Studies in Society and History*, 29(1),24–55.

Bloch, M. (1973). The long term and the short term: The economic and political significance of the morality of kinship. In J. Goody (Ed.), *The Character of Kinship* (pp. 75–87). Cambridge: Cambridge University Press.

Carney, M. (2005). Corporate governance and competitive advantage in family-controlled firms. *Entrepreneurship Theory and Practice*, 29(3),249–265.

Carney, M., & Gedajlovic, E. (2002). The co-evolution of institutional environments and organizational strategies: The rise of family business groups in the ASEAN region. *Organization Studies*, 23(1),1–29.

Carsten, J. (2000). Introduction: Cultures of relatedness. In J. Carsten (Ed.), *Cultures of Relatedness: New Approaches to the Study of Kinship* (pp. 1–36). Cambridge: Cambridge University Press.

Carsten, J. (2004). Introduction: After kinship? In J. Carsten (Ed.), *After Kinship* (pp. 1–30). Cambridge: Cambridge University Press.

Carsten, J. (2013). What kinship does – and how. *Hau: Journal of Ethnographic Theory,* 3(2),245–251.

Carsten, J. (2020). Imagining and living new worlds: The dynamics of kinship in contexts of mobility and migration. *Ethnography,* 21(3),319–334.

Carter, S., Kuhl, A., Marlow, S., & Mwaura, S. (2017). Households as a site of entrepreneurial activity. *Foundations and Trends in Entrepreneurship,* 13(2),81–190.

Carter, S., & Ram, M. (2003). Reassessing portfolio entrepreneurship. *Small Business Economics,* 21(4),371–380.

Combs, J. G., Shanine, K. K., Burrows, S., Allen, J. S., & Pounds, T. W. (2020). What do we know about business families? Setting the stage for leveraging family science theories. *Family Business Review,* 33(1),38–63.

Cruz, C., Justo, R., & De Castro, J. O. (2012). Does family employment enhance MSEs performance? Integrating socioemotional wealth and family embeddedness perspectives. *Journal of Business Venturing,* 27(1),62–76.

Danes, S. M., Lee, J., Stafford, K., & Heck, R. K. Z. (2008). The effects of ethnicity, families and culture on entrepreneurial experience: An extension of sustainable family business theory. *Journal of Developmental Entrepreneurship,* 13(3),229–268.

Daspit, J. J., Chrisman, J. J., Ashton, T., & Evangelopoulos, N. (2021). Family firm heterogeneity: A definition, common themes, scholarly progress, and directions forward. *Family Business Review,* 08944865211008350.

Dieleman, M., & Sachs, W. M. (2008). Coevolution of institutions and corporations in emerging economies: How the Salim Group morphed into an institution of Suharto's crony regime. *Journal of Management Studies,* 45(7),1274–1300.

Dieleman, M., & Boddewyn, J. J. (2012). Using organization structure to buffer political ties in emerging markets: A case study. *Organization Studies,* 33(1),71–95.

Dyer, W. G., Nenque, E., & Hill, E. J. (2014). Toward a theory of family capital and entrepreneurship: Antecedents and outcomes. *Journal of Small Business Management,* 52(2),266–285.

Eriksen, T. H. (2004). Place, kinship and the case for non-ethnic nations. *Nations & Nationalism,* 10(1/2), 49–62.

Eriksen, T. H. (2015). *Small Places, Large Issues: An Introduction to Social and Cultural Anthropology* (4th ed.). London: Pluto Press.

Fletcher, D., De Massis, A., & Nordqvist, M. (2016). Qualitative research practices and family business scholarship: A review and future research agenda. *Journal of Family Business Strategy,* 7(1),8–25.

Fortes, M. (1972). Kinship and the social order: The legacy of L.H. Morgan. *Current Anthropology,* 13(2),285–296.

Fox, R. (1983). *Kinship and Marriage.* Cambridge: Cambridge University Press.

Franklin, S., & McKinnon, S. (2000). New directions in kinship study: A core concept revisited. *Current Anthropology,* 41(2),275–279.

Freeman, D. (1973). Kinship, attachment, and the primary bond. In J. Goody (Ed.), *The Character of Kinship* (pp. 109–119). Cambridge: Cambridge University Press.

Furstenberg, F. F., Harris, L. E., Pesando, L. M., & Reed, M. N. (2020). Kinship practices among alternative family forms in western industrialized societies. *Journal of Marriage and Family,* 82(5),1403–1430.

Ge, J., Carney, M., & Kellermanns, F. (2019). Who fills institutional voids? Entrepreneurs' utilization of political and family ties in emerging markets. *Entrepreneurship Theory and Practice*, 43(6),1124–1147.

Geertz, C. (1973.) *The Interpretation of Cultures: Selected Essays by Clifford Geertz*. New York: Basic Books.

Hamilton, E., Cruz, A. D., & Jack, S. (2017). Re-framing the status of narrative in family business research: Towards an understanding of families in business. *Journal of Family Business Strategy*, 8(1),3–12.

Harrington, B., & Strike, V. M. (2018). Between kinship and commerce: Fiduciaries and the institutional logics of family firms. *Family Business Review*, 31(4),417–440.

Harris, I. C. (2009). Ethnicity effects on the family business entrepreneurial process: Commentary and extension. *Family Business Review*, 22(3),293–296.

Iyer, G. R. (2004). Ethnic business families. *International Research in the Business Disciplines*, 4, 243–260.

Jaskiewicz, P., & Dyer, W. G. (2017). Addressing the elephant in the room: Disentangling family heterogeneity to advance family business research. *Family Business Review*, 30(2),111–118.

Jaskiewicz, P., Neubaum, D. O., De Massis, A., Holt, D. T. (2020). The adulthood of family business research through inbound and outbound theorizing. *Family Business Review*, 33(1),10–17.

Karra, N., Tracey, P., & Phillips, N. (2006). Altruism and agency in the family firm: Exploring the role of family, kinship, and ethnicity. *Entrepreneurship Theory and Practice*, 30(6),861–877.

Keesing, R. M. (1990). Kinship, bonding, and categorization. *The Australian Journal of Anthropology*, 1(2),159–167.

Khayesi, J. N. O., George, G., & Antonakis, J. (2014). Kinship in entrepreneur networks: Performance effects of resource assembly in Africa. *Entrepreneurship Theory and Practice*, 38(6),1323–1342.

Koning, J. (2013). Generational change in Chinese Indonesian SMEs. In T. Menkhoff, Chay Yue Wah, H-D. Evers & Hoon Chang Yau (Eds.), *Catalysts of Change: Chinese Business in Asia* (pp. 231–250). Singapore: World Scientific Publishing.

Kuper, A. (2018). We need to talk about kinship. *Anthropology of this Century*, 23, 1–12.

Le Breton-Miller, I., & Miller, D. (2018). Beyond the firm: Business families as entrepreneurs. *Entrepreneurship Theory and Practice*, 42(4),527–536.

Madison, K., Eddleston, K. A., Kellermanns, F. W., & Powell, G. N. (2021). Kinship and gender in family firms: New insights into employees' organizational citizenship behavior. *Family Business Review*, 08944865211008062.

Mckinnon, S. (2016). Doing and being. In S. Coleman, S. B. Hyatt, & A. Kingsolver (Eds.), *The Routledge Companion to Contemporary Anthropology* (pp. 161–182). London: Routledge.

Miller, D. (2007). What is a relationship? Is kinship negotiated experience? *Ethnos*, 72(4),535–554.

Morris, M. L., & Kellermanns, F. W. (2013). Family relations and family businesses: A note from the guest editors. *Family Relations*, 62(3),379–383.

Murithi, W., Vershinina, N., & Rodgers, P. (2020). Where less is more: Institutional voids and business families in Sub-Saharan Africa. *International Journal of Entrepreneurial Behaviour and Research*, 26(1),158–174.

Nordqvist, M., Hall, A., & Melin, L. (2009). Qualitative research on family businesses: The relevance and usefulness of the interpretive approach. *Journal of Management and Organization*, 15(3), 294.

O'Brien, K. E., Minjock, R. M., Colarelli, S. M., & Yang, C. (2018). Kinship ties and employee theft perceptions in family-owned businesses. *European Management Journal*, 36(3),421–430.

Peletz, M. G. (1995). Kinship studies in late twentieth-century anthropology. *Annual Review of Anthropology*, 24(1),343–372.

Peletz, M. G. (2001). Ambivalence in kinship since the 1940s. In S. Franklin & S. McKinnon (Eds.), *Relative Values: Refiguring Kinship Studies* (pp. 413–444). Durham: Duke University Press.

Peng, Y. (2004). Kinship networks and entrepreneurs in China's transitional economy. *American Journal of Sociology*, 109(5),1045–1074.

Peredo, A. M. (2003). Nothing thicker than blood? Commentary on "help one another, use one another": Toward an anthropology of family business. *Entrepreneurship Theory and Practice*, 27, 397–400.

Ram, M., & Holliday, R. (1993). Relative merits: Family culture and kinship in small firms. *Sociology*, 27(4),629–648.

Redding, S. G. (1990). *The Spirit of Chinese Capitalism*. New York: Walter de Gruyter.

Rosa, P., & Caulkins, D. D. (2013). Entrepreneurship studies. In D. D. Caulkins and A. T. Jordan (Eds.), *A Companion to Organizational Anthropology* (pp. 98–121). Oxford: Blackwell Publishing.

Sahlins, M. (1972). *Stone Age Economics*. Chicago: Aldine-Atherton.

Sahlins, M. (2011). What kinship is (part one). *Journal of the Royal Anthropological Institute*, 17(1),2–19.

Schneider, D. M. (1984). *A Critique of the Study of Kinship*. Ann Arbor: University of Michigan Press.

Steier, L. P., Chrisman, J. J., & Chua, J. H. (2015). Governance challenges in family businesses and business families. *Entrepreneurship Theory and Practice*, 39(6),1265–1280.

Stewart, A. (1991). A prospectus on the anthropology of entrepreneurship. *Entrepreneurship Theory and Practice*, 16(2),71–91.

Stewart, A. (2003). Help one another, use one another: Toward an anthropology of family business. *Entrepreneurship Theory and Practice*, 27(4),383–396.

Stewart, A. (2010a). Sources of entrepreneurial discretion in kinship systems. *Advances in Entrepreneurship, Firm Emergence and Growth*, 12, 291–313.

Stewart, A. (2010b). Skeptical about family business: Advancing the field in its scholarship, relevance, and academic role. *Advances in Entrepreneurship, Firm Emergence and Growth*, 12, 231–241.

Stewart, A. (2014). The anthropology of family business: An imagined ideal. In L. Melin, M. Nordqvist, & P. Sharma (Eds.), *The SAGE Handbook of Family Business* (pp. 66–82). Los Angeles: Sage.

Stewart, A. (2020). Family control, ambivalence, and preferential benefits. *Journal of Family Business Strategy*, 100352.

Stewart, A., & Hitt, M. A. (2010). The *yin* and *yang* of kinship and business: Complementary or contradictory forces? (And can we really say?). *Advances in Entrepreneurship, Firm Emergence and Growth*, 12, 243–276.

Stewart, A., & Hitt, M. A. (2012). Why can't a family business be more like a nonfamily business? Modes of professionalization in family firms. *Family Business Review*, 25, 58–86.

Stewart, A. & Miner, A. S. (2011). The prospects for family business in research universities. *Journal of Family Business Strategy*, 2(1),3–14.

Strathern, M. (2014). Out of context: The persuasive fictions of anthropology. *Modernist Anthropology*, 28(3),80–130.

Suddaby, R., & Jaskiewicz, P. (2020). Managing traditions: A critical capability for family business success. *Family Business Review*, 33(3),234–243.

Verver, M. J. (2016). *Chinese Capitalism in Cambodia: An Anthropological-Institutional Approach to Embedded Entrepreneurship* (PhD dissertation). Zutphen: CPI Koninklijke Wöhrmann.

Verver, M., & Koning, J. (2018). Toward a kinship perspective on entrepreneurship. *Entrepreneurship Theory and Practice*, 42(4),631–666.

Welter, F. (2019). *Entrepreneurship and context*. Cheltenham: Edward Elgar Publishing.

Wright, M., Chrisman, J., Chua, J. H., & Steier, L. (2014). Family enterprise and context. *Entrepreneurship Theory and Practice*, 38(6),1247–1260.

Yu, X., Stanley, L., Li, Y., Eddleston, K. A., & Kellermanns, F. W. (2020). The invisible hand of evolutionary psychology: The importance of kinship in first-generation family firms. *Entrepreneurship Theory and Practice*, 44(1),134–157.

Zellweger, T. M., Nason, R. S., & Nordqvist, M. (2012). From longevity of firms to transgenerational entrepreneurship of families: Introducing family entrepreneurial orientation. *Family Business Review*, 25(2),136–155.

Part II: **Business Families with Multiple Businesses**

Navneet Bhatnagar and Kavil Ramachandran

7 Influence of Next-Generation Family Champions on New Venture Creation by Business Families: An Indian Perspective

Abstract: New venture creation is critical to sustain transgenerational family entrepreneurship. Business families with diversified businesses perceive emergent opportunities distinctly from those perceived by family firms engaged in a single line of business. Driven by passionate next-generation family champions, the scope of venture creation for business families goes beyond business, including creation of social ventures. This probe examines four in-depth case studies of new venture creation by four business families in India. The study probes the drivers, the process, key players, and the dynamics of new venture creation by these business families. The study observes that the nature, intensity, and direction of the influence of family champions varies across business families, leading to different venture choices and outcomes. Interests and inclinations of next-generation members distinctly shapes business families' venture creation and resource allocation decisions. Some business families create new *business ventures* for strategic depth, competitive advantage, growth and providing career path to family members. In contrast, other business families create new *social ventures* for a lasting family legacy or to support a social cause espoused by the next-generation family champion. Based on the observations of their new venture creation decisions and strategies followed, business families are classified into two categories: the guarded *Conservatives* and the adventurous *Pathfinders*. The chapter presents a typology of new venture creation by business families and concludes with implications for theory and practice.

Keywords: new venture creation, business families, family champion, opportunity, exploration, transgenerational family entrepreneurship, next-generation leadership

Introduction

New venture creation is crucial for growth and long-term sustenance of business (Shepherd, Souitaris, & Gruber, 2021; Davidsson, Recker, & von Briel, 2020; Timmons & Spinelli, 2009). In the family business context, formation of new ventures is significant for growth, survival, and family continuity across generations (Minola, Brumana,

Navneet Bhatnagar, IIMRaipur and Kavil Ramachandran, Indian School of Business

https://doi.org/10.1515/9783110727968-007

Campopiano, Garrett, & Cassia, 2016; Schjoedt, Monsen, Pearson, Barnett, & Chrisman, 2013). Creation of multiple ventures over time, eventually transforms a family business into a business family with a portfolio of firms. Therefore, new venture creation must be examined from the perspective of a business family (Zellweger, Nason, & Nordqvist, 2012). Business scholars are increasingly interested in further probing and enhancing our understanding of the *process* of new venture creation (Davidsson & Gruenhagen, 2020; Nair, Gaim, & Dimov, 2020; Kleinhempel, Beugelsdijk, & Klasing, 2020; Kier & McMullen, 2020). This chapter addresses that call in the context of business families and specifically examines how next-generation family members, who champion the new venture idea, influence the family's new venture decisions. In this chapter, we study the characteristics of and motivations for new ventures created during the last two decades by four prominent business families in India. In contrast to the conventional deductive methods, we employ the abductive approach of multiple case-study method, which provides a broader scope to probe and understand this phenomenon and its dimensions.

Employing these case studies, the chapter examines the process, family members' role, and the dynamics, involved in new venture creation. The business family perspective permits the examination of the expanded scope of new ventures created and the motivations that lead to their establishment. More specifically, we focus on the influence of next-generation family members who champion a commercial or a social cause, on the business family's new venture decisions. Based on the case-study analyses, the paper presents a typology of new ventures that business families create. According to the varying nature of influence of next-generation champions on new venture decisions made by the families, two categories of business families are identified: the *conservatives* and the *pathfinders*. The chapter concludes with the discussion on implications of the study, for theory and practice.

The Paradigm Shift: "Family Business" to "Business Family" Perspective

New venture creation has been predominantly studied from the perspective of entrepreneurship and start-up firms (Kier & McMullen, 2020). The nuanced processes of new venture creation need to be examined in-depth (Davidsson & Gruenhagen, 2020). Specifically, there is a need to improve our understanding of the dynamics involved in new venture creation, from a business family perspective (Brinkerink, Rondi, Benedetti, & Arzubiaga, 2020; Bhatnagar, Ramachandran, & Ray, 2018). While assessing the longevity of family business, Zellweger, Nason, & Nordqvist (2012) advised that "business family" is a more appropriate level of analysis because families create or close several ventures across multiple generations. Since then, the study of business families attracted the attention of several scholars (Le Breton-Miller & Miller, 2018;

Jaskiewicz & Dyer, 2017; Jennings, Breitkreuz, & James, 2014). However, a recent schol-arly review observed that the business family phenomenon has been examined with a narrow focus that covered only four aspects: (1) *family member relationships* (cohesion or conflict); (2) *family member roles* (such as parent/child/sibling); (3) *family transitions* (such as marriage/divorce); and (4) *linking constructs between business and family* (such as work-family role/identity conflict, succession, and performance) (Combs, Sha-nine, Burrows, Allen, & Pounds, 2020). Hence, business families need to be examined extensively.

The business families' perspective presents to scholars a vastly under-explored domain of entrepreneurship research. Several aspects of business families remain under-examined. Specifically, scientific enquiry from the business family perspec-tive is distinct from that of the traditional family business perspective, since it presents a comprehensive view of three aspects leading to novel observations (con-figurational issues, scope issues and identity issues), as elaborated below.

Configurational Issues

These issues pertain to research questions related to the nature of a business fam-ily's constitution and the influence exerted by its constituents. For instance, how does the family/members' *purpose* distinctly shape their businesses? Or how does a specific configuration of family members (father-daughter/father-son teams/female leaders) differently manage the business? Similarly, another underexplored area is, how does the purpose and specific configurations of family members distinctly in-fluence new venture creation by business families? The boundary between the fam-ily and business sub-systems and their overlap is another area of deeper probe. For instance, how various resources are shared between the family and the ventures it creates. How does that determine the influence of the family over a venture? An-swers to these inquiries are likely to enrich our understanding of business families and their new venture creation process.

Scope Issues

The business family perspective also broadens the scope to study several other fac-tors that could result in different scenarios in the business and family. For instance, how does the quality of family governance affect the transgenerational continuity of the family business? What factors motivate business families to create new ventures? How do next-generation members influence new venture decisions of business fami-lies? How does the presence of a dominant leader affect a business family's new ven-ture decisions? It also broadens the scope of gender issues that affect the family and business. For instance, how women outside the main business may influence key decision-makers and strategic decisions in the business, say in, succession planning. Daughters who were traditionally not seen as successors, have now begun to lead business or social ventures. Another issue related to scope is the variety of businesses that a business family is involved in. A business family operating across industries also has the challenge of dealing with different industry-specific issues, while each industry is passing through a different stage in its life cycle. These issues need to be managed in different ways using a calibrated approach. Hence, a business family perspective helps in effectively decoding the overall complexity involved in business and family decision-making.

Identity Issues

These issues relate to how a business family identifies itself. A business family perceives its organizational identity different from that perceived by a family business, which results in their distinct behavioural responses and outcomes (Brinkerink, Rondi, Benedetti, & Arzubiaga, 2020). In a family business, the core identities of the business (i.e., "what we do") and family (i.e., "who we are") have a major overlap. Hence, a family business strongly identifies the family with its core business activities ("we are what we do"). In contrast, a business family engaged in several businesses, has an "*elastic organizational identity*" with respect to their business (i.e., "we do many things") but a distinct and enduring identity of the family (i.e., "what the family stands for" – family beliefs, values, and practices reflected in business and non-business activities). Due to this difference in self-perception, a family business may view an uncertain, high-risk scenario, such as an emergent disruptive innovation, as an existential threat. However, a business family may view the same scenario as an opportunity for new venture creation. Hence, the business family perspective provides scholars and practitioners with the comprehensive understanding of the dynamic nature of transgenerational family entrepreneurship.

Families often invest in new ventures and on several occasions they sell out or close down older businesses that no longer remain profitable or strategically important. Even the families having business presence in a single industry, go through various stages of product life cycle and industry life cycle wherein they witness periodic expansion/contraction in product lines and emergence/extinction of markets and competitors. All these changes require carefully calibrated responses. Hence, it is advisable to move beyond the debate between these two perspectives and treat all family businesses as entrepreneurial business families.

Next-Generation Champions and New Venture Creation

The most unique and invaluable resource of a business family is its human capital (Dawson, 2012; Danes, Stafford, & Haynes, 2009; Sorenson & Bierman, 2009). The next-generation members are the key constituents of family human capital (Murphy, Huybrechts, & Lambrechts, 2019; Sirmon & Hitt, 2003). Their commitment to entrepreneurship has a significant bearing on family business growth and performance (Barbera, Stamm, & DeWitt, 2018; Sharma & Irving, 2005). Next-generation members may emerge as strong family champions of certain business/product ideas (De Massis et al., 2016) or social/philanthropic objectives (Bhatnagar, Sharma, & Ramachandran, 2020). However, family members may vastly differ in their aspirations, capabilities, and risk-taking capacity (Kellermanns, Eddleston, Barnett, & Pearson, 2008). They may also vary in their entrepreneurial imaginativeness (Kier & McMullen, 2020). Driven by their varying goals and aspirations, the next-generation members may either decide to join the family's existing business or setup new internal ventures as subsidiaries of their family business (Cabrera-Suárez, García-Almeida, & De Saá-Pérez, 2018; Mazzola, Marchisio, & Astrachan, 2008). Alternatively, they may create new ventures that are totally unrelated to the existing family business (Ramírez-Pasillas, Lundberg, & Nordqvist, 2021; Pittino, Visintin, & Lauto, 2018). Hence, distinct characteristics and motivations of different next-generation members are likely to uniquely shape their family's new venture creation choices and strategic decisions. However, we have little understanding of how a next-generation family champion influences the venture decisions of their families. This study seeks to probe that. In addition, the paper also examines how intergenerational issues, especially, the presence of a strong senior-generation leader, affect those decisions.

Redefined Expanse of Business Family's New Ventures

A business family has a significant influence on the entrepreneurial activities and decisions of its members (Edelman, Manolova, Shirokova, & Tsukanova, 2016; Chang, Memili, Chrisman, Kellermanns, & Chua, 2009). Conversely, the passions pursued by individual members also influence a business family's collective decisions and their venture creation outcomes (de Mol, Cardon, de Jong, Khapova, & Elfring, 2020). Entrepreneurial families create several business ventures across generations (Minola, Brumana, Campopiano, Garrett, & Cassia, 2016). In some instances, these new ventures are closely related to the existing business. For example, a business family may create a new venture that engages in the backward or forward integrated activities within the value-chain of the existing business. In other cases, these new ventures are diversifications into a completely new line of business that is unrelated to the existing business activities. Business families are also known for the creation of social ventures for the purpose of philanthropy (Bhatnagar et al., 2020). Therefore, the "business family" perspective allows for broadening of the scope in which the new venture creation process is traditionally perceived and examined. It expands beyond the limited scope of setting up a business venture and includes the creation of social ventures focused on serving social or philanthropic causes. Hence, this study considers within its ambit both the business and social new ventures created by business families.

Next-Generation Champions and New Venture Creation by Indian Business Families: Exemplar Case Studies

India has many established multi-generational business families, which have been growing their businesses and establishing several new ventures (Manikutty, 2000). In recent years, several Indian business families have witnessed the emergence of next-generation leaders who have championed new ventures. Therefore, India presents an appropriate context to ascertain the scope and nature of new venture creation by business families (Bhatnagar, Ramachandran, & Ray, 2018). With this objective, we identified 30 family firms included in the Nifty-50 index of the National Stock Exchange (Nifty-50 firms are significant contributors to and representatives of the Indian economy). From these 30 family firms the cases of four large renowned business families were selected that had a history of successful new venture creation. The ventures included in the study were all setup within the past two decades (i.e., 2000–2019). This period witnessed business growth and expansion in India. It had also been a significant period for the emergence of next-generation leadership in many established Indian business families. The four exemplar cases included in this study are: *(1) JSW Paints Private Limited* launched by industrialist, Sajjan Jindal and family; *(2) Svatantra Microfin Private Limited* setup by Aditya Vikram Birla group; *(3) Cipla Foundation* launched by the Hamied family that owns the pharmaceutical company, Cipla; and *(4) Azim Premji Foundation*, established by Azim Premji, ex-Chairman of the computer software firm, Wipro. All data were sourced from published and publicly reported information. One limitation of this method is that it represents only the publicly sanctioned parts of venturing dynamics in these families, possibly leaving out any adverse commentary. However, we have attempted to overcome this limitation by collecting information from multiple, independent media sources.

Case 1: JSW Paints Private Limited (JSW Group)

The JSW Group, controlled by industrialist, Sajjan Jindal and family, launched their new venture, JSW Paints Private Limited in May 2019. The *Sajjan Jindal Family Trust* owns 88% in this venture, while another group entity owns the remaining 12% stake. JSW Paints is headed by Sajjan's son, *Parth Jindal*, who joined the family business after an MBA from the Harvard Business School. The venture aims to tap the Indian paints market, which is growing at a CAGR of 15%. JSW Paints has a consumer division that makes water-based decorative paints. Besides consumer paints, it also has an industrial paints division, which mainly serves another group firm, JSW Steel Coated Product Limited, which is India's largest colour coated steel coils and sheets producer. Therefore, the company has a robust business model based on in-house consumption.

Source

- John, S., & Gaur, V. (2018). A 28-year-old scion is earning the spurs at $13 billion JSW Group. *The Economic Times* (August 8).

Case 2: Svatantra Microfin Private Limited (AV Birla Group)

Svatantra Microfin Private Limited, a microfinance venture that commenced operations in 2013, was founded by *Ananya Birla*, the daughter of Indian businessman Kumar Mangalam Birla. Ananya, who studied economics and management at Oxford, established Svatantra with an aim to achieve financial inclusion of the under-privileged rural Indian women excluded by the existing banking system. The firm provides financial solutions that empower women with opportunities to make themselves financially independent. Though the larger goal is societal development, the business is professionally managed as a self-sustainable commercial venture. The firm achieved break even in 2017 with a net profit of INR 40 million and had a loan book of INR 2.6 billion with a default rate of less than one percent. In 2019, Svatantra acquired a micro-housing finance business to extend its operations to rural housing finance. Energized by Ananya's passion, the venture continues to grow towards becoming a major microfinance venture in the country.

Sources

- Mandavia, M., Kalesh, B., & Vijayraghavan, K. (2016). How these famous heirs are carving their own paths of success. *The Economic Times*.
- Hetavkar, N. (2017). Svatantra Microfin reached break even in FY17. *Business Standard*.
- https://svatantramicrofin.com/about-svatantra-microfinance.html

Case 3: Cipla Foundation (Hamied Family – Cipla Limited)

Cipla Foundation was established in 2011 as the CSR arm of the Indian pharmaceutical company Cipla Limited, controlled by the Hamied family. Third generation family member, *Rumana Hamied* is the Managing Trustee of Cipla Foundation and a permanent invitee to the CSR Committee meetings of Cipla Limited. She is passionate about social responsibility initiatives. The foundation works across India and South Africa, where Cipla has its business presence. CSR initiatives of Cipla are mainly undertaken through the Cipla Foundation, which operates in four key areas: health, skilling, education, and disaster response. The foundation manages a palliative care and training centre. It also supports maternal health services. The Cipla foundation supports school improvement programmes and provides scholarships to children from economically weaker sections. It assists skill building and vocational training initiatives to strengthen the employability of students from remote villages. The foundation also undertakes disaster relief and rehabilitation works to help communities affected by natural disasters.

Sources

- https://www.cipla.com/ciplafoundation/annual-report/index.html
- http://www.iiserpune.ac.in/news/inauguration-of-the-cipla-foundation
- https://indiacsr.in/csr-cipla-spends-rs-36-cr-towards-community-development-projects-in-fy-2020/
- CSIR-IICT, Cipla Foundation team up for distribution of masks in Telangana, *The Hindu Business Line*, Aug. 4, 2020.
- Cipla pledges Rs 25 cr donation to government for fighting COVID-19 crisis, *Business Standard*, Apr. 21, 2020.

Case 4: Azim Premji Foundation (Premji Family – Wipro)

Azim Premji Foundation was established in 2001 by Azim Premji, the founder of IT services firm, Wipro. The primary objective of the foundation was to facilitate universal primary education ensuring its equity and quality. Azim Premji's second son, *Tariq Premji* joined the foundation in 2012. Passionate about philanthropic initiatives in the education sector, Tariq has been serving the board of the foundation since 2016. He manages various activities of the foundation, which is not only a grant making organization but is directly involved in improving the education sector. Independent of the Wipro business, the foundation is deeply engaged with several state governments across India in curriculum reforms, textbook development, capacity development of education functionaries, and promoting institutions for learning. The foundation has established the Azim Premji University, which aims to develop professionals for the education and development sectors. The foundation also undertakes several philanthropic initiatives such as serving vulnerable groups and improving child nutrition.

Sources

- https://azimpremjifoundation.org/about/who-we-are
- Sood, V. and Sen, A. (2018). Second sonrise at Wipro as Tariq Premji joins board. *Livemint.com*
- Krishnan, R. (2020). Schools, girls' rights, Covid relief – what India's top philanthropist Azim Premji spends on. *ThePrint.in*

Findings and Discussion

Next-generation members are one of the key drivers of new venture creation by business families (Nordqvist & Melin, 2010). Especially, when they obtain high-quality education and global experience, they have high growth aspirations. They come up with their own new venture ideas or plans for growth and expansion of the family business (Pittino et al., 2018). Often, business families support those venture ideas if found promising, financially viable, and a good strategic fit with the future growth objectives of the overall family business (Bhatnagar et al., 2018). The

JSW Paints case exemplifies these considerations. The JSW group is a well-established business group with strong earnings and capital reserves. Steel and Cement are the two main businesses of the group. Their next-generation family member, Parth Jindal obtained his education at Brown University and did his MBA from the Harvard Business School. Groomed meticulously by his father, Parth gained outside work experience at JFE Steel, Japan. He joined the family business as an analyst in 2012 and then headed the group's cement business in 2014 (John & Gaur, 2018). As part of his grooming, Sajjan had asked Parth to turnaround a lossmaking steel plate and pipe mill. Family champions are known to drive change in their family firms (Salvato, Chirico, & Sharma, 2010). Exemplifying that, Parth modernized the plant, focused on making better products at lower costs and turned it around in a few years (Mandavia, 2015). In 2019, under Parth's leadership the group launched the paints venture. Parth played a critical role in recognition of new business opportunities, especially with the strategic goal of moving into higher value-added industries from the commoditized steel business. The paints venture had a strategic connection with the steel and cement businesses of the group, which catered to the construction sector of the Indian economy.

> You need steel and cement to build a house and finally you need to paint it, explained Parth. (John, 2021)

JSW Steel, their core business, was the largest producer of colour coated steel in India. Therefore, JSW Paints had the benefit of ready in-house demand from JSW Steel for nearly 40,000 kilolitres of paints per year (Gaur, 2019). Parth's father, Sajjan Jindal, had spent his life in the steel business. Sajjan was passionate about the family's steel business and was focused on growing it. Parth was fully aware of the importance of his family's steel business and the implied compulsion it brought on him of not trying something very different from the existing line of the family's business.

> Steel is the group's bread and butter. All the funds that have been used to start new businesses have come from steel, Parth underscored. (Thomas, 2019)

However, being a champion for value creation, Parth was determined to move up the value chain from the commoditized steel business to a more consumer-centric paints business.

> A steel company stock trades at seven-to-eight times its price to earnings ratio. At the same time, a paint and cement stock trades at 60 times and 35–40 times, respectively. JSW Steel has been able to build strong brand equity which we can leverage (to build greater value), said Parth. (Thomas, 2019)

Family champions create value through innovation (De Massis et al., 2016). Led by Parth, JSW Paints focused on innovating and exploring new hygiene-centric product offerings. It launched anti-bacterial paints during COVID-19 pandemic times of 2020. JSW Paints also introduced the innovative pricing concept of "Any Colour,

One Price", which contrasted with the pricing policy of existing competitors in Indian paints sector, who charged more for shades that used more pigments, that is, more vibrant and dark colours (Jayakumar, 2019). It aimed to leverage the distribution strengths of the group and had ambitious growth plans.

> We have launched antibacterial paint called JSW Paints Halo Safe Home. Our range of antibacterial paints are for all three surfaces – wall, wood, and metals. We are leveraging our group businesses' retail distribution. We plan to double our distribution network by taking the retailers' count to 2,000 and treble the number of contractors, said A. S. Sundaresan, the Joint Managing Director and CEO of JSW Paints. (Sen, 2020)

Though Parth aimed high, he was also grounded and was mindful of his limitations. He was aware of the big challenge he faced to successfully establish the new venture.

> I am extremely new to the industry and new to running a business. It has been just two-and-a-half to three years. For me, the challenge is in actually building a substantial business, said Parth. (Thomas, 2019)

Next-generation members can be passionate about a business idea that is not directly related to the existing business(es) of the family (Ramírez-Pasillas et al., 2021). Business families do support such new venture proposals, especially when those are financially viable (Bhatnagar et al., 2018). In addition to serving as a source of fulfilment of personal aspirations and purpose, such ventures also become a good training ground before the next-generation member takes up bigger responsibilities in the business. For instance, Ananya Birla, the daughter of Kumar Mangalam Birla, Chairman of the Aditya Birla group, developed a passion to extend financial services to rural women entrepreneurs who were not served by the banking system. A business family undertakes corporate venturing when its next-generation members enter their working age (Minola et al., 2016). Ananya had studied economics at the Oxford University and was keen to setup a venture. With financial support from the family, she established Svatantra Microfin, a micro-finance venture in 2013, when she was 17 years old. Kumar Mangalam was very supportive to Ananya's new venture and assigned senior executives as her mentors. New venture outcomes are positive when parents encourage and support next-generation champions (Pittino et al., 2018). This was proven in the case of Svatantra Microfin. By July 2017, the company had a loan portfolio of $40 million and served 300,000 clients (Agarwal, 2017). Svatantra was recognized for technological innovation. The company launched a mobile app to facilitate digital transactions. The business was run as a commercial venture. Since the beginning it had a negligible client default rate. The business achieved a break even in 2017.

> Svatantra's loan book has grown at a compounded annual growth rate (CAGR) of 220 per cent since inception and it has achieved break-even in 2017, said Ananya. (Hetavkar, 2017)

Forming an effective team to manage a new venture is crucial for its success (Schjoedt et al., 2013). Aware of this, Ananya ensured that she had an effective and cohesive team at Svatantra. She gave them the freedom to operate, while she herself focused more on strategy and long-term objectives.

> I love setting up the business and then finding a great team to look after it from execution and implementation, elements which I monitor. I then get into a more strategic role, said Ananya. (Agarwal, 2017)

However, this journey was quite challenging for Ananya as reaching out to the unbanked women clients in pockets of deeper rural India was not easy. Ananya underscored, how support from the family was critical to her success.

> I used to have days when I would feel that this is just not working out. My mother then said there is no looking back now. She gave me the strength to persevere, said Ananya. (Mandavia, Kalesh, & Vijayraghavan, 2016)

Aiming to grow Svatantra into a bank one day, Ananya takes pride in facilitating a societal change: not by charity, but by providing financial services on a commercially viable manner.

> I don't like it when people say we are helping them. Our clients are rural women entrepreneurs who are helping themselves, said Ananya. (Mandavia, Kalesh, & Vijayraghavan, 2016)

Transgenerational entrepreneurship succeeds when the incumbent generation successfully passes on family values and entrepreneurial legacy to the next generation (Jaskiewicz, Combs, & Rau, 2015). Besides her passion for societal change, a key reason for the success of Svatantra was Ananya's deep-rooted connection to family values that her father and the family lived by – specifically, preserving wealth and employing it judiciously to achieve desired business objectives.

> I am very conscious of money and how privileged I am. I use it for the right purposes. Today, banks are lending to Svatantra, because Svatantra is doing well. To me every single rupee counts. I have seen it in rural India. I have seen how much it matters, said Ananya. (Agarwal, 2017)

In some instances, it was observed that the new ventures which business families create are outside the purview of for-profit commercial activities. These are social ventures that may take the form of a foundation or trust that may be operated as a corporate social responsibility (CSR) arm of the business. The activities undertaken by these social ventures, often led by a family champion for a cause, may be related to the core business. For instance, the pharmaceutical firm Cipla Limited, established the Cipla Foundation in 2011 for palliative care of terminally ill cancer patients. Social identity theory point towards natural inclination of women for creating social ventures (Lortie et al., 2017). This is exemplified by Rumana Hamied, who manages the Cipla Foundation. Daughter of M. K. Hamied, Vice Chairman of Cipla Limited, Rumana is a third-generation family member. She is passionate about societal welfare and providing healthcare access to the needy and terminally ill patients (*Source:* https://www.cipla.com/ ciplafoundation/annual-report/index.html). She is especially focused on palliative care and its need in India.

> By integrating palliative care into the healthcare system, we can achieve holistic wellbeing for communities, avert catastrophic expenditure and address unnecessary suffering. Palliative Care puts the patient at the centre, not the disease, said Rumana. (Mascarenhas, 2021)

Though the foundation has its own organization structure and office, it operates as the CSR arm of the pharmaceutical business, Cipla Limited. Rumana Hamied is supported by a team of corporate professionals who manage the foundation's work. In business families, fathers are likely to support capable and passionate daughters (Akhmedova et al., 2020). Rumana is a strong family champion for the cause of providing palliative healthcare to the needy. Her father and uncle help and encourage her for welfare efforts. The Cipla Foundation has not only established its own palliative care facility but also supported several other healthcare and research organizations. It also supports certain schools, skill development projects and other philanthropic initiatives. However, the foundation is financially dependent on the corporate expenditure by Cipla Limited on CSR activities. Hence, the Cipla foundation works in close coordination with Cipla Limited.

Yet another form of new venture business families create, is a completely independent social venture such as a trust or family foundation to achieve specific welfare objectives (Lungeanu & Ward, 2012). Such a venture may be driven by a senior-generation member or a next-generation family champion who is strongly committed to a particular cause. For instance, the Azim Premji Foundation was established in 2000 by Azim Premji, the founder chairman of the computer software firm, Wipro Limited. Premji created the foundation by donating a part of his stake in Wipro. The foundation's main objective is to improve the education system and quality of its delivery across India. The foundation began to operate in South India aiming to improve the elementary education system in rural areas. By 2010, it extended computer-aided education to over 16,000 schools. In 2012, Tariq Premji, Azim's second son, joined the foundation. Since then, Tariq has been enthusiastically managing the foundation's activities. Tariq kept a low profile and was keenly focused on the foundation's tasks. He was brought on the foundation's board in 2016 (Sood & Sen, 2018). The foundation established demonstration schools at several semi-urban/rural locations, which provided free education to children in the local community. Its field institutes in over 40 districts operate across six Indian states. The foundation has a well-structured organization that is operated by non-family professionals (https://azimpremjifoundation.org/). In 2010, the Azim Premji University was set up as a not-for-profit institution to provide inclusive and high-quality higher education.

Even though the Premji family had many years of business experience, managing philanthropic activities were a major challenge, especially because these activities were quite different from their software business.

> Our success in business has taught us many things. But, in social issues, we have to all start afresh. You have to be prepared for the processes of consensus, development of discovering large complexity and execution, and deeply conflicting but equally valid demands, very often not even knowing the next step forward. We do learn and we will contribute but need much more patience and humility than in business, said Azim Premji. (Babu, 2020)

The energy behind the foundation was the Premji family's deep sense of responsibility towards the society and its welfare.

> All of us have a duty to contribute to society. The practice of moral leadership will help us in this; it will also help us in business. We need to work together to develop the India that we have envisioned in our Constitution – an idea that is equitable, humane and sustainable, said Premji. (Babu, 2020)

Though all these new ventures created by business families were managed by next-generation family champions, they were distinct on various counts. Key characteristics of these ventures and business families' motivations for creating these, were identified by analysing the case studies. The specific factors studied include, the new venture's Organization, its conceptualization, scope of activities, leadership team configuration, family involvement, motivations and objectives, resource mobilization, governance practices and outcomes. These are described in Table 7.1.

We observed from the analyses of these exemplar case studies that Indian business families created different kinds of new ventures in their multi-generational lifespan. Broadly, these new ventures included: *1. Business Ventures,* and *2. Social Ventures.* Most importantly, these new ventures were driven and managed by the *next-generation family champions* who were passionate about the causes they espoused, whether business or social. All the next-generation family champions had high growth aspirations for their ventures. Another significant observation was that all these next-generation champions were deeply rooted in family values and aimed to continue their family's legacy.

The cases revealed that the senior-generation leaders played a crucial role in establishing the new venture and mentoring the next-generation champions, either directly or through expert non-family professionals. The business families significantly contributed to the resources-capabilities mix of their ventures including finances, mentoring and family human capital. Heterogeneity was observed in the way these ventures were structured, operated, and governed. The exemplar cases studied brought forth the nuanced distinctions. While some business families created new ventures that closely related to their existing business(es), other families created ventures quite distinct from their traditional business(es) (see Figure 7.1). These venture choices depended predominantly on interests and inclinations of the next-generation family champion and the incumbent leader of the senior generation. In families where the

Table 7.1: Key characteristics that emerged from the case study analysis of New Ventures Created by prominent business families in India.

Key Characteristics of New Venture Created	Case 1: JSW Paints Private Limited JSW Group	Case 2: Svatantra Microfin Private Limited AV Birla Group	Case 3: Cipla Foundation Hamied Family (Cipla Limited)	Case 4: Azim Premji Foundation Premji Family (Wipro)
Venture's Nature	– Business Venture	– Business Venture	– Social Venture	– Social Venture
Venture's Organization	– Subsidiary of Existing Business	– Separate Business Entity	– CSR Arm of Existing Business	– Separate Foundation
Conceptualization	– Conceptualized as an extension/supporting activity of the existing business	– Conceptualized as a completely distinct/ unrelated business	– Conceptualized as an entity embedded in/social "face" of the existing business	– Conceptualized to serve a distinct social cause that the founder/ business family is truly passionate about
Scope of Activities	– Existing business is the major customer	– Started as a small venture but now it is the fastest growing microfinance business in India	– CSR initiatives in healthcare and skill building are closely integrated to the Hamied family's pharmaceutical business	– Completely disentangled from the existing business in information technology
Leadership Team Configuration	– Father/Son	– Father/ – Daughter	– Father/Uncle – Daughter/ Niece	– Father/Son

Family Involvement	– Set up by the family – Led and managed by the next-generation member	– Established and managed by the Next-generation member	– Established by the Business Board/Hamied family and managed by the next-generation member	– Set up by the founder as a Special purpose organization for improvement of education system and managed by the next generation
Motivations and Objectives	– To extend support to the expansion of existing business activity – Offer products and services that complement the existing ones (thus becoming a full-service player)	– To fulfil the aspirations of the next-generation member passionate about financial inclusion of rural under-privileged women – To manage rural microfinance business as a profit-making commercial venture	– To serve the social cause of healthcare and education around the areas of business operations – Improvement of Corporate Image – Statutory compliance of mandatory CSR expenditure required to be incurred on social causes	– Driven by the higher order cause of doing the larger good, that is, giving back to the society by improving the education system. – Service to mankind: social transformation – through universal, good quality education at all levels.
Resource Mobilization	– Capital and working capital from existing business – The subsidiary/ venture was a profit centre	– One-time investment from family corpus – The new venture became a profit centre in its own	– Annual Resource generation: 2% – of net profits of Cipla as stipulated by CSR guidelines – High Dependence on the business (hence resource mobilization constrained)	– One-time resource mobilization: corpus fund created by the founder who gave part of his stake in Wipro – Self-sustaining model (foundation generates its own income)

(continued)

Table 7.1 (continued)

Key Characteristics of New Venture Created	Case 1: JSW Paints Private Limited JSW Group	Case 2: Svatantra Microfin Private Limited AV Birla Group	Case 3: Cipla Foundation Hamied Family (Cipla Limited)	Case 4: Azim Premji Foundation Premji Family (Wipro)
Governance Practices and Outcomes	– Standard corporate governance structure with a board of directors and its committees – High focus on establishing and growing the business – Attempt to establish using innovative product and pricing strategy	– Small management and governance team, hence decision making is quick – Nimble, fast-growing business in rural micro-finance category – Scope extended to include rural micro-housing finance	– Corporate professionals are involved in managing the foundation – Activities tied to the CSR Committee of the business – Contributes to the government's social development schemes – Provides funding support to Programs run by other NGOs	– Well-structured governance mechanisms and systems. – Facilitated educational services through facilities/institutions established by the foundation itself

next-generation champion was trained and oriented towards business, s/he developed keen interest in creating a business venture. This was aided if the incumbent senior-generation leader also ambitiously aimed to grow the business as was the case with Jindal and Birla families. In contrast, business families in which the next-generation champions aimed to pursue societal welfare goals, created social ventures. This was aided if the incumbent senior-generation leader had already completed a very long phase of successful business leadership and wanted to devote efforts and money to social causes. It was evident in Hamied and Premji families.

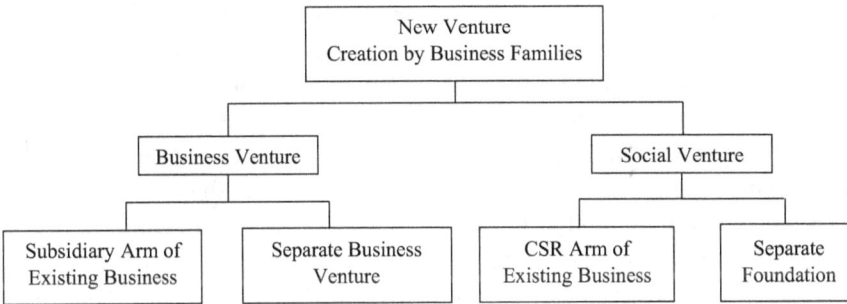

Figure 7.1: Categories of new ventures.

Heterogeneity in Business Families and New Venture Typology

Based on the comparative analysis of the case studies, we find that business families are heterogenous in their new venture choices. They can be classified into two categories:

The Conservatives

These business families create new ventures that are related to their existing line of business(es) and are guarded in to venturing out in a very distinct line of business. Even while creating social ventures, these families set up a venture that is related to their existing operations. Scope for growth in existing or adjoining businesses, economies of scale, familiarity and experience, rich and relevant capabilities set, and high cost of failure are the crucial factors due to which these business families decide to remain in a familiar zone. Also, when the incumbent leader is a strong, proven, and ambitious individual who aims to grow the existing lines of business, then the next-generation champions also limit their zone of opportunity exploration and plan to create a new venture in related areas. This was evident in the Jindal and Hamied families in which the incumbent leaders related strongly with their steel and pharmaceutical businesses, respectively. Hence, they created new ventures in related areas.

The Pathfinders

These business families explore new opportunities in a wider perspective. Hence, they create new ventures in areas that may not be closely related to their existing line of business(es). They are adventurous in nature and even when they create a social venture, it may be quite unrelated or distant from their existing business. More promising growth opportunity in emergent sectors, ability to risk failure, extraordinary pay-outs, and ability to extend resources and capabilities needed in the new venture area are some of the factors that give courage to these business families for venturing into unfamiliar territories. Another factor that facilitates this is when the incumbent leader has a long tenure to serve, then his/her risk-taking capacity is high, hence s/he permits the next-generation champion to explore new areas of growth. This was evident in the Birla case. Alternatively, even when the incumbent leader has had a long tenure, if the cost of failure is not very high, or the family has a wide safety net to protect its wealth through better governance and investment planning mechanisms, then the risks are hedged, hence, the family may create ventures in unrelated areas. This was evident in the Premji family case, which created a foundation to improve the quality of education.

Typology of New Ventures Business Families Create

Based on the structural/operational proximity of the new venture to the existing business and the domain in which the venture operates (business or social), we present a *typology of four distinct kinds of new ventures that business families create* (Figure 7.2). We find that each category of new venture creation is driven by distinct motivations and addresses a different need.

1 Embedded New Business Venture

These are new commercial ventures created by business families in areas which are closely related with the existing business(es). They may share the resources, structures and governance practices with other businesses controlled by the family. These may be created to provide career opportunity to a next-generation family member and/or to fulfil his/her aspiration to enter a new-age business that offers a promising growth opportunity. This was exemplified by the JSW Paints case, where the Harvard educated, next-generation member was passionate about chasing a growing paints market. In this case, his objectives were aligned with that of the business family, which saw synergy between the paints business and the colour coated steel coils and strips business.

2. *Extended new business venture:* These are new commercial ventures that business families establish in areas that are distinct, new, or unrelated to the group's existing business(es). They may lend the resources from other businesses controlled by the family or from a common pool. Such unrelated venture is often created to address the aspirations of a family member who wants to passionately pursuit that business idea, as exemplified by the Svatantra Microfin case in which the next-generation member, Ananya Birla wanted to empower the rural under-privileged women who were out of the existing banking system. However, she was determined to achieve this in a commercially viable and sustainable way. With determination and family support she was able to achieve that objective.

3. *Embedded new social venture:* These are new social ventures created by business families to address a social cause. However, these ventures are more related to or embedded in the existing business(es), for instance, a subsidiary that acts as CSR arm of an established firm. These may take the form of a foundation or a trust or a not-for-profit company. Most often, these are headed by a family member who is passionate about the social cause it espouses. The case of Cipla Foundation, which operates as the CSR arm of Cipla, exemplifies this.

4. *Extended new social venture:* These are also new social ventures that business families create to address a social problem, but these ventures are independent of the family's existing business(es). They may be set up as an independent trust or a foundation, not entangled with any of the existing businesses of the family. Often a passionate family member, such as the founder or a women or next-generation member in the family heads it. The case of Azim Premji Foundation exemplifies this category.

Besides the typography presented in this chapter, the following *three key themes emerged from the qualitative assessment of the exemplar cases* of new venture creation by business families:

1. **Influence of senior generation leader on business family's new venture decisions**
   - A more secure founder/senior-generation leader may support the next-generation members to become more entrepreneurial and allow them to venture on their own with business ideas they are passionate about. Such a business family would see more of independent business ventures coming up. For

Business Family Heterogeneity

The Conservatives	The Pathfinders

Structural and Operational Proximity to Existing Business

		Related	Distinct
Operational Domain of the New Venture	**Business Venture**	*Embedded* *New Business Venture*	*Extended* *New Business Venture*
	Social Venture	*Embedded* *New Social Venture*	*Extended* *New Social Venture*

Figure 7.2: Heterogeneity in business families and their new venture creations.

instance, Ananya's father, Kumar Mangalam Birla, supported her to follow her passion and establish the microfinance venture.

– Senior generation leaders who focused on next-generation capability building were instrumental in new venture creation by their families. Besides technical capabilities, such senior leaders also ensured the intergenerational transmission of family values and continuity in the organizational culture. These leaders were also found to emphasize on the next-generation members' exposure and learning through outside work experience. For instance, Parth Jindal was groomed by his father, Sajjan Jindal, for business leadership and effective management.

– A founder/senior leader with strong desire for social welfare and betterment may often separately devote wealth and resources to develop an entity distinct from the business, such as a foundation that aims at serving the society. They are likely to have an over-arching influence in determining the aims and objectives of such foundation. This was observed in the cases of Cipla and Azim Premji Foundation. While at Cipla, Rumana, who was passionate about social and healthcare causes was motivated and supported by the senior generation leaders, the Azim Premji Foundation was primarily driven by Premji's zeal for societal welfare.

2. **Influence of strategic objectives and family values on new venture decisions**
   - Business families aim to expand and grow, for which new venture creation is essential. Businesses setup their subsidiaries to provide allied products and services. In several cases, these new businesses were established to block the competitors by providing a full-service portfolio or total solution to customers. For instance, the JSW Paints venture enabled the group to establish their presence across categories within the construction materials segment. Since the group had a large in-house demand for paints for color coated steel, it found the paints venture a good strategic fit with existing businesses.
   - New ventures can also be created in areas unrelated to existing business (es), especially when a next-generation member wishes to pursue his/her passion in a distinct field. For instance, in several cases the next-generation members perceived their family's existing business as boring and non-glamorous, with which they could not relate! Instead, they created new-age, technology-driven modern ventures that made business/social impact. Creation of such new ventures support transgenerational entrepreneurship in the family, which is crucial for transgenerational continuity of family legacy. For instance, Ananya was passionate about sustainable societal welfare. The micro-finance venture not only allowed her to pursue that passion but also trained her for bigger responsibility in the future.
   - As they create new ventures, business families also need to meticulously plan the ownership structure. Otherwise, it may become a sore issue in the future as these ventures become large and successful. Family intrapreneurs may demand sweat equity and aspire for ownership rights as performance rewards of "their" ventures even if the investment is made from the family corpus. To promote entrepreneurial spirit, business families need to strike the right balance between concentrated ownership and incentivizing family intrapreneurship. For instance, Ananya's venture received funding from the family, but it had a systematic ownership and governance structure. Periodic performance review was conducted, and measures for improvement were identified and implemented.
   - Traditionally, Indian business families had adopted a family trust model or a family holding company structure for managing the ownership of different ventures. However, tightly coupled families with highly concentrated firm ownership structures face the threat of disintegration by third or later generation. In the Indian context, third or later generation business families had been forced to untangle business ownership because different family branches demanded direct ownership control of the ventures they managed. Therefore, formulating a clear policy and structure for new venture ownership safeguards the long-term interests of the business family. For instance, JSW Paints was incorporated as a distinct legal entity with its own board of directors and governance mechanism. The Jindal family trusts held the ownership of the venture.

- Power dynamics and distribution, especially the dilution of patriarchy and the shift towards nuclear family has broadened the scope of new ventures. Gender equality and change acceptance in leadership succession trend (i.e., successor choice no more limited to the eldest male child) has also diversified the nature of new ventures created. Intergenerational relationship in nuclear families has become much closer. Conversely, the cost of successor-failure has also increased. For instance, in each of these cases, the next-generation leaders had very close and strong relationships with their senior generation leaders. They only had one or two siblings; hence the family had limited choice for a successor. Therefore, the cost of failure for those next-generation members was very high. They were aware of this and hence made conscious efforts to lead the ventures effectively.
- Businesses establish their CSR arms as they become (or want to portray themselves as) more socially responsible. These CSR arms may be mainly functional in and around the areas of their business operations. They may mainly aim at fulfilling the mandatory CSR norm (profit-making Indian firms need to spend 2% of net profit on CSR activities) or engage in social welfare initiatives in association with other NGOs. Some CSR ventures may also be established with strategic objectives, for instance, a business operating in a highly polluting industry may set up a CSR arm that promotes sanitation and recycling. However, in this study, it was found that there was a genuine desire for societal welfare among the next-generation leaders, which was reflected in Cipla and Svatantra cases.
- New venture creation choices are significantly influenced by the owner family's purpose and values. In cases where the business family has a deeper belief to work for societal well-being and development, they may setup a separate foundation with clear aims and objectives. Separate funds to support its activities, may be allocated to the foundation either from family wealth or may be sourced from existing business(es). The foundations are likely to adopt a self-sustaining model. Usually, these foundations are driven by a family member's passion for some higher-order objective(s). This member may be the founder or senior generation leader or the spouse or the daughter/son of the business leader. For instance, in the Premji foundation case, the philanthropic efforts were initiated by the founder and carried forward by his son who was passionate for societal welfare.

3. **Influence of the Next-Generation Members on New Venture Decisions**
   - Sometimes, the next-generation members may not want to join the existing business, which they may view as "old-fashioned". In addition, they may be motivated by a new-age, technology-oriented business. Hence, to fulfil their aspirations, the business families may support new ventures in unrelated areas. For instance, after getting world-class education, Parth wanted to explore options

beyond the traditional family business of steel; paints, and cement ventures offered him that, while providing a good strategic fit with existing business.
- In some cases, a family member (more often a women) may have a passion to pursue a social cause. Therefore, the business family may establish a social venture to fulfil those needs. In some cases, the family may drive this initiative and setup a distinct body. While in other cases, the family member may become the head of the CSR arm of the business, just as Rumana did in the case of Cipla.
- Daughters have been becoming very active in creating new ventures. Sometimes such ventures may be a hybrid of social and business ventures. In several cases, their social venture experience may provide a next-generation member with the necessary experience and training required to make a successful entry into the business. In this study, this was observed in the case of Ananya Birla, who got groomed for the group's larger business leadership role.

Conclusion

New venture creation strategies and choices made by Indian business families continue to evolve with time. We observe that business families boldly venture into unrelated business areas where they see promise of growth and an untapped opportunity. However, unlike in the olden times when this diversification was necessitated due to artificial caps on capacity placed by regulatory authorities, Indian business families now plan their new venture in a more systematic and well-planned manner. They are also more open to hire the services of experts and outside professional talent to build the talent pool and capabilities required to successfully manage the new venture. Planning for next-generation members' capability development is becoming very crucial. The next-generation members of the business families are playing a key role in identifying the new venture opportunities in areas that are high-tech or underserved markets/product/service categories.

In essence, this study makes three significant contributions to extant literature on new venture creation by business families. First, it identifies heterogeneity in business families based on variations in proximity of their new ventures to their existing business(es). Two categories of business families, that is, the guarded *conservatives* and the adventurous *pathfinders* are identified and underlying reasons for their distinct decision behaviour are discussed. Second, expanding the nature and scope of new ventures, the study observes that new ventures created by business families can either be a business or social venture. It also identifies the family-level drivers of these choices. Finally, the study identifies the influence next-generation family champions exert on new venture decisions of business families. It underlines how this influence is moderated by the motivations and inclinations of the incumbent senior-generation leader as families make their new venture choices. The typology of new venture creation by business families presented in the study extends the literature on new venture creation by distinguishing new ventures on account of the domain in which they operate and their proximity to existing business(es) of the family.

Some of the drivers of new venture choices, especially, social ventures, may be context dependent, due to the unique cultural/spiritual influences on next-generation family members (Bhatnagar et al., 2020). However, we believe that the key findings would apply to business families in similar cultural contexts, especially in the emerging economies across Asia. The typology of new ventures established by business families presented in this study is likely to apply globally, because the variations in structural and operational proximity to existing business and operational domain of the new venture are likely to exist regardless of the geo-economic context. Juxtaposing these two factors in any macro-economic setting is likely to result in the four categories depicted in the suggested typology framework. The study also presents interesting avenues for future research. The typology we present and the underlying factors determining new venture choices made by business families can be validated by large sample studies across different geographic contexts. Further probe of individual-level influences on venture decisions are a fertile ground of study. For instance, whether and how family members not involved in business influence venture decisions, especially, the invisible women. The role of macro-environment and regulatory factors in determining new venture decisions of business families, is another area that may provide new insights.

Business families play a critical role in orchestrating the necessary mix of capabilities, financial, and human capital, essential to exploit new venture opportunities. With rising concerns for ensuring sustainable and equitable ways of life, business families are increasingly creating new business and social ventures to address societal needs. Next-generation champions in business families are increasingly playing the vital role of catalysts for this positive change.

References

Agarwal, S. (2017). Ananya Birla: Every single rupee counts. *Mint* (Sep. 16).

Akhmedova, A., Cavallotti, R., Marimon, F., & Campopiano, G. (2020). Daughters' careers in family business: Motivation types and family-specific barriers. *Journal of Family Business Strategy*, 11(3), 100307.

Babu, G. (2020). Azim Premji finds philanthropy much more complex than running a business. *Business Standard* (Jan. 17).

Barbera, F., Stamm, I., & DeWitt, R. L. (2018). The development of an entrepreneurial legacy: Exploring the role of anticipated futures in transgenerational entrepreneurship. *Family Business Review*, 31(3), 352–378.

Bhatnagar, N., Ramachandran, K., & Ray, S. (2018), The role of familial socio-political forces on new venture creation in family business, *Cross Cultural and Strategic Management*, 25(4), 550–577.

Bhatnagar, N., Sharma, P., & Ramachandran, K. (2020). Spirituality and corporate philanthropy in Indian family firms: an exploratory study. *Journal of Business Ethics*, 163(4), 715–728.

Brinkerink, J., Rondi, E., Benedetti, C., & Arzubiaga, U. (2020). Family business or business family? Organizational identity elasticity and strategic responses to disruptive innovation. *Journal of Family Business Strategy*, DOI: 10.1016/j.jfbs.2020.100360, 1–12.

Cabrera-Suárez, M. K., García-Almeida, D. J., & De Saá-Pérez, P. (2018). A dynamic network model of the successor's knowledge construction from the resource-and knowledge-based view of the family firm. *Family Business Review*, 31(2), 178–197.

Chang, E. P., Memili, E., Chrisman, J. J., Kellermanns, F. W., & Chua, J. H. (2009). Family social capital, venture preparedness, and start-up decisions: A study of Hispanic entrepreneurs in New England. *Family Business Review*, 22(3), 279–292.

Combs, J. G., Shanine, K. K., Burrows, S., Allen, J. S., & Pounds, T. W. (2020). What do we know about business families? Setting the stage for leveraging family science theories. *Family Business Review*, 33(1), 38–63.

Danes, S. M., Stafford, K., Haynes, G., & Amarapurkar, S. S. (2009). Family capital of family firms: Bridging human, social, and financial capital. *Family Business Review*, 22(3), 199–215.

Davidsson, P., & Gruenhagen, J. H. (2020). Fulfilling the process promise: A review and agenda for new venture creation process research. *Entrepreneurship Theory and Practice*, DOI: 1042258720930991

Davidsson, P., Recker, J., & von Briel, F. (2020). External enablement of new venture creation: A framework. *Academy of Management Perspectives*, 34(3), 311–332.

Dawson, A. (2012). Human capital in family businesses: Focusing on the individual level. *Journal of Family Business Strategy*, 3(1), 3–11.

De Massis, A., Kotlar, J., Frattini, F., Chrisman, J. J., & Nordqvist, M. (2016). Family governance at work: Organizing for new product development in family SMEs. *Family Business Review*, 29(2), 189–213.

de Mol, E., Cardon, M. S., de Jong, B., Khapova, S. N., & Elfring, T. (2020). Entrepreneurial passion diversity in new venture teams: An empirical examination of short-and long-term performance implications. *Journal of Business Venturing*, 35(4), 105965.

Edelman, L. F., Manolova, T., Shirokova, G., & Tsukanova, T. (2016). The impact of family support on young entrepreneu's' start-up activities. *Journal of Business Venturing*, 31(4), 428–48.

Gaur, V. (2019). JSW Paints aims at Rs 2,000 crore revenue over three years. *The Economic Times* (May 2).

Hetavkar, N. (2017). Svatantra Microfin reached break even in FY17. *Business Standard* (June 30).

Jaskiewicz, P., Combs, J. G., & Rau, S. B. (2015). Entrepreneurial legacy: Toward a theory of how some family firms nurture transgenerational entrepreneurship. *Journal of Business Venturing*, 30(1), 29–49.

Jaskiewicz, P., & Dyer, W. G. (2017). Addressing the elephant in the room: Disentangling family heterogeneity to advance family business research. *Family Business Review*, 30, 111–118.

Jayakumar, PB (2019). JSW Group enters paints business with 'Any Colour, One Price' USP. *Business Today* (May 3).

Jennings, J. E., Breitkreuz, R. S., & James, A. E. (2014). Theories from family science: A review and roadmap for family business research. In L. Melin, M. Nordqvist, and P. Sharma (Eds.), *SAGE Handbook of Family Business* (pp. 25–46). London, England: Sage.

John, N. (2021). Grasim, JSW, Reliance face off in paint world. *Business Today* (January 27).

John, S., & Gaur, V. (2018). A 28-year-old scion is earning the spurs at $13 billion JSW Group, *The Economic Times* (August 8).

Kellermanns, F. W., Eddleston, K. A., Barnett, T., & Pearson, A. (2008). An exploratory study of family member characteristics and involvement: Effects on entrepreneurial behavior in the family firm. *Family Business Review*, 21(1), 1–14.

Kier, A. S., & McMullen, J. S. (2020). Entrepreneurial imaginativeness and new venture ideation in newly forming teams. *Journal of Business Venturing*, 35(6), 106048.

Kleinhempel, J., Beugelsdijk, S., & Klasing, M. J. (2020). The Changing Role of Social Capital During the Venture Creation Process: A Multilevel Study. *Entrepreneurship Theory and Practice*, DOI: 10.1177/1042258720913022, 1–34.

Le Breton-Miller, I., & Miller, D. (2018). Beyond the firm: Business families as entrepreneurs. *Entrepreneurship Theory and Practice*, 42(4), 527–536.

Lungeanu, R., & Ward, J. L. (2012). A governance-based typology of family foundations: The effect of generation stage and governance structure on family philanthropic activities. *Family Business Review*, 25(4), 409–424.

Lortie, J., Castrogiovanni, G. J., & Cox, K. C. (2017). Gender, social salience, and social performance: how women pursue and perform in social ventures. *Entrepreneurship and Regional Development*, 29(1–2), 155–173.

Mandavia, M., Kalesh, B. & Vijayraghavan, K. (2016). How these famous heirs are carving their own paths of success. *The Economic Times* (Feb. 4).

Mandavia, M. (2015). Parth Jindal with new ideas, sets out to diversify JSW Group. *The Economic Times* (Sep. 2015).

Manikutty, S. (2000). Family business groups in India: A resource-based view of the emerging trends. *Family Business Review*, 13(4), 279–292.

Mascarenhas, A. (2021). #AshaHamesha campaign bats for palliative care to manage cancer during Covid-19. *The Indian Express* (Feb. 2).

Mazzola, P., Marchisio, G., & Astrachan, J. (2008). Strategic planning in family business: A powerful developmental tool for the next generation. *Family Business Review*, 21(3), 239–258.

Minola, T., Brumana, M., Campopiano, G., Garrett, R. P., & Cassia, L. (2016). Corporate venturing in family business: A developmental approach of the enterprising family. *Strategic Entrepreneurship Journal*, 10(4), 395–412.

Murphy, L., Huybrechts, J., & Lambrechts, F. (2019). The origins and development of socioemotional wealth within next-generation family members: An interpretive grounded theory study. *Family Business Review*, 32(4), 396–424.

Nair, S., Gaim, M., & Dimov, D. (2020). Toward the Emergence of Entrepreneurial Opportunities: Organizing Early-phase New-venture Creation Support Systems. *Academy of Management Review*, DOI: 10.5465/amr.2019.0040

Nordqvist, M., & Melin, L. (2010). Entrepreneurial families and family firms. *Entrepreneurship and Regional Development*, 22(3–4), 211–239.

Pittino, D., Visintin, F., & Lauto, G. (2018). Fly away from the nest? A configurational analysis of family embeddedness and individual attributes in the entrepreneurial entry decision by next-generation members. *Family Business Review*, 31, 271–294.

Ramírez-Pasillas, M., Lundberg, H., & Nordqvist, M. (2021). Next-generation external venturing practices in family-owned businesses. *Journal of Management Studies*, 58(1), 63–103.

Salvato, C., Chirico, F., & Sharma, P. (2010). A farewell to the business: Championing exit and continuity in entrepreneurial family firms. *Entrepreneurship and Regional Development*, 22(3–4), 321–348.

Schjoedt, L., Monsen, E., Pearson, A., Barnett, T., & Chrisman, J. J. (2013). New venture and family business teams: Understanding team formation, composition, behaviors, and performance. *Entrepreneurship Theory and Practice*, 37(1), 1–15.

Sen, S. (2020). JSW Paints to invest aggressively in home hygiene, launch more COVID-safe products. *The New Indian Express* (June 5).

Sharma, P., & Irving, P. G. (2005). Four bases of family business successor commitment: Antecedents and consequences. *Entrepreneurship Theory and Practice*, 29(1), 13–33.

Shepherd, D. A., Souitaris, V., & Gruber, M. (2021). Creating new ventures: A review and research agenda. *Journal of Management, 47*(1), 11–42.

Sirmon, D. G., & Hitt, M. A. (2003). Managing resources: Linking unique resources, management, and wealth creation in family firms. *Entrepreneurship Theory and Practice, 27*(4), 339–358.

Sood, V., & Sen, A. (2018). Second sonrise at Wipro as Tariq Premji joins board. *Livemint.com*

Sorenson, R. L., and Bierman, L. (2009). Family capital, family business, and free enterprise. *Family Business Review, 22*(3), 193–195.

Thomas, P. M. (2019). Parth Jindal's $8 billion ambition, *Moneycontrol.com* (November 29) (Retrieved from https://www.moneycontrol.com/news/business/companies/parth-jindals-8-billion-ambition-4682341.html).

Timmons, J. A., & Spinelli, S. (2009), *New Venture Creation, Entrepreneurship for the 21st Century*, 8th ed., McGraw-Hill Higher Education, Irwin.

Zellweger, T. M., Nason, R. S., & Nordqvist, M. (2012). From longevity of firms to transgenerational entrepreneurship of families: Introducing family entrepreneurial orientation. *Family Business Review, 2*(2), 136–155.

Nava Michael-Tsabari

8 "All My Firms?" Managing SEW Affective Endowments in Business Family Portfolios

Abstract: SEW is defined as a "stock of affect-related value that the family has invested *in the firm*" (Berrone, Cruz, Gómez-Mejía, & Larraza-Kintana, 2010, p. 106). However, the singular reference to *the* family firm contradicts findings that describe most family firms as controlling multiple firms. How than does the family manage the SEW stock when it is distributed between multiple firms, with various ages, sizes, and importance? Extending Zellweger and Dehlen's (2012) AIM model of affect infusion, this chapter conceptualizes about how a business family owner manages his or her emotional endowment with a cluster of firms.

Keywords: socioemotional wealth, affect infusion, portfolio, cluster, business family owner, stock, flow

Introduction

In Arthur Miller's masterpiece play *"All my sons"*, Joe Keller's character was a war profiteer who sold defective cylinder heads to the American Air Force during World War II. This directly caused the death of 21 pilots, and indirectly the suicide, out of shame, of his own pilot son. At the end of the play, learning about the suicide, Joe Keller acknowledges that *"Sure, he was my son. But I think to him they were all my sons. And I guess they were, I guess they were"* (Miller, 1949, Act III), *italics added.*

The essence of what differentiates family firm phenomenon from that of other organizational forms is believed to be its Socioemotional Wealth (SEW). SEW is defined as an affective endowment, or a "stock of affect-related value that the family has invested *in the firm*" (Berrone, Cruz, Gómez-Mejía, & Larraza-Kintana, 2010, p. 106) [italics added]. This stock of affect-related value is the result of a family's continuous non-economic goal pursuance (Westhead & Howorth, 2007).

Unlike the singular count of one-family-one-firm implicitly implied to by the SEW definition, family firms are found to be better described as one-family-multiple-firms, namely owning a portfolio (Sieger, Zellweger, Nason, & Clinton, 2011; DeTienne & Chirico, 2013). There is already a widespread recognition describing families as owners of portfolios of firms (e.g., Discua-Cruz, Howorth, & Hamilton, 2013; Sieger et al., 2011), whether interconnected businesses (Carney & Gedajlovic, 2002) or a cluster of different organizations (Michael-Tsabari, Labaki, & Zachary, 2014). For example,

Nava Michael-Tsabari, Tel Aviv University

https://doi.org/10.1515/9783110727968-008

family firms own an average of 1.58 publicly listed firms (Carney & Child, 2013), and/ or 3.4 different firms (Zellweger, Nason, & Nordqvist, 2012). A family may keep and hold its original core business, however, over the firm's life cycle and across genera- tions, a family may also choose to sell, cash-out, invest, and buy business units, thereby directing a much more complicated, "messy and complex" portfolio of assets (Rosa, 1998, p. 44). This portfolio, or cluster model of firms, is the result of entrepre- neurial business activities over time.

The complex reality of the business family's cluster of firms raises the question of how the family manages the "stock of affect-related value" when it is distributed between *multiple* firms, which are characterized by various ages, histories, sizes, and importance in the portfolio. Since only a minority of family firms manage a sin- gle firm over time (Zellweger et al., 2012b), the SEW terminology has yet to consider new, shifting, and/or changing firms in the portfolio. Therefore, in this chapter I address the question of *how does a business family owner manage his or her affective SEW endowments within a portfolio of firms*? Is the business family owner emotion- ally attached to each firm in the portfolio in the same way? Are all the firms "his [or her] firms", in the same meaning of belonging and affect as Joe Keller's character has eventually found out about "all his sons"?

Looking into SEW endowments of firms in a portfolio, this chapter has three important contributions to the literature. First, scholars have already argued that "not all firms in a family firm portfolio have similar levels of SEW"(DeTienne & Chirico, 2013, p. 1298), but have not yet addressed this source of "heterogeneity within". I conceptualize the process of how owners develop their SEW assessments regarding each single firm in their portfolio. Second, the current SEW literature has largely theorized based on how SEW stocks affect economic flows (such as short- term profits). Since flows may lead to the accumulation of stocks, the SEW terminol- ogy has not yet modeled how affective SEW flow variables influence stocks of SEW (Chua, Chrisman, & De Massis 2015). I discuss flow and stock SEW considerations for a business family portfolio. Third, as suggested by Chua et al. (2015), the rela- tionship between stocks and flows of SEW may be an important source of heteroge- neity among family firms. I discuss the various possible variables influencing this relationship, which may result in heterogenous "among firms" SEW perceptions. Extending Zellweger and Dehlen's (2012) Affect Infusion Model (AIM) and SEW to a portfolio of firms, I explore the implications for family firm owners and SEW, and suggest fertile ways forward for future research.

Theoretical Background: SEW Flow and Stock

Family firms are characterized as firms with economic and noneconomic goals (Westhead & Howorth, 2007). Distinguishing between flows and stocks, family firms engage in activities attempting to achieve economic goals for profit (a flow), to accumulate financial wealth (a stock), as well as pursuing non-economic goals for family benefits (a flow), which accumulates over time to SEW (a stock) (Chua et al., 2015). This distinguishment between flows and stocks is important because the strategic management literature indicates that only stocks are a source of competitive advantage or value, whereas only flows can be adjusted in the short term to maintain or create value (Chua et al., 2015; Dierickx & Cool, 1989). In their review of SEW, Chua et al. (2015) clearly state that while Gómez-Mejía and his colleagues (Gómez-Mejía, Haynes, Núñez-Nickel, Jacobson, & Moyano-Fuentes, 2007; Gómez-Mejía et al., 2011) have moved the field forward by defining SEW as a stock of affect, "we still have not come to grips with the implications for how the stocks and flows of noneconomic benefits or utilities should be treated in family business studies" (p. 175). Responding to this call, I start with Zellweger and Dehlen's (2012) Affect Infusion Model (AIM) of SEW perceptions and move on to discuss definitions and descriptions of organic and portfolio family firms, core and peripheral types of firms within a cluster, and the SEW stock of emotional endowment related to each type.

Zellweger and Dehlen's (2012) Affect Infusion Model (AIM)

Looking at the first decade of SEW studies, Jiang, Kellermanns, Munyon, and Morris (2018) build their review on the FIBER concept, conceptualizing the SEW endowment along five dimensions of *Family* control and influence, *Identification* with the firm, *Binding* social ties, *Emotional* attachment, and *Renewal* of family bonds to the firm throughdynastic succession (Berrone, Cruz, & Gómez-Mejía, 2012). The emotional dimension is described as "a distinctive attribute of family firms" resulting from the general "intermingling of emotional factors originating from family involvement with business factors" (Berrone et al., 2012, p. 263). However, in spite of the emotional centrality and distinctiveness in the family firm context declared by family firm scholars, Jiang et al. (2018) note that "recognizing that affect is a key aspect of what creates and constitutes SEW, it is surprising to find that affective arguments are adopted with the least breadth and depth of all five psychological tenets that we examined across the SEW literature, typically only being scantly mentioned in 29.9% of the 421 peer-reviewed papers included in this review" (p. 135). The question of why the specific variable expressed in the title of *affective* flows and endowments is under studied, is beyond the scope of this chapter. However, I therefore believe that understanding affective processes in business families is important and wish to extend the Affect Infusion Model (AIM) suggested by Zellweger and Dehlen (2012). Figure 8.1 describes my extended model for the relationship between SEW flows of affect related to one firm in the portfolio and SEW's stock of emotional endowment of this one firm, mediated by target, personal, and situational features.

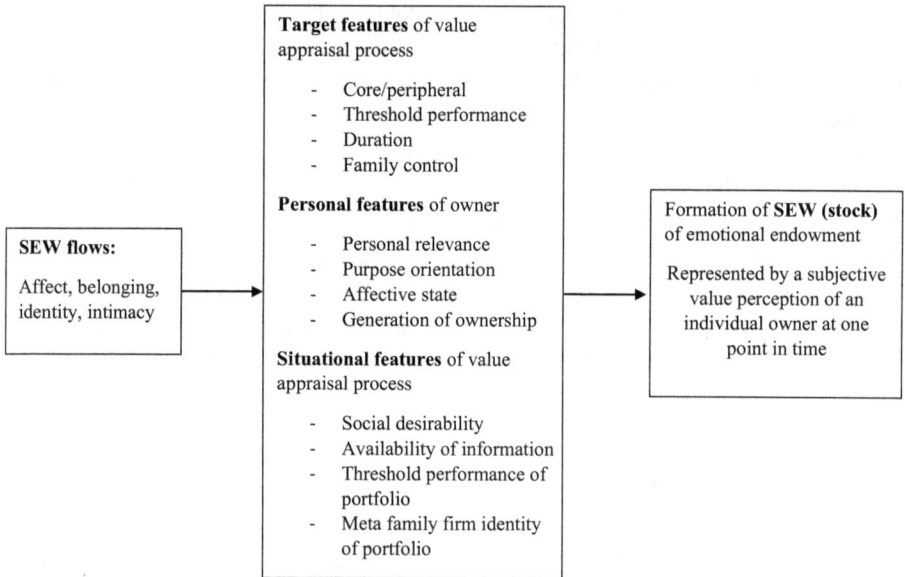

Figure 8.1: A relationship between SEW flows of affect related to one firm in the portfolio and SEW's stock of emotional endowment of this one firm, mediated by target, personal, and situational features.

Looking at the full assets owned by a family firm in a singular count of one-family-one-firm, Zellweger and Dehlen (2012) suggest a conceptual model of SEW value formation based on the AIM of cognitive psychology (Forgas, 1995). The AIM seeks to explain how does affect come to influence perceptions and judgements (Forgas, 1995), making it a good candidate to understand decision making and the formation of SEW perceptions. Specifically, affect infusion is defined as "the process whereby affectively loaded information exerts an influence on and becomes incorporated into the judgmental process, entering into the judge's deliberations and eventually coloring the judgmental outcome" (Forgas, 1995, p. 39). AIM is part of emotion regulation processes, by which individuals influence which emotions they have, when they have them, and how they express and experience these emotions (Gross, 1998). Emotions are included in the wider umbrella concept of affect, are elicited by a particular cause or target, often include physiological reactions and action sequences, and change over time (Barsade & Gibson, 2007; Frijda, 1986). The AIM assumes that affective states and emotional responses interact with and inform cognitive processes and judgements by influencing the availability of cognitive structures used in the constructive processing of information (Forgas, 1995). As SEW perceptions can also be seen as reference points guiding owners' strategic decision-making (Nason, Mazelli, & Carney, 2019), the AIM promises a good foundation in understanding the influence of affective components on the formation of the cognitive SEW perceptions. Referring to target, personal, and situational features in the subjective valuation that owners do for a single-family firm they own, a heterogenous SEW spectrum is suggested. I wish to extend Zellweger and Dehlen's (2012) model to apply for the value formation of each firm within a portfolio of firms.

SEW Perceptions and Flows

The SEW terminology is founded on behavioural agency theory (Wiseman & Gómez-Mejía, 1998), which argues that preferences are shaped by existing endowments (Miller & Le Breton-Miller, 2014). Referring to SEW as a stock of affective endowments, SEW studies have only indirectly shown evidence for its existence (Zellweger, Keller-manns, Chrisman, & Chua, 2012). This is important because SEW endowments are actually preferences and perceptions created by individual owners at specific points in time, which serve as a reference point for firm decision-making (Jiang et al., 2018; Nason et al., 2019). Scholars have already argued that different family owners within one family may have varying degrees of SEW attached to the same firm owned by the family, based on their generational belonging or various other personal characteristics or own life stages (De Tienne & Chirico, 2013; Miller & Le Breton-Miller, 2014; Jiang et al., 2018). While still referring to one monolithic SEW reference point per family generation, Nason et al. (2019) nevertheless suggest that SEW reference points are dynamic and include various forward versus backward and inward versus outward considerations. This means that SEW perceptions and priorities may vary and or change across the life cycle of a firm and the individual family owners, for example, "founders may desire a robust business to pass on to later generations, whereas later generations may wish to benefit from the wealth and community status wrought by their family firm" (Miller & Le Breton-Miller, 2014, p. 714). The "antithetic views" regarding the exit from the historical steel business held by different quarreling descendants of the Italian Falck family demonstrate this heterogeneity (Salvato et al., 2010, p. 334), as well as the different emotions tied to the core firm by the second versus the third-generation members of the Pery family (Michael-Tsabari et al., 2014).

The multiple SEW reference points, levels of analysis and changing nature over time are summed up by Jiang et al. (2018) concluding that

> Causal arguments in the SEW literature tend to include several crucial but generally unspecified and unmeasured family member activities at multiple levels of analysis. Indeed, authors often allude to SEW as something that family members can both *individually* and *collectively* feel,

possess, and change through their involvement in and control of a firm, which then affects their interactions in the firm and various firm-level outcomes. (italics in the original)

My model therefore describes the process of the unspecified SEW flows, namely family-owned activities of relational components, such as affect, belonging, intimacy (Gómez-Mejía et al., 2007; Zellweger et al., 2012), and the relationship of these flows on the creation of SEW stocks of emotional endowment.

Although the various variables included in Gómez-Mejía and his colleagues SEW lists include "both stock *and* flow components" (Chua et al., 2015, p. 174, italics added), I suggest that relational variables that develop over time, such as intimacy, affect, and belonging, characterize the SEW flows that start the perception AIM process. Specifically, as the proverb "out of sight out of mind" implies, "a person stops thinking about something or someone if he or she does not see that thing or person for a period of time"[1] (Merriam-Webster Dictionary). I contend that the SEW endowment will be created with direct SEW flows of affect resulting from attention, information, and involvement which an owner will experience at the individual level. With no involvement or connection to a firm or a portfolio of firms, "out of sight", no relational SEW flows can influence SEW perceptions. For example, Warren Buffett and six other founders of multi-billion firms have announced that their assets will not be inherited by their next generation heirs (Martin, July 6, 2017). Leaving his three children each $2 billion, only a fraction of his estate, Buffett declares "Leave the children enough so that they can do anything, but not enough that they can do nothing" (Vega, 21.6.2021). I contend that Warren Buffett's children's identity, affective attachment, and intimacy with the rest of his portfolio should become non-existent, or at least questionable, after years of their father's declaration, in SEW flow and stock terminology. Without relational affective and identity flows, Berkshire Hathaway Company should be an economic financial investment now, and not a stock of affect-related value for Howard, Susan, and Peter Buffett, even though Howard sits on the board or if earlier in their life they still had SEW flows towards their father's firm, leading to the following propositions:

Proposition 1: *Only SEW flows of affect attachment, belonging, intimacy and identity created with a firm or portfolio create a process of SEW stock formation. Without SEW flows, the firm or portfolio will remain financial investments for the individual owner.*

Proposition 2: *The SEW flows of affect attachment, belonging, intimacy, and identity directed at a firm or portfolio change over time for the individual owner.*

---

1 In some languages, like in Hebrew, for example, this proverb says, "out of sight out of heart", referring to an affective relationship rather than a cognitive one.

The relationship between SEW flows and the formation of a SEW stock is mediated by various target, personal, and situation characteristics. The perception of SEW endowment, which is a result of this process, is made individually by each owner at specific points in time. This process will be described in the following sections. I start with the definitions of portfolio, organic, core, and peripheral firms and their SEW considerations.

A Portfolio of Firms

A portfolio entrepreneur is defined as "an individual who currently has majority or minority ownership stakes in two or more independent businesses that are either new, purchased and/or inherited" (Westhead, Ucbasaran, & Wright, 2005, p. 73). This definition has an individual level perspective, since most studies focus solely on entrepreneurs and new firms rather than looking at families over time or generations (Aldrich & Cliff, 2003; Chang, Memili, Chrisman, Kellermanns, & Chua, 2009). One exception is Michael-Tsabari et al. (2014) who describe one family over 80 years and propose the Cluster model as a better description of family firm assets. Looking at entrepreneurial activity at the family level of analysis and over time needs to address multiple firms, as only less than 11% of family firms own a single firm (Zellweger et al., 2012b). Unlike the singular count of one-family-one-firm implicitly implied by the SEW definition, Zellweger et al.'s (2012b) study on entrepreneurship in family firms shows that these firms, on average, control 6.1 firms, create 5.4 firms, add 2.7 firms through merger and acquisitions, spin off 1.5 firms, and shift industry focus 2.1 times. Therefore, a portfolio owned by a business family, defined at the family level of analysis is also defined as a cluster, when "multiple business entities [are] owned by the family" (Michael-Tsabari et al., 2014, p. 176).

Organic Versus Portfolio Family Firms

Michael-Tsabari et al. (2014) differentiate between organic and portfolio types of family firms. Organic family firms differ from portfolio family firms not only because of a technical count of the number of firms owned, but they significantly differ, for example, in their entrepreneurial mindset. This distinction between core and portfolio family firms is built on Habbershon and Pistrui's (2002) earlier suggestion to differentiate between a "family-in-business" mindset, which differs from a "family-as-investor". The family-in-business mind set, like the organic family firm, includes a particular business that is the focus of managerial efforts that lead a family "to think of itself as a particular type of a family (a "brewery family" or a "manufacturing family"), which in turn locks it into path-dependent corporate strategies and family traditions that dictate its capital asset strategies" (Habbershon & Pistrui, 2002, p. 231). Kikkoman and Zildjian are two examples of organic family firms operating across several generations (Michael-Tsabari et al., 2014). This means that Kikkoman is known as "the Soy" family firm, where the Kikkoman family's interests and strategies are intertwined with one business of soy production, until their identity overlaps. So much so that even history scholars acknowledge this fusion of identities and identify Kikkoman as "the family as a firm and the firm as a family" (Fruin, 1980). Zildjian is a "Music percussion" family firm (Michael-Tsabari et al., 2014, p. 179), where the 13th generation of the Zildjian family owners are still leading cymbal and percussion manufactures after doing that for almost four hundred years (Anwar & Tariq, 2011). Other well-known examples of organic family firms, where the family owns one major firm that gives the family firm its intertwined identity, serve as the first introductory sentences in many family firm studies. For example, Daspit, Long, and Pearson (2019) start their study acknowledging that "Hoshi Ryokan, a family-owned hotel in Komatsu, Japan, was founded in the year 718 and is currently overseen by the 46th generation of family. The Antinori family has produced wine since 1385 in Tuscany, and the Beretta family has manufactured firearms since 1526" (p. 133). These three examples of successful transgenerational family firms could be defined as organic firms, mainly known for one business focus of hotel, wine, and firearms, respectively.

Actually, this type of an organic family firm, with its identity and mind set focused mainly on one business, was the type of firm that the SEW construct was based on. In their seminal study introducing SEW, Gómez-Mejía et al. (2007) use a sample of "all olive oil mills that have operated in the province of Jaén (Spain) during the period between 1944 and 1998" (p. 114). These firms can be defined as organic family firms, since the authors specifically explain that "the mills extract and store virgin olive oil, *with extraction being the fundamental activity*" (p. 114) [italics added]. Olive oil mills are agricultural businesses. Small family firms comprise a larger share of rural economies (Brewton, Danes, Stafford, & Haynes, 2010), which is manifested in the study's majority of 1,407 olive oil family firms versus 549 non-family firms (Gómez-Mejía et al., 2007). Rural family firms differ in their perceptions of the family business compared to urban ones (Brewton et al., 2010), and may succeed to reach a very long age (e.g., an average of 11 generations for the wineries in Jaskiewicz, Combs, & Rau, 2015), however, I wish to point at the implicit *singular* count of one-family-one-firm, which characterizes the Gómez-Mejía et al. (2007) data.

Investigating these organic rural family firms with one main business activity lies at the foundation of the SEW construct, leading Gómez-Mejía and his colleagues to define it as a "stock of affect-related value that the family has invested *in the firm*" (Berrone et al., 2010, p. 106) [italics added]. With a focus on one business, the emotional endowment and the identification of the family are clear. However, this type of family firm, which is devoted and intertwined with one main business focus, describes the minority of family firms, not characterizing the majority of them.

The second more common type is the portfolio family firm, where "a family owns more than one firm" (Michael-Tsabari et al., 2014, p. 179). These business families have a family-as-investor mindset, committed to wealth creation while pursuing capital allocation strategies. These strategies are responsive to the market, not necessarily manifested in "a particular business entity or legacy asset" (Habbershon & Pistrui, 2002, p. 231). The German Franz Haniel & Cie. GmbH family firm is an example of a portfolio family firm (Michael-Tsabari et al., 2014). The Haniel family firm is more than 250 years old and operates in 50 countries. Contrary to Zildjian or Kikkoman, this family spun off several firms during its long history and has changed industries of operation: from trade to industry then mining and shipping, and now consumer goods and pharmaceuticals (Haniel, 2008; James, 2009). In their 2018 annual report the Haniel family firm openly states its strategic family-as-investor mindset declaring that "Haniel has EUR 1.4 billion for the further expansion of the portfolio. Clear criteria determine which companies are considered for selection: The contribution to further diversification of the portfolio plays just as much a role as does future capability and an orientation towards sustainability" (Haniel Website, 2021). Obviously, this is a business family managing a portfolio of various firms with an investor's mindset guided by strategic decisions. The definition itself of a business family includes this investor's mindset, moving from a family firm in the first generation to a group of decision-makers who manage an estate: "the business-owning family level of analysis, which refers to the coalition of decision makers who control the strategy and future of at least one firm and are related by either consanguinity, marriage, or other relationships that provide inheritance rights in the descendants' estate" (Nason et al., 2019, p. 846). The fundamental differentiation between organic and portfolio family firms leads to the following propositions:

Proposition 3: *The SEW flow and stock perceptions in an organic family firm relate to one single firm owned by the family.*

Proposition 4: *The SEW flow and stock perceptions in a portfolio business family relate to multiple firms owned by the family.*

The question then arises how is the emotional endowment, namely SEW, divided between multiple peripheral firms? What happens to SEW flow and stock when firms change in the portfolio?

Core Versus Periphery Firms in the Cluster

Looking at entrepreneurial activity of families over time most family firms start as a bivalent "one family-one firm" type at the early stages of the first generation (Michael-Tsabari et al., 2014). While a minority of family firms stay in this form and therefore can be characterized as organic family firms, the majority evolve over time and across generations into a cluster structure of "one family holding more than one firm", defined as portfolio family firms (p. 180). When a family owns and manages more than one firm, a distinction between *core* and *peripheral* firms is made: a core business is "the primary area or activity that a company was founded on or focuses on in its business operations" (Kotler & Keller, 2009, p. 179), while other peripheral firms evolve later in time (Michael-Tsabari et al., 2014). The core business not only comes earlier in time within a portfolio of a business family, but it is usually also the biggest firm and main source of wealth for the family (Cruz & Justo, 2017; Ward, 2004), for example, on average making up roughly three quarters of total sales of the family-owned business activity in Zellweger et al.'s (2012b) sample. This leads to the suggestion that "in a portfolio context, it is likely to expect that family owners will be strongly attached to the core business and less attached to other firms (e.g., subsequent businesses that are part of the family's extended portfolio of business activity" (DeTienne & Chirico, 2013, p. 1306). Therefore, changing the core business would not be a common event for a family firm: indeed, when the Haniel family changed their main business focus after the first 50 years of operation it was termed "the most important step that the Haniels had ventured up to that time – the merchants had turned into industrialists" (Haniel, 2008, p. 8).

Similarly, Salvato et al. (2010) describe the difficult shift that the Italian Falck family went through, moving from being known for producing steel for over a century, to entering the renewable energy and real estate fields. Having to shift the "emotional anchoring in the founder's business", the family is described as changing a strong identification with the steel industry by "reinventing the firm's entrepreneurial story" in the new field (p. 323). However difficult at the time, after only a while, the transition into renewable energy was interpreted "as 'natural' for Falck" (p. 339). Another case where an original core business identification had to be changed is the Beretta family, which has begun with a business focus of being merchants of barrels. Only later from the 19th century, they changed their activity by starting as a manufacturer of rifles and guns, which is the core firm they are known for today (Paris, 2016). The Falck and Beretta examples suggest that changing a core firm in a family's portfolio is a hard and significant event, requiring an identity shift (Salvato et al., 2010). However, these two stories also show that with a considerable investment of time and identity shaping, the firearms and renewable energy "new" activities have become core firms for the Beretta and Falck families, with SEW affective endowments attributed to them once again. This shows that the process of SEW shaping of stock may be dynamic and changing over time, a result of family efforts of various relational flows, such as intimacy and identity.

Types of Firms in a Family Cluster and Various SEW Affective Endowments

The attachment between a family and its core business may be stronger than other peripheral businesses (DeTienne & Chirico, 2013; Michael-Tsabari et al., 2014). Describing the core business founded by the first generation, there is a well-established recognition that the identity of the family is intertwined with the identity of the firm, with overlap as a defining characteristic (Tagiuri & Davis, 1996). This identity overlap is also the foundation of the traditional SEW definition, which describes family owners as individuals "whose identity is inextricably tied to the organization" (Berrone et al., 2010, p. 87). Regarding the first generation-core business-SEW endowment implicit triple Gordian knot, Chua et al. (2015) wondered whether stocks of SEW are "endowed in family firms at birth or do they all need to be developed through investment flows over time? For example, the stock of SEW attached to family control could accompany the establishment of the firm, or could only become manifest after the firm has reached some threshold of success" (p. 175). The questions of immediate founding SEW or the threshold of success are beyond the scope of this chapter. However, as my model describes, because emotional attachment grows with time (Zellweger et al., 2012a) I theorize that flows of SEW over time, namely investing identity, affect, personal sacrifices of career and energy (Salvato et al., 2010), mediated by the considerations of target, personal and situation, lead to forming a subjective SEW perception of emotional stock.

Gómez-Mejía, Patel, and Zellweger (2018) refer to peripheral firms added to a family's portfolio over time as "unrelated" acquisitions, implicitly terming core activities as "related". They explain the lower SEW endowments tied to unrelated peripheral firms because they "lead to losses in familial control, water down the family firm's identity, and weaken social ties linked to the firm" (Gómez-Mejía et al., 2018, p. 1371).

The centrality and importance of the core firm compared to other peripheral businesses is anecdotally described by scholars. Carter and Ram (2003, p. 378) term peripheral firms "satellites",[2] and wonder what would be "the relationship between the core business and its new satellites"? Cruz and Justo (2017, p. 575) discuss the ability to grow through adding firms to the portfolio "while keeping the core business intact". This special care of the core business is also described with emotional terms, as the family's attachment to the historical first firm is unique. For example, comparing the core ice cream firm to a new peripheral ice cream factory recently added to the portfolio, a non-family CFO described the founder's difficulties: "(after the purchase) for Mrs. Pery it was always 'them' and 'us', and I would tell her, 'It's also us, it's the

---

2 This terminology would make the core firm a mothership, which is an interesting observation in our context.

same pocket' and she would say 'Yes, I understand, but' . . . I think that logically the brain would understand, she was aware of it, she was a business woman, but the heart never accepted it, I think" (Michael-Tsabari et al., 2014, p. 177). This means that the founder, Mrs. Pery, had a strong emotional attachment to the core firm, and not to the later acquired firm, even when both were ice-cream firms, demonstrating that owners feel differently to core compared to peripheral firms.

Another example testifying for a stronger emotional attachment to a core firm than to other firms in the portfolio is the repurchase of the French champagne Taittinger. A 3rd generation family owner repurchased the 80-year-old champagne core firm only, and not the hotels and luxury goods businesses in the family empire, after the other 38 family owners sold the portfolio to an American private-equity fund (Frank, 2006; Pier Taittinger, 2021). The emotional attachment to the champagne business was his explanation, declaring that "It was not for my ego. I was in love with my customers, my staff and our growers" (*The Irish Times*, 23.2.2008). However, this strong level of emotional attachment to the champagne business, which is the core determinant of the SEW stock, was not equally shared by the whole group of Taittinger owners. This story once again demonstrates that the owning family is not a homogeneous entity regarding SEW perceptions. In fact, business families may have heterogeneous ownership of shares, with family members differentiated by ownership stakes (Michael-Tsabari et al., 2014; Salvato et al., 2010) and attachments to various firms owned. This insight is included in my model (see Figure 8.1) by referring to the outcome of SEW stock of emotional endowment in the individual level, as each owner among one business family develops his or her own SEW perception, and leads to the following propositions:

Proposition 5: *SEW stock perceptions of a core firm are higher than SEW stock perceptions of peripheral firms in the portfolio owned by the business family.*

Proposition 6: *SEW stock perceptions are individual level, therefore there could be heterogeneity among owners from one family regarding the same one firm in a portfolio.*

In the next section I discuss how the literature addresses points of one single firm's entrance to or exit from a portfolio.

Entrance and Exit Points of Firms from a Portfolio

Though SEW considerations have not yet been discussed for a portfolio of *existing* firms owned by a business family, scholars have begun to study the entrance or exit points of *one* firm in or out of the cluster (Cruz & Justo, 2017; Sieger et al., 2011). The firm exit point refers to "the process by which owners remove themselves, in varying degrees, from the firm" (DeTienne, 2010, p. 203). SEW scholars have rarely discussed cases where "part of the SEW stock" is lost (Chua et al., 2015, p. 179), as would happen with a sale of one firm out of a portfolio, and have rather focused on situations characterized by a total loss of all SEW endowment, as happens with a sale of the total assets (Kim, Hoskisson, & Zyung, 2019; Zellweger et al., 2012a), referred to as "SEW extinction" (Berrone et al., 2012, p. 261) by SEW scholars. Interestingly, a partial exit from a core firm is actually the case with the Gómez-Mejía et al. (2007) olive oil firms, which had a choice between full ownership and joining a co-op (partial ownership). Pointing to this choice, Zellweger et al. (2012a, p. 861) comment that giving up a portion of SEW (namely joining a co-op) "may be viewed in an entirely different way" than giving up all the SEW endowment. Nevertheless, scholars have yet to better understand which firms in a portfolio the business family owners would prefer to keep to minimize the partial loss of SEW stock (Kim et al., 2019).

Chirico, Gómez-Mejía, Hellerstedt, Withers, and Nordqvist (2020) hypothesize that family owners are less likely to exit their firm under distressed conditions, since exiting implies an immediate loss of SEW, whereas non-family owners wish to cut their losses through divestment and thus, with only financial considerations, have a stronger preference for exiting. They find that family owners differ also in their mode of exit, when this alternative is chosen, and prefer a mode that involves at least some future SEW preservation (a merger) compared to a loss of all SEW (a complete sale).

Looking at partial sales of a family portfolio, scholars have studied divestiture decisions. Family firms are found as less likely than non-family firms to undertake divestitures, especially when these companies are managed by family rather than non-family-CEOs (Feldman, Amit, & Villalonga, 2016). Feldman et al. (2016) explain these results claiming that family owners fail to fully exploit available economic opportunities, potentially because they pursue financial as well as familial objectives. Akhter, Sieger, and Chirico (2016) study how family firms prefer to exit a peripheral firm in their portfolio, also terming these investments "satellite firms" (p. 372). They find that owners prefer to shut down a peripheral business rather than sell it, which is primarily explained by identity considerations. This finding supports the notion that peripheral firms still have SEW stock considerations made by family owners.

Kim et al. (2019) compare between family CEOs who are supposed to include SEW considerations in their decision-making, with non-family CEOs, who may be more objective towards divestitures because they employ "rational-calculative decision criteria" (Carney, 2005, p. 255) to maximize financial wealth. They find that SEW considerations do indeed drive decisions: family CEOs, as opposed to non-family CEOs, prefer to retain majority- and wholly-owned foreign subsidiaries, but not minority- and equally owned ones, and prefer to retain subsidiaries in host countries where their families have already lost subsidiaries through past divestitures. However, to fully understand family owners' contemplation regarding the sale of one firm out of a portfolio we need to go beyond the context of foreign multi-national investments, because divestiture decisions are biased towards more impersonal, economic, and universalistic decision-making, to begin with (Kim et al., 2019).

Looking at the point of entrance, family entrepreneurs are found to be more likely to add new firms to their portfolio than non-family entrepreneurs (Cruz & Justo, 2017). This finding is stronger for older, female, and ethnic family entrepreneurs. Another study finds that when a family firm invests in a new peripheral business abroad, if the new local firm is also a family firm, a joint venture is preferred, while if only the investing firm is a family firm, a wholly owned subsidiary is more likely (Sestu & Majocchi, 2020).

Sieger et al. (2011) qualitatively study human, social, and reputational resources which a business family uses in the process of adding new firms to their portfolio, and how these change over time. They differentiate between two stages of portfolio enlargement, where the first stage is industry specific, helping to build the family's specific reputation, while the second stage is beyond the original industry, when the family develops a meta-industry reputation and learns how to manage a portfolio of firms. I build on their distinction between firm-specific and meta-industry in our next discussion of portfolio meta SEW identity.

Portfolio Meta SEW Identity

Not only do current SEW studies not theorize about single firms in a business family's portfolio, they also do not discuss the SEW transformation from a firm specific emotional endowment to a portfolio of investments, which could or could not include the original historical core firm. One path to start theorizing this question has been suggested by Gómez-Mejía, Campbell, Martin, Hoskisson, Makri, and Sirmon (2014), who have updated the SEW construct moving beyond the idea that the family owners only try to avoid SEW losses when making decisions under risk, by suggesting a mixed gamble perspective. This means that family owners estimate both possible SEW gains as well as SEW losses. This integrated SEW refinement describes family owners as facing a dilemma in their strategic entrepreneurial decision making by having to assess the likelihood of gains and losses of their actions in terms of financial *and* SEW considerations in tandem (Gómez-Mejía et al., 2018). This integrated approach overcomes the prevailing conservative view of family owners, which focuses on their wish to only avoid SEW losses (Cruz & Justo, 2017), and adds the point of entrance to a portfolio.

Looking at the entry point of one new firm into an existing portfolio, Cruz and Justo (2017) build on the mixed gamble suggestion and argue that families have financial as well as SEW motives. Differentiating between family and business antecedents to entrepreneurial strategic changes, family motives may be more prevalent compared to business ones (Michael-Tsabari et al., 2014). For example, as a next generation business owner explained the reason for splitting one firm into five separate companies: "The company was split not because there was any demand from the market for such a move, it was just to give them [the brothers] something to do" (Ram, 1994, p. 89, cited in Carter & Ram, 2003, p. 376).

Gómez-Mejía et al. (2018) describe the dilemma family owners face as whether to engage in acquisitions, and in particular peripheral ones, in the pursuit of future financial gains, or to refrain from acquisitions, in particular peripheral ones, to preserve current SEW. They find that family owners with below-level-aspiration performance will tend be more inclined to prioritize financial over SEW considerations, which is reflected in the acquisition of peripheral targets. This finding supports the claim that financial and SEW considerations co-exist in owners' assessments, and that they can prioritize or downplay considerations based on their needs or understanding, leading to the following proposition:

Proposition 7: *When a new firm is added to the portfolio (by acquisition or founding), the decision will be made to maximize the combination of financial and SEW stock perceptions.*

Proposition 8: *When a firm is deleted from the portfolio (by divestment or cash out), the decision will be made to minimize the combination of financial and SEW stock perceptions.*

If new peripheral firms added to the portfolio may have mainly lower SEW endowments and "losses" in the familial identity with a core firm (Gómez-Mejía et al., 2018, p. 1371), how then is SEW preserved over time in a family cluster? If the Haniel family has a SEW endowment today, as the SEW terminology suggests, how was it kept over time, if today the family does not own any of its original core firms, only peripheral "unrelated" acquired firms? In a family firm with multiple financial acquisitions, such as the current Haniel, can the relationship with the various firms in their portfolio not be similar to "more distant, transitory . . . and utilitarian" one, which Gómez-Mejía and colleagues attribute only to nonfamily owners (Berrone et al., 2012, p. 260)? Isn't "distant, transitory and utilitarian" a fair description of financial economic considerations? Even in family firms? How then is the emotional SEW endowment kept when the business family mainly employs a more "rational-calculative decision criteria" (Carney, 2005, p. 255) to maximize financial wealth in later generations?

Already discussed was how in the first core business founded by the first generation of the family owners, the identity of the family is intertwined with the identity of the firm, as indicated by the traditional SEW definition (Tagiuri & Davis, 1996; Berrone et al., 2010). Moving to a portfolio owned by a business family, the identity is no longer attributed to a specific firm. Shepherd and Haynie (2009) describe this transformed identity as a meta identity of *family business*. This is a higher-level identity that represents the intersection of the *family* and the *firm* lower identities, defined as "who we are as a family business" (Shepherd & Haynie, 2009, p. 1253). This meta identity is created in case of an identity conflict between the two lower *family* and *firm* identities and serves to conjointly inform family members as to how the two lower identities intersect. As long as the two lower identities overlap and do not conflict, a higher meta identity of *family business* will not be created.

Compatible with my discussion of a new acquisition of a peripheral firm, which differs from the earlier core activity, Shepherd and Haynie (2009) claim that the family business meta identity is created when a family has to decide about a new entrepreneurial activity, which they define as "an opportunity", and "a situation conducive to introducing future goods and services for gain" (p. 1253). The identity conflict is created because the new activity is dissimilar with the family's activities in the past. This definition complies with my discussion of peripheral financial considerations of firms, which are different from known core ones, in a family's previous history. The conflict is resolved by transforming the meta family business identity, to fit with the newly acquired activity.

Moreover, each deliberation of a new opportunity is idiosyncratic and specific for a certain time and context, so there is an ongoing process for the business family with each new activity through the interaction of family owners (Shepherd & Haynie, 2009). Moving over time from a firm-specific identity to a meta identity complies with Sieger et al.'s (2011) finding of a shift from "industry-specific" to "meta-industry", as well as with Salvato et al.'s (2010) description of the Falck's family identity shift. From a firm-specific identity, the family has moved to a higher identity of the family's DNA of entrepreneurial spirit, as described by a Falck's long-time board member:

> I believe the Falck family has always had an entrepreneurial vision which went beyond steel, the specific business in which they had been active since the beginning . . . *It's in their blood, in their DNA*; it's the bloodline which prevails – they just don't surrender. You can feel the activism, the resolution to persist, always struggling to improve . . . *It's the family's entrepreneurial spirit.* (Filippo Tamborini, president of Falck's Advisory Board since 1976, p. 338–339), italics added

This shift demonstrates "who we are as a family business" (Shepherd & Haynie, 2009, p. 1253), referring to the family's DNA, *family-specific*, and not to a firm-specific identity.

Transferring SEW from firm-specific to family-specific warrants a clarification of levels of analysis. I discuss the SEW flow and stock in this chapter as affective relational perceptions and actions performed by an individual owner. During the first generation, this could apply to the founder, or to single owners such as in the Beretta model of a single heir per generation. However, when the family grows and includes multiple owners, their SEW assessments performed at the individual level, need to be aggregated to the family level of analysis. As affective and identity phenomena are conceptualized and studied also at the group level (Barsade & Knight, 2015; Wielsma & Brunninge, 2019), family firm scholars have yet to develop conceptual models to explore and understand how various individual SEW judgements join to form one family/group level construct. The current use of a single-family re-spondent in SEW studies is, for example, explained by Cruz and Justo (2017, p. 579) because they wish to refer to "a dominant actor" and not to "family dynamics":

> Following a longstanding tradition in research about portfolio entrepreneurship (MacMillan, 1986; Scott & Rosa, 1996), we use the individual as the unit of analysis (instead of the family) acknowledging that even though the family unit *"refers to a collective of individuals, there is typi-cally a dominant actor or a coalition of actors that represent a vision which, more than other vi-sions, determines the future of the family's entrepreneurial activities (Chua, Chrisman, & Sharma, 1999)"* (Nordqvist & Melin, 2010, p. 223). This is more so the case in SME contexts, in which ex-tant evidence reveal that central role is played by owners preferences in the decision making process (Brockman & Simmonds, 1997; Jennings & Beaver, 1997). Furthermore, we believe that such level of analysis is indeed appropriate when the research interest lies in explaining the drivers that push family owners to engage in portfolio entrepreneurship in the first place, rather that the family dynamics taking place once the portfolio is operational (italics in the original).

As the Taittinger, Pery, and Falck examples demonstrate, the multiple and different SEW judgements held by individual owners converged to a collective family decision in the Pery and Falck stories, but to divergent actions in the Taittinger case. Under-standing how family dynamics drive preferences and decision-making is actually an exciting future area for research, understanding engagement in *and* operation of port-folio entrepreneurship. Whether an individual perception or a group level aggregate, as the business family and the portfolio of firms grow and become organizationally complex, the family owners will rely more heavily on the family-specific meta-identity as a systematic way of dealing with SEW perceptions in a way akin to a decision heu-ristic (Shepherd & Haynie, 2009). This leads to the next proposition:

Proposition 9: *When a business family owns a portfolio mainly consisting of periph-eral firms, the SEW endowment perceptions will refer to a meta-identity of family-specific "who we are as a family business" and not to a specific firm.*

The Full AIM of SEW Endowments

Introducing the AIM, Forgas (1995) laid the theoretical foundation to explain the processes through which affectively loaded information influences cognitive judg-ments and becomes incorporated into an individual's deliberations. Zellweger and Dehlen (2012) use this model to describe the degree of affect infusion in the forma-tion of owners' subjective ownership value assessments of their firm. Extending the model to the evaluation of multiple firms in a portfolio, an owner assesses his or her SEW perceptions, which depend on (a) the target firm features; (b) the personal features of the owner assessing the SEW; and (c) the situational features under which the SEW is determined (Forgas, 1995; Zellweger & Dehlen, 2012). In other words, my model suggests that SEW flows of relational components (such as intimacy, attachment of affect and identity) exert influence on individual level SEW stock perceptions through target, personal, and situational features of the evaluation process. This means that target, personal, and situational features are mediators linking SEW flows to SEW stock endowments.

Target Features in Determining Family Owners SEW Perceptions

In the assessment of how SEW flows influence SEW stocks, the specific firm attributes of core versus peripheral, threshold performance, duration in the portfolio, and family control, have already been argued to have mediating influence. Mode of ownership (e.g., majority- and wholly owned but not minority- and equally owned) investments have been found to influence SEW considerations (Kim et al., 2019). Some studies argue that a longer duration in a portfolio have a positive influence on SEW (Zellweger et al., 2012a), while others do not replicate this finding (Kim et al., 2019). Tying the longer time horizon in family ownership and resource allocation, family owners are also argued to reduce the family's threshold of performance (DeTienne & Chirico, 2013), which leads to the next proposition:

Proposition 10: *The process of shaping SEW stock from SEW affective flows is mediated by target firm's features of core versus peripheral, threshold performance, duration in the portfolio, and family control.*

Personal Features in Determining Family Owners SEW Perceptions

In the assessment of how SEW flows influence SEW stocks, the personal attributes of the individual owner performing the assessment itself, namely his or her characteristics of personal relevance, purpose orientation, affective state, and generation of ownership are suggested to mediate the SEW stock outcome. Personal relevance of a specific firm may be determined by the size of ownership stake represented within the owner's total wealth, with a more important role given to a larger fraction (Zellweger & Dehlen, 2012). Personal relevance and or purpose orientation may be dependent on an owner's identification needs and nonfinancial goals. The AIM suggests that a judge's affective state may influence the process, for example, an owner's good mood is believed to elicit more positive value assessments whereas a negative mood more negative assessment (Zellweger & Dehlen, 2012). The owner's generation has long been argued to influence the SEW process: decreasing SEW between Stage I of "founding-family-controlled-and-managed", Stage II of "non-founding extended family owned and managed") to Stage III "extended family owned and professionally managed", in the original oil firms' study (Gómez-Mejía et al., 2007, p. 125), up to a different set of "next-generation values and vision" incorporated into a different SEW reference point shift (Nason et al., 2019, p. 847). Referring to the meta identity shift, Shepherd and Haynie (2009, p. 1256) argue that "it is likely that different generations perceive the intersection of family and business differently in the context of opportunity evaluation", leading to the following proposition:

Proposition 11: *The process of shaping SEW stock from SEW affective flows is mediated by owner's personal features of personal relevance, purpose orientation, affective state, and generation of ownership.*

Situational Features in Determining Family Owners SEW Perceptions

The last source of influence in the assessment of how SEW flows influence SEW stocks, are situational attributes of the value appraisal process, namely social desirability, availability of information, threshold performance of portfolio, and meta family firm identity of portfolio. Social desirability norms may differ for salient stakeholders with pure financial goals, influencing owners to consider their emotional attributes to a lesser or an extended degree (Zellweger & Dehlen, 2012). For example, cultural norms to display emotions vary between countries, making the American context as the most extreme one to hold norms for the exclusion of affect from a business organization in the name of "acting professional" (Uhlmann, Heaphy, Ashford, Zhu, & Sanchez-Burks, 2013). The size and the performance of the whole portfolio may influence SEW formation, as, for example, in the Warren Buffett case, where the exceptional size of the family's assets raises questions of social responsibility and philanthropical endeavors, leading to my last proposition:

Proposition 12: *The process of shaping SEW stock from SEW affective flows is mediated by situational attributes of the value appraisal process, namely social desirability, availability of information, threshold performance of portfolio, and meta family firm identity.*

Conclusion

In this chapter, I have discussed the process of affective SEW flows creating perceptions of SEW stocks, influenced by target, personal and situational features of the owner who is making the SEW assessment. My model extends Zellweger and Dehlen's (2012) model of AIM from the value process of one single firm to a portfolio of firms owned by a business family. The propositions suggested review a full range of theoretical dilemmas, ranging from the acknowledgement of SEW as a cognitive perception resulting from affective antecedents, from affective antecedents to the changing process over time, the "heterogeneity within" one family's assets, where individual owners assess the SEW stock of affect they relate to their portfolio. Integrating the AIM theory of affective deduction, portfolio of firms in a cluster owned by business families, identity shifts and available research, this chapter has three contributions.

First, I theorize the process of how owners develop their SEW assessments regarding a single firm in their portfolio. Differentiating between core and peripheral firms I argue that owners do not treat their firms equally as "all their firms" implied to in the title of this study, but rather develop particular and time specific SEW stock perceptions. These perceptions are influenced by the existence of SEW flows of affective and relational components of intimacy, attachment, and identity, and then mediated by the AIM features of target, personal, and situation.

Second, I extend the specificity and distinction between SEW flows and SEW stock. Although flows may lead to the accumulation of stocks, the SEW terminology has not yet modeled how affective SEW flow variables influence stocks of SEW. Elaborating on the development over time from a single core family firm to a complicated business family portfolio, I discuss flow and stock SEW considerations for a business family portfolio and for individual owners. Third, my discussion contributes to the understanding of heterogeneity sources among family firms, among different owners of one family, and between different points in time for a single individual owner.

Many questions are still open, as even the level of SEW stocks over time, as increasing or decreasing – is still debated. Relating to the examples in this chapter, did the Falck family owners sell the historic steel core firm before or after they shifted into their meta-family identity? How does the dominant coalition of a family firm drive these changes among all owners? Does it take an exceptionally long horizon of about two hundred years until a new acquisition becomes a core firm, like in the Beretta family firm? Did Pierre-Emmanuel Taittinger have higher chances of repurchasing the champagne core business from the venture fund his relatives sold it to because he actively worked in the champagne firm, and not in the other peripheral businesses owned by his family? Did Howard, Susan, and Peter Buffet have a SEW stock earlier in their life, losing it only after their father's announcement about not transferring his firm to them? Pursuing the quest of emotional flows and stocks, future studies will have to further explain the complex and interesting phenomenon of the affective attributes that influence decision-making in family firms.

References

Akhter, N., Sieger, P., & Chirico, F. (2016). If we can't have it, then no one should: Shutting down versus selling in family business portfolios. *Strategic Entrepreneurship Journal*, 10(4), 371–394.

Aldrich, H. E., & Cliff, J. E. (2003). The pervasive effects of family on entrepreneurship: Toward a family embeddedness perspective. *Journal of Business Venturing*, 18(5),573–596.

Anwar, S. T., & Tariq, S. M. (2011). Evolution of entrepreneurship and organizational configurations at Zildjian, 1623–2010. *Journal of International Entrepreneurship*, 9(3), 175–194.

Barsade, S. G., & Gibson, D. E. (2007). Why does affect matter in organizations? *Academy of Management Perspectives*, 21(1), 36–59.

Barsade, S. G., & Knight, A. P. (2015). Group affect. *Annual Review of Organizational Psychology and Organizational Behavior*, 2(1), 21–46.

Berrone, P., Cruz, C., Gómez-Mejía, L. R., & Larraza-Kintana, M. 2010. Socioemotional wealth and corporate responses to institutional pressures: Do family-controlled firms pollute less? *Administrative Science Quarterly*, 55(1),82–113.

Berrone, P., Cruz, C., & Gómez-Mejía, L. R. (2012). Socioemotional wealth in family firms: Theoretical dimensions, assessment approaches, and agenda for future research. *Family Business Review*, 25(3), 258–279.

Brewton, K. E., Danes, S. M., Stafford, K., & Haynes, G. W. (2010). Determinants of rural and urban family firm resilience. *Journal of Family Business Strategy*, 1(3), 155–166.

Carney, M. (2005). Corporate governance and competitive advantage in family–controlled firms. *Entrepreneurship Theory and Practice*, 29(3), 249–265.

Carney, R. W., & Child, T. B. (2013). Changes to the ownership and control of East Asian corporations between 1996 and 2008: The primacy of politics. *Journal of Financial Economics*, 107(2), 494–513.

Carney, M., & Gedajlovic, E. (2002). The co-evolution of institutional environments and organizational strategies: The rise of family business groups in the ASEAN region. *Organization Studies*, 23(1), 1–29.

Carter, S., & Ram, M. (2003). Reassessing portfolio entrepreneurship. *Small Business Economics*, 21(4), 371–380.

Chang, E. P. C., Memili, E., Chrisman, J. J., Kellermanns, F. W., & Chua, J. H. (2009). Family social capital, venture preparedness, and start-up decisions. *Family Business Review*, 22(3),279–292.

Chirico, F., Gómez-Mejía, L. R., Hellerstedt, K., Withers, M., & Nordqvist, M. (2020). To merge, sell, or liquidate? Socioemotional wealth, family control, and the choice of business exit. *Journal of Management*, 46(8), 1342–1379.

Chua, J. H., Chrisman, J. J., & De Massis, A. (2015). A closer look at socioemotional wealth: Its flows, stocks, and prospects for moving forward. *Entrepreneurship Theory and Practice*, 39(2),173–182.

Cruz, C., & Justo, R. (2017). Portfolio entrepreneurship as a mixed gamble: A winning bet for family entrepreneurs in SMEs. *Journal of Small Business Management*, 55(4), 571–593.

Daspit, J. J., Long, R. G., & Pearson, A. W. (2019). How familiness affects innovation outcomes via absorptive capacity: A dynamic capability perspective of the family firm. *Journal of Family Business Strategy*, 10(2), 133–143.

DeTienne, D. R. 2010. Entrepreneurial exit as a critical component of the entrepreneurial process: Theoretical development. *Journal of Business Venturing*, 25(2),203–221.

DeTienne, D. R., & Chirico, F. (2013). Exit strategies in family firms: How socioemotional wealth drives the threshold of performance. *Entrepreneurship Theory and Practice*, 37(6), 1297–1318.

Dierickx, I. & Cool, K. (1989). Asset stock accumulation and sustainability of competitive advantage. *Management Science*, 35(12),1504–1511.

Discua Cruz, A., Howorth, C., & Hamilton, E. (2013). Intrafamily entrepreneurship: The formation and membership of family entrepreneurial teams. *Entrepreneurship Theory and Practice*, 37(1), 17–46.

Feldman, E. R., Amit, R., & Villalonga, B. (2016). Corporate divestitures and family control. *Strategic Management Journal*, 37(3), 429–446.

Forgas, J. P. (1995). Mood and judgment: the affect infusion model (AIM). *Psychological Bulletin*, 117(1), 39.

Frank, M. (2006). Taittinger Heirs and French Bank Buy Back Champagne House, *Wine Spectator*, Taittinger Heirs and French Bank Buy Back Champagne House | Wine Spectator, retrieved on 19.9.2021.

Frijda, N. H. (1986). *The Emotions*. Cambridge, UK: Cambridge, University Press.

Fruin, W. M. (1980). The family as a firm and the firm as a family in Japan: The case of Kikkoman Shoyu Company Limited. *Journal of Family History*, 5(4), 432–449.

Gómez-Mejía, L. R., Campbell, J. T., Martin, G., Hoskisson, R. E., Makri, M., & Sirmon, D. G. (2014). Socioemotional wealth as a mixed gamble: Revisiting family firm R&D investments with the behavioral agency model. *Entrepreneurship Theory and Practice*, 38(6), 1351–1374.

Gómez-Mejía, L. R., Cruz, C., Berrone, P. & De Castro, J. (2011) The bind that ties: Socioemotional wealth preservation in family firms, *Academy of Management Annals*, 5(1),653–707.

Gómez-Mejía, L. R., Haynes, K. T., Núñez-Nickel, M., Jacobson, K. J., & Moyano-Fuentes, J. (2007). Socioemotional wealth and business risks in family-controlled firms: Evidence from Spanish olive oil mills. *Administrative Science Quarterly*, 52(1), 106–137.

Gómez-Mejía, L. R., Patel, P. C., & Zellweger, T. M. (2018). In the horns of the dilemma: Socioemotional wealth, financial wealth, and acquisitions in family firms. *Journal of Management*, 44(4), 1369–1397.

Gross, J. J. (1998). The emerging field of emotion regulation: An integrative review. *Review of General Psychology*, 2(3), 271–299.

Habbershon, T. G., & Pistrui, J. (2002). Enterprising families domain: Family-influenced ownership groups in pursuit of transgenerational wealth. *Family Business Review*, 15(3),223–237.

Haniel, F. (2008). *A Haniel Chronology 1756–2008*. Duisburg, Germany. https://haniel-2018.corpo rate-report.net/en/ (accessed September 14, 2021.

James, H. (2006). *Family Capitalism: Wendels, Haniels, Falcks, and the Continental European Model*. Cambridge, Massachusetts: The Belknap Press.

Jaskiewicz, P., Combs, J. G., & Rau, S. B. (2015). Entrepreneurial legacy: Toward a theory of how some family firms nurture transgenerational entrepreneurship. *Journal of Business Venturing*, 30(1), 29–49.

Jiang, D. S., Kellermanns, F. W., Munyon, T. P., & Morris, M. L. (2018). More than meets the eye: A review and future directions for the social psychology of socioemotional wealth. *Family Business Review*, 31(1), 125–157.

Kim, H., Hoskisson, R. E., & Zyung, J. D. (2019). Socioemotional favoritism: Evidence from foreign divestitures in family multinationals. *Organization Studies*, 40(6), 917–940.

Kotler, P., & Keller, K. L. (2009). *Marketing Management* (13th ed.). Upper Saddle River, NJ: Prentice Hall.

Martin, E., (July 6, 2017). Billionaires who won't leave their fortunes to their kids (cnbc.com), retrieved on 28.9.2021.

Merriam-Webster. (n.d.). Out of sight, out of mind. In *Merriam-Webster.com dictionary*. Retrieved September 28, 2021, from https://www.merriam-webster.com/dictionary/out%20of%20sight %2C%20out%20of%20mind

Michael-Tsabari, N., Labaki R., & Zachary, K. R., (2014). Towards the cluster model: The family firm's entrepreneurial behavior over generations. *Family Business Review*, 27(2), 161–185.

Miller, A. (1949). *All My Sons (1947)*. Na.

Miller, D., & Le Breton-Miller, I. (2014). Deconstructing socioemotional wealth. *Entrepreneurship Theory and Practice*, 38(4),713–720.

Nason, R., Mazzelli, A., & Carney, M. (2019). The ties that unbind: Socialization and business-owning family reference point shift. *Academy of Management Review*, 44(4), 846–870.

Paris, I. (2016). Product diversification in a survival family firm: The case of Fabbrica d'Armi Pietro Beretta (1946–1996). *Revista de Historia Industrial*, 25(65), 151–180.

Pierre Taittinger Wikipedia webpage, Pierre Taittinger – Wikipedia, retrieved on 21.9.2021.

Rosa, P. (1998). Entrepreneurial processes of business cluster formation and growth by "habitual" entrepreneurs. *Entrepreneurship Theory and Practice*, 22(4), 43–61.

Salvato, C., Chirico, F., & Sharma, P. (2010). A farewell to the business: Championing exit and continuity in entrepreneurial family firms. *Entrepreneurship & Regional Development*, 22(3–4), 321–348.

Sestu, M. C., & Majocchi, A. (2020). Family firms and the choice between wholly owned subsidiaries and joint ventures: A transaction costs perspective. *Entrepreneurship Theory and Practice*, 44(2), 211–232.

Shepherd, D., & Haynie, J. M. (2009). Family business, identity conflict, and an expedited entrepreneurial process: A process of resolving identity conflict. *Entrepreneurship Theory and Practice*, 33(6), 1245–1264.

Sieger, P., Zellweger, T. M., Nason, R. S., & Clinton, E. (2011). Portfolio entrepreneurship in family firms: A resource-based perspective. *Strategic Entrepreneurship Journal*, 5(4),327–351.

Tagiuri, R., & Davis, J. (1996). Bivalent attributes of the family firm. *Family Business Review*, 9(2), 199–208.

The Irish Times, 23.2.2008, Bubbly Taittinger back at helm of champagne firm (irishtimes.com), retrieved 19.9.2021.

Uhlmann, E. L., Heaphy, E., Ashford, S. J., Zhu, L., & Sanchez-Burks, J. (2013). Acting professional: An exploration of culturally bounded norms against nonwork role referencing. *Journal of Organizational Behavior*, 34(6), 866–886.

Vega, N. (2021, June 23). Warren Buffett is 'halfway' through giving away his massive fortune. Here's why his kids will get almost none of his $100 billion. *CNBC*. https://www.cnbc.com/2021/06/23/why-warren-buffett-isnt-leaving-his-100-billion-dollar-fortune-to-his-kids.html (accessed October 26, 2021).

Ward, J. (2004). *Perpetuating the Family Business: 50 Lessons Learned from Long Lasting, Successful Families in Business*. Palgrave Macmillen, UK.

Westhead, P., & Howorth, C. (2007). "Types" of private family firm: An exploratory conceptual and empirical analysis. *Entrepreneurship Regional Development*, 19(5),405–431.

Westhead, P., Ucbasaran, D., & Wright, M. (2005). Experience and cognition: Do novice, serial and portfolio entrepreneurs differ? *International Small Business Journal*, 23(1), 72–98.

Wielsma, A. J., & Brunninge, O. (2019). "Who am I? Who are we?" Understanding the impact of family business identity on the development of individual and family identity in business families. *Journal of Family Business Strategy*, 10(1), 38–48.

Wiseman, R., & Gómez-Mejía, L. (1998). A behavioral agency model of managerial risk taking. *Academy of Management Review*, 23(1),133–153.

Zellweger, T. M., & Dehlen, T. (2012). Value is in the eye of the owner: Affect infusion and socioemotional wealth among family firm owners. *Family Business Review*, 25(3), 280–297.

Zellweger, T. M., Kellermanns, F. W., Chrisman, J. J., Chua, J. H. (2012a) Family control and family-firm valuation by family CEOs: The importance of intentions for transgenerational control. *Organization Science*, 23(3),851–868.

Zellweger, T. M., Nason, R. S., & Nordqvist, M. (2012b). From longevity of firms to transgenerational entrepreneurship of families: Introducing family entrepreneurial orientation. *Family Business Review*, 25(2),136–155.

Sophie Bacq and Robert S. Nason

9 Business Family Reputation, Internal Markets, and Holdup Agency Costs

Abstract: Recent research has drawn attention to the distinct agency costs of owner-managed firms. We focus on the problem of holdup, where employees are disincentivized to make firm-specific investments (e.g., hone specific skills necessary to perform their job at that particular firm). Research contends that holdup may be exacerbated in family firms since family owner-managers have incentive and discretion to favour family employees over non-family employees. We argue that business families – families who own multiple firms – have critical advantages relative to single-family firms in addressing holdup-related agency costs. Specifically, we discuss why and how family ownership of multiple businesses may provide (1) ex-ante credible signals through inimitable reputations; and (2) ex-post institutional controls through internal labor markets, which mitigate the problem of holdup.

Keywords: holdup, agency cost, business family reputation, family firm employees

Introduction

Scholars have long recognized the agency paradox that prevails in family businesses. On the one hand, corporate governance theorists advance that agents may impose costs on owners, known as the principal-agent problem (Eisenhardt, 1989; Jensen & Meckling, 1976). Such costs take the form of monitoring expenditures or expensive performance plans and incentive systems. Owner-management, such as in family businesses, may thus mitigate these costs as ownership and management belong to the same hands. On the other hand, there is increased recognition that family business owners have owner-manager incentives to engage in behaviours that may increase agency costs (Schulze, Lubatkin, Dino, & Buchholtz, 2001; Schulze & Zellweger, 2021). Indeed, per agency theory predictions, owner-managers have residual rights of control, which gives them both the incentive and discretion to exercise behavioural opportunism and pursue self-interested or particularistic goals that do not align with the firm's goal of sustained competitive advantage (Carney, 2005; Gedajlovic & Carney, 2010). As a result, family owner-managers may engage in behaviours that are costly for the firm, such as the pursuit of family-centred non-financial goals

Sophie Bacq, Indiana University
Robert S. Nason, McGill University

https://doi.org/10.1515/9783110727968-009

(Gómez-Mejía, Haynes, Núñez-Nickel, Jacobson, & Moyano-Fuentes, 2007; Zellweger, Nason, & Nordqvist, 2012). Behavioural opportunism of owner-managers disincentivizes key stakeholders such as employees from making firm-specific investments (FSIs) – a problem known as holdup (Hoskisson, Gambetta, Green, & Li, 2018). Holdup is a critical problem since, according to the resource-based view (Barney, 1991), a firm achieves sustained competitive advantage through unique bundles of resources that are often created by key stakeholder FSIs (Hoskisson et al., 2018; Wang & Barney, 2006).

FSIs made by non-family employees are critical for the development of a family business competitive advantage (Tabor, Chrisman, Madison, & Vardaman, 2018). Indeed, there has been much concern and research in the family business literature about the asymmetric treatment and possible neglect of non-family employees relative to family employees, known as bifurcation bias (Jennings, Dempsey, & James, 2018; Verbeke & Kano, 2012). Family firms have been found to hire under-qualified family members (Kidwell, Kellermanns, & Eddleston, 2012; Schulze et al., 2001), give family members undeserved pay (Gómez-Mejía, Larraza-Kintana, & Makri, 2003; Lubatkin, Schulze, Ling, & Dino, 2005), provide family members with protective contracts (Cruz, Gómez-Mejia, & Becerra, 2010), and retain family managers despite poor performance (Gómez-Mejía, Nunez-Nickel, & Gutierrez, 2001). At the same time, family firms may scapegoat non-family members for performance declines (Gómez-Mejía et al., 2001). The consensus is that family members tend to receive preferential treatment in critical human resource practices, such as personnel selection and performance appraisal (Jennings et al., 2018). This bifurcation bias reduces the incentive for non-family employees to make FSIs which, in turn, threatens the family firm's achievement of sustained competitive advantage. It is thus key for a family business that aims to remain competitive to incentivize such key stakeholders to make FSIs.

Holdup research has identified a range of mechanisms to induce FSIs by critical stakeholders (Hoskisson et al., 2018). Firms can encourage FSIs by sending credible and reassuring signals, or coerce them by establishing institutional controls. For instance, firms may use ex-ante property rights contracts such as profit sharing, or ex-post-resource depreciation controls such as diversification (Hoskisson et al., 2018). However, family business research has argued that family businesses may not have the interest or ability to implement such signals and controls, or those devices such as profit-sharing conflict with overarching family goals (Gómez-Mejía, Cruz, Berrone, & De Castro, 2011). Unable to mitigate the problem of holdup, family businesses face unaddressed employees' concerns of owner-opportunism which may translate into costly ex-ante adverse selection (i.e., family businesses are not able to attract the best talent) and ex-post moral hazards (i.e., key stakeholders such as non-family employees shirk and do the bare minimum at their job) (Schulze & Zellweger, 2021).

In this chapter, we explore the issue of holdup in family firms and contend that families with multiple businesses may have unique advantages that allow them to mitigate and potentially overcome the problem of holdup, which is supposedly exacerbated in family firms. Specifically, we examine how business families may provide ex-ante credible signals through inimitable reputations, and ex-post institutional controls through internal labor markets.

Business Families: Prevalence and Idiosyncrasies

While heterogeneity prevails among family firms, this fact is too infrequently incorporated into family firm theorizing (Chua, Chrisman, Steier, & Rau, 2012; Melin & Nordqvist, 2007). One important delineation to recognize is that successful owner-managed "family firms" may transition into "business families" (Steier, Chrisman, & Chua, 2015; Zellweger et al., 2012). In line with serial and portfolio entrepreneurship research that distinguishes between novice entrepreneurs and habitual entrepreneurs (e.g., Westhead & Wright, 1998; Wiklund & Shepherd, 2008), families who start and own a single business are distinct from families who have made a habit of founding, acquiring, and divesting multiple businesses (Combs, Shanine, Burrows, Allen, & Pounds, 2020; Michael-Tsabari, Labaki, & Zachary, 2014; Zellweger et al., 2012). Business families have unique structures, characteristics, and strategic mindsets (Le Breton-Miller & Miller, 2018; Nason, Mazzelli, & Carney, 2019).

Business families are likely to have family wealth and business survival as their primary aim as opposed to maintaining control of any individual business entity (Zellweger et al., 2012). As a result, family wealth is not concentrated in any individual business but rather is spread across a broad range of business assets and financial instruments (Steier et al., 2015). Further, business families tend to have patient financial capital and a longer-term time horizon (Le Breton-Miller & Miller, 2018), which enables them to make a larger array of investments. Business families are also likely to diversify their social networks and accumulate several types of capital (e.g., social, cultural) beyond financial capital. Indeed, business families develop relationships that expand into the community, politics, and upper echelons of wealthy society (Kaplan & Rauh, 2013; Le Breton-Miller & Miller, 2018). This social and cultural capital is utilized to continually grow wealth and preserve their position in the status hierarchy (Carney & Nason, 2018; Nason et al., 2019). In all, because of their portfolio approach to business ownership, business families benefit from increased size and scope, and a lack of total dependence on any individual firm. For example, the Hériard Dubreuil family manages and owns the Rémy Cointreau group, a French spirits family-owned business group whose origins date back to 1724. With multiple subsidiaries and several well-known liquor and whisky brands, the family manages the financial performance of its conglomerate, selling (e.g., Piper-Heidsieck and Charles Heidsieck champagnes, sold in 2011) and acquiring (e.g., Seattle-based Westland Distillery, acquired in 2017) companies as makes sense for the financial health of the group.

We focus on two primary attributes of business families that may alleviate agency costs related to holdup in family firms. Specifically, we discuss how business families may provide ex-ante credible signals through inimitable reputations, and ex-post institutional controls through internal labor markets. These safeguards not only attenuate the agency costs related to holdup in business families compared to single-family firms but may also confer advantages in the attraction and retention of skilled employees relative to non-family firms. Figure 9.1 illustrates our arguments.

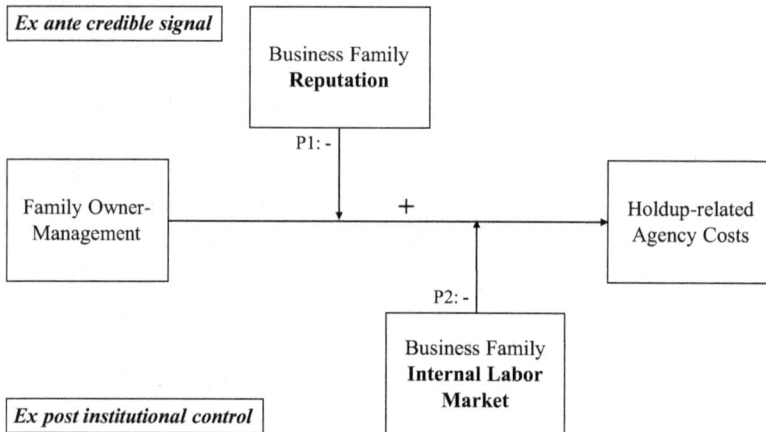

Figure 9.1: Mitigating factors of holdup-related agency costs in business families.

Business Family Reputation

Reputation – "stakeholders' perceptions about an organization's ability to create value relative to competitors" (Rindova, Williamson, Petkova, & Sever, 2005, p. 1033) – is a key inimitable asset to any organization (Deephouse & Jaskiewicz, 2013; Villalonga & Amit, 2010). Yet, it is difficult to form since it develops incrementally and idiosyncratically over time (Barney, 1991; Dierickx & Cool, 1989). Business families are uniquely capable of cultivating inimitable reputations that combine competency and citizenship. First, by virtue of their size and scope, business families often earn reputations as highly competent (Gorji, Carney, & Prakash, 2020). It is primarily highly qualified and successful family firms that can transition their industry-specific skills into a portfolio of businesses and become a business family. Over the course of structural evolution from a successful single firm to diversified operations, business families become endowed with perceptions of exceptional operations and professional business acumen.

The overlap between the family identity and the business identity creates a strong incentive for any family whether they own one or multiple businesses to preserve and enhance their reputation (Dyer & Whetten, 2006; Zellweger, Nason, Nordqvist, & Brush, 2013). We suggest that the standing as a business family provides the ability to expand a reputation for competency in a way that single-family firms may not. Indeed, families who own multiple firms are highly concentrated in the 1% wealthiest households, which confers the tremendous advantages of elite status (Carney & Nason, 2018). For instance, business families have the requisite financial resources to invest in professionalizing the family firm by sending offspring to leading educational institutions before returning to manage family operations (Stavrou & Swiercz, 1998), and by hiring world-class consulting experts.

Moreover, business families have social capital and industry-leading positions that facilitate collaboration with other high-status partners (Sieger, Zellweger, Nason, & Clinton, 2011). These factors allow business families to foment reputations for long-term orientation, good business partnership, and entrepreneurial spirit across industries (Clinton, Nason, & Sieger 2013; Le Breton-Miller & Miller, 2018). This track record of success has reinforcing effects over time as it facilitates the accumulation of additional valuable resources, including exceptional human capital (Zimmerman & Zeitz, 2002). Business families' competitive market positions (Miller & Le-Breton Miller, 2006) and longstanding community stature (Le Breton-Miller, Miller, & Steier, 2004) send signals of success and professionalism to prospective employees.

Second, business families may combine their reputation as competent with a citizenship-oriented reputation derived from their status as family owners. Whereas competency-based reputation may distinguish business families from the majority of single-family firms, citizenship-based reputation may differentiate business families from non-family firms. Large business families often actively promote their family ownership and management to instill values of loyalty and stability, and cultivate an employee-friendly environment (Jaskiewicz, Lutz, & Godwin, 2016). In this way, business families may be particularly adept at creating commitment-based human resource configurations (Lepak & Snell, 1999).

The citizenship-grounded reputation of business families is further reinforced by business families' potential scale of social impact, which serves as an increasingly decisive criterion for contemporary employees who seek meaning in their work (Net Impact, 2012). Recent research has highlighted the propensity of some family firms towards high social performance (Berrone, Cruz, Gómez-Mejía, & Larraza-Kintana, 2010; Cruz, Larraza-Kintana, Garcés-Galdeano, & Berrone, 2014; Van Gils, Dibrell, Neubaum, & Craig, 2014). We suggest that business families retain this disposition towards social performance and are in fact even more equipped than single-family firms to engage in impactful citizenship behaviours because they have the maturity and financial means to support their social goals in a way that achieves both impact depth and breadth (Desa & Koch, 2014). Indeed, the financial success associated with business families (Sieger et al., 2011) increases their capacity to invest in programs that expand the range or quality of services for a particular group of beneficiaries (impact depth). Additionally, business families have the potential to increase the number of beneficiaries or geographic reach, across their relatively larger economic footprint (impact breadth).

Reputation generally serves as an attractive attribute for individuals to incorporate into their self-concept (Whetten & Mackey, 2002). Individuals incorporate organizational attributes into their self-concept by accepting employment positions and increasing identification with the organization (Ashforth & Mael, 1989; Pierce, Kostova, & Dirks, 2001). Both competency and citizenship are attractive attributes, and we argue that business families may be uniquely positioned to fuse both into their reputations.

On the one hand, whereas single-family firms often have perceptions as dysfunctional and nepotistic (Gómez-Mejía et al., 2011), by virtue of their success, business families develop reputations as highly competent professionals. On the other hand, in an unpredictable job market characterized by a decline in job security and benefits (Kalleberg, 2011), the citizenship-oriented reputational attributes of business families may serve as a particularly meaningful signal to prospective employees, in contrast to professional non-family firms that may be seen as unsympathetic and unrelenting to non-family employee needs. Business families can leverage their family-derived perceptions of loyalty and credible high scale of social impact to contrast with perceptions of independent family firms and faceless corporations.

Thus, we propose that the hard values of professionalism and success blended with the soft values of loyalty and trustworthiness combine in a way that likely resonates positively with contemporary workers who seek challenge, stability, and purpose. In this way, the carefully cultivated and uniquely fused reputation of business families may serve as an ex-ante credible signal to recruit talented non-family employees to business families. Stated more formally, we propose:

Proposition 1: *The reputation of a business family mitigates holdup-related agency costs.*

Business Family Internal Labor Market

Business families have unique organizational structures (Steier et al., 2015). As they evolve from a single business to a portfolio of companies, they develop their internal markets (Carney et al., 2011). Most research to date has focused on families creating internal financial markets for themselves, especially in institutional voids (La Porta,

Lopez-de-Silanes, & Shleifer, 1999). Internal markets allow families to decrease reliance on external financial institutions and manage operations to maximize family-level rather than firm-level wealth (Almeida & Wolfenzon, 2006; Khanna & Rivkin, 2001). However, business families' internal markets not only facilitate the flow of financial resources but also of highly qualified human resources. Indeed, family business groups can compensate for undeveloped labor pools by investing in training and development (Khanna & Palepu, 2000; Lincoln & Gerlach, 2004) and sending talent to appropriate subsidiaries (Lincoln & Gerlach, 2004). We suggest that these internal labor markets not only buffer business families from labor constraints but may also serve as a viable retention strategy for non-family employees, mitigating the holdup problem ex-post.

First, internal labor markets incentivize employees to invest in firm-specific skills by reducing the sunk cost risks associated with firm-specific effort. When employees commit to an organization, they develop skills that may not be readily transferrable, thus limiting their ability to get full market value for those skills. Internal labor markets provide a viable means for employees to progress on their career trajectory horizontally (Wang & Barney, 2006) while incentivizing them to invest in specialized assets (Hoskisson et al., 2018). Further, internal labor markets allow for professional advancements with continuity across different employee preferences: dual career partners may benefit from the dispersed job location advantages of internal labor markets, whereas ambitious yet grounded employees may benefit from the upward career trajectory without having to relocate.

Second, internal labor markets may offer business families' employees several psychological benefits, which may increase non-family employee retention. Internal labor markets provide employment security (Delaney & Huselid, 1996), which contributes to employees' mental and physical health (Sverke, Hellgren, & Näswall, 2002). Career progress and promotion prospects may increase employees' perceptions of opportunities for personal development and imply longer employee tenure in the business family group, which engenders ownership feelings in non-family employees (Sieger, Bernhard, & Frey, 2011). Since psychological ownership generates a strong sense of identification and high commitment towards the firm (Pierce et al., 2001), employees' enhanced self-identification with a business family thus serves as an impetus to make specialized investments.

In sum, we suggest that through internal labor markets, business families can create a unique institutional infrastructure that allows for job security and job diversity. This combination is likely to be attractive to high-quality current employees who value stability, but also seek the challenge to grow their skills and careers. Internal labor markets provide opportunities for skill transfer and engender increased psychological ownership allowing business families to improve talented employee retention. A standalone family firm may be reluctant to implement safeguards against the holdup threat, such as profit sharing or ownership transfer because it conflicts with family control interests (Schulze & Zellweger, 2021). However, for business families, internal labor markets naturally serve to alleviate holdup as they align with business family interests to expand in size and scope. Stated more formally:

Proposition 2: *The internal labor market in a business family mitigates holdup-related agency costs.*

Discussion

There is growing recognition that owner-managers may generate self-inflicted agency costs (Schulze & Zellweger, 2021), including the potential for holdup due to asymmetric treatment of non-family employees (Daspit, Chrisman, Sharma, Pearson, & Long, 2017; Verbeke & Kano, 2012). In this chapter, we have examined factors that moderate family firm-induced holdup costs. Specifically, we have considered the case of business families and their unique abilities to attract high-quality employees due to inimitable reputational assets, and to retain talented employees through internal labor markets.

It is important to recognize, however, that while single-family firms may try to mimic these mechanisms by working on their reputation and diversify their activities across industries, these same factors that are advantageous for business families may exacerbate the holdup problem in single-family firms. Indeed, the literature shows evidence of standalone family firms developing harmful reputations as self-interested, unprofessional, and controlling micro-managers (Binz, Hair, Pieper, & Baldauf, 2013). Family firms may also intentionally restrict expansion and limit managerial positions in a manner that prevents non-family employees from experiencing career growth (Klein & Bell, 2007). Yet, recent research on talent acquisition in family firms points to differential perceptions of family firm characteristics depending on prospective employees' values: those who value conservation or self-transcendence are particularly attracted to working in a family firm, while those who favour openness to change or self-enhancement are less attracted (Hauswald, Hack, Kellermanns, & Patzelt, 2016). This recent evidence opens future avenues for research to consider communication strategies according to different prospective employee profiles to mitigate the cost of holdup ex-ante.

Future research could also investigate the family firms' dedicated support of social issues through corporate social responsibility programs (Cruz et al., 2014; Van Gils et al., 2014). While one can argue that business families may have the maturity and financial means to support large non-family-centred non-economic goals – for instance by supporting economic development initiatives, underwriting efforts to assist the needy, or becoming benefactors of cultural improvement – this behaviour is not uniform across business-owning families. Indeed, Miller and Le Breton-Miller

(2021) argue that family businesses are a breed of extremes. Some families have leveraged this idiosyncratic capacity (Carney, 2005) to bring about tremendous social impact from community development to disease eradication. Other family-owned businesses have been culpable in some of the greatest corporate and environmental scandals – from aggressive tax evasion to political corruption to environmental degradation. Much more research is needed into the nature and authenticity of social issue initiatives undertaken by family-owned enterprises. Further, the success of business families is also associated with increased professionalization and focus on wealth management (Steier et al., 2015). These economic imperatives may come in tension with non-family-centred non-economic goals such as social impact. In this case, a single-family firm may thus be more favourable to the support of non-family-centred non-economic goals, especially if the family firm has built strong ties with the community (Lumpkin & Bacq, 2022).

Such an organizational focus on non-family-centred non-economic goals could engender a strong sense of identification and high-value commitment towards the firm amongst non-family employees (Pierce et al., 2001; Zellweger et al., 2013). Highly identified stakeholders such as employees will have self-continuity incentives to behave in accordance with organizational interests and to support the family firm would it face a social performance crisis (Cooper & Fazio, 1984; Nason, Bacq, & Gras, 2018; Zavyalova, Pfarrer, Reger, & Hubbard, 2016). Hence, the firm identification mechanism could further reinforce non-family employees' commitment to the firm by making FSIs, thereby mitigating the holdup problem ex-post.

Additionally, future research could think of other ex-post institutional controls that mitigate holdup through increased firm identification of key stakeholders. Family firms and business families likely build organizational identities on a mix of family-related and other identity features. While business families' reputation blending competency and citizenship might be what mitigates adverse selection ex-ante, organizational identities explicitly centred around positive values, or values that fit with non-family employee's profiles (Hauswald et al., 2016), may act as ex-post controls of the holdup problem. Furthermore, one element our model did not account for is the economic environment in which the family firm operates, which may of course affect the firm ability to attract and retain talent. Therefore, future research should examine the contextual factors that moderate and strengthen, or diminish the effectiveness of the mechanisms we have discussed in the propositions above.

Finally, rather than painting broad strokes around common tendencies of family firms, we intended to use a more fine-grained approach to the reality of family businesses and stress their heterogeneity, which could manifest in important agency cost differentials. We also call for further investigations of the holdup problem beyond the family business context. The insights developed in this chapter could for instance trigger reflection on mechanisms mitigating agency costs in other owner-CEO situations, such as small businesses and start-ups. Indeed, while much research on agency costs in owner-managed contexts has taken place within the frontiers of family business research (e.g., Chrisman, Chua, & Litz, 2004), there is ample room for development in other organizational contexts. In particular, scholars studying owner-managed organizations that blend very different values at their core, including social enterprises (Vedula, Doblinger, Pacheco, York, Bacq, Russo, & Dean, 2022), hybrid (Battilana & Lee, 2014; Smith & Besharov, 2019) and pluralistic organizations (Denis, Lamothe, & Langley, 2001; Mitchell, Weaver, Agle, Bailey, & Carlson, 2016), could pursue that research avenue by exploring the problem of holdup in settings marked by systems in tension.

Conclusion

We hope that this chapter stimulates further conversation regarding the distinctive agency costs in private ownership and family firms. We proffer that business families may be able to move beyond the paternalistic small business owner stereotype that too often dominates the family firm literature, into a professionalized organizational structure. In doing so, business families may cultivate blended reputations for competency and citizenship, and build internal labor markets. This unique combination may allow for holdup protection that neither single-family firms nor non-family firms are incentivized or able to achieve. These distinctive features can resonate with contemporary workers and may confer advantages both in terms of employee attraction and retention. Thus, we conclude that holdup is not an inexorable problem in family firms but varies quite dramatically across the heterogeneous family business landscape.

References

Almeida, H. V., & Wolfenzon, D. (2006). A theory of pyramidal ownership and family business groups. *The Journal of Finance*, 61(6), 2637–2680.

Ashforth, B. E., & Mael, F. (1989). Social identity theory and the organization. *Academy of Management Review*, 14(1), 20–39.

Barney, J. (1991). Firm resources and sustained competitive advantage. *Journal of Management*, 17(1), 99–120.

Battilana, J., & Lee, M. (2014). Advancing research on hybrid organizing: Insights from the study of social enterprises. *Academy of Management Annals*, 8(1), 397–441.

Berrone, P., Cruz, C., Gómez-Mejía, L. R., & Larraza-Kintana, M. (2010). Socioemotional wealth and corporate responses to institutional pressures: Do family-controlled firms pollute less? *Administrative Science Quarterly*, 55(1), 82–113.

Binz, C., Hair, J. F., Pieper, T. M., & Baldauf, A. (2013). Exploring the effect of distinct family firm reputation on consumers' preferences. *Journal of Family Business Strategy*, 4(1), 3–11.

Carney, M. (2005). Corporate governance and competitive advantage in family–controlled firms. *Entrepreneurship Theory and Practice*, 29(3), 249–265.

Carney, M., Gedajlovic, E. R., Heugens, P. P., Van Essen, M., & Van Oosterhout, J. H. (2011). Business group affiliation, performance, context, and strategy: A meta-analysis. *Academy of Management Journal*, 54(3), 437–460.

Carney, M., & Nason, R. S. (2018). Family business and the 1%. *Business & Society*, 57(6), 1191–1215.

Chrisman, J. J., Chua, J. H., & Litz, R. A. (2004). Comparing the agency costs of family and non-family firms: Conceptual issues and exploratory evidence. *Entrepreneurship Theory and Practice*, 28(4), 335–354.

Chua, J. H., Chrisman, J. J., Steier, L. P., & Rau, S. B. (2012). Sources of heterogeneity in family firms: An introduction. *Entrepreneurship Theory and Practice*, 36(6), 1103–1113.

Clinton, E., Nason, R. S., & Sieger, P. (2013). Reputation for what? Different types of reputation and their effects on portfolio entrepreneurship. In P. Sharma, P. Sieger, R. S. Nason, A.C. Gonzalez, & K. Ramachandran (Eds.), *Exploring Transgenerational Entrepreneurship: The Role of Resources and Capabilities*. Northampton, UK: Edward Elgar Publishing, 172–191.

Combs, J. G., Shanine, K. K., Burrows, S., Allen, J. S., & Pounds, T.W. (2020). What do we know about business families? Setting the stage for leveraging family science theories. *Family Business Review*, 33(1), 38–63.

Cooper, J., & Fazio, R.H. (1984). A new look at dissonance theory. *Advances in Experimental Social Psychology*, 17, 229–266.

Cruz, C. C., Gómez-Mejía, L. R., & Becerra, M. (2010). Perceptions of benevolence and the design of agency contracts: CEO-TMT relationships in family firms. *Academy of Management Journal*, 53(1), 69–89.

Cruz, C., Larraza-Kintana, M., Garcés-Galdeano, L., & Berrone, P. (2014). Are family firms really more socially responsible? *Entrepreneurship Theory and Practice*, 38(6), 1295–1316.

Daspit, J. J., Chrisman, J. J., Sharma, P., Pearson, A. W., & Long, R. G. (2017). A strategic management perspective of the family firm: Past trends, new insights, and future directions. *Journal of Managerial Issues*, 29(1), 6–29.

Deephouse, D. L., & Jaskiewicz, P. (2013). Do family firms have better reputations than non-family firms? An integration of socioemotional wealth and social identity theories. *Journal of Management Studies*, 50(3), 337–360.

Delaney, J. T., & Huselid, M. A. (1996). The impact of human resource management practices on perceptions of organizational performance. *Academy of Management Journal*, 39(4), 949–969.

Denis, J. L., Lamothe, L., & Langley, A. (2001). The dynamics of collective leadership and strategic change in pluralistic organizations. *Academy of Management Journal*, 44(4), 809–837.

Desa, G., & Koch, J. L. (2014). Scaling social impact: Building sustainable social ventures at the base-of-the-pyramid. *Journal of Social Entrepreneurship*, 5(2), 146–174.

Dierickx, I., & Cool, K. (1989). Asset stock accumulation and sustainability of competitive advantage. *Management Science*, 35 (12), 1504–1511.

Dyer, W. G., & Whetten, D. A. (2006). Family firms and social responsibility: Preliminary evidence from the S&P 500. *Entrepreneurship Theory and Practice*, 30(6), 785–802.

Eisenhardt, K. M. (1989). Agency theory: An assessment and review. *Academy of Management Review*, 14 (1), 57–74.

Gedajlovic, E., & Carney, M. (2010). Markets, hierarchies, and families: Toward a transaction cost theory of the family firm. *Entrepreneurship Theory and Practice*, 34(6), 1145–1172.

Gómez-Mejía, L. R., Cruz, C., Berrone, P., & De Castro, J. (2011). The bind that ties: Socioemotional wealth preservation in family firms. *Academy of Management Annals*, 5(1), 653–707.

Gómez-Mejía, L. R., Haynes, K. T., Núñez-Nickel, M., Jacobson, K. J., & Moyano-Fuentes, J. (2007). Socioemotional wealth and business risks in family-controlled firms: Evidence from Spanish olive oil mills. *Administrative Science Quarterly*, 52(1), 106–137.

Gómez-Mejía, L. R., Larraza-Kintana, M., & Makri, M. (2003). The determinants of executive compensation in family-controlled public corporations. *Academy of Management Journal*, 46(2), 226–237.

Gómez-Mejía, L.R., Nunez-Nickel, M., & Gutierrez, I. (2001). The role of family ties in agency contracts. *Academy of Management Journal*, 44(1), 81–95.

Gorji, Y., Carney, M., & Prakash, R. (2020). Indirect nepotism: Network sponsorship, social capital and career performance in show business families. *Journal of Family Business Strategy*, 11(3), 100285.

Hauswald, H., Hack, A., Kellermanns, F. W., & Patzelt, H. (2016). Attracting new talent to family firms: Who is attracted and under what conditions? *Entrepreneurship Theory and Practice*, 40(5), 963–989.

Hoskisson, R., Gambeta, E., Green, C., & Li, T. (2018). Is my firm-specific investment protected? Overcoming the stakeholder investment dilemma in the resource-based view. *Academy of Management Review*, 43(2), 284–306.

Jaskiewicz, P., Lutz, E., & Godwin, M. (2016). For Money or Love? Financial and Socioemotional Considerations in Family Firm Succession. *Entrepreneurship Theory and Practice*, 40(5), 1179–1190.

Jennings, J. E., Dempsey, D., & James, A. E. (2018). Bifurcated HR practices in family firms: Insights from the normative-adaptive approach to stepfamilies. *Human Resource Management Review*, 28(1), 68–82.

Jensen, M. C., & Meckling, W. H. (1976). Theory of the firm: Managerial behavior, agency costs and ownership structure. *Journal of Financial Economics*, 3(4), 305–360.

Kalleberg, A. (2011). *Good Jobs, Bad Jobs: The Rise of Polarized and Precarious Employment Systems in the United States, 1970s to 2000s*. New York: Russell Sage Foundation.

Kaplan, S. N., & Rauh, J. D. (2013). Family, education, and sources of wealth among the richest Americans, 1982–2012. *American Economic Review*, 103(3), 158–162.

Khanna, T., & Palepu, K. (2000). Is group affiliation profitable in emerging markets? An analysis of diversified Indian business groups. *The Journal of Finance*, 55(2), 867–891.

Khanna, T., & Rivkin, J.W. (2001). Estimating the performance effects of business groups in emerging markets. *Strategic Management Journal*, 22(1), 45–74.

Kidwell, R. E., Kellermanns, F. W., & Eddleston, K. A. (2012). Harmony, justice, confusion, and conflict in family firms: Implications for ethical climate and the "Fredo effect". *Journal of Business Ethics*, 106(4), 503–517.

Klein, S. B., & Bell, F.A. (2007). Non-family executives in family businesses: A literature review. *Electronic Journal of Family Business Studies*, 1(1), 19–37.

La Porta, R., Lopez-de-Silanes, F., & Shleifer, A. (1999). Corporate ownership around the world. *The Journal of Finance*, 54(2), 471–517.

Le Breton-Miller, I., & Miller, D. (2018). Beyond the firm: Business families as entrepreneurs. *Entrepreneurship Theory and Practice*, 42(4), 527–536.

Le Breton-Miller, I., Miller, D., & Steier, L. P. (2004). Toward an integrative model of effective FOB succession. *Entrepreneurship Theory and Practice*, 28(4), 305–329.

Lepak, D. P., & Snell, S. A. (1999). The human resource architecture: Toward a theory of human capital allocation and development. *Academy of Management Review*, 24(1), 31–48.

Lincoln, J. R., & Gerlach, M. L. (2004). *Japan's Network Economy*. Cambridge, UK: Cambridge University Press.

Lubatkin, M. H., Schulze, W. S., Ling, Y., & Dino, R. N. (2005). The effects of parental altruism on the governance of family-managed firms. *Journal of Organizational Behavior*, 26(3), 313–330.

Lumpkin, G. T., & Bacq, S. (2022). Family business, community embeddedness, and civic wealth creation. *Journal of Family Business Strategy*, 13(2), 100469.

Melin, L., & Nordqvist, M. (2007). The reflexive dynamics of institutionalization: The case of the family business. *Strategic Organization*, 5(4), 321–333.

Michael-Tsabari, N., Labaki, R., & Zachary, R.K. (2014). Toward the cluster model the family firm's entrepreneurial behavior over generations. *Family Business Review*, 27(2), 161–185.

Miller, D., & Le Breton-Miller, I. (2006). Family governance and firm performance: Agency, stewardship, and capabilities. *Family Business Review*, 19(1), 73–87.

Miller, D., & Le Breton-Miller, I. (2021). Family firms: A breed of extremes? *Entrepreneurship Theory and Practice*, 45(4), 663–681.

Mitchell, R. K., Weaver, G. R., Agle, B. R., Bailey, A. D., & Carlson, J. (2016). Stakeholder agency and social welfare: Pluralism and decision making in the multi-objective corporation. *Academy of Management Review*, 41(2), 252–275.

Nason, R.S., Bacq, S., & Gras, D. (2018). A behavioral theory of social performance: Social identity and stakeholder expectations. *Academy of Management Review*, 43(2), 1–25.

Nason, R., Mazzelli, A., & Carney, M. (2019). The ties that unbind: Socialization and business-owning family reference point shift. *Academy of Management Review*, 44(4), 846–870.

Net Impact. (2012). *Talent Report: What Workers Want in 2012*.

Pierce, J. L., Kostova, T., & Dirks, K. T. (2001). Toward a theory of psychological ownership in organizations. *Academy of Management Review*, 26(2), 298–310.

Rindova, V. P., Williamson, I. O., Petkova, A. P., & Sever, J. M. (2005). Being good or being known: An empirical examination of the dimensions, antecedents, and consequences of organizational reputation. *Academy of Management Journal*, 48(6), 1033–1049.

Schulze, W. S., Lubatkin, M. H., Dino, R. N., & Buchholtz, A. K. (2001). Agency relationships in family firms: Theory and evidence. *Organization Science*, 12(2), 99–116.

Schulze, W., & Zellweger, T. M. (2021). Property rights, owner-management, and value creation. *Academy of Management Review*, 46(3), 489–511.

Sieger, P., Bernhard, F., & Frey, U. (2011). Affective commitment and job satisfaction among non-family employees: Investigating the roles of justice perceptions and psychological ownership. *Journal of Family Business Strategy*, 2(2), 78–89.

Sieger, P., Zellweger, T., Nason, R. S., & Clinton, E. (2011). Portfolio entrepreneurship in family firms: A resource-based perspective. *Strategic Entrepreneurship Journal*, 5(4), 327–351.

Smith, W. K., & Besharov, M. (2019). Bowing before dual gods: How structured flexibility sustains organizational hybridity. *Administrative Science Quarterly*, 64(1), 1–44.

Stavrou, E. T. & Swiercz, P. M. (1998). Securing the future of the family enterprise: A model of offspring intentions to join the business. *Entrepreneurship Theory and Practice*, 23(2), 19–21.

Steier, L. P., Chrisman, J. J., & Chua, J. H. (2015). Governance challenges in family businesses and business families. *Entrepreneurship Theory and Practice*, 39(6), 1265–1280.

Sverke, M., Hellgren, J., & Näswall, K. (2002). No security: A meta-analysis and review of job insecurity and its consequences. *Journal of Occupational Health Psychology*, 7(3), 242–264.

Tabor, W., Chrisman, J. J., Madison, K., & Vardaman, J. M. (2018). Nonfamily members in family firms: A review and future research agenda. *Family Business Review*, 31(1), 54–79.

Van Gils, A., Dibrell, C., Neubaum, D. O., & Craig, J. B. (2014). Social issues in the family enterprise. *Family Business Review*, 27(3), 193–205.

Vedula, S., Doblinger, C., Pacheco, D., York, J. G., Bacq, S., Russo, M. V., & Dean, T. J. (2022). Entrepreneurship for the public good: a review, critique, and path forward for social and environmental entrepreneurship research. *Academy of Management Annals*, 16(1), 391–425.

Verbeke, A., & Kano, L. (2012). The transaction cost economics theory of the family firm: Family-based human asset specificity and the bifurcation bias. *Entrepreneurship Theory and Practice*, 36(6), 1183–1205.

Villalonga, B., & Amit, R. (2010). Family control of firms and industries. *Financial Management*, 39(3), 863–904.

Wang, H., & Barney, J. B. (2006). Employee incentives to make firm specific investment: Implications for resource-based theories of corporate diversification. *Academy of Management Review*, 31(2), 466–476.

Westhead, P., & Wright, M. (1998). Novice, portfolio, and serial founders: Are they different? *Journal of Business Venturing*, 13(3), 173–204.

Whetten, D. A., & Mackey, A. (2002). A social actor conception of organizational identity and its implications for the study of organizational reputation. *Business & Society*, 41(4), 393–414.

Wiklund, J., & Shepherd, D. A. (2008). Portfolio entrepreneurship: Habitual and novice founders, new entry, and mode of organizing. *Entrepreneurship Theory and Practice*, 32(4), 701–725.

Zavyalova, A., Pfarrer, M. D., Reger, R. K., & Hubbard, T. D. (2016). Reputation as a benefit and a burden? How stakeholders' organizational identification affects the role of reputation following a negative event. *Academy of Management Journal*, 59(1), 253–276.

Zellweger, T. M., Nason, R. S., & Nordqvist, M. (2012). From longevity of firms to transgenerational entrepreneurship of families introducing family entrepreneurial orientation. *Family Business Review*, 25(2), 136–155.

Zellweger, T. M., Nason, R. S., Nordqvist, M., & Brush, C. G. (2013). Why do family firms strive for nonfinancial goals? An organizational identity perspective. *Entrepreneurship Theory and Practice*, 37(2), 229–248.

Zimmerman, M. A., & Zeitz, G. J. (2002). Beyond survival: Achieving new venture growth by building legitimacy. *Academy of Management Review*, 27(3), 414–431.

Ramzi Fathallah and Georges Samara

10 The Transformative Function of Weak Institutional Environments: The Case of Business Families in the Arab Middle East

Abstract: This chapter examines how business families operating in a weak and complex institutional environment internationalize their business and family asset portfolios. We discuss the case of business families from the Arab Middle East. We argue that business families have unique capacities to adapt to difficult institutional environments and expand their operations to more stable institutional environments through a process of institutional borrowing and arbitrage. Business families' internationalization approach in this context reveals a bright side of SEW where non-economic goals are catalyzing and reinforcing economic objectives.[1]

Keywords: institutional environments, Arab Middle East, institutional borrowing, arbitrage, internationalization, family asset portfolios

Introduction

Al Mansour Group, a business family that originated from Egypt, has witnessed many challenges due to the complex institutions of the region but now operates in more than 100 countries all over the world and employs around 60,000 people (Mansour Group (a), 2021). Many business families emerging from home countries characterized by weak and complex institutions, such as some countries in the Arab Middle East, are increasingly pursuing internationalization strategies and expanding their operations to other countries in the Arab Middle East and even to other western and non-western contexts where they are diversifying their business portfolio and flourishing (Samara, 2021). Despite the importance of the topic, the question of how and why business families internationalize despite the risk of loss of their Socioemotional Wealth (SEW) while expanding is still not well explored in the current literature.

The majority of the family business literature thus far has indicated that family businesses may be reluctant to pursue internationalization strategies due to higher

---

[1] We are grateful to our research assistant Jessica Hajjar for her outstanding work in supporting our research project.

Ramzi Fathallah, University of Ottawa
Georges Samara, University of Sharjah

https://doi.org/10.1515/9783110727968-010

risk aversion adopted by family leaders and because of the potential resultant loss of SEW. SEW is defined as the affective endowments that the family gains from their involvement in the business (Gomez-Mejia et al., 2007; Samara & Arenas, 2017) and has been decomposed into five main dimensions, namely a desire to preserve family influence and control, the identification of family owners with the business, binding social ties, emotional attachment of family members, and renewal of family bonds through dynastic succession (Berrone, Cruz, & Gomez-Mejia, 2012). While these SEW dimensions have initially been conceptualized as static and common to all family firms, recent advances in the family business literature, particularly the literature addressing family business heterogeneity, indicates that different family firms may grant different importance levels to these dimensions (Debicki et al., 2016; Samara, Jamali, & Parada, 2021). For example, while some family firms may have their priorities tilted towards maintaining absolute family influence and control over the business and a restrictive emotional attachment to the business, others may grant priority to building, maintaining and expanding their social ties and establishing a family dynasty through building an international business reputation (Samara, Jamali, & Parada, 2021). In parallel, international business research shows that internationalization is an imperative that allows businesses to stay competitive over time through exploring opportunities and exploiting non-location bound firm-specific advantages (Debellis, Rondi, Plakoyiannaki, & De Massis, 2021).

In this chapter, we aim to explore some of the drivers behind the internationalization strategies of business families embedded in weak and complex institutional environments taking some countries in the Arab Middle East as the empirical setting. In fact, the institutional diversity of the countries embedded in the Arab Middle East (Jamali et al., 2020; Samara, 2021), and the importance of international expansion to maintain local and global competitiveness, makes exploring the internationalization strategies of business families in the Arab Middle East important and timely. This work therefore allows to get rich information on the drivers of internationalization of business families, by zooming in on how weak institutional infrastructures affect internationalization decisions and on how SEW translates and manifests in business families to affect internationalization decisions.

We argue that business families in the Arab Middle East grant high importance to binding social ties and to building an international reputation, insofar that they prioritize these dimensions over maintaining absolute influence and control and other restrictive factors of SEW. Particularly, the desire of family firms to expand their operations to more stable institutional environments through a process of institutional borrowing and arbitrage, the capacity of business families to adapt to difficult institutional environments, in addition to their family investment strategy, all serve to reveal a bright side of SEW where non-economic goals are catalyzing and reinforcing economic objectives (Samara, 2021).

Below, we review the literature on family firms and internationalization, we discuss the particular case of business families in the Arab Middle East, and we illustrate our arguments with publicly available information on three businesses families originating from Egypt, Saudi Arabia, and Yemen.[2]

Internationalization and Family Firms

Internationalization of family firms has been a topic of research for many years now and many recent reviews have attempted to synthesize our knowledge of the "why, who, when, where and how" family firms venture into foreign markets (Bau et al., 2017; Carney et al., 2014; Debellis et al., 2021; Pukall & Calabrò, 2014).

Some family firms are reluctant to internationalize as they are afraid to incur additional costs due to inexperience of the family and risk of losing their SEW that could translate into a loss of absolute control of the business (Gomez-Mejia et al., 2011). Other family firms are motivated to internationalize in their aim to diversify the risk of investing only in their home country, as well as to have access to expand their operations and therefore have access to a wider range of suppliers and customers from different contexts (Kogut, 1985).

Examining the role of institutional factors in the internationalization processes of family firms, studies show that weak and informal institutions in developing countries affect the reputation of family firms and consequently the quality of their products (Chen, Saarenketo, & Puumalainen, 2016). Moreover, the home country institutional structure has an important influence on family firms internationalization strategy and success (Eddleston, Jaskiewicz, & Wright, 2019). For example, family firms in developed and pro-reform market countries have significant higher growth rates than non-family businesses, and studies show that their growth potential is stronger in a stable political environment where there are rules of law, strong regulated national institutions, and low corruption levels (Miroshnychenko et al., 2020).

In tandem, recent research calls for a better understanding of the interrelationship between the family, organization, and institutions especially that family firms are founded and managed by families that are embedded in the home institutional environment (Eddleston, Jaskiewicz, & Wright, 2019). Debellis and colleagues (2020) also argue also that the host country institutional characteristics are important factors that shape family firms' internationalization decisions. While some family firms seek to enter countries that undergo pro-market development or reforms, others look for countries with weak institutions. Despite increased calls for new research accounting for institutional factors of home and host countries to understand better family firms internationalization and to move beyond the unsatisfactory status quo of the literature (Debellis et al., 2020; Eddleston, Jaskiewicz, & Wright, 2019), studies

---

2 We use the public available information to illustrate our points, but we do not claim that our arguments represent the views of the business families mentioned in the chapter.

employing institutional perspectives remain surprisingly scarce with few exceptions (cf., Carney & Gedajlovic, 2002; Carney, Dieleman, & Taussig, 2016; Deephouse, & Jaskiewicz, 2013; Xu & Hitt, 2020). Also, most studies focus on firm characteristics and tend to overlook the role of the family in these internationalization decisions. We believe that internationalization decisions become more complex and critical when we examine business families that operate different businesses in a complex institutional environment.

Business Families

Business families (BFs) are families that established more than one business, still own several enterprises in different industries and markets, and plan to involve family members in the future (Le Breton-Miller & Miller, 2018). Their objective is not only to generate business profits but also to manage the family wealth on the long run (Brinkerink et al., 2020; Michael-Tsabari, Labaki, & Zachary, 2014). They are known to be quite entrepreneurial, experiencing rapid growth through internationalization and diversifications (Bjornberg, Elstrodt, & Pandit, 2015). Hence, BFs form economic entities that rely on their drive and resources to create value for the family wealth and the multiple businesses (Le Breton-Miller & Miller, 2018; Zellweger, Nason, & Nordqvist, 2012).

Unlike family businesses where the focus is on generating profit and managing the growth of a single business (Steier, Chrisman, & Chua, 2015), BFs are flexible in their diversification strategy. They have the capacity and willingness to let go of an entity that is no longer fit for the family enterprise's objectives and to enter a new market or product that is aligned with their future vision. The diversification and expansion strategies push the enterprise into becoming more complex and differently structured than the original business (Habbershon & Pistrui, 2002). BFs are entrepreneurial in nature and are constantly searching for new ventures and evaluating existing ones (Steier, Chrisman, & Chua, 2015). Thus, we assume that families in complex institutional environments are continuously looking for opportunities in similar and/or different institutional context to sustain and grow their business activities as well as their family wealth.

An Institutional Perspective to Business Families Internationalization

Institutions are defined as "the humanly devised constraints that structure political, economic and social interactions" (North, 1991, p. 97). They consist of formal rules (such as laws and property rights) as well as informal norms of behaviour (e.g., cultural values). These rules and cultural norms vary across countries, and they are therefore of substantial importance for internationalizing firms and multi-national corporations. For example, high quality formal institutions (i.e., a legal system that is transparent, impartial, and effective; public institutions that are honest as well as credible; and policies that support competition and openness to international trade) can be characterized by lower levels of uncertainty for economic activities and can help firms grow and develop (Zaman et al., 2021). Firms would also consider internationalizing into countries with regulated markets and strong institutions, as they provide an environment for growth (Valentino et al., 2019). When transparency, free markets, openness to trade, competition, and rule of law reign in a country, firms are more likely to develop, and the economy is less likely to go through uncertainties (Valentino et al., 2019). Similarly, within the family business scholarship, research indicates that firms grow faster in countries with more democracy, government effectiveness, regulatory quality, rule of law, corruption control, and political stability (Miroshnychenko et al., 2020).

In parallel, research also finds that weak institutions or the absence/underdevelopment of regulations and control-enforcing mechanisms (institutional voids) are very common in developing economies (Eze et al., 2020; Khanna & Palepu, 2010; Peng et al., 2018) and provide many challenges to firms when they pursue internationalization. However, many businesses were able to adapt to these environments and have developed certain capabilities in managing and adapting to these institutional voids (Khanna & Palepu, 2006). In fact, firms that originate from similar challenging contexts can learn how to adapt to difficult and weak institutional environments and are therefore more equipped to operate within institutional voids (Khanna & Palepu, 2006). Family firms, and family conglomerates in particular, are widely known in taking role of filling those institutional voids and outperforming non-family firms in these markets due to their familiness, translated into the unique resources and capabilities incorporated in the family firm's culture and social capital; hence, they become rare and difficult to imitate (Peng et al., 2018).

International business scholars found that multi-national firms emerging from these challenging institutional environments also attempt to internationalize to more regulated institutional markets in foreign countries to escape their home country's weak and ineffective institutional context (Boisot & Meyer, 2008; Luo & Wang, 2012; Witt & Lewin, 2007) and diversify their risks of operating only in contexts of institutional and political instabilities (Krammer, Strange, & Lashitew, 2018; Cuervo-Cazurra, 2016).

Multi-nationals from emerging markets are also known to follow distinct strategies in going global, particularly related to their choice of location. Scholars described the internationalization behaviours of these firms as institutional arbitrage, whereby businesses exploit the differences between institutional arrangements operating in different jurisdictions (Boisot & Meyer, 2008; Fathallah, Branzei, & Schaan, 2018). Firms may want to exploit and leverage their competencies gained in their difficult institutional environments by expanding to less institutionally developed countries (Cuervo-Cazurra & Genc, 2008; Holburn & Zelner, 2010). Alternatively, they may consider internationalizing to more institutionally developed countries to escape home country challenges or diversify the risks (Luo & Wang, 2012; Witt & Lewin, 2007). In other words, some firms rely on their acquired knowledge and experience in operating in weak institutional settings to internationalize in countries with similar contexts by taking advantage of their capabilities of doing business in environments of institutional uncertainty (Luiz, Stringfellow, & Jefthas, 2017). However, some scholars argue that when the institutional uncertainty increases, firms become more pressured to internationalize into more stable countries in order to diversify their risks, hedging against their exposure to the uncertain institutional environments and voids (Luiz et al., 2017) rather than escape from home country, as the domestic context remains a significant part of their operations (Fathallah et al., 2018; Luiz et al., 2017).

The Arab Middle Eastern BFs as an Exploratory Case

Going back to the roots of entrepreneurship, "the earliest accounts point to the Phoenicians' trading skills (Wingham, 2004) and to the Assyrians' inherited system of private enterprise in Sumer and Babylon (Butler, 2004)" in the Middle East (Krueger et al., 2021, p. 3). The entrepreneurial spirit was transferred from generation to generation in families, and Middle Eastern families are known of their business acumen (Field, 1985). These families are historically characterized by a long-lasting entrepreneurial spirit and retailing and trading is the most popular sector in the Arab Middle East (Booz&co, 2009).

Family businesses are considered the backbone of economic and social development in this region (Samara, 2021). According to multiple reports, family businesses constitute 90% of the companies in the Middle East generating more than 60% of its GDP and employing more than 70% of the workforce in the region (Ernst & Young, 2014; PWC, 2016).

The Arab Middle Eastern context does not form a homogeneous group of countries, but rather a diversity of identities, cultures, political systems, and geographies (Fathallah, Sidani, & Khalil, 2020; Jamali et al., 2020; Samara, 2021), which makes it a particular context to study (Krueger et al., 2021; Zahra, 2011). In fact, while many countries are characterized by complex, ongoing economic turmoil, and unstable environments, others are more economically and politically stable and provide more developed institutions. These facts make countries in the Arab Middle East an ideal comparative context to study how families, business and institutions interact (Krueger et al., 2021; Samara, 2021).

As mentioned earlier, we define institutionally complex environments as contexts of relatively weak institutions, low institutional trust (Jaskiewicz et al., 2021), and where organized systems might act unpredictably through instability and unclear laws. There is little guarantee against uncertainty and risk (and political stability) in these environments (Jaskiewicz et al., 2021; Shapiro, 1987).

For example, OECD (2019) characterized Egypt as a fragile context, while Yemen and Iraq as extremely fragile. Within the Middle East, countries differ in the extent of perceived corruption and the degree to which governments uphold the rule of law (Jamali et al., 2020). For instance, in 2012, the percentile rank of government effectiveness was 83 in the UAE, 34 in Algeria, and 25 in Egypt (Cammett, 2017; "Databank | Worldwide Governance Indicators", n.d.). War-torn and/or politically turbulent countries such as Iraq, Lebanon, and Yemen have particularly poor measures, while the Gulf oil monarchies exhibit relatively low levels of corruption and greater respect for the rule of law (Cammett, 2017).

The diversity, richness, and complexity of the institutional environment of the Middle East, therefore, offers an ideal laboratory to explore the heterogeneity among family firms and how the institutional environment shapes family dynamics and firm behaviours. In this region, dealing with the family businesses started to differ between the Arabian Gulf countries and the Levant and North African countries. In the GCC, family businesses are in stage where they are developing succession, governance, and growth strategies unlike the Levant and North African family firms, which are facing economic and political instability (FFI Practitioner, 2016). According to FFI Practitioner article, family business owners based in this region prioritize the growth, diversification and internationalization of the business to address the region's political and economic uncertainty (FFI Practitioner, 2016).

Many Arab Middle Eastern family firms desire to maintain family influence and control; thus, they may be reluctant to internationalize as this decision involves a significant amount of investment and uncertainty (Samara, 2021). At the same time, many Arab Middle Eastern countries face harsh situations in the home country, stemming from weak state institutional structures and some countries being hurdled with turbulence, war, and corruption (Zahra, 2011). Under such circumstances, family firms may shift their attention to international markets to secure family wealth and sustainability of the business (Samara, 2021). According to PWC (2016), some of the motives that pushed Middle Eastern family businesses into internationalization are: the slowed economies that were affected by the instability in the region, local saturated markets, and broader investment and growth opportunities internationally, as well as owning the "trading" mindset (PWC, 2016). Looking into the BFs of this region, studies noted that most of these families are present in multiple sectors and geographies, but they have yet to establish meaningful presence outside their home country (Björnberg, Elstrodt, & Pandit, 2015). Hence, examining the way business families view and engage in internationalization strategies may help shed light on how SEW could be enacted in those business families and how SEW could interact with the wider institutional milieu to impact the family mindset and the resultant firm behaviour.

The cases that we explore in the sections on institutional borrowing and institutional arbitrage, taken from public sources, highlight several general themes that enabled and motivated business families to internationalize. These business families show a high degree of SEW driving their internationalization decisions, albeit manifesting in positive directions to affect internationalization decisions. SEW, in the cases below, is translated into a strong desire to diversify risks, build, and maintain social ties with internal and external stakeholders, and expand the family's business legacy and reputation. These factors, coupled with experience in the home country, motivate business families to internationalize and allow them to gain the necessary legitimacy and trust to partner with foreign multi-nationals.

Inward Internationalization: Institutional Borrowing

Many of the BFs in the Middle East have emerged from a trading history in their home country. These families were first to initiate contacts with foreign multi-national enterprises to represent their products and services in the region. Through early interactions with foreign suppliers and partners, these BFs started to get involved with international business activities by importing products and services from the developed markets and acting as licensees or franchisees in the region.

One illustrative case is Mansour Group, a global Arab family business founded by Loutfy Mansour, that emerged in Egypt in 1952 and expanded to more than 100 countries around the world, employing more than 60,000 people (Mansour Group, n.d.-a). Starting as a cotton company, Mansour Group became the second largest conglomerate in Egypt and the largest General Motors dealership in the world (Lead Foundation, 2016), passing its legacy on to all three family generations. Mansour Group leveraged its early relational capital with international companies and became a $7 billion international conglomerate with six subsidiary companies operating in various sectors, including automotive, healthcare, transportation, real estate, among others (Haine, 2021).

In 1964, the nationalization of the cotton industry in Egypt, during the reign of President Abdel Naser, led to the confiscation of the company's assets; however, against this institutional adversity, the founder decided immediately to move the business to Switzerland. He founded a cotton brokerage firm in Geneva, with connections in Sudan (Mansour Group, n.d.-b). The group built up its empire in the hybrid-half-market, half-command – economy which emerged following President Sadat's "open door" policy of the 1970s. Then, foreign multi-nationals were encouraged to invest in Egypt, but could not own their companies outright nor repatriate profits freely. The family acted as a partner to foreign multi-nationals, which desired to gain a foothold in the Egyptian market (Guha, 1997). The BF had sole rights to distribute and service General Motors cars and trucks and was Egypt's sole dealer in Caterpillar construction machinery. Over the years, Mansour Group became a leading BF in Egypt and gained the trust of foreign multi-national corporations and communities, while playing a considerable role in the Egyptian economy (Lead Foundation, 2016).

Another example comes from Saudi Arabia. Founded in 1945 as a small trading business by Sheikh Abdul Latif Jameel (ALJ), ALJ acquired Toyota distribution agency in 1955 in the Kingdom of Saudi Arabia and became the largest vehicle distribution network in the kingdom. ALJ acquired extensive experience in the automotive field then expanded into diversified sectors (Energy and environment, Real estate, and Advertising and Media . . .) and built strong networks in the region in around 30 countries (Abdul Latif Jameel, n.d.-a).

Similarly, the Bazara family established its business in 1956 as the sole Toyota distributor in Yemen. When the family imported the first Land Cruiser to Aden port, Toyota cars became the most popular vehicles among Yemeni locals (Development Aid, n.d.). In the 1960s, the popularity of Toyota grew even bigger in Yemen (Development Aid, n.d.) and the family business became the employer of over 3,000 people in different locations in Yemen (*Tharawat Magazine*, 2016). The Bazaras were traders for over 200 years before formally establishing the first business in 1956. They used to trade in timber and foodstuff, until they switched to automotive in the 1950's and 1960's when they started importing harvesters and trucks from the US and other types of Skoda cars (Development Aid, n.d.). The family also acquired the agency of Yanmar Marine Diesel Engines from Japan and diversified its market to operate in different sectors such as: banking, insurance, steel and gases manufacturing, education (Yemeni Business Club YBC, n.d.).

Many BFs in the Arab Middle East made sure to educate quite early their next generation in the western or foreign system to learn from foreign multi-nationals and borrow the ways of doing good business into their local BFs operations in the Middle East. Having been brought up or educated in the western system gave legitimacy to next generation business leaders who became familiar with clear institutions, laws, regulations, and ways of doing business in the West, which motivated foreign enterprises to work with these families. Of course, there was more specific knowledge-sharing at later stage of the relationship between local BFs and foreign partners, but the next generation's early exposure to western and foreign developed institutions was key in initiating and developing their business relationships and business models. When enforcement institutions are weak in the local market, businesses are likely to look for mechanisms elsewhere – in other words, through institutional borrowing – where partners bring strong legal institutions into weak legal institutional environments (Pinkham & Peng, 2017). The cases show that this borrowing could happen due to the family members' early exposure to these strong institutions through education or training in the developed and/or western world.

Just like their father, Mohamed Mansour and his brothers (second generation) lived an international experience and developed an international western business mentality, which undoubtedly affected their decisions in terms of transparency, sponsorship investment, and establishing and maintaining long-term partnerships (Haine, 2021). The Mansours's big opportunity came when they set up a General Motors dealership, "GM were talking to banks about possible partners, and they said there were these three American-educated brothers in Alexandria", Mansour Junior told the *Financial Times* in his first ever interview (Hazlehurst, 2016). The founder sent his sons to learn the textile business at North Carolina State University in 1960 with the understanding that they would come back to work in the cotton trade. He continued, "My father and uncles understood the US mentality, which was always to be transparent, to be clear if you can do something or not, but more importantly to build the partnership for the long term" (Hazlehurst, 2016). His father quickly became known as "Mr. Mansour Chevrolet" (Moukheiber, 2011). The father shared, "It wasn't easy and we were learning as we went along, but it helped that we were US-educated and so we understood the mentality of the General Motors and the Caterpillars of this world" (Haine, 2021).

Similarly, the three sons of ALJ graduated from international universities (Mohammed from MIT, Hassan from Sophia University in Tokyo and London Business School, and Fady from Sophia University in Tokyo, Japan). Hassan Jameel told Mckinsey Publishing: "We're following the Toyota way, using approaches of kaizen [continuous improvement] and genchi genbutsu – which means go out to the field and experience it yourself" (Schwartz & Youssef, 2020).

Ahmed, one of the Bazara's brothers, completed his higher education in the United States in Computer Sciences and Business Management and came back to work on the diversification of the company while his brothers stayed engaged in the core business. As the Bazara family has a large third generation, most of them are getting their higher education in the US in order to be more prepared to enter the family business (*Tharawat Magazine*, 2016).

We argue that through their education and experience these families were able to attract foreign multi-nationals that were interested in the institutionally complex environments of the Middle East such as Egypt, Yemen, and Saudi Arabia but lacked the capabilities to operate directly in this region. From a small and limited portfolio of representing foreign companies, these BFs were able to expand their enterprises and act as agents of multiple foreign firms across nationalities and industries.

For example, Mansour acquired the sole rights to sell Philip Morris in the country then acquired the McDonald's franchise for Giza (part of Cairo) and Alexandria (ElDeeb, 2020). Then, Mansour partnered with British American Tobacco after their partnership ended in 2014 with Philip Morris. Similarly, ALJ started growing to become the agent for international brands like Toshiba, Sharp, Apple, White-Westinghouse, Alpine, Westinghouse, Bosch, and Dora in Saudi Arabia and many other countries (Abdul Latif Jameel, 2019; Abdul Latif Jameel, n.d.-c).

In addition, the next-generation family members were learning from their parents how to conduct business with suppliers, customers, and other partners. For example, Loutfy Mansour shared in his FT interview: "I listened to my father speak on the phone, saw how he conducted a meeting, went to presentations. He'd ask me, 'What did you learn? What did you find interesting? What did you think of this?' Slowly, I learnt" (Hazlehurst, 2016).

Business Families and Institutional Arbitrage

Building on their relational capital and home-grown capabilities to do business in complex institutional markets, BFs were expanding into other challenging markets with unclear and complex institutions. Family firms domiciled in countries with institutional voids of less-developed countries may convey images of operating in inefficient, uncertain, and unregulated markets (Chen, Saarenketo, & Puumalainen, 2016, p. 47; Eddleston, Jaskiewicz, & Wright, 2019). Nevertheless, BFs may exploit their superior relational capabilities in countries with institutional voids, as they are known to build close relationships based on trust in emerging markets (Debellis et al., 2020). Here again, we note that the binding social ties dimension of SEW becomes dominant and manifests into learning and adapting to operate in an institutional setting similar to that of the home country.

BFs were leveraging their relationships with multi-national enterprises as well as their capabilities of navigating complex environments into regions where multinationals needed trusting partners. This is a particular characteristic of families in business as they can transmit their relationships and know-how across generations. BFs sustain their reputation as a family of doing reliable and trustworthy business with suppliers and partners (Le Breton Miller & Miller, 2018). They have developed a reputation as a reliable supplier of products or services for major, diversified clients; thus, they may more easily branch out into supplying other offerings for the same clients, often for different international markets (Galbraith, 1999; Le Breton Miller & Miller, 2018).

Indeed, these families had developed "institutional capabilities" through a long-term learning process of operating in challenging environments that could be leveraged in other challenging contexts (Carney, Dieleman, & Taussig, 2016). These capabilities such as trust building, relational contracting that depends on individuals or families making personal credible commitments where formal institutions are weak, and maintenance of enduring relationships with partners (Carney, Dieleman, & Taussig, 2016) are family-specific, thus relatively easy to transfer across family members and generations.

Despite the large impact of the Arab Spring and the resultant crisis in Egypt in 2011, Mansour family considered this crisis as an additional chapter in a tumultuous saga for Egypt and, in parallel, for the Mansour family (Moukheiber, 2011). One of the Mansour key family members shared in an interview, "We've always got challenges. We take country by country; some countries the challenge is security for our people, another country the challenge is the foreign exchange devaluation, [another country], the mining industry is hurting" (Trenwith, 2015). He continued, "But what does this give us versus somebody who's sitting comfortably in his comfort zone? A balance: if I'm in 100 countries, not all 100 are going to go through a difficult time, so some are going to have difficulty, some are going to be up, some down and it's a balance. But we just need to be prudent and wise about how we invest" (Trenwith, 2015). In this case, the family's pursuit of minimizing risk is translated into a diversification strategy, which eventually led to a notable resilience against institutional disruption and adversity.

The Mansours won the Caterpillar franchise for six African countries – Nigeria, Ghana, Sierra Leone, Kenya, Uganda, and Tanzania early in their internationalization. Sub-Saharan Africa was a remote area of which the Mansours had no knowledge: "A lot of people in my company said 'but Mr Mansour we know very little about Sub-Saharan Africa'. Egyptians by nature have always stuck to the Delta, around the Nile, we don't travel much . . . [But] I said 'no, we'll do it' and we did it and we've grown that business from $170m turnover for Caterpillar in Africa in 1996 to $2bn today. You can see how phenomenal the growth has been." He continued, "I pestered Caterpillar again. I said 'what other territories do you have?' It was Russia" (Trenwith, 2015).

"This was Russia in the late 1990s, with [former president] Boris Yeltsin in charge," he says. "Everyone said Russia was unsafe. We were told [by advisors] we would lose $5 million a year. Imagine Egyptians [accustomed to 40-degree Celsius] clad in winter coats and boots and working in minus 40 °C temperatures in eastern Siberia. "But we were profitable from year one and many of our earliest managerial hires are still working there, very happily" (Wilson, 2016). He also explained, "We have an edge in that we have been in Africa since 1996, so we know it well. We're in a lot of very difficult countries by the way; Africa is not easy from the security standpoint; you had Ebola this year; the price of oil has dropped so the GDP will be affected in Nigeria" (Trenwith, 2015).

Mansour Group market expansion continued when GM officially appointed their agency for Al Mansour Automotive in Iraq in 2004 and in Libya in 2006 and the Hero Motorcorp in 2019, forming Mantrabike and entering the Ugandan market (Mansour Group, n.d.-b). We noted how this BF case was able to leverage its capability to operate in complex institutional environment by expanding into similar or more complex institutional contexts. According to their public website, "The Mansour Group's long-term, patient capital approach has helped Mantrac Group navigate economic cycles and other challenges such as falling commodity prices. Its experience of operating in Africa has also helped Mantrac overcome political instability and bureaucracy, as well as health and safety concerns in the regions it operates in" (Mantrac Group, n.d.).

Similarly, ALJ expanded its Toyota distribution to Algeria in 1993, Morocco in 1995, and China in 1998 (Abdul Latif Jameel, n.d.-a; Abdul Latif Jameel, n.d.-g). Under Commercial Vehicles and Equipment business, ALJ started representing Hino trucks in Algeria in 2007 (Abdul Latif Jameel, 2019; Abdul Latif Jameel, n.d.-e). ALJ also expanded to automotive after-market manufacturing in China and Malaysia in 2011 (Abdul Latif Jameel, 2019; Abdul Latif Jameel, n.d.-b). Under the automotive engineering and manufacturing business, ALJ established a joint venture with DENSO in KSA in 2001 with distribution to North Africa, and in 2014 the joint venture expanded its operations to Turkey (Abdul Latif Jameel, n.d.-d).

Research has developed the institutional arbitrage logic under which lay the two following factors: many firms get involved in foreign direct investment to diversify away from the institutional voids and instability present in their home countries, and others seek to leverage their competencies (gained in their home countries) in weak institutional environments. In other words, firms rely on the institutional advantages that benefit them in their choice of the host countries.

To preserve the continuity of the enterprise across generations as well as to diversify the risk of operating in complex institutional markets, we argue that BFs had to resort to more developed institutional countries. For example, in 2005, Mansour Group entered the real estate business and founded Palm Hills Developments (PHD) that was listed on both the Egyptian and the London stock exchange markets. Operating in more developed institutional markets also helped them to build legitimacy with another multi-national. In 2012, ALJ went into the auto manufacturing sector, investing in Rivian electric-vehicle manufacturer in the US for several reasons: getting into the US-western market and taking part in the disruption of a sector rather than being disrupted (Schwartz & Youssef, 2020). For ALJ, entering this field allowed it to gain the necessary knowledge and competencies in time (Schwartz & Youssef, 2020). In addition, as the environment and sustainable energy global issues are big concerns for the family, ALJ took a strategic decision that allowed it to enter new diversified markets in new regions. In 2015, ALJ acquired Fotowatio Renewable Ventures FRV, a solar-energy company in Madrid addressing a global market and reaching up to 18 countries in Europe, Latin America, and Australia (Abdul Latif Jameel, n.d.-f).

Due to the heterogeneity in the institutional development in the Arab Middle East, some BFs were able to arbitrage better institutions of those in their home countries in more developed markets in the Middle East such as the UAE. Relatively to war-torn Iraq, Al Handal International Group HIG, founded in 1975 in Baghdad as a trading company expanded into the UAE and Turkey through different subsidiaries ("Al Handal International Group", n.d.). HIG currently operates in several sectors such as: Construction, Banking and Investment, Protection, Distribution, Media, and Travel (AlHandal, n.d.-b). The family relocated its headquarters to Dubai, UAE ("Al Handal International Group", n.d.).

However, this institutional arbitrage practice was built on family businesses presence in their home countries such as in Egypt, Iraq, or Saudi Arabia, as they had no intention to leave the home country. On the contrary, they had plans to expand in these markets. Operating in more than 100 countries, the Mansours knew that their strategic decisions would provide a balance for the business between the stable and unstable countries and markets. A member of the third generation expressed that whatever happens politically, the family is committed to Egypt: "Of course, the situation [in Egypt] has been a concern, but we've seen many cycles over the years. As a business we try to navigate those . . . We have a presence in over 100 countries, so when one country is down, another is up – it's all part of our diversification strategy and long-term approach, which allows us to mitigate short-term noise. It means we're not thinking of the exit. We've been investing in Egypt for decades" (Hazlehurst, 2016). Similarly, HIG believes that having survived all the difficult situations would attract foreign companies that desire to invest in the region, "Iraq is now back on the business capital market, and multi-national firms will be searching for investment opportunities to 'build new partnerships and forge new alliances'" (AlHandal, n.d.-a). The family believes that they will attract foreign investment opportunities into the family business through the offices present in UAE and Turkey (*Tharawat Magazine*, 2020).

Family Investments

BFs are known to have investments that go beyond their businesses (Le-Breton Miller & Miller, 2018). Families in complex institutional environments explore opportunities for investments to preserve, increase, and sometimes protect their financial wealth through investments in more developed institutional environments where there is less risk, and some invest in higher risk institutions to grow their wealth. We believe BFs in the Arab Middle East have portrayed a similar approach of institutional arbitrage for their family and non-business investments.

For example, while the Mansour BF was still expanding globally, Man Capital was founded in 2010, to protect, preserve, and reinvest the family's wealth (Wilson, 2016). Man Capital was established in London because "we decided that we wanted to diversify our risk and to build new 'verticals' for the group" said the third generation Loutfy Mansour (Hazlehurst, 2016). The growth of Man Capital continues through investing in different countries in Europe, MENA, and Asia, in sectors ranging from logistics, technology, and education, to telecommunication, and oil and gas (Mansour Group, n.d.-b). The diverse international team is made of 10 people from US, France, UK, India, Switzerland, and China (Hazlehurst, 2016). Man Capital's co-founders Mohamed Mansour and his son Loutfy also consider London "their second home" (Wilson, 2016). They saw moving to London a strategic move, Loutfy Mansour commented:

"Man Cap was founded in 2010, before the Egyptian Revolution. The family office is an integral part of the Mansour Group's strategy for future growth and London is the best place for expanding internationally" (Hazlehurst, 2016).

Man Capital has access to foreign assets and opportunities in more stable countries and well-known multi-nationals. For instance, Man Capital started by investing in marine logistics firms that provides operations for oil and gas offshore companies and acquired Vanguard Logistical Services in 2012 (Lead Foundation, 2016). Man capital was also an early investor in Uber, Facebook, Airbnb, Spotify, and more recently in Snowflake and Adyen (Lead Foundation, 2016). To run its tech investments, Man Capital launched 1984 Ventures, based in California as a venture capital fund (Mansour Group, n.d.-a). In 2016, Man Capital opened its second office in Washington D.C. to reinforce Mansour Group's growth in the US and ensure long-term commitment with its US partners (Man Capital, 2016).

According to the National News, Mohamed Mansour now calls London home: "I love London, ask me why, because I will tell you it is a country where there is the rule of law. That's why I came here. Rule of law, nobody gives a damn who you are. I mean not a damn, but it is not because you are . . . you abide by the law, people are polite, civilized" (Haine, 2021).

Foreign Citizenship: Another Investment Incentive for BFs?

Another phenomenon we would like to shed light on in this chapter is the increasing popularity of foreign citizenship acquisition by nationals of the Arab Middle East. Foreign citizenship by investment is a relatively recent phenomenon that highlights the desire of affluent individuals to gain another citizenship in developed countries, many of which are entrepreneurs or family business owners in unstable and complex economies (Hendrickson, 2017). These families are willing to leverage their business investments or wealth to earn citizenship or foreign passport to secure their individual and family well-being and access to safety in more stable institutional environments. We believe this is a very interesting phenomenon that has not been captured yet in the international business or family business fields. Through an arbitrage logic, affluent families based in complex institutional environments resort to this practice and might use an international business opportunity to get access to a citizenship from a western nation with advanced institutions and stability.

Economic citizenship, or second passports, is a multibillion-dollar industry, and one that is growing faster in the Middle East than in any other part of the world because of the political and economic instability that is recurrent or persistent in some countries (Underwood, 2015). These residents are seeking safety and financial security in a second citizenship.

These programs offer secondary residency/foreign passports to wealthy individuals and families without having to relocate from their home country. We argue that this is a practice that provides an arbitrage opportunity for business families where they can exploit their business presence in complex institutional environments but have access to family residency in more stable institutions that could help them protect their assets and, more importantly, ensure a secure and prosperous future for themselves and their families or, in turn, open up opportunities for their businesses or family investments. It is noted that many do not plan to move away from their home country, where their main businesses operate and where they have built great wealth and relationships with the community. But these second citizenships give them other options to operate under the governance of better institutions for their family and assets as well as open-up the opportunity to increase their social capital and expand the family legacy (Buller, 2020). A second passport provides a plethora of new opportunities for travel, investment, and business ventures. For example, BFs could own second homes and investment properties abroad.

Conclusion

While the family business literature has traditionally considered SEW as an inhibitor of internationalization (e.g., Kraus et al., 2016; Xi et al., 2015), our chapter explores how SEW manifests in a particular family business form, namely business families embedded in the Arab Middle East. Doing so, we add to the literature on how and why family businesses differ from each other (Eze et al., 2020) by honing in on the heterogeneity that comes from being a business family (Steier, Chrisman, & Chua, 2015) embedded within the Arab Middle Eastern context (Samara, 2021). We argue that SEW reveals its bright side (Kellermanns, Eddleston, & Zellweger, 2012) when it is manifested in business families embedded in weak and complex institutions. These home institutions play a transformative function by equipping business families with the necessary knowledge and resources to expand to more turbulent contexts, while also incentivizing them to pursue internationalization opportunities in more stable environments, as they are seeking the family's wealth protection, business family diversification, and family's environmental security.

Our chapter, therefore, contributes to both the international business literature and the family business literature in important ways. Within international business, weak institutions or institutional voids have been portrayed as restrictive factors when it comes to the internationalization of businesses. Our findings indicate that embeddedness in weak institutional environments allows the business family to familiarize itself with operating in such turbulent contexts and therefore provides an incentive for the family to pursue internationalization through a process of institutional borrowing and institutional arbitrage. Also, within the dominant negative connotation of SEW when related to internationalization, we find that business families in the Arab Middle East grant higher importance to increase and cultivate their international, regional and local social ties and that operating in a complex or risky environment is actually fueling their desire for international expansion either to capitalize on their unique acquired knowledge of navigating difficult environments (when they move to similar or more challenging institutional environments), or to pursue the security and well-being of their offspring and diversify their operations (when they expand to countries that have a strong institutional environment).

It is our hope that this chapter provides a step forward towards further exploring the business family phenomenon, how it differs from the traditional family business, and how multiple institutional, organizational, and individual forces combine to affect micro-family behaviour and meso-family business outcomes.

References

Abdul Latif Jameel. (2019, June). *Our History*. ALJ. Retrieved from https://www.alj.com/app/up loads/2019/06/20190619-ALJ-Corporate-Timeline-June-2019-EN.pdf

Abdul Latif Jameel. (n.d.-a). About Us and Our Diversified Businesses | Abdul Latif Jameel®. Retrieved from https://www.alj.com/en/about/story/

Abdul Latif Jameel. (n.d.-b). Aftermarket Vehicle Services | Abdul Latif Jameel®. Retrieved from https://www.alj.com/en/transportation/expanded-vehicle-services/

Abdul Latif Jameel. (n.d.-c). Consumer Products and Electronics | Abdul Latif Jameel®. Retrieved from https://www.alj.com/en/consumer-products/

Abdul Latif Jameel. (n.d.-d). Engineering and Manufacturing | Abdul Latif Jameel®. Retrieved from https://www.alj.com/en/engineering-manufacturing/

Abdul Latif Jameel. (n.d.-e). Material Handling, Heavy Equipment and Machinery | Abdul Latif Jameel®. Retrieved from https://www.alj.com/en/transportation/commercial-vehicles-equipment/

Abdul Latif Jameel. (n.d.-f). Renewable Energy and Environmental Services | Abdul Latif Jameel®. Retrieved from https://www.alj.com/en/energy-and-environmental-services/energy-overview/

Abdul Latif Jameel. (n.d.-g). Transportation | Abdul Latif Jameel®. Retrieved from https://www.alj.com/en/transportation/transportation-overview/

Al Handal International Group. (n.d.). Retrieved from https://www.linkedin.com/company/al-handal-international-group/

AlHandal. (n.d.-a). Home – AlHandal. Retrieved from https://alhandal.me/?page_id=2

AlHandal. (n.d.-b). Home – AlHandal. Retrieved from https://alhandal.me/?page_id=8

Bau, M., Block, J., Discua Cruz, A., & Naldi, L. (2017). Locality and internationalization of family firms. *Entrepreneurship & Regional Development*, 29(5–6), 570–574. doi: 10.1080/08985626.2017.1315501

Berrone, P., Cruz, C., & Gomez-Mejia, L. (2012). Socioemotional wealth in family firms: Theoretical dimensions, assessment Approaches, and Agenda for future research. *Family Business Review*, 25(3), 258–279. doi: 10.1177/0894486511435355

Björnberg, Å., Elstrodt, H., & Pandit, V. (2015, July). Joining the family business: An emerging opportunity for investors. *McKinsey & Company*. Retrieved from https://www.mckinsey.com

Boisot, M., & Meyer, M. W. (2008). Which way through the open door? Reflections on the internationalization of Chinese firms. *Management and Organization Review*, 4(3), 349–365.

Booz&co. (2009). *GCC Family Businesses Face New Challenges*. New York: Booz & Company.

Brinkerink, J., Rondi, E., Benedetti, C., & Arzubiaga, U. (2020). Family business or business family? Organizational identity elasticity and strategic responses to disruptive innovation. *Journal Of Family Business Strategy*, 11(4), 100360. doi: 10.1016/j.jfbs.2020.100360

Buller, A. (2020, June 4). UAE-based Arab and Indian expats snap up US residency through Grenada. *Arabian Business*. Retrieved from https://www.arabianbusiness.com

Butler, J. S. (2004). The science and practice of New business ventures: Wealth creation and prosperity through entrepreneurship growth and renewal. In D. H. B. Welsh (Ed.), *Entrepreneurship: The way ahead*, 43–54, New York: Routledge.

Cammett, M. (2017). Development and underdevelopment in the Middle East and North Africa. In C. Lancaster & N. Van de Walle (Eds.), *The Oxford handbook of politics of development*. Oxford: Oxford University Press. Retrieved from http://www.oxfordhandbooks.com/view/10.1093/ox fordhb/9780199845156.001.0001/oxfordhb-9780199845156-e-25

Carney, M., & Gedajlovic, E. (2002). The Co-evolution of Institutional Environments and Organizational Strategies: The Rise of Family Business Groups in the ASEAN Region. *Organization Studies*, 23(1),1–29. https://doi.org/10.1177/0170840602231001

Carney, M., Dieleman, M., & Taussig, M. (2016). How are institutional capabilities transferred across borders? *Journal of World Business*, 51(6), 882–894.

Carney, M., Fathallah, R., Gedajlovic, E. R., & Shapiro, D. (2014). The internationalization of ethnic Chinese family firms. In *Handbook of East Asian Entrepreneurship* (pp. 132–143). Routledge.

Chen, J., Saarenketo, S., & Puumalainen, K. (2016). Internationalization and value orientation of entrepreneurial ventures – A Latin American perspective. *Journal of International Entrepreneurship*, 14(1), 32–51. doi: 10.1007/s10843-016-0169-9

Cuervo-Cazurra, A. (2016). Multilatinas as sources of new research insights: The learning and escape drivers of international expansion. *Journal of Business Research*, 69(6), 1963–1972.

Cuervo-Cazurra, A., & Genc, M. (2008). Transforming disadvantages into advantages: Developing-country MNEs in the least developed countries. *Journal of International Business Studies*, 39(6), 957–979.

Databank Worldwide Governance Indicators. (n.d.). Retrieved from https://databank.worldbank. org/source/worldwide-governance-indicators

Debellis, F., Rondi, E., Plakoyiannaki, E., & De Massis, A. (2021). Riding the waves of family firm internationalization: A systematic literature review, integrative framework, and research agenda. *Journal of World Business*, *56*(1), 101144. doi: 10.1016/j.jwb.2020.101144

Debicki, B. J., Kellermanns, F. W., Chrisman, J. J., Pearson, A. W., & Spencer, B. A. (2016). Development of a socioemotional wealth importance (SEWi) scale for family firm research. *Journal of Family Business Strategy*, 7(1), 47–57.

Deephouse, D. L., & Jaskiewicz, P. (2013). Do family firms have better reputations than non-family firms? An integration of socioemotional wealth and social identity theories. *Journal of Management Studies*, 50(3), 337–360.

Development Aid. (n.d.). Automotive & Machinery Trading Centre-AMTC. Retrieved from https://www. developmentaid.org/organizations/view/15855/automotive-machinery-trading-centre-amtc

Eddleston, K., Jaskiewicz, P., & Wright, M. (2019). Family firms and internationalization in the Asia-Pacific: The need for multi-level perspectives. *Asia Pacific Journal of Management*, 37(2), 345–361. doi: 10.1007/s10490-018-9608-6

ElDeeb, L. (2020, November 8). Egyptian Billionaire Mohamed Mansour gives his two cents on investment to Bloomberg. *WAYA*. Retrieved from https://waya.media

Ernst & Young. (2014). *Family business in the Middle East / Facts and figures*. EY. Retrieved from https://familybusiness.ey-vx.com/pdfs/page-65-66.pdf

Eze, N., Nordqvist, M., Samara, G., & Parada, M. (2020). Different strokes for different folks: The roles of religion and tradition for transgenerational entrepreneurship in family businesses. *Entrepreneurship Theory and Practice*, 45(4), 792–837. doi: 10.1177/1042258720964428

Fathallah, R., Branzei, O., & Schaan, J. L. (2018). No place like home? How EMNCs from hyper turbulent contexts internationalize by sequentially arbitraging rents, values, and scales abroad. *Journal of World Business*, 53(5), 620–631.

Fathallah, R., Sidani, Y., & Khalil, S. (2020). How religion shapes family business ethical behaviors: An institutional logics perspective. *Journal of Business Ethics, 163*(4), 647–659.

FFI Practitioner. (2016, August 3). The Evolving Perception of Family Businesses in the Middle East and North Africa (MENA). *FFI Practitioner*. Retrieved from https://ffipractitioner.org

Field, M. (1985). *Merchants, The Big Business Families of Saudi Arabia and the Gulf States*. New York: Overlook Press.

Galbraith, J. (1999). *Designing the Global Corporation*. San Francisco: Jossey-Bass.

Gomez-Mejia, L. R., Cruz, C., Berrone, P., & De Castro, J. (2011). The bind that ties: Socioemotional wealth preservation in family firms. *Academy of Management Annals*, 5(1), 653–707.

Gomez-Mejía, L. R., Haynes, K. T., Núñez-Nickel, M., Jacobson, K. J., & Moyano-Fuentes, J. (2007). Socioemotional wealth and business risks in family-controlled firms: Evidence from Spanish olive oil mills. *Administrative Science Quarterly*, 52(1), 106–137.

Guha, K. (1997). Empire set for opportunity and challenge. *Financial Times*.

Habbershon, T. G., & Pistrui, J. (2002). Enterprising families domain: Family-influenced ownership groups in pursuit of transgenerational wealth. *Family Business Review*, 15(3), 223–237.

Haine, A. (2021, February 4). Mohamed Mansour, the billionaire who doesn't measure success in zeroes. *The National*. Retrieved from https://www.thenationalnews.com

Hazlehurst, J. (2016, March 8). Loutfy Mansour – The rising son. *Financial Times*. Retrieved from https://www.ft.com

Hendrickson, V. L. (2017, May 7). Golden Visas Offer Residency, Tax Breaks for Buyers and Boons for Participating Countries. *Mansion Global*. Retrieved from https://www.mansionglobal.com

Holburn, G. L., & Zelner, B. A. (2010). Political capabilities, policy risk, and international investment strategy: Evidence from the global electric power generation industry. *Strategic Management Journal*, 31(12), 1290–1315.

Jamali, D., Jain, T., Samara, G., & Zoghbi, E. (2020). How institutions affect CSR practices in the Middle East and North Africa: A critical review. *Journal of World Business*, 55(5), 101127.

Jaskiewicz, P., Block, J., Wagner, D., Carney, M., & Hansen, C. (2021). How do cross-country differences in institutional trust and trust in family explain the mixed performance effects of family management? A meta-analysis. *Journal of World Business*, 56(5), 101196.

Kellermanns, F. W., Eddleston, K. A., & Zellweger, T. M. (2012). Article commentary: Extending the socioemotional wealth perspective: A look at the dark side. *Entrepreneurship Theory and Practice*, 36(6), 1175–1182.

Khanna, T., & Palepu, K. G. (2006). Emerging giants: Building world-class companies in developing countries. *Harvard Business Review*, 84(10).

Khanna, T., & Palepu, K. G. (2010). *Winning in Emerging Markets: A Road Map for Strategy and Execution*. Harvard Business Press. Boston, MA.

Kogut, B. (1985). Designing global strategies: Comparative and competitive value-added chains. *Sloan Management Review (pre-1986)*, 26(4), 15.

Krammer, S. M., Strange, R., & Lashitew, A. (2018). The export performance of emerging economy firms: The influence of firm capabilities and institutional environments. *International Business Review*, 27(1), 218–230.

Kraus, S., Mensching, H., Calabrò, A., Cheng, C. F., & Filser, M. (2016). Family firm internationalization: A configurational approach. *Journal of Business Research*, 69(11), 5473–5478.

Krueger, N., Bogers, M. L., Labaki, R., & Basco, R. (2021). Advancing family business science through context theorizing: The case of the Arab world. *Journal of Family Business Strategy*, 12(1), 100377.

Le Breton-Miller, I., & Miller, D. (2018). Beyond the firm: Business families as entrepreneurs. *Entrepreneurship Theory and Practice*, 42(4),527–536

Lead Foundation. (2016). Partners: Lead Foundation. Retrieved August 13, 2021, from https://lead.org.eg/partners

Luiz, J., Stringfellow, D., & Jefthas, A. (2017). Institutional Complementarity and Substitution as an Internationalization Strategy: The Emergence of an African Multinational Giant. *Global Strategy Journal*, 7(1), 83–103. doi: 10.1002/gsj.1143

Luo, Y., & Wang, S. (2012). Foreign direct investment strategies by developing country multinationals: A diagnostic model for home country effects. *Global Strategy Journal*, 2(3), 244–261. doi: 10.1111/j.2042-5805.2012.01036.x

Man Capital. (2016, March 21). *Man capital opens office in Washington D.C* [Press release]. Retrieved from https://www.man-capital.com/news/man-capital-opens-office-in-washington-dc/

Mansour Group. (2021a). Who We Are –. Retrieved from https://www.mansourgroup.com/who-we-are/

Mansour Group. (2021b). Who We Are –. Retrieved from https://www.mansourgroup.com/who-we-are/#content

Mantrac Group. n.d. Discover Mantrac – Mansour Group –. Retrieved from https://www.man tracgroup.com/en-lr/discover-mantrac/mansour-group/

Michael-Tsabari, N., Labaki, R., & Zachary, R. K. (2014). Toward the cluster model: The family firm's entrepreneurial behavior over generations. *Family Business Review*, 27(2), 161–185.

Miroshnychenko, I., De Massis, A., Miller, D., & Barontini, R. (2020). Family business growth around the world. *Entrepreneurship Theory and Practice*, 45(4), 682–708. doi: 10.1177/1042258720913028

Moukheiber, Z. (2011, February 9). Crosshairs of History. *Forbes*. Retrieved from https://www.forbes.com

North, D. C. (1991). Institutions. *Journal of Economic Perspectives*, 5(1), 97–112.

OECD. (2019). *How Arab Countries and Institutions finance Development*. Development Co-operation Directorate. Retrieved from https://www.oecd.org/dac/dac-global-relations/Development_finance_Arab_countries_institutions.pdf

Peng, M., Sun, W., Vlas, C., Minichilli, A., & Corbetta, G. (2018). An Institution-Based View of Large Family Firms: A Recap and Overview. *Entrepreneurship Theory and Practice*, 42(2), 187–205. doi: 10.1177/1042258717749234

Pinkham, B. C., & Peng, M. W. (2017). Overcoming institutional voids via arbitration. *Journal of International Business Studies*, 48(3), 344–359.

Pukall, T. J., & Calabrò, A. (2014). The internationalization of family firms: A critical review and integrative model. *Family Business Review*, 27(2), 103–125.

PWC. (2016). *Keeping it in the family: Family firms in the Middle East*. Author. Retrieved from https://www.pwc.com/m1/en/publications/family-business-survey/middle-east-family-business-survey-2016.pdf

Samara, G. (2021). Family businesses in the Arab Middle East: What do we know and where should we go? *Journal of Family Business Strategy*, 12(3), September 2021, 100359. https://www.sci encedirect.com/science/article/pii/S1877858520300863

Samara, G., & Arenas, D. (2017). Practicing fairness in the family business workplace. *Business Horizons*, 60(5), 647–655.

Samara, G., Jamali, D., & Parada, M. J. (2021). Antecedents and outcomes of bifurcated compensation in family firms: A multilevel view. *Human Resource Management Review*, 31(1), 100728.

Schwartz, D., & Youssef, A. (2020, January 23). How LJ – A '75-year-old start-up' – leads with purpose. *McKinsey & Company*. Retrieved from https://www.mckinsey.com

Shapiro, S. P. (1987). The social control of impersonal trust. *American Journal of Sociology*, 93(3), 623–658.

Steier, L., Chrisman, J., & Chua, J. (2015). Governance Challenges in Family Businesses and Business Families. *Entrepreneurship Theory and Practice*, 39(6), 1265–1280. doi: 10.1111/etap.12180

Tharawat Magazine. (2016, May 12). Family Business Interview with Ahmed Bazara, Yemen. *Tharawat Magazine*. Retrieved from https://www.tharawat-magazine.com

Tharawat Magazine. (2020). Al Handal International Group: Building a Culture of Continuity with the Family Office. *Tharawat Magazine*. Retrieved from https://www.tharawat-magazine.com

Trenwith, C. (2015, October 16). How one Egyptian family's $6bn enterprise has spanned the globe. *Arabian Business*. Retrieved from https://www.arabianbusiness.com

Underwood, M. (2015, April 30). Passport for sale: Instability in the Middle East leaves many seeking second citizenship. *The National*. Retrieved from https://www.thenationalnews.com

Valentino, A., Schmitt, J., Koch, B., & Nell, P. (2019). Leaving home: An institutional perspective on intermediary HQ relocations. *Journal of World Business*, 54(4), 273–284. doi: 10.1016/j.jwb.2018.08.004

Wilson, E. (2016, April 25). Patience is key for family-run Mansour Group. *The National*. Retrieved from https://www.thenationalnews.com

Wingham, D. W. (2004). Entrepreneurship through the ages. *Entrepreneurship: The Way Ahead*, 27–42, New York: Routledge.

Witt, M. A., & Lewin, A. Y. (2007). Outward foreign direct investment as escape response to home country institutional constraints. *Journal of International Business Studies*, 38(4), 579–594.

Xi, J. M., Kraus, S., Filser, M., & Kellermanns, F. W. (2015). Mapping the field of family business research: past trends and future directions. *International Entrepreneurship and Management Journal*, 11(1), 113–132.

Xu, K., & Hitt, M. A. (2020). The international expansion of family firms: The moderating role of internal financial slack and external capital availability. *Asia Pacific Journal of Management*, 37(1), 127–153.

Yemeni Business Club YBC. (n.d.). Ahmed Bazara. Retrieved from https://www.ybc-yemen.com/about/member/37

Zahra, S. A. (2011). Doing research in the (new) Middle East: Sailing with the wind. *Academy of Management Perspectives*, 25(4), 6–21.

Zaman, S., Arshad, M., Sultana, N., & Saleem, S. (2020). The effect of family business exposure on individuals' entrepreneurial intentions: An institutional theory perspective. *Journal of Family Business Management*, 11(4), pp. 368–385.

Zellweger, T. M., Nason, R. S., & Nordqvist, M. (2012). From longevity of firms to transgenerational entrepreneurship of families: Introducing family entrepreneurial orientation. *Family Business Review*, 25(2), 136–155.

Peter Rosa and Zografia Bika

11 Evolutionary Long-Term Entrepreneurial Processes in Business Families

Abstract: This chapter draws on socio-economic evolutionary theories of organizational change to explain transgenerational continuity and growth issues of successful long-lived entrepreneurial business families. We suggest that wider political, social, and economic forces that cannot be predicted, act as selective mechanisms at different levels of resolution (within a firm; within a group of firms, on a whole industry, or even on the fabric of the whole business family). The complex interaction of these evolutionary processes is illustrated in two contrasting empirical cases from Scotland and Uganda. There are challenges to researchers in integrating emergent evolutionary changes (based on evolutionary theory) with those associated with planned strategy-based theories stressing the role of strategic long-term entrepreneurial orientation in transgenerational business families.

Keywords: evolutionary theories, transgenerational continuity, entrepreneurial processes, entrepreneurial orientation

Introduction

There has been a proliferation of interest in transgenerational entrepreneurship in long-lived family businesses in the last decade. Much of this research is based on strategy theory, that the long-term survival and success of a family business is causally linked to developing and perpetuating, over generations, a long-term strategic orientation (LTO) and commitment to entrepreneurial renewal and growth (Lumpkin, Grigham, & Moss, 2010). This is a more dynamic theoretical perspective than older theories of long-lived family business success based on stewardship, that is the strategic commitment by senior family members to conserve the business and pass it on to the next generation intact and viable (Eddleston & Kellermanns, 2007; Eddleston, Kellermanns, & Sarathy, 2008; Zahra, Hayton, Neubaum, Dibrell, & Craig, 2008). It is thus fundamentally expansive rather than defensive as is the case with stewardship.

Long-term strategizing, however, may be more an intention than a predictable route to success, as in the longer term the family business inevitably will encounter traumatic events that cannot be predicted in advance. Such events may occur at any time and be either external (such as the Wall Street crash of 1929, two world

Peter Rosa, University of Edinburgh
Zografia Bika, University of East Anglia

https://doi.org/10.1515/9783110727968-011

wars, most recently the emergence of COVID-19 and its subsequent economic recession), or internal "critical incidents" such as the sudden deaths of key family members, family feuds and conflicts, and divorces. This is a different viewpoint that raises important questions: Do family businesses consciously have generic long-term conscious strategies designed to safeguard against uncertain or unpredictable future challenges and the strategic ability to quickly access new opportunities (Rauch, Wiklund, Lumpkin, & Frese, 2009; Lumpkin & Bingham, 2011; Zellweger, Nason, & Nordqvist, 2012)? Or are there underlying emergent mechanisms that produce successful outcomes at a less conscious level? The central theorem of biological evolution is the existence of mechanisms that ensure survival of the fittest. Do similar mechanisms exist in the context of family business continuity that operate in unpredictable and competitive business environments, and override any strategic orientations or intentions?

In this chapter we suggest that micro-economic and social evolutionary theory could provide insights into how underlying emergent processes act on business families. Micro-economic evolutionary theory is based on the concept that forces of selection act upon the routines and systems of firms to create new forms (Dosi & Marengo, 2007). Further insights are provided by socio-psychological evolutionary theory proposed by Campbell (1965), which can also be applied to firms and business organizations. We discuss how these theories could be applied to the context of change and long-term longevity of transgenerational business families. Finally, we illustrate the possibilities of applying evolutionary theory through an analysis of the complex development of two business families since the early 20th century, the McKay Family in Scotland, and the Madhavi family in Uganda. We conclude by pointing out the complementarity of the evolutionary and strategy-based theoretical perspectives for our understanding of the adaptation of transgenerational business families to shifting environments.

Literature Review

Economic Evolutionary Theory and Business Groups

Micro-evolutionary theory has been developing since the 1930s, partly as a reaction to neo-classical economics, with its assumptions of perfect, information and competition, and the rationality of actors and agents. There is now a substantial literature on economic change and evolution (Dosi & Marengo, 2007), particularly in the fields of the firm and business organizations. The greatest challenge in applying biological evolutionary theory at the level of firms and organizations has been to identify a meaningful and rigorous unit of analysis. This has been achieved by integrating evolutionary theory with behavioural theories of the firm (Cyert & March,

1963; Nelson & Winter, 1982). In the development of evolutionary economics by these authors and their followers, the unit of analysis is theorized as routines within an organization, on which primary mechanisms of variation and selection act upon them to bring about new, improved, or hybridized forms. These mechanisms are bounded rationality, productive knowledge and information acquisition and learning, and unresolved conflict arising from uncertainty (Dosi & Marengo, 2007), which can be treated as equivalents of evolutionary mechanisms and processes in the biological sciences. For example, injections of new information and knowledge could be conceived as an equivalent of biological natural selection based on differential attrition and mortality.

Additionally, Aldrich and Kenworthy (1999) signpost the seminal contribution of Donald Campbell, a psychologist who proposed an evolutionary theory of blind variation, selection and retention that combine to produce a selection system leading to a better fit of social order (Campbell, 1965, p. 26 in Aldrich, 2011, p. 47). These are firstly, the occurrence of *variations* in the social order (such as creative ideas, innovations), which can arise "blindly" or haphazardly (the equivalent of mutations in biology). Secondly, the existence of consistent *selection criteria* leading to the retention of improved or better forms, and the disappearance of less fit forms (equivalent to natural selection mortality and fertility). Thirdly, a mechanism of *retention*, allowing for the replication and preservation of the new form. In a dynamic environment there is always a tension, as Campbell emphasized, between replacement and retention. Without the presence of all three elements, there can be no successful evolution towards better fit. The random nature in the emergence of many new cultural and social variations was stressed by Campbell and are encapsulated in the use of his term "blind variation", which he preferred to randomness which has a more precise statistical meaning in the biological sciences (Aldrich & Kenworthy, 1999).

The Unit of Analysis Problem

Evolutionary economists, as explained earlier, have identified management routines as the primary unit of analysis for theorizing evolutionary processes in organizations. How such a perspective integrates with other theoretical perspectives has become an important challenge for organizational researchers (Dosi & Marengo, 2007). These authors, discuss how theories based on resource capabilities (Penrose, 1959) and dynamic capabilities (Teece, Pisano, & Shuen, 1997), could also be considered from an evolutionary perspective. Dynamic capabilities, form from the organization's activities, rather than from a stock of library knowledge, and this results in dynamic modifications of routines (ultimately the unit of analysis from an evolutionary viewpoint). If capabilities and resources could be subsumed under the generic label "routines", then routines remain the primary mechanism of variation of organizational evolution. However, capabilities and resources could each be treated as distinct kinds of variants, and this adds complexity in theorizing evolutionary dynamics within organizations.

Teece, Pisano, and Shuen (1997) in their seminal article, emphasize that strategic management has an important role in shaping and establishing managerial processes, the breaking of established routines, in directing new paths for new activities, and in how far existing routines can be replicated without modification. This implies that the processes of change in resource-based and dynamic capability theories, are not randomly or impersonally determined as in biological evolutionary theory, because conscious strategic planning by management of some kind is involved. Complexity is added by the fact that innovations in routines are not usually unique to a firm but are commonly introduced by a pioneer within an industry. Early pioneers, through experimentation, discover the best fit for the innovation and this is then copied and diffused to other competitors within the industry, who must adopt it to remain competitive. In this case, selection forces operate on routines at the industry rather than the firm level, and there is considerable isomorphism between firms in how they react to change. The evolutionary introduction of superior new routines that disrupts or even replaces older routines within the industry is not usually predictable.

The firm itself, as the primary evolutionary unit of analysis, has been explored by Aldrich (2010) in the context of birth and survival of new firms by nascent entrepreneurs in the US (Reynolds, Miller, & Maki, 1993; Reynolds & Curtin, 2009). He notes the high volatility of new firm formation in the US, with high failure rates, and failed firms constantly being replaced by a stream of new entrants each year. Of those selected to survive, only a small percentage grow fast into sizeable firms. "Selection criteria are set through the operation of market forces, competitive pressures, the logic of internal organizational structuring, conformity to institutionalized norms, and other forces" (Aldrich & Wiedenmayer, 1993, p. 5). These selection forces vary not only in space (from one regional context to another) (Bika & Rosa, 2022) but also over time (Bika & Frazer, 2021). Evolutionary change could thus be researched in terms of firms as units on which evolutionary change acts upon without having to examine the evolution of routines within firms as the primary unit of selection.

Changing the Unit of Analysis from the Firm to the Entrepreneur

Aldrich (2011, p. xiv) stresses that it is the "struggle by entrepreneurs and organizations to obtain resources, both social and physical, [that] drives evolutionary processes". This adds an implicit focus on the entrepreneur as well as the firm. The motivations, social status, and networks, personal knowledge are new kinds of social and psychological variants relating to an entrepreneur who starts a firm, not the firm as an organization. This may not appear to be an important distinction when considering new firm dynamics associated with novice entrepreneurs, but it becomes much more problematic when the equation of a single firm with the entrepreneur does not apply, as is the case when an entrepreneur owns a group of firms.

Viewing routines as the central focus of evolutionary theory in organizations becomes increasingly complex once the focus is switched to the portfolio entrepreneur who is no longer an organization, but a social actor who owns and manages a series of organizations (Rosa, 1998; Iacobucci & Rosa, 2010). From the portfolio entrepreneur's perspective, the units of concerns are his or her firms, which can be divested and closed, and replaced or added to by new ones. External forces of selection and the speed of change that they impose can determine the volatility and dynamics of the business group. The business group could therefore be conceived, in the longer term, as a visible symptom of evolutionary dynamics when the portfolio entrepreneur becomes the unit of analysis even though it does not replace routines, capabilities and resources as the building blocks of organizational evolution, as these forces are simultaneously still acting within each company in the group.

Complexities from Family

A business family is a group of family members who collectively own or manage a single or a group of firms. It is only recently that organizational researchers have begun to appreciate that family business groups not only exist but are more complex than corporate groups (Carney, Gedajlovic, Heugens, Van Essen, & Van Oosterhout, 2011). A business family possesses potentially, from the viewpoint of Campbell's theory, a greater natural pool of entrepreneurial variants than the single entrepreneur. In time this can lead to the evolution of large complex business portfolios, with diverse combinations of family founders and shareholding (Rosa, Howarth, & Discua-Cruz, 2014; Rautiainen, Rosa, Pihkala, Parada, & Discua-Cruz, 2019). It could be argued that the business assets of the whole business family could be treated as a single business, with its constituent firms and other business elements constituting sub-entities. Thus, from an economic evolutionary perspective it would be valid to treat the overall business as a complex bundle of routines and variants at different levels of resolution on which internal and external selection pressures are acting upon.

We suggest that in the case of business groups owned and managed by business families, evolutionary mechanisms acting of a "firm's routines and forms" becomes more difficult to conceptualize and research. At one level each firm in a business group, has its own specific evolutionary dynamics based on its own routines but at the business group level, it is the firm in a portfolio that can also be the unit of selection. In entrepreneurial families displaying portfolio entrepreneurship, new business opportunities are typically not introduced as new routines within a single firm, but by starting new firms. Important threats do not just lead to changes in routines within a single firm but can be dealt with by closing or divesting an affected firm or even a sub-group of firms leading to its extinction within the business group. This necessitates a realignment of family ownership where family members have a differential stake in firms within the family business portfolio. There may thus be a case for researching complex family business groups in terms of firm volatility within the group as the primary evolutionary focus.

In contrast, however, where a business family predominantly owns and manages a single firm, the only way evolutionary mechanisms can act upon the development of the family firm (without its extinction) is through the evolution of routines within the family firm. Entrepreneurship may still be important in the long-term survival of the firm, through the ability of the family to seek and implement new business opportunities and innovations within the firm. Where this involves the introduction of new lines of business or changes of focus into new markets, this may lead to radical changes or shifts in production and managerial priorities, systems, and routines.

In researching evolutionary mechanisms in business families, therefore, it could be productive to distinguish empirically between single family businesses, or businesses with a single core business and subsidiaries related to the core, from large family business groups or entrepreneurial family conglomerates with complex business portfolios. In the case of the former, evolution can be analyzed from the perspective of routines and systems. In the latter they can be analyzed more conveniently from the perspective of the evolution of trading firms within the business group.

Long-Term Evolutionary Processes in Two Business Families

In this section we present a preliminary overview on how evolutionary processes may have affected two contrasting business families. The first is the McKay[1] family from Scotland (see Table 11.1) who have specialized in one industry, construction, and housing since the 1920s. Until the 2,000s they had not developed a diverse business group but had, nevertheless, experienced considerable changes in markets and routines since its foundations. The second is the Madhvani family from Uganda (see Table 11.2), one of East Africa's most entrepreneurial and successful business families. Since their founders started their first business enterprise in 1908, their business interests have evolved diversified business groups in Uganda and overseas. Tables 11.1 and 11.2 provide a summarized overview of the main events and changes that have affected the two families, and the evolutionary

---

1 The McKay family name has been disguised to preserve confidentiality and anonymity as it involves personal interviews by the researchers (Bika, Rosa, & Karakas, 2019). The Madhvani name is not changed as the case, as described, is derived primarily from secondary sources in the public domain and published research (Madhvani & Foden, 2008; Balunywa, 2009).

processes that have influenced their business developments. The detailed picture is more complex and difficult to map accurately for some decades, particularly in the pre-war decades dating before living family recall.

The McKay Family

The events described in Table 11.1 demonstrate that over the years the family has faced many unpredictable threats and challenges from external events, which at times have threatened the survival of the family business. These were ultimately caused by disruptive world events such as the two world wars, the depression of the 1930s, the oil crisis of 1973 that resulted in sudden high rates of inflation and a deep recession in the UK. Some of these events such as World War II could have been predicted, but not their full impact and severity on the construction sector. It is the reaction of government to these events that appears repeatedly to have impacted most directly and immediately on the prosperity of the family and its business. From Table 11.1, we highlight:

- The unexpected crises that occurred when the government withdrew subsidies to house building in 1933. This forced the family to change its strategic focus, production, resources, and management routines into private renting and customized homeowner housing rather than council housing.
- The enforced stopping of all private building at the outbreak of World War II. A new focus had to be developed quickly to building war works, which required new production and management routines, new kinds of knowledge and new resources to invest in the changes.
- Penal death duties based on taxing a substantial proportion of business assets crippled the family's ability to expand in the 1960s, and better meet the competition of large English construction firms. This again needed a shift in focus to more customized and limited home building.

At the same time, however, many of the disruptive government policies opened new opportunities to replace the old, which the family readily exploited. We highlight from Table 11.1:

- Government subsidies after World War I to boost housing.
- Encouraging Building Society mortgages in the 1930s to make it easier to buy high-cost housing.
- Encouragement of construction firms to switch their expertise to war work construction.
- Lifting of restrictions on housing developments in the 1950s.
- Tax exemption for manufacturing companies in the 1960s (re-classification of many of its activities in timber frame construction as "manufacturing").

Table 11.1: The Key Events in the McKay Business Family, Scotland.

	Venture/Activity/ Critical Incidents	Family Members	Reason	Entrepreneurial Evolutionary Mechanism
1890s	Ryan McKay was in business as wood merchant and builder. Engaged in some land speculation.	Nephew, Anthony McKay Snr. (AM) joined the business as apprentice.	Details not known.	
1902	Jonathan Ross (JR), chief accountant of wood business forms new partnership with AM.			
1909	A forms venture of his own and splits from JR but rejoins JR in 1910 as a manager.		Details not known.	
1924	JM goes into voluntary liquidation.		Not known.	
1925	McKay and Ross Ltd created by JMR's son, also Jonathan, and AM.		To exploit new government subsidies to boost housing stocks through contracts with builders.	Reaction to new emergent opportunity.

Table 11.1 (continued)

	Venture/Activity/ Critical Incidents	Family Members	Reason	Entrepreneurial Evolutionary Mechanism
1925–	Legally separate firm established in names of syndicate of partners' wives as a land bank (buying stocks of land to build to).	AM's son Frederick joins firm.	To separate land assets from business and protect them from insolvency. To ensure land is always available to build on in the future. Long term policy established of buying up green land around urban areas for eventual development for housing.	None: Planned risk management in keeping up with practices of similar building firms in the UK.
1933	Diversification within the business into private renting sector and building homeowner occupied homes.	AM's son Donald joins firm.	Forced following withdrawal of government subsidies.	Adverse change forcing entry into alternative lines of business and new building routines.
1930s	Refocusing of emphasis on high-cost housing.		Growth in availability of Building Society Mortgages.	Reaction to new emergent opportunity requiring changes of routines and resources.
1940–1945	Crisis as building stops altogether on outbreak of war.	Frederick and Donald in armed forces.	Switch to war work (building hospitals, war factories, shelters, bomb repairs).	Radical change forcing entry into new lines of business and changes in routines
1943	Ross family leave firm and are bought out by the McKay family.			

Table 11.1 (continued)

	Venture/Activity/ Critical Incidents	Family Members	Reason	Entrepreneurial Evolutionary Mechanism
1945–1957	Diverse contract work for government post war rebuilding.		Little scope for private housing because of restrictions on the sector.	Forced small scale survivalist diversification
1957–	Start of private house building again as restrictions lift.			Pull opportunistic diversification.
1961 1962		Frederick McKay dies; AM dies.	Penal estate duties caused by the deaths precipitate financial and survival crisis. Little spare resources to fund new lines of business (15 years to resolve).	Sudden drastic drain on resources leads to survivalist re-organization of goals and production routines and practices
Early 1960s	Change in focus from large-scale housing development to selective building, with a new environmental focus introduced by Derek M., grandson of AM.		Competition of large English-based house builders into Scotland.	Competitors force changes in business focus and routines.
1966	Firm re-organized and manufacturing aspects segregated into separate firm McKay Products Ltd.		Reacting to new government company levy exemption for manufacturing companies.	Reaction to new emergent opportunity requiring changes in organizational structure.

Table 11.1 (continued)

	Venture/Activity/ Critical Incidents	Family Members	Reason	Entrepreneurial Evolutionary Mechanism
1960s–1990s	Complex trends as severe recessions and decline hit the UK and frequent restructuring of the business both in terms of business and personnel. Series of companies acquired. 1990s were especially traumatic. Some diversifications into biochemicals and even formula 1 racing.	Entry of outsiders into the firm – notably Jack G. David, Frederick's son and Bill, Donalds's son join business.	Complex economic trends in the construction sector leading to periodic crises.	Uncertainty and volatility in business environment cause frequent realignments of company structures and focuses. The family reacts by adding small satellite businesses to its ownership portfolio. Some do better than others, causing failure and divestment in some subsidiaries (evolutionary churn).

Table 11.1 (continued)

	Venture/Activity/ Critical Incidents	Family Members	Reason	Entrepreneurial Evolutionary Mechanism
2000s to present	Complex series of collaborative and innovative ventures into urban regeneration and environmentally sensitive green field building. New firms acquired and partnerships established with other building firms resulting in a diverse business group. This currently has seven divisions: – Home building – Commercial property development – Timber frame construction – Contract building services – Private renting – Strategic land holdings – An investment fund with investments in projects and companies in energy, construction, healthcare, technology, service, and leisure sectors	David's son Alan joins firm. Other outsider Ethan M joins board. Bill McKay's children Mary and Rob join board. Radical re-socialization of family members. Unlearning outmoded attitudes and best practice which they were raised under.	Economic recovery sees profits soar in response to chronic housing shortages in the UK, the need for greener housing, and new construction innovations.	Reorganization into a full-scale business group to capitalise on new opportunities emerging from changes in the business environment. Younger generation brings in new and radical modern styles of management.

Source: Bika, Rosa, and Karakas (2019).

- Successive government initiatives since 2000 have encouraged urban regeneration and greener building practices and sought to address a chronic shortage of housing in the UK. These recent policies have led to diverse new opportunities within the broad umbrella of the construction sector. This has resulted in the McKay family changing from predominantly a one firm company to a business group comprising seven diversified divisions (see Table 11.1).

The Madhvani Family

In the mid to late 19th century Indians began to migrate to East Africa during the establishment of Britain's East African colonies and protectorates in the late 19th and early 20th century. In this early period one Indian entrepreneur, Alladina Vishram, developed, from small beginnings, a large conglomerate in East Africa. He became the role model that inspired the next generation of East African Indian entrepreneurs. The pioneering Madhvanis (Vithaldes, Muljibhai, and Nanjibhai) rapidly built-up capital through establishing shops, which were badly needed to serve the influx of European administrators, adventurers, and Indian migrants into East Africa. After surviving difficult economic conditions during World War I, the Madhvani family managed to create a thriving group of agricultural plantations and processing plants by the end of the 1920s. This was a response to opportunities driven by two policies by the Ugandan colonial administration. Firstly, the need to develop products and industries to make Uganda economically self-supporting. Secondly, discouragement of European agricultural settlement in Uganda, which were not applied to Indians.

Following two decades of limited economic opportunities in East Africa after the depression of the 1930s and World War II, they spectacularly recovered in the 1950s and 1960s to become one of East Africa's largest and most diverse commercial group of companies. They were able to do this in response to the British administration's policy to accelerate development of the Ugandan economy in preparation for independence, and subsequently, the need of the new Ugandan independent government for rapid economic development. They also managed to diversify overseas. Their overseas enterprises helped limit the devastating impact of the loss of all their Ugandan companies in 1972 when they were confiscated by the dictator Idi Amin.

In the mid-1980s, the family was able to return to Uganda and re-establish their sugar plantation at Iganga in Uganda. From this base they have grown a large business group with 33 Ugandan companies, and additional new overseas ventures. These businesses are associated with opportunities arising from the rapid economic regeneration of Uganda in the 1990s and 2,000s. To date they are still expanding their business group in Uganda, but have moved increasingly away from agriculture and manufacturing, to include tourism, hotels, and real estate.

Table 11.2: The Key Events in the Madhvani Business Family, Uganda.

	Venture/Activity/ Key episode	Family members	Reason	Entrepreneurial Evolutionary Mechanism
1890s–1914	Madhvani pioneers Vithaldes and Nanjibhai and latterly Muljibhai in 1908 emigrate to East Africa and establish shops. Success provides capital to start a coffee plantation.		Retail opportunities for retailing and agricultural production from rapidly expanding colonial administration and, its costs.	Opportunistic reaction to new emergent opportunities.
1914–1920	Concentration on local products and retrenchment.		Deterioration of trading conditions during World War I. Large losses after coffee prices plummeted in 1919.	Survivalist contraction and divestment of coffee business.
1918–early 1920s	Sugar plantation started and developed (becoming Ugandan Kakira Sugar Works Ltd.).		Muljibhai identified sugar as a more profitable industry.	Entrepreneurial discovery and change of routines to grow sugar.
Later 1920	Family established portfolio of three more companies, Vithaldas Harridas and Co. Ltd., Nile Industries and Tobacco Companies Ltd., and Uganda Cotton Brokers Ltd. Muljibhai starts sugar processing factory of his own in Uganda.		With no white settlers permitted in Uganda, there were significant and unique opportunities for enterprising Asians in the growing Uganda Protectorate.	Entrepreneurial diversification into new crops and into the processing of crops once their potential was discovered. Reorganization of managerial and production routines.
1930s and 1940s	Little expansion – details unknown.		The Great Depression, World War II.	Survivalist retrenchment.

Table 11.2 (continued)

	Venture/Activity/ Key episode	Family members	Reason	Entrepreneurial Evolutionary Mechanism
1947	Business relaunched under new name.	Family partnership dissolved with Vithaldes branch.		
1950–1958	Original Sugar company expanded to seven by Muljibhai.	Muljibhai dies. Succeeded by two of five sons, Jayant and Manubhai.	Better economic conditions of East African countries encouraged by British government preparing them for independence.	Opportunistic expansion of business group.
1958–1971	Expansion of group to largest commercial group throughout East Africa. By 1971 owned 70 companies employing 22,000 people throughout East Africa. Muljibhai Madhvani, buys Maliban Glass in Bekaa, Lebanon in 1964. Change of emphasis from agricultural production to manufacturing.	Death of Jayant 1971.	Seizing opportunities created by newly independent country's needs to develop and grow fast and create jobs. Overseas glass to participate in Lebanon's golden age of prosperity.	Rapid reactions to rapidly expanding new opportunities in manufacturing. Focus shifts from agribusiness to manufacturing, and radical changes in production and managerial routines and practices.
1972	Loss of all Ugandan companies severely affecting whole family and group of companies.		Expulsion of Asians by Idi Amin and seizure of all their assets in Uganda.	Sudden, unexpected, and dramatic adverse change in the business environment.

Table 11.2 (continued)

	Venture/Activity/ Key episode	Family members	Reason	Entrepreneurial Evolutionary Mechanism
1979	Madhvani International SA Inc. (MISA) established after overthrow of Amin.	Headed by Nitin, son of Jayant.	To recover, rehabilitate and manage the assets that were seized by Ugandan government.	Forced diversification into other countries.
1984	Return to Uganda when family invited back by new president, Musevani.	Mayurbhai, Muljibhai youngest son, takes over as CEO. Traumatic family disputes over ownership of family assets.	Family anxious to reclaim their heritage, particularly their emotional core business, the Kakira Sugar plantation and factory. They were invited back by the Ugandan president to revive their companies.	Reaction to opportunities created by a sudden reversal of policy.
1985–2021 Uganda	33 new companies created in Uganda in agricultural, manufacturing, hospitality, and service sectors under the "Madhvani Group". Many companies are different from those in the business group established in 1960s, but the core Kakira Sugar estate, the original company remains the emotional home of the family.	Headed by Manubhai and Mayurbhai.	Revival of Uganda economy threw up plentiful and unique opportunities in all sectors of the Ugandan economy.	Reactions and adjustments to waves of new opportunity. New focuses have emerged from manufacturing to tourism, hospitality, and real estate. There has been some churn with divestment of manufacturing companies.

Table 11.2 (continued)

	Venture/Activity/ Key episode	Family members	Reason	Entrepreneurial Evolutionary Mechanism
1980s to present Overseas	Expansion of overseas companies world-wide; India, Belgium, Africa, North America, and the Middle East. 2007 the Maiban Glass factory in Lebanon was lost when bombed by the Israelis.	Most headed by Nitin – president of Madhvani International (MISA). Revival of family disputes by Nitin in 2020 are reinforcing independence of his companies from those of the family groups.	Taking advantage of opportunities thrown up by globalization.	Opportunistic diversification but limited by reorganization of family governance and cohesiveness following ownership disputes.

Source: Madhvani and Foden (2008); Balunywa (2009).

Case Study Analysis and Discussion

In both cases it is noticeable that there have been waves of opportunity and re-trenchment caused by external political and economic forces, which often emerged with little warning. While global events such as world wars, economic depressions, forces that brought an end to the European empires were ultimately responsible for the radical changes to business environments, the most immediate and, arguably, the most traumatic triggers of change were the reactions of governments to these events. They initiated policies, usually with little warning, which created large shifts in either entrepreneurial opportunity or threats to survival. The most dra-matic were the sudden confiscation of the Madhvani companies by the Idi Amin re-gime, and the enforced cessation on the McKay business of housing construction at the beginning of World War II by the British government. Tables 11.1 and 11.2 clearly highlight the important effects of government policy changes and initiatives in both cases. This is keeping in line with Aldrich (2010) when he identifies institutional change as a particularly potent source of evolutionary change.

Darwinian evolutionary theory predicts that if there is a sudden change to the environment, organisms must react and adapt, or die. The two cases have survived and adapted to the challenges brought about by change during different generations, but in the overall picture we must also consider the large number of family busi-nesses that ceased to trade during these crises. In a macro sense, dramatic shifts in business environments does produce high rates of mortality of firms as the less fit are forced out of business (Aldrich & Wiedenmayer, 1993). However, non-macro theories of evolutionary change, as outlined earlier in the article, are also relevant in explaining how business organizations adapt to dynamic business environments. In our two cases these become relevant as they have survived and adapted successfully over several generations to successive waves of crises and opportunity.

The central unit of analysis in micro economic evolutionary theory is forms or routines on which mechanisms of variation and selection act upon. Campbell (1965) defined the essence of the evolutionary process as comprising three forms, *"blind" variation* (the regular emergence of variations in the economic and social order, often occurring haphazardly and unpredictably); the existence of *selection* criteria leading to new and better forms replacing the old; and *retention*, the ability of the new form to be replicated and preserved in the organization long enough to act beneficially. But how far do these mechanisms reflect the experience of the McKay and Madhvani business families?

The occurrence of blind variations is commonly associated with the rapid appearance and diffusion of disruptive new technology, which makes older routines less efficient, and increasingly redundant. There is no direct historical evidence from the two cases of the detailed effect that the introduction of innovations in production, administrative routines, or business models has had on their organizational routines. However, we can assume that throughout their business history the families have kept abreast and embraced the many improvements and developments in their industries, which would have resulted in frequent production and managerial adjustments of routines. Information from the current generations, however, illustrate their commitment to responding to innovations. Both the McKay and Madhvani families since the 1990s have demonstrated a series of radical modernization initiatives, which have completely aligned their businesses to the latest production, managerial and family ownership governance trends. The period since the millennium has witnessed an increasingly rapid introduction of changes in keeping up with the exponential acceleration of global innovation.

More important, however, has been the need to quickly change routines and forms because of entering new lines of business, often at short notice. When, for example, the Madhvani family switched from coffee to sugar in the 1920s, or the McKays from housing construction to construction for the war effort, radical new organizational forms and routines had to be established, and former ones were run down, mothballed, or discarded. New kinds of knowledge of production, markets and resourcing had to be quickly developed. Switching to new lines of business was frequent throughout the history of the two families but was especially prominent for the Madhvani family when they expanded their business interests to form large business groups when economic conditions were favourable. Each of the 33 companies in the current Madhvani portfolio requires its own set of efficient managerial and production routines. Running a safari lodge is radically different from running a sugar factory, for example. The financial and knowledge resources needed for acquiring and running a glass factory are quite different from sugar growing. Within each company there is an internal modernization process of routines adapting to the latest innovations. The reorganization of family governance to cope with an expanding business group has also involved its own evolutionary processes. Even if operating within the same industry over several generations, as the McKay family has, a switch in market focus (such as, e.g., from large-scale housing to selective high value housing in the early 1960s), still required considerable changes in organizational routines and forms. In terms of selection and retention, changing routines to increase efficiency in line with industry norms has been a constant feature in each family (fewer fit routines have been discarded or modified). There is no evidence that either family viewed consciously the retention of new routines as a major preoccupation, but we can assume that if the new routines worked, they would not be changed unless new forces of change occurred.

Competition for resources is a primary selection mechanism in biological evolutionary ecology. In the current cases, however, it appears (when viewed in the long term) as having played a lesser role than might be expected. In only one instance (when large English firms forced the McKay family to abandon large scale housing in the 1960s) was competition from rivals a primary selective effect. We can assume that business competitors would have played a constant role throughout their histories in adjusting their organizational forms, but these forces were less important than the macro government policy forces that affected their day-to-day competitors, too. For example, the conditions that opened new opportunities for sugar, cotton, and tea plantations in the 1920s in Uganda were shared with other competing Indian business families who also established plantations at the time. The competitors also had to adjust quickly when the recession of the 1930s caused a need for retrenchment. The same families were also quick at entering new manufacturing businesses in the 1950–1960s. In the two decades these same families have, like the Madhvani family, turned away from manufacturing to hotels and real estate. A similar picture emerges when analysing the McKay history where other families in construction share the same opportunities and threats and reacted to them in similar ways. Thus, industry isomorphism is an important factor, indicating that selective forces are often operating directly on the whole industry, before being diffused into the family's businesses.

Hence, switching the unit of analysis from the firm to the family, it is organizations associated with lines of business rather than firms themselves that have shown the greatest evolutionary volatility. This is most clear when lines of business are organized as separate companies forming business groups. The Madhvani case shows that over the generations there has been a churn of companies, established in response to new opportunities, and divested or forced out of business when political conditions changed. At the business group level of analysis, it is the companies within the group that are the units that selective forces act upon. In families where lines of businesses are not legally separated, the same evolutionary churn can also be observed.

This case study analysis highlights the complexity of evolutionary processes acting upon transgenerational business families. The complexity is caused by the fact that evolutionary change is occurring at different levels of resolution: (a) within each firm/production unit (routines, organizational forms, knowledge, and resources); (b) on lines of business within a complex single business or within business groups; (c) on the very existence of the family itself as an integrated business family (family governance forms, family conflicts, and ownership disputes); and (d) on the whole industry and family business community (common pressures leading to industry wide selective pressures and isomorphic reactions to these pressures at an industry and societal level). This makes researching such processes particularly challenging.

Proactive Transgenerational Strategizing

The long-term transgenerational survival and growth of successful business families is being theorized by family business researchers dominantly in terms of strategy-based theories, particularly those stressing the role of long-term entrepreneurial orientation in a business family's success (Lumpkin & Brigham, 2011). Evolutionary theory, however, contains no direct role for long-term strategizing, as it is the selective action of impersonal and largely unpredictable wider economic and social forces that are the main drivers of outcomes. Yet long-term orientations do exist, and these are detectable on the two cases.

The McKays have demonstrated a long-term commitment to confining its activities to the construction industry. This has been reinforced by a conscious strategy (common to most UK construction companies) of ensuring a long-term supply of land around urban settlements for housing developments. This was formalized by establishing a legally separate land company in 1925. However, there is no evidence in the McKay family of a conscious strategic long-term entrepreneurial orientation of seeking new opportunities or establishing routines and resources designed to establish new opportunity-based business ventures. Throughout their history the family has reacted rather than been proactive to the wider forces of change. Its management routines have been changing regularly adapting to the new market focus of the day.

The Madhvanis, however, have employed a conscious strategy, common to older East African Indian families, of growing through establishing business groups by adding new diversifications and companies to exploit the opportunities of the day (Rosa & Balunywa, 2017). (e.g., these were plantations in the 1920s, manufacturing in the 1950–1960s, currently hotels and tourism). At the same time, they have diversified since their early days into investments overseas in case of political instability in East Africa. The family has a strong family identity centred around their original company, the Kakira sugar works, and the cultivation of a family reputation for business and social integrity, which has provided credibility when the need to borrow resources has occurred. In deciding what to invest in, however, they too have reacted to opportunities as they have emerged, in line with what their competing Indian families were doing, rather than proactively anticipating them.

The cases thus demonstrate that evolutionary forces have been operating within a long-term umbrella of loose but detectable family strategic orientations. The relationship between strategic orientation and evolutionary mechanisms is thus an interesting field of future theorizing and research.

Conclusion

This chapter demonstrates that it is possible to analyze real business families from the standpoint of evolutionary theory (see Figure 11.1 for a visual summary representation of the components of this). However, a key concern remains, is evolutionary theory anything more than an attractive analogy, or does it have the potential of explanatory power in helping us to understand the complexities of the business activities of entrepreneurial transgenerational business families? Does it offer new insights to the current strategy-based theories of long-term entrepreneurial orientation? Evolutionary theory does present challenges to the appropriateness of long-term strategic planning such as LTO, which is being increasingly criticized (Nordqvist & Melin, 2010). It has more in common with emergent strategy, where strategic thinking is "intuitive and creative", and involves "messy processes of informal learning" (Mintzberg, 1994, p. 108).

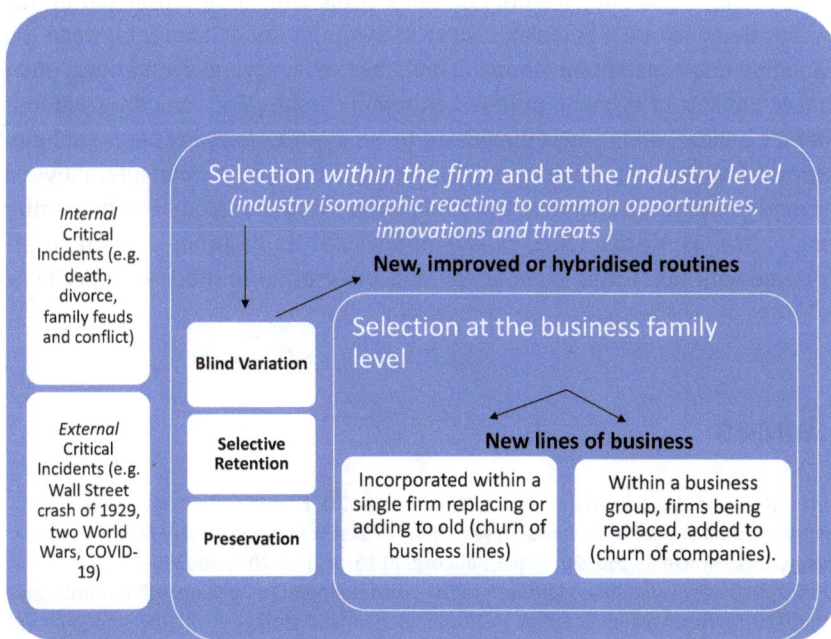

Figure 11.1: How forces of natural selection act upon entrepreneurial routines and systems of firms in transgenerational business families.

We conclude that it may be profitable to research a wide range of transgenerational business families from an evolutionary perspective. The cases reveal a complex interaction of forms that can be subject to selection forces. Within firms and single firm-focused family businesses there are routines, production, and management systems that are vulnerable to new innovative systems that supersede the old and render them less competitive. Within business families the firms within their business group are constantly changing to respond to new external business opportunities and threats. In all business families, even single firm-focused ones, new business opportunities and lines of business are similarly being subject to forces of selection and may be considered as a basic entrepreneurial form to base research on evolutionary change. The family itself also has its own evolution of family members, who die and are replaced. Just as significant, however, may be the need to research how family strategies, orientations, attitudes, and capabilities evolve across generations, when faced with wide ranging social change in the wider external society, and how these impact on the business family (Aldrich, Brumana, Campopiano, & Minola, 2021) without assuming a single and simplified long-term entrepreneurial orientation.

Aldrich (2011, p. iv) suggests that: "the fundamental axiom of evolutionary analysis is that outcomes result from the interactions of organizations and environments, rather than being attributable to either organizations or environments taken separately". This insight resonates with the findings of the two cases considered in this study, which demonstrate a complex history of evolutionary dynamics between the business family and constant environmental changes over several generations, often through mechanisms of evolving portfolio entrepreneurship. Focusing on evolutionary theory we believe, adds a new dimension to explain the complex nature of long-lived business families, but we do not claim it should be treated as an alternative to other currently researched theories. The value of an evolutionary approach to entrepreneurship, lies, as Aldrich (2011, p. xiv) emphasized, in its promise as an "overarching framework permitting comparison and integration to other social science theories".

References

Aldrich, H. E., Brumana, M., Campopiano, G., & Minola, T. (2021). Embedded but not asleep: Entrepreneurship and family business research in the 21st century. *Journal of Family Business Strategy*, 12(1), article no 100390. https://doi.org/10.1016/j.jfbs.2020.100390

Aldrich, H. E. (2011). *An Evolutionary Approach to Entrepreneurship*. Cheltenham, UK: Edward Elgar.

Aldrich, H. E. (2010). Beam me up Scott(ie)! Institutional theorists' struggles with the emergent nature of entrepreneurship. *Institutions and Entrepreneurship Research in the Sociology of Work*, 21, 329–364.

Aldrich, H. E., & Kenworthy, A. (1999). The accidental entrepreneur: Campbellian antinomies and organizational foundings. In J. A. C. Baum & B. McKelvey (Eds.), *Variations in Organization Science: In Honor of Donald T. Campbell* (pp. 19–33). Newbury Park, CA.: Sage.

Aldrich, H. E., & Wiedenmayer, G. (1993). From traits to rates: An ecological perspective on organizational foundings. In J. Katz & R. Brockhaus (Eds.), *Advances in Entrepreneurship, Firm Emergence, and Growth* (pp. 145–195). Greenwich, CT: JAI Press.

Balunywa, W. (2009). *Portfolio Entrepreneurs and Growth: The Case of Uganda*, PhD thesis, University of Stirling.

Bika, Z., & Frazer, M.L. (2021). The affective extension of 'family'in the context of changing elite business networks. *Human Relations*, 74(12): 1951–1993.

Bika, Z., & Rosa, P. (2022). Regional economic performance and the differential prevalence of corporate and family business. *Journal of Enterprising Communities*, 16(2): 238–259.

Bika, Z., Rosa, P., & Karakas, F. (2019). Multilayered socialization processes in tyransgenerational family firms. *Family Business Review*, 32(3), 233–258.

Campbell, D. T. (1965). Blind variation and selective retention in socio-cultural evolution. In H. R. Barringer, G. I. Blanksten, & R. W. Mack (Eds.), *Social Change in Developing Areas: A Reinterpretation of Evolutionary Theory* (pp. 19–48). Cambridge MA: Schenkman.

Carney, M., Gedajlovic, E. R., Heugens, P. P., Van Essen, M., & Van Oosterhout, J. (2011). Business group affiliation, performance, context, and strategy: A meta-analysis. *Academy of Management Journal*, 54(3), 437–460.

Cyert, R. M., & March, J. G. (1963). *A Behavioral Theory of the Firm*. Englewood Cliffs, NJ.: Prentice Hall.

Dosi, G., & Marengo, L., (2007). Perspective on the evolutionary and behavioral theories of organizations: A tentative roadmap. *Organization Science*, 18(3), 491–502.

Eddleston, K. A, Kellermanns, F. W., & Sarathy, R. (2008). Resource configurations in family firms: Linking resources, strategic planning and technological opportunities to performance. *Journal of Management Studies*, 45(1), 26–50.

Eddleston, K. A. & Kellermanns, F. W. (2007). Destructive and productive family relationships: A stewardship perspective. *Journal of Business Venturing*, 22(4), 545–565.

Iacobucci, D., & Rosa, P. (2010). The growth of business groups by habitual entrepreneurs: the role of entrepreneurial teams. *Entrepreneurship, Theory and Practice*, 34(2), 351–377.

Lumpkin, G. T., & Brigham, K. H. (2011). Long-term orientation and intertemporal choice in family firms. *Entrepreneurship Theory and Practice*, 35(6), 1149–1169.

Lumpkin, G. T., Grigham, K., & Moss, T.W., (2010). Long-term orinetation: Implications for the entrepreneurial orientation and performance of family business. *Entrepreneurship and Regional Development*, 22(34), 241–264.

Madhvani, M., & G. Fodan (2008). *Tide of Fortune: A Family Tale*. India: Random House.

Mintzberg, H. (1994). The fall and rise of strategic planning. *Harvard Business Review*, 72(1), 107–114.

Nelson, R.R., & Winter, S.G. (1982). The Schumpeterian tradeoff revisited. *American Economic Review*, 72(1), 114–132.

Nordqvist, M., & Melin, L. (2010). The promise of the strategy as practice perspective for family business strategy research. *Journal of Family Business Strategy*, 1(1), 15–25.

Penrose, E. (1959). *The Theory of the Growth of the Firm*. Oxford: Basil Blackwell.

Rauch, A., Wiklund, J., Lumpkin, G. T., & Frese, M. (2009). Entrepreneurial orientation and business performance: An assessment of past research and suggestions for the future. *Entrepreneurship Theory and Practice*, 33, 761–787.

Rautiainen, M., Rosa, P., Pihkala, T., Parada, M. J. & Discua-Cruz, A. (Eds.) (2019). *The Family Business Group Phenomenon*. Switzerland, AG.: Springer.

Reynolds, P. D., Miller, B., and Maki, W. (1993). Regional characteristics affecting business volatility in the United States 1980–84. In Karlsson, C., Johannisson, B. and Storey, D.J. (Eds.) *Small Business Dynamics: International, National and Regional Perspectives* (pp. 78–114). London: Routledge.

Reynolds, P.D., & Curtin, R.T. (2009). *New Firm Creation in the United States*, Switzerland AG. : Springer.

Rosa, P., & Balunywa, W. (2017). Placing the Ugandan entrepreneurship paradox in context. In M. Ramirez-Pasilla, E. Brundin, and M. Markowska (Eds.). *Contextualizing Entrepreneurship in Emerging and Developing Countries* (pp. 235–250). Cheltenham, UK.: Edward Elgar.

Rosa, P.; Howarth, C., & Discua-Cruz, A. (2014). Habitual and portfolio Entrepreneurship and the family business. In L. Melin, M. Nordqvist, and P. Sharma (Eds.). *The Sage Handbook of Family Business* (pp. 364–383). London: Sage Publishing.

Rosa, P. (1998). Entrepreneurial processes of business cluster formation and growth by 'habitual' entrepreneurs. *Entrepreneurship, Theory and Practice*, 22(4), 43–62.

Teece, D. J., Pisano, G., & Shuen, A. (1997). Dynamic capabilities and strategic management. *Strategic Management Journal*, 18(7), 509–533.

Zahra, S., Hayton, J., Neubaum, D., Dibrell, C., & Craig, J. (2008). Culture of family commitment and strategic flexibility: the moderating effect of stewardship. *Entrepreneurship, Theory and Practice*, 32(6), 1035–1054.

Zellweger, T. M., Nason, R. S., & Nordqvist, M. (2012). From longevity of firms to transgenerational entrepreneurship of families: Introducing family entrepreneurial orientation. *Family Business Review*, 25(2), 136–155.

Andrea Colli

12 Entrepreneurial Multi-Business Families – Evidence from Continental Europe

Abstract: The chapter is focusing on European entrepreneurial families, multi-generational, actively investing in multiple directions by means of entities, which are in between a family office, a financial holding, and a private equity company. These entrepreneurial families usually leverage on their reputation for fostering the expansion of their business. They are often collaborating with both family and non-family international investors such as SWFs. They are frequently employing professionals, not belonging to the family, who enjoy a high degree of freedom and autonomy. The chapter analyses, with a qualitative case-based approach borrowing from business history literature, entrepreneurial families in Italy, France, Germany, Spain, and Scandinavia. Drawing on several of these cases and borrowing from the available literature on entrepreneurial households, the chapter will also go beyond narratives proposing some stylized facts.

Keywords: entrepreneurial families, Europe, business history, multi-business families

Introduction

This chapter deals with family entrepreneurship from the perspective of *entrepreneurial multi-business families*. Entrepreneurial families, that is, families who diversify their entrepreneurial initiatives, not only within the timeframe of a single generation but also in the medium to long term and often across several generations, are now a subject of study in family business literature (Nordqvist & Melin, 2010; Habbershon, Nordqvist, & Zellweger, 2010; James et al., 2020), even if the "multi-business" perspective is analyzed only superficially. This behaviour confers on entrepreneurial business families a specific trait, that is, *longevity* in business, as well as *resilience*, which is the ability to survive downturns and periods of crisis, particularly when family ownership is positively connected to innovative behaviour. Longevity and resilience are different – albeit interconnected concepts. In the following analysis, they will be used in some cases as quasi-synonyms to highlight a company's ability to successfully meet exogenous challenges (resilience) in order to achieve a successful chance of long-term survival (longevity).

Andrea Colli, Bocconi University

https://doi.org/10.1515/9783110727968-012

As this chapter will show in greater detail, entrepreneurial families as described above are not an exception. Limiting the analysis to continental Europe that – given the nature of its capitalist tradition of which family firms are a "pillar" – is a kind of privileged observatory for understanding the nature of this phenomenon, entrepreneurial multi-business families are an important component of every nation's corporate landscape.

As anticipated, this chapter focuses on family dynasties that demonstrate a remarkable tendency towards diversification strategies pursued in the medium to long term, that is, entrepreneurial multi-business families. *Entrepreneurial attitudes and behaviour*, therefore, are considered here as the main resources and capabilities of these family dynasties; it is obvious, as noted by existing literature, that the focus here is shifting from the firm dimension to the family dimension (Zellweger et al., 2012; Michael-Tsabari, Labaki, & Kay Zachary, 2014).

Based on the narrative and qualitative historical method,[1] this chapter aims to provide more detailed understanding of the main stylized features of these dynastic entrepreneurial multi-business families involved in long-term diversification strategies. The chapter consists of seven sections. Following this Introduction, the section on entrepreneurial multi-business families will discuss some "dimensions" of the analytical framework that is useful to interpret the nature of "entrepreneurial multi-business families": the scope of their activity, the available resources, and the longevity and sustainability of this family business model. The next section entitled "A Widespread Phenomenon" provides some empirical evidence of entrepreneurial multi-business families operating in continental Europe between the 18th and 20th centuries. The next section entitled "Why Diversification" concerns the drivers for non-related diversification, while the subsequent section on the Bonomi family outlines the case of a five-generation Italian entrepreneurial family, with its development across different historical periods and sectors of activity up to the foundation of a global private equity company. The section on shared destines discusses a set of traits common to continental Europe's entrepreneurial multi-business families. The final section is the Conclusion.

---

1 This chapter is based on information collected from different sources, including business histories, press articles. and interviews with local experts. I must acknowledge the support received from my colleagues Bram Bouwens, Hartmut Berghoff, Ludovic Cailluet, Jari Ojala, Paloma Fernandez Perez, Ewout Hasken, Christina Lubinski, Andrea Schneider, Hans Sjögren, and Knut Sogner. Rania Labaki and Carlo Salvato provided fundamental suggestions for improvements. Of course, I alone am responsible for any errors or omissions.

Entrepreneurial Multi-Business Families: The Analytical Framework

Generally speaking, the entrepreneurial family model described in this chapter ideally includes dynasties that have progressively diversified from their initial area of activity into multiple entrepreneurial ventures in different industries, perhaps also in different geographical locations (for a very recent review see Hafner, 2021); they have undertaken this process across several generations; they have been able to mobilize and accumulate a considerable amount of resources in financial terms (Bierl & Kammerlander, 2019) and in terms of reputation and human capital – resources that constitute a sort of immaterial endowment of the family in its investment activity, and allow stable and sustainable development over time (Hafner, 2021, p. 546; Step, 2017, pp. 14–15; Zachary, 2011, p. 32).

Of course, not all multi-generational family companies – or entrepreneurial families in general – as analyzed by the current literature correspond to this framework, and it is therefore useful to clarify its components in more detail.

Scope of Activity

A first area concerns the effective *scope of activities* that fall within the range of the "family". By their nature, "entrepreneurial families" tend to broaden their range of entrepreneurial initiatives into fields that are (sometimes extremely) distant from their original sphere. In other cases, however, the degree of diversification, albeit important, tends to be limited to broad areas with a certain "homogeneity", for instance, in terms of consumption styles (e.g., luxury). The diversification process can be also "radical" (i.e., it is difficult to identify a prevalent business in the portfolio of activities) or "marginal" (i.e., the diversification strategy is limited to a range of activities, which in terms of relevance/dimensions complement a core business) (for a review of diversification strategies in family firms see Hafner, 2021, p. 534).

Of course, the diversification process is also intended in geographical terms; some entrepreneurial dynasties tend to limit their range of diversification to a single country, although the international (if not global) dimension is much more frequent, particularly when it comes to the later generations. Finally, the flow of both *intrage*nerational and *inter*generational entrepreneurial initiatives is the outcome of different factors, some of which are quite "standard" in nature (from the presence of institutional voids to the willingness to diversify risk), while others are related to a completely different set of issues, such as the capabilities and competences of different components of the family. Additionally, the fact that entrepreneurial families are characterized by the reiteration of entrepreneurial initiatives over several generations means that the technological, socio-cultural, and institutional context plays a key role in providing the necessary incentives and opportunities (James et al., 2020).

Resources

As highlighted by current family business literature, the resources available to family-run companies (and entrepreneurial families) include various kinds of capital: financial, reputational, and human/social (Habbershon & Williams, 1999; Arrègle et al., 2007; Danes et al., 2009)

Finance

A first cluster of resources belongs to the financial aspect of business, specifically to the sources of finance that entrepreneurs can mobilize by investing both their own means and other resources available to them. The variation in the sources of finance and in the use of financial instruments is one of the most evident differences, particularly over time, between the generations within the same family, given the evolution in (learning the) use of sophisticated financial instruments by these entrepreneurial families. An important issue here is to distinguish between the entrepreneurial families who move towards pure financial entrepreneurship (for instance, through the creation of a family office investing in several directions for pure capital gain, without any direct involvement in managerial activities), and those investing financial resources with the explicit purpose of direct operational involvement, taking an entrepreneurial role in several industries.

Of course, financial resources are not collected only on financial markets. An important part of the resource-scouting activity of entrepreneurial families occurs through the involvement of a number of different co-investors, ranging from institutional investors to individuals and other entrepreneurial families interested in sharing ventures and activities.

Reputation

The presence of this typology of co-investors introduces a number of other important aspects, mainly concerning relations, which are largely based upon a further typology of resources: *reputation* and *reputational capital*. Therefore, it is crucial for entrepreneurial families to develop and nurture their own reputations as entrepreneurs and investors as a key resource in order to maximize the possibility of involving strategic partners in their activities. One important component in this process of reputation building is clearly the *multi-generational* nature of these entrepreneurial families, which in some cases deliberately emphasize the longitudinal nature of their diversified entrepreneurial experience in order to reassure and attract potential partners in their activities.

In the case of entrepreneurial multi-business families, co-investors can be seen not only in their role as providers of financial resources, but also as providers of expertise and competences and – indirectly – of additional reputational input. For instance, this is the not infrequent case of an entrepreneurial multi-business family able to involve an institutional investor as an investment partner in a new venture, for example, a sovereign wealth fund, which can in turn provide managerial expertise and competence in a specific field and act as a flagship investor for the aggregation of other investors, as in the case of private-equity initiatives.

Human Capital

Financial resources, reputational capital and partnerships are important but complementary assets to be exploited by entrepreneurial multi-business families. Over time, they also face the issue of involvement and interaction with professional management, which is necessary for managing a wide range of activities in different fields. The role, nature, and contribution of professional managers to the activities of entrepreneurial families is still an under-researched area of analysis in the resources available for this particular form of organization. However, almost all the empirical evidence available shows that non-family members provide an essential contribution to the process of diversifying and expanding the range of business activities under the leadership of family members. The way in which these professional figures are recruited, and above all how they are connected to the family members and put in charge of significant sections of the family holdings is especially important. It is frequently these professionals who help entrepreneurial multi-business families to widen their range of activities and competences, providing not only the necessary human capital but also other resources and networking.

However, this mention of professionals introduces another important aspect of the resources possessed by entrepreneurial multi-business families: the presence of multiple family members involved in the diversification of activities. The "demographic" of the generations involved in running the business is important, since empirical evidence again shows that the range of activities within the range of the family's interests is very often a variable that depends on the number of family members available.

Longevity, Stability, and Sustainability

A third key aspect of entrepreneurial families concerns their longevity, stability and general sustainability in the long run (Olson et al., 2003). Entrepreneurial families rarely develop their activities within the space of a single generation; the life-cycle of an entrepreneurial family normally spans several generations, and it may pass through different stages before it achieves the status of a multi-business entrepreneurial family. There are several courses that can be taken, as represented and summarized in Figure 12.1. A family business spanning several generations can evolve in different ways over time. A first and very frequent situation is depicted in Pattern 1, where a multi-generational family company passes from generation to generation and remains in what is basically the same area of activity. Here, the knowledge assets mentioned under resources above are exploited in order to enlarge the business in terms of scale, internationalization, and specialization in the same area of activity as that of the company when it was founded. Pattern 2 describes another quite frequent situation, which is when a multi-generational company starts to diversify in fields that are related, albeit different to its original area of activity. For instance, this is the case of family companies that expand their scope of operations by investing in vertical backward and forward integration, employing the resources available – including family members – in this growth strategy (Basco et al., 2019; Nordqvist & Melin, 2010).

Finally, Pattern 3 describes the genesis of an "entrepreneurial multi-business family", and its possible developments. An entrepreneurial multi-business family has its quite obvious origins in a mono-business activity, and may follow Pattern 2 of related diversification for some time (one or two generations), or may take a completely different path by starting to invest in areas barely related to its original sphere of activity, using all its available resources, including family members, to expand in multiple fields and areas. This process may take a long time to unfold but may also develop quite rapidly, depending on a set of factors that include contextual factors (for instance, technological opportunities) and the availability of the resources mentioned above (Hafner, 2021, p. 554). The assumption on which Figure 12.1 is based, which is derived from the qualitative analysis contained in the following paragraphs, is that continental Europe's entrepreneurial families do not start the process of diversification (related or even non-related) immediately after the company's foundation. This strategy is implemented after a period of successful consolidation in the original business and may follow a generational shift, which provides the human resources, motivation, and willingness necessary to initiate a process of diversification. In this respect it is possible to notice a difference between the behaviour of entrepreneurial families in Europe and, for instance, those in Asia. The process of diversification may start very soon after the foundation of a company in Asia, due to a set of area-specific factors like environmental uncertainty, government developmental pressures, or simply because of the opportunities provided by fast-developing markets – a situation that is quite different from that historically characterizing the economies of continental Europe (see, e.g., Carney & Dieleman, 2008).

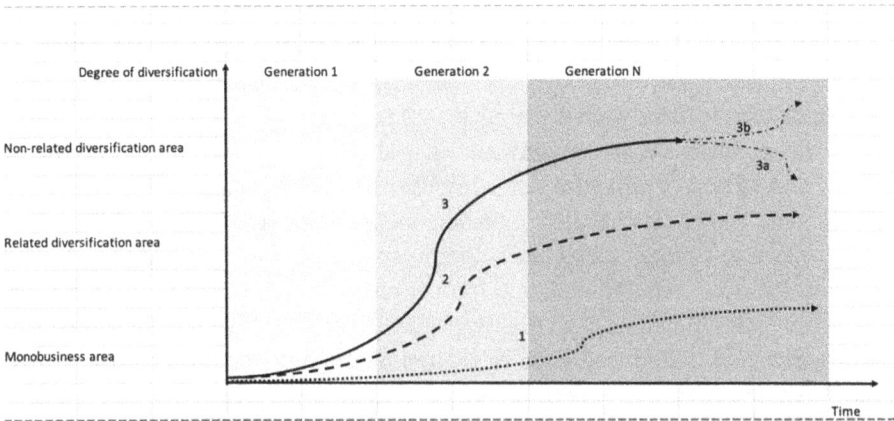

Figure 12.1: The multiple patterns of entrepreneurial and entrepreneurial multi-business families.

Of course, Figure 12.1 is (extremely) schematized and it represents a much more complex process, which takes very different forms and shapes from case to case. For instance, the graph deliberately describes a "progressive" approach to related and non-related diversification in Patterns 2 and 3, whereas some of the cases mentioned in the following paragraphs show that the decision to diversify follows a sudden change in the external context, for example, when privatizations or nationalizations occur (see, for instance, the examples of the Wendel family and Benetton family described in the section "Why Diversification?").

However, Figure 12.1 helps to introduce the (little-investigated) area of multi-business activity within family businesses, which is extremely frequent.

The patterns described in Figure 12.1 do not help a great deal in the discussion regarding longevity and sustainability of the different business models. While the relationship between successful intergenerational transmission and longevity is a commonplace in family business studies, it is unclear whether this relationship holds true and valid when intergenerational transmission is accompanied by the diversification of the entrepreneurial activities into areas unrelated to the original one (Hafner, 2021, p. 553). Empirical evidence put forward by business historians (James, 2006) seems to corroborate the intuition that, under certain circumstances (e.g., the degree of maturity of a given industry), the chances of survival and therefore the longevity of a family business pass through diversification of its activities into areas that are completely unconnected with the area in which the family may have been active for a long time (Gomez-Mejia et al., 2010). Conversely, the reluctance of the new generations to explore new ventures, and their determination to continue in the original area of business at any cost, may in certain circumstances lead to crisis and decline.

Therefore, sustainability and longevity can – in several cases – be positively connected to the process of non-related diversification in the long term. A relevant point to note here is that while available literature on the emergence and functioning of business groups stresses the importance of contextual drivers in explaining the existence of this peculiar governance structure (Morck, 2005; Khanna & Yafeh, 2007; Colpan, Hikino, & Lincoln, 2012; Colpan & Hkino, 2018), this chapter puts the emphasis largely (but not exclusively) on elements that are endogenous to the business family.

The three patterns described in Figure 12.1 also raise different issues in terms of the sustainability and potential longevity of the family "company", meaning the range of activities in which family members are involved. The higher the degree of diversification, the more crucial and important becomes the issue of managing the necessary financial, reputational, and human resources. This may result in two diverging outcomes in Pattern 3 on the right side of Figure 12.1, where the diversification process may be reduced back to related diversification and perhaps mono-business strategies (3a), or may be increased even more in terms of the conglomeration level (3b).

A Widespread Phenomenon

Entrepreneurial multi-business families are relatively widespread today, particularly in areas where industrialization began long ago. This is of course the case of western continental Europe, including Scandinavia, where family dynasties have traditionally been present and consolidated since the beginning of industrialization, and where the contextual aspects, such as the maturation of the industries in which the original investment took place, are more clearly at work.

A non-systematic review of some European cases highlights some well-known and other less-known family companies that – more or less recently – have adopted strategies of non-related diversification, substituting or accompanying their initial "core" activity with others in different fields, developed by the same generation or by those following.

Available examples of multi-generational entrepreneurial multi-business families confirm the impression (to be corroborated by further research) that the phenomenon is "explained" by a wide range of factors, and not simply by risk mitigation strategies.

The longitudinal perspective of this chapter makes it possible to identify some examples of entrepreneurial families that at a certain point in time during their life cycle started a process of diversification in several fields of activity. To provide just a few examples, some of Italy's entrepreneurial multi-business families are among the leaders of the country's industrialization. These include the Agnelli family (mainly known for the Fiat automobile brand and now controlling Exor, a Netherlands-based listed investment holding with a market capitalization of around $20 billion and approximately $900 million of assets under management), the Falck family (leading iron and steel producers until the 1990s), and more recent cases like the Caprotti family (mass distribution), and the Benetton family, with its family investment holding Edizione (a turnover of $22.5 billion). There are many examples of medium-sized family companies, which in some cases have demonstrated a remarkable ability to reorient their business according to changes in technologies and in market demand, such as the Fumagalli family's transition from industrial gases to healthcare and biotechnology, or the De'Longhi family's transition in the late 1990s from the production of heaters and air conditioners to household appliances.

Similar examples can easily be found in other European countries. France's Wendel family originally operated in the iron and steel industry but has diversified into a vast range of industries through its listed Wendel Participations SE, with a market capitalization of around $6 billion and a turnover of $9 billion. Other more recent cases from France are the Bouygues diversifying from infrastructures to services), Lagardère and Bolloré (a conglomerate ranging from electricity to communications and logistics), Daher (from shipping to equipment for nuclear power stations and aircraft), and Mulliez (a conglomerate present in several industries connected to retail) families.

In Spain, the Basque Ybarra Careaga family is another multi-investor, with activities in a dozen industries that include mobile communications, agribusiness, energy, and logistics. Another Spanish family, the Ortega family, started with the global textile group Inditex and has now invested in a varied range of industries that include gas distribution, with an investment holding (Pontegadea) that has a total turnover of $32.5 billion.

In Germany, prominent cases include the Haniel family, which moved from steel into a wide range of investments in different industries now controlled through Franz Haniel Cie GmbH, with a turnover of nearly $4 billion in 2020. There is also Bertelsmann, a family company that operated originally in the media business, but has now diversified much more into digital business services (Berghoff & Köhler, 2021).

Germany's Heraeus Holding GmbH, which has a turnover of $25 billion and has moved from its origins as a pharmacy into several businesses involving precious and rare materials, is an extremely unusual case (IDCH, 130, pp. 254–260). The same is true for William Prym Holding GmbH, Germany's oldest family company, which is present in sectors ranging from textiles to fashion, fastening systems and electromechanical solutions. One of Germany's richest families, the Reimanns, trace their history back to the chemical industry in the early decades of the 19th century, but their family holding JAB (with a turnover of about $820 million) is now a direct and active investor in five areas that range from pet care to coffee, cosmetics, beauty, and luxury (Shotter, 2016).

Entrepreneurial multi-business families are also present in northern Europe, where the traditional involvement in trade and commercial activities probably underlies the tendency of some family companies to pursue a constant process of diversification into different activities. The Dutch SHV (with a total turnover of nearly $26.5 billion) is a family-owned (Fentener van Vlissingen) conglomerate founded over 100 years ago, which has progressively invested in various areas such as energy, logistics, wholesale distribution, pet food, oil, and gas. In a similar way, the Swiss-based COFRA Holding is fully controlled by the Dutch Brenninkmeijer family, which originally operated in textiles but during a century of activity across six generations has diversified into several areas and now operates in private equity. The Finnish Hartwall Capital (with a turnover of $169 million) is another very good example of a successful family company; having operated in the beverage industry for over 150 years, it then sold its original activity and invested the financial resources from the sale in an investment company that is present in a wide range of sectors. The rather secretive Ehrnrooth family (Jensen-Heriksen, Hilpinen, & Forsén, 2020), also Finnish, controls an investment "vehicle", Structor SA (now Caverion Corporation) that is present in a vast array of industries including construction and telecommunications among others. Norway is home to several interesting cases. These include the Andresen family, which embodies a multi-investing, active, long-term approach of an entrepreneurial multi-business family, with six generations of business activity in a wide range of sectors and now a company (Ferd) with a turnover of over $2 billion). Sweden is generally identified with the Wallenberg family, another traditionally diversified powerful dynasty that has been active across generations. It carries out a wide range of activities via its holding company, Investor AB, a giant with $43 billion of market capitalization and a turnover of almost $4.8 billion (Lindgren, 2012); other less-known cases include the Stenbeck family, a multi-investor since the very beginning of its business activity in 1936, whose holding company (Kinnevik) is listed with $9.5 billion of market capitalization and a turnover of nearly $1.5 billion; it originally operated in industries ranging from pulp to paper and chocolate, then shifted to television, and more recently the third generation has moved into e-commerce (Sjögren, 2018, pp. 82–83; IDCH, 136, pp. 249–254). Axel Johnson has a similar story (with a turnover of more than $9.5 billion); currently run by the fourth generation after approximately 150 years as a diversified investor in industry and trade, it now acts as an accelerator for companies in high-tech and digital services at the global level (Sjögren, 2018, pp. 49–50; IDCH, 126, pp. 57–61).

Why Diversification?

Since non-related diversification is widespread among European entrepreneurial multi-business families of the present and of the past, it would be useful to understand what makes such a strategy attractive, and also whether some drivers in this process are a particular feature of family firms.

The drivers of non-related diversification may actually be very different in nature. Table 12.1 tentatively summarizes some of the drivers that may underlie the decision to pursue a diversification strategy outside the company's original main area of activity. Some of these drivers are common to family and non-family firms, while others are specific and idiosyncratic to family firms. It is also important to stress that the decision to undertake a non-related diversification strategy can of course be the outcome of several drivers acting simultaneously.

Table 12.1: Drivers of Non-Related Diversification
By Family Firms.

a)	Technological change
b)	Market opportunities
c)	Surplus financial resources
d)	Risk diversification
e)	Serendipity
f)	Institutional changes
g)	Political determinants
h)	Generational will (∗)
i)	Availability of competences in new generations (∗)
j)	Generational dimension (∗)
k)	Family-related dynamics (∗)

(∗) indicates idiosyncratic family business drivers

Non-idiosyncratic Drivers

a) Among the diversification drivers that are non-specific to family firms, technological change (or stagnation) is of course a key element, particularly when the original activity has reached a high degree of maturity and low levels of real growth. The case of iron and steel producers Wendel, Haniel, and Falck is particularly relevant in this perspective. All three families share common origins in the Alsace region, and all have a long history dating back to the 18th and early 19th centuries; they started out in the iron trade, then invested in industrial activities and benefited from the spread of second industrial revolution technologies of steel production in the first half of the 20th century (James, 2006). This process of consolidation lasted for around three to four generations until the 1960s, when the increasing degree of maturity of the steel industry in continental Europe created the premises for a radical change of strategy. Of course, exit from a mature industry is not always a smooth and predictable process. Germany's Haniel family progressively implemented an exit strategy from the steel industry starting in the 1960s; this radically transformed the company, which is still family-owned, into an investment holding active in different industries including mass distribution, operating as a proactive investor thanks to the activity of skilled professionals (IDCH, 225, pp. 155–161). When the French government nationalized steel production in the 1970s, the Wendel family was forced to concentrate its interests in companies ranging from healthcare to IT services; it followed the shifting technological opportunities that arose with the advent of the third industrial revolution to become what is today one of Europe's most active investment companies, with a long-term, active approach (IDCH, 145, pp. 451–456). The Italian Falck family suffered the most, due to its reluctance to relinquish its investments in the steel industry. Eventually, in the 1990s it began to diversify into the field of renewable energy, enabled also by long-standing experience in the hydroelectric industry that had been created to serve the steel industry. (Salvato, Chirico, & Sharma, 2010)

The inescapable maturation and decline of the coal industry led SHV (mentioned in the section "A Widespread Phenomenon" above), a Dutch trading company controlled by the third generation of the van Vlissingen family, to diversify into energy-related industries like oil and gas; from the 1970s it also moved into increasingly non-related fields like Makro (a global cash-and-carry chain), distribution of consumer goods, technical installations, construction, shipping, technical equipment, and metal recycling.

b) Market opportunities or radical changes in the pattern of consumption and the availability of new technologies can make the difference, particularly when coinciding with a generational transition (Konig et al. 2013). Several of the cases mentioned here show that generational transitions have frequently coincided with changes in consumption styles that create new market opportunities, thus prompting a diversification of the family investments. The Ortega family is a clear case in point: starting from textiles, the change in its investment pattern has been accelerated by the second generation's involvement in top-level management of the group. The same can be said of the Ybarra Careaga group, which has constantly diversified its investments and entrepreneurial initiatives, starting out in the 19th century with mining in Spain's Basque country; it moved into the iron and steel industry at the beginning of the 20th century, then into shipping and banking, and has more recently become involved in other areas that include mobile communications and renewables. A combination of market opportunities and new technologies explains the investment diversification process undertaken by the third generation of the Italian Annoni-Fumagalli family. In the 1920s, the first generation started a successful business producing oxygen and hydrogen for industrial use. The second generation followed with successful diversification of this core activity into production of other gases, benefiting from advances in chemical research in order to widen the applications of gas, while the third generation has made massive investments in healthcare and now in biotechnologies. The entire story of Kinnevik AB, the company controlled by the Swedish Stenbeck family (IDCH, 136, pp. 249–254), is a succession of diversification strategies in non-related fields. Starting with investments in iron, steel, and woodworking, the next area of investment was the food sector, with controlling stakes in the chocolate industry. After World War II, investments in the automotive industry became important in the company's portfolio, followed in the 1990s by mobile communications and media. Today the company is a multiple investor in internet-related industries, including online distribution via the Zalando brand.

c) This is also the case when the core business of the family generates a considerable amount of financial resources that make diversification possible, also within the framework of . . .

d) . . . a risk-diversification policy. This is for instance the very unusual case of the Benetton family in Italy. The company was founded in the mid-1950s by four siblings headed by Luciano, the charismatic eldest brother; it successfully interpreted radical changes in consumer tastes, and in two decades grew to become one of Italy's most successful enterprises. When listed in the mid-1980s, the company's already considerable cash flows were increased by vast financial resources now added to the company's investment capacity; this allowed diversification into a wide – although not always successful – range of activities in related industries (footwear and sportswear), and also in increasingly distant fields, like infrastructures and supermarkets (Colli, 2017). The already-mentioned case of the Finnish Hartwall family must be included in the same category as the Benetton family: following the successful sale of Oy Hartwall AB in 2008, its multi-generational family beverage company established in 1836, the family then began a strategy of stable active investment across a wide range of industries, thus developing from a single-business family company into a multi-business investment company committed to the development of established entrepreneurial initiatives. A particularly interesting case in this respect is that of the Norwegian Andresen family (Sjögren 2018, p. 104). The family company started out in the mid-19th century with the purchase of the Tiedemanns tobacco company, which immediately provided the necessary (and abundant) cash flow required for diversification into shipping, packaging, consumer products, logistic services, and other areas. A combination of changing consumption habits (see point b on market opportunities) and changes in the laws on tobacco consumption drove the Andresens to sell off their assets in tobacco and establish Ferd, which is an investment company that acquires important stakes in a wide range of sectors with the purpose of active ownership, based also on a set of values the family aims to transmit to the financed companies. A similar case is the quite complex story of the Dutch SHV Holding, established by coal traders towards the end of the 19th century as a syndicate company under the charismatic leadership of Frederik Hendrik Fentener van Vlissingen; not only was he the company CEO and its main owner, but he also drove its diversification into a wide range of activities in the energy, shipping, chemical, and airline industries through an investment vehicle called Unitas (IDCH, 125, pp. 344–347). However, the best example of an investment holding emerging from a dominant activity is probably the Istituto

Finanziario Italiano (IFI) of Italy's Agnelli family. Established in 1927, almost three decades after the foundation of Fiat, it managed business ventures in the areas of consumer goods, industrials, leisure, and tourism, which were radically different from the family's core business of automobile manufacturing. In the 1960s, IFI became IFIL and started a new cycle of investments in industries related to consumption and distribution, still backed by the dominant business (Castronovo, 1999). More recently, now transformed into Exor, the Agnelli family's investment holding has been investing through direct control of companies and partnerships in a wide range of sectors, including publishing, fashion, and luxury goods. In the Agnelli-Exor story, the converging drivers of diversification are the presence of a dominant resource-generating activity, changes in market and consumption styles, and a considerable amount of serendipity.

e) Serendipity, that is, the unexpected chance or opportunity for new investments in new fields of activity, must not be overlooked as a possible driver. In other words, families may diversify just because good opportunities present themselves and diversification appears to be a good opportunity for risk diversification. One original example is provided by the history of La Rinascente, one of Italy's major department stores, whose origins date back to a family company, the Magazzini Bocconi, which was established in Milan in the late 19th century. Problems in the passage from one generation to the next saw the company sold in 1917 to another powerful family, the Borletti, who possessed enormous financial resources derived from its precision mechanics activity supplying Italy's armed forces. Although this was a completely different area of business for the Borletti family, they decided to invest in the profitable department stores also in order to benefit from the Italian government's abolition of taxation on reinvested profits. Several decades later, in 1969, the same serendipity brought La Rinascente under the ownership of another major Italian family, the Agnelli, whose IFIL company had been managing their extremely diversified holdings since 1964. (Amatori, 2017)

f) Changes in the institutional/legal framework may result in the decision either to end the activity or else to radically transform it into something new (Hafner, 2021, pp. 546–547). One clear example of this is when institutional changes forcibly drive towards the search for an alternative, for instance with nationalization of the "core business", or on the contrary, with the opportunities some entrepreneurial families found in the privatization of state assets during the 1990s. The cases of France's Wendel family and Italy's Benettons both proceed very markedly in this direction. The Wendels started a process of multi-business diversification in the mid-1970s, when the French government was faced with a structural crisis in the industry and nationalized the entire steel industry. This forced a redirection of the family's operations towards non-steel activities, including IT services and healthcare (James, 2006; IDCH, 145, pp. 451–456). For the Benetton family, on the other hand, the opportunity for non-related diversification arrived in the second half of the 1990s, when the

Italian government undertook a radical process of liberalization and privatization of state-owned assets in several industries. This opportunity combined with the availability of considerable financial resources and very independent skilled professionals, allowing the family to diversify radically from knitwear into infrastructures (highways and airports), motorway catering, and supermarkets (all of which had previously belonged to the huge state-owned conglomerate IRI), followed by investments in the liberalized telecom sector (Colli, 2017). Similarly, a change in the laws allowing banks to own industrial stakes in 1916 led the powerful Swedish Wallenberg dynasty, owner of the Stockholm Enskilda Bank, to create an investment holding, Investor AB, which has been present since then as the controlling shareholder in some of the Sweden's leading companies in several industries.

g) It must also be considered that in some cases (not infrequent in the case of continental Europe), the privatization of formerly state-owned assets through the diversification of family companies into completely non-related activities has been incentivized by the very same governments, in order to avoid the (politically unacceptable) sale of strategic activities to unwelcome investors. France is a quite obvious example in this respect. During the late 1980s and early 1990s, when both conservative and progressive French governments opted for the privatization of national assets, they shared the intention of involving private French investors, who thus became "guarantors" of French interests in strategic assets. In some cases, such as that of the Bouygues family, this led to a process of diversification, even if not in a completely unrelated field, with the acquisition of the electro-mechanic company Alstom. Founded soon after World War II as "Entreprise Francis Bouygues", the company expanded as a general contractor for public works in the following two decades, operating mainly in Paris but also abroad, and starting a process of acquisitions that made Bouygues the world leader in public works. In late 1987, however, the company's diversification strategy changed. Besides public works, and in the midst of handing over to the second generation, Bouygues acquired Télé France 1 (TF1) from the French government. In 1994 it launched Bouygues Télécom, and in 2006 it acquired a controlling stake in the recently privatized (and strategic) Alstom, a leader in the electro-mechanic industry.

The intricate history of the Lagardère group, founded by an energetic engineer and initially active in the aerospace industry, combines the careful exploitation of technological opportunities offered by the digital revolution in the publishing industry with the exploitation of political connections. In the mid-1960s, Jean-Luc Lagardère headed Matra Aviation, a private French company with a leading role in the production of jet engines, satellite systems and other high-tech solutions; in 1980 Matra took control of ultra-centenarian French publishing house Hachette, which had already diversified into several branches of the media industry, including television. These two apparently distant industries actually found synergic opportunities in the multimedia industry launched in the mid-1990s, before the Lagardère group was asked by the French government to become a major investor in the privatization of the European

Aeronautic Defense and Space Company (EADS). In 2003, the transition to the second generation, represented by the founder's son Arnaud, led to intense refocusing in the area (broadly intended) of entertainment, sports, event management, multimedia, and travel retail, progressively moving away from involvement in the aerospace industry.

Drivers Specific to Family Firms

In any case, it is important to note how these non-family firm-specific drivers impact on family firms in a very specific way; the (quite strong) hypothesis here is that the presence of considerable socio-emotional wealth makes the drive towards non-related diversification *even stronger* among family firms (Hafner, 2021, pp. 531), given the willingness of new generations to keep the entrepreneurial involvement of the family alive – sometimes at any cost (Muñoz-Bullon, Sanchez-Bueno, & Suárez-González, 2018, p. 42; for a review of different perspectives, see Hafner, 2021, p. 531).

In addition to these drivers that are common to family and non-family firms, it is necessary to include another series of drivers that are peculiar to family firms (Hafner, 2021, p. 535).

h) A first group of drivers are those labeled as "generational will", which includes the willingness of new generations to undertake fresh entrepreneurial initiatives, usually without openly challenging the established business practice of the previous generations (Hafner, 549). A very interesting – and in some ways unusual – case history is that of the already mentioned Fentener van Vlissingen family. As stressed above under risk diversification policy, the diversification of the (initially) energy-based group SHV was carried out by the second generation, and above all by the third generation of the family, consisting of the three brothers, John, Paul, and Fritz. John, however, was never directly involved in the family holding's affairs; at the start of his career, he chose to concentrate on independent management of a completely different business involved in travel, leisure, and tourism, which he founded in 1975. His BCD Group has become a global market leader in travel services. In his own words, the decision to diversify into a radically different business area was a kind of conscious reaction to his family's overall established strategy:

> In reaction to all this high-minded, Calvinist striving, Mr. van Vlissingen turned into something of a black sheep. When he was 16, he was sent to a boarding school in England "because my father thought I was having too much fun. He thought I had to get serious." Within an hour of arrival, he was in detention. Nor did he bother with university, unlike his brothers. Worse was to come. Instead of joining the family business – "my father was in shock; he couldn't accept it" – Mr. van Vlissingen took off to Wall Street to learn about what really interested him: the gyrations of the financial markets. But the family genes were stronger than he imagined, and working for someone else proved unsatisfying. Even while he was still a banker, Mr. van Vlissingen convinced his employers – at that point Pierson, a Dutch broker – to let him set up his own business as a sideline. (*The Economist*, April 19, 2001)

Apart from this quite extreme case, other case histories show how frequently the diversification process has been a much less conflictual – but efficient – way to solve or control conflicts that potentially threaten the unity and well-being of the family (Colli 2018). Edoardo Agnelli, born in 1892, was the only son born to Giovanni Agnelli, the founder of Fiat. With a strong personality that was quite different from that of his father, Edoardo was progressively but slowly involved in the main family business area of automotives; this was still firmly managed by his father, who treated him as his natural designated successor. Before Edoardo's premature death in a plane accident in 1934, he had shown his entrepreneurial and organizational capabilities by managing two ventures that were extremely distant from the family's core business, but which would become increasingly important with time. The first was Turin's Juventus soccer club, which he began to manage in an increasingly entrepreneurial way, and the second venture was the creation in 1931 of the first Alpine resort for summer and winter mass-holidays at Sestrière, in Piedmont's Susa Valley, fully controlled by the Fiat group. Until very recently, the second generation of the Benetton family had no direct involvement in managing the investments belonging to the family holding (Edizione). For this reason, Alessandro, the second son of Luciano Benetton who is the eldest of the company's four original founding siblings, began his own career in private equity, where he remains active.

i) The availability of competences in the new generations – perhaps due to specific educational patterns and/or field experiences – may result in the decision to embark on new ventures in completely different industries. For example, a combination of problems connected to the maturity of the family's core activity and to the availability of new competences underlie the fascinating entrepreneurial history of Bernardo Caprotti. Although destined to inherit a well-established family cotton business immediately after World War II, after a formative trip to the US Caprotti used his own capital and finance from US investors to invest in what was a promising and completely new field for Italy by founding a successful supermarket chain (Esselunga).

j) Another idiosyncratic driver for diversification (in this case, not necessarily unrelated), is the size of the incoming generation, which may be crucial in providing the incentive for younger family members to create new initiatives (Michael-Tsabari, Labaki, & Kay Zachary, 2014). The diversification of the above mentioned Fentener van Vlissingen family into non-related fields has also been fostered by the presence of three brothers (two directly involved in the company) in the generation that took over company leadership after World War II.

k) A fourth group of determinants for diversification consists of the opportunities for new initiatives stemming from family dynamics, for instance when marriages bring an established business into the family. This can also happen in the opposite case, that is, when family tensions and feuds are prevented or resolved through a *de facto* separation of relatives, with each one dedicated to their own business and responsibilities. In the cases of the Swedish Wallenberg family and the Finnish Ehrnrooth family, a common practice has been to "relocate" family members, especially the younger generations, in positions of responsibility in the group's companies, effectively maximizing the opportunities for crucial training of this human capital, while at the same time clearly separating their spheres of responsibility, and thereby avoiding potential clashes. (Komulainen & Siltala, 2016; Sjögren, 2018, pp. 84–85)

One Case in Detail: The Bonomi Family, Italy

What emerges with clarity from the stories mentioned in the previous section is that the nature of entrepreneurial multi-business families is extremely idiosyncratic and that heterogeneity dominates (Nordqvist et al. 2014). The differences depend on several factors, among which may be included institutional factors, including the legal system within which companies operate, cultural factors, and factors related to the "family ingredient", including the personal expectations and competences of individual members. The identification of a stylized model able to provide an exhaustive account of the "entrepreneurial multi-business family" is therefore particularly problematic. This means that instead of seeking simplification, it is necessary to make extensive use of available evidence in order to supplement our present knowledge of the phenomenon. Luckily, business history provides plenty of such evidence. One case spanning five generations may help to clarify some of the aspects highlighted in the previous paragraphs. The story of the Bonomi family dates back to the early 1870s, when widowed Maria Bergamaschi decided to invest the family capital in the tax collection in the city of Milan, and thereby obtained sufficient financial resources to expand this activity to include other Italian cities. The income derived from tax collection was subsequently used by three of Maria Bergamaschi's sons, Angelo, Carlo, and Ambrogio Bonomi, to found a company that operated in construction and real estate, and benefited greatly from the city's urban expansion that began in the last decade of the 19th century. Carlo, the second son, soon took over leadership of "Fratelli Bonomi" as its operations steadily expanded, focusing on the construction industry and acting also as general contractors for public works, such as Milan's Central Station. When Carlo died, he left his daughter Anna one of Italy's largest fortunes. This gave her enough resources to become very active in a wide range of sectors, including financial speculation on the Milan Stock Exchange, also with the help of professional advisors and managers. Her entrepreneurial interests, backed by the constant cash flow from her real estate assets, ranged from insurance to matches, from banking to cotton, from electricity to chemicals, from mail order to real estate, contracting and public works, and were managed through two holdings, Beni Immobili Italia (real estate) and Invest. When

Anna retired in the early 1980s, the family holding created by the merger of the two holdings mentioned above and listed on the Milan stock exchange, Bi-Invest, was therefore a sort of "conglomerate" with controlling interests in a wide range of industries. From the early 1980s, this conglomerate was managed by Anna's youngest son, Carlo. The first member of the dynasty to have completed formal higher education, with a degree and an MBA, Carlo was in turn trained and then assisted by executives with long-term positions in the company. Following a hostile takeover, Carlo sold Bi-Invest and transferred most of the family activities abroad to Spain and the UK, beginning to invest in a wide range of industries. The family assets have then formed the basis of another entrepreneurial "turning point" initiated by the fifth generation, consisting of Carlo's two sons Andrea and Carlo Umberto. Since the 1990s they have managed InvestIndustrial, a private-equity company that invests actively and stably in dozens of companies in different sectors both in Italy and abroad, with a strong activist and entrepreneurial orientation.

In this shortened and oversimplified account, some of the previously discussed drivers are at work simultaneously. For a significant part of the family's history (the first two generations), there was a dominant activity, which consisted of real estate investments and public works. This dominant activity allowed the accumulation of sufficient financial resources to enable the third generation to diversify and expand into completely non-related fields by creating a holding and involving professional managers. Therefore, the fourth generation found itself at the head of a conglomerate, with quite a similar level of diversification to those in vogue during the same period in the USA. A hostile takeover stripped the family of its historical assets in real estate but provided additional capital, and most importantly it motivated the fifth generation to develop the family's investment approach into a modern private-equity company. InvestIndustrial invests in a wide range of industries and involves dozens of professionals; it openly emphasizes that the aim of developing the companies in its portfolio transcends the aim of merely reaping financial returns.

Shared Destines

Notwithstanding the radical differences in their histories, environments and cultures, a very common outcome in the evolution of the entrepreneurial multi-business families analyzed in this chapter is that sooner or later they create more or less sophisticated investment holding companies. These are actively committed to being a stable presence in the companies they invest in, providing capital but providing above all the competences, expertise, and resources essential for the promotion of corporate development and efficiency (Sieger & Zellweger, 2012; Calabrò et al., 2017). Almost all the cases mentioned above have evolved – or are now evolving – in this direction. Some develop into corporate structures similar to integrated business groups with a very strong corporate identity that is transversal to all the units included in the group itself. This is for instance the case of the German family holding, Heraeus, which is an unrelated diversifier in high-tech industries and holds controlling stakes in dozens of companies; these are grouped into eleven business units and have all been "re-branded" with the prefix "Heraeus". Some of these investment holdings act as "pure" investment holdings, committing the family's resources to the acquisition of long-term shareholding, as in the case of the Haniel and Wendel families (proudly defining them-selves *investisseurs de long terme* on their websites). Ybarra Careaga's Onchena and Benettons' Edizione are also very good examples in this sense, since they hold control-ling shares in companies and take an active approach, instead of simply seeking finan-cial returns as in the case of a standard family office. The websites of the Norwegian Andresen family's Ferd, the Dutch SHV, and the Swedish Kinnevik all openly empha-size a strategy of "value creation" through long-term shareholdings.

However, an investment company is just one of the possible legal solutions for managing the unrelated diversification strategy of entrepreneurial multi-business families. One very interesting example is provided by JAB. Named after the founder of the family's original chemical business Johann Adam Benckiser and owned by the co-founding Reimann family, JAB is a conglomerate investment company organized on five investment platforms in different industries and activities. The investment ex-pertise and competence possessed by the corporate offices, however, led to the estab-lishment in 2014 of the JAB Consumer Fund (JCF), an aggregation of investors (institutional investors, foundations, family offices) pooling around €15 billion in-vested in controlling stakes of consumer goods companies around the world, and managed alongside the other JAB investments as a kind of private-equity fund. The Norwegian Ferd established a private-equity fund in 2002 that was rebranded as Herkules Capital in 2008 and legally separated from the main company's activ-ity, which is headed by Ferd owner Johan Andresen (IDCH, 156, pp. 123–128).

The transition towards private equity is indeed another possible outcome, exem-plified by the case history of InvestIndustrial and of the Bonomi family. Even in its "continental European" version, the private-equity approach is of course different from that of an investment company that holds controlling stakes in companies over a long period of time. Based on funds created in order to invest in a portfolio of com-panies, a private-equity company should in principle be mainly oriented towards its funds' financial returns. In the case of InvestIndustrial, this is again combined with a strong orientation towards the industrial efficiency of the portfolio companies, pursued through "our innate entrepreneurial spirit", as the company website de-clares, explicitly referring to its origins in family competence in managing multiple investments in non-related businesses (Hafner, 2021, p. 545). Similarly, the Agnelli family's Exor traces its entrepreneurial competence back to the family's long-term in-dustrial approach: "Our approach to new investments is based on our long experi-ence of building companies". (https://www.exor.com/pages/companies-investments/companies/approach.); and again "As a fifth-generation family-led business, we have shown we are builders not traders. (https://www.exor.com/pages/companies-invest ments/investments/seeds). The Swedish Axel Johnson group openly emphasizes that its main asset is the capability of managing a set of very different activities:

> The Axel Johnson AB group has changed share over its more than 140-year history. No one knows exactly what the group will look like in the future. With our shared culture and basic values, we within Axel Johnson will continue to build, transform, and develop profitable businesses. And we will continue to believe in the family company as a form of ownership for good, long-term business (https://www.axinter.com/who-we-are/)

This is even more explicitly declared by Haniel on its company website:

> As a family-equity company, Haniel is building a portfolio with market-leading companies. The rule is: We combine the professionalism of a private equity investor with the understanding of the values of a family business (https://www.haniel.de/en/company/).

Whatever the corporate form (holding of participations, holding of investments, family office, or private equity or even venture capital – Ljungqvist & Boers, 2017; Sieger & Zellweger, 2012), in all cases entrepreneurial multi-business families rely on the contribution of professionals and managers to run their multiple investments. The cases analyzed in this paper provide mixed but consistent evidence of a progressive detachment of the families from executive roles, even if there are some cases of family members still to be found in top executive roles. Quite understandably, and with very few exceptions, the direct involvement of family members is inversely proportional to the "age" of the company in terms of generations. The fourth-fifth generation is normally the "turning point" that marks the final detachment of the family from direct management of business activity through dual governance structures. For instance, this has been the case of both the Haniel family, composed of over 700 shareholders, which limits its presence to four representatives on the company's supervisory board, and of the Wendel family, which has over a thousand shareholders grouped into Wendel Participations SA., the main shareholder in the Wendel Group, which nominates six members of the supervisory board. At JAB, no family members are directly involved in management of the holding. Since 2014, the Dutch investment holding SHV has been managed exclusively by professionals, while the Benetton family's Edizione holding company has been managed since the early 1990s by a small team of professionals not belonging to the family, with just one of the four original founding siblings, Gilberto, in the (very much honorary) role of Chairman of the Board. The Dutch Brenninkmeijer family, now entering the sixth generation, has taken a different approach. Out of over 60 descendants, only a few are selected after a rigorous period of apprenticeship to join the Board of Directors of COFRA Holding, which is in any case managed by a CEO not belonging to the family. Just one member of the Finnish Hartwall family sits on the Board of Hartwall Capital. A slightly different case is that of InvestIndustrial, headed by Andrea Bonomi, who is supported by a dozen other partners. Different again is the case of Exor, where the Agnelli family is still very present, with four family members of the board, of which three are non-executive and one executive (John Elkann, who is also the main shareholder of Giovanni Agnelli BV, the family holding that ultimately controls Exor) in the position of Chairman and CEO. The presence of professional teams is also an important prerequisite for the "standing" of these investment companies, which enables them to attract a range of other investors of a different nature. The JAB Consumer Fund mentioned above is a very interesting case: in addition to JAB Holding, other participants in the fund, which in 2019 had a capital under management of around $16 billion, are university endowments, other wealthy families through their family offices, and sovereign wealth funds.

Conclusions: Entrepreneurial Multi-Business Families as a Model?

Privately family-owned and controlled investment holdings and companies of all sizes and dimension are plentiful today in continental Europe. Most show a remarkable level of diversification into non-related businesses and a remarkable ability in the management of conglomerate structures, not only on the basis of pure financial indicators but with an openly stated willingness to be active investors, able to influence the management and the overall performances of the companies they control.

The stories analyzed in this chapter display a number of analogies, but also appreciable differences. Evidence available from research does not allow the identification of clear and homogeneous patterns beyond those described in the first part of the paper, particularly in Figure 12.1. Entrepreneurial multi-business families are, however, a quite idiosyncratic version of family entrepreneurship; their approach is radically different from that of families that remain in the same business across generations with little or no deviation from their established pattern of activity. They are also different from those families that opt for wealth management practices through the establishment of a family office in charge of managing and investing the family wealth, diversifying risk, and granting a decent return on capital invested in multiple financial products. Entrepreneurial multi-business families have as a common characteristic the intention to invest their own resources (and those entrusted by other investors on the basis of mutual trust) in acquiring significant stakes in other companies with the purpose of being "active" investors. They are authoritative and trustworthy due to their multi-generational entrepreneurial competence and their teams of skilled professionals, and they have various means of influencing the decisions and practices of corporate management concerning the adoption of value-enhancing practice, for instance, ESG.

Another important trend that is still to be investigated is the impact on the leadership structure. The most successful cases (in terms not only of financial performance, but also of longevity and enduring family leadership) present at least two shared patterns of behaviour. The first is an accurate selection of the family members responsible for investment company strategy. Generation after generation, family members provide not only an increasing quantity of adequate human resources, but are also endowed with a much higher level of formal education than that of the previous generations. Formal education is not only relevant in "technical" terms – that is, for the practicalities of the business itself – but is also functional to the second pattern of behaviour. Family members who are directly involved in managing investment understand very well that the complexity of active multi-investment strategies that are not purely financially driven requires the top-level involvement and collaboration of professional figures, who are normally elevated to the rank of partners (not simply salaried managers). This has a strong impact on the nature of leadership, but also on the way the family perceives its formal involvement in company activity (Hafner, 2021, p. 543; Muñoz-Bullon et al., 2018). The outcome of this is an extremely delicate balance between the impact of family history and values on controlled companies and partners, and the autonomy of skilled professionals, who ensure high performance standards and a good international reputation.

References

Amatori, F. (Ed.). (2017). *100 anni della Rinascente*. Milano: Egea.

Arrègle, J., Hitt, M. A., Sirmon, D. G., & Very, P. (2007). The development of organizational social capital: Attributes of family firms, *Journal of Management Studies*, 44(1), 73–95.

Basco, R., Calabrò, A., & Campopiano, G. (2019). Transgenerational entrepreneurship around the world: Implications for family business research and practice, *Journal of Family Business Strategy*, 10(4), 100249.

Berghoff, H., & Köhler, I. (2021). *Varieties of Family Business. Germany and the United States, Past and Present*. Frankfurt/New York: Campus Verlag.

Bierl, P., & Kammerlander, N. (2019). Family equity as a transgenerational mechanism for entrepreneurial families. *Journal of Family Business Management*. DOI: 10.1108/JFBM-09-2018-0043

Calabrò, A., Campopiano, G., Basco, R., & Pukal, T. (2017). Governance structure and internationalization of family-controlled firms: The mediating role of international entrepreneurial orientation. *European Management Journal*, 35(2), 238–248.

Carney, M., & Dieleman, M. (2008). Heroes and Villains. "Ethnic Chinese Family Business in Southeast Asia", in Phillip H. Phan and John E. Butler (Eds.). *Theoretical Developments and Future Research in Family Business*. Charlotte, NC: Information Age Publisher, pp. 49–76.

Castronovo, V. (1999). *Fiat 1899–1999. Un secolo di storia italiana*. Milano: Rizzoli.

Colli, A. (2017). *Edizione. The History of the Benetton Holding Company, 1986-present*. London: Profile Books.

Colli, A. (2018). A theory of emotions and sentiments in family firms: A role for history. *Entreprise et Histoire*, 91(2), 126–137.

Colpan, A., Hikino, T., & Lincoln, J. R. (eds). (2012). *The Oxford Handbook of Business Groups.* Oxford University Press.

Colpan, A., & Hikino, T. (2018). *Business Groups in the West. Origins, Evolution and Resilience.* Oxford University Press.

Danes, S. M., Stafford, K., Haynes, G., & Amarapurkar, S. S. (2009). Family capital of family firms: Bridging human, social, and financial capital. *Family Business Review*, 22(3), 199–215.

Gomez-Mejia, L. H., Makri, M., & Kintana, M. L. (2010). Diversification decisions in family-controlled firms. *Journal of Management Studies*, 47, 223–252.

Habbershon, T., & Williams, M. L. (1999). A resource-based framework for assessing the strategic advantages of family firms. *Family Business Review*, 12(1), 1–25.

Habbershon, T, Nordqvist, M., & Zellweger, T. M. (2010). Transgenerational entrepreneurship, in Mattias Nordqvist and Thomas M. Zellweger (Eds.). *Transgenerational Entrepreneurship. Exploring Growth and Performance in Family Firms Across Generations*, Ch. 1.

Hafner, C. (2021). Diversification in family firms: A systematic review of product and international diversification strategies. *Review of Managerial Science*, 15, 529–572.

IDCH: *International Directory of Company Histories*, St. James Press, n. Volume.

James, H. (2006). *Family Capitalism. Wendels, Haniels, Falcks, and the Continental European Model.* Cambridge: Belknap Press.

James, A., Hadjielias, E., Guerrero, M., Cruz, A. D., & Basco, R. (2020). Entrepreneurial families in business across generations, contexts and cultures. *Journal of Family Business Management*. DOI:10.1108/JFBM-01-2020-0003

Khanna, T., & Yafeh, Y. (2007) Business groups in emerging markets: Paragons or parasites? *Journal of Economic Literature*, 2, 331–372.

Komulainen, A., & Siltala, S. (2016). How to Build a Business Dynasty: A Comparative Study of the Business Families Ehrnrooth and Wallenberg", conference paper, EBHA, Bergen.

Konig et al., 2013: Andreas König, Nadine Kammerlander and Albrecht Enders, "he family innovator's dilemma: how family influence affects the adoption of discontinuous technologies by incumbent firms. *Academy of Management Review*, 38, 418–441.

Morck. R. (Ed.). (2005). *A History of Corporate Governance Around the World: Family Business Groups to Professional Managers*. Cambridge: NBER Books.

Muñoz-Bullon, F., Sanchez-Bueno, M. J., & Suárez-González, I. (2018). Diversification decisions among family firms: The role of family involvement and generational stage. *Business Research Quarterly*, 21, 39–52.

Nordqvist, M., Sharma, P., & Chirico, F. (2014). Family firm heterogeneity and governance: A configuration approach. *Journal of Small Business Management*, 52, 192–209.

Nordqvist, M., & Melin, L. (2010). Entrepreneurial families and family firms. *Entrepreneurship and Regional Development*, 22(3–4), 211–239.

Jensen-Eriksen, N., Hilpinen, S., & Forsén, A. (2020). Nordic noblemen in business: The Ehrnrooth family and the modernisation of the Finnish economy during t[he] lat[e] 19th century. *Business History*. DOI: 10.1080/00076791.2020.1828868

Lindberg, H. (2012). "The Long-Term Viability of the Wallenberg Family Business Group: The Role of a 'Dynastic Drive'", in Anders Perlinge and Hans Siögren (Eds.). *Biographies in the Financial World*. Hedemora: Gidlunds.

Ljungqvist, T., & Boers, B. (2017). Another hybrid? Family businesses as venture capitalists. *Journal of Family Business Management*, 7(3), 329–350.

Michael-Tsabari, N., Labaki, R., & Zachary, R. K. (2014). Toward the cluster model: The family firm's entrepreneurial behavior over generations. *Family Business Review*, 27(2), 161–185.

Olson, P. D., Zuiker, V. S., Danes, S. M., Stafford, K., Ramona, K. Z. H., & Duncan, K. A. (2003). The impact of the family and the business on family business sustainability. *Journal of Business Venturing*, 18, 639–666.

Salvato, C., Chirico, F., & Sharma, P. (2010). A farewell to the business: Championing exit and continuity in entrepreneurial family firms. *Entrepreneurship and Regional Development*, 22(3–4), 321–348.

Shabir, A., Rosmini, O., & Quoquab, F. (2021). Family firms' sustainable longevity: the role of family involvement in business and innovation capability. *Journal of Family Business Management*, 11(1), 86–106.

Shotter, J. (2016). Germany's intensely private and immensely wealthy Reimann family. *Financial Times*, March 11.

Sieger, P. & Zellweger, T. (2012). *From a Family Enterprise to an Entrepreneurial Family*. Credit Suisse AG.

Sjögren, H. (2018). *Family Dynasties. The Evolution of Global Business in Scandinavia*. London: Routledge.

Step. (2017). STEP, *Understanding Transgenerational Entrepreneurship Practices in European Family Businesses*. Babson College. https://digitalknowledge.babson.edu/sumrep/18

The Economist, April 19. (2001). Flying Dutchman: John Fentener van Vlissingen fled a powerful family dynasty. But he has not been able to escape questions of family ownership and succession.

Zachary, R. K. (2011). The importance of the family system in family business. *Journal of Family Business Management*, 1(1), 26–36.

Zehrer, A., & Leiß, G. (2019). Family entrepreneurial resilience – An intergenerational learning approach. *Journal of Family Business Management*. https://doi.org/10.1108/JFBM-09-2018-0037

Zellweger, T. M., Nason, R. S., & Nordqvist, M. (2012). From longevity of firms to transgenerational entrepreneurship of families: Introducing family entrepreneurial orientation. *Family Business Review*, 25(2), 136–155.

Part III: **Governing the Business Family**

Rania Labaki and Neus Feliu

13 Introducing "Top Governance Teams": Towards an Extension of the Family Business Cluster Model

Abstract: The nexus of governance and ownership has received limited attention in the family business literature, particularly in relation to the Family Business Cluster (FBC) Model. We extend the exploration of the FBC Model by opening its governance "black box" with a focus on the owning family. Integrating the Agency, Stewardship and Upper Echelon theoretical perspectives, we organize the fragmented research on the nature of agency problems in FBCs and the mechanisms to address them from a team perspective. Based on an exploratory study of two FBCs cases, we introduce the terminology "Ownership – Top Governance Team" (O-TGT) and propose a conceptual model on the underlying conditions for its effective collaboration and contribution. From a design and purpose perspective, we suggest that the O-TGT is a hybrid team, composed formally and/or informally by family owners and non-family members, committed to the sustainability of the FBC ownership system as its complexity increases over time. The O-TGT can contribute to preventing or managing the FBC agency problems, such as ensuring an alignment of interests (financial wealth and SEW) among the FBC owners. Effective collaboration among the O-TGT members likely requires common motivations in relation with identification and emotional attachment to the FBC, the development and the use of specific competencies (governance, ambidexterity, and emotion management), and a process based on shared effort norms, cohesion, and cross-functional coordination (at the governance, ownership, and family levels). The limitations of this chapter open avenues for new research directions on O-TGTs in FBCs.

Keywords: agency relations, collaboration, Family Business Cluster Model, family business, Latin America, Ownership Governance, Socio-Emotional Wealth (SEW), Top Management Team (TMT)

Introduction

Ever since the emblematic *"Agency problems in large family business groups"* by Morck and Yeung (2003), research on governance has proliferated in the family business field (Gersick & Feliu, 2014; Suess-Reyes, 2017). According to the classical Three-Circle

Rania Labaki, EDHEC Business School
Neus Feliu, Lansberg·Gersick & Advisors

https://doi.org/10.1515/9783110727968-013

Model, family businesses are composed of three interacting systems – the business, the family, and the ownership (Tagiuri & Davis, 1996). To the extent of the lack of separation between their management and ownership, family businesses are typically viewed as organizations with low or zero agency cost (Ang, Cole, & Lin, 2000; Dalton & Daily, 1992). However, their evolution changes the agency equation. Over time, the business tends to grow beyond the core entity and to expand through the creation, the merger and acquisition, or the spin-off of several businesses (Zellweger, Nason, & Nordqvist, 2012). The family tends also to span several generations and increase in membership while the ownership tends to move from "founder-owned businesses" to "siblings partnerships" and to "cousin consortiums" (Gersick, Davis, McCollom Hampton, & Lansberg, 1997). As a result, the family gradually controls more than one business, reaching an average of 6.1 firms according to the study of Zellweger, Nason, and Nordqvist (2012), and has to manage a much more complicated portfolio of assets (Michael-Tsabari, Labaki, & Zachary, 2014). Scholars have coined the concept "Family Business Cluster (FBC) Model" (Michael-Tsabari, Labaki, & Zachary, 2014) to extend the Three-Circle Model and emphasize the increasing complexities and emotional dynamics of families controlling several businesses at once. However, the main research efforts still overlook the specificities of family business groups, including the processes driving and enabling the effectiveness of their governance, albeit a few exceptions (e.g., Carney & Gedajlovic, 2002; Discua Cruz, Howorth, & Hamilton, 2013; Piana, Vecchi, & Jimenez, 2018).

In fact, as the family, management and ownership systems are often interlinked and interdependent, family businesses require special governance (Nordqvist & Melin, 2002). Whereas trust and informal structures stand as the prevailing governance mechanisms in the early stages of family businesses, more formalized structures are initiated in the later stages to deal with the increasing potential for agency costs (Labaki, 2011; Steier, 2001; Van Aaken, Rost, & Seidl, 2017). These costs are due to the emergence of different principal-agent-principal relationships, characterized by conflicts of interest, asymmetry of information, and altruism. Looking into these agency problems, research has highlighted distinct corporate governance and family governance systems in family businesses as compared to other organizations (Gersick & Feliu, 2014; Suess, 2014). Empirical studies did not, however, address in-depth the specificities of FBCs in terms of complexity which is their underlying feature. Overall, researchers have associated corporate and family governance with a series of outcomes relative to financial and socio-emotional wealth (SEW) components (Suess, 2014). On the corporate governance level, they highlighted the characteristics of board governance, in terms of structure, composition, and processes that lead to the board functional performance, and subsequent performance on the organizational level (Federo, Ponomareva, Aguilera, Saz-Carranza, & Losada, 2020). On the family governance level, they focused on the typology of mechanisms, in terms of structures, agreements, and processes, that lead to family cohesion and harmony (Mustakallio, Autio, & Zahra, 2002), and subsequently influence corporate governance, organizational outcomes, and strategies (Suess, 2014). Governance at the ownership level (Gersick & Feliu, 2014) has not received sufficient attention as it was mainly included as part of the family governance. This gap is surprising as ownership issues are particularly relevant in FBCs where more diverse agency relations emerge (Zellweger & Kammerlander, 2015) because of the weakening of the emotional attachment to the business(es) and the increasing divergence of interests among different types of owners (Labaki, 2007, 2011; Michael-Tsabari, Labaki, & Zachary, 2014). Including ownership governance in the analysis has the potential, therefore, to offer a complementary and broader understanding of FBC governance.

In line with these considerations, we engage in the exploration of ownership governance by focusing on the team driving it. While a significant stream of research has studied how management teams thrive in the accomplishment of their tasks and impact organizational outcomes (Cannella, Finkelstein, & Hambrick, 2008), there is a lack of studies that delve into teams at the ownership governance level, in family businesses in particular. Our object of study is the top team leading the ownership governance of the Family Business Cluster Model, representing the existing portfolio of businesses controlled by an enterprising family (Michael-Tsabari, Labaki, & Zachary, 2014).

First, we bridge the theoretical focus of the family business governance research on Agency and Stewardship with the Top Management Teams (TMT) research on the Upper Echelon Theory. We extend the exploration of the FBC Model by opening the governance "black box" with a focus on "the owning family". Second, we build on vignettes of two FBCs to introduce and illustrate the novel concept of Ownership Top Governance Team (O-TGT). This top governance team, including family and/or non-family members, tends to operate at the highest level of the family control while being interlinked with other governance and/or management teams of the existing businesses. Our premise is that by exploring the ownership top governance team, in terms of purpose, design, process, characteristics, and contribution, we set the stage for a more exhaustive picture of effective family business governance at the intersection of the family, business, and ownership in FBCs. Based on the insights from these family business cases and the organization of the fragmented arguments and findings from prior research, we provide an initial examination and conceptualization of the O-TGTs, we distill what is unique about these teams, which tasks effectively establish their decision-making for the management of the FBC affairs, their dynamics, and their outcomes in the FBC. We derive a series of propositions from our analysis and suggest a research agenda on O-TGT towards further developments.

Theoretical Background and Literature Review: The Nexus of Governance and Ownership in the Family Business Cluster (FBC) Model

The Nature of Agency Dynamics in the Family Business Cluster

Agency Theory stems from the likelihood of asymmetric information and misalignment of interests between principal (e.g., owner) and agent (e.g., manager) in organizations characterized by a separation between management and ownership (Jensen & Meckling, 1976). By setting up corporate governance bodies, mechanisms and processes, these organizations monitor, incentivize, and make the agent accountable for actions in line with the principal's interests, thereby reducing agency risks. In family businesses, the agent and the principal are often family members whose roles overlap, although to different degrees, which reduces the likelihood of agency sources or makes them almost non-existent (Ang, Cole, & Lin, 2000; Dalton & Daily, 1992). Stewardship behaviours tend also to prevail in these businesses, in reference to Stewardship Theory (Davis, Schoorman, & Donaldson, 1997), with family business managers acting as stewards of the business rather than engaging with opportunistic behaviour (Miller & Breton-Miller, 2006).

Still, research has shown that agency sources exist in family businesses albeit with other nuances. First, family businesses tend to develop more diverse forms of agency conflicts along their life cycle. As families tend to control more than one business over time (Zellweger, Nason, & Nordqvist, 2012), eventually the business expands into a cluster model of businesses (Michael-Tsabari, Labaki, & Zachary, 2014), leading to the emergence or proliferation of agency problems. Research on business groups in general suggests that group diversification leads to simultaneous and dual agency problems between controlling and minority shareholders (principal–principal) and shareholders and managers (principal–agent) in affiliated firms (Purkayastha, Pattnaik, & Pathak, 2021). The principal–principal conflict can be explained by the predominant effect of control rights over ownership rights leading controlling owners to divert firm resources for personal uses (Morck & Yeung, 2003) or expropriate value from minority shareholders (Shleifer & Vishny, 1997). The principal-agent conflict can emerge given the greater difficulty or impossibility for controlling owners to predict and observe the opportunistic behaviour of the affiliate managers of diversified business groups, as their attention is concentrated in the flagship businesses in the group (Purkayastha, Pattnaik, & Pathak, 2021). In addition, corporate diversification that is common in business groups can be fostered by managers who operate opportunistically in the interest of deriving private benefits such as power, prestige, and compensation to the detriment of shareholders (Jensen, 1986), leading to Agency Type I. It can be also fostered by controlling shareholders acting opportunistically to diversify their risk at the cost of minority shareholders, leading to Agency Type II, which negatively affects firm value (Young, Peng, Ahlstrom, Bruton, & Jiang, 2008) although to a lesser extent in the case of controlling family business groups (Villalonga & Amit, 2006).

In the family business cluster, the principal – agent conflicts are conflicts between family or non-family manager(s) and family owner(s) (Agency Type I) and the principal-principal agency conflicts are conflicts among majority family owners and minority family or non-family owners as well as variations within (agency problem type II). In their study, Villalonga and Amit (2006) distinguish three family business categories by exclusively considering the Agency Type II in the presence of non-family minority owners. (1) Family businesses with Agency problem II and without Agency problem I are those who have control-enhancing mechanisms (dual-share classes, pyramids, crossholdings, or voting agreements) and a family CEO; (2) Family businesses with Agency problems I and II are those who have control-enhancing mechanisms but no family CEO; (3) Family businesses with no Agency problems are those who have a family CEO but no control-enhancing mechanisms.

Agency problems in the FBC can, however, also occur in family principal-principal relations. Due to different strategic preferences, goals, and identities, family owners can be subject to Agency conflicts Type II, such as in relation to growth expectations (Calabrò, Campopiano, & Basco, 2017). The attention of family owners can vary depending on their level of identification to the core business in comparison with the other businesses within the cluster (Ramachandran, Manikandan, & Pant, 2013), as well as on their managerial role in the different businesses. This might create discrepancies in resource allocation to and across businesses and divergence of alignment in terms of interests (Agency Type II). Second, an additional type of agency source has been specifically identified in family businesses, that is, asymmetric altruism (Schulze, Lubatkin, & Dino, 2003). According to Lubatkin, Schulze, Ling, and Dino (2005), the influence of altruism changes as the ownership evolves along the family business life cycle model, from the "controlling owner" (a single individual, usually the founder and household head) to the siblings ("sibling partnership"), and from the siblings to the extended family ("cousins consortium") (Gersick, Davis, McCollom Hampton, & Lansberg, 1997). Particularly, parental altruism influences the ability of the family owner-manager to exercise self-control and might not be reciprocated by the next generation members of the family. This can increase the risk of Agency Type I at the controlling and siblings' ownership stage, to which Agency Type II is added at the cousin consortium stage (Labaki, 2008; Lubatkin, Schulze, Ling, & Dino, 2005).

The ownership structure stands therefore as an important determinant of the likelihood of agency problems and requires appropriate governance systems to address them. In light of the evolving and additional types of agency conflicts, we adopt the definition of governance as "the means of stewarding the multi-generational family organization . . . [as it] establishes the processes whereby strategic goals are set, key relationships are maintained, the health of the family is safeguarded, accountability is maintained, and achievement and performance are recognized" (Goldbart & DiFuria, 2009, p. 7).

Ownership Governance: The Overlooked Dimension of the FBC Ownership System

Business ownership can endorse different meanings depending on the theories and disciplines that define it. Looking at theories in economics and finance,[1] ownership is viewed as "a tool that, when deployed correctly, aligns incentives among parties and leads to high economic value creation" (Foss, Klein, Lien, Zellweger, & Zenger, 2021, p. 306).[2] In their essay "Developing a Theory of the Firm for the 21st Century", Alvarez, Zander, Barney, and Afuah (2020) acknowledge, however, that this view is evolving and suggest a revision towards a contemporary meaning of business ownership that matches the current environment. They particularly emphasize the "money with attitude" ownership, and refer to "active", "situated", "ethical", or "responsible" ownership that entails not just exercising faceless on-paper-only controlling from afar but exercising responsibility beyond the economic considerations and in line with sustainability issues.

This is particularly relevant in family businesses, where the ownership goals can extend the creation and perpetuation of the classical financial wealth towards socioemotional wealth (Gomez-Mejia, Haynes, Nunez-Nickel, Jacobson, & Moyano-Fuentes, 2007). Family businesses are not, however, static neither homogeneous, but evolve over time along with their goals which may vary among family owners (Labaki & Hirigoyen, 2020). Several definitional and operationalization efforts of ownership have been made in the literature. According to Daspit, Chrisman, Sharma, Pearson, and Mahto (2018), the ownership of family businesses can vary along six dimensions at least, which often interact, including (i) the number of families or family members involved in ownership; (ii) the proportion of family ownership; (iii) the dispersion of ownership among families or family members; (iv) the relationships that exist among owners; (v) the demographic characteristics of owners; and (vi) the nature of involvement of owners in governance bodies such as the board of directors, advisory board, family council, and family office.

These governance bodies are not restricted to the business and the family though (Gersick & Feliu, 2014). In the business system, governance serves the operating companies. In a FBC, each operating entity has its own governance system that supports and oversees managerial leadership and performance, in line with

---

1 Agency, Incomplete Contracting, and Property Rights Theories.

2 As a comprehensive review of the "ownership" concept in the fields of management, finance, and economics is beyond the scope of this chapter, we invite the reader to refer to Foss, Klein, Lien, Zellweger, and Zenger (2021).

the overall objectives of the owners (Gersick & Feliu, 2014). In the family system, governance attends to the demands and rewards of the family, who shares a psychological and emotional sense of ownership in relation to the FBC (Gersick & Feliu, 2014). In the ownership system, the role of governance is to care for the actual owners, protecting both the security of the asset base and the return on those assets. Whereas this role is often carried out by a board of directors, it can also be assigned to other forums, such as partners, trustees, the sole owners, or a group of owners who are representative of shareholders (Gersick & Feliu, 2014).

Scarce research exists in the family business at the nexus of ownership and governance. Going back to the standard ownership concepts and theories, Foss, Klein, Lien, Zellweger, and Zenger (2021) observe that they focus on incentive effects and do not convey an exhaustive picture of ownership. In an effort to fill the gap, they introduce the multidimensional concept of "ownership competence" (what, how, and when to own) which they define as the skills with which asset owners exercise matching, governance, and timing competence. They suggest that this concept captures the means through which ownership can be instrumentalized, towards matching judgment about resource use and governance with the evolving environment of the business and subsequently creating value. The authors seem to make a distinction between ownership and governance, by first considering that "ownership is fundamental to governance", then by presenting "governance competence" as one of the dimensions of "ownership competence" (how to own). We take this argument further by suggesting that looking at the nexus of ownership and governance, through the ownership governance, requires a close-up examination of the team, which is formally or informally in charge of ownership governance.

Governance Teams at the Heart of the Mechanisms that Address Agency Dynamics

Research on business groups, viewed as a network of independent companies held together by a core owner, suggests that a major factor in their effectiveness is a formal management layer called "the group centre" organized around the office of the group chairperson to oversee the companies (Ramachandran, Manikandan, & Pant, 2013). This mechanism helps smart business groups spot more opportunities and capitalize on them while retaining their identity and values (Ramachandran, Manikandan, & Pant, 2013). Transposing such a configuration to the FBC, we argue that for governance to contribute to preventing or reducing agency problems, it requires a governance team that stands at the top level of the FBC and effectively collaborates across systems. Different from other organizations, the FBCs comprise the family, businesses, and ownership systems. Despite the increasing research on corporate and family governance, the focus remains on the characteristics of effective corporate and family governance in the board of directors and other family governance structures (Suess, 2014) with little attention to the teams operating in the FBC ownership system. Ownership governance can therefore be held by a formal or informal team of individuals (family and non-family members; owners and non-owners) who collaborate on related governance tasks towards ensuring that the FBC ownership goals are achieved. The purpose and the nature of the tasks that the FBC ownership governance team pursues and the extent to which they can differ from those of other top management teams or governance bodies have not been yet explored. This leads us to refer to the initial learnings from the TMT and corporate governance literatures as a reflection basis on the characteristics of effective ownership governance teams in FBCs.

The Upper Echelon perspective (Hambrick & Mason, 1984) stands as the predominant theory in this regard, stating that organizational outcomes are partially predicted by the managerial background characteristics of the top level management team. The executives' experience, values, and personalities greatly influence their interpretations of the situations they face and, in turn, affect their choices (Hambrick & Mason, 1984). While the definition of TMT varies in the TMT literature, Hambrick and Mason (1984) refer to "the dominant coalition" or "the powerful actors in an organization" while Pettigrew (2008, p. 163) refers to the "managerial elites" concept, as "those who occupy formally defined positions of authority, those at the head of, or who could be said to be in strategic positions", including the board of directors, executive committees, or TMTs. The extension of the Upper Echelon Theory to the family business literature by Ensley and Pearson (2005) has built on a comparison of the behavioural dynamics of TMTs in family and non-family new ventures, with a focus on cohesion, conflict, potency, and consensus. The authors found that "the family business creates a unique management situation that results in both advantages and disadvantages to the firm" (Ensley & Pearson, 2005, p. 267). Based on a literature review, D'Allura (2019) suggests specifying the TMT concept by looking at the Family-TMT as a top management team in which the family's influence, in terms of goals, aspirations, and emotions, is taken into consideration and effectively shape strategic and organizational decisions. Family business scholars have overall bridged Upper Echelon Theory with other theories such as Agency Theory, Stewardship Theory, Internationalization theories, Entrepreneurial Orientation, and Social Capital Theory to highlight the impact of TMT features on different organizational outcomes, such as the quality of decision-making (Vandekerkhof, Steijvers, Hendriks, & Voordeckers, 2018), innovation (Röd, 2019), entrepreneurial orientation, performance, and internationalization (Alayo, Maseda, Iturralde, & Arzubiaga, 2019) and task-related and relationships conflicts (Sciascia, Mazzola, & Chirico, 2013). They did not explore, however, the teams at the governance level. As for the literature on corporate governance, including family businesses, it highlights the boards characteristics in terms of structure, composition, and processes, that influence the board functional performance, and subsequent performance on the organizational level (Federo, Ponomareva, Aguilera, Saz-Carranza, & Losada, 2020). Considering the lack of research on ownership governance teams in FBCs, we suggest an exploratory study from which we derive a series of propositions.

The "Ownership Top Governance "Team" (O-TGT) Concept: An Exploratory Study

Our study of ownership governance builds on selective case vignettes of two FBCs, leading us to introduce and characterize the concept of Ownership Top Governance Team (O-TGT) concept through a series of propositions, represented in the model in Figure 13.1. These propositions revolve around five salient dimensions of the O-TGT underlying conditions of effective collaboration and contribution: the purpose and the design (i.e., what constitutes an O-TGT and what purpose do the members have in relation with the FBC ownership?); the characteristics (i.e., what motivations and competencies characterize the O-TGT members?); the process (i.e., how does the O-TGT members operate and strive to achieve their purpose in the FBC?); and the contribution (i.e., what are the O-TGT contributions to the FBC)?

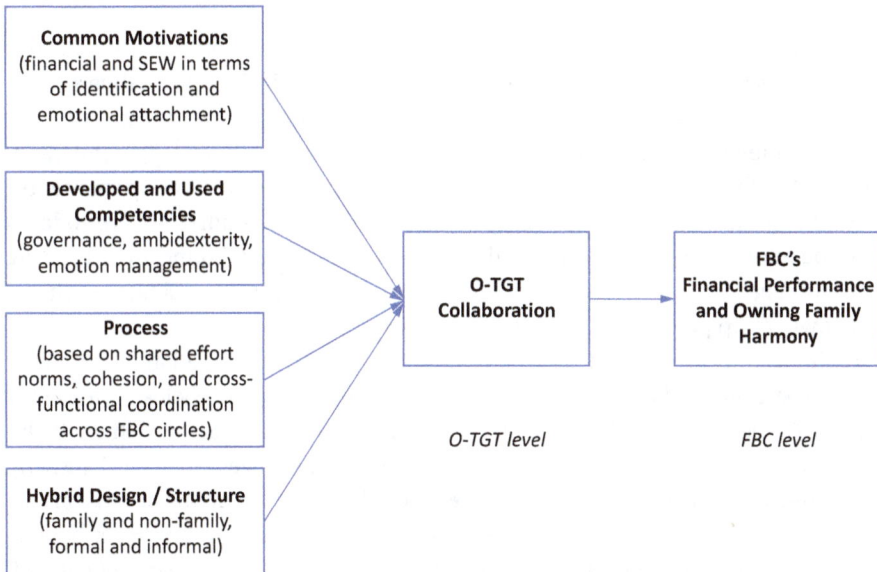

Figure 13.1: Conceptual model of O-TGT.

Case Vignettes Description

As "single case studies are capable of developing and refining generalizable concepts [. . .]" (Pettigrew, 1985, p. 66), we engage in an exploratory study that builds on two single cases of FBCs. This research strategy allows us to focus on understanding the "dynamics of single settings and to contribute to early theory development efforts (Eisenhardt, 1989), particularly relevant for the study of family business governance (Steier, 2001). Based on qualitative data collected via in-depth interviews with multiple respondents, we developed two case vignettes[3] as an illustration of the ownership governance in FBCs based in Latin America (LATAM). While these two cases are not generalizable, they offer insights into common FBC configurations in the LATAM region, where family businesses are considered as the predominant mode of business groups' ownership (La Porta, Lopez-de-Silanes, & Shleifer, 1999; Morck & Yeung, 2003).

Vignette 1: Rodriguez Family Business Cluster

Founded in 1919 as a department store in a LATAM country, the family business grew into six departments stores and shopping centres with a presence in all Central American countries. Parallel to the business expansion, four family members of the third generation (among 18 members distributed in five branches) lead four other businesses in retail, real state, manufacturing, with the aim to diversify by geography and industry. The rationale behind was to mitigate risks (country risk), increase value creation for growing ownership, and harness knowledge and capabilities of family owners, as "necessity is one of the basic motives of entrepreneurs" according to the family CEO of one of the businesses. The Rodriguez are today a family business group, with a portfolio of businesses legally bound by a Holding Company. Figure 13.2 represents the Rodriguez Family Business Cluster with the family ownership percentage in the different businesses.

Each business has its own governance and is led by third-generation family CEOs, who have been successful entrepreneurs and leaders, increasing shareholders' value over the years. As the four family CEOs approached their retirement age (as stated in the Rodriguez's Shareholders Agreement), traditional succession challenges emerged (Lansberg, 1988) as well a realization that businesses were heavily dependent on them. Tensions between autonomy, alignment, and integration of the businesses with the cluster became more and more evident and challenging to navigate. "*Our cousins have made of the businesses they manage their fiefdoms. They do not understand that they are managing our*

---

3 For confidentiality reasons, the names of the families and family businesses as well as their location have been disguised. Given the limited space allocation and the exploratory nature of the study, we choose the vignettes presentations as illustrative cases in line with other works in the family business field (e.g., Labaki, Michael-Tsabari, & Zachary, 2013; Sharma, 2004; Steier, 2001).

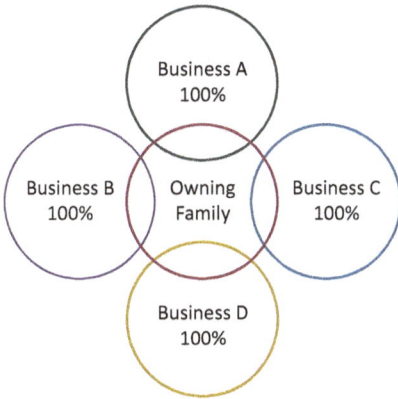

Figure 13.2: The Rodriguez family business cluster.

capital and that we, owners, have a voice", according to a third-generation owner. As ownership passed on to the fourth generation, the complexity of the family remarkably increased with more than a hundred shareholders. The dispersion of ownership was echoed by a dispersion of the shareholders' backgrounds, interests, values, expectations and capacities, and a need to reconcile them as explained by the Chair of the Family Council: *"We need a group of people who represent all shareholders and align their interests and expectations, so that we can have one sole ownership vision and same business standards as a group."* The board of the holding, with a majority of family directors (eight family directors and three independent directors), took this ownership role. It became a strategic architect with the responsibility of setting the expectations of the owners regarding critical variables, such as the level of growth, risk, liquidity, debt of the business group, and the monitoring of their compliance. In addition, it aims to inject into the business group the values, purpose, and family's vision of the FBC. This holding board, including family directors, acts as the Rodriguez's Top Governance Team.

Vignette 2: Richardson Family Business Cluster

The Richardson's family business group started as a bank in a Latin American country and expanded over just one generation into a multi-national and multi-industry portfolio of businesses. Its main industries are banking (A), hospitality (B), pharmaceutical (C), and supermarkets (D). The controlling owner is a visionary entrepreneur and a leader who has managed to develop a good team of executives, loyal to his vision, and with strong managerial capacities. Figure 13.3 illustrates the Richardson Family Business Cluster with the family ownership percentage in the different businesses.

The complexity of the different businesses, the dependency of the business group on the founder, and the growing needs of his five children, mostly shareholders with a non-executive role, with different backgrounds and expertise, became crucial challenges for the family business group. As a top executive of the pharmaceutical company

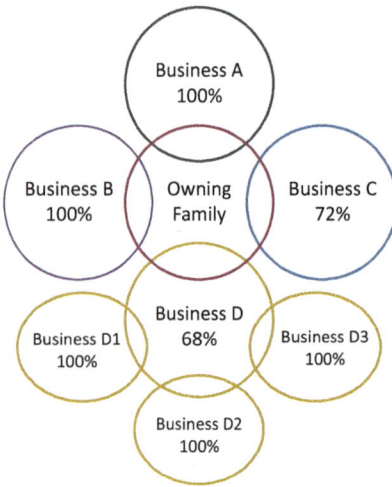

Figure 13.3: The Richardson family business cluster.

explained: "It was clear that we needed to strengthen the governance so that we reduce the dependency of the group on Mr. Richardson. Besides, we decided to develop governance capacity at the ownership and strategic levels as a way to protect the continuity and dynamism of the group." The "top governance team" was created with the participation of the founder and four of his five children, in addition to two non-family members who are highly trusted former executives of the group. Those external members had also a bridging function between generations and between the family and the group. The "top governance team" was a governance forum that is not supported by any legal vehicle and who had two main roles. On the one hand, it oversees and coordinates the activities of all the companies within the group. On the other hand, it instills the family DNA in key and strategic family business group decision-making. As one of the siblings puts it, *"this team is key for us as owners, particularly because no one among us works in any of the businesses. We want the leading team [the operating board and the management team] of each business to focus on the operations. We, as owners want to be responsible for the decisions that are strategic, protect our investment and reputational capital, and have a long-term impact on the businesses we own."* Another sibling added, *"We are anticipating the ownership challenges that our third generation will face. The increase in the number and dispersion of our owners' group will make this team even more relevant. In the end, when facing difficulties all the operating boards turn to us and ask "what does the (owning) family think?"*

Following the categorization of Daspit, Chrisman, Sharma, Pearson, and Mahto (2018) presented earlier in this chapter, Table 13.1 describes the ownership dimensions of the Rodriguez and the Richardson Family Business Clusters.

As suggested by Chrisman, Chua, Le Breton-Miller, Miller, and Steier (2018), while formal governance mechanisms inside family businesses have unique characteristics, informal governance mechanisms may be equally important, and can profoundly influence

Table 13.1: Ownership Dimensions – The Rodriguez and the Richardson Family Business Clusters.

Ownership Dimensions	The Rodriguez FBC	The Richardson FBC
Number of families or family members involved in ownership	104 shareholders (2G, 3G, and 4G).	7 shareholders, the founder (1G), and 5 of the children (2G).
Proportion of Family Ownership	– The family holds 100% of the group ownership. – Ownership is dispersed among the 104 shareholders. The 18 shareholders of the 3G have already distributed shares to their children, through different legal vehicles (private foundations, trusts and/or *fideicomisos*). – No one family owner (3G) together with her/his 4G own more than the 11% of the equity.	– The family holds 100% of the group ownership, except for two businesses of the cluster that have minority non-family shareholders (the supermarkets and the hospitality businesses). – The founder holds the majority of the equity, which will be distributed equally to the 3G in the future.
Dispersion of ownership among families or family members	– Unequal dispersion of ownership due to demographics and family executives rewarded with convertible stock options.	– In the 1G, the founder has the majority of ownership. – In the 2G, shareholders will have equal ownership.
Relationships that exist among owners	– Intergenerational and family blood ties.	– Intergenerational and family blood ties.
Demographic characteristics of owners	– Gender diversity. – Nationality diversity (mainly US, Latin American country of origin, and other Latin American countries). – Different life stages (adults, mid-lifers, post-mid-lifers and senior-adults (according to Levinson (1986)'s life stages). – Diverse backgrounds with high level education.	– Gender diversity. – Same nationality, except for one sibling that has double nationality (US and country of origin). – Similar life stages (two siblings are mid-lifers with adolescent children at university, and two are adults with small kids (according to Levinson's (1986) life stages)). – Very similar background with high level education.

Table 13.1 (continued)

Ownership Dimensions	The Rodriguez FBC	The Richardson FBC
The Nature of involvement of owners in governance bodies	– In Family and Ownership governance, participation is based on branch representation and the representatives are selected by the branches, based on a defined and agreed profile. – In the Businesses governance, participation is determined by a selection process based on merits and business-related expertise.	– In Family and Ownership Governance, all 2G participate, with no predetermined profile and/or selection process. – In the Businesses governance, three siblings participate on the operating boards and two of them hold the Chair role.

Note: G = generation (e.g., 1G = First Generation).

the behaviour and performance of family businesses. We present in Table 13.2 the governance system's characteristics of the Rodriguez and the Richardson FBC cases, following the categorization by Gersick and Feliu (2014).

Next, we present a series of propositions with illustrative quotes from each case to conceptualize the O-TGT in FBCs.

Propositions on O-TGT: Purpose, Design, Characteristics, Process, and Contribution

The Richardson and the Rodriguez case vignettes suggest that as family businesses evolve to a family business cluster, their ownership demands also extend to the cluster level. Independent of the legal ownership structure of the cluster, the different businesses are subject to coordinated action and the control of a single owner, a person or a group, that imposes lines of common governance among them (Del Giudice, 2017). Based on the cases, we observed that complexity increases in the FBC not only relative to new operating businesses but also to other entrepreneurial and philanthropic initiatives or to formalizing existing ones. Thus, in the FBC we can find operating businesses, asset-holding companies, family offices, as well as philanthropic foundations which were founded as part of the owners' shared interests. As such, the denomination Family "Business" Cluster can be extended to Family "Enterprises" Cluster (FEC) to include other types of entities that might fall under the control of the family, although it does not have the same

Table 13.2: The Governance System of the Rodriguez and the Richardson Family Business Clusters.

Governance Dimensions	The Rodriguez FBC	The Richardson FBC
Ownership Governance	**O-TGT:** *Line of authority:* – Directly derived from the legal structure of the FBC. *Composition:* – Holding board with legally bound subsidiaries. – Members: Family owners (selected by and representing each of the family branches) and independent directors. – Family CEOs (upon invitation) exerting relevant influence in an informal way. **Shareholder Agreement:** – Regulates owners' issues and governance framework.	**O-TGT:** *Line of authority:* – Derived from the ownership of the FBC. *Composition:* – A governance forum that is not supported by any legal vehicle. – Members: The founder and four of his five children, along with two external members (highly trusted, selected by the founder). **Shareholder Agreement in progress:** – The Owning Family is finalizing a shareholder agreement that will, once approved, be replicated to each of the businesses within the cluster (all shareholders have similar rights, obligations, and arrangements regarding how the businesses should be governed and operated).
Business Governance	**Operating board of directors in each business:** *Composition:* – Members: Family owners and independent directors. – Dual role: CEOs and Chairs. – Board committees (mainly Audit and Nomination and Remuneration committees).	**Operating board of directors in each business:** *Composition:* – Members: One family director who holds the Chair role in each of the boards (except for one business) and independent directors. – Two of the businesses of the cluster have non-family shareholders (minority), the supermarket business and the hospitality one. These shareholders participate as board members in the operating board.

Table 13.2 (continued)

Governance Dimensions	The Rodriguez FBC	The Richardson FBC
		– The hospitality business has three subsidiaries governed by a sole administrator. – Governance committees: Audit, and Finance, and Philanthropy Committees.
Family Governance	– Family Council, with branch representation and with no external members. – Family Protocol that organizes and manages the role of the family in the FBC.	– Family Council, where all siblings and their mother – the founder's spouse – participate. – There is no family protocol or constitution.
Philanthropy Governance	– Board of the Family Foundation with only family participation.	– Two family foundations, each of which has its own board, with family and non-family directors, and is led by one of the sisters, as a chairperson.
Relationship between the structures	*Formal:* – The Chairman of the Holding Board/O-TGT is the channel of communication with the Boards of Directors of the Businesses, the Family Council and the Board of the Family Foundation. *Informal:* – Informal meetings and conversations between owners involved in different structures and roles. – Pre-agreements of relevant issues within branches.	*Formal:* – Two siblings (2G) are chairpersons of two of the operating businesses. The eldest is Chair of the core and legacy business, the bank, and the sister is Chair of the pharmaceutical group. – Another sister is "director of training" in a third business, following a developmental plan as director and future Chair. – In the businesses where any 2G member are part of the Board, the owning family appoints a trusted person to be either director or chair, in order to keep control and communication open with all businesses. *Informal:* – Informally, the founder and the eldest child – the son – meet regularly with the management and the board of all the businesses.

legal and operational characteristics.[4] There is a value added in the coordination between the different enterprises although the level of coordination and/or alignment can differ greatly depending on the type of enterprise, their business relationships, the economic and geopolitical context, as well as the purpose and the vision of the owners in relation with the cluster.

Both cases highlight the need to address ownership tasks in a systemic approach for all enterprises within the cluster. On the one hand, owners aim to imprint their values, purpose, and vision on the group (and on the entities that are part of it) and to enhance a sense of belonging. This leads to benefiting from the group's assets and resources and to greater cohesiveness among the FBC owners based on psychological factors such as solidarity, long-term vision, and a sense of entrepreneurial tradition. On the other hand, shared ownership leads to different expectations among owners (such as family owners who are employees and/or members of governance structures and those who are not involved); confusion between family and business roles; rivalry among leaders of the different business units; and succession-related challenges, that may jeopardize performance and continuity. To address both the ownership tasks and the ownership challenges that the FBC faces, the Rodriguez Family and the Richardson Family selected a "top ownership governance team" combining formal and informal processes, with the mission to collaborate on ownership governance tasks related to the cluster. Given this, we present our first proposition pertaining to the conceptualization of O-TGT.

The Emergence of O-TGT: Purpose and Design

Proposition 1: *The O-TGT is a hybrid team, composed by family owners and non-family members, that is likely to be formed in informal or formal ways and variations within, in family businesses facing an increasing complexity of their cluster in order to prevent or to address agency challenges at the ownership level.*

Owning families whose business evolves into a cluster of businesses may face challenges in terms of resource allocation and competing needs between businesses within the portfolio and other types of enterprises. In both cases, the financial capital and human capital, required to manage and govern existing enterprises but also to start new entrepreneurial ventures, became scarcer resources as the FBCs were evolving. Additionally, risk was a competing consideration, as the owning family can only assume a certain limited degree of risk at the cluster level, having to expand its risk ceiling among the businesses that comprise it. The Rodriguez family has been successful in developing a culture that supports entrepreneurship at the operating

---

4 An in-depth exploration of the nuances between the different identified entities comprising the FEC is, however, beyond the scope of this chapter, which focuses on the FBC.

business level while retaining the long-term and strategic decisions at the cluster level. This approach has allowed each business within the cluster to promote the attitudes and practices that have made the business innovative, proactive and able to exploit the opportunities it has encountered or generated (Miller, 1983; Sirmon & Hitt, 2003). As each business has required different leadership styles, cash flow needs, and knowledge, the O-TGT has played a critical role. On the one hand, it has facilitated business access to highly diverse resources (such as networks, business opportunities, synergies between businesses and shared expert knowledge and talent). On the other hand, it has provided direction to the businesses so that resources and risk are distributed based on the owners' vision and aligned concerns for the cluster. Through its role, the O-TGT has enhanced the cluster's access to a highly diverse pool of resources, the owners' cohesion (preventing different interests from generating conflict between the family CEOs of each business), and long-term commitment to the group.

The Rodriguez O-TGT is accountable to the cluster's core owners and thus strives to find a balance between empowering businesses to develop their operations, according to their own expertise and leadership style, and maintaining the owners' values and vision for the cluster. The Richardson O-TGT aims to share responsibility for the leadership of the businesses within the cluster as the transition between the founder and the second generation evolves. *"No one can succeed our father as leader. He has been a visionary, but also an executive leader. The complexity of the group today, and the complexity of each of the businesses that we own, requires a diverse group of people, with [the owners] authority, who offer a clear mandate to each of the operating board of directors, so that they can pass it on to their executive teams. If we fail to do this, we will not make a successful transition"*, stated the eldest son of the Richardson family. The Richardson's O-TGT distilled the decisions that the founder made at the time, and the issues he used to address. The O-TGT ensured that by design they had, as a team, the appropriate capabilities and roles so that they could, collectively, deal with them. They progressively reduced dependence on the founder and generated trust in the cluster and its other governance structures. Each member of the team participated in one of the operating boards of the businesses, entrepreneurial initiatives and/or foundations, so that they could understand the knowledge, expertise, and experience that they (as a governance team) should have to add value to the different entities. As for the Foundations, even though they do not have a legal ownership relationship (as foundations do not have owners), the members of the O-TGT represent the owners who provide the funds to the foundations, directly or through the companies and entities of the cluster, as well as influence the definition of the vision, management, and governance model. The siblings wanted to prevent the legal independence and industry specialization of each of the cluster ventures which could set off centrifugal forces reducing the cluster to little more than a portfolio of stocks, with no emotional value and attachment to them as owners.

Given this, O-TGTs emerge in FBCs with an increasing potential for agency problems type I related to the evolving needs, resource allocation, and risk-taking considerations.

P1.1: *The O-TGT is likely to be formed in family businesses facing an increasing complexity of their cluster in terms of competing entrepreneurial needs, resource allocation discrepancies, and risk-taking divergence between owners and enterprises.*

As the ownership circle evolves from controlling owner, to sibling partnership, then to cousin consortium (Gersick, Davis, McCollom Hampton, & Lansberg, 1997) and advanced cousin consortium, the owners tend to increasingly diverge in terms of financial interests (Labaki, 2011), need for family control and influence as well as identification and emotional attachment to the cluster and to the businesses within the cluster differ (Michael-Tsabari, Labaki, & Zachary, 2014). Members of the Rodriguez Family agree that *"we are a 'retail family' and this is where our heart is. In the rest of the businesses we own, we are investors, therefore our patience with poor performance, our flexibility and our long-term commitment to them are more limited."* In addition, as ownership dipersed in both the Rodriguez and Richardson cases, the financial needs diverged between owners who have an executive or a governance role in the cluster and receive compensation, and those who don't. This affected the extent of SEW which typically requires alignment of the rising generation on a shared vision that incorporates their aspirations for the family business cluster. According to one of the Richardson's siblings, *"as family members' interests differ, it will be more difficult to transmit our father's entrepreneurial spirit and "his/our way of doing business" across family members, board members and executives".* For one of the third generation CEO of the Rodriguez FBC, *"when the business was passed on to us [cousins in the third generation], we realized that we needed to have a team with formalized processes at the owner's level, who could collaborate, make decisions based on alignment of opinions, and set the tone for the businesses within the portfolio".* In a similar line, the Rodriguez O-TG stated *"one of our tasks is to preserve the family bonds among branches and individuals. We are a representative group of the owning family, our collaboration fosters collaboration among branches and family members."*

Given this, O-TGTs also emerge in FBCs with an increasing potential for agency problems type II related to divergent interests among family owners.

P1.2: *An O-TGT is likely to be formed in family businesses facing an increasing complexity of their cluster in terms of growing and divergent SEW and financial needs among family owners.*

O-TGT Characteristics

The analysis of the family business clusters allows us to identify two main charac-teristics of the O-TGTs members which seem pivotal in having them successfully collaborate: common motivations and specific competencies.

O-TGT motivations

The O-TGT members display clear and shared motivations that stand as the guiding principles for their behaviours, in alignment with the purpose of the FBC. One of the members of the Richardson O-TGT describes the relationship among team members in the following way: *"we understand the motivations that each of us individually and us, as a team, have and their impact on the dynamics of the team"*. Members of the O-TGT of the Rodriguez agree that *"we are committed and some of us even passionate about the purpose that the owners share and the impact that we [the team] can make to fulfill it"*. *"We act as a control and monitoring centre of the purpose, mission, vision and values of the family enterprise group."* These motivations are connected to the O-TGT identifica-tion with the FBC, which is a relevant dimension of socioemotional wealth that stimu-lates the creation and sustainability of the FBC (Michael-Tsabari, Labaki, & Zachary, 2014). The FBC represents the legacy, the source of pride, and the identity of the best glue for the family to stay connected. One of the members of the third generation of the Rodriguez family described it as follows: *"My father and uncles always worked as a team, first in one store, then in the different businesses that were created. They always had the good of the family and of the employees in mind. Each one had his own area of responsibility, and they respected each other. Even when they disagreed, they always man-aged to reach an agreement for the good of each of them, and for the good of all, which they saw as interrelated. The Rodriguez have grown up like that, it is an important part of the legacy they have left us."* Members of the O-TGT showed transgenerational intentions (Berrone, Cruz, & Gomez-Mejia, 2012) to harvest the sacrifices of past generations, repre-senting another dimension of motivation related to a sense of stewardship of the O-TGT members. *"We are not investors, but owners"*, as one of the Rodriguez third generation cousins stated. This commitment to the team and ultimately to the FBC is a significant asset to pursue and achieve SEW. In addition, the fact that most of the eighteen cousins of the Rodriguez third generation have worked in the businesses with their fathers and have shared family vacations makes them feel very connected with the family, the leg-acy enterprise, and the new businesses. All the cousins have been spectators of the cre-ation of the businesses and of how their four cousins who took the leadership were growing their businesses and adding value to the group. There was a sense of pride to-wards cousins and siblings. For the 3G, they felt their identity, as a family but also as individuals, was very tied to the cluster and to the concept of being "entrepreneurs". However, we have also observed that this identity can be endangered when loyalty and commitment are greater in or exclusively dedicated to a business within the cluster, where a family member is involved as an executive or director or where his/her father or sibling leads that business. In the view of potential multiple identities (one per each business) in the FBC, the O-TGT is motivated to create a robust and meaningful identity of the cluster and maintain the emotional attachment to its different constituents. "*We need to think like one group*", as one director of the Rodriguez O-TGT said.

Given this, we suggest the following proposition.

Proposition 2: *The O-TGT is characterized by common motivations, articulated around shared SEW dimensions of emotional attachment and identification to the FBC.*

O-TGT competencies

In both the Rodriguez and the Richardson FBCs cases, we have identified three areas of competencies that may be key to fulfilling the O-TGT purpose: FBC governance, ambidexterity, and emotional management competencies.

First, the O-TGT team members showed expert and business-related knowledge and experience including corporate and family governance. The transfer of tacit knowledge was highlighted in both cases a key factor. One of the O-TGT members of the Richardson family explained, "*as a second generation, we are gaining and developing knowledge specific to our group, through our own education and experience within and outside the group. We are all in a process of development where we learn directly from our father and his trusted executives, some of whom already retired but have been part of the group expansion.*"

Second, ambidexterity was identified as highly relevant to the O-TGT. One member of The Rodriguez O-TGT stated, "*as the top governance team, we need to be sensible to the impact the decisions we make have on the different constituencies within the cluster, not only on the family and the branches, but also on a specific business or executive team. If we are not able to do so, we won't help the group to work together towards one shared vision.*" On the one hand, ambidexterity allows the team to balance and synthesize polarizing needs of the family, the owners, and the businesses. On the other hand, it enables the team to articulate and disseminate a shared understanding of the whole cluster. This is deemed necessary for nurturing collaborative capacity among the O-TGT members; for encouraging empathetic understanding across the different entities within the cluster; for navigating multiple businesses and organizations environments with potentially contradictory norms; and for gaining the confidence of the FBC owners and managers.

Third, the O-TGT members acknowledged the importance of being aware of the impact of their own emotions on the team dynamics and as consequence, on its performance. One of the siblings of the Richardson family points out that "*at the beginning, it was difficult for them [O-TGT members] to put aside issues that they were facing as siblings, so they needed to put their emotions to rest in order to focus on the task".* We also found that emotional competencies are particularly valuable when the family members of the O-TGT differ in the opinions, skills, and strengths they bring to the table, allowing the team to learn to manage differences and align perspectives. By using and/or developing their emotion management competencies, the O-TGT members managed to handle emotionally charged situations in a constructive way and to contribute with a more balanced rational and emotional approach to the team decision-making. As one member of the Rodriguez O-TGT observed, *"each of us is able to bring her/his skills and strengths to the team. Then, with all the diverse perspectives, we are capable of challenging each other's opinions, and we are learning to give feedback to each other in a constructive way."*

These three competencies, when developed and commonly used among the team members, appear as the aggregate competencies of the O-TGT. Given this, we make the following proposition:

Proposition 3: *The O-TGT is characterized by governance, ambidextrous, and emotion management competencies.*

O-TGT Process

In addition to the importance of shared motivations and competencies within the O-TGT, our interviews with the Rodriguez and Richardson O-TGTs suggest that their collaboration process builds on committing efforts in line with their role, maintaining the cohesion of the team, and acting cross-functionally within the cluster.

Firstly, within Richardson's O-TGT, all members agreed that their commitment to the role was key to working together as a team, based on their knowledge, skills, and abilities as one of them pointed out, *"we all dedicate the required time, effort, and commitment to the team".* Research in family business has already shown evidence of "board" effort norms, representing a group's shared beliefs regarding the level of effort each individual (including outside directors) is expected to show inside the boardroom (Bettinelli, 2011; Wageman, 1995). Our testimonials echo these findings as they also identify the presence of "O-TGT" effort norms as part of the process.

Secondly, team cohesion was identified as necessary for the members to collaborate effectively. Although not sufficiently studied at the board and the TMT levels in family businesses, team cohesion is conceptualized as the bonding within management or governance groups that may be both positive and negative for the family business in as much as they could lead to groupthink (Bettinelli, 2011). One of the family members of the Rodriguez's O-TGT referred to it as follows *"belonging to the family with all the history behind us brings us together and helps us focus on working as a team and carrying out the tasks that our shareholders have entrusted us with. The non-family members of this team, while not yet family, also feel part of this collective project and share our priorities."* As for the Richardson family, the older brother illustrated it as follows: *"We have shared a lot as siblings, at a family level but also at the business family level, wanting to support our father, develop ourselves and contribute to the group of businesses, each one of us with our own possibilities. The non-family members have known and seen us in this developmental process. This has made us very aware of the need to have clear and shared goals as a team, and that getting along well will be key in collaborating."* In our two cases, team cohesion was considered as a positive feature of the collaboration process that the O-TGTs actively strives to maintain.

Thirdly, we realized that the O-TGT in both FBCs works in two directions: upwards, by keeping the values of the owners alive and coordinating education and social initiatives that serve to transfer the values, beliefs, and family identity to the succeeding generation of owners; and downwards, by acting as the custodian of values across the cluster. The O-TGT defines the group systems that will ensure proper communication of the FBC identity and values, embedding them across the businesses so that they can be part of the organizational identity. It strives to reaffirm the cluster identity and manages its alignment with key strategic decisions.

While in both cases cross-functionality is an O-TGT feature that is still in progress and needs to be improved, it appears as an integral part of the O-TGT process. As of today, the appointed non-family members in both O-TGTs contribute to the pool of valuable knowledge resources. They were either former relevant executives in one of the businesses of the cluster or qualified professionals with a particular expertise strategically relevant to the group. The family members in both O-TGTs have participated in the governance of different businesses within the cluster, therefore contributing to the cross-functionality of the design of the team. Cross-functionality can be achieved in both formal and informal ways. Looking at the formal cross-functionality in the Rodriguez Family, the Chair of the O-TGT (Holding Board) meets regularly with the Chairs of the different governance structures within the cluster. In addition, the CEOs of all businesses are invited to present regularly on specific issues to the O-TGT. Another way through which the O-TGT introduces cross-functionally is by having members serve in different teams within the governance forums of the cluster. As interlocking directorates, their presence on different teams can help them in sharing competencies and harmonizing practices among them. Informally, the O-TGT team members regularly meet with the owners, Chairs and directors of the businesses, whether family or non-family, to learn about their perspectives and receive input on the issues they are handling as a team.

Given this, we suggest the following:

Proposition 4: *The O-TGT collaborates based on shared effort norms, cohesion, and cross-functional coordination across FBC circles.*

O-TGT Contribution to the FBC

For teams to function effectively, certain basic elements need to exist in the working conditions, the extent of which increases the chances of a successful team outcome (Farrington, Venter, & Boshoff, 2012). As suggested by our interviews, effectiveness at the team level seems determined by hybrid team members with a common purpose, motivated by high FBC identification and emotional attachment, using and developing competencies relative to an adequate distribution of roles, operating in a cross-functional and cohesive way, and in line with team effort norms. In family business, team effectiveness can be measured by perceived financial performance and family harmony (Farrington, Venter, & Boshoff, 2012), which are also relevant for O-TGT to assess its contribution to the FBC. The O-TGT can have a profound impact on the FBC direction, by aligning the composition of a broad business portfolio with the owners' values. Moreover, it can help the cluster meet simultaneously the economic, business-related goals, and the non-economic, family-centred goals. This influence can be exercised directly on the owners through the O-TGT itself, and indirectly through the influence of the O-TGT on the operating boards of the different entities within the cluster, whether the O-TGT members are board members or not.

In their recent article titled "Collaboration or Clash?", Medina, Ramachandran, and Daspit (2019) explain how internal team dynamics, in particular conflict, have notable effects on the outcome of the team, and consequently on the enterprise. Referencing different studies, they imply that the cross-functional design of a top management team (TMT) creates a pool of valuable knowledge resources potentially beneficial to firm innovativeness and performance, and when shared, lead to better quality decisions. To add value and achieve these goals, the O-TGT guides activities along two parallel dimensions. On the one hand, the team members engage in work on strategic matters and leverage the group capabilities driving financial performance, and, on the other hand, they engage in work on identity driving family harmony. The Rodriguez O-TGT agreed that "*owners feel they are well-represented by the team. We represent the different facets, perspectives, opinions, genders, generations, and roles within our family business group. And they trust us to make ownership decisions. Business managers respect us and accept that we challenge the assumptions they hold.*" One of the siblings who is member of the Richardson's O-TGT of added "*we encourage leaders of the businesses to think strategically and as a group (i.e., shepherding cross-business opportunities and synergies), to think with the ownership vision in mind, and to set their sights higher*". Family members can contribute in a different way to non-family members. They have a deeper understanding of the family values and legacy and, most importantly, an ability to inject their perspective into strategic conversations and decisions typical of governance forums. The O-TGT team members are role models for the rest of the family about how to collaborate and make decisions effectively.

Both the Rodriguez and the Richardson families pointed out the added value that the O-TGT offers to the cluster through leveraging capabilities. In the words of the

Chairman of the Rodriguez O-TGT *"the knowledge that we have in the team at the systemic level of the cluster allows us to suggest practices and policies to the different businesses, that have the potential to create synergies among them. For instance, one of our businesses developed an information system, which proved efficient and was replicated in most of the other businesses of the portfolio. This allowed us to share the cost of investment between businesses, resulting in great savings for us, the final owners. In addition, it opened the possibility for the cluster, in the future, to create new synergies in knowledge and data management practices."* In a similar line, another member of the O-TGT of the Richardson family added, *"One of the roles of the TGT is to identify potential synergies that typically wouldn't be apparent to individual businesses and propose initiatives that foster the exchange of capabilities and ideas"*.

Our observation is that the unique value creation potential of the cluster of businesses, from the owners' perspective, lies in the ability to build and combine internal resources (to the cluster) and external resources under a sole ownership vision, which refers to "dynamic capabilities" (Chirico & Nordqvist, 2010). In the first or second-generation, this task is traditionally handled by the founder who relies on her/ his personal character, or an inner circle of trusted executives, interlocking directorates, and sometimes on informal mechanisms such as family loyalties, informal interactions among leaders and/or directors of the different businesses. However, in later generations, leadership in the cluster is shared among a group of leaders and/or governance structures hindering the effectiveness of the informal coordination methods. In addition, FBCs increasingly aim for clear and professionalized corporate governance standards. The O-TGT contributes to clarifying the lines of authority and accountability of the businesses and their boards to the family owners. As such, the TMTs within each business report to their own board of directors, and the board reports to the O-TGT, as a delegate and representative forum of the core owners. The O-TGT also contributes to the foundations in the same way as it does to the businesses. It provides guidelines in terms of purpose and vision, management and governance criteria, and distribution of resources within the cluster. As the Chairman of the Rodriguez family O-TGT described, *"the mission of the Foundation reflects the social concerns of the owning family, as part of the legacy we received from our father and uncles. A portion of the profits of the companies of the cluster is annually destined to the Foundation. The O-TGT ensures that all businesses meet this commitment, that the Foundation is governed according to legal standards of good governance, and also nominates family directors to serve on its board."*

Given these considerations, we suggest the following proposition.

Proposition 5: *Effective O-TGT collaboration enhances the ability of the FBC to leverage capabilities, which affects outcomes such as the FBC financial performance and the owning family harmony.*

Discussion, Limitations, and Future Directions: Towards a Conceptual Model of O-TGT in FBCs

According to Ramachandran, Manikandan, and Pant (2013), multi-generational business groups are the ones that have been successful in increasing their governance and management capacity to run both the traditional and the new businesses, explore synergies between them, forge strategic plans, and counteract the forces of fragmentation. Looking at family-influenced ownership groups, Habbershon and Pistrui (2002) suggest that the family-as-investor type is committed to wealth creation, pursuing capital allocation strategies and structures that are responsive to the market. This mindset leads family members *"to be stewards of their resources and capabilities and not necessarily of a particular business entity or legacy asset"* (Habbershon & Pistrui, 2002, p. 231), in contrast to owners or managers who act opportunistically and expropriate other owners.

As teams are known for being an essential pillar of effective management, whether permanent or temporary, through their novel combination of members enabling work on new problems and dealing with relevant decisions (Huse & Cummings, 1985), we posit that at the group governance level, family influence also exists and impacts (as it does at the management level) strategic and organizational decisions (D'Allura, 2019). Our propositions suggest that stewardship can be echoed in a TGT at the owners' level, which requires a unified purpose and common motivations in terms of identification and emotional attachment to the FBC. One of the most important challenges of the O-TGT is the potentially different aspirations of autonomous businesses within the cluster. When the FBC expectations are clear and shared among family owners, they facilitate the strategic decision-making at the group level, lending stability, and continuity to the group despite the environment changes, and setting the boundaries within which the individual businesses can articulate their own identities. In FBCs, the additional challenge is to maintain the entrepreneurship orientation and effectiveness in spotting new opportunities and capitalizing on them, while retaining the cluster's values and identity and responding to the needs of a larger family shareholders' group. According to the Family Business Cluster Model, both the business and the (predominant) family challenges are the roots of the entrepreneurial behaviour that allows a family enterprise to become a group of businesses (Michael-Tsabari, Labaki, & Zachary, 2014). The TMT literature suggests that the top management is the "dominant coalition" (Hambrick & Mason, 1984). In FBCs where business and ownership systems are highly differentiated, we suggest that the O-TGT are the "powerful actors" of the cluster, operating within the top ownership structure, formed by a team of members, trusted by and representing the owning family, and which can have different labels, such as "Owners Council", "Holding Board", and "Trustees".

On the practical level, our observations suggest that owners can design their O-TGT by deciding on the profile and the place of their members in the FBC in terms of scope and authority in order to optimize the process of collaboration addressing strategic challenges. As such, they can prevent or deal with agency problems and contribute to the continuity of the FBC.

This article is not exempt from limitations that open avenues for research directions. We have built our propositions on two cases of O-TGTs that were successful in adding value to the ownership governance, and consequently to the FBC's performance and owning family's harmony, albeit facing challenges in implementing and empowering the O-TGT. We also observed that high levels of cohesion characterize the effective O-TGTs whereas the literature is more nuanced regarding the dysfunctional impact of extremely high levels of family owners' cohesion (Jaskiewicz, Combs, Shanine, & Kacmar, 2017; Labaki & Hirigoyen, 2020). We suggest expanding the number of case studies to include cases of dysfunctional O-TGTs, which failed to positively impact the FBC.

Extant research on TMTs emphasizes the influence of TMT interaction processes such as the different types and intensities of team conflicts and the organizational performance. Cognitive and process conflicts tend to have a positive impact at moderate levels and negative impact at high and low levels (Caputo, Marzi, Pellegrini, & Rialti, 2018; Kellermanns & Eddleston, 2004), while relational or affective conflicts tend to have a negative impact whatever their level, such as on team cohesion (Ensley & Pearce, 2001) and effectiveness (De Dreu & Weingart, 2003), decision-making quality (Olson, Parayitam, & Bao, 2007), and family business performance (Eddleston & Kellermanns, 2007). As Medina, Ramachandran, and Daspit (2019) recently observed, there is very little literature examining the outcomes of these types of TMT conflicts; this warrants further investigation on their impact within the O-TGT and on the FBC.

We have explored two FBC cases from Latin America, where according to the literature, FBCs are more common than non-family business groups (Morck & Yeung, 2003), though scarcely researched to date (Botero, Cruz, & Müller, 2018). We have responded to recent calls to overcome the predominant lack of context research in family business (Krueger, Bogers, Labaki, & Basco, 2021), in line with the suggestion by Aguinis, Villamor, Lazzarini, Vassolo, Amorós, and Allen (2020) that the conditions and timing are right to conduct management research in LATAM, including testing predictions of existing theories, such as agency theory (family principal–family agent conflicts). Still, the cultural and institutional nuances in other contexts might offer another perspective, ranging from the design to the contribution of the O-TGTs. Therefore, we suggest exploring the O-TGT concept in other cultural contexts as a future research direction.

Furthermore, the O-TGTs of both our FBC cases are formed by family owners and non-family members whereas other compositions of O-TGTs can offer different insights. Similar to research suggesting the positive role played by outside directors on the family business boards (Bettinelli, 2011), albeit under certain conditions (Uhlaner, Massis, Jorissen, & Du, 2020), the non-family members appeared as positive contributors to the O-TGT. They played the role of facilitators and bridges between generations and/or between family members with different positions and opinions regarding certain issues and decisions that the O-TGT had to address, or when decisions and or discussions were emotionally charged. Given these considerations, we suggest extending the concept of "governance competencies" considered as part of the ownership competencies, according to Foss, Klein, Lien, Zellweger, and Zenger (2021), to the O-TGT members, both family and non-family. We invite future studies to build on the competencies that we have identified and to delve further in them, towards mapping those that the O-TGT should develop at the individual (member) level and at the team level to be able to foster the O-TGT collaboration. Among these competencies, we highlighted the emotion management of the O-TGT. Recently, Labaki and D'Allura (2021) suggested an integrated framework of emotion governance in the family business, viewed as a set of formal and informal mechanisms, which influence the explicit emotion management strategies of family business members and consequently the family business continuity. Exploring how and to what extent the O-TGT can be an integral part of the emotion governance mechanisms of the FBC, leveraging its emotion management competencies and its cross-functionality features, warrants another promising avenue of research.

We also selected typical FBCs controlled by one family whereas FBCs can be also controlled by multi-families, with nuances regarding the agency relationships, as suggested recently by Chrisman, Madison, and Kim (2021). We invite scholars to explore how O-TGTs emerge and how collaboration develops across owning families to deal with agency problems.

Other FBCs can have a diverse composition of minority owners who might also contribute to the O-TGT. It would be relevant to explore the O-TGTs variations across ownership compositions in FBCs. As research has also looked at the optimal point beyond which family ownership does not contribute to entrepreneurial strategies (Sciascia, Mazzola, Astrachan, & Pieper, 2012), it would be interesting to explore the optimal O-TGT features that correspond to this threshold or optimal ownership concentration in the entrepreneurial behaviours of the FBCs.

Another possible extension could be moving from the owners' view to the stakeholders' view; that is exploring how the O-TGT can also address conflicts of interests, including other stakeholders and strive to balance their negative perceptions of owners expropriation and their positive perception of "social dividends" as coined by Sachs, Dieleman, and Suder (2008).

Our analysis of the cases has put forward the presence of different entities in the cluster that go beyond businesses, such as family offices or family foundations, that we labelled as Family Enterprises Cluster (FEC) by extending the Family Business Cluster (FBC) denomination. We invite future research to consider the nature of these different entities and their relationships with top governance teams.

Lastly, whereas our focus was on the O-TGTs directed towards ownership, we invite scholars to extend the exploration of "the ownership concept" by including "psychological ownership", that is, the extent to which family members or stakeholders feel that the family business is "ours" although they do not hold legal property rights (Mustafa, Labaki, & Henssen, 2022; Pierce & Jussila, 2010). We also encourage the exploration of formal and/or informal TGTs in the family governance and other governance systems.

Conclusion

Based on the reflections from the case vignettes and the integration of the fragmented research on corporate governance and on TMTs, the conceptual model on O-TGTs that we suggest revolves around the following arguments, yet to be explored in more depth.

From a design and purpose perspectives, O-TGTs are collaborative teams composed formally and/or informally by family owners and non-family members, some of whom may hold governance and/or managerial positions, and who are committed to the ownership system of the Family Business Cluster (FBC) model. The O-TGTs strives towards achieving sustainability of the family control of the FBC as its complexity increases over time. Preventing or managing the FBC agency problems, such as ensuring an alignment of interests (financial wealth and SEW) among the FBC owners, can be facilitated by the O-TGT effective collaboration. From the perspective of underlying conditions, it appears that the O-TGT collaboration requires common motivations in relation with identification and emotional attachment to the FBC, the development and the use of specific competencies, a process based on shared effort norms, cohesion, and coordination of activities in a cross-functional manner (at the governance, ownership, and family levels).

Carney (2005) argues that the competitive advantage of family businesses arises from their system of corporate governance. Extending this assertion to ownership governance, our chapter suggests an initial conceptualization of O-TGTs that we hope will inspire future qualitative and quantitative research investigations towards a more exhaustive understanding of sustainable FECs.

References

Aguinis, H., Villamor, I., Lazzarini, S. G., Vassolo, R. S., Amorós, J. E., & Allen, D. G. (2020). Conducting management research in Latin America: Why and what's in it for you? *Journal of Management*, 46(5), 615–636.

Alayo, M., Maseda, A., Iturralde, T., & Arzubiaga, U. (2019). Internationalization and entrepreneurial orientation of family SMEs: The influence of the family character. *International Business Review*, 28(1), 48–59.

Alvarez, S. A., Zander, U., Barney, J. B., & Afuah, A. (2020). Developing a theory of the firm for the 21st century. *Academy of Management Review*, 45(4), 711–716.

Ang, J. S., Cole, R. A., & Lin, J. W. (2000). Agency costs and ownership structure. *The Journal of Finance*, 55(1), 81–106.

Berrone, P., Cruz, C., & Gomez-Mejia, L. R. (2012). Socioemotional wealth in family firms: Theoretical dimensions, assessment approaches, and agenda for future research. *Family Business Review*, 25(3), 258–279.

Bettinelli, C. (2011). Boards of directors in family firms: An exploratory study of structure and group process. *Family Business Review*, 24(2), 151–169.

Botero, I. C., Cruz, A. D., & Müller, C. G. (2018). Introduction. In Müller, Botero, Cruz, & Subramanian (Eds.), *Family Firms in Latin America*. Routledge.

Calabrò, A., Campopiano, G., & Basco, R. (2017). Principal-principal conflicts and family firm growth: The moderating role of business family identity. *Journal of Family Business Management*, 7(3), 291–308.

Cannella, B., Finkelstein, S., & Hambrick, D. C. (2008). *Strategic Leadership: Theory and Research on Executive, Top Management Teams, and Boards*: Oxford University Press.

Caputo, A., Marzi, G., Pellegrini, M. M., & Rialti, R. (2018). Conflict management in family businesses: A bibliometric analysis and systematic literature review. *International Journal of Conflict Management*, 29(4), 519–542.

Carney, M., & Gedajlovic, E. (2002). The co-evolution of institutional environments and organizational strategies: The rise of family business groups in the ASEAN region. *Organization Studies*, 23(1), 1–29.

Carney, M. (2005). Corporate governance and competitive advantage in family-controlled firms. *Entrepreneurship Theory and Practice*, 29(3), 249–265.

Chirico, F., & Nordqvist, M. (2010). Dynamic capabilities and trans-generational value creation in family firms: The role of organizational culture. *International Small Business Journal*, 28(5), 487–504.

Chrisman, J. J., Chua, J. H., Le Breton-Miller, I., Miller, D., & Steier, L. P. (2018). Governance mechanisms and family firms. In SAGE Publications: Los Angeles, CA.

Chrisman, J. J., Madison, K., & Kim, T. (2021). A dynamic framework of noneconomic goals and inter-family agency complexities in multi-family firms. *Entrepreneurship Theory and Practice*. doi:https://doi.org/10.1177/10422587211005775

D'Allura, G. M. (2019). The leading role of the top management team in understanding family firms: Past research and future directions. *Journal of Family Business Strategy*, 10(2), 87–104.

Dalton, D. R., & Daily, C. M. (1992). Financial performance of founder-managed versus professionally managed corporations. *Journal of Small Business Economics*, 30, 25–34.

Daspit, J. J., Chrisman, J. J., Sharma, P., Pearson, A. W., & Mahto, R. V. (2018). Governance as a source of family firm heterogeneity. *Journal of Business Research*, 84, 293–300.

Davis, J. H., Schoorman, F. D., & Donaldson, L. (1997). Toward a stewardship theory of management. *Academy of management review*, 22(1), 20–47.

De Dreu, C. K., & Weingart, L. R. (2003). Task versus relationship conflict, team performance, and team member satisfaction: A meta-analysis. *Journal of Applied Psychology*, 88(4), 741.

Del Giudice, M. (2017). *Understanding Family-Owned Business Groups: Towards a Pluralistic Approach*. Springer.

Discua Cruz, A., Howorth, C., & Hamilton, E. (2013). Intrafamily entrepreneurship: The formation and membership of family entrepreneurial teams. *Entrepreneurship Theory and Practice*, 37(1), 17–46.

Eddleston, K. A., & Kellermanns, F. W. (2007). Destructive and productive family relationships: A stewardship theory perspective. *Journal of Business Venturing*, 22(4), 545–565.

Eisenhardt, K. M. (1989). Building theories from case study research. *Academy of Management Review*, 14(4), 532–550.

Ensley, M. D., & Pearce, C. L. (2001). Shared cognition in top management teams: Implications for new venture performance. *Journal of Organizational Behavior: The International Journal of Industrial, Occupational and Organizational Psychology and Behavior*, 22(2), 145–160.

Ensley, M. D., & Pearson, A. W. (2005). An exploratory comparison of the behavioral dynamics of top management teams in family and nonfamily new ventures: Cohesion, conflict, potency, and consensus. *Entrepreneurship Theory and Practice*, 29(3), 267–284.

Farrington, S. M., Venter, E., & Boshoff, C. (2012). The role of selected team design elements in successful sibling teams. *Family Business Review*, 25(2), 191–205.

Federo, R., Ponomareva, Y., Aguilera, R. V., Saz-Carranza, A., & Losada, C. (2020). Bringing owners back on board: A review of the role of ownership type in board governance. *Corporate Governance: An International Review*, 28, 348–371.

Foss, N. J., Klein, P. G., Lien, L. B., Zellweger, T., & Zenger, T. (2021). Ownership competence. *Strategic Management Journal*, 42(2), 302–328.

Gersick, K. E., Davis, J., Mccollom Hampton, M., & Lansberg, I. (1997). *Generation to Generation: Lifecycles of the family business*. Boston: Harvard Business School Press.

Gersick, K. E., & Feliu, N. (2014). Governing the family enterprise: Practices, performance and research. In Melin, Nordqvist, & Sharma (Eds.), *The SAGE Handbook of Family Business* (pp. 196–225). London: Sage Publications.

Goldbart, S., & Difuria, J. (2009). Money and meaning. *Journal of Practical Estate Planning*, 11(6), 7–9.

Gomez-Mejia, L. R., Haynes, K. T., Nunez-Nickel, M., Jacobson, K. J. L., & Moyano-Fuentes, J. (2007). Socioemotional Wealth and Business Risks in Family-controlled Firms: Evidence from Spanish Olive Oil Mills. *Administrative Science Quarterly*, 52(1), 106–137.

Habbershon, T. G., & Pistrui, J. (2002). Enterprising families domain: Family-influenced ownership groups in pursuit of transgenerational wealth. *Family Business Review*, 15(3), 223–237.

Hambrick, D. C., & Mason, P. A. (1984). Upper echelons: The organization as a reflection of its top managers. *Academy of Management Review*, 9(2), 193–206.

Huse, E. F., & Cummings, T. G. (1985). Organization Development and Change, St. Paul: West Publishing Co.

Jaskiewicz, P., Combs, J. G., Shanine, K. K., & Kacmar, K. M. (2017). Introducing the family: A review of family science with implications for management research. *Academy of Management Annals*, 11(1), 309–341.

Jensen, M. C., & Meckling, W. H. (1976). Theory of the firm: Managerial behavior, agency costs and ownership structure. *Journal of Financial Economics*, 3(4), 305–360.

Jensen, M. C. (1986). Agency costs of free cash flow, corporate finance, and takeovers. *The American Economic Review*, 76(2), 323–329.

Kellermanns, F. W., & Eddleston, K. A. (2004). Feuding families: When conflict does a family firm good. *Entrepreneurship Theory and Practice*, 28(3), 209–228.

Krueger, N., Bogers, M. L., Labaki, R., & Basco, R. (2021). Advancing family business science through context theorizing: The case of the Arab world. *Journal of Family Business Strategy*, 12 (1), 1–6. doi: https://doi.org/10.1016/j.jfbs.2020.100377

La Porta, R., Lopez-De-Silanes, F., & Shleifer, A. (1999). Corporate ownership around the world. *The Journal of Finance*, 54(2), 471–517.

Labaki, R. (2008). Le rôle de l'altruisme dans la gouvernance de l'entreprise familiale: Un état de l'art. *Journal des Entreprises Familiales*, 1(2), 81–116.

Labaki, R. (2007). *Contribution à la connaissance des liens familiaux dans les entreprises familiales françaises cotées: Renforcement versus atténuation* (PhD Dissertation), University of Montesquieu Bordeaux IV, Bordeaux.

Labaki, R. (2011). The Nova Group case study: Family dynamics in a multigenerational French family business. *International Journal of Management Cases*, *13*(1), 27–42.

Labaki, R., Michael-Tsabari, N., & Zachary, R. K. (2013). Exploring the emotional nexus in cogent family business archetypes. *Entrepreneurship Research Journal*, 3(3), 301–330.

Labaki, R., & Hirigoyen, G. (2020). The strategic divestment decision in the family business through the real options and emotional lenses. In Palma-Ruiz, Barros, & Gnan (Eds.), *Handbook of Research on the Strategic Management of Family Businesses* (pp. 244–279). Hershey, PA: IGI Global.

Labaki, R., & D'Allura, G. (2021). A governance approach of emotion in family business: Towards a multi-level integrated framework and research agenda. *Entrepreneurship Research Journal*, 11(3), 119–158.

Lansberg, I. (1988). The succession conspiracy. *Family Business Review*, 1(2), 119–143.

Levinson, D. J. (1986). A conception of adult development. *American Psychologist*, 41(1), 3–13.

Lubatkin, M. H., Schulze, W. S., Ling, Y., & Dino, R. N. (2005). The effects of parental altruism on the governance of family-managed firms. *Journal of Organizational Behavior*, 26, 313–330.

Medina, M. N., Ramachandran, I., & Daspit, J. J. (2019). Collaboration or clash? Mapping the effects of top management team conflict on firm absorptive capacity. *International Journal of Innovation Management*, 23(03), 19500231–195002329.

Michael-Tsabari, N., Labaki, R., & Zachary, R. K. (2014). Toward the cluster model: The family firm's entrepreneurial behavior over generations. *Family Business Review*, 27(2), 161–185.

Miller, D. (1983). The correlates of entrepreneurship in three types of firms. *Management Science*, 29(7), 770–791.

Miller, D., & Breton-Miller, L. (2006). Family governance and firm performance: Agency, stewardship, and capabilities. *Family Business Review*, 19(1), 73–87.

Morck, R., & Yeung, B. (2003). Agency problems in large family business groups. *Entrepreneurship Theory and Practice*, 27(4), 367–382.

Mustafa, M., Labaki, R., & Henssen, B. (2022). Psychological Ownership in Heterogeneous Family Firms: A Promising Path and a Call for Further Investigation. *Entrepreneurship Research Journal*. doi:https://doi.org/10.1515/erj-2022-0156

Mustakallio, M., Autio, E., & Zahra, S. A. (2002). Relational and contractual governance in Family firms: Effects on strategic decision making. *Family Business Review*, 15(3), 205–222. doi:10.1111/j.1741-6248.2002.00205.x

Nordqvist, M., & Melin, L. (2002). The dynamics of family firms: An institutional perspective on corporate governance and strategic change. In *Understanding the Small Family Business* (pp. 108–124): Routledge.

Olson, B. J., Parayitam, S., & Bao, Y. (2007). Strategic decision making: The effects of cognitive diversity, conflict, and trust on decision outcomes. *Journal of Management*, 33(2), 196–222.

Pettigrew, A. M. (1985). Contextualist research and the study of organizational change processes. In Lawler (Ed.), *Research Methods in Information Systems* (pp. 222–274). San Francisco: Jossey-Bass.

Pettigrew, A. M. (2008). On studying managerial elites. *The Value Creating Board*, 179–207.

Piana, B. D., Vecchi, A., & Jimenez, A. (2018). Embracing a new perspective on the governance of family business groups: A cross-cultural perspective. *European Journal of International Management*, 12(3), 223–254.

Pierce, J. L., & Jussila, I. (2010). Collective psychological ownership within the work and organizational context: Construct introduction and elaboration. *Journal of Organizational Behavior*, 31(6), 810–834.

Purkayastha, A., Pattnaik, C., & Pathak, A. A. (2021). Agency conflict in diversified business groups and performance of affiliated firms in India: Contingent effect of external constraint and internal governance. *European Management Journal*. doi:https://doi.org/10.1016/j.emj.2021.05.004

Ramachandran, J., Manikandan, K., & Pant, A. (2013). Why conglomerates thrive (outside the US). *Harvard Business Review*, 91(12), 110–119.

Röd, I. (2019). TMT diversity and innovation ambidexterity in family firms. *Journal of Family Business Management*, 9(4), 377–392. doi:https://doi.org/10.1108/JFBM-09-2018-0031

Sachs, W. M., Dieleman, M., & Suder, G. G. S. (2008). Expropriation of minority shareholders or social dividend? Beware of good corporate citizens. In *International Business under Adversity: A Role in Corporate Responsibility, Conflict Prevention and Peace* (pp. 57–72): Cheltenham, UK and Northampton, MA: Elgar.

Schulze, W. S., Lubatkin, M. H., & Dino, R. N. (2003). Toward a theory of agency and altruism in family firms. *Journal of Business Venturing*, 18(4), 473–490.

Sciascia, S., Mazzola, P., Astrachan, J. H., & Pieper, T. M. (2012). The role of family ownership in international entrepreneurship: Exploring nonlinear effects. *Small Business Economics*, 38(1), 15–31.

Sciascia, S., Mazzola, P., & Chirico, F. (2013). Generational involvement in the top management team of family firms: Exploring nonlinear effects on entrepreneurial orientation. *Entrepreneurship Theory and Practice*, 37(1), 69–85.

Sharma, P. (2004). An overview of the field of family business studies: Current status and directions for the future. *Family Business Review*, 17(1), 1–36.

Shleifer, A., & Vishny, R. W. (1997). A survey of corporate governance. *The Journal of Finance*, 52(2), 737–783.

Sirmon, D. G., & Hitt, M. A. (2003). Managing resources: Linking unique resources, management, and wealth creation in family firms. *Entrepreneurship Theory and Practice*, 27(4), 339–358.

Steier, L. (2001). Family firms, plural forms of governance, and the evolving role of trust. *Family Business Review*, 14(4), 353–367.

Suess-Reyes, J. (2017). Understanding the transgenerational orientation of family businesses: The role of family governance and business family identity. *Journal of Business Economics*, 87(6), 749–777.

Suess, J. (2014). Family governance – Literature review and the development of a conceptual model. *Journal of Family Business Strategy*, 5(2), 138–155.

Tagiuri, R., & Davis, J. (1996). Bivalent attributes of the family firm. *Family Business Review*, 9(2), 199–208.

Uhlaner, L., Massis, A. D., Jorissen, A., & Du, Y. (2020). Are outside directors on the small and medium-sized enterprise board always beneficial? Disclosure of firm-specific information in board-management relations as the missing mechanism. *Human Relations*, 1–38. doi:https://doi.org/10.1177/0018726720932985

Van Aaken, D., Rost, K., & Seidl, D. (2017). The substitution of governance mechanisms in the evolution of family firms. *Long range planning*, 50(6), 826–839.

Vandekerkhof, P., Steijvers, T., Hendriks, W., & Voordeckers, W. (2018). Socio-emotional wealth separation and decision-making quality in family firm TMTs: The moderating role of psychological safety. *Journal of Management Studies*, 55(4), 648–676.

Villalonga, B., & Amit, R. (2006). How do family ownership, control and management affect firm value? *Journal of Financial Economics*, 80(2), 385–417.

Wageman, R. (1995). Interdependence and group effectiveness. *Administrative Science Quarterly*, 145–180.

Young, M. N., Peng, M. W., Ahlstrom, D., Bruton, G. D., & Jiang, Y. (2008). Corporate governance in emerging economies: A review of the principal–principal perspective. *Journal of Management Studies*, 45(1), 196–220.

Zellweger, T., & Kammerlander, N. (2015). Family, Wealth, and Governance: An Agency Account. *Entrepreneurship: Theory & Practice*, 39(6), 1281–1303. doi:10.1111/etap.12182

Zellweger, T. M., Nason, R. S., & Nordqvist, M. (2012). From longevity of firms to transgenerational entrepreneurship of families: Introducing family entrepreneurial orientation. *Family Business Review*, 25(2), 136–155.

Carole Howorth, Martin R. Kemp, and Timothy J. Nichol

14 Codes of Governance for Family Businesses

Abstract: In this chapter, we critically review national governance codes and guidance developed for family businesses. Governance codes tend to state that their aim is business improvement and focus on individual companies, with little recognition of the intertwining of businesses and shadow decision-making structures that can occur within business families. This is surprising considering that most guidance and codes were compiled by family business associations or networks. Governance codes for family businesses tend to provide recommendations and advice based on moral, quasi-legal or practical principles rather than evidence-based findings.

Keywords: governance codes, corporate governance, family governance, locus of decision-making, expropriation, governance principles, transparency

Introduction

Some countries have developed governance codes with the aim of ensuring responsible company management. However, governance codes and guidance developed for publicly-owned companies with dispersed shareholdings might not be applicable to more closely-held family businesses. Codes developed for private companies focus on corporate governance, particularly the board of directors, with little reference to the governance context for family businesses. A small number of countries have developed governance codes or practice guidance specifically for family-owned and family-run businesses, but mostly focused on individual company level with no consideration of the interconnectedness of business families.

Business families with sizable portfolios can have a powerful influence within their communities and on local or national politics (ten Kate, Kuepper, & Piotrowski, 2021; Roscoe, Discua Cruz & Howorth, 2013), as well as within the realms of their businesses. Large private companies make significant contributions to the economy and wield power as major employers within their communities (Morck, 2005; Pindado & Requejo, 2015); the social and environmental impact of their business operations can be substantial and, on occasion, devastating (ten Kate, Kuepper & Piotrowski, 2021).

Carole Howorth, University of York
Martin R. Kemp, IFB Research Foundation
Timothy J. Nichol, Liverpool John Moores University

https://doi.org/10.1515/9783110727968-014

Governance of the business interests of business families is therefore relevant not just to their immediate stakeholders but also for wider society.

Weak governance might lead to company scandals, malpractices, and corporate failures, with knock-on effects for employees, supply chains, economies, and society's trust in the business sector. National governments tend to control business governance risks through legislation, for example, specifying statutory reporting requirements and duties of directors. Governance codes provide recommendations of good practice alongside legislation, usually on the basis of "comply or explain", which requires businesses to report on each element of a code, whether/how they have complied with it and if not, why not. There are over a hundred national codes of corporate governance, with some countries having separate codes for listed and private companies. Business families with international interests could therefore be subject to an array of governance codes, depending on the countries they operate in and whether they have private or listed companies.

Much business governance legislation and regulation focuses on the listed company sector but in recent years, there has been growing concern and increasing regulation around the governance of private companies. To our knowledge, there is no governance legislation aimed specifically at family-owned businesses or business-owning families. Governance presents additional challenges for family-owned businesses as they negotiate family relationships intertwined with business imperatives, therefore governance encompasses family governance as well as corporate governance. Family relationships can bring love, commitment, and passion for the business, but can also drive nepotism, rivalries, conflict, and power struggles (Tagiuri & Davis, 1996). With multiple generations, family relationships can become increasingly complex and more challenging to manage, particularly where there are competing objectives and varying levels of interest and involvement across different branches of a family. For business families with intertwined ownership structures across a portfolio of companies and assets, such complexity is multiplied. There is very little in law that recognizes the intertwining of businesses that might exist in families, other than an obligation for directors to declare conflicts of interest. Family ownership aspects are more likely to be encapsulated within governance codes rather than legislation. From the early 21st century, there has been an increase in countries developing governance codes specifically for family businesses.

In this chapter, we examine family business governance codes to understand their purported purpose and content. It is important to understand the purpose, design, and content of governance codes before their effectiveness can be assessed, particularly as assessments of the effectiveness of governance codes have proved challenging (Chaher & Blume, 2016) due to variation among codes, and lack of consensus about what the dependent variable should be.

Our analysis identifies that most family business governance codes are focused on enhancing business performance, and protection of investors, with an emphasis on corporate governance guidelines, many of which are already enshrined in law or other corporate governance codes. The content across codes is very similar with little to indicate variations in cultural context. Family business governance codes pay little attention to responsibilities towards society or a broader group of stakeholders. Codes rarely considered the potential for stewardship, long-term perspectives, psychological ownership, and altruism to influence governance approaches and requirements. In some business families, attitudes of trust, love and commitment may make positive and responsible business behaviours more likely and reduce the need for formal controls or regulation. In such circumstances, the application of strong controls might stimulate perceptions of not being trusted, leading to tensions, self-serving behaviours, and a downward spiral of trust.

The reviewed governance codes failed to consider that business owning families may be complex, interwoven, social organizations. Governance codes did not recognize that family shareholders may use relational as well as contractual governance mechanisms to retain power and influence over corporate decision-making. Governance codes did not acknowledge the potential risks arising from the substantial influence that some dynastic business families may exert within interconnected businesses and wider society. The effectiveness of governance codes in relation to business families is undermined because they fail to recognize that the locus of decision making is likely to be at group level.

Definitions and Development of Governance Codes

It is interesting that the development of corporate governance codes, in the UK, can be traced back to a powerful business family, exemplifying the influence, and impact that individual members of business owning families can have politically and in society. Sir Adrian Cadbury, former chairman (1965–1989) of Cadbury Ltd (which became Cadbury Schweppes), was a director of the Bank of England and IBM, and Chancellor of Aston University, when he chaired the Cadbury Committee (Cadbury, 1992) tasked with reviewing financial reporting and accountability aspects of corporate governance, focusing on listed companies. The "Cadbury Report" (1992) provided an important foundation for the development of corporate governance regulation. Cadbury stated the need for corporate governance thus:

> The country's economy depends on the drive and efficiency of its companies. Thus the effectiveness with which their boards discharge their responsibilities determines Britain's competitive position. They must be free to drive their companies forward, but exercise that freedom within a framework of effective accountability. This is the essence of any system of good corporate governance. (Cadbury, 1992, p. 10)

For Cadbury, governance was about the board of directors being efficient, effective, and competitive, as well as responsible and accountable. Subsequent reports (Greenbury, 1995: Hampel, 1998; Turnbull, 1999) explored aspects of governance not initially covered by the Cadbury Committee, leading to the Combined Code: Principles of Good Governance and Code of Best Practice (FRC, 2000). Periodically revised, the current iteration is the 2018 UK Corporate Governance Code. Following Cadbury's 1992 report, legislation and codes around the world led to similar provisions in other jurisdictions. For example, in 1994, Canada released the Toronto Report on Corporate Governance and in the same year, the American Law Institute in the US published their Principles of Corporate Governance. Brazil was one of the first emerging markets to issue a corporate governance code, in 1999 (Santos et al., 2020). The Organization for Economic Cooperation and Development (OECD) Principles of Corporate Governance, first issued in 1999 and re-issued in 2004 and 2015, provides an international benchmark, summarizing the need for good governance thus:

> Good corporate governance is not an end in itself. It is a means to support economic efficiency, sustainable growth and financial stability. It facilitates companies' access to capital for long-term investment and helps ensure that shareholders and other stakeholders who contribute to the success of the corporation are treated fairly. (OECD, 2015)

In the US, the Sarbanes-Oxley Act was introduced in 2002, its main purpose being protection of investors following high-profile corporate scandals including Enron and WorldCom. In 2006, the United Nations published their Guidance on Good Practices in Corporate Governance Disclosure (UNCTAD, 2006), providing a list of 52 items around financial transparency, corporate responsibility and compliance, audit, shareholding structure and control rights, and board management structures and processes. Following the financial crisis of 2008, there was an increase in countries adopting codes of corporate governance, still aimed mainly at publicly-listed companies. Variations in national codes arose because the institutional contexts varied and because countries differed in which groups or institutions developed the codes. For example, codes were driven by the financial sector in the UK, businesses in France and India, accountants in Hong Kong, the government in Spain, and investors in the Netherlands (Cadbury, 2000a; Cuomo et al., 2016). Cadbury suggests that countries need to learn from each other:

> there is no single right corporate governance model . . . the best approach is to start from whatever system is in place and to seek ways of improving it. In this search for improvement, every country can learn from the experience of others. (Cadbury 2000a, p. 7)

The basic premise of governance is to provide oversight and ensure accountability. Definitions of governance often include how rules, norms, and actions are regulated and people or organizations held accountable. There are various definitions but the OECD (2004) provides a broad, internationally adopted definition of corporate governance as:

> Procedures and processes according to which an organisation is directed and controlled. The corporate governance structure specifies the distribution of rights and responsibilities among the different participants in the organisation – such as the board, managers, shareholders and

other stakeholders – and lays down the rules and procedures for decision-making. (OECD, 2004, Glossary)

The OECD definition emphasizes rights and responsibilities of a range of stakeholders. The implementation of a governance structure requires power and authority to ensure it is effective. Corporate governance emphasises the directors' accountability to shareholders (Cadbury, 1992). There is often very little consideration of the accountability of shareholders, particularly major or dominant shareholders as might be found in business families. It is frequently assumed that power and authority lie with the board of directors but in business families particularly, relational governance mechanisms can provide individuals or groups of shareholders with significant power (Nichol, 2021).

Governance for Family-Owned Businesses

Agency theory is dominant in corporate governance guidance based on an assumption of separate ownership and control. It is frequently assumed that for many business families, agency theory is silent because they do not have separation of ownership and control. However, business families may face agency issues if they have major and minor shareholders, dominant family executives, inactive or distant shareholders, or indeed any circumstance where one group of family members (agents) are acting on behalf of others (principals). There is little consideration however of family governance or the rights and responsibilities of business-owning families in early governance codes. Sir Adrian Cadbury followed the 1992 report with guidance specifically for family businesses (Cadbury, 2000b) but this was not taken up formally and the UK, like the majority of countries, does not currently have a code of governance specifically tailored to family businesses.

Codes of practice and corporate governance legislation aimed at publicly listed companies (PLCs) are based on a market model that expects companies to have a widely dispersed shareholder base and a majority of independent non-executive board members. The typical family-owned business has a concentrated group of shareholders from one or more business families and, frequently, family members are active in management and on the board (Westhead & Howorth, 2007). Many family-owned businesses are privately owned, and some avoid debt, so are not subject to the external governance that comes through financial markets (Tappeiner, Howorth et al., 2012; Shyu & Lee, 2009; Croci et al., 2011). The relevance of governance codes developed for PLCs may be questioned by business families. The UK's Institute of Directors note that:

> [For privately held companies] copying the widely-recognized principles of best practice for listed companies is . . . not a viable solution, as the corporate governance challenges of listed companies are distinct from those of unlisted companies. (IoD, 2010, p. 9)

Some countries have developed codes of governance for privately owned businesses, for example, *Code Buysse* II in Belgium (Buysse, 2009). In 2010, the European Confederation of Directors' Associations (ecoDa) developed governance guidance for unlisted European firms (updated, 2021). In the UK, all companies over 2,000 employees or £2 million turnover have been required since 2019, to state which code of governance they adhere to and explain any deviations. Alongside this statutory requirement, government and business representatives developed the Wates Corporate Governance Principles for Large Private Companies (FRC, 2018). The six Wates Principles all relate to the role of the board of directors and state that they aim to provide a flexible approach to corporate governance for large private firms "without being unduly prescriptive" (FRC, 2018, p. 5).

Most governance codes emphasise principles of impartiality; transparency; trust; probity; fairness and equity; representation, and accountability. Codes aimed at private companies focus on corporate governance, and particularly the role of the board of directors. Guidance designed for unlisted or private firms rarely acknowledges or provides recommendations on the particular governance challenges faced by family firms; nor does it have much to say on the rights and responsibilities of owners. Some countries have developed voluntary codes and national level guidance specifically for family-owned businesses, following concerns by commentators such as Lane et al. who argued that governance codes and guidance developed for publicly owned companies could be "detrimental" to family-owned businesses and that:

> many of these recommendations may harm family unity or might be too complex for private firms, and many are applicable only to very large, public companies with dispersed ownership. As a result of these differences, many . . . laws and recommendations may actually be harmful to family-owned businesses. (Lane et al., 2006, p. 147)

A family constitution (a.k.a. charter, protocol) is one mechanism unique to family business governance. The implementation of a family constitution has been associated with improvements in financial returns, particularly for small family businesses facing increased complexity, for example, later generations, multiple owners and non-family CEOs (Arteaga & Menéndez-Requejo, 2017). Family constitutions tend to be premised on separating "family issues" from business ones, managing family conflict and the notion of professionalization. A more nuanced approach would define the disposition of decision-making power in and around a family's businesses (Nichol, 2021).

To provide more insight into these issues, we analysed codes of governance developed specifically for family-owned businesses, as explained in the following sections.

Code Selection and Analysis

Governance codes and guides developed specifically for family firms were identified for eleven countries. Of these, eight were available in English translation (Arab Gulf countries, Finland, Germany, Italy, Netherlands, Pakistan, Spain, Switzerland) and included in our analysis. Three countries' codes (Columbia, Morocco, and Saudi Arabia) were excluded because they were not available in an English translation. Table 14.1 provides basic characteristics of the selected codes. All eight guides or codes were compiled between 2003 and 2017. Most were written by, or in collaboration with, national family business associations or networks, many of whom were member associations of the international Family Business Network (FBN). Legal and business experts from advisor institutions produced codes for Pakistan and Switzerland.

Analysis was qualitative and aimed to capture, compare, and contrast the elements of each code within the context of how and why each code was developed. Matrices, notes, and discussions between the researchers formed the main tools of our analysis.[1]

Aim and Purpose of Codes

Four of the eight guidance documents called themselves "codes", and four were presented as "guidance" on good governance practices. They were all written for family-owned or controlled companies in their respective countries and covered family as well as corporate governance to varying degrees; their intended audience, stated purpose and specific scope varied.

The codes and guidance targeted either large and medium-sized family firms (Germany, Italy, Pakistan, Switzerland) or family firms of any size (Finland, Gulf countries, Netherlands, Spain). Most of the codes were aimed at unlisted family firms. The Swiss code was directed towards all family firms irrespective of their legal form, and explicitly mentioned family members and business officers working in medium-sized and large firms. The codes developed in Germany and the Gulf countries were written for owners of family firms. The Finland guidance identified the different roles that family and non-family members might have in relation to governance of a family business, for example, active and non-active owners, active non-owning family members, and non-family members. Interestingly, the Finland guidance identified, in addition, that family members not active in the business (e.g., next generation, spouses)

---

1 An earlier version of this analysis was prepared for the Institute of Family Business Research Foundation and published in the report: Howorth, C. and Kemp, M. (2019) "Governance in Family Business: Evidence and Implications" London: IFB Research Foundation.

Table 14.1: Description of Codes.

Country	Year	Title (Reference)	Contributors
Arab Gulf countries	2016	The GCC Governance Code: Governance Guidance for Family Businesses (FBCG, 2016)	The Family Business Council – Gulf (FBCG), representing family firms in Saudi Arabia, Kuwait, the United Arab Emirates, Qatar, Bahrain, and Oman
Finland	2009	Good Corporate Governance in Family Business: Governance of Ownership, Business and Family (FFFA, 2009)	Finnish Family Firms Association (PL)
Germany	2015	Good Governance in the Family Business: Guidelines for the responsible management of family businesses and business-owner families (May et al., 2015)	INTES (the Academy for Family Businesses), FBN, and Die Familienunternehmer (ASU)
Italy	2017	Principi per il Governo della Società Non Quotate a Controlla Familiare: Codice di Autodiscipling/Corporate Governance Principles for Unlisted Family-Controlled Companies: Code of Corporate Governance (AIDAF, 2017)	AIDAF (Italian Association of family firms) with Bocconi University
Netherlands	2003	The Family Business Governance Report: Practices and Recommendations (FBNed, 2003)	FBNed (The Dutch Association of Family Firms): The FBNed Committee for Good Governance in Family Businesses
Pakistan	2008	The Corporate Governance Guide: Family-Owned Companies (CIPE, 2008)	Pakistan Institute of Corporate Governance, The Institute of Chartered Accountants, and Centre for International Private Enterprise
Spain	2005	Good Governance in the Family Business/Buen Gobierno en la Empresa Familiar (Casado et al., 2005)	El Instituto de la Empresa Familiar (IEF)
Switzerland	2008	Code G Family: Business: Environment: Governance Guide for Families and their Businesses (Continuum & Prager Dreifuss, 2008)	Continuum AG and Prager Dreifuss (lawyers and advisers)

were relevant to the governance of their businesses. The Netherlands guidance helpfully indicated which stakeholders each recommendation applied to senior or junior family members, executives, board members, or shareholders. This enabled different stakeholders to identify guidance specific to their position.

Most of the codes and guidance stated that their aim was business improvement. For example, the Finland guide stated aims around improving understanding and "to help family firms develop their corporate governance practices and thereby improve their competitiveness" (FFFA, 2009, p. 6). The Netherlands guidance provided recommendations that sought to promote a "healthy vital business". Without presenting evidence, the codes and guidance suggested that improvements in corporate governance would improve the performance of businesses and employed this as part of the argument for adopting their guidance.

There was recognition that working through the guidance would enable family businesses to assess their current practices and structures. The Swiss Code was described as a "regulatory framework for governance", intended to help "determine the power, management and control structure for the family (family governance), the company (corporate governance), and their conduct towards external stakeholders (public governance)" (Continuum and Prager Dreifuss, 2008, p. 3). The German code sought to offer 'family-owned companies and their environment (stakeholders) a reliable framework for the assessment and optimization of their individual governance structures' (May, Haub and Goebel, 2015: prelim). The code for the Gulf countries sought to codify best governance practice and provide "a common compass to help family businesses navigate through their own process" (FBCG, 2016, p. 3). The Pakistan guidance stressed the need for good governance to reduce conflict, which was assumed to be higher in family-owned businesses.

The ability to tailor recommendations to specific circumstances was recognized in most codes and guidance. The German code stated that guidance should be "tailored to the situation specific to the business and the family involved" (May et al., 2015, p.8). The Spanish guidance sought to offer "practical instruments to family businesses which help to answer a series of challenges which cannot be dealt with through laws or self-regulation", presented as "a set of principles and actions which [. . .] may contribute to improving the long–term feasibility of family businesses, independently of their size, sector or origin" (Casado et al., 2005, p. 16). The Gulf code emphasized heterogeneity of family firms and gave them a series of questions to consider. The Netherlands guidance also acknowledged variation and provided advice around the governance challenges faced by different types of family business (owner-managed, family-managed, family-controlled). The Italian code set out principles and guidelines for family firms to examine and improve governance and then "to report the (even partial) adoption of the recommendations and behaviours set out in the Code in its Annual Report or in any other similar document" (AIDAF, 2017, p. 6). The Pakistan guide stated the need for flexibility in adoption as follows:

> The Guide includes different recommendations for various types of family-owned companies; given the wide variety of company attributes such as size, age of the company, the nature of business, the composition of shareholders, and family dynamics. Therefore, not all provisions of this Guide are applicable to all companies across the board, and the Guide may be adapted in accordance with the needs of individual businesses. (CIPE, 2008, p. 3)

Content of Guidance and Codes

Most of the guidance analysed included a conceptual element, albeit fairly descriptive, setting out general principles and definitions, followed by specific practical recommendations. The more sophisticated ones integrated general principles into their recommendations. The less sophisticated guides focused on practical recommendations with a bit of tailoring to family firms. All the reviewed codes and guidance provided recommendations for the board of directors and typically provided detailed guidance on family governance structures and mechanisms such as family councils, family charters, and the relationship between the family and the company. All texts covered family governance as well as corporate governance, but varied considerably in the extent to which they addressed governance issues relating to owners and shareholders, management, the external environment and societal responsibilities. Texts varied in accessibility, readability, and ease of navigation, with lengths between 19 and 40 pages.

The Swiss code was structured into separate recommendations for each of the family, "business players", and external stakeholders. The German guidance started by discussing the role of family firm owners, their rights and obligations, and then defined the role of the [supervisory] board, followed by advice on management, ownership, and family governance. The German guidance included a useful glossary with definitions of key terms and concepts.

The Italian code identified the behaviours or governance practices believed to characterise a well-functioning governance system, organized around 20 principles and 10 articles, with clear definitions of key concepts and scope. Each "article" included principles with recommendations for how to apply them. Topics included the "management of the ownership structure, succession plans, involvement of non-family managers, and balance between company and family interests" (AIDAF, 2017, p. 7).

The Netherlands guidance was schematic, structured around the familiar tripartite model (family, business, ownership), the "three pillars" of a "healthy vital business". The Netherlands guidance provided a detailed analysis of what constitutes good governance in a family business context. This guidance was atypical in that it designated advice as recommended, advisable, or to be considered, and specified relevance for different types of family firms or stakeholder groups.

Similarly, the Finland guidance used Tagiuri and Davis (1996) "three circles model" to structure their guide. The style was more discursive with explanations and reflections on why the included principles and practical recommendations were important. The content ranged from specific practical advice (e.g., tax deductibility of family governance expenses) to high level concepts (e.g., the power of majority owners).

The Spanish guidance adopted a theoretical approach, employing systems theory to consider the complexity of family firms in relation to governance guidance. The tripartite family-business-ownership system was also used here to organize recommendations but with emphasis on relationships within that system (e.g., between business and family, shareholders, and board).

The Pakistan code started each section with a prescriptive statement (e.g., the board should . . .) and then provided very succinct descriptions of each constituent part. A series of "Annexures" included a simplistic explanation of three stages in the lifecycle of family-owned businesses, tips for independent directors and a glossary of terms.

The code developed for the Gulf countries was unusual among those reviewed in that corporate governance received less attention than family governance. "Questions to consider" focused on ownership governance-legal structure, governing policies (such as shareholder agreements) and governing bodies (shareholder council, shareholder assembly), as well as wealth governance, public engagement and succession planning.

Some of the codes or guidance documents included recommendations on implementation. The Swiss code included a separate section on how to implement the recommendations, with a comprehensive checklist. Similarly, the Gulf countries code included a useful checklist, with steps needed to achieve an effective governance system for family businesses.

Corporate Governance

Corporate governance recommendations in the codes and guidance included definitions of corporate governance and the rationale for it, plus advice about boards of directors including the purpose, structure and composition of boards, and the recruitment and remuneration of directors. Corporate governance in the guides and codes varied in the attention given to the relationship between corporate and family governance, and in addressing corporate governance beyond board structure and duties.

Corporate governance in the Swiss code centred on management, including recommendations and advice on vision and strategic orientation; the structure of the business; the board of directors (board composition, chair, duties); shareholders (relationship with board, engagement); management (decision-making, duties, reporting, remuneration, compliance); corporate culture and motivation; and managing generational change and succession planning.

The German guidance discussed the role of the supervisory board, its purpose, and responsibilities. It also provided recommendations on reporting remuneration, composition of the supervisory board, and the selection of board members (including family membership).

The Finnish guidance also recognized the value of a supervisory board. This guidance explained the reasons and implications of a range of recommendations for boards of directors including rewarding and motivating directors, structure of boards, and committees. It included sections on communication and employing family members. The guidance recognized that requirements change with the size of company.

The Spanish guidance considered the role of the board in the context of the "family business system of governance" and provided advice on board regulations; board structure and function; size and composition; directors' competences, duties, and remuneration.

The Gulf countries code stressed the importance of defining relationships between family and business. A definition of corporate governance was followed by scope and elements of good corporate governance including vision, legal structures and governing bodies, the board of directors and their responsibilities, board composition, and committees. Advice included having "well-qualified family" members on the board and that at least one-third of the board should be independent. It also discussed the benefits of a having a board that was entirely external or expert based.

The Italian code stated that:

> a well-functioning system of governance has to favour the dynamic achievement of two objectives: (i) the ability of the owner family to express a clear vision of the future of the company/subsidiary group; (ii) the possibility of (family or non-family) management to implement said vision using the best available resources on the market. (AIDAF, 2017, p. 4)

The Italian code focused on corporate governance and business management, with less attention to family governance. The code highlighted the advantages of adopting a corporate governance system in which:

> powers are balanced and the interests of the company in respect to all interests, both proprietary and not, are represented, are aimed at ensuring continuity and growth, thus characterizing a modern concept of sound and responsible entrepreneurship. (AIDAF, 2017, p. 7)

Similarly, the Pakistani guidance focused most attention on corporate governance and business management. The advice was prescriptive and little explanation provided, but included practical recommendations in line with legislation around the duties of directors.

Corporate governance guidance across all the countries included advice on the duties, size, composition and operation of the board, the chair's role and the role of independent directors – their selection and remuneration.

Family Governance

Typically, guidance was provided on family governance structures and mechanisms such as family councils, family constitutions (charters, protocols), and the relationship between the family and the company. Some also included guidance on succession decisions and process, family employment, communication, and preventing or managing conflict.

The Swiss guidance stressed control mechanisms, and suggested family governance requirements depended on how much influence the family had on the business. Family governance was expected to ensure business stability and protect against issues arising within the business owning family. Recommendations included defining family goals and values and expressing these in a family charter, producing a clear wealth strategy, organizing family reunions and establishing a family council, formulating a clear communication policy, and developing strategies for succession and for involving the next generation in the business.

The code for German firms claimed that family governance had two main goals: first, "to strengthen and foster long-term consolidation of the feeling of cohesion on the part of the owner family and their identification with the company – in the sense of a common project"; and, second, "to avoid potential conflicts or help resolve them" (May et al., 2015, p. 31). One chapter in the code covered principles and activities for achieving "solid family governance".

The Netherlands guidance on family governance aimed to achieve a "functional entrepreneurial family". It recommended, for example, producing an historical narrative of the family business and working with family members to define the family's mission and its vision for the business. The guidance detailed how to encourage good communication and consensus among family members, and how to establish a family council. The guidance also included recommendations for the business family regarding family leadership; engaging the next generation, successful succession, involving family members in the business, and preventing and managing family conflict.

The guidance for Spanish family firms explained the purpose of family governance, then detailed advice on family councils, family assemblies, and the relationship between them. Given the systems approach underpinning this guidance, it emphasized the family-business relationship and the relationship between family and corporate governance structures, for example, how the board and family council should interact, recommending a formal "family protocol" document to help clarify and manage the relationship and governance arrangements.

The Finnish guidance explained why and how owners' councils and family councils should be formed. The owners' council was seen as distinct from the family council, with a narrower remit. The guidance also discussed raising the next generation as an aspect of family governance.

The Pakistani guidance on family governance focuses on the rights of shareholders and states that these "should be respected and protected by forming a functioning family council" (CIPE, 2008, p. 9). Family governance in the Pakistani guide did not go beyond basic guidance on representation on the family council and management of conflict.

Family governance was not covered separately in the Italian code; instead, the guidance on corporate governance was tailored to the particular circumstances of unlisted family-controlled firms.

Management

Interwoven within governance guidance were recommendations relating to business management. Guidance typically included advice on recruitment and remuneration, the role of executives in governance, and the involvement of family members in running the business.

The Swiss guidance for family businesses included a chapter on business management, with recommendations on strategy and structure, decision-making, reporting, compliance, remuneration, corporate culture, and ensuring professional qualifications not family membership were the basis of recruitment. The guidance for German firms also included a chapter dedicated to management that started by defining the responsibilities and duties of company management, providing advice on composition, remuneration, family involvement, and employment in the firm. The Pakistani guidance included a section on the management of employees that provided simple statements of how they should be treated. The Finnish guidance included warnings and advice on the employment of family members. The Netherlands guidance also included advice on business operations, particularly where they came into conflict with "family traditions and values" or the priorities of individual family members. The recommended family firms should be professionally managed to remain "sufficiently entrepreneurial and innovative" and cautioned against conservatism and continuing with non-profitable activities where the motivation may be "family pride", stating "this conservative attitude can be a grave handicap in business terms" and "sticking to the closed character of the family business can have important negative consequences for its own development" (FBNed, 2003, pp. 24–25).

Social and Environmental Responsibilities

Guidance relating to the external environment, stakeholder engagement, and societal responsibilities did not figure strongly in the codes, which notably focused on internal controls and governance. An exception was the Swiss guidance, which included advice on "public governance" and effective cooperation with external stakeholders to preserve and promote the company's public reputation. The code advised family businesses to "demonstrate an active concern for the public and the environment", providing recommendations on reporting, the treatment of employees, the mitigation of negative environmental impacts, effective management of resources, philanthropy, and community engagement. The guidance advocated reporting on environmental and social goals and activities, noting that "information and reporting on economic, social, and ecological performance can boost long-term success and the reputation of the company" (Continuum and Prager Dreifuss, 2008, p. 29).

There was a small section on transparency and corporate responsibility in the Spanish guidance, covering reporting, annual accounts, relationships with non-family members, social and environmental responsibility. The Gulf countries code included a section on "engaging the public", highlighting the importance of philanthropy. The Pakistani guidance included a section on "Ethics, Disclosure and Transparency" but this did not go much beyond statutory audit and reporting requirements.

Discussion

It is interesting that governance codes for family businesses, without exception, take the individual company as the object in focus. None of the codes or guidance acknowledged that business families could have a portfolio of interconnected companies, other than nods towards declaring conflicts of interest. Clearly, this is a major omission. Some individuals, and particularly business families, might yield enormous power and influence through interconnected roles, shareholdings, and dependencies that on their own might not be viewed as significant. Whilst from an entrepreneurial perspective, business families can provide increased opportunities, resources, and support that improve chances of success (Discua Cruz, Howorth, & Hamilton, 2013), from a governance perspective they can present opaque decision-making, expropriation risks, and increased opportunities to hide malpractice. Power structures within business families can allow certain family members to influence decision-making behind the scenes, informally and formally.

By treating each firm as a separate family business, governance codes ignore the reality that business families operating as a formal family business group frequently make decisions at the group level rather than in individual firms' boardrooms. Different firms may be implicitly connected through family stakes and leadership positions leading to expropriation risks for minority shareholders and creditors. Related party transactions, which enable such expropriation, are of concern to stock exchange regulators but they do not feature in any of these codes. Furthermore, in the worst cases, business families' group structures can be used to conceal malpractice and environmental wrongdoing, through obfuscation and distancing the main firm from their affiliates (ten Kate et al., 2021).

A key element in effective governance is identifying the locus of decision-making power and attenuating potential abuses of power. By not addressing or even acknowledging shadow decision-making, expropriation risks or the potential to hide malpractice through complex structures in business families, the very purpose of family business governance codes is undermined as they cannot assure transparency nor accountability.

The reason for this omission appears to be partly because governance codes for family businesses are presented in terms of improving the performance of individual companies. The authors of codes tended to family business associations, networks or advisers whose main purpose is to educate and advocate for family businesses, rather than hold them to account. The recommendations provided were usually sensible but, in most cases, based on moral, quasi-legal or practical principles rather than evidence-based findings. The codes and guidance implicitly, and sometimes explicitly, suggested that adopting their advice and recommendations would lead to improvements in business performance, with assumptions about subsequent increases in shareholder wealth left unsaid. Indeed, the Finland guide opens with "Good corporate governance strengthens and clarifies the activities of the family firm while improving its competitiveness". In many cases, a business case underpins the argument for adopting good governance with implications of "you will make more money" rather than "you need to act responsibly and be accountable for your actions". This is at odds with increasing recognition and emphasis on stewardship principles within some business families. The underlying (agency) theory of corporate governance assumes a separation of ownership and control and individuals who are self-serving, assumptions that do not necessarily apply to more socially-oriented organizations, including some business families. Family managers and owners may act as stewards, doing what they believe is best for the business, the family or indeed the environment. Nevertheless, most guides stated their aims in terms of business improvement rather than accountability, responsibility or indeed stewardship.

The codes/guidance varied considerably in the extent to which they addressed ownership and shareholders, management, environmental, and social responsibilities. Management recommendations were often interwoven with governance recommendations. Management is about processes, structures and arrangements that mobilize resources whereas governance, broadly defined, is about ensuring "accountability, transparency, responsiveness, rule of law, stability, equity and inclusiveness, empowerment, and broad-based participation" (UNESCO, 2021). Most codes did not go beyond internal governance and paid little attention to responsibilities towards the external environment, stakeholder engagement and corporate social responsibility, perhaps with the exception of the Swiss code.

Codes and guidance were shaped by the country context and some minor variations could be linked to legal and regulatory requirements. Some of the recommendations in the Dutch guidance cite Dutch company law, and the authors of the Italian code referred to the Italian Civil Code. The Swiss code was compiled by a working group of Swiss corporate and legal experts and therefore represents their perspective on how to achieve good governance in family firms. There was little mention or consideration of how family businesses might vary in their country and the implications for governance. Carney (2005) argued that the institutional context could have a direct bearing on any competitive advantage that might be obtained through "good" governance. Analysis of the codes and guidance here suggest that countries around the world may tend towards an Anglo-Saxon conception of good governance despite variations in their political and economic environments, the structure of their industries, society, and culture. Underpinning the Anglo-Saxon model is individualism, common law, strong institutions, and developed economies, which are clearly not the case for business families in many parts of the world (Gupta & Levenburg, 2010). Business families in different countries vary in their conception of ownership; for example, Latin American families may have a more collectivist approach (Gupta et al., 2008). Some countries are dominated by concentrated ownership often within dynastic families (Koh & Lee, 2020). For business families operating in some parts of South America, transparency could increase risks of kidnap or worse (Sandino Vargas, 2020) and governance is within a context of protecting family and property. There were strong similarities across the recommendations in the guides we reviewed, with emphasis on a managerial approach to governance, individual companies, controls, and hierarchical structures, similar to Cadbury's 1992 report. Family governance was an addendum to the managerial model, emphasizing control and risk management with little attention to the positive aspects of family ownership. Our sample selection could have made this more likely, but we would suggest that the influence of Cadbury and the UK system on governance codes around the world is substantial.

Our analysis also highlights that family business researchers and academics could do more to ensure that their thoughtful, nuanced conceptualizations of business families are shared with the objects of their research and fed into policy and practice.

Conclusion

Whilst it is encouraging that governance codes and guidance have been developed specifically for family businesses, it is disappointing that they rarely acknowledge the prevalence of business families with interconnected portfolios of businesses and assets, and often, significant influence. Codes were very inward looking and there was little consideration of business families' relationships with, and responsibilities towards, the societies and environments that enable and support them. Although not mentioned explicitly, the maxim of maximizing shareholder wealth was implicit in the way that codes and guidance were presented. Whilst this may help to convince some business families of the value of adopting the advice, it means that codes and guidance risk being self-serving and failing to deliver accountability regarding business families' wider responsibilities.

Good governance processes and structures clarify relationships, rights, and responsibilities to ensure that businesses are governed effectively and responsibly, whereas inadequate corporate governance is often a factor in corporate scandals and failures (Cuomo et al., 2016; Mallin, 2018). While poor governance might constrain or destroy a business and it is assumed well-governed businesses may create more value, there is limited evidence on the impacts of 'good' governance. Occasionally, the guidance we reviewed drew on evidence to support claims but, typically, the recommendations and advice tended to be unsupported, normative, and prescriptive. This is not surprising, as assessments of the impact of governance measures are challenging. Cadbury (2000a) emphasized that quantitative measures, for example, on the composition of boards, do not capture how effective or competent directors are, nor do they give insights into effectiveness of processes. Studies that examine individual business performance fail to capture the business interconnectivity that occurs in business families and within society. It is difficult to tease out shadow decision-making and relational governance measures in business families (Nichol, 2021). Some codes provided thoughtful comments about issues that family businesses might face, and they drew on the experiences of a range of participants. However, a thorough understanding is needed of the effectiveness of different governance mechanisms in particular circumstances.

Governance codes aim to improve trust in businesses, providing mechanisms that increase transparency and accountability, alongside or in addition to legal and regulatory requirements. If governance is about responsibility, transparency, and accountability, perhaps we should not be assessing individual business (financial) performance but instead assessing reductions in business failure, longevity and survival, reduction in corporate scandals, and improvements in societal and environmental impacts of businesses. However, we must first acknowledge the intertwining of businesses within business families and address the resulting governance issues. Moreover, guidance needs to be clear on the purpose of "good" governance. There is clearly scope for anchoring governance guidance more firmly in research, employing more evidence and getting to grips with conceptual understandings and the realities of business families.

References

AIDAF (2017). *Corporate Governance Principles for Unlisted Family-Controlled Companies: Code of Corporate Governance. Italian Association of Family Businesses (AIDAF)*. Milan: University of Bocconi.

Arteaga R, Menéndez-Requejo S. (2017). Family constitution and business performance: Moderating factors. *Family Business Review*, 30(4), 320–338.

Buysse, Baron (2009). *Buysse Code II: Corporate Governance Recommendations for Non-Listed Enterprises*. Belgium: Code Buysse.

Cadbury (1992). *Report on Financial Aspects of Corporate Governance*. Cadbury Committee. London: Gee and Company Ltd.

Cadbury, Sir A. (2000a). The Corporate Governance Agenda. *Corporate Governance: An International Review*, 8 (1) 7–15.

Cadbury, Sir A. (2000b). *Family Firms and Their Governance: Creating Tomorrow's Company from Today's*. London: Egon Zehnder International.

Carney, M. (2005). Corporate governance and competitive advantage in family-controlled firms. *Entrepreneurship Theory and Practice*, 29(3) 249–265.

Casado, F., Olcese, A., Nueno, P., & Roure, J. (2005). Good Governance in the Family Business/ Buen Gobierno en la Empresa Familiar. Barcelona: Instituto de la Empresa Familiar, IESE.

Chaher, S., & Blume, D. (2016). *Strengthening Corporate Governance Codes in Latin America. 2016 Meeting of the Latin American Corporate Governance Roundtable, San Jose, Costa Rica*. Paris: OECD Publishing.

CIPE. (2008) The Corporate Governance Guide: Family-Owned Companies. Karachi: Centre for International Private Enterprise.

Continuum and Prager Dreifuss. (2008). *Code G Family: Business: Environment: Governance Guide for Families and their Businesses*. Zurich: Continuum AG and Prager Dreifuss.

Croci, E., Doukas, J. A., & Gonenc, H. (2011). Family control and financing decisions. *European Financial Management*, 17(5), 860–897.

Cuomo, F., Mallin, C., & Zattoni, A. (2016). Corporate governance codes: A review and research agenda. *Corporate Governance: An International Review*, 24(3), 222–241.

Discua Cruz, A., Howorth, C., & Hamilton, E. (2013). Intrafamily entrepreneurship: The formation and membership of family entrepreneurial teams. *Entrepreneurship Theory and Practice*, 37(1), 17–46.

FBCG. (2016). *The GCC Governance Code: Governance Guidance for Family Businesses*. Dubai: The Family Business Council-Gulf.

FBNed (2003). *The Family Business Governance Report: Practices and Recommendations. The FBNed Committee for Good Governance in Family Businesses*. Tilburg: Familiebedrijven Nederland.

FFFA (2009). *Good Corporate Governance in Family Business: Governance of Ownership, Business and Family. Finnish Family Firms Association*. Helsinki: Perheyritysten Liitto.

FRC. (2000). *Combined Code: Principles of Good Governance and Code of Best Practice*. London: Financial Reporting Council.

FRC. (2018). *The Wates Corporate Governance Principles for Large Private Companies*. London: Financial Reporting Council.

Greenbury, Sir R. (1995). *Directors Remuneration: Report of a Study Group. Confederation of British Industry*. London: Gee and Company Ltd.

Gupta, V., Levenburg, N., Moore, L. L., Motwani, J., & Schwarz, T.V. (2008). *Culturally Sensitive Models of Family Business in Latin America: A Compendium Using the GLOBE Paradigm*. Hyderabad: Icfai University Press.

Gupta, V., & Levenburg, N. (2010). A thematic analysis of cultural variations in family businesses: The CASE project. *Family Business Review*, 23(2), 155–169.

Hampel, R. (1998). *Committee on Corporate Governance: Final Report*. Financial Reporting Council. London: Gee Publishing Ltd.

Howorth, C., & Kemp, M. (2019). *Governance in Family Business: Evidence and Implications*. London: IFB Research Foundation.

IoD. (2010). *Corporate Governance Guidance and Principles for Unlisted Companies in the UK*. London: Institute of Directors.

Koh, A., & Lee, J. (2020). *Asian Family Businesses: Succession, Governance and Innovation*. Singapore: World Scientific Publishing.

Lane, S., Astrachan, J., Keyt, A., & McMillan, K. (2006). Guidelines for family business boards of directors. *Family Business Review*, 19(2), 147–167.

Mallin, C.A. (2018). *Corporate Governance, 6th Edition*. Oxford University Press.

May, P., Haub, K-E. W., & Goebel, L. (2015). *Good Governance in the Family Business: Guidelines for the Responsible Management of Family Businesses and Business-Owner Families*. Bonn: INTES Akademie fur die Familienunternehmen.

Morck, R. K. (2005). *A History of Corporate Governance Around the World: Family Business Groups to Professional Managers*. Chicago: University of Chicago Press.

Nichol, T. J. (2021). *Keeping it in the Family: A Case Study-Based Inquiry into the Role of Governance Mechanisms in the Maintenance of Family* Power *and* Influence in Fifth or More Generation Private Family Companies. Unpublished PhD thesis. University of York.

OECD. (2004). *Glossary of Statistical Terms: Corporate Governance*. Paris: OECD Publishing.

OECD. (2015). *G20/OECD Principles of Corporate Governance*. Paris: OECD Publishing.

Pindado, J., & Requejo, I. (2015). Family business performance from a governance perspective: a review of empirical research. *International Journal of Management Reviews*, 17(3), 279–311.

Roscoe, P., Discua Cruz, A., & Howorth, C. (2013). How does an old firm learn new tricks? A material account of entrepreneurial opportunity. *Business History*, 55(1), 53–72.

Sandino Vargas, E. (2020). Capturing the antecedents and aftermath of a family business process: The entrepreneurial journey of a displaced agricultural family in Colombia, PhD thesis. *Jönköping International Business School, Centre for Family Entrepreneurship and Ownership*.

Santos, A. A., Crispim, S. F., Oliva, E. C., & Dornelles, M. (2020). Codes of corporate governance of Latin American countries: Analysis of UN practices. *Revista de Administração Mackenzie*, 21(6), 1–28.

Shyu, Y. W., & Lee, C. I. (2009). Excess control rights and debt maturity structure in family-controlled firms. *Corporate Governance: An International Review*, 17(5), 611–628.

Tagiuri, R., & Davis, J. (1996) Bivalent attributes of the family firm. *Family Business Review*, 9(2), 199–208.

Tappeiner, F., Howorth, C., Achleitner, A. K., & Schraml, S. (2012). Demand for private equity minority investments: a study of large family firms. *Journal of Family Business Strategy*, 3(1), 38–51.

Ten Kate, A., Kuepper, B., & Piotrowski, M. (2021). Several Large Indonesian Palm Oil Companies Also Have Risky Mining Businesses. August 2021. Chain Reaction Research. https://chainreactionresearch.com/wp-content/uploads/2021/08/Chain-Reaction-Research-Several-Large-Indonesian-Palm-Oil-Companies-Also-Have-Risky-Mining-Businesses-2021.pdf (accessed November 16, 2021).

Turnbull, N. (1999). *Internal Control: Guidance for Directors on the Combined Code. The Turnbull Committee*. London: Institute of Chartered Accountants England and Wales (ICAEW).

UNCTAD (2006). *Guidance on Good Practices in Corporate Governance* Disclosure. *United Nations Conference on Trade and Development*. UNCTAD/ITE/TEB/2006/3 Geneva and New York: United Nations.

UNESCO (2021). Concept of Governance. UNESCO International Bureau of Education. http://www.ibe.unesco.org/en/geqaf/technical-notes/concept-governance (accessed September 29, 2021).

Westhead, P., & Howorth, C. (2007). 'Types' of private family firms: An exploratory conceptual and empirical analysis. *Entrepreneurship and Regional Development*, 19(5), 405–431.

Myung-Seon Song

15 Family Office Research: A Primer

Abstract: Although the practical importance of family office is rising to sustain the dynastic wealth of business families, there is comparatively little academic research on such phenomena. In this chapter, I explore the evolution of family office research through (1) development and classification of family offices, (2) a review of previous literature on family offices in the management field, and (3) suggestions on possible future family office research. First, I clarify that family offices are distinguished from other professional financial services in terms of holistic/long-term approach, higher personal attention to families, and close cooperation with other types of trusted advisors. I then explain that family offices function as tools for wealthy families to regenerate themselves while continuously maintaining their elite class formation. Second, I thoroughly review previous literature on family offices in the management field in terms of four main research streams: (1) governance; (2) succession, legacy, and education; (3) advice and investment; and (4) family entrepreneurship. Lastly, based on the comprehensive literature review, I identify five possible future research topics on the family office. All these descriptions imply that ample room exists for researchers to explore family office topics in the future in terms of theoretical and empirical perspectives.

Keywords: family office, wealth management, elite class formation, family entrepreneurship, trusted advisors

Introduction

Family offices have expanded exponentially in recent decades. According to Campden Research (2019), it is estimated that there were 7,300 single family offices worldwide, up a significant 38% from 2017. Also, Beech (2019) reported that the total estimated assets under the management of family offices amount to $5.9 trillion. Notably, family offices are increasingly entering high growth emerging markets, which often have a number of business families that are frequently underserved by financial services. Rebecca Gooch, who is a director of Campden research, remarked, "In Asia, where we have seen a remarkable 44% increase in the number of family offices from 2017 to 2019, there has been a surge of growth in business which is leading to a rise in the ultra-high net worth population."

Myung-Seon Song, National University of Singapore

https://doi.org/10.1515/9783110727968-015

While there is substantial professional practitioner interest in the family offices, there is comparatively little academic research on such phenomena. In this chapter, I explore the evolution of family office research through (1) development and classification of family offices, (2) a review of previous literature on family offices in the management field, and (3) suggestions on possible future family office research. As such, I seek to offer a balanced perspective and insightful synthesis on family office research based on a comprehensive review of recent professional developments and academic publications.

Development and Classification of Family Offices

Wealthy families with investable assets in excess of US$100 million often establish family offices (Wessel et al., 2014). Generally, family offices are borne out of family businesses. According to a longitudinal study sample conducted by US Trust and Campden Research on family offices, over 70% reported that the source of family wealth originated from the core family business, with 60% having an ongoing operating business (e.g., operating revenue from family businesses). Other respondents reported that they established family offices after a windfall from a partial or full sale of a family business or IPO. Other significant wealth-transferring events (e.g., lottery winning, mega-divorce proceeding) could also trigger the establishment of a family office.

According to Rosplock (2014), a family's financial affairs are managed internally by employees of the business at a family firm's early evolutionary stages. As the family assets grow in tandem with the growth of the family business, requirements for managing the family's finances, taxes, estate planning, and investments become more complex. Consequently, employees within family businesses become increasingly compromised, and a conflict of interest arises as they become more involved and responsible for managing the personal and financial affairs of family members while serving their operational duties to the family. Furthermore, as the personal financial affairs of a family grow in complexity, the family's interest in privacy also increases. To address the aforementioned issues, the family realizes the need to isolate certain responsibilities from the management of the business, which, in turn, leads to the creation of a family office (Rosplock, 2014).

Consisting as one element of a family enterprise – along with family business, family council, and family foundation – a family office is a professional organization dedicated to serving the financial and personal needs of the family (Kenyon-Rouvinez & Park, 2020) (see Figure 15.1). Specifically, family offices undertake activities that are largely classified into three types: (1) investment-related (e.g., asset allocation, manager selection and monitoring, investing, investment performance measurement, and education of family members); (2) family-related (e.g., philanthropy, risk management, insurance, concierge services, security); and

(3) administrative-related activities (e.g., banking, financial administration, legal services, trust accounting, technology solution, and support) (Amit & Liechtenstein, 2012). These activities differ depending on each family's objectives, values, and culture (Amit & Liechtenstein, 2012; Rosplock, 2014). Taken together, the ultimate purpose of the family office is to preserve and possibly grow the family's financial and non-financial wealth (e.g., socio-emotional wealth) through serving its unique needs.

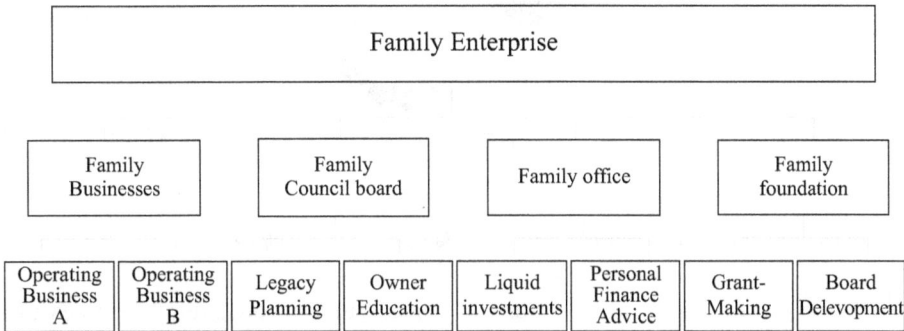

```
┌─────────────────────────────────────────────────────────────┐
│                      Family Enterprise                       │
└─────────────────────────────────────────────────────────────┘

┌──────────────┐  ┌──────────────┐  ┌──────────────┐  ┌──────────────┐
│   Family     │  │   Family     │  │              │  │   Family     │
│  Businesses  │  │ Council board│  │ Family office│  │  foundation  │
└──────────────┘  └──────────────┘  └──────────────┘  └──────────────┘

┌──────────┬──────────┐┌──────────┬──────────┬──────────┬──────────┐┌──────────┬──────────┐
│Operating │Operating ││          │          │          │ Personal ││          │          │
│Business  │Business  ││ Legacy   │ Owner    │ Liquid   │ Finance  ││ Grant-   │  Board   │
│   A      │   B      ││ Planning │Education │investments│ Advice  ││ Making   │Delevopment│
└──────────┴──────────┘└──────────┴──────────┴──────────┴──────────┘└──────────┴──────────┘
```

Figure 15.1: The four pillars of the family enterprise ecosystem.
Source: Danielle and Hamilton (2013).

While some family offices employ an entire office with accountants, lawyers, and investment professionals to manage their assets (Rowley, 2018), not all have their own in-house team. In such cases, family offices use external service experts such as accountants, lawyers, investment advisors, bookkeepers, tax specialists, or real estate specialists (Jain & Lotia, 2009). Through collaborating with experts in their respective fields, family members formulate their strategic decisions. It is worthwhile to note that whether some activities are managed in-house or outsourced, family offices first evaluate every investment opportunity suggested by external experts to prioritize the interests of the family (Jain & Lotia, 2009).

In Figure 15.2, I provide a diagram illustrating the relationship between family firm, family, and family office. To elaborate, families accumulate wealth by receiving dividends or salaries from their operating family businesses in exchange for investing their financial and human capital. Otherwise, families can also accumulate wealth by liquidating their family firms through partial/complete sales or IPO. Families then centralize the management of a significant family fortune by establishing family offices that provide a wider range of private wealth management services (e.g., other business or investments, tax services, family expenses, charitable giving). Accordingly, as Figure 15.2 indicates, the financial wealth originating from family firms flows into families, and families establish family offices to centralize their wealth management and related functions.

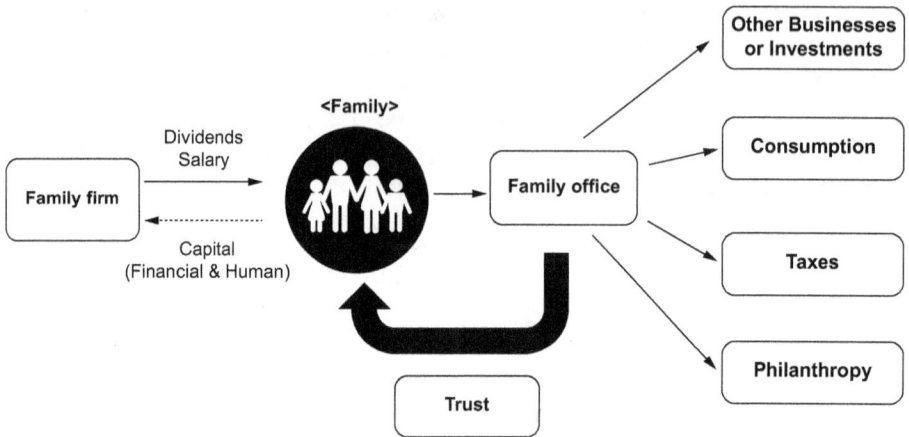

Figure 15.2: The relationship between family firm, family, and family office.

Distinguished from other financial service institutions, family offices are uniquely positioned to provide long-term, customized strategic planning that aligns well with the family's personal and financial needs (Jain & Lotia, 2009; Kenyon-Rouvinez & Park, 2020). For example, regarding the question of why a wealthy family chooses a family office instead of another form of wealth management, Curtis (2001) quoted a remark from one manager in single family office: "The most fundamental reason has to do with the challenge of stewardship: no one will take your issue as seriously as you will take them yourself". Furthermore, family offices are characterized as private, anonymous, and confidential, which families highlight as a benefit of operating such offices (Amit et al., 2008; Jain & Lotia, 2009).

Moreover, several scholars have argued that family offices serve as the "most trusted advisors" within family firms, providing advice to wealthy families owning and operating a business based on long-term relationships and trust built over years of repeated interactions (Strike & Rerup, 2016; Strike, Michel, & Kammerlander, 2018). More specifically, Strike, Michel, & Kammerlander (2018) classified family offices as group-based advisors, which are new categories of advisors in the family business literature in addition to expertise-based advisors (i.e., those who are externally hired by the family or firm and who are either content or process experts) and trust-based advisors (i.e., formal or informal advisors that may also include family members and firm members). Strike (2012) further illustrated that the advisor administering the family office coordinates content experts who provide counsel on investments, taxes, and trusts, all with a focus on preserving the family wealth, history, and legacy. Such a practice indicates that family offices closely cooperate with other types of the most trusted advisors.

There are typically two types of family office: the single-family office and the multi-family office. A single-family office exclusively focuses on managing the wealth of a single individual or family, while multi-family office manages the wealth of at least two families who pool their investable capital together for a more formal/institutional arrangement (Wessel et al., 2014). A single-family office is usually managed by a family member who has previous experience in finance and management (Jain & Lotia, 2009). Compared to multi-family offices, single family offices are more long-term oriented and offer more customized services with a higher degree of control, privacy, and confidentiality (Kenyon-Rouvinez & Park, 2020). Other factors that differentiate single family offices from other structures include a lack of conflicts of interest, a flexible structure, exclusivity, and discretion (Rivo-Lopez et al., 2017). Figure 15.3 summarizes the characteristics of single-family offices, multi-family offices, and financial service institutions.

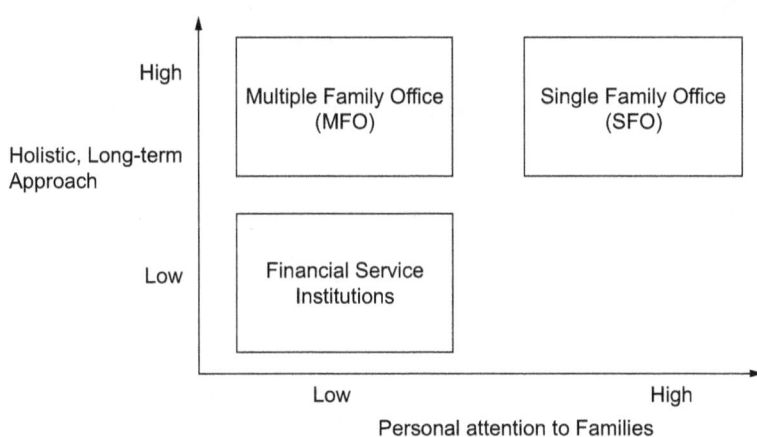

Figure 15.3: Characteristics of SFOs, MFOs, and financial service institutions.
Source: Kenyon-Rouvinez and Park (2020).

Like family businesses, family offices are under direct family influence and involvement. Kenyon-Rouvinez and Park (2020) identified family involvement as one feature that differentiates family office operations from other financial organizations.

> Family dynamics play an integral role in every facet of the family office-from its set up, functions, and governance to its resulting success in the effective management of the family wealth. Family offices at a nascent stage are characterized by intense levels of family control combined with a low level of governance structure. In some cases, even family members without appropriate expertise want to participate in the investment process, either as an informal contributor or as a member of the investment committee. Thus, a high level of family involvement does not always lead to optimal performance. However, it is undeniably a priority for most owner families to be involved in the investing and operating decisions of the family office, to ensure it fulfils the family's unique needs over the long term. (Kenyon-Rovinez & Park, 2020, p. 7).

Previous Literature in the Management Field on Family Offices

According to the family office exchange (FOX), it is estimated that more than 3,000 families in the US have family offices, and at least twice that number is embedded inside private operating companies (Rosplock, 2014). Although family offices have been increasing, the topic remains underexplored in family business studies due to the difficulty of accessing information and lack of a universally accepted definition of family office (Amit et al., 2009) (see Table 15.1). Such scarce management attention on family offices is in stark contrast to the extensive streams of research exploring how family-owned businesses differ from non-family businesses in terms of managerial processes (e.g., succession, professionalization), strategic choices (e.g., R&D, diversification, acquisition), organizational governance (e.g., role of the board, agency contract), and stakeholder management (e.g., stakeholder relationships, corporate social responsibility) (Gomez-Mejia et al., 2011).

The following question then remains: *Why should management researchers pay academic attention to family offices beyond family businesses?* Regarding such a fundamental question, Dunn (1980) suggested that family office functions as a "kinecon" group a group representing kinship bonds and shared economic interests, which helps the family maintain a cohesive family unit through successive generations, through control of their business, and through political, cultural, and religious influence. Specifically, previous literature has emphasized that family offices play an active role in resolving conflicting interests among family members. For example, Brown and Jaffe (2009) viewed the adoption of the family office unit as an "institutional vehicle", which helps develop and improve the family business operation and ownership by creating an integrated corporate and family control system.

Further advanced from this perspective, several sociology scholars have viewed family offices as institutional mechanisms for perpetuating wealth inequality and class-making. Such a radical perspective started from Harrington (2012), who argued that professionals such as trust and estate planners contribute to creating and maintaining socio-economic inequality on a global scale by sheltering their clients' assets from taxation to preserve private wealth for future generations. In line with such arguments, Glucksberg and Burrows (2016) viewed family offices as contemporary institutionalized infrastructures that take the role of reproducing family wealth over generations. By doing so, family offices support the dynasty-making process of wealthy families by helping them not only to manage their daily lives, but also to sustain family cohesion. Similarly, Roure et al. (2013) proposed that the family office plays a critical role in expanding family wealth over generations and achieving continuity as a family business. In summary, family offices function as a means for families to continuously reinvest and regenerate themselves over generations, which has practical importance in sustaining family enterprises and dynastic wealth.

Table 15.1: Inconsistent Definition of Family Office.

Author	Definition
File, Prince, & Rankin (1994)	Investment management firms that families own and create to manage their assets
Langsberg (1996)	An independent operational entity that manages the relationship between family and business, by means of investment of the family wealth as a whole, which has advantages that include increased market power and reduced financial management costs because of the centralized viewpoint for decision-making
Curtis (2001)	A structure which has as its main goal for the management of the assets belonging to a family with great resource
Wolosky (2002)	An organization to support a specific family's financial needs from strategic asset allocation to record keeping and reporting
Avery (2004)	A centre of influence and stability to help exceptionally wealthy families ensure the preservation and growth of their financial assets and family heritage
Bowen (2004)	An organization dedicated to serving wealthy individuals and/or families in a diverse range of financial, estate, tax, accounting, and personal family needs
Jaffe & Lane (2004)	An administrative structure that provides services to family members and monitors family investment
Amit (2006)	A professional centre dedicated to serving the financial and personal needs of an affluent family
Ward (2008)	Professional organization whose aim is to manage family wealth and family matters and which makes it possible to redefine the operation of effective management in business families on the basis of three pillars: firm, family, and wealth
Amit et al. (2009)	A unique family business that is created to provide tailored wealth management solutions in an integrated fashion while promoting and preserving the identity and values of the family

Table 15.1 (continued)

Author	Definition
Fermadez-Moya & Castro-Balaguer (2011)	A private office for managing and preserving the wealth of the proprietary family
Decker & Lange (2013)	An administrative body that exercises control over complex financial and personal issues, and which provides advice to its clients
Roure et al. (2013)	An entity created to provide continuity, planning, and execution of investment and wealth management activities of a family that promote, perpetuate, and preserve its wealth, values, and legacy
Family Office Exchange (FOX) (2016, 2018)	An organization that is created, often after the sale of a family business or realization of significant liquidity, to support the financial needs of a specific family group

Source: Rivo-López, Villanueva-Villar, Vaquero-García, and Lago-Peñas (2017).

Consequently, researchers need to pay more academic attention to family offices, as the portfolio of holistic business activities that family offices oversee beyond core family businesses enables the growth and continuity of family enterprises, as well as wealth accumulation (Habbershon & Pistrui, 2002; Zellweger, Nason, & Nordqvist, 2012).

Although the literature on family offices is scarce, previous family office literature within the management field can be classified into four main research streams: (1) governance; (2) succession, legacy, and education; (3) advice and investment; and (4) family entrepreneurship (Rivo-Lopez, Villanueva-Villa, & Vaquero-Garcia, 2016).

1. First, previous research has revealed that family offices usually operate as a family governance mechanism (Rivo-Lopez et al., 2017). For example, Jaffe and Lane (2004) proposed that family offices are created not only for the family's own interest, but also as an alternative to the traditional governance structure to improve asset and investment management. Suess (2014) also viewed the family office as a governance mechanism for the family business and considered this structure within the scope of family governance. In line with this view, Zellweger and Kammerlander (2015) considered family offices as intermediary governance structures that separate families from their businesses and assets. More specifically, the authors argued that embedded family offices, which are a hybrid two-tier structure established to manage family affairs by hiring a fiduciary from within the existing asset structure, have a low level of separation between the family and its assets. On the other hand, single family

offices, which are separate legal entities entirely dedicated to managing single family affairs, indicate a high level of separation between the family and its assets. More-over, the authors maintained that embedded family offices solve family blockholder conflicts only to a limited extent while incurring some level of double-agency costs. However, single family offices also directly address family blockholder conflicts, be-cause single family offices formalize investment guidelines and delegate all wealth management tasks to one professional fiduciary. Family offices are also susceptible to double-agency costs, depending on the degree of alignment between family offi-cers and family interests. Furthermore, Strike, Michel, and Kammerlander (2018) classified family offices as group-based advisors, which are new categories of ad-visors in the family business literature. Related to the governance structure of family offices, Amit and Liechtenstein (2012) argued that the stronger performance of European single-family offices can be attributed to their more developed gover-nance structure, which is characterized as a higher presence of committees, ad-vanced documentation use, and frequent communication policy.

2. Second, previous research has found that family offices contribute to "soft" re-sponsibilities, such as preparing for succession planning, maintaining family leg-acy, and providing education programs for younger generations. It is noted that family offices play an essential role in training successors and organizing activities that help the family unite (Hall, 1988; Gilding, 2005). Grote (2003) argued that fam-ily offices are established to avoid business failures during the succession period by separating the business and the family, thereby contributing to a minimum of po-tential conflicts during the succession process. In particular, family offices provide ed-ucation that serves as an effective tool for planning succession and training the next generation as future shareholders, board members, or managers (Hall, 1988). More-over, through education programs, family offices facilitate transferring family knowl-edge, culture, and legacy to future generations. As such, the family office ideally has a higher purpose of bridging generations to create continuity and cohesion among family members around their wealth (Rosplock, 2014). Moreover, File, Prince, and Rankin (1994) maintained that family offices are designed to place greater emphasis on the en-trepreneurial education of the next generation.

3. Third, previous research has highlighted that family offices provide a coordinated, managed, and consistent investment process aimed at sustaining and growing the family wealth across multiple generations (See Figure 15.4). Jaffe and Lane (2004) argued that business families worldwide have started to pay heightened attention to creating de-veloped structures of accountability to effectively manage their wealth. This is because as family generation moves beyond the first generation, it becomes crucial to maintain shared control over the family's highly diversified financial and business assets. In this regard, they proposed that the family office is the governance and administrative struc-ture that provides services to family members and monitors family investments. In this line of research, scholars investigated the investment patterns, financial strategies, and

cash management of family offices (Hamilton, 1992; File, Prince, & Rankin, 1994; Kaye & Hamilton, 2004). Notably, considering that the influence of family is inherently high, a family office may reflect the founder's investment preference, risk tolerance, and interest in financial matters (Kenyon-Rouvinez & Park, 2020).

Moreover, depending on the objectives regarding family wealth management (e.g., preserving wealth vs. growing wealth), family offices may organize some of their investments through investment partnerships, whereby they pool a portion of individual family members' capital to invest in selected asset classes or direct investments. For example, the asset allocation of family offices can be based on a combination of public equity, venture capital funds, hedge funds, private equity, or real assets (Kenyon-Rouvinez & Park, 2020). Notably, Kenyon-Rouvinez & Park (2020) highlighted that a family office sometimes makes unusual decisions that external investment professionals would not have made due to the influence of owner family. For example, if a family has developed their business through a close relationship with the local community over the generations, family members may influence the family office to make a financially suboptimal investment to maintain its community contribution. In addition, Tse, Sola, and Gheorghita (2011) proposed three determinants of family wealth management strategy: (1) family mission, (2) family characteristics, and (3) macro-economic and asset performance. Specifically, family mission includes maintaining the core business and planning for the family wealth (e.g., wealth preservation or wealth growth). Family characteristics include the number of decision-makers, the presence of the business founder/family patriarch, and the number of generations and attitude towards wealth. Macro-economic and asset performance incorporates economic conditions and asset class performance. While the first two categories are associated with family dynamics, the third is more related to financial modern portfolio management. As a concluding remark, the authors highlighted that family wealth advisors are responsible for reconciling all the aforementioned factors and crafting successful investment strategies for wealthy families.

Another line of research has investigated how family office investment practices differ from those of other private equity investors. For example, Davis, Cieniewski, and Birenbaum (2016) illustrated the differences between private equity minority investments made by family offices and private equity funds. More specifically, unlike a private equity fund that only caters to its own investors (i.e., limited partners), family offices are focused on satisfying the family needs. In terms of investment periods, although the authors reported that private equity funds have a restricted period of investment requiring a certain degree of capital returns to its investors, a family office is much more flexible in determining the investment period and generally has a much longer investment period than private equity funds. However, the authors also pinpointed that while private equity funds move quickly because they are highly focused on meeting the timelines a business owner is seeking, family offices move much more slowly. In addition, Block et al. (2019) also compared the investment criteria of private equity investors with family offices, business angels, venture capital funds, growth equity funds, and leverage buyout funds. Using an experimental conjoint analysis, they found that family offices, growth equity funds, and leveraged buyout funds place a higher value on profitability relative to business angels and venture capital funds. Similarly, drawing upon capital structuring theory and behavioural agency theory, Schickinger et al. (2021a) found that single family offices are less likely to raise debt than private equity firms when making direct entrepreneurial investments. Moreover, they found that the relationship between single family office and debt financing is reinforced by the idiosyncrasies of entrepreneurial families, such as higher levels of owner management and higher firm age.

4. Finally, previous research has examined the role of family offices from entrepreneurship perspectives. For example, Welsh et al. (2013) highlighted that family offices are also involved in entrepreneurial practices to elevate the family's wealth. Zellweger, Nason, and Nordqvist (2012) proposed that family offices function as financing entrepreneurial activities in addition to being a structure for creating transgenerational wealth. Distinguished from the previous research examining entrepreneurial orientation at the organization level, the authors emphasized the family as the key level of analysis for transgenerational value creation. Related to this, Cruz and Nordqvist (2012) asserted that while founders' entrepreneurial attributes are vital to the first generation of family firms, later generations are dependent on non-family resources as drivers of entrepreneur orientation. Such an approach helps scholars understand the family's transition from a family enterprise into an entrepreneurial family, which implies the family as an institution or social structure that can drive and constrain entrepreneurial activities (Nordqvist & Melin, 2010; Zellweger & Sieger, 2012). In addition, Randerson and researchers (2015) argued that family offices function in diverse ways to support family entrepreneurship. Specifically, the authors suggested that based on a resource-based view, family offices can provide resources needed for entrepreneurship. Furthermore, network theory can be applied in analyzing family offices from entrepreneurship perspectives in that the social ties of the family members are the means of enabling resources for any envisaged entrepreneurship. Also, drawing on social capital theory, the authors argued that moral infrastructure that establishes the relationships between family members could influence the financing of new entrepreneurial projects from the family office.

Moreover, families provide financial resources to venture capital funds that promote the formation and growth of startups (Decker & Gunther, 2016) and support the entrepreneurial activities of their next generation through their family offices even if the ideas differ from those of generations managing the family business (Zellweger and Sieger, 2012, Zellweger et al., 2012). For example, Decker and Gunther (2016) provided anecdotal evidence that family offices can support wealth owners' entrepreneurial endeavours beyond their traditional family businesses. In this regard, the authors suggested that family offices act as coordinators of families' entrepreneurial activities. Similarly, Roure et al. (2013) examined family offices from the vantage point of an entrepreneurial process, focusing on how multi-generational families move from managing a family business to running a family office as if the latter was its main business for wealth creation. Specifically, the authors proposed a conceptual model of the family office process, noting that the success of the family office model depends on a dynamic fit between the family individual's vision, strategy, and entrepreneurial profiles. Thus, the family's collective entrepreneurial profile may determine whether the family office will invest in riskier high-growth assets such as venture capital or less-risky alternatives. Schickinger and researchers (2021b) examined the entrepreneurial investment behaviour of single-family offices through interviews with 109 German-speaking families owning single family offices. Based on the socio-emotional emotional wealth and agency theory combined with the explorative interviews, they suggested that families operating single family offices while still owning original family firms engage less in direct entrepreneurial investment compared to those who sold their original family firm. In addition, they postulated that first-generation single-family offices engage more in direct entrepreneurial investments than those of later generations. Simply put, the authors proposed how the entrepreneurial investment behaviour of single-family offices may vary depending on family characteristics.

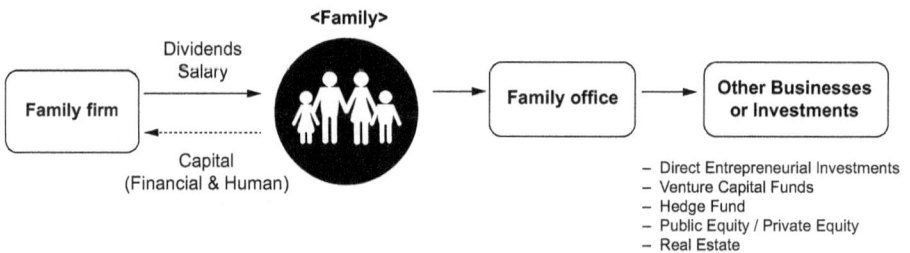

Figure 15.4: Family office and financial investments.

Possible Future Research on Family Offices

Extended from the previous literature on family offices, management scholars can further explore the role that familial capitalism plays in the entrepreneurial investment process.

1. First, from a theoretical standpoint, little systematic knowledge exists on the logic that investment-portfolio entrepreneurial families apply to administer family assets and investments. Distinguished from other private investors, family members operating family offices have specialized knowledge and expertise in the family business domain. However, research has yet to fully explore *whether* and *how* family businesses that wealthy families own or operate impact direct entrepreneurial investments of family offices. Specifically, it remains unknown whether family offices invest in venture firm

sectors that are similar or dissimilar from their core family businesses. Theoretically, two competing arguments generate the opposite prediction. On the one hand, in line with modern portfolio theory, family offices may diversify their venture firm investment sectors away from family businesses to mitigate the systematic risks involved in the overall investment portfolio. On the other hand, drawing on the knowledge literature, family offices may choose venture firm sectors that are similar or adjacent to their family business. More specifically, the family's creation or holding of the core business results in deep expertise, strategic knowledge, and industry insight in family business domains, which provide competitive advantages in selecting and evaluating venture firms in related sectors. Despite conflicting theoretical arguments on direct entrepreneurial investments by family offices, research has yet to explore such a research puzzle. Researchers address this lack of research by testing competing views to determine the investment-portfolio logic family offices apply when configuring their entrepreneurial investment portfolio.

2. Second, prior studies on family offices have been largely premised upon the implicit assumption that family offices have no direct/indirect impact on the strategy formation of family businesses. Specifically, several studies have examined whether and how family businesses influence family office operation. For example, according to the longitudinal study on family office investing conducted by US Trust and Campden Research, there appears to be an "operating company effect" whereby those families with operating companies are larger when it comes to assets under management and number of staff, and tend to be younger in age, serve few family members, direct their investing from in-house, and invest more aggressively (Rosplock, 2014). Further, family offices connected to families with an operating company have lower family office cost structures and high expectations that the office will be profitable (Rosplock, 2014). This line of research suggests that a privately held family business has a significant impact on the investment performance, management, and function of a family office. However, scholars have been silent on whether family offices can influence the performance, management, or operation of family businesses in reverse. Although several studies suggest that wealth growth facilitated by family offices can increase investments in the family enterprise (Aldrich & Cliff, 2003; Welsh & Raven, 2006), the research exploring the impact of family offices on family businesses is missing. Accordingly, researchers can investigate whether family offices can function as an "elongated workbench" or "external source of innovation", which supports the existence and expansion of the family business (Decker & Gunther, 2016). More specifically, future research can explore the relationship between direct entrepreneurial investment of family offices, CVC investments, or acquisition behaviour of family businesses.

3. Third, another knowledge gap is whether family offices engage in more socially responsible investing compared to non-family, financial institutions. More specifically, prior studies on family business have mixed and contradictory findings on whether

family firms are more socially responsible than their non-family counterparts. For example, drawing on socioemotional wealth theory, Berrone et al. (2010) found that family-controlled public firms have a better environmental performance than their non-family counterparts. Similarly, Cennamo et al. (2012) argued that family firms are more likely to adopt proactive stakeholder management activities to preserve and enhance their socio-emotional wealth. Bingham et al. (2011) showed that family firms have a higher corporate social performance compared to their non-family counterparts. On the other hand, Dyer and Whetten (2016) found no significant differences between family and non-family firms regarding positive social initiatives. Furthermore, Neckerbrouck and researchers (2018) argued that family firms are worse organizational stewards than their non-family counterparts. More specifically, the authors provided empirical evidence that family firms provide lower compensation and invest less in employee training, which collectively leads to higher employee voluntary turnover and lower labour productivity. Moreover, the authors indicated that such a negative impact of family on employment practices worsens as firm age and family involvement increase. However, to the best of my knowledge, there is no research examining whether such arguments can be extended into family office contexts. Specifically, there is a growing argument in the literature suggesting that family offices also aim to achieve non-financial goals along with managing financial wealth. Socially responsible investing represents a unique combination of financial and social objectives, while other standard investment decisions are concentrated solely on financial returns. Thus, given that socially responsible investing can satisfy the families' desire to achieve both financial and non-financial aspects, researchers can explore whether family offices engage in more socially responsible investing compared to non-family, financial institutions.

4. Fourth, scholars need to examine the factors driving the rapid growth of family offices around the world in more critical terms and particularly focus upon the perpetuation of dynastic wealth. Practitioner literature has attributed the recent growth of family offices merely as the response to accommodate demands from an increasing population of ultra-high-net-worth individuals (Rosplock & Hauser, 2014). However, growing sociological literature on elites and the global inequalities driven by their wealth accumulation view the rapid growth of family offices more critically. For example, tracing back to Piketty's (2014) seminal work on capital accumulation in the 21st century that analyzed the return of inheritance as the principal mechanism for wealth accumulation among the global elite in contemporary societies, Glucksberg and Burrows (2016) framed family offices as contemporary infrastructures of dynastic wealth, which have begun to emerge as institutions for contemporary elite formation since 2008. In addition, with the resurgence of patrimonial forms of capitalism (Piketty, 2014), Harrington (2016) suggested that wealth inheritance is not an automatic or purely transaction process, but rather socially and culturally dependent and bound up in relationships of family and kinship. Related to this perspective,

Sklair and Glucksberg (2021) argued that philanthropy activities that family offices undertake function as affective practices to ensure the success of inheritance and family business succession planning, as wealth moves down generations of dynastic families. More specifically, the authors suggested that such philanthropic activities as affective wealth management strategies frame wealthy families as custodians of both private capital and the common good, thereby publicly demonstrating the legitimacy of their growing wealth. As Kuusela (2018) argued, future research can explore what other sociological, economic, and cultural factors facilitate the rising creation of family offices, and how family offices administer the social dynamics through which dynastic family wealth has managed to persist and contribute to class-making.

5. Lastly, from an empirical standpoint, there have been few quantitative studies examining the family office (Rivo-Lopez et al., 2017). Indeed, most of the research has been based on descriptive and qualitative methods, such as case studies (e.g., Lopez, Lopez, & Sanchez, 2013; Roure et al., 2013), ethnography (e.g., Glucksberg & Burrows, 2016), surveys (e.g., Amit, et al., 2008; Roure et al., 2013), and in-depth interviews (e.g., Decker & Gunther, 2016) that all rely on relatively small samples or merely propose conceptual propositions (e.g., Rivo-Lopez et al., 2013; Wessel et al., 2014). To increase the generalizability of theoretical arguments and empirical findings, researchers need to conduct large-sample quantitative research to statistically examine the financial investments made by family offices. In addition, because the theoretical definition of family office is not consistent among researchers, the empirical boundaries of the family office are also controversial. For example, according to Kenyon-Rouvinez and Park (2020), when Bloomberg (2014) published a list of the 50-largest family offices based on their assets under management, Zeuner, Lagomasino, and Ulloa (2014) critiqued the data, arguing that most of the top-listed firms were not family offices but traditional financial service firms positioning themselves as family offices. To mitigate such a classification concern, researchers need to make extra efforts to conduct a thorough search and confirm whether family offices are founded by family members and are genuinely dedicated to serving the unique needs of single- or multi-families.

Taken together, scholars can fill the aforementioned theoretical and empirical gaps existing in family office research by answering the five interrelated questions as follows:

1. What investment logic do family offices rely on when making direct entrepreneurial investments?
2. How do direct entrepreneurial investments made by family offices impact the strategy formation of family businesses (e.g., CVC investment or acquisition behaviour)?
3. Do family offices more actively engage in socially responsible investing compared to other non-family, financial institutions?
4. What factors are driving the rapid growth of family offices around the world?

5. How should one conduct critical-based research mitigating the methodological limitations with family offices, such as heightened privacy and non-transparency?

Although the practical importance of family office is rising to sustain the dynastic wealth of business families, the academic literature shedding light on such phenomenon is scarce. In this chapter, I first provide an overview regarding the professional development and classification of family offices. Notably, I clarified that family offices are distinguished from other professional financial services in terms of holistic/long-term approach, higher personal attention to families, and close cooperation with other types of trusted advisors. I then explain why researchers should further expand their academic attention from family businesses to family offices, arguing that family offices function as tools for wealthy families to regenerate themselves while continuously maintaining their elite class formation. In addition, I thoroughly review previous literature on family offices in the management field, ranging from both practical and academic papers. Lastly, based on the comprehensive literature review, I identify five possible future research topics on the family office. All these descriptions imply that ample room exists for researchers to explore family office topics in the future in terms of theoretical and empirical perspectives.

References

Aldrich, H. E., & Cliff, J. E. (2003). The pervasive effects of family on entrepreneurship: Toward a family embeddedness perspective. *Journal of Business Venturing*, 18(5), 573–596.

Amit, R. (2006). Family Offices in the US. Working document.

Amit, R., Liechtenstein, H., Prats, M. J., Millay, T., & Pendleton, L. P. (2008). Single family offices: Private wealth management in the family context, Technical report, 2008, Wharton School, University of Pennsylvania, Philadelphia, PA.

Amit, R., Liechtenstein, H., Prats, M.J., Millay, T., & Pendleton, L.P. (2009). Single family office: identifying the performance drivers, Technical report, Wharton School, University of Pennsylvania, Philadelphia, PA.

Amit, R., & Liechtenstein, H. (2009). Report highlights for benchmarking the single family office: Identifying the performance drivers. Wharton School, University of Pennsylvania.

Amit, R. and Liechtenstein, H. (2012). Report Highlights for Benchmarking the Single Family Office: Identifying the Performance Drivers, (Technical Report), Wharton School, University of Pennsylvania, Philadelphia, PA.

Avery, H. (2004). Keeping it in the family. *Euromoney*, 35(425), 236–246.

Bingham, J. B., Dyer, W. G., Smith, I., & Adams, G. L. (2011). A stakeholder identity orientation approach to corporate social performance in family firms. *Journal of Business Ethics*, 99(4), 565–585.

Beech, J. (2019, July 18). Global family office growth soars, manages $5.9 trillion. Campden FB. Retrieved September 26, 2021, from https://www.campdenfb.com/article/global-family-office -growth-soars-manages-59-trillion.

Berrone, P., Cruz, C., Gomez-Mejia, L. R., & Larraza-Kintana, M. (2010). Socioemotional wealth and corporate responses to institutional pressures: Do family-controlled firms pollute less?. *Administrative Science Quarterly*, 55(1), 82–113.

Block, J., Fisch, C., Vismara, S., & Andres, R. (2019). Private equity investment criteria: An experimental conjoint analysis of venture capital, business angels, and family offices. *Journal of Corporate Finance*, 58, 329–352.

Bloomberg (2014). Bloomberg Brief: Family Office. Retrieved September 26, 2022, from www.bloombergbriefs.com/content/uploads/sites/2/2014/06/Family_Office_Supplement.pdf.

Bowen, J. (2004). In the family way. *Financial Planning*, 8, 31–33.

Brown, F.H., & Jaffe, D.T. (2009). Overcoming Entitlement and Raising Responsible Next Generation Family Members. Boston: Family Firm Institute.

Cennamo, C., Berrone, P., Cruz, C., & Gomez–Mejia, L. R. (2012). Socioemotional wealth and proactive stakeholder engagement: Why family–controlled firms care more about their stakeholders. *Entrepreneurship Theory and Practice*, 36(6), 1153–1173.

Cruz, C., & Nordqvist, M. (2012). Entrepreneurial orientation in family firms: A generational perspective. *Small Business Economics*, 38(1), 33–49.

Curtis, G. (2001). Establishing a family office: A few basics. Greycourt White Paper, 10.

Daniell, M., & Hamilton, S. (2010). Family Legacy and Leadership: Preserving True Family Wealth in Challenging Times. John Wiley and Sons.

Davis, E., Cieniewski, S., & Birenbaum, J. (2016). The Smart Money: When a Private Equity Minority Investment Can Be Better Than a Bank Loan (and What about a Family Office?). *The Journal of Private Equity*, 20(1), 21–24.

Decker, C., & Gunther, C. (2016). Coordinating family entrepreneurship: when money seeks opportunity. *International Journal of Entrepreneurial Venturing*, 8(1), 46–61.

Decker, C., & Lange, K. S. (2013). Exploring a secretive organization: What can we learn about family offices from the public sphere. *Organizational Dynamics*, 42(4), 298–306.

Dunn, M. G. (1980). The family office as a coordinating mechanism within the ruling class. *Insurgent Sociologist*, 9(2–3), 8–23.

Dyer, W. G., & Whetten, D. A. (2006). Family firms and social responsibility: Preliminary evidence from the S&P 500. *Entrepreneurship Theory and Practice*, 30(6), 785–802.

The Family Office Quick Guide. The Family Office Quick Guide | Family Office Exchange. (2016). Retrieved September 26, 2022, from https://www.familyoffice.com/family-office-quick-guide.

The Family Office Quick Guide. The Family Office Quick Guide | Family Office Exchange. (2018). Retrieved September 26, 2022, from https://www.familyoffice.com/family-office-quick-guide.

Fermadez-Moya & Castro-Balaguer (2011). Looking for the perfect structure: The evolution of family office from a long-term perspective. *Universia Business Review*, 32, 82–93.

File, K. M., Prince, R. A., & Rankin, M. J. (1994). Organizational buying behavior of the family firm. *Family Business Review*, 7(3), 263–272.

Gilding, M. (2005). Families and fortunes: Accumulation, management succession and inheritance in wealthy families. *Journal of Sociology*, 41(1), 29–45.

Glucksberg, L., & Burrows, R. (2016). Family offices and the contemporary infrastructures of dynastic wealth. *Sociologica*, 10(2), 1–23.

Gomez-Mejia, L. R., Cruz, C., Berrone, P., & De Castro, J. (2011). The bind that ties: Socioemotional wealth preservation in family firms. *Academy of Management Annals*, 5(1), 653–707.

Grote, J. (2003). Conflicting generations: a new theory of family business rivalry. *Family Business Review*, 16(2), 113–124

Habbershon, T. G., & Pistrui, J. (2002). Enterprising families domain: Family-influenced ownership groups in pursuit of transgenerational wealth. *Family Business Review*, 15(3), 223–237.

Hall, P. D. (1988). A historical overview of family firms in the United States. *Family Business Review*, 1(1), 51–68.

Hamilton, S (1992). Research note: A second family business-patterns in wealth management. *Family Business Review*, V(2), 181–188.

Harrington, B. (2016). *Capital Without Borders: Wealth Managers and the One Percent*. Cambridge, MA: Harvard University Press.

Harrington, B. (2012). Trust and Estate Planning: The Emergence of a Profession and its Contribution to Socioeconomic Inequality 1. In *Sociological Forum*, 27(4), 825–846). Oxford, UK: Blackwell Publishing Ltd.

Jaffe, D. T., & Lane, S. H. (2004). Sustaining a family dynasty: Key issues facing complex multigenerational business-and investment-owning families. *Family Business Review*, 17(1), 81–98.

Jain, M., & Lotia, H. (2009). Family Offices in Asia with Special Focus on Singapore. Available at SSRN 1448613.

Kaye, K., & Hamilton, S. (2004). Roles of Trust in consulting to financial families. *Family Business Review*, XVII 17 (2), 151–163

Kenyon-Rouvinez, D., & Park, J. E. (2020). Family office research review. *The Journal of Wealth Management*, 22(4), 8–20.

Kuusela, H. (2018). Learning to own: Cross-generational meanings of wealth and class-making in wealthy Finnish families. *The Sociological Review*, 66(6), 1161–1176.

Lansberg, I. (1999). Succeeding Generations: Realizing the Dream of Families in Business. Harvard Business Review Press.

López, E. R., López, N. R., & Sánchez, B. G. (2013). The family office in Spain: An exploratory study. *Management Research: Journal of the Iberoamerican Academy of Management*.

Neckebrouck, J., Schulze, W., & Zellweger, T. (2018). Are family firms good employers? *Academy of Management Journal*, 61(2), 553–585.

Nordqvist, M., & Melin, L. (2010). Entrepreneurial families and family firms. *Entrepreneurship and Regional Development*, 22(3–4), 211–239.

Piketty, T. (2014). Capital in the 21st Century. Cambridge, MA and London, England: Harvard University Press.

Randerson, K., Bettinelli, C., Fayolle, A., & Anderson, A. (2015). Family entrepreneurship as a field of research: Exploring its contours and contents. *Journal of Family Business Strategy*, 6(3), 143–154.

Rivo-López, E., Villanueva-Villar, M., & Vaquero-García, A. (2016). *Family Office: A New Category in Family Business Research?* (No. 1601). Universidade de Vigo, GEN-Governance and Economics Research Network.

Rivo-López, E., Villanueva-Villar, M., Vaquero-García, A., & Lago-Peñas, S. (2017). Family offices. What, why and what for. *Organizational Dynamics*, 46(4), 262–270.

Rosplock, K. (2014). *The Complete Family Office Handbook: A Guide for Affluent Families and the Advisors Who Serve Them*. John Wiley & Sons.

Rosplock, K., & Hauser, B. R. (2014). The family office landscape: Today's trends and five predictions for the family office of tomorrow. *The Journal of Wealth Management*, 17(3), 9–19.

Roure, J., Segurado, J. L., Welsh, D. H., & Rosplock, K. (2013). Toward a conceptual model of the role of entrepreneurship in the family office. *Journal of Applied Management and Entrepreneurship*, 18(4), 42.

Rowley, J. D. (2018, March 26). Charting The Adoption of Direct Startup Investments by Family Offices. Retrieved December 12, 2019, from https://news.crunchbase.com/news/charting-adoption-direct-startup-investments-family-offices/.

Schickinger, A., Bertschi-Michel, A., Leitterstorf, M. P., & Kammerlander, N. (2021a). Same, but different: capital structures in single family offices compared with private equity firms. *Small Business Economics*, 1–19.

Schickinger, A., Bierl, P. A., Leitterstorf, M. P., & Kammerlander, N. (2021b). Family-related goals, entrepreneurial investment behavior, and governance mechanisms of single family offices: An exploratory study. *Journal of Family Business Strategy*, 100393.

Sklair, J., & Glucksberg, L. (2021). Philanthrocapitalism as wealth management strategy: Philanthropy, inheritance and succession planning among the global elite. *The Sociological Review*, 69(2), 314–329.

Strike, V. M. (2012). Advising the family firm: Reviewing the past to build the future. *Family Business Review*, 25(2), 156–177.

Strike, V. M., & Rerup, C. (2016). Mediated sensemaking. *Academy of Management Journal*, 59(3), 880–905.

Strike, V. M., Michel, A., & Kammerlander, N. (2018). Unpacking the black box of family business advising: Insights from psychology. *Family Business Review*, 31(1), 80–124.

Suess, J. (2014). Family governance–Literature review and the development of a conceptual model. *Journal of Family Business Strategy*, 5(2), 138–155.

Tse, T., Sola, D., & Gheorghita, R. (2011). Factors determining the investment strategies of family wealth: Cases from western Europe. *International Journal of Management Cases*, 13(1), 101–110.

Ward, J. L. (2008). How values dilemmas underscore the difficult issues of governing the large, enterprising family. In *Family Values and Value Creation* (pp. 102–124). London: Palgrave Macmillan.

Welsh, D. H., & Raven, P. (2006). Family business in the Middle East: An exploratory study of retail management in Kuwait and Lebanon. *Family Business Review*, 19(1), 29–48.

Welsh, D. H., Memili, E., Rosplock, K., Roure, J., & Segurado, J. L. (2013). Perceptions of entrepreneurship across generations in family offices: A stewardship theory perspective. *Journal of Family Business Strategy*, 4(3), 213–226.

Wessel, S., Decker, C., Lange, K. S., & Hack, A. (2014). One size does not fit all: Entrepreneurial families' reliance on family offices. *European Management Journal*, 32(1), 37–45.

Wolosky, H. (2002). Family offices come downtown. *Practical Accountant*, 35(3), 23–27.

Zellweger, T., & Kammerlander, N. (2015). Article commentary: Family, wealth, and governance: An agency account. *Entrepreneurship Theory and Practice*, 39(6), 1281–1303.

Zellweger, T. M., Nason, R. S., & Nordqvist, M. (2012). From longevity of firms to transgenerational entrepreneurship of families: Introducing family entrepreneurial orientation. *Family Business Review*, 25(2), 136–155.

Zellweger, T., & Sieger, P. (2012). Entrepreneurial orientation in long-lived family firms. *Small Business Economics*, 38(1), 67–84.

Zeuner, M., Lagomasino, M. E., & Ulloa, S. (2014). A family office by any other name. *The Journal of Wealth Management*, 17(3), 20–26.

Nadine Kammerlander and Alexandra Bertschi-Michel

16 Family Wealth Governance and the Role of Advisors

Abstract: In this chapter we aim at reviewing the literatures on family wealth, in particular that on family offices, its related governance implications as well as the literature on family business advisors. Subsequently, we discuss the findings from these literature streams to reveal interdependencies and relationships between family offices, governance aspects and advisors. Finally, we conceptually integrate those results into a holistic model on advisor involvement in the unique context of family offices. Hence, in this chapter we reveal how the traditional family business research is moving towards other disciplines such as family offices and their interrelated, family external parties such as professional advisors. In doing so, we aim at contributing to the literatures on family wealth, in particular family offices, governance and that on advisors by bridging the so far mostly isolated sub-disciplines within family business research and by providing an integrated model thereof.

Keywords: family governance, family office, family business advisors, family wealth, enterprising families

Introduction

Since its inception in the late 1980s, the business(es) of enterprising families have been at the centre of academic research on family businesses and business families. Further family-related constructs, such as conflicts, emotions, and family dynamics, have been added to the picture. However, one important piece of the puzzle has largely been ignored: *family wealth* and its governance. Family wealth is an important aspect of family business and business family research, as it constitutes the source of families' enterprising activities (Bierl & Kammerlander, 2019). Moreover, the aim to accumulate wealth is one of the reasons why families decide to engage in entrepreneurial activities and continue to do so over generations. However, family wealth and its distribution can also be the source of important family conflicts. In recent years, academics and practitioners have increasingly started to focus on topics related to family wealth as family offices have become more visible. Family offices, legal asset management and investment structures are often created after the sales of the original family firm (i.e., the exit of the family from the family

Nadine Kammerlander, WHU – Otto Beisheim School of Management
Alexandra Bertschi-Michel, University of Bern

https://doi.org/10.1515/9783110727968-016

business) or in cases where the family has accumulated substantial wealth through dividend payouts over time (Schickinger, Bertschi-Michel et al., 2022). Such family offices are set up to maintain or increase family wealth and to provide a governance structure to the family (Schickinger, Bierl et al., 2021). While research on family offices and their governance structures is slowly growing, one important aspect is still not sufficiently understood: the role of advisors of family offices and family wealth governance.

This is surprising, as evidence from practice as well as some prior academic studies suggest that in the context of family offices, advisors play an important role in supporting family members when making crucial decisions regarding their wealth preferences and investment strategies (Lowenhaupt, 2008; Wessel et al., 2014). Interestingly, to date, academic research lacks a conceptually established and theoretically validated model of advisor involvement in family offices (Zellweger & Kammerlander, 2015). This is unfortunate because in other family business disciplines, advisors have been found to be of great value for family owners and their firms (Reay et al., 2013; Strike, 2012; Strike et al., 2018). However, one can assume that advising family businesses is different from advising family offices, as the latter requires different competencies (financial and legal aspects rather than business operations), is characterized by unique challenges (e.g., the task of increasing the next generation's commitment to a "product-free" family office rather than a family business), and is embedded in a globally connected environment (family office investments are not restricted per se to certain countries or even industries). Moreover, the competitive landscape of family offices (competing with other financial investors such as private equity [PE] funds or holding companies) is different from that of family businesses.

A large number of studies on advisors in family businesses focus on the context of intergenerational succession by emphasizing the importance of having a formal third-party advisor supporting incumbents and successors throughout the entire succession process (Bertschi-Michel et al., 2021). Advisors, for example, may facilitate successor leadership development (Salvato & Corbetta, 2013) or engage in emotion mediation activities (e.g., Bertschi-Michel et al., 2020), eventually resulting in improved firm performance (Naldi et al., 2015). Other studies on family business advisors largely focus on specific behaviours and techniques of advisors in their interaction with family businesses, such as knowledge sharing (Su & Dou, 2013), trust building (de Groote & Bertschi-Michel, 2020), facilitating collective attention followed by certain actions (Strike, 2013), or inducing a mediated sensemaking process within the family business owner, allowing doubt and rethinking of extant positions (Strike & Rerup, 2016).

In the following, we aim to review the literature on family wealth, particularly on family offices, its related governance implications and the literature on family business advisors. Subsequently, we discuss the findings from these literature streams to reveal interdependencies and relationships between family offices, governance aspects, and advisors. Finally, we conceptually integrate those results into a holistic model of advisor involvement in the unique context of family offices and compare those with that of advisors involved in family businesses. Hence, with this chapter, we aim to contribute to the literature on family wealth, in particular, family offices, governance, and advisors by bridging the most isolated subdisciplines within family business research to date and providing an integrated model thereof. In doing so, we also show that the frontiers of the traditional family business research are moving into relatively new fields such as family offices and thereby are going beyond investigating just the roles of the founding family but of other interrelated actors such as their professional advisors.

Theoretical Background

Family Wealth and Governance

Many business families, over generations of being active in the firm, generate substantial wealth at the family level. To administer this wealth, many business families currently decide to set up a so-called family office, a legal entity that is dedicated to maintaining and increasing family wealth. Families can decide to set up their own family office, solely dedicated to their family (a so-called single-family office, or SFO) or join forces with other families (in a so-called multiple-family office or MFO that is steered by either one or a few families, a service provider, or even a bank). The scope of responsibilities of family offices can vary widely, from strategizing and implementing family investment strategies to philanthropic activities or even dealing with family issues (e.g., next-generation education). Similarly, the legal structure (e.g., as a holding) and size of family offices (from one to dozens of employees) vary substantially. While the idea of having a dedicated "office" to take care of one's wealth goes back to medieval merchants, for business families, it was the traditional "house bank" that helped with wealth governance issues for many decades. However, this trend has changed from banks towards family offices in the early 2000s, stemming from decreased trust in institutions after the financial crisis as well as the desire of business families to remain "entrepreneurial" even after the potential sale of the family business.

According to a 2019 study by Campden, the number of single-family offices worldwide has grown to 7,300 entities with total assets of US$5.9 billion under management.[1] Family offices are often seen as viable vehicles to administer the family's wealth and, in particular, to diversify asset classes and reduce risks. A

---

1 https://www.campdenfb.com/article/global-family-office-growth-soars-manages-59-trillion#:~:text=The%20total%20estimated%20assets%20under,a%20significant%2038%25%20from%202017

recent SFO study in the German-speaking part of Europe (Bierl et al., 2018) shows that families diversify their assets across different asset classes (see Figure 16.1). While most business families possess company shares from stock-listed firms as well as real estate, roughly half of the firms directly invest in established companies, thereby being active in the PE market. As a recent wealth report by UBS[2] shows, the COVID-19 pandemic proved that (most) SFOs have a robust investment strategy, with returns ranging between minus 7 and plus 20% during the crisis, with the lower end of the performance mostly attributable to investments in specific sectors such as gastronomy and tourism that were hit hard by regional lockdowns.

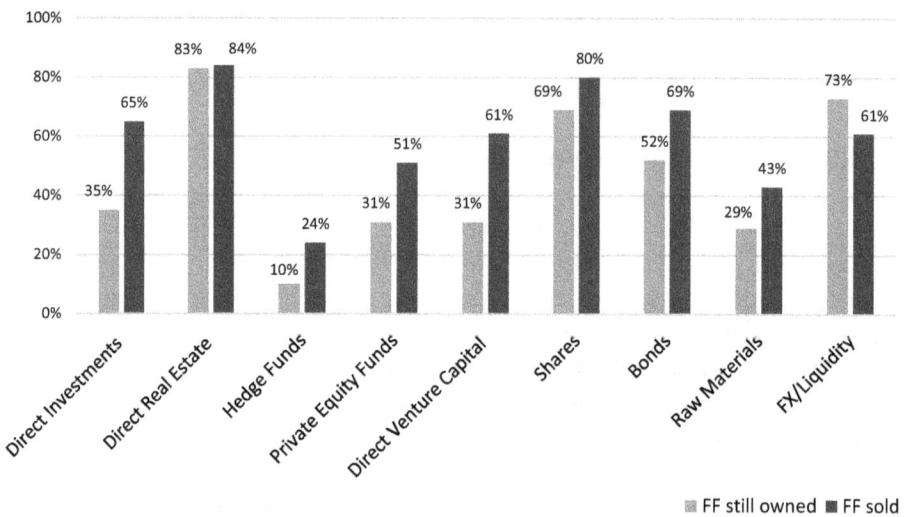

Figure 16.1: Percentage of SFOs with activities in the respective asset class.
Source: Bierl, Schickinger, Leitterstorf, & Kammerlander, 2018.

As the UBS report shows, family offices, on average, have so far navigated successfully through the crisis. Nevertheless, managing family wealth and setting up a family office are accompanied by many challenges. In particular, it is important to obtain the "right governance" of family wealth. As Zellweger and Kammerlander (2015) argue in their conceptual article, a lack of family wealth governance might lead to a "Michael Jackson-like dispute" over family wealth; once the patriarch or matriarch has passed away, (potential) heirs may start fighting over the existing wealth, resulting in chaos and eventually leading to a substantial reduction of the existing financial and non-financial family wealth.

---

2 https://www.ubs.com/global/en/global-family-office/reports/global-family-office-report-2020.html

As already indicated in this section above, a family office, set up as a separate legal entity with defined tasks, rights, and liabilities, might help govern such wealth. In particular, when setting up a family office to administer family wealth, individual family members need to agree on their overall goals and investment principles. For instance, some family members might prioritize risk mitigation, while others might focus on profit maximization. Moreover, some family members might constrain their investments by certain moral boundaries (e.g., exclusion of certain industries such as tobacco or alcohol, investments only in vegan or carbon-neutral firms, etc.). All these guiding principles must be thoroughly discussed and agreed upon. Other questions important for family wealth governance include the following: Does the family invest as an entity or do members invest individually? Or a mixture? What are the conditions under which the family office invests in a family member's venture? Who should run the family office? Are family members considered for the family office team, and, if so, under what conditions? Are family-external individuals considered for the family office team, and, if so, under what conditions? How open and transparent should the conversation with the family office be? What are the scope and criteria for working together with external partners? What should the reporting look like (e.g., in terms of frequency and depth)? How will the family deal with potential conflicts over family wealth and related investments? Who can become part of the family office (e.g., what about spouses)? What is the role of the next generation? How could or should they be involved? How can the family office serve as the new "entrepreneurial nucleus" of the business family, in particular in case the original family firm has been sold? How shall the family office interact with the family business (if still existent)? What is the role of philanthropy within the family office?

Advisors in Family Firms

Owing to the huge challenges family firms face in an increasingly uncertain world characterized by immense challenges such as the recent COVID-19 pandemic (De Massis & Rondi, 2020; Shepherd, 2020), family firm research has recently drawn attention to the crucial role played by advisors (e.g., Reay et al., 2013; Strike, 2012; Strike et al., 2018). Advisors can be defined as a business-external source that provides objective and subtle advice to the owners of a family firm. Objective advice includes expert knowledge, such as answers to technical questions related to financial, organizational, or tax issues, whereas subtle advice involves the advisor's tactics and behaviour to influence the attention of the advised individuals in a certain direction (Strike, 2013). Moreover, advice can be provided either on a formal, hired basis or, in contrast, on an informal friendship-like basis (Strike, 2012). As outlined above, extant research on family firm advisors mainly focuses on the context of succession as well as on specific behaviours and tactics of advisors when advising a family firm.

Within the context of family firm succession, advisors have also been found to facilitate transitional leadership, meaning an advisor may support leadership skill development in a successor, and at certain points perhaps even assume leadership ad interim until the successor has grown into his or her new role (Salvato & Corbetta, 2013). Moreover, an advisor closely guides incumbents and successors throughout the succession process by providing both parties equally with crucial information (Michel & Kammerlander, 2015) and by unearthing and alleviating upcoming emotions and thus engaging in mediation activities. In doing so, an advisor can speed role adjustments and thereby advance the succession process (Bertschi-Michel et al., 2020).

Such behaviour, also referred to as tertius iungens behaviour connecting group members with one another and thereby increasing the whole group's advantages (Obstfeld, 2005), has been found to enhance the incumbent's and successor's overall satisfaction with the succession process as well as the family firm's performance post-succession (Bertschi-Michel et al., 2021). Relatedly, the study by Naldi et al. (2015) finds support for an inverted U-shaped relationship between the number of family advisors and family firm performance, proposing that too few or too many family advisors leads to worse performance outcomes, whereas a "right" amount of advice enhances performance. Furthermore, the study finds that such an inverted U-shaped relationship is moderated by the generation in charge, which is a positive relationship between advisors and performance in first-generation family firms, whereas in later-generation family firms, the relationship turns into an inverted U-shape.

Regarding an advisor's behaviours and techniques, one of the first studies on advisor interaction with family firms emphasized the importance of an advisor's ability to assume adaptive behaviour, meaning that an advisor can promptly react to feedback received from the family to tailor his or her advice to the needs of the firm (Davis et al., 2013). Thereby, knowledge sharing was identified as one central mechanism to tailor advice to the family firm, as it improves the accuracy of issue identification and supports the systematic analysis to arrive at an integrated solution of high credibility (Su & Dou, 2013). In addition to providing credible advice, advisors also pursue mentoring activities, for example, to support the development of a protégé (Distelberg & Schwarz, 2015).

On a more subtle basis, advisors were found to use specific techniques, such as capturing attention and becoming attuned to family firm members, to influence and aid family members in mindfully collaborating and governing the firm. Thus, an advisor also serves as a facilitator of an environment of collective attention (Strike, 2013). Relatedly, advisors induce internal processes such as adaptive sense-making among family firm owners by slowing down the action and allowing feelings of doubt. This fosters a critical rethinking of existing positions and manifests itself in a mediated sensemaking process guided by the advisor (Strike & Rerup, 2016). Hence, such internal processes require an advisor's close acquaintance, which increases the more he or she is embedded within the family firm (Barbera & Hasso, 2013). Trust and trust-building processes thereby serve as key constructs allowing advisors to interact with family firms in intimate ways, as described in this section above (Strike, 2012). To build such trusting relationships, an advisor pursues a nonlinear process of trust building starting with an intention to trust that develops into perceived trust and eventually manifests itself as behavioural trust (de Groote & Bertschi-Michel, 2021) to ultimately become a trusted advisor (Strike, 2013).

Discussion

Our literature review reveals that business families frequently rely on advisors. Anecdotal evidence shows that this is also true regarding the management and preservation of their wealth by setting up family offices to gain access to expert knowledge related to, for example, tax issues, strategic changes, or succession (Reay et al., 2013; Zellweger & Kammerlander, 2015). The extant literature of both disciplines, that on family offices and advisors in family firms, stresses that trust serves as a key construct determining the collaboration of the family with externals such as an advisor (de Groote & Bertschi-Michel, 2021; Welsh et al., 2013). Family firm literature has already developed the concept of the most trusted advisor (MTA), first introduced and defined by Strike (2013) as those advisors being closest to family firm members and exercising the strongest influence; this concept has been further refined by numerous authors (e.g., Michel & Kammerlander, 2015; Reay et al., 2013; Strike & Rerup, 2016). In the following, we aim to synthesize the literature on family offices and family advisors. In doing so, we extend the crucial concept of the MTA by introducing a more fine-grained distinction between the *most trusted wealth advisor* (MTWA) and the *most trusted business advisor* (MTBA). In particular, we identify six major areas in which we compare and discuss the tasks and roles that both types of advisors assume. In a subsequent step, we develop an integrated model of how MTWAs and MTBAs differ yet are complementary to each other and eventually derive important avenues for future research on the so far understudied field of MTWAs as an outcome of our model.

Syntheses of MTWA and MTBA

From our previous literature analyses, we define six major areas to compare and discuss the roles and tasks of the MTWA and the MTBA. In particular, we look first at the *services* they provide to the family office and the family firm, second at *collaboration*, third at *conflict* management, fourth at the involvement of the *next generation*, fifth at the impact on *digitalization* and finally, at the relationship with *performance*.

Regarding the provision of *services*, MTWAs in family offices dedicate significant effort to managing the wealth of the family. In doing so, they make crucial investment decisions to implement and achieve families' investment goals, which might include economic but also social and environmental goals (Block et al., 2019; Decker & Lange, 2016). This requires broad and deep expertise of different asset classes but also market and environmental developments (Zellweger & Kammerlander, 2015). The MTBA also provides services to the family, but whereas the MTWA's primary focus is related to the families' wealth, the MTBA's focus often lies in the provision of expertise to the family firm related to certain tasks (such as tax or legal questions) or processes (Strike, 2012). In doing so, the MTBA provides knowledge that the family firm lacks as well as an external perspective and thus can help overcome the frequent problem of family inertia (Michel & Kammerlander, 2015; Naldi et al., 2015). In sum, we assume that both functions, that of the MTWA and that of the MTBA, require broad expertise. However, we conclude from our review that the provision of services related to the management of families' private wealth requires even deeper levels of expertise in a highly complex and dynamic environment of financial investments. In particular, MTWAs need to possess a deep understanding of the risk considerations of family members, including potentially different assessments of variability and bankruptcy risk (Kempers et al., 2019), which become much more salient in the case of family offices.

In the way MTWAs *collaborate* with families, particularly in family offices, the definition of clear governance principles is crucial. Therefore, clear rules of participation as well as of how investments are made and how the family interacts with the MTWA have to be defined (Zellweger & Kammerlander, 2015). In contrast, the MTBA often interacts with the family firm more on an informal, or project-related, basis (de Groote & Bertschi-Michel, 2021; Strike, 2012). Nevertheless, the MTBA also needs to ensure that all stakeholders are equally involved by connecting family members. The MTBA achieves this by assuming a tertius iungens behaviour whereby s/he increases collaboration among group members (Bertschi-Michel et al., 2021; Strike, 2013). As such, we find that for both roles, that of the MTWA and that of the MTBA, open communication is key to successfully collaborate with the family. However, our analysis also reveals that, particularly in the context of family offices where collaboration entails sensitive issues regarding families' wealth, clear rules and governance mechanisms are needed. One important aspect in this regard is the question of which family members need to be included in the conversation. Whereas the answer to this question is often rather clear for MTBAs (in the first place those family members who are active in the firm), the scope of family stakeholders to be included becomes much broader for MTWAs, including passive family investors.

As *conflicts* frequently emerge within families, both types of advisors have to engage in conflict management (Frank et al., 2011). For MTWAs, such conflicts frequently stem from disagreements regarding wealth goals (preservation vs. growth) or investment decisions (pure growth vs. goals related to sustainability, social engagement, etc.). Therefore, MTWAs place much emphasis on the definition of criteria regarding investment decisions (Decker & Lange, 2016) – a task for which a family constitution or family office constitution might be of great support (Arteaga & Menéndez-Requejo, 2017). Additionally, proactive and transparent reporting can help keep family members informed, build trust, and avoid any conflicts in the case of unsuccessful investments. The MTBA, again, interacts with the family firm in a more informal way where s/he ensures an equal provision of information, provides support on role transitions in a succession context, and engages in emotion mediation activities where upcoming feelings are unearthed and addressed (Bertschi-Michel et al., 2020). As such, both types of advisors frequently face highly emotional conflicts. However, as conflicts, especially in family offices, are highly related to family internal and private wealth issues, we assume that an MTWA needs even greater sensitivity when addressing such conflicts than an MTBA. In particular, MTWAs need to possess sensitivity for the personal and private needs of the various family members (e.g., study loans; dependency on dividend payments) and take them into consideration while potentially not addressing them explicitly.

Another crucial topic for both MTWAs and MTBAs is the involvement of the *next generation,* either from a wealth perspective (MTWA) or in the family firm (MTBA). The extant literature predicts that one crucial task of the MTWA is a clear definition of roles and rules for young family members determining whether and under which conditions they might join the family office. Furthermore, the MTWA also engages in achieving commitment to participation among next-generation family members, as they frequently have divergent interests and goals (Zellweger & Kammerlander, 2015). For instance, anecdotal evidence shows that next-generation members are particularly interested in impact investment and making a positive societal and/or ecological impact. In this context, an MTWA often arranges education possibilities to prepare the next generation for their future involvement in the family office (Gray, 2005). In a similar vein, in the context of family firm succession, the MTBA frequently engages in a leadership skill development of the future successor that might even include ad interim management to support leadership transition (Salvato & Corbetta, 2013). In doing so, the MTBA provides crucial knowledge on the succession process to the family firm and closely coaches the successor within his or her transition role (Michel & Kammerlander, 2015). We propose that, order to fulfill this role, both functions, that of the MTWA and that of the MTBA, require trust of the family and in particular from the next generation/successor. Yet while in case of the MTBA especially *interpersonal* trust between the family members/successor and the advisor is important, for the MTWA impersonal trust manifesting itself as *institutional* trust becomes relevant as those advisors are likely to be institutionalized through corporations

(David et al., 2013). Institutional trust is defined as "an individual's expectation that some organized system will act with predictability and goodwill" (Maguire & Phillips, 2008, p. 372). Such trust is required as in the MTWA context, the family cannot always observe what is going on inside the advising organization due to bureaucracy and invisibility with the organization. Therefore, we assume that introducing the next generation into the families' private wealth management might require even deeper levels of trust in case of MTWA compared to guiding designated successors into their new role in the family firm by the MTBA.

Whereas the provision of advice regarding the involvement of the next generation is a well-known area where families frequently require external support, the current *digitalization* wave is a novel field where families need advice. In family offices, currently, the establishment of digital investment platforms and the use of algorithms to make investment decisions and/or to monitor the evolution of ongoing investments is a key factor of success (Hassani et al., 2018). Moreover, digital platforms that allow for co-investments and club deals have become increasingly popular. Additionally, the provision of digital wealth reports to family members is a future challenge of the MTWA. In a similar vein, MTBA increasingly provide advice to digitalize family firm internal processes, products, and business models – something family firms have been found to be somewhat reluctant to do (Kammerlander & Ganter, 2015). A recent study in the family firm context finds that dynamic capabilities essentially drive digital business model innovation. In particular, knowledge exploitation fosters, among other firm innovations, digital business model innovation and is thus a crucial success factor for family films (Soluk et al., 2021). Hence, digitalization seems to be a new core topic relevant for both MTWAs and MTBAs. In family offices, it is rather a mean to achieve higher-quality investment decisions, whereas in family firms, it is more an outcome positively affecting efficiency, productivity, and competitive advantage. However, as new technologies of digitalization and corresponding data access actively seem to determine the investment success of a family office, we conclude that for the MTWA digitalization is particularly crucial to innovate and thus improve the quality of investment decisions.

Finally, advisors are eventually involved in increasing *performance*. MTWAs, for example, invest much work in the observation and measurement of the achievement of defined wealth targets. Therefore, for MTWAs, it is of utmost importance to be part of a broad network. In fact, intimate financial network access is necessary to obtain timely information on financial and market changes (Zellweger & Kammerlander, 2015). Such information and knowledge is then required to be able to make timely portfolio adaptations and investment decisions if, for example, the performance of a certain asset class is declining (Decker & Lange, 2016). Thus, establishing and maintaining a broad network to achieve financial performance is one primary goal of MTWAs, and the family usually requires regular performance reports on the family offices' investment performance. In family firms, in contrast, MTBAs often strive to increase performance, not as the actual goal, but rather as the result of their interventions. Extant research has found, for example, that advisors' tertius iungens behaviour in a succession context eventually positively affects financial post-succession performance (Bertschi-Michel et al., 2021). However, research also indicates that there is an inverted U-shaped relationship between the number of advisors involved and financial performance, meaning that too many advisors in family firms might lead to even worse performance outcomes (Naldi et al., 2015). Moreover, in addition to such financial performance outcomes, mostly with regard to advising by the MTBA (and in contrast to MTWAs), the literature also frequently mentions the importance of non-financial performance achievements such as advisee satisfaction (Bertschi-Michel et al., 2020) or outcomes related to increasing firms' socioemotional wealth (SEW) (Perry et al., 2015). Thus, we conclude that performance is important to both MTWAs and MTBAs. However, whereas the primary goals of MTWAs are related to achieving financial performance for the family office (with non-financial goals setting the boundaries), MTBAs also aim to achieve nonfinancial goals in family firms. The MTBA frequently advises the family firm as a sole and independent advisor, as too many advisors have been found to be counterproductive. The MTWA, in contrast, strongly requires a broad and well-established network to have access to timely market information and to achieve increased financial performance. Table 16.1 provides a summary of our findings on the roles and tasks of MTWAs and MTBAs.

To summarize, our synthesis of the literature on MTWAs in family offices and on MTBAs in family firms has revealed that both types of advisors face similar challenges. However, we also reveal that, particularly in the most delicate context of family offices managing a family's private wealth, the MTWA requires more *expertise* on financial issues, more *governance mechanisms* to manage the family involvement, more *sensitivity* in dealing with family issues, more *trust* in involving the next generation, more *innovation* in using new digital possibilities, and finally more *network* access to achieve performance. Figure 16.2 visualizes these findings on MTBAs and MTWAs.

Research Gaps and Future Research

While our literature synthesis and conceptual model show many similarities between MTWAs and MTBAs, as well as some particularities of MTWAs, several important research gaps remain. Addressing these research questions will be important to advance our understanding of MTWAs – an endeavor equally important for theory and practice.

Table 16.1: Roles and Tasks of MTWA and MTFA.

MTWA *Most Trusted Wealth Advisor*	MTBA *Most Trusted Business Advisor*
Services to the family office – Provision of wealth management services – Implementation of investment goals – Evaluation of impact of investment decisions	*Services to the family business* – Provision of expert knowledge – Provision of an external view – Challenge of family inertia
Collaboration in the family office – Governance principles – Definition of rules of participation – Open communication among members	*Collaboration via tertius iungens behaviour* – Equal involvement of all stakeholders – Connection of family members – Open communication among family
Wealth conflicts – Family dissonance on wealth goals – Definition of goals regarding investments – Family constitution defines (investment) decision processes	*Family conflicts* – Equal provision of information on goals – Emotion mediation (unearthing & alleviating upcoming emotions) – Manage role transitions within the family
Next generation involvement – Definition of roles and rules – Achieving commitment of participation – Education arrangements	*Succession* – Support in leadership transition – Provision of (process) information – Leadership skill development
Digitalization as a means – Establishment of digital platforms for investments – Algorithms for investment decisions – Digital provision of wealth reports	*Digitalization as a result* – Provision of advice to digitalize family business processes – Innovation via digitalization – Digital knowledge sharing
Performance as a goal – Measurement of achievement of wealth targets – Investment adaptations after regular performance evaluation – Performance reports to the family	*Performance as a result* – Inverted U-shaped relationship between number of advisors and performance – Tertius iungens behaviour promotes performance – Advised successions increase post-succession performance

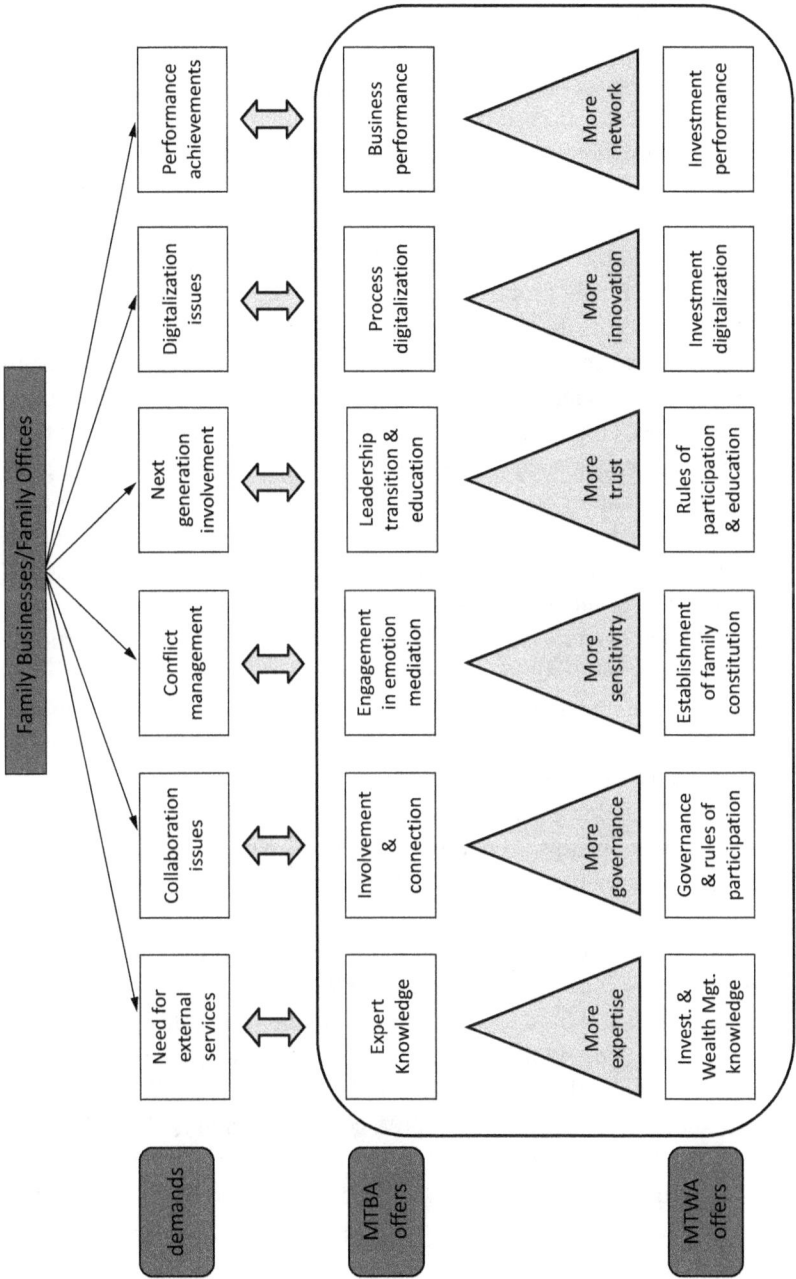

Figure 16.2: Integrated model of MTBAs in family firms versus MTWAs in family offices (own illustration).

MTWA Skill-building

Our chapter showed that MTWAs need specific content-related competencies as well as more subtle skills to succeed in their work as trusted advisors for members of family offices. To date, however, the education programs for MTWAs are limited (with some notable exceptions such as the CFWA program of the Family Firm Institute). Bankers and financial experts are often trained in their subject matters yet lack a deeper understanding of family matters. Indeed, the second author's experience as an educator for family firm advisors, in particular in an in-house program for a major German bank, showed that trust of family members, an emphasis on nonfinancial aspects, and the long-term nature of the family-advisor relationship are often undervalued by financial advisors. At the same time, trained family (business) advisors often focus on "soft" issues and smoothening processes rather than providing advice on investment decisions. As Zellweger and Kammerlander (2015) showed, it is often the (former) CFO of the (former) family business that takes on an important (advising) role in the family office. This is problematic, as such a person typically lacks the breadth of financial experience (e.g., in various asset classes not associated with the core family firm) as well as in-depth family knowledge – an aspect, which has already been raised by early family business research that studied the phenomena from ethnographic (Marcus & Hall, 1992) and sociology (Dunn, 1980) perspectives. In such cases advisors who already share relationships in one domain with family members (i.e., as the CFO of the family firm) begin interacting with the family members in a second domain (i.e., wealth advising). Hence, they cross multiple social domains – a phenomenon known as transposition leading to so called multiplex relationships (Li & Piezunka, 2020). What is special in our research field is that those relationships are not intra-familiar, yet cross the familiar borders.

In sum, these observations indicate that more education programs targeted at MTWAs are required, focused especially on bridging gaps between the different roles and combining soft and hard aspects. Related studies could, for instance, answer the following questions: What are necessary and what are helpful characteristics of MTWAs? What should an educational curriculum for MTWAs look like? What should (national or international) MTWA certifications look like? How can MTWAs be trained to be more effective? What contingencies (e.g., focusing on one specific aspect vs. multiple aspects; being hired on a project basis vs. a long-term employment contract; being employed internally vs. externally) increase the likelihood of MTWA success?

Innovation in Family Offices

Whereas the literature on family firm innovation is flourishing (e.g., Kammerlander et al., 2020; Röd, 2016), there is a dearth of research on innovation in family offices. Family offices are often associated with pure wealth management. However, as Bierl and Kammerlander (2019) argue, family offices might often serve as nuclei for further entrepreneurial activities. Practice supports this claim. For instance, the German platform "bridges+links" relates family (office) investors with innovative startups. An increasing number of family offices, such as Knauf, emphasize the importance of having a promising startup portfolio. The abovementioned trend towards digitalization further underlines this necessity. The first platforms, such as the real estate investment platform LINUS, build on digital technology to enable highly profitable deals for family offices. Nevertheless, much is to be learned in this area: How innovative are family offices in general? How can innovation be fostered and what is the role of advisors in this regard? How can the advisor's network help to become more innovative? What are different modes of innovation – starting from launching new ventures (e.g., Riar et al., 2021) to investing in promising startups? How can the innovativeness of family offices be measured?

Family Wealth Governance

Governance is important not only for family businesses (and hence MTBAs) but also for family offices (and hence MTWAs). The larger the family and more complex the investment portfolio, the more governance mechanisms are required. Governance can make the implicit explicit, the informal formal. It helps to set up rules of communication and decision-making and might prevent conflicts from escalating. Indeed, it can be seen as a playbook providing solutions and answers to many of the challenging situations that may arise for family businesses. This is the reason why an increasing number of MTWAs promote the establishment of family charters and family governance codices. However, some anecdotal evidence suggests that not all governance codices are equally effective. Indeed, some governance guidelines might be time- and money-consuming without reaching the desired level of stability and agreement among family members. Hence, research studying the success factors of certain governance structures is required. Moreover, researchers might consider the institutional perspective – in particular the institutional trust associated with MTWAs – when addressing governance issues. Harrington (2012), for example, has controversially done much work in this area and her work, as well as the research published in the *Journal of Professions and Organization*, might be a good starting point for family business researchers who are interested in answering the following questions: How can MTWAs steer the family office governance processes in the most effective way? How can (and must) the different generations (and family members in different spheres of the family) be included to achieve the highest possible levels of acceptance of governance arrangements? How do governance structures (positively or negatively) influence emotions? What are the best practices for establishing governance mechanisms for family offices? What should the (advisory) board of the family office look like? What skills (and which diversity levels) are required? What role does institutional trust play for defining effective governance measures?

Impact Measurement of Family Offices

Adequate reporting remains one of the core challenges for family offices and, thus, also for MTWAs. On the one hand, (financial) reporting is a key priority in family offices. Unlike the family business, an owner-manager of a family office cannot easily understand financial performance by looking at few numbers. Instead of simple revenue and cost/profit numbers, MTWAs need to help family members of family offices establish more complex reporting formats, covering all asset classes and all relevant geographies, highlighting not only cost and profit but also risk and potential developments. MTWAs need to support the responsible families to find a level of frequency and granularity that suits them. What is important to note here is a potential variance among family stakeholders; while some possess the education and experience to understand more complex and fine-grained KPIs, others need information on a more general and easier-to-digest level. The same is true for reporting cycles. Moreover, we see that an increasing number of members of the next generation care about the social and ecological impact of their investment. Interestingly, initial evidence of a study conducted at the second author's chair shows that many next gens feel that they lack competent MTWAs to help them choose the right impact investment vehicles. In particular, questions about measuring the impact of investment decisions remain unclear. Hence, research needs to answer the following questions: How can enterprise value calculations be amended by societal and ecological impacts? How can important externalities be quantified? How can family firms develop and use pragmatic tools to measure their societal, ecological, and human footprints?

Conclusion

Most business families realize, over time, that external advice by qualified advisors can help them achieving their financial and non-financial goals. While research in the family firm field has started to thoroughly examine the role of the MT(B)A, we propose a closer look at the MTWA – the advisor supporting family offices. Given the globally increasing number of family offices and the idiosyncratic challenges associated with them, a deeper understanding of the tasks, required skills, and challenges of such MTWAs is required. In our chapter, we provide a comprehensive framework based on a literature review and our own work as researchers and consultants that outline the similarities of and differences between MTBAs and MTWAs.

References

Arteaga, R., & Menéndez-Requejo, S. (2017). Family constitution and business performance: Moderating factors. *Family Business Review*, 30(4), 320–338. https://doi.org/10.1177/0894486517732438

Barbera, F., & Hasso, T. (2013). Do we need to use an accountant? The sales growth and survival benefits to family SMEs. *Family Business Review*, 26(3), 271–292. https://doi.org/10.1177/0894486513487198

Bertschi-Michel, A., Kammerlander, N., & Strike, V. M. (2020). Unearthing and alleviating emotions in family business successions. *Entrepreneurship Theory and Practice*, 44(1), 81–108. https://doi.org/10.1177/1042258719834016

Bertschi-Michel, A., Sieger, P., & Kammerlander, N. (2021). Succession in family-owned SMEs: the impact of advisors. *Small Business Economics*, 56(4), 1531–1551. https://doi.org/10.1007/s11187-019-00266-2

Bierl, P., & Kammerlander, N. H. (2019). Family equity as a transgenerational mechanism for entrepreneurial families. *Journal of Family Business Management*. Advance online publication. https://doi.org/10.1108/JFBM-09-2018-0043

Bierl, P. A., Schickinger, A., Leitterstorf, M. P., & Kammerlander, N. (2018). *Family Office, Family Equity und Private Equity – Unternehmerisches Investieren und generationsübergreifendes Unternehmertum; Praxisreport*.

Block, J., Fisch, C., Vismara, S., & Andres, R. (2019). Private equity investment criteria: An experimental conjoint analysis of venture capital, business angels, and family offices. *Journal of Corporate Finance*, 58(8), 329–352. https://doi.org/10.1016/j.jcorpfin.2019.05.009

David, R. J., Sine, W. D., & Haveman, H. A. (2013). Seizing opportunity in emerging fields: How institutional entrepreneurs legitimated the professional form of management consulting. *Organization Science*, 24(2), 356–377. https://doi.org/10.1287/orsc.1120.0745

Davis, W. D., Dibrell, C., Craig, J. B., & Green, J. (2013). The effects of goal orientation and client feedback on the adaptive behaviors of family enterprise advisors. *Family Business Review*, 26(3), 215–234. https://doi.org/10.1177/0894486513484351

de Groote, J. K., & Bertschi-Michel, A. (2021). From intention to trust to behavioral trust: trust building in family business advising. *Family Business Review*, 34(2), 132–153. https://doi.org/10.1177/0894486520938891

De Massis, A., & Rondi, E. (2020). Covid-19 and the future of family business Research. *Journal of Management Studies*, 57(8), 1727–1731. https://doi.org/10.1111/joms.12632

Decker, C., & Lange, K. S. G. (2016). The global field of multi-family offices: An institutionalist perspective. *Journal of Financial Services Marketing*, 21(1), 64–75. https://doi.org/10.1057/fsm.2015.24

Distelberg, B. J., & Schwarz, T. V. (2015). Mentoring across family-owned businesses. *Family Business Review*, 28(3), 193–210. https://doi.org/10.1177/0894486513511327

Dunn, M. G. (1980). The family office as a coordinating mechanism within the ruling class. *Insurgent Sociologist*, 9(2–3), 8–23. https://doi.org/10.1177/089692058000900202

Frank, H., Kessler, A., Nosé, L., & Suchy, D. (2011). Conflicts in family firms: state of the art and perspectives for future research. *Journal of Family Business Management*, 1(2), 130–153. https://doi.org/10.1108/20436231111167219

Gray, L. P. (2005). How family dynamics influence the structure of the family office. *The Journal of Wealth Management*, 8(2), 9–17. https://doi.org/10.3905/jwm.2005.571004

Harrington, B. (2012). Trust and estate planning: The emergence of a profession and its contribution to socioeconomic inequality. *Sociological Forum* 27(4), 825–846. https://doi.org/10.1111/j.1573-7861.2012.01358.x

Hassani, H., Huang, X., & Silva, E. (2018). Banking with blockchain-ed big data. *Journal of Management Analytics*, 5(4), 256–275. https://doi.org/10.1080/23270012.2018.1528900

Kammerlander, N., & Ganter, M. (2015). An attention-based view of family firm adaptation to discontinuous technological change: Exploring the role of family CEOs' Noneconomic Goals. *Journal of Product Innovation Management*, 32(3), 361–383. https://doi.org/10.1111/jpim.12205

Kammerlander, N., Patzelt, H., Behrens, J., & Röhm, C. (2020). Organizational ambidexterity in family-managed firms: The role of family involvement in top management. *Family Business Review*, 33(4), 393–423. https://doi.org/10.1177/0894486520961645

Kempers, M., Leitterstorf, M. P., & Kammerlander, N. (2019). Risk behavior of family firms: A literature review, framework, and research agenda. In E. Memili & C. Dibrell (Eds.), *The Palgrave Handbook of Heterogeneity among Family Firms* (pp. 431–460). Palgrave Macmillan.

Li, J. B., & Piezunka, H. (2020). The uniplex third: Enabling single-domain role transitions in multiplex relationships. *Administrative Science Quarterly*, 65(2), 314–358. https://doi.org/10.1177/0001839219845875

Lowenhaupt, C. A. (2008). Freedom from wealth and the contemporary global family: A new vision for family wealth management. *The Journal of Wealth Management*, 11(3), 21–29. https://doi.org/10.3905/jwm.2008.11.3.021

Maguire, S., & Phillips, N. (2008). 'Citibankers' at Citigroup: a study of the loss of institutional trust after a merger. *Journal of Management Studies*, 45(2), 372–401. https://doi.org/10.1111/j.1467-6486.2007.00760.x

Marcus, G. E., & Hall, P. D. (1992). *Lives in Trust: The Fortunes of Dynastic Families in Late Twentieth-Century America*. Westview Press.

Michel, A., & Kammerlander, N. (2015). Trusted advisors in a family business's succession-planning process – An agency perspective. *Journal of Family Business Strategy*, 6(1), 45–57. https://doi.org/10.1016/j.jfbs.2014.10.005

Naldi, L., Chirico, F., Kellermanns, F. W., & Campopiano, G. (2015). All in the family? An exploratory study of family member advisors and firm performance. *Family Business Review*, 28(3), 227–242. https://doi.org/10.1177/0894486515581951

Obstfeld, D. (2005). Social networks, the tertius iungens orientation, and involvement in innovation. *Administrative Science Quarterly*, 50(1), 100–130. https://doi.org/10.2189/asqu.2005.50.1.100

Perry, J. T., Ring, J. K., & Broberg, J. C. (2015). Which type of advisors do family businesses trust most? An exploratory application of socioemotional selectivity theory. *Family Business Review*, 28(3), 211–226. https://doi.org/10.1177/0894486514538652

Reay, T., Pearson, A. W., & Gibb Dyer, W. (2013). Advising family enterprise. *Family Business Review*, 26(3), 209–214. https://doi.org/10.1177/0894486513494277

Riar, F., Wiedeler, C., Kammerlander, N., & Kellermanns, F. (2021). Venturing motives and venturing types in entrepreneurial families: A corporate entrepreneurship perspective. *Entrepreneurship Theory and Practice*. Advance online publication. https://doi.org/10.1177/10422587211006427

Röd, I. (2016). Disentangling the family firm's innovation process: A systematic review. *Journal of Family Business Strategy*, 7(3), 185–201. https://doi.org/10.1016/j.jfbs.2016.08.004

Salvato, C., & Corbetta, G. (2013). Transitional leadership of advisors as a facilitator of successors' leadership construction. *Family Business Review*, 26(3), 235–255. https://doi.org/10.1177/0894486513490796

Schickinger, A., Bertschi-Michel, A., Leitterstorf, M. P., & Kammerlander, N. (2022). Same, but different: capital structures in single family offices compared with private equity firms. *Small Business Economics*, 58(3), 1407–1425. https://doi.org/10.1007/s11187-021-00448-x

Schickinger, A., Bierl, P. A., Leitterstorf, M. P., & Kammerlander, N. (2021). Family-related goals, entrepreneurial investment behavior, and governance mechanisms of single family offices: An exploratory study. *Journal of Family Business Strategy*. Advance online publication. https://doi.org/10.1016/j.jfbs.2020.100393

Shepherd, D. A. (2020). COVID 19 and entrepreneurship: Time to pivot? *Journal of Management Studies*, 57(8), 1750–1753. https://doi.org/10.1111/joms.12633

Soluk, J., Miroshnychenko, I., Kammerlander, N., & De Massis, A. (2021). Family influence and digital business model innovation: The enabling role of dynamic capabilities. *Entrepreneurship Theory and Practice*. Advance online publication. https://doi.org/10.1177/1042258721998946

Strike, V. M. (2012). Advising the family firm. *Family Business Review*, 25(2), 156–177. https://doi.org/10.1177/0894486511431257

Strike, V. M. (2013). The most trusted advisor and the subtle advice process in family firms. *Family Business Review*, 26(3), 293–313. https://doi.org/10.1177/0894486513492547

Strike, V. M., Michel, A., & Kammerlander, N. (2018). Unpacking the black box of family business advising: Insights from psychology. *Family Business Review*, 31(1), 80–124. https://doi.org/10.1177/0894486517735169

Strike, V. M., & Rerup, C. (2016). Mediated sensemaking. *Academy of Management Journal*, 59(3), 880–905. https://doi.org/10.5465/amj.2012.0665

Su, E., & Dou, J. (2013). How does knowledge sharing among advisors from different disciplines affect the quality of the services provided to the family business client? An investigation from the family business advisor's perspective. *Family Business Review*, 26(3), 256–270. https://doi.org/10.1177/0894486513491978

Welsh, D. H.B., Memili, E., Rosplock, K., Roure, J., & Segurado, J. L. (2013). Perceptions of entrepreneurship across generations in family offices: A stewardship theory perspective. *Journal of Family Business Strategy*, 4(3), 213–226. https://doi.org/10.1016/j.jfbs.2013.07.003

Wessel, S., Decker, C., Lange, K. S.G., & Hack, A. (2014). One size does not fit all: Entrepreneurial families' reliance on family offices. *European Management Journal*, 32(1), 37–45. https://doi.org/10.1016/j.emj.2013.08.003

Zellweger, T., & Kammerlander, N. (2015). Family, wealth, and governance: An agency account. *Entrepreneurship Theory and Practice*, 39(6), 1281–1303. https://doi.org/10.1111/etap.12182

Toshio Goto

17 How Can a Family Control its Business Without Ownership Influence? A Case Study of Suzuki Corp

Abstract: This chapter investigates a unique family business type, namely family-managed but not family-owned for generations, in order to find out the legitimacy of family control. In response to calls for studies on the heterogeneity of the family business and the longitudinal research, this chapter presents a summary of the author's three researches; first, a thorough investigation of all family-managed-but-not-owned family firms listed in Japan; second, their analysis from the resource-based theory perspective; and third, an in-depth case study of Suzuki Corp, the 11th largest automaker in the world, which has maintained such a status since 1949. The author concludes that family capital, composed of financial, human, and social capital, is instrumental to maintain the family influence on the family firm, and specifically that social capital is essential for a business family to control its firm without ownership influence. The research contributes to the literature in three ways. First, it fills a gap in the research of family business heterogeneity. Second, the research presents an alternate way for business families to maintain managerial influence without ownership influence. Third, it implies a new meaning of the family's ownership, while arguing that heavy reliance upon family ownership is potentially detrimental to long-term survival.

Keywords: family control without ownership, suzuki, type-C, family capital, social capital, family influence

Introduction

How can a family business survive for generations? Business families certainly dream to sustain their business to last forever, but for many, this dream will die. Ward (1987) posited that "Family businesses fail because they allow themselves to be destroyed, slowly but surely, by the action – or more accurately, the inaction – of their owner/managers."

This research aims to contribute to the family business longevity over generations by discussing the case of Suzuki Motor Corporation from the resource-based perspective. The Suzuki Motor Corporation is the 11th largest automaker in the world, which is at its fifth generation since its foundation in 1909. This family

Toshio Goto, Japan University of Economics

https://doi.org/10.1515/9783110727968-017

business is unique because it has not been owned but managed by the family for generations. The research question is, "How can a family control its business without ownership influence over generations?", which is composed of "How can a family control its business without ownership influence?" and "How can a family keep such an unique situation over generations?"

Longevity is central to family business research, and the factors involved in sustaining firm vitality continue to receive growing attention. Challenging the traditional "family-owned and controlled" notion, the research sheds light on the family business heterogeneity. As shown in the section entitled "Case study of Suzuki Motor Corporation", Suzuki is not the only "not owned but managed" family business in Japan. More than one hundred listed family businesses exist, which are managed without family ownership influence in Japan.

Suzuki is chosen for this case study because this corporation has maintained such a status for the longest period. The literature showed that the family dilutes its ownership in accordance with the growth of the business, the increase of the capital, and specifically after going public. The automobile industry is a typical industry that experienced significant growth in the last decades. We will longitudinally reveal the transformation process of the firm and the factors substantial to remain as a family firm after losing familial ownership influence for more than 70 years.

This research is positioned as the first step towards the comprehensive analysis of the overall mechanism of the family influence transformation and the maintenance of the family business status after losing the ownership influence. We analyze Suzuki Motor Corporation, from the resource-based view, focusing on its process of the erosion of the family influence and then the factors substantial to maintain the family firm status after losing familial ownership influence.

The research aims to contribute to the literature by filling in the gap in the research of family business heterogeneity. Although studies in this field traditionally focused on the difference between family and non-family firms, they paid little attention to family firms not family-owned empirically or theoretically. The present paper is one of the pioneering attempts to shed light on this topic, firstly identifying such heterogeneous family businesses (not owned but managed), secondly analyzing the mechanism of family management maintenance after losing the ownership influence over generations, and thirdly presenting its theoretical explanation.

The rest of the paper is composed of the literature review, a Suzuki Motor case study, discussion, implications before arriving at the conclusions.

Literature Review

Family business, broadly defined as any firm under a family's influence (Neubauer & Lank, 1998), has quickly gained considerable attention in developing and developed countries. The main reasons for this attention include but are not limited to the major role that family business plays in the national economy globally, its superior performance, and unique characteristics.

Family firms are conservatively estimated to comprise between 65% and 80% of all existing firms worldwide (Acs et al., 2004). Among the big firms, family firms also take a significant share. In the US, for example, 35% of the S&P firms (excluding financial institutions) are family firms. Family businesses are well known to outperform other types of firms (Anderson & Reeb, 2003), and Japan is no exception in this regard. According to the Family Business Yearbooks of Japan, comprising 97% of all firms and 53.1% of all listed firms, family firms outperform non-family ones in profitability (ROA) and stability (FBC, 2016, 2018). ·

The literature addressed the unique characteristics of the family business from various viewpoints. A family business is typically presented as a three-circle model (Gersick et al., 1997), namely, composed of family, ownership, and business subsystems. The family's involvement and its influence on the ownership and management make the family business distinct from other types of organizations.

In the last decades, a series of new approaches has been presented, which enriched the research of this field, by departing the more restrictive "single family influencing a single business" idea that characterizes much of the extant literature. These approaches include the introduction of the reciprocal institution – business families, where individuals connected by family ties could have multiple entrepreneurial activities, not necessarily limited to one business (Litz, 2008: Le Breton-Miller & Miller, 2018: Brinkerink et al., 2020). Several important calls were also made to enrich the research of this field, including the call for the non-dichotomy definition of the family business (Astrachan et al., 2002), a study of the heterogeneity of the family business (Chua et al., 2012: Memili & Dibrell, 2019), and the longitudinal research (Sharma et al., 2014).

Responding to these calls, several papers were published, and of which, those relevant to the present research are reviewed underneath. First is the definition of a family business, which remained a major problem in family business research. Chua et al. (1999, p. 20) pointed that although some definitions do not require family ownership, those that do imply, explicitly or implicitly, controlling ownership. The interpretation of the controlling ownership widely varies among the researchers who propose the definition, such as 60% (Donckels & Frohhch, 1991), the majority (Miller& Le Breton-Mille, 2005; Smyrnios & Odgers, 2002), 15% (Poza, 2004, p. 6), 5% (Anderson & Reeb, 2003), and legal control (Lansberg et al., 1988, p. 2).

By addressing several shortcomings of the traditional family firm definition, Astrachan et al. (2002) proposed an alternative method for assessing the extent of family influence on the enterprise and enabling family impact to be measured according to successes, failures, strategies, and operations, calling for studies on the non-dichotomic definition. They presented the family power, experience, and culture (F-PEC) model to assess the family's influence using a continuous scale rather than categorically. F-PEC's claim of non-dichotomy is notable. However, F-PEC has not been operationalized.

Goto (2012, p. 3) presented a new non-dichotomic definition. That is, a family firm is defined as any business entity having more than two members of a family either as its board members and/or shareholders, based on the three-circle model, as an extension of Newbauer and Lank (1998) and other preceding works. A different level of family ownership is an important factor of the family business diversity, which the non-dichotomous definition can observe and quantitatively analyze. This definition is operationalized as presented later in this section, which this paper goes with.

In this definition, "two members" can appear sequentially or simultaneously. Sequential appearance means multiple family members participate in different generations, such as a grandparent as a founder followed by his/her offspring in the latter generations. Simultaneous appearance means that multiple family members (e.g., husband and wife) participate in the firm during the same period.

A family member is defined as a linear blood relative within the six degrees and a relative by affinity within the third degree as defined by the Civil Code (Goto, 2012, p. 3). Furthermore, a family is not limited to the founding family, and any family taking over the firm is also recognized as a family as far as complying with the above-mentioned definition. This consideration is natural as we research the family business under the family influence and not necessarily the founding family influence.

Second is the heterogeneity of the family business. Chua et al. (1999) categorized family business into three combinations: (i) family-owned and family-managed, (ii) family-owned but not family-managed, and (iii) family-managed but not family-owned. The literature focused mostly on (i) and (ii), not (iii), and Chua et al. (1999) either did not address category (iii) in depth.

The present research fills in the gap by shedding light on the family firm without the family's ownership influence and broadens our research perspective of the family business heterogeneity. The strength of the new definition is its capability to grasp the level of the family's influence on its firm based on the magnitude of the family's influence on the ownership and control, which is a non-dichotomy definition of the family business as requested by Astrachan et al. (2002). From this definition, FBC (2016, pp. 6–7) categorized a family business into six different types based on the level of the family influence on the ownership and management as follows (see Figure. 17.3 on page 383): In Type A, the subject family is the largest shareholder and represented in the board of the directors. In Type <a>, the subject family is among the major shareholders and on the board, whereas in Type B, the subject family is the largest shareholder, not on the board. In Type <b>, the subject family is among the major shareholders in total, not on the board. In Type C, the subject family is on the board as the CEO, not among the main shareholders. In Type <c>, the subject family is on the board (not as the CEO), not among the main shareholders. Type C corresponds to the family-managed but not family-owned firms as specified by Chua et al. (2012).

The above-mentioned definition and categorization are operationalized to find the diversity of the family business listed in Japan. By identifying the number and the magnitude of the listed family businesses in each type as of 2015 and 2017, respectively, FBC (2016, 2018) presented a new landscape of family business heterogeneity, ranging from Type A with the highest level of the family influence to Type C with its lowest level. Such a diverse landscape of the family business becomes available by employing the non-dichotomy definition proposed by Goto (2012) and operationalized by FBC (2016, 2018).

Dichotomy definitions with some cut-off level of the family ownership narrow the landscape of the family business to eliminate family-managed but not family-owned family firms (Type C). The newly developed non-dichotomous definition broadens our perspective to encompass various types of family firms and facilitate the development of the heterogeneity study in this research field. From the viewpoint of the current research, one of the most important findings of FBC (2018) is that 77 Type C firms exist, accounting for 2.2% of all listed firms in 2017.

Third, three longitudinal studies were conducted on the family firms listed in Japan, both on the macro and micro levels. On the macro level, Goto (2016b) analyzed the transformation of the listed family firms between 1922 and 2015. The author found that among 113 family businesses listed in 1922, only two remained as a family business in 2015, whereas 66 became non-family firms, and 69 firms phased out (Goto, 2016b; FBC, 2018, pp. 119–120).

On the micro-level, two case studies were conducted. First, the transformation process of three automakers (Toyota, Suzuki, and Mazda[1]) was analyzed starting from their foundation to 2015 (Goto, 2016a). Second, Nippon Crucible Co.[2] was analyzed as a case that has maintained the family's influence in management and ownership from 1885 to 2017 (Goto, 2018).

The major findings of these studies are summarized as follows: (1) Maintaining the family business status is quite difficult. (2) Family capital is essential to maintain the family business status, which requires conscious and continuous efforts of the family members. (3) Erosion of the family financial capital is the most important force that causes transformation. (4) The major causes of the transformation include the decision-making at the business expansion phase, separation of ownership and management, disposal of the shares, and resignation from the board of

---

1 Mazda Motor Corporation is a Japanese multi-national automaker, founded in 1920. It has been under Mazda family's influence until 1977. From 1974, Mazda had a partnership with the Ford Motor Company. At its dissolvement in 2015, the company signed an agreement with Toyota to form a "long-term partnership".

2 Nippon Crucible Co., Ltd. is a listed family business, engaging in the manufacture and sale of graphite crucibles and refractory materials since its foundation in 1887 by Kawamura family. The family evolved from Kawamura to Mogi, Fujisaki, Okada, and the current Okubo families, all of which are related by either marriage or adoption (Goto, 2018).

directors. (5) The transformation process to the non-family status, once occurred, is seldom reversible (Goto, 2021).

This research, positioned as the fourth micro-level one, is an in-depth case study of Suzuki Motor Corporation, which has remained as Type C, family-managed but not owned, for over 60 years. Staying as Type C in such a long period is rare despite the decrease of the ownership influence of the family, while many lose the family business status in accordance with the decrease of the family influence. Thus, Suzuki Motor is chosen for the case study to find the answer to the following research question: "How can a family control its business without ownership influence?" Focusing on Suzuki Motor, family-managed but not family-owned for generations, this research aims to present the mechanism of the long-term survival and the legitimacy of the family management without ownership influence over generations.

Case Study of Suzuki Motor Corporation

This section presents the Suzuki case, starting with its overview, followed by the brief history over five generations, longitudinal changes in the family's involvement in management and ownership, and stakeholders' relationship.[3]

Overview

Starting as a textile machinery manufacturer in 1909 in Hamamatsu City, Shizuoka Prefecture, Suzuki Motor Corporation has grown into a Japanese multi-national corporation, with over 45,000 employees, 35 production facilities in 23 countries, and 133 distributors in 192 countries. The corporation is the 11th biggest automaker by production worldwide, its worldwide sales volume of automobiles is the world's 10th largest, and the domestic sales volume is the third largest in the country after Toyota and Nissan.[4] Its consolidated sales revenue is 3,488 billion JYN, comprising 91.2% in automobile business (light, sub-compact, and standard-sized vehicles) and 6.6% in the motorcycle business. Marketwise, the overseas segment accounts for 70% of its total sales. The company has been listed in Tokyo Stock Exchange since 1949.

---

3 Descriptions of the firms and families are based upon the companies' history books unless otherwise remarked.

4 Nissan Motor Co., Ltd. a Japanese multi-national automobile manufacturer, was founded in 1914. Since 1999, It has been part of the Renault–Nissan–Mitsubishi Alliance, with 43.7% shares owned by Renault as of March 2020.

Brief History Over Five Generations

This section presents the personal background and business involvements of each generation head as summarized in Figure. 17.1, based on the following information sources unless otherwise specified: Suzuki jidosha kogyo kabushikigaisha 40-nen-shi hensan iinkai (1960), Suzuki jidosha kogyo kabushikigaisha Shashi hensan iinkai (1970), Chunichishinbun Tokai honsha hodo-bu-hen (1987), Suzuki jidosha kogyo kabushikigaisha keiei kikaku-bu koho-ka-hen (1990), and Suzuki (2009).

	Presidency
1909 Loom machinery production started	
1922 Suzuki Loom Ltd. established	Michio Suzuki
1936 Automobile R&D started	(1909-1957)
1949 Listed in Tokyo Stock Market	
1950 Labor dispute	Shunzo Suzuki
1951 Two cycle motor bicycle (36 cc) developed	(1957-1973)
1953 Automobile R&D officially started	Jitsujiro Suzuki
1954 Name changed to Suzuki Motors	(1973-1978)
1955 Kei car Suzulight (360 cc) launched	Osamu Suzuki
1979 Alto, best-selling small car (550 cc), launched	(1978-2000)
1981 Alliance with GM (1981-2003)	Masao Toda
1982 Joint venture agreed with Indian government	(2000-2003)
1980' Local production started in India/Pakistan (1982), Spain(1985) and Canada (1986)	Hiroshi Tsuda
1990 Local production in Hungary: The 1ˢᵗ establishment of Japanese automotive makers in Eastern Europe Name changed to Suzuki Corp.	(2003-2008) Osamu Suzuki (2008-2015)
2009 Alliance with VW (2009-2011)	Shunzo Suzuki
2017 A memorandum of understanding for a business alliance signed with Toyota	(2015-present)

Figure 17.1: Brief history of Suzuki Corp.
Source: Compiled by the author.

First Generation

Michio Suzuki (1887–1982) founded Suzuki Loom Manufacturing Company as a manufacturer of looms, textile machinery in 1909. Born as a son of a cotton farmer, Michio preferred more skillful work and chose to start a seven-year apprenticeship under the strict guidance of a carpenter. During this period, he acquired the knowledge and skills of loom manufacturing and inspiration for his later innovations. Later, he grew as an inventor who during his lifetime got 120 patents, which is comparable to Sakichi Toyoda (1867–1930), the founder of the Toyota automotive group in the nearby village. Finishing his apprenticeship in 1908 at the age of 21, he acquired control of his family's silkworm farm. He quickly turned it into a loom manufacturing workshop as the foundation of his company, which grew to gain international fame a decade later with the production of a punch card loom, which was exported across Southeast Asia, owing to its effectiveness in weaving sarongs. He was meanwhile elected as a member of the Hamamatsu City Council in 1930 and served eight years in the municipal government.

Not content with restricting his innovations to the manufacture of looms, Michio decided to diversify the company's product range to include light passenger motor vehicles and started developing automotive technology in 1936. This endeavor was unfortunately halted by the Japanese government during World War II. After the war was over, the company resumed research and development in the motor vehicle field. Listing the company on the Stock Exchanges in 1949, he changed its name to Suzuki Motor Co., Ltd. in 1954, to manifest his strong commitment to the automobile business. In the next year, Suzulight (360 cc, two strokes), the first front-wheel drive, four-wheel independent suspension, and rack-and-pinion steering, was produced, which took the lead in the rapid growth of compact car commercialization. One of the toughest moments during his presidency was the labor dispute in 1950, which lasted for half a year, and the company was almost at the brink of bankruptcy.[5] Michio was succeeded by Shunzo Suzuki (1903–1977) at the age of 70 and passed away five years later.

Second Generation

Shunzo Suzuki served as the president until 1973, to become the first chairman of Suzuki Motor. Born as the third son of Kimura Zensuke, he joined Suzuki Looms Manufacturing in 1931, after he married Michio's eldest daughter and became Michio's adopted son. One of his earlier contributions to the company as an engineer was the development of "Power Free", a 36-cc motorcycle motor in 1952, which boosted the sales, recovered the company from the cumulative deficit and prompted the company's diversification to the automotive arena. His achievement in the four-wheel drive included Suzulight (2 cycles, 360 cc) and Suzulight Carry (truck), which maintained the top sales position in the truck category starting in 1971 for 14 consecutive years.

Management modernization is another area, in which Shunzo took initiative before and during his presidency, including the modernization of the governance by introducing the decision-making system of the top management and staff organization to assist the top management in 1957, corporate identity in 1958, and corporate precept in 1962. Its "Mission statement" sets products of superior value as its primary

---

5 https://www.city.hamamatsu.shizuoka.jp/documents/31552/02.pdf [Online available as of September 21, 2021].

goal, where all employees are making daily efforts in creating value-packed products. He died in 1977 at the age of 74.

Third Generation

Shunzo was succeeded in 1973 by Jitsujiro Suzuki (1913–1994), who served as the third president between 1973 and 1978. Born as the fourth son of the Nakanishi family, a farmer, he graduated from Hamamatsu College of Technology the same as Shunzo and joined the Ministry of Telecommunication. He joined Suzuki Looms manufacturing after he married Michio's third daughter and became Michio's adopted son, the same with Shunzo, his brother-in-law. During his presidency, the company faced an oil crisis in 1973 and emission regulation and environmental issues. The delay in the development of the new engine to meet the regulation brought serious financial crisis, from which the company recovered again with support from the Toyota Group. Jitsujiro got ill in 1977 and retired the following year.

Fourth Generation

In 1978, Osamu Suzuki (1930–) succeeded the presidency from his aunt-in-law, Jitsujiro Suzuki. He served as either the president, chairperson, or CEO of the company until 2021. Under his strong leadership, the firm's annual revenue expanded ten-fold until his retirement in 2021. Born as the fourth son of the Masuda family, he joined Suzuki in 1958 when he married Shoko Suzuki, the granddaughter of Michio Suzuki, and as an adoptee, and he took up the family name of Suzuki. His achievements before taking the presidency include the launching of Jimny, a four-wheel-drive jeep, and Alto, a 550-cc two-cycle three-door passenger car, which laid the foundation for Suzuki's four-wheeled vehicles.[6]

Osamu made major decisions to lay down the foundation for the domestic and overseas markets to establish today's Suzuki (Nagai, 2011).[7] Domestically, he established a nationwide sales network. With relatively limited resources, he chose to add sales capability to its repair companies, which currently account for 80% of its domestic sales. As for the overseas business, he strategically pursued the top position in the niche market, as shown in India, Pakistan, and Hungary. He advocated "Don't do what others do. Even in small markets, we will always strive to be number one in what we do (Saito, 2017)." The local production of passenger cars started

---

6 https://car.watch.impress.co.jp/docs/news/168413.html [Online available as of September 21, 2021].

7 https://www.sankeibiz.jp/workstyle/news/210312/wsa2103120559001-n1.htm [Online available as of September 21, 2021].

in India and Pakistan (1982), Spain (1985), Canada (1986), and Hungary (1990). Although its Spanish joint venture was dissolved in 1995, projects in the developing countries have been successful.

In India, a joint venture was agreed upon between the Indian government and Suzuki in 1982, and the local production of the Maruti 800 (Alto) started together with the state-owned Maruti Udyog. After the liberalization of the Indian economy in 1991, Suzuki increased its stake in Maruti from 26% to 50% and then 54.2% in 2002. In the 2017 fiscal year, Suzuki sold 1,643,467 units to maintain a 50.0% share of the passenger car market in India (Kudo, 2020).

In Hungary, Suzuki signed a car production contract and established Magyar Suzuki in 1990 as the first Japanese automobile manufacturer to enter Eastern Europe one year after Hungary became a democratic parliamentary republic. After Hungary joined the European Union in 2004, the local production capacity increased from 50,000 to 300,000 units per year, and 90% of its production is exported (Saito, 2017). Suzuki's stake at Magyar Suzuki increased from the original 40% to 97.5%.

Another goal Osamu has quested is the global alliance, facing fierce competition. The first cooperation started in 1981 with General Motors (GM). GM's stake in Suzuki increased from 5.3% to 20% in 2000. However, facing the financial crisis and Chapter 11 reorganization, GM divested its stake in 2008. Suzuki then chose a "comprehensive partnership" with Volkswagen in 2009, in which Suzuki acquired a 2.5% voting stake in Volkswagen and VW purchased 19.89% of Suzuki shares. This partnership was practically dissolved in 2011 when Suzuki gave notice to Volkswagen regarding the termination of partnership, and an international arbitration court ordered Volkswagen to sell the stake back to Suzuki in 2015.

In 2017, Suzuki and Toyota Motor concluded a memorandum of understanding towards business partnership, and both companies announced their agreement to begin considering concrete collaboration in new fields in 2019. Toyota invested 96 billion yen and owns approximately 5% of Suzuki shares, and Suzuki also invested 48 billion yen to acquire Toyota shares (approximately 0.2%).

In February 2021, the company announced that Osamu will retire in June 2021 and become an adviser at the age of 91. Prior to this, Osamu might have retired on some occasions. Under his chairpersonship were two non-family presidents: Masao Toda between 2000 and 2003 and Hiroshi Tsuda between 2003 and 2008. In 2001, Hirotaka Ono (1955–2007), retiring as a senior executive of the Ministry of Economy, Trade, and Industry and married to Osamu's eldest daughter, joined Suzuki as solicited by Osamu Suzuki, to re-establish the companies' strategy in the midst of the global competition. He, however, unexpectedly passed away at the age of 52 in 2007. Reports showed that when Osamu met Hirotaka for the first time, he intuitively felt that Hirotaka could become the president at the age of 52. To Osamu, the loss of Hirotaka was a great loss for his successor (Nakanishi, 2015). During his funeral service, President Tsuda revealed publicly that Osamu Suzuki and he were considering Mr. Ono as the next president.[8]

Fifth Generation

Osamu's son Toshihiro Suzuki (1959–) first joined Nihon Denso, one of the major Toyota Group companies, in 1983. Joining Suzuki in 1994, he was appointed the president and CEO of Suzuki underneath Osamu's Chairpersonship in 2015. At his inauguration, the company expressed its intent to shift to a more teamwork-based management style from his predecessor's charismatic one.

Longitudinal Changes in the Family's Involvement

Management

Rosters of the board members show the changes in the family's involvement in the management. In 1909, Suzuki Looms Manufacturing started with eight board members, which included five family members (Michio, his cousin, brothers, and brother-in-law) constituting 62.5%. In 1926, the company was established as a joint-stock limited corporation, with no changes in the board members. Among board members, family members stayed around five up to 2005 when the total number of the board members expanded to 35, indicating that the ratio of family members slowly declined in accordance with the expansion of the board. In 2019, among the 13 board members, two are from the family, namely, Osamu Suzuki, Chairman, and Michihiro Suzuki, president.

Ownership

Rosters of all shareholders were made public before 1949, some of which are missing. In 1909, Suzuki Looms Manufacturing started with 73 shareholders, but its roster is not found. The earliest roster of shareholders available is in 1925 with 73 shareholders holding 20,000 stocks in total, and of which, Michio Suzuki was the largest shareholder with 11,910 stocks. In total, 22 family members held 15,893 stocks, which accounted for 79.5% of all stocks issued. The total capital amount doubled in 1939 and 1941, when the total number of shareholders increased to 279 and 365, respectively. Rosters of all shareholders are available

---

8 https://toyokeizai.net/articles/-/110 [Online available as of September 21, 2021].

in 1941 when the Japan Conscription Insurance emerged as the largest shareholder with 17,300 stocks (33.2% of all stock issued), followed by Michio Suzuki
(9,610 stocks, 18.4%), Shunzo Suzuki (5,000 stocks, 9.6%), and others. Suzuki
family members held 44,245 stocks in total, which accounts for 55.3% of all
stocks issued.

The next roster is available in 1946, which shows a total number of shareholders
of 791 holding 180,000 stocks (capital amount as 9 million JYN). The top two largest
shareholders were institutions; Daiwa Life Insurance (22,500 stocks, 12.5% of all
stocks issued) and Japan Stock Exchange (8,490, 4.7%). Seventy-one family members
held 48,960 stocks (accounting for 27.2% of all stocks issued), including Michio Suzuki (6,210 stocks, 3.4%) as the largest shareholder, followed by Shunzo Suzuki
(4,000 stocks, 2.2%). In 1949, when the Japanese stock market re-opened, the company went public. As its preparation, the company increased the capital from 36 million
JYN to 54 million JYN. Institutions occupy the new roster of the top 10 shareholders.[9]
which include Daiwa Life Insurance (18,000 stocks, 5.0%), Chiyoda Life Insurance
(18,000 stocks, 5.0%), Tokyo Marine Fire Insurance (10,000, 2.8%) Hikari Life Insurance (10,000 stocks, 2.8%), and Meiji Life Insurance (10,000 stocks, 2.8%). Since
then, family shareholders have disappeared from the top 10 largest largest shareholders (Figure. 17.2).

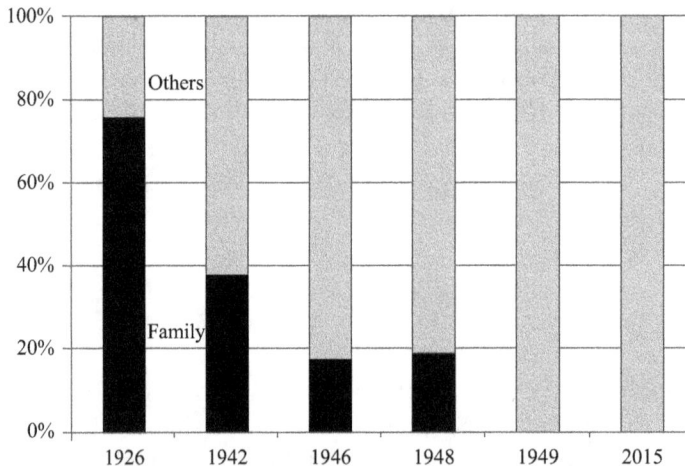

Figure 17.2: Suzuki's top 10 shareholders: 1926–2015.
Note: Major shareholders denote the second to the 10th shareholders.
Source: Compiled by the author.

---

9 Since the reopening of the stock market, disclosure of the shareholders' information was limited
to the top 10.

Currently, the top 10 shareholders are all institutions as of 2019, and no family shareholders are among the top 10. The most recent annual report shows the top largest shareholders of Suzuki Corp as follows: Master Trust Bank of Japan (owning 8.41%), Japan Trustee Services Bank (6.32%), Tokio Marine & Nichido Fire Insurance (4.07%), MUFG Bank (3.62%), Shizuoka Bank (3.08%), Resona Bank (2.94%), JPMorgan Chase Bank (2.91%), Sompo Japan Nipponkoa Insurance (1.76%), NIPPON STEEL CORP (1.76%), and Japan Trustee Services Bank (1.71%) in this order.

Stakeholders' Relationship

This section presents Suzuki's long-term relationship with its major stakeholders, that is, shareholders, partners, and customers in this order. First, among the 10 largest shareholders, Tokio Marine & Nichido and Sompo Japan Nippon-koa have been holding Suzuki's stocks since Suzuki went public in 1949. MUFG and Resona have holding since 1960, and Shizuoka Bank and JPMorgan Chase Bank since 2000. In total of the issued stocks owned by the 10 largest shareholders, 33.9% have been kept by the shareholders for over 50 years, and the majority (50.2%) have been kept by the same shareholders for over 10 years.

The same annual report carries a list of the stocks owned by the Suzuki Corp. A comparison between this list and the major shareholders' list as shown under the ownership section above reveals the cross-ownership[10] relationship among Suzuki Corp and MUFG Bank, Resona Bank, Shizuoka Bank, Sompo Japan Nipponkoa, and NIPPON STEEL CORPORATION. The purpose of holding their stock is explained as "to reinforce business relationships" either with the main banks or vendors.[11] Cross ownership is a method of reinforcing business relationships by owning stock in the companies with which a given company does business.

Second, among its partners, Suzuki has maintained a close connection with Toyota Motor Corp. since its founder's, which has been beneficial for Suzuki's survival facing several critical situations. First, in 1950, when a storm of labor disputes broke out across the country, Suzuki's cash flow deteriorated sharply. The founder, Michio Suzuki, relied on Toyota Industries, to survive with a loan of 20 million yen. Taisuke Ishida, the president of Toyota Industries, reportedly visited Suzuki and said to its employees, "I have no intention of interfering Suzuki's management, so I want you to work with peace of mind."

---

10 Suzuki Corp keeps 60 companies' stocks, of which 50 companies are cross holding.
11 Suzuki Corp Annual report, pp. 62–65, 2019.

In 1976, when the first photochemical smog pollution occurred in Tokyo, exhaust gas regulations were tightened. Suzuki was unable to make cars because of the delays in complying with exhaust gas regulations and fell into the most serious business crisis since its founding. At this time, Osamu, then the managing director, asked Eiji Toyoda, the fifth president of Toyota, for emergency assistance. Suzuki had a narrow escape from bankruptcy with the supply of engines by Daihatsu Motor Co., Ltd., a Toyota Group company. Shunzo Suzuki, the father-in-law of Osamu and the second president of Suzuki, left behind the words to Osamu, "If something serious happens, ask Mr. Toyoda." Most recently, Toyota and Suzuki agreed to explore a possible partnership in 2016 soon after Suzuki's partnership with Germany's Volkswagen ended. Osamu personally introduced his son, Toshihiro, to the top management of Toyota, when Toshihiro became the president in 2018.[12]

Third, with Suzuki's car dealers, Osamu has established a strong personal relationship nationwide. His strong relationship was witnessed during the 2008 Suzuki's Annual Car Dealer Conference. Its banquet after the study session was televised, where many wives of the dealer executives waited in a long line to meet and hug him, and some ladies begged for his eyebrows as a precious souvenir. Osamu, while pouring beer, called them by name and conversed about their families, which indicates his serious consideration of each one of them.[13]

Osamu Suzuki, as televised, makes it custom to sending New Year's cards every year with his handwriting. This sincere attitude shown to thousands of customers, employees and vendors certainly left a deep impression on the recipients. The current author also witnessed such a sincere and impressive behaviour whenever I interviewed him. As soon as he recognized me approaching, he swiftly stood up and bowed deeply before I did. These actions may be trivial to the westerners, which, however, the Japanese culture takes quite seriously and views them as evidence of his serious care for stakeholders.

Discussion

This section analyzes Suzuki's case to figure out how the Suzuki family can control its business without ownership influence for generations from the resource-based perspective. The discussion starts with the analysis of the family influence erosion, followed by the mechanism to maintain family influence after losing ownership influence, and a trust-based relationship with the stakeholders as its foundation.

---

12 "Toyota, Suzuki explore technology partnership" Reuters, October 12, 2016. https://www.reuters.com [Online available as of September 21, 2021].

13 "Squeeze out profit!" Cumbria Palace. 3–2–2009, TV Tokyo.

Family Influence and its Erosion

Suzuki Motor started as Suzuki Looms Manufacturing in 1909, and the ownership was in its early stage concentrated at his family (79.5% in 1925), which was gradually decreased in accordance with the business growth and capital increase to 55.3% in 1941 and then 27.2% in 1946. The largest shareholder position, kept by the family until 1941, was lost to the emerging institutional shareholders in 1946. In 1949, the company went public when the family dropped from the top 10 largest shareholders. Since then, Suzuki Motor has been in Type C status, or managed but not owned, until present, with its family not in the top 10 shareholders.

According to the categorization of family firms by family influence in ownership and management (FBC, 2016), Suzuki Motor stayed as Type A since 1909 until 1941, moving down to Type <a> in 1946, and Type C in 1949 until the present (Figure. 17.3). This transformation process coincides with the literature (Goto, 2016a; Goto, 2017; FBC, 2018; Goto, 2018), which pointed out that the transformation process towards the non-family status, once occurred, is seldom reversible. Our finding supports the "Family Influence Erosion Model" and the concept of the gravity and resistance power as presented by FBC (2016, pp. 17–20).

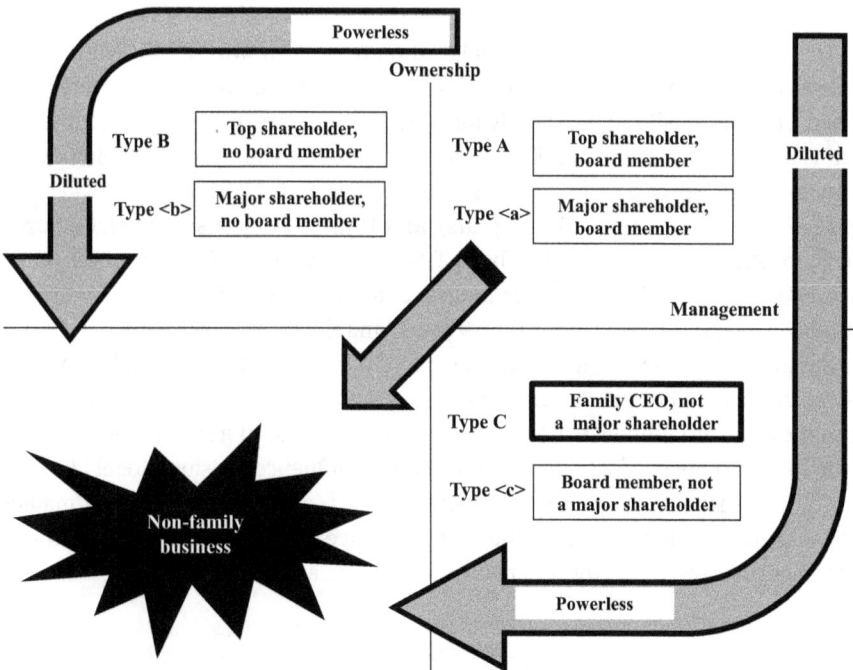

Figure 17.3: Family influence erosion model.
Source: Goto (2016, 2017).

The model posits the following: (1) a family business, mostly starting as Type A, experiences the dilution of its ownership and loss of the management control to eventually become a non-family business. (2) Three routes exist to become a non-family business, namely, Type A–Type C–non-family business, Type A–Type B-non-family business, and Type A-non-family business. (3) Gravity erodes the family influence, while resistance power maintains the family influence.

Gravity (G) is the power to erode the family influence over the firm, which is named after the natural gravity to explain the status quo of the downward transformation, which include but are not limited to dilution of the ownership, loss of management control, and sell-out. Resistance power (Rp) maintains and increases the family influence, with the increase of human, financial, and social capitals. The difference between the gravity and the resistance power (Rp minus G) defines the direction (up/down) and the speed of the change of the family influence and, as its result, the transformation of the family business towards the non-family business. Gravity is produced naturally during a lapse of time, particularly at the time of the business expansion just like natural gravity, whereas resistance power is produced only with the conscious and continuous efforts of the family members. Thus, the family business tends to erode the family influence over the firm and eventually become a non-family business unless the family continues the conscious efforts to maintain the family influence.

The breakdown of 77 Type C firms listed on 2016 as shown in FBC (2016) and its backward trace leads to the following findings: (1) The majority of them were transformed from those with higher family influences in either ownership and/or management (Type A/a). (2) Among 77 Type C firms in 2016, the duration of keeping Type C status is widely spread as follows: 18 firms (0–9 years), 13 firms (10–19 years), 21 firms (20–29 years), 15 firms (30–39 years), and 11 firms (40 years or over). (3) Suzuki Motor, together with Canon,[14] has been Type C for the longest period of 68 years[15] since 1949. (4) With 68 years as the longest and 3 years as the shortest, the average duration of keeping Type C status is 26.9 years, and the mean is 28 years.

Based upon the above data and the "Family Influence Erosion Model", we can answer the first half of the research question, "How can a family control its business without ownership influence"? as following: Type C firms, in general, are positioned as the intermediate configuration on the "Family Influence Erosion Model" to move from family business to non-family business status, and that families can manage Type C firms after loosing the ownership influence temporarily until their gravity overcomes their resisting power to make the business as non-family business.

---

14 Canon Inc. one of the major Japanese multi-national family businesses, specializing in optical, imaging, and industrial products, was founded in 1937 by Mitarai family.
15 Suzuki Motor maintains Type C status for 72 years as of this writing in 2021.

As shown by the "Family Influence Erosion Model", maintaining the family business status is quite difficult, and family influence, once diluted, is seldom reversible particularly in its ownership influence. However, as shown by the above-introduced data, 77 Type C firms have maintained such status for generations, with the average duration of keeping such a status is 26.9 years, and the mean is 28 years, and Suzuki, together with Canon, has so far the longest record of accomplishment.

In order to answer the second half of the research question, "How can a family keep such an unique situation over generations?", the next section analyzes its mechanism to keep family influence after losing its ownership influence, not temporarily but over generations.

Family Capital: Financial and Human Capitals

The resource-based view considers the bundle of resources as the source of the firm's competitiveness (Barney, 1986). From this perspective, family capital is an important resource of the family business, which is defined as the total resources of owning family members with components of human, social, and financial capital (Danes et al., 2009).

A change in the family capital is a factor of a change in the family influence over its firms as shown in its analysis. When the gravity exceeds the resistance power, the family firm loses the family capital and ultimately becomes a non-family firm (FBC, 2016, pp. 19–20). For a family business to remain as Type C for generations, human and social capital plays an important role as the financial capital is easily lost as shown in the literature. We review the Suzuki family's survival from the human, social, and financial capital perspective in this order.

Financial Capital

As the shareholder, family influence steadily and constantly erodes in accordance with the dilution of the financial capital as a result of the gravity minus resistance power, as addressed by FBC (2016, pp. 19–20) and supported by Goto (2016a, 2018). Gravity functions are similar to the natural gravity during the lapse of time unless conscious efforts are made to prevent erosion. Gravity, related to the financial capital, includes the dilution of ownership, loss of management control, and sell-out. The dilution of ownership is caused by succession (ownership split, stock dispersion, and inheritance tax), business expansion (capital increase, third-party allotment), and cash needs (cash deficit, investment to other firms, start-up of new business, and other personal needs). The dilution of ownership is explained theoretically by FBC (2016, pp. 19–20) and empirically by Goto (2016a, 2018).

The Suzuki family is a typical case of financial capital dilution, which has been caused by the gravity related to the business expansion, capital increase, and going public. Family ownership was high at the early stage at 79.5% in 1926, which was diluted to 55.3% in 1942. In 1948, one year before going public, family ownership was 30.5%, but at the time of going public and thereafter, a family member has not been on the top 10 shareholders.

Human Capital

To continue the family influence over the firm, having qualified people both in the quality and quantity is essential. The above-mentioned history of Suzuki Corp proves that the Suzuki family's continuous maintenance and exertion of the family's human capital is one of the main reasons for its involvement in the management of Suzuki Corp for four generations.

In quantity, the Suzuki family did not have sufficient human capital, which was supplemented with three adult adoptions, indicating how seriously the family tried to get involved continuously in the management. The Japanese Civil Code defines the relationship through adoption that "From the time of adoption, the relationship between an adopted child and an adoptive parent (and his/her relative by blood) shall be deemed to be the same as that between relatives by blood" (Article 727). While the adoptee is legally recognized the same as a natural child, unfair treatment is not unusual, so that adoptees are under the pressure to perform the best to meet the expectation of the family, as shown in the Suzuki case.

Osamu Suzuki was adopted from the Matsuda family and joined the company in 1958 at the age of 28. Elected as a board member in 1963, he had to manifest his ability and contribute to the firm for 20 years until elected president. He was not necessarily welcome in the company and had to gain the trust of the board and family members before getting the presidency. His private conversation with Shunzo, his father-in-law, shows how sensitive they are to the emotion and reaction of the adopting family.[16] Under such a hostile environment, Osamu Suzuki contributed to recover the firm from the serious recession to grow into one excellent automaker.

In quality, the Suzuki family has maintained its human capital for generations. The founder's innovativeness has been kept high through generations as witnessed, which is quite visible in Osamu Suzuki. In his book and other occasions, Osamu Suzuki often remarks, "I'm the head of a SME firm"[17] to tighten the belt to overcome the fierce competition, domestically and globally. He still sees himself as a small-

---

16 "Never forget we are adoptees. Be sensitive always to what the Suzuki family thinks", Sankei Shinbun, 2015.5.2.
17 Suzuki (2009) I'm the head of SME firm. Nihon Keizai Shinbun Shuppansha.

business owner although his firm is now one of the big global manufacturers with an annual turnover exceeding 4 trillion JYN. He makes it a rule to walk through the assembly line of the plants, domestic and overseas. He considers it critical for employees to keep the persistence just as if the ancestors had to overcome the series of hardships.

Family Capital and Family Influence: Social Capital

Social capital is often referred to as social connections and the attendant norms and trust. Among various definitions, the current paper stays with Putnam (1995), who defined social capital as a usable resource created by open, collective, and cooperative networks, built on relationships of trust. The author also argued that social capital is in essence a result of trust and shared norms among actors within a social structure (Goto, 2013). In addition, social capital is distinguished from other types of capital, such as human capital and financial capital, as it derives from, and depends on, interactions among social actors and is not inherent independently in a single actor (Bourdieu, 1985; Nahapiet & Ghoshal, 1998). As relevant to every aspect of human existence, social capital is widely applied to social, political, economic, educational, and environmental issues. In organization and management studies, researchers focused on the role of trust in promoting network relationships and collaborations (Child, 1998), reducing conflicts and transaction costs (Manolova et al., 2007), and integrating individual objectives for common interests (Discua Cruz et al., 2013), among others.

Family social capital (FSC) best distinguishes family firms from other types of firms in the family social (Sorenson & Bierman, 2009) primarily because of the characteristics of the family business, including but not limited to the long-term family relationships (Chrisman et al., 2003) and local community embeddedness (Berrone et al., 2012; Zellweger et al., 2013). Family firms are stronger than non-family ones in terms of social capital, offsetting the weaknesses in human and financial capital to show the same or even superior performance as suggested by Levie and Lerner (2009). A family business has social capital in two layers, one at the family level as FSC and another at the organizational level as organizational social capital (OSC); of which, strong FSC is suggested to facilitate OSC (Arrregle et al., 2007). Community-level social capital (CSC) is an important reason for the survival and persistence of family firms (Lester & Cannella, 2006). Therefore, long-lived family firms, such as Suzuki Motors, are likely to have developed their OSC and CSC through FSC to foster their longevity in the embedded community.

Social capital is typically important with Type C family firms, in which the families, after losing the family's influence as the shareholder, made the best of their social capital to build their trust-based relationship with various stakeholders, resulting in keeping their influence over their shareholders and the board members.

Trust-based Relationship

Trust is widely accepted as a major component of human social relationships and, as such, has been studied from various disciplines, including but not limited to sociology (Helbing, 1994; Mollering, 2002; Molm et al., 2000), psychology (Rotter, 1967; Cook et al., 2005), and economics (Granovetter, 1985; Huang, 2007). In 1998, the *Academy of Management Review* devoted its entire issue to the role of trust in society, principally in economic relationships, as working together involves interdependence, and people must therefore depend on others in various ways to accomplish their personal and organizational goals (Mayer et al., 1995). At the organizational level, The Nature of the Firm (Coase, 1937) defines a firm as the system of relationships, and in such relationships, trust is viewed as critical for efficient transactions (Arrow, 1972). As discussed already, social capital can be considered a system composed of a network and value, and value, such as trust, is shared among the relevant members connected via the network. Since the social capital literature first emerged (e.g., Bourdieu, 1985), trust has consistently been regarded as an important form of social capital.

Although research on trust has produced "no single consensus definition" (Welter, 2012) to date, common themes can be pointed out among definitions, which include the existence of trustor and trustee and the relationship between them with potential vulnerability. For example, Mayer et al. (1995) defined trust as "the willingness of a party to be vulnerable to the actions of another party based on the expectation that other will perform a particular action important to the trustor, irrespective of the ability to monitor or control that other party". In their trust relationship, the trustor risks being vulnerable to the trustee based on positive expectations of the trustee's intentions or behaviour (Rotter, 1967).

The literature presented several models of organizational trust, and among which, Mayer et al. (1995), reviewing Butler (1991), Mishra (1996), and Sitkin and Roth (1993), presented a model of organizational trust. This model posits that three characteristics of a trustee (ability, benevolence, and integrity) as perceived, together with the trustor's propensity to trust, foster the trustor's sense of trust for the trustee. Then, trust leads to risk-taking in a relationship, with perceived risk as a moderator.

Following the model of Mayer et al. (1995), we now analyze the organizational trust in the case of Suzuki Motor focusing on the ability, benevolence, and integrity of the trustee as the most critical facets of trustworthiness.

1. First, ability refers to the trustee's skills, competencies, and characteristics that enable the trustee (Suzuki) to have an influence on some specific domains. The domain of the ability is specific because the trustee may be highly competent in some technical areas, affording the trustor (Suzuki's stakeholders) trust in the trustee's tasks related to that area (Mayer et al., 1995). In the specific domain of the automotive business, the trustee's ability is highly valued by the trustors

(stakeholders), in manufacturing and marketing. Akio Toyoda (trustor) publicly remarked, "We would like to learn Suzuki's challenger's spirit in the partnership with Suzuki (trustee)" at the joint press conference to commemorate the joint development and production between Toyota and Suzuki.[18] With the sense of impending crisis about the big company disease,[19] Akio is eager to learn Suzuki's cost competitiveness and market penetration.

2. Second, benevolence is the extent to which a trustee is believed to want to do good to the trustor, aside from an egocentric profit motive. As the perception of a positive orientation of the trustee toward the trustor, benevolence suggests that the trustee has some specific attachment to the trustor (Mayer et al., 1995). In the Suzuki family, we identify three factors that account for its benevolence, namely, non-financial goal orientation, its type C status, and adoptees for generations.

    a. The non-financial goals, such as customer satisfaction, employee satisfaction, corporate citizenship, and others, are considered more embracing by the family business than non-family business (Tagiuri and Davis, 1992). The main reason is that the family sees the business as an extension of the family (Dyer and Whetten, 2006), and pursuit of such goals without a direct monetary value is related to the preservation of the family and business reputation, including the social status of the family in the community. Family firm reputation does matter, and family identification leads the firm to adopt value creation goals specific to the family or non-financial goals (Cabrera-Suárez et al., 2014). Suzuki Motor and its family are no exception, as indicated by the above case study.

    b. The Type C status, managing the firm without ownership influence, puts the family under tension to perform best to satisfy the stakeholders, including but not limited to the shareholders. The Suzuki family's top priority is the best performance, customer satisfaction, and contribution to the community, leaving no room for an egocentric profit motive. Benevolence is, in a sense, a logical consequence of the Type C status.

    c. Adoptee position puts Suzuki executives under another pressure to suffice the adopting family. Osamu, the fourth adopted CEO, recalling his conversation with Toshio Suzuki, his father-in-law, and the third adopted CEO, told[20]

---

18 "Toyota and Suzuki agree to start discussions on joint projects related to development and production" Homepage May 25, 2018 https://global.toyota/jp/newsroom/corporate/22684616.html [Online available as of September 21, 2021].

19 Full-year financial results briefing for the fiscal year ending March 2018, https://car.watch.impress.co.jp/docs/news/1120932.html [Online available as of September 21, 2021].

20 The evaluation of "light car" has changed with the times – Osamu Suzuki, chairman and president of Suzuki. 2015.01.06 https://www.nippon.com/ja/people/e00072/ [Online available as of September 21, 2021].

that the adoptees' mission is nothing but to satisfy the adopting family and its company with dedicated efforts, and they are always overseen. As specified by the Civil Code, the acquired status of the adoption (Article 727) shall come to an end by dissolution of adoptive relation (Article 729). Once the adoptive relations are dissolved, the adoptee loses all legal rights including the property succession.

3. Third, the integrity of the trustee is the most critical facet of trustworthiness as the relationship between integrity and trust involves the trustor's perception that the trustee adheres to a set of principles that the trustor finds acceptable (Mayer et al., 1995). Adherence to and acceptability of the principles are important because following some set of principles defines personal integrity, as suggested by McFall (1987). Such issues as the consistency of the party's past actions, credible communications about the trustee from other parties, belief that the trustee has a strong sense of justice, and the extent to which the party's actions are congruent with his or her words all affect the degree to which the party is judged to have integrity (Mayer et al., 1995).

The Suzuki family's integrity is manifested in the maintenance of its stakeholder relationship and its Type C status over generations. Trust serves as an organizing principle for family firms as contended by Eddleston et al. (2010, p. 1044) and plays a critical role in strategic decision-making, networking and relationship building, resource acquisition and organization, and opportunity creation and exploitation (Shi, 2014). Trust can be an important source of competitive advantage for family businesses (Arregle et al., 2007; Steier, 2001) and therefore needs to be sustained to benefit the firm's performance in the long run (Sundaramurthy, 2008). The Suzuki family's persistence in the trustworthy relationship with its stakeholders has acquired the trustor's positive perception, to which its tension as being Type C and adoptee has been substantial. Its trustor risks being vulnerable to the trustee based on positive expectations of the trustee's intentions or behaviour (Rotter, 1967; Tyler, 1990; Rousseau et al., 1998).

Based on our discussion, we conclude that various stakeholders' trust in the family is the foundation of the legitimacy of the families without ownership influence. Such a trustworthy long-term relationship with various stakeholders is the legitimacy of Suzuki and other Type C families without ownership influence, which has been made possible by the continuous efforts of the family. The lack of ownership influence does not only impair the family's legitimacy but also solidify it through the tension caused by the loss of the ownership influence.

Implications

This section addresses the academic and practical implications of this research.

1. Academically, the present paper first widens our perspective to further study the heterogeneity of family business. The discovery of family-managed but not family-owned family firms is contrary to the general tendency to focus on family-owned firms (Chua et al., 2012). Further study of the overall mechanism of the family influence transformation and the maintenance of the family business status after losing the ownership influence is expected to present a new horizon to the research of the heterogeneity of family business.

2. Second, further study of Type C firms may provide new perspectives about the tensions under which the family manages the firm. This paper analyzed them from the trustworthy relationship with the stakeholders, but the subject family may find other ways to maintain the family business status, such as leveraging its management influence to increase its power.

3. Third, this research provides a significant implication to the meaning of the family's ownership, which constitutes the core of agency theory (Jensen & Meckling, 1976). The literature revealed the dark side of family ownership, such as too much concentrated ownership negatively affects the financial performance of the family business (Morck et al., 1988; Anderson & Reeb, 2003), nepotism (Vinton, 1998), and a new type of agency problems, such as minority shareholders (Shleifer & Vishny, 1997). The current author envisions that a further study of Type C family business will present a new perspective about the family's ownership, which contrasts with the conventional notion that the family business has the family's legitimacy in its ownership.

The practical implication of the paper is the importance of the maintenance of the family capital to achieve steady and healthy growth of the family business under the family's influence for generations. Business families' aspiration for their business longevity can be achieved as long as they are trusted by the stakeholders, which is made possible by the family and its executives who serve for the welfare of the stakeholders.

Conclusion

To answer the research question, "How can a family control its business without ownership influence over generations?", this paper first identified 77 Type C family businesses as of 2017, and empirically analyzed the case of Suzuki Motor, in which the founding family-maintained management after losing the ownership influence for 68 years.

Theoretically, it first explained the Type C firms, in general, positioned as the intermediate configuration on the "Family Influence Erosion Model" to move from family business to non-family business status, and that families can manage Type C firms after losing the ownership influence temporarily until their gravity overcomes their resisting power to make the business as non-family business.

The mechanism of maintaining the management influence after losing the ownership influence over generations was then explained from the resource-based perspective, as the balance between the gravity and the resistance power both influencing the family capital, and the important contribution of the trust of the stakeholders including its shareholders, to maintain the management influence after losing the ownership influence over generations.

The research showed that after losing ownership influence caused by the gravity in its financial capital, the family pursues to maintain the resistance power in its human and social capitals, of which, the latter is instrumental to gain the trust of the stakeholders including its shareholders, to maintain the management influence after losing the ownership influence over generations.

The research fills the gap in the research of the family business heterogeneity with its focus on a family-managed but not owned family firm. This paper is expected to further advance a comprehensive analysis of the overall mechanism of the family influence transformation in various types of family business. The extended research may also shed light on the nature and the meaning of ownership in the family business in general.

Despite its major contribution to the literature, the paper has several limitations, including the absence of the statistical analysis and comparative studies of other countries to determine the universal applicability of the findings of the paper, segregating any cultural and institutional factors specific to Japan.

References

Acs, Z. J., Arenius, P., Hay, M., & Minniti, M. (2004). *Global entrepreneurship monitor*. Babson College.

Anderson, R. C., & Reeb, D. M. (2003). Founding-family ownership and firm performance: evidence from the S&P 500. *The Journal of Finance*, 58(3),1301–1328.

Arregle, J. L., Hitt, M. A., Sirmon, D. G., & Very, P. (2007). The development of organizational social capital: Attributes of family firms. *Journal of Management Studies*, 44(1), 73–95.

Arrow, K. J. (1972). Gifts and exchanges. *Philosophy and Public Affairs* 1(4), 343–362.

Astrachan, J., Klein, S., and Smyrnios, K. (2002). The F-PEC scale of family influence: a proposal for solving the family business definition problem. *Family Business Review*, 15(1), 45–58.

Barney, J. B. (1986). Organizational culture: Can it be a source of sustained competitive advantage?" *Academy of Management Review*, 11, 656–665.

Berrone, P., Cruz, C., & Gómez-Mejia, L. R. (2012). Socioemotional wealth in family firms: Theoretical dimensions, assessment approaches, and agenda for future research. *Family Business Review*, 5(3), 258–279.

Bourdieu, P. (1985). The social space and the genesis of groups. *Social Science Information*, 24(2), 195–220.

Brinkerink, J., Rondi, E., Benedetti, C., & Arzubiaga, U. (2020). Family business or business family? Organizational identity elasticity and strategic responses to disruptive innovation. *Journal of Family Business Strategy*, 11(4), 100360.

Butler Jr., J. K. (1991) Toward understanding and measuring conditions of trust: Evolution of a conditions of trust inventory. *Journal of Management*, 17(3), 643–663.

Cabrera-Suárez, M. K., Déniz-Déniz, M. D. L. C., & Martín-Santana, J. D. (2014). The setting of non-financial goals in the family firm: The influence of family climate and identification. *Journal of Family Business Strategy*, 5(3), 289–299.

Child, J. (1998). Trust and international strategic alliances: the case of the sino-foreign joint ventures. In C. Lane and R. Bechmann (Eds.), *Trust Within and Between Organizations: Conceptual Issues and Empirical Applications* (pp. 241–272). Oxford University Press.

Chrisman, J. J., Chua, J. H., & Sharma, P. (2003). Current trends and future directions in family business management studies: Toward a theory of the family firm. *Coleman White Paper Series*, 4(1), 1–63.

Chua, J. H., Chrisman, J. J., & Sharma, P. (1999). Defining the family business by behavior. *Entrepreneurship Theory and Practice*, 23(4), 19–39.

Chua, J. H., Chrisman, J. J., Steier, L. P., & Rau, S. B. (2012). Sources of heterogeneity in family firms: An introduction. *Entrepreneurship Theory and Practice*, 36 (6), 1103–1113.

Chunichishinbun Tokai honsha hodo-bu-hen. (1987). Suzuki jiko monogatari (Story of Suzuki Motor Ltd. In Japanese). Suzuki jidosha kogyo kabushikigaisha; Hamamatsu-Shi.

Coase, R. H. (1937). The nature of the firm. *Economica* 4, 33–55.

Cook, K. S., Yamagishi, T., Cheshire, C., Cooper, R., Matsuda, M., & Mashima, R. (2005). Trust building via risk taking: A cross-societal experiment. *Social Psychology Quarterly*, 2, 68, 121–142

Danes, S., Stafford, K., Haynes, G., & Amarapurkar, S. (2009). Family capital of family firms bridging human, social, and financial capital. *Family Business Review*, 22(3),199–215.

Discua Cruz, A., Howorth, C., & Hamilton, E. (2013). Intrafamily entrepreneurship: the formation and membership of family entrepreneurial teams. *Entrepreneurship Theory and Practice*, 37(1), 17–46.

Donckels, R., & Fröhlich, E. (1991). Are family businesses really different? European experiences from STRATOS. *Family Business Review*, 4(2),149–160.

Dyer Jr., W. G., & Whetten, D. A. (2006). Family firms and social responsibility: Preliminary evidence from the S&P 500. *Entrepreneurship Theory and Practice*, 30(6),785–802.

Eddleston, K. A., Chrisman, J. J., Steier, L. P., & Chua, J. H. (2010). Governance and trust in family firms: An introduction. *Entrepreneurship Theory and Practice*, 34(6),1043–1056.

FBC *(Famiri Bijinesu Hakusho Henshuu Iinkai)*. (2016). *Famiri Bijinesu Hakusho (Family business yearbook 2015* in Japanese). Tokyo, Doyukan.

FBC *(Famiri Bijinesu Hakusho Henshuu Iinkai)*. (2018). *Famiri Bijinesu Hakusho (Family business yearbook 2018* in Japanese). Tokyo, Hakuto Shobo.

Gersick, K., Davis, J., & Hampton, M. and Lansberg, I. (1997). *Generation to Generation: Life Cycles of the Family Business*. Harvard Business School Press: Cambridge.

Goto, T. (2012). *Famiri bijinesu: Shirarezaru jitsuryoku-to kanousei (Family business: Its capability and potential* in Japanese). Hakuto shob: Tokyo.

Goto, T. (2013) Secrets of family business longevity in Japan from social capital perspective. in K. Smyrnios, P. Poutziouris & S. Goel, (Eds), *Handbook Of Research On Family Business*, second Edition. Edward Elgar Publishing, 2013:554–587.

Goto, T. (2016a). Jigyo-shokei ni okeru sogyouke eikyoryoku-no suii: juryoku-to kouryoku (Transformation of the founding family's influence: gravity& resistance power in Japanese) *Jigyo-shokei*, 5. 36–49.

Goto, T. (2016b). Family firms' transformation to non-family firms during 1920's-2015. *Journal of Japanese Management*, 1(1), 44–59.

Goto, T. (2018). Shinzoku-nai jigyo shokei to famirī shihon: Nihonrutsubo (kabu) ni okeru Motegi-ka no yakuwari o chūshin ni. (Business succession within relatives and family capital: Focusing on the role of the Motegi family in Japan Crucible Co., Ltd in Japanese). *Jigyo shokei*, 7, 153–166.

Goto, T. (2021). Longevity and disruption: Evidence from Japanese family businesses. In Yan, H. D., & Yu, F. L. T. (Eds.) *The Routledge Companion to Asian Family Business: Governance, Succession, and Challenges in the Age of Digital Disruption*. Routledge: Abingdon.

Granovetter M. (1985). Economic action and social structure: The problem of embeddedness. *American Journal of Sociology*, 91, 481–510.

Helbing, D. (1994). A mathematical model for the behavior of individuals in a social field. *The Journal of Mathematical Sociology*, 19(3), 189–219.

Huang, F. (2007). Building social trust: A human-capital approach. *Journal of Institutional and Theoretical Economics*, 163(4), 552–573.

Jensen, M. C., & Meckling, W. H. (1976). Theory of the firm: Managerial behavior, agency costs and ownership structure. *Journal of Financial Economics*, 3(4), 305–360.

Kudo, T. (2020). Suzuki ga Indo de shea 50-pāsento-cho o iji suru riyū: Sekai 5-i no dai ichiba de hanbai daisū wa Toyota no 10-bai (Why Suzuki Maintains Over 50% Share in India: Sales volume is 10 times that of Toyota in the world's 5th largest market in Japanese). *Toyo Keizai*, 2020/05/15.

Lansberg, I. (1988). The succession conspiracy. *Family Business Review*, 1(2), 119–143.

Le Breton-Miller, I., & Miller, D. (2018). Beyond the firm: Business families as entrepreneurs. *Entrepreneurship Theory and Practice*, 42(4), 527–536.

Lester, D. L., & Parnell, J. A. (2006). The complete life cycle of a family business. *Journal of Applied Management and Entrepreneurship*, 11(3), 3.

Levie, J., & Lerner, M. (2009) Resource mobilization and performance in family and nonfamily businesses in the United Kingdom. *Family Business Review*, 22(1), 25–38.

Litz, R. A. (2008). Two sides of a one-sided phenomenon: conceptualizing the family business and business family as a möbius strip. *Family Business Review*, 21(3), 217–236.

Manolova, T. S., Gyoshev, B. S., & Manev, I. M. (2007). The role of interpersonal trust for entrepreneurial exchange in a transition economy. *International Journal of Emerging Markets*, 2(2), 107–122.

Mayer, R. C., Davis, J. H., & Schoorman, F. D. (1995). An integrative model of organizational trust. *Academy of Management Review*, 20(3), 709–734.

McFall, L. (1987). Integrity. *Ethics*, 98(1), 5–20.

Memili, E., & Dibrell, C. (Eds.). (2019). *The Palgrave handbook of heterogeneity among family firms*. Cham. Palgrave Macmillan.

Miller, D., & Le Breton-Miller, I. (2005). *Managing for the long run: Lessons in competitive advantage from great family businesses*. Harvard Business Press: Cambridge.

Mishra, A. K. (1996) Organizational responses to crisis: The centrality of trust. In R. M. Kramer & T. Tyler (Eds.), *Trust in organizations: Frontiers of theory and research*. SAGE Publications, Inc.

Mishra, S. N., & Chand, R. (1995). Public and private capital formation in Indian agriculture: Comments on complementarity hypothesis and others. *Economic and Political Weekly*, A64-A79.

Mollering, G. (2002). The nature of trust: From Georg Simmel to a theory of expectation, interpretation and suspension. *Sociology*, 35(2), 403–420.

Molm, L. D., Takahashi, N., & Peterson, G. (2000). Risk and trust in social exchange: An experimental test of a classical proposition. *American Journal of Sociology*. 105(5), 1396–1427.

Morck, R., Shleifer, A., & Vishny, R. (1988). Management ownership and market valuation: An empirical analysis. *Journal of Financial Economics*, 20, 293–315.

Nagai, T. (2011). Ningenchikara de Suzuki o gurobaru kigyo ni shita karisuma kha suzuki osamu-shi shirizoku (Osamu Suzuki, a charismatic manager who made Suzuki a global company with human power, retires in Japanese). *Sankei Biz*, 2021.3.12,

Nahapiet, J., & Ghoshal, S. (1998). Social capital, intellectual capital, and the organizational advantage. *Academy of Management Review*, 23(2), 242–266.

Nakanishi, T. (2015). Suzuki no dai gosan, 'VW to no teikei' o motometa riyū (Suzuki's big miscalculation, the reason for asking for 'tie-up with VW' in Japanese) *Nikkei Bizgate*, https://bizgate.nikkei.co.jp/article/DGXMZO31138780300052018000000?page=3. 2015/12/17 [Online available as of September 21, 2021].

Neubauer, F., & Lank, A. G. (1988). *The Family Business: Its Governance for Sustainability*. Palgrave Macmillan: London.

Neubauer, F., & Lank, A. G. (1998). Stages of evolution of family enterprises. *In The Family Business* (pp. 26–55). Palgrave Macmillan, London.

Poza, E. J. (2004). *Family Business*, 2nd edition. Thomson South-Western: Mason.

Putnam R. (1995). Tuning, tuning out: The strange disappearance of social capital in America P.S. *Political Science and Politics*, 28, 664–683.

Rotter, J. B. (1967). A new scale for the measurement of interpersonal trust. *Journal of Personality*, 35(4),651–665.

Rousseau, D. M., Sitkin, S. B., Burt, R. S., & Camerer, C. (1998). Not so different after all: A cross-discipline view of trust. *Academy of Management Review*, 23(3), 393–404.

Saito S. (2017). Suzuki no hatten (Development of Suzuki in Japanese). *Senshū manejimento jānaru*, 7(1), 49–62.

Sharrma, P., Salvato, C., & Reay, T. (2014). Temporal dimensions of family enterprise research. *Family Business Review*, 27(1), 10–19.

Shleifer, A. & Vishny, R. (1997). A survey of corporate governance. *Journal of Finance*, 52(2),737–783.

Shi, H.X. (2014), *Entrepreneurship in Family Business: Cases from China*, Springer, New York, NY.

Shi, H. X., Shepherd, D. M., & Schmidts, T. (2015). Social capital in entrepreneurial family businesses: The role of trust. *International Journal of Entrepreneurial Behavior & Research*. 21(6), 814–841.

Sitkin, S. B., & Roth, N. L. (1993). Explaining the limited effectiveness of legalistic "remedies" for trust/distrust. *Organization Science*, 4(3), 367–392.

Smyrnios, K., & Odgers, J. (2002). An exploration of owner and organizational characteristics, and relational marketing and opportunity search variables associated with fast-growth family versus nonfamily firms. In: *Proceedings of the Family Business Network 13th Annual World Conference*, Helsinki, Finland. Lausanne, Switzerland: FBN, 239–256.

Sorenson, R. L., & Bierman, L. (2009). Family capital, family business, and free enterprise. *Family Business Review*, 22(3), 193–195.

Steier, L. (2001). Family firms, plural forms of governance, and the evolving role of trust. *Family Business Review*, 14(4), 353–368.

Sundaramurthy, C. (2008). Sustaining trust within family businesses. *Family Business Review*, 21(1), 89–102.

Suzuki jidosha kogyo kabushikigaisha 40-nen-shi hensan iinkai. (1960). *Suzuki jidosha kogyo kabushikigaisha 40-nen-shi (Suzuki Motor Co., Ltd. 40 Year History* in Japanese). Suzuki jidosha kogyo kabushikigaisha: Hamatsu-Shi.

Suzuki jidosha kogyo kabushikigaisha Shashi hensan iinkai. (1970). *Suzuki jidosha kogyo kabushikigaisha 50-nen-shi (Suzuki Motor Co., Ltd. 50 Year History* in Japanese). Suzuki jidosha kogyo kabushikigaisha: Hamatsu-Shi.

Suzuki jidosha kogyo kabushikigaisha keiei kikaku-bu koho-ka-hen. (1990). 70-nen-shi (*70 Years History* in Japanese). Suzuki jidosha kogyo kabushikigaisha: Hamatsu-Shi.

Suzuki O. (2009). Ore wa chūshokigo no oyaji (*I am the father of a small and medium-sized enterprise* in Japanese). Nihonkeizaishinbun shuppan: Tokyo.

Tagiuri, R., & Davis, J. A. (1992). On the goals of successful family companies. *Family Business Review*, 5(1), 43–62.

Tyler, T. (1990), *Why People Obey the Law*, Yale University Press, New Haven and London.

Vinton, K. L. (1998). Nepotism: An interdisciplinary model. *Family Business Review*, 11(4),297–303.

Ward, J. (1987). *Keeping the Family Business Healthy: How to Plan for Continued Growth, Profitability and Family Leadership*. Jossey-Bass: San Francisco.

Welter, F. (2012). All you need is trust? A critical review of the trust and entrepreneurship literature. *International Small Business Journal*, 30(3), 193–212.

Zellweger, T. M., Nason, R. S., Nordqvist, M., & Brush, C. G. (2013). Why do family firms strive for nonfinancial goals? An organizational identity perspective. *Entrepreneurship Theory and Practice*, 37(2), 229–248.

Yasaman Gorji and Nastaran Simarasl

18 How Business Families Advance Their Members' Careers: The Case of Show Business Families

Abstract: Business families operate in a wide variety of industries around the world and are powerful forces that drive local, national, and regional economies. Specifically, within the domain of entrepreneurship and family business research, there is a growing recognition of the various roles that families play in their members' career development. In this chapter, we focus on show business families and their role in the career development of their members across generations. We discuss the family mechanisms ranging from hands-on approach to spillover effects in supporting family members' career trajectories. The unique feature of show business families is that they rarely own firms; instead, they generate economic rents from roles in project-based organizations. In this context, the *hands-on approach* involves the recruitment of family members in the businesses or projects operated by family members. In the *mediatory approach*, the members of show business families use their industry reputation and legitimacy to serve as brokers and sponsors to advance their family members' careers through their social network. In the *spillover approach*, family members' careers benefit from their family embeddedness through reputational spillover effects.

Keywords: business families, career development mechanisms, project-based industries, network brokerage, spillover effect

Introduction

Labor markets have become very competitive over time, and individuals are using various strategies to gain a competitive advantage in landing jobs that offer advancement opportunities. In entrepreneurship and family business research, family embeddedness has been vastly discussed as a source of support in the provision of various resources needed for starting and running a business (Aldrich & Cliff, 2003). Whereas some research has mostly focused on the emotional support provided by family members when one tends to start a business, others have emphasized other instrumental resources offered by family to facilitate venturing, such as

Yasaman Gorji, ESSCA School of Management
Nastaran Simarasl, California State Polytechnic University

https://doi.org/10.1515/9783110727968-018

labor, money, and information (Hanlon & Saunders, 2007; Rooks et al., 2016). In other family business research, the social family dynamics that impact the processes and performance outcomes of family businesses are investigated to shed light on the factors that give family-owned businesses a competitive advantage compared to their non-family counterpart (Simarasl et al., 2020; Cruz et al., 2012; Pearson et al., 2008). By and large, this chapter draws on three gaps in past family business research. First, past studies have not given sufficient credit to industry features that impact the family businesses and business families' outcomes at the individual and firm levels (King & Peng, 2013). Second, even though there is no consensus on the definition of business families in the literature (Combs et al., 2020) most of them lean towards business-owning and controlling families (Gorji et al., 2021). This limits our scope of investigation into the different aspects of families and their implications for business. Third, there is a slim body of research on the career trajectories of members of show business families, which mostly focuses on intergenerational succession within families (Gorji et al., 2020; Zhao et al., 2020; Pittino et al., 2018); but the influence of family businesses and business families on the career trajectories of their members, within and outside the family and business have not been sufficiently investigated (Zellweger al., 2011; Schröder et al., 2011).

That said, our work makes three contributions: first, we bring attention to industry heterogeneity in family business scholarship by focusing on business families in the entertainment or, more specifically, the Hollywood industry, an industry structured around project-based work (e.g., movies, etc.) where the transferability of social networks and reputational assets play a significant role in incumbents' career outcomes (Gorji, 2020; Rossman et al., 2010). In the second contribution, we extend the definition of business families (Uhlaner, 2006) to "families in business" who may not necessarily own and control firms but who are deeply ingrained in the industry. This characteristic gives a competitive edge to these families and their members' career advancement by allowing the show business families to get their family members involved in their temporary projects (e.g., specific movies) or by promoting their appointment to projects owned by other influential industry incumbents. We believe this is an important contribution as research findings about project-based economy is generalizable to the rising gig economy, which is built on projects and contracts business and business families can serve as a nexus of contract (Gorji et al., 2021). Third, we provide a typology of business family mechanisms that help to advance family members' careers. Our proposed typology comprises three mechanisms that differ in family engagement and commitment towards family members' career advancement in the movie industry. In the hands-on approach, show business family members directly hire their family members in their ventures. In the mediatory approach, family members do not necessarily employ their family members, but they use their social capital to provide visibility and sponsorship in their family members' careers. Finally, in the spillover approach, the family is not directly involved in their members' career advancement, but the reputational resources of the business-owning family members spill over to other family members in the same industry (Gorji, 2020; Rossman et al., 2010). Figure 18.1 illustrates the typology of business families' mechanisms that help to advance members' careers. We discuss our typology and each of the proposed mechanisms with the help of real-world cases and examples from well-known show business families in Hollywood.

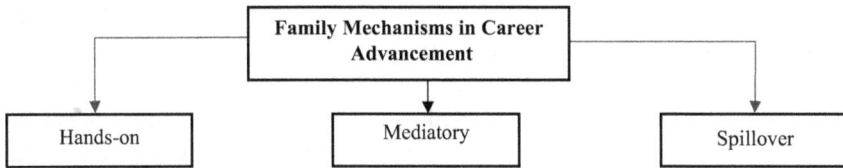

Figure 18.1: Family mechanisms that advance members' careers in show business families.

Family Mechanisms in Show Business Family Members' Career Advancement

Hands-on Approach: Appointment of Family Members

Being born in a business family is assumed to provide individuals with various resources when it comes to choosing and developing their careers. Raising the next generation in a family with industry knowledge and relevant and powerful social capital can encourage the children to pursue their parents' careers and to prolong their family name and reputation. After all, parents are the most significant source of career advice and tacit knowledge transfer to their children (Ayoobzadeh & Gorji, 2017; Michaeli et al., 2016). Furthermore, family members' occupations, educational attainments, family expectations and aspirations, family relationships, and support have been shown to impact members' career choices and outcomes (Whiston & Keller, 2004; Oren et al., 2013). In addition, the selective hiring and appointment of family members to key organizational positions, nepotism, has been identified as important in how business families help advance their members' careers.

Nepotism is a form of preferential treatment or favouritism in terms of employment and the distribution of other benefits exclusively granted to individuals connected to one by blood (Jaskiewicz et al., 2013). Nepotism is prevalent in contexts where market mechanisms are not well-developed or cultural, and industry norms assign great importance to family relationships (Taşdemir et al., 2017; Corak, 2013). In family businesses, nepotism is exercised in direct or indirect ways. In the direct approach, family members are assigned to organizational roles without regard for their competence and professional fit. In contrast, in indirect nepotism, a family appointment occurs only when family members demonstrate the required job-related capabilities (Gorji et al., 2020). Families' willingness to hire from their members is positively influenced by the level of trust that they have in each other to manage the business resources efficiently (Urassa, 2016).

Show business families provide excellent examples of selective hiring from close family members. Because the entertainment industry is structured around project-based work, show business families lean towards assigning family members to their show business projects (e.g., specific movies or series), or they may assign their family members to work at or lead certain departments in their movie production companies. It is usually assumed that the next generation acquires the required skills through experiential learning and mentorship from their older family members who have established a strategic position for themselves and their show business in the industry. This further incentivizes the decision-makers in show businesses to cast their family members in their movies.

The Coppola family, an influential show business family, is an example of selective hiring of family members in the show business. Casting several family members at a very young age in movies such as *The Godfather* and *Apocalypse Now*, which are regarded as the greatest films of all time, has doubtlessly been a kickstart that paved the way for a fast-track flourishing career path. Sofia Coppola, Francis Ford Coppola's daughter, the director, and the scriptwriter of *The Godfather*, was cast in her father's movie, *The Godfather (I)*, as early as one year old. This trend did not stop following the tremendous success of *The Godfather (I)*. Along with Sofia, other Coppolas cast in *The Godfather Saga* are Carmine, Gian-Carlo, Italia, and Roman Coppola (LoBrutto & Morrison, 2012). Based on the information from the International Movie Database (IMDb), the movie was a complete success with an average estimated budget of $6 million and a cumulative worldwide gross income of $246 million. In terms of artistic achievements, the movie brought several prestigious awards such as the Academy Award and the Golden Globes to Francis Ford; moreover, the movie ranks as the second-best movie of all time in the IMDb's top 250 movies list. We speculate that these early achievements further accelerated Sofia Coppola's career advancements in the entertainment industry. She got nominated for the prestigious award of Cannes Palm d'Or at the age of 28 in her first directed feature film, *The Virgin Suicides*. Four years later, she won the Academy Award for the Best Original Script for *Lost in Translation* in her next feature film. Another example is the Warner Brothers Studios, where close family members have been appointed to the finance, production, and technical departments.

We refer to the appointment of family members in show business projects as a hands-on career advancement mechanism exercised by show business families. Once family members are hired, their careers will benefit from the accumulated reputation of the show business and other reputable family members, in addition to exposure to key organizational positions (Gorji et al., 2020; Deephouse & Jaskiewicz, 2013).

By and large, it is possible to conclude that membership and embeddedness in business show families play an essential role in members' career advancement through getting them involved in creative projects that are not equally accessible to non-family members. Therefore,

Proposition 1: *In show business families, members' career advancement is positively associated with their recruitment in their family members' artistic projects.*

The Mediatory Approach: Borrowing Family Members' Social Capital

The value of social networks and social capital as mechanisms for individual economic outcomes and career advancement is well established (Di Maggio & Garip, 2012; Granovetter, 2005; Granovetter, 2018, Seibert et al., 2001). A well-positioned network is specifically important in industries such as entertainment and Hollywood, where the individual and organizational-level networks play an important role in boosting individual and organizational performance. Social networks provide a variety of benefits such as information access (Walter et al., 2007), enhanced performance (Sparrowe et al., 2001; Cattani & Ferriani, 2008), and legitimacy (Hawdon, 2008; McPherson et al., 2001; Carlisle & Flynn, 2005). Establishing these networks take a long time and require significant effort (Bourdieu, 1986); therefore, individuals tend to borrow the social capital of those who know and trust them. Network brokers bridge the structural holes across networks by making connections between otherwise unconnected individuals (Burt, 1992; 2001). Sometimes establishing the connection between two previously unconnected individuals, bridging the structural hole, is enough to kickstart one's career on a fast pedal. This is realized by enhancing the novices' visibility to others who can advance their careers after learning about their skills and capabilities as a result of forged connections. But in many circumstances, the introduction and exposure do not support the novices' career success per so; that is, they are more beneficial when made by high-status industry members whose advocacy can provide significant visibility and legitimacy to lower-status ones (Berger et al., 1998). In other words, high-status individuals lend their social capital to the lower-status ones, giving the latter more legitimacy and visibility, especially if their personal characteristics do not convey their competence to third parties (Burt, 2000; Gorji et al., 2020). Also referred to as sponsorship, it tends to boost individuals' careers, especially during one's early career stages when the novice's quality signals are weak or not adequately developed (Turner, 1960). Not unexpectedly, in both network brokerage and sponsorship, their intensity and effectiveness depend on the broker's or sponsor's familiarity with or access to information about the novice.

Hollywood is a complex ecosystem of diverse players, including large public corporations (e.g., movie studios) and social evaluators (e.g., Oscars & Cannes Film Festival) in powerful positions to influence perceptions, judgments, and hiring preferences of the internal and external industry stakeholders (Lutter, 2015). More specifically, in Hollywood, due to the inherent ambiguity in identifying and appraising qualified creative talent, evaluators rely on social evaluations and other non-performance markers of merit when making hiring decisions (Le Breton-Miller & Miller, 2015; Lehman et al., 2019). Therefore, individuals' career advancement in Hollywood depends on their social capital, especially their family network, which is more readily accessible than their non-family network. In other words, in an industry like Hollywood, where reputational resources are crucial to one's career progress, activating family brokers and sponsors who are willing to provide visibility and put their credibility on the line to make critical introductions is indispensable. For instance, a reputable member of a show business family may make a favourable recommendation or referral for a relative for a promising role in a movie or an employment opportunity in a movie production company. This gives the recommended individuals more visibility and the possibility of being shortlisted for critical positions (roles) (Taşdemir et al., 2017). Particularly, this might help women crack the glass ceiling in a male dominant industry (Grugulis & Stoyanova, 2012) and potentially get more executive positions in movie projects (Gorji et al., 2021).

For instance, it seems that Tom Hanks, who has established a strong relationship with the movie director, Stephen Spielberg, has been able to successfully advance his son's career through his relationship with the prominent director. Not only did Spielberg cast Tom Hanks in five of his productions, but also, he has cast Tom Hanks' son, Chet Hanks, a minor role in the movie *Indiana Jones and the Kingdom of the Crystal Skull* in 2008, which marked the second movie in Chet Hank's filmography at the age of 18 (Ojomu & Aulak, 2021). Thus, we reason that the relationship between Spielberg and Tom Hanks has provided Chet Hanks with increased visibility and has ultimately provided him with opportunities to make giant leaps early in his career. In other words, the interactions between the influential industry players and the members of show business families are likely to be beneficial to their family members' careers, be it through bursts of random exposures where Spielberg was able to get familiar with and learn about Chet Hanks's acting skills (information exchange through brokering structural holes), and also through proactive advocacy of their family members (sponsorship).

Although both brokerage and sponsorship lead to favourable career outcomes for members of business show families, they are governed by two different mechanisms. We contend that in network brokerage, family members can increase the likelihood of interactions (i.e., interactions between Spielberg and Chet Hanks in the context of Spielberg's and Tom Hanks's relationship), and information exchange between the business show family members and influential figures in the industry (Kwon et al., 2020), giving exposure to their lesser-known and younger family members, and increases their chances of being invited in different projects outside their business show family or family business (Burt, 1992).

Based on the project-based nature of Hollywood, members of show business families have ample opportunities to sponsor (advocate) each other based on the exchange of benefits with influential others and expectations of reciprocity, or fear of social sanctions in future projects (Trivers, 1971; Weber et al., 2018). Members of business family shows may boost their access to sponsors if their business family is connected to the members of other show businesses with whom they can engage in an exchange of career benefits (Jaskiewicz et al., 2013). Reciprocity motives dominate social relationships when the industry resources are valuable, rare, and hard to obtain (Ashton et al., 1998). This commonly occurs in the Hollywood industry, where the number of qualified industry players outweighs the number of available roles in box office movies or production companies. In addition, such benefits may exponentially grow when individuals marry another individual in the same industry. In these cases, each person may actively promote their spouse's career goals by lending and sharing their social network, resulting in social capital synergies (Gorji, 2018; Jaskiewicz et al., 2013). One example can be the case of Michelle Pfeiffer, the three-time Oscar nominee, with other 25 wins and 62 nominations in prestigious industry awards. She used to have limited appearance and roles in the not-so-highly-rated movies before her marriage in 1981. Similarly, Peter Horton, Michele Pfeiffer's husband, also had a meager appearance in few TV series. Interestingly, the couple experienced a leap in their careers post marriage. Two years after their marriage, Michelle Pfeiffer played the lead actress role against Al Pacino in *Scarface* and her husband got leading roles in television series (Gorji et al., 2021).

Overall, in project-based labor markets, such as the entertainment industry and more specifically in Hollywood, social capital brokerage and sponsorship are essential means for the members of the show business families to advance their careers through enhanced exposure and visibility (Gorji et al., 2020). One mechanism is when show business family members provide visibility to their novice family members, for instance, by taking them along or inviting them to social events where meetings of influential industry incumbents occur so that their talents and capabilities are exposed. The other way is when show business families become sponsors by advocating their family members' relevant skills and capabilities in the eyes of powerful industry leaders to establish trust and confidence. Therefore,

Proposition 2: *In show business families, members' career advancement is positively associated with the extent to which their family members serve as network brokers and sponsors.*

Spillover Approach: Reputational Effects

Reputation spillover is another way the show business families impact family members' career advancement. By reputation spillover effects, we refer to the flow of reputational benefits that flow from the prominent members of a show business family to their family members (Reschke et al., 2018). We consider this a passive approach because such effects occur without the direct involvement and commitment of family members towards promoting their family members' careers. Operating in an industry where entertainment and creative arts overlap, show business families can attain reputational assets by winning the minds and hearts of the public and industry critics. From the reputational perspective, winning the Oscars have real implications at the box office and, becoming the best picture laureate/winner helps the individual earn significantly higher earnings compared to the non-winners (Nelson et al., 2001). Such significant achievements positively impact industry incumbents' collective assessments of industry players' competencies and govern their expectations about the individuals' future performance (Weigelt & Camerer, 1988). We propose that in addition to the winner, these reputational indicators impact the career trajectories of the individuals who are connected to the winner through the spillover effects (Rossman et al., 2010; Kim & King, 2014). More specifically, this is likely to happen in industries, such as entertainment, where the subjective and artistic nature of the industry products, in addition to the prevailing uncertainty and ambiguity around one's future performance, pose challenges to the objective assessment of individuals' performance outcomes in the future (Yu & Lester, 2008). Under such circumstances, observable qualities such as association with prize-winning family members, especially for novice actors, are likely to positively impact the critics', judges', and movie directors' evaluations of relevant competencies through signaling effects (Azoulay et al., 2014). Such associations that are induced by family membership occur under the assumption that younger family members naturally inherit their winning family members' talents and capabilities (Kaye, 1999). In addition, younger family members are considered to receive ongoing informal training and mentorship from their older family members, preparing them for taking on an active role in the industry (Ayoobzadeh & Gorji, 2017; Boyd et al., 1999).

An example from a multi-generational show business family, the Barrymores, helps to show how reputational spillover effects may be ubiquitous in Hollywood. The Barrymores have been active in the entertainment industry for 150 years. Maurice, the patriarch of the Barrymore family, was a stage actor in the 1870s. In the realm of Barrymore royalty, which includes several highly recognized members, it is fair to expect that their reputation has spilled over to the other family members. Maurice's son, Lionel, won a Best Actor Academy Award for *A Free Soul* in 1931. His Daughter, Ethel, is a one-time Academy Award winner and a three-time nominee. His third son, John, an actor himself, married Dolores Costello, known as "the Goddess of the Silent Screen" The third generation did not shine as bright as its predecessors; however, the fourth generation of the Barrymore family includes Drew Barrymore, a one-time Golden Globe winner. He has received several nominations in prestigious awards such as BAFTA and Primetime Emmy (Furman & Furman, 2008).

Another example is the Farrow family. The director, the producer, and writer, John Farrow, received several awards and nominations, the most prestigious of which was the Academy Award. His daughter, Mia Farrow, is also the recipient of several awards such as the Golden Globe and several others. The Farrow's extended family also includes award-winning actors and producers such as Woody Allen, who was nominated for Oscar twenty-five times and won it four times, in addition to their other award-winning relatives. This trend continues to the third generation, John Farrow's grandson, Ronan Farrow, who has received a nomination in 2021 for the Best-Spoken Word Album (a Grammy Award), for his work on Harvey Weinstein's repugnant activities. Ronan Farrows received positive reviews for his work's impact (Cooke, 2019). By and large, we argue that among the members of show business families, being associated with reputable family members such as award-winning parents can positively impact individuals' career advancement in the entertainment industry. This occurs through reputational spillover effects. We can back up this argument concerning a few examples of show business families in Hollywood where family members experienced a significant and positive shift in their careers. We argue that this is at least partially attributable to reputational spillover effects in their families.

Proposition 3: *In show business families, members' career advancement is positively associated with their family members' reputational assets through spillover effects.*

Discussion and Conclusion

In this chapter, we provide a typology of family mechanisms that help celebrities who are associated with show business families advance their careers. Using real-world examples and cases that we have adopted from multi-generational show business families in Hollywood, we have shown how show business families help advance their members' careers, including the hands-on, mediatory, and spillover mechanisms. In the hands-on approach, the owners and founders of the show business families directly support their family members' careers by hiring them in their show businesses. Throughout their career, an individual may play a role in a feature movie directed by their family members. Depending on the film's success, this may mark a significant achievement in their career, an opportunity that was less likely to occur without their family affiliation. In the second mechanism, the mediatory approach, the show business family members use their social network that includes other industry gatekeepers and stakeholders to advance their family members' careers. Under these circumstances, influential and accomplished family members can become a means to expose their family members to others or serve as career sponsors by becoming their family members' advocates, making introductions, and promoting their careers in front of others. Finally, in the third mechanism, the spillover approach, the show business families' reputational assets leak to other family members; hence, play a key role in their career advancement (Rossman et al., 2010). We believe that our typology lends itself to further empirical examination.

In comparison to the second and third mechanisms, there is usually stigma of nepotism around the exercise of the hands-on approach. This is likely to signal the beneficiaries' unmerited advancement regardless of their suitability for the position. When the mediatory (network brokerage and sponsorship) or spillover mechanisms are in place, advancing family members' careers does not occur through their kin directly. For instance, when actor and producer, Will Smith, cast his son, Jaden Smith, in a leading role in his 2013 movie, *After Earth*, he was accused of direct nepotism and faced a considerable backlash from viewers and critics (Meek, 2013; Schulz, 2015). This can partially explain why the movie became a box-office flop. As explained before, this was not the case for Chet Hanks as his career leaped, at least partially due to Tom Hanks' relationship with Spielberg, even though later, Chet vandalized his career due to his controversial behaviours (Ojomu & Aulak, 2021).

Although all the three mechanisms lead to family members' career advancement, they may differ in terms of the time required for their effect to take place. For instance, for an individual who cannot benefit from the hands-on approach or one whose families' reputational assets are not outstanding, career advancement based on borrowing their show business family members' social capital is critical since it may take novice players a long time to develop their personal industry network especially in an industry where aging is not viewed in a positive light when it comes to appointment to key movie roles, etc. We suggest that future research investigates these mechanisms from a temporal perspective and investigates the factors that impact the length of time that these approaches need before making an impact on a family members' career outcomes.

Furthermore, future researchers can longitudinally examine the three proposed mechanisms and the types of impact they have on members' career outcomes among show business families, and in other similar industries with strong reputational and social network effects. In addition, it is worthy to study which family members are better positioned to serve as career sponsors for their family members and what factors determine which family members' careers benefit the most from each of these mechanisms. We speculate that family members' gender and their relationship to the focal member in the show business family moderate these relationships. In addition, it is crucial to study the possible negative impacts of the proposed mechanisms on the career prospects of affiliated family members.

References

Aldrich, H. E., & Cliff, J. E. (2003). The pervasive effects of family on entrepreneurship: Toward a family embeddedness perspective. *Journal of Business Venturing*, 18(5), 573–596.

Ashton, M. C., Paunonen, S. V., Helmes, E., & Jackson, D. N. (1998). Kin altruism, reciprocal altruism, and the Big Five personality factors. *Evolution and Human Behavior*, 19(4), 243–255.

Ayoobzadeh, M., & Gorji, Y. (2017). Does parental support influence offspring's short-and long-term career outcomes? In *Academy of Management Proceedings*, 2017(1), 10902. Briarcliff Manor, NY: Academy of Management.

Azoulay, P., Stuart, T. & Wang, Y. (2014). "Matthew: Effect or fable?" *Management Science*, 60, 92–109.

Berger, J., Ridgeway, C. L., Fisek, M. H., & Norman, R. Z. (1998). The legitimation and delegitimation of power and prestige orders. *American Sociological Review*, 63(3), 379–405.

Bourdieu, P. (1986). The forms of capital. In J. G. Richardson (Ed.), *Handbook of Theory and Research for the Sociology of Education* (pp. 241–258). Greenwood Press.

Boyd, J., Upton, N., & Wircenski, M. (1999). Mentoring in family firms: A reflective analysis of senior executives' perceptions. *Family Business Review*, 12(4), 299–309.

Burt, R. S. (1992). *Structural Holes*. Cambridge, Harvard University Press.

Burt, R. S. (2000). The network structure of social capital. *Research in Organizational Behavior*, 22, 345–423.

Burt, R. S, (2001). Social capital of structural holes. In M. Guillen, R. Collins, P. England, M. Meyer, (Eds.). *New Directions in Economic Sociology* (pp. 202–247). New York: Russell Sage Foundation.

Carlisle, E., & Flynn, D. (2005). Small business survival in China: Guanxi, legitimacy, and social capital. *Journal of Developmental Entrepreneurship*, 10(01), 79–96.

Cattani, G., & Ferriani, S. (2008). A core/periphery perspective on individual creative performance: Social networks and cinematic achievements in the Hollywood film industry. *Organization Science*, 19(6),824–844.

Combs, J. G., Shanine, K. K., Burrows, S., Allen, J. S., & Pounds, T. W. (2020). What do we know about business families? Setting the stage for leveraging family science theories. *Family Business Review*, 33(1), 38–63.

Cooke, R., (2019) Catch and Kill by Ronan Farrow review – How the great white predators stick together, *The Guardian*. https://www.theguardian.com/books/2019/oct/20/catch-and-kill-ronan-farrow-review

Corak, M. (2013). Income inequality, equality of opportunity, and intergenerational mobility. *The Journal of Economic Perspectives*, 27(3), 79–102.

Cruz, C., Justo, R., & De Castro, J. O. (2012). Does family employment enhance MSE's performance? Integrating socioemotional wealth and family embeddedness perspectives. *Journal of Business Venturing*, 27(1), 62–76.

Deephouse, D.L. & Jaskiewicz, P. (2013). Do family firms have better reputations than non-family firms? *Journal of Management Studies*, 50(3), 337–360.

DiMaggio, P., & Garip, F. (2012). Network effects and social inequality. *Annual Review of Sociology*, 38, 93–118,

Furman, L., & Furman, E. (2008). *Happily Ever After: The Drew Barrymore Story*. New York: Ballantine Books.

Gorji, Y. (2018). All in the Family: Three Studies on Kinship, Networks and Career Outcomes (Doctoral dissertation, Concordia University).

Gorji, Y. (2020). Do Family Members of Oscar Winners Win Too? A Status-Shift Spillover Effect Analysis. *Nordic Journal of Media Management*, 1(4), 481–493.

Gorji, Y., Carney, M., & Prakash, R. (2020). Indirect nepotism: Network sponsorship, social capital, and career performance in show business families. *Journal of Family Business Strategy*, 11(3), 1–10.

Gorji, Y., Carney, M., & Prakash, R. (2021). Celebrity Couples as Business Families: A Social Network Perspective. *Family Business Review*, 34(4), 365–384.

Granovetter, M. (2005). The impact of social structure on economic outcomes. *Journal of Economic Perspectives*, 19(1), 33–50.

Granovetter, M. (2018). *Getting a Job: A Study of Contacts and Careers*. Chicago: The University of Chicago Press.

Grugulis, I., & Stoyanova, D. (2012). Social capital and networks in film and TV: Jobs for the boys? *Organization Studies*, 33(10), 1311–1331.

Hanlon, D., & Saunders, C. (2007). Marshaling resources to form small new ventures: Toward a more holistic understanding of entrepreneurial support. *Entrepreneurship Theory and Practice*, 31(4), 619–641.

Hawdon, J. (2008). Legitimacy, trust, social capital, and policing styles: A theoretical statement. *Police Quarterly*, 11(2), 182–201.

Jaskiewicz, P., Uhlenbruck, K., Balkin, D. B., & Reay, T. (2013). Is nepotism good or bad? Types of nepotism and implications for knowledge management. *Family Business Review*, 26, 121–139.

Kaye, K. (1999). Mate selection and family business success. *Family Business Review*, 12(2), 107–115.

Kim, J. W., & King, B. G. (2014). Seeing stars: Matthew effects and status bias in major league baseball umpiring. *Management Science*, 60(11), 2619–2644.

King, R., & Peng, W. Q. (2013). The effect of industry characteristics on the control longevity of founding-family firms. *Journal of Family Business Strategy*, 4(4), 281–295.

Kwon, S. W., Rondi, E., Levin, D. Z., De Massis, A., & Brass, D. J. (2020). Network brokerage: An integrative review and future research agenda. *Journal of Management*, 46(6), 1092–1120.

Le Breton-Miller, I. & Miller, D. (2015). The arts and family business: Linking family-related resources to the market environment. In *Academy of Management Proceedings* (Vol. 2015, No. 1, p. 13248). Briarcliff Manor, NY 10510: Academy of Management. Learning & Education.

Lehman, D. W., O'Connor, K., Kovács, B., & Newman, G. E. (2019). Authenticity. *Academy of Management Annals*, 13(1), 1–42.

LoBrutto, V., & Morrison, H. R. (2012). *The Coppolas: A Family Business*. ABC-CLIO.

Lutter, M. (2015). Do women suffer from network closure? The moderating effect of social capital on gender inequality in a project-based labor market, 1929 to 2010. *American Sociological Review*, 80(2), 329–358.

McPherson, M., Smith-Lovin, L., & Cook, J. M. (2001). Birds of a feather: Homophily in social networks. *Annual Review of Sociology*, 27(1), 415–444.

Meek, T. (2013), "After Earth": Nepotism gone awry on an Erath gone bad. *Cambridge Day*. https://www.cambridgeday.com/2013/06/01/after-earth-nepotism-gone-awry-on-an-earth-gone-bad/

Michaeli, Y., Dickson, D. J., & Shulman, S. (2016). Parental and nonparental career-related support among young adults: Antecedents and psychosocial correlates. *Journal of Career Development*, 45(2), 150–165.

Nelson, R. A., Donihue, M. R., Waldman, D. M, & Wheaton, C. (2001). What's an Oscar Worth. *Economic Inquiry*, 39, 1–6.

Ojomu, N. & Aulak, S., (2021). Controversial Chet: Who is Tom Hanks' son? *The Sun*. https://www.the-sun.com/entertainment/528460/tom-hanks-cleveland-guardians-son-born/

Oren, L., Caduri, A., & Tziner, A. (2013). Intergenerational occupational transmission: Do offspring walk in the footsteps of mom or dad, or both? *Journal of Vocational Behavior*, 83(3), 551–560.

Pearson, A. W., Carr, J. C., & Shaw, J. C. (2008). Toward a theory of familiness: A social capital perspective. *Entrepreneurship Theory and Practice*, 32(6), 949–969.

Pittino, D., Visintin, F., & Lauto, G. (2018). Fly away from the nest? A configurational analysis of family embeddedness and individual attributes in the entrepreneurial entry decision by next-generation members. *Family Business Review*, 31(3), 271–294.

Reschke, B. P., Azoulay, P., & Stuart, T. E. (2018). Status spillovers: The effect of status-conferring prizes on the allocation of attention. *Administrative Science Quarterly*, 63(4), 819–847.

Rooks, G., Klyver, K., & Sserwanga, A. (2016). The context of social capital: A comparison of rural and urban entrepreneurs in Uganda. *Entrepreneurship Theory and Practice*, 40(1), 111–130

Rossman, G., Esparza, N., & Bonacich, P. (2010). I'd like to thank the Academy, team spillovers, and network centrality. *American Sociological Review*, 75(1), 31–51.

Schröder, E., Schmitt-Rodermund, E., & Arnaud, N. (2011). Career choice intentions of adolescents with a family business background. *Family Business Review*, 24(4), 305–321.

Schulz, L. (2015) Will Smith Calls 'After Earth' the 'Most Painful Failure' of His Career. *Variety*. https://variety.com/2015/film/news/will-smith-after-earth-comment-most-painful-failure-of-his-career-1201432773/

Seibert, S. E., Kraimer, M. L., & Liden, R. C. (2001). A social capital theory of career success. *Academy of Management Journal*, 44(2), 219–237.

Simarasl, N., Jiang, D. S., Kellermanns, F. W., & Debicki, B. J. (2020). Unmasking the Social Ghost in the Machine: How the Need to Belong and Family Business Potency Affect Family Firm Performance. *Family Business Review*, 33(4), 351–371.

Sparrowe, R. T., Liden, R. C., Wayne, S. J., & Kraimer, M. L. (2001). Social networks and the performance of individuals and groups. *Academy of Management Journal*, 44(2), 316–325.

Taşdemir, D. Ç., Çayırağası, F., & Güven, G. G. (2017). A conceptual study on nepotism and effects in family enterprises. *International Journal of Innovation and Economic Development*, 3(5), 59–64.

Trivers, R. L. (1971). The evolution of reciprocal altruism. *The Quarterly Review of Biology*, 46(1), 35–57.

Turner, R. J. (1960). Sponsored and contest mobility and the school system. *American Sociological Review*, 25(6), 855–867.

Uhlaner, L. M. (2006). Business family as a team: Underlying force for sustained competitive advantage. *Handbook of research on family business*, 125, 144.

Urassa, G. (2016). Effects of nepotism and family conflicts on the performance of family-owned firms in Tanzania: contrasting views. *Business Management Review*, 18(1), 45–69.

Walter, J., Lechner, C., & Kellermanns, F. W. (2007). Knowledge transfer between and within alliance partners: Private versus collective benefits of social capital. *Journal of Business Research*, 60(7), 698–710.

Weber, T. O., Weisel, O., & Gächter, S. (2018). Dispositional free riders do not free ride on punishment. *Nature communications*, 9(1),1–9.

Weigelt, K., & Camerer, C. (1988). Reputation and corporate strategy: A review of recent theory and applications, *Strategic Management Journal*, 9(5), 443–454.

Whiston, S. C., & Keller, B. K. (2004). The influences of the family of origin on career development: A review and analysis. *The Counseling Psychologist*, 32(4), 493–568.

Yu, T., & Lester, R. H. (2008). Moving beyond firm boundaries: A social network perspective on reputation spillover. *Corporate Reputation Review*, 11(1), 94–108.

Zellweger, T., Sieger, P., & Halter, F. (2011). Should I stay or should I go? Career choice intentions of students with family business background. *Journal of business venturing*, 26(5), 521–536.

Zhao, J., Carney, M., Zhang, S., & Zhu, L. (2020). How does an intra-family succession effect strategic change and performance in China's family firms? *Asia Pacific Journal of Management*, 37(2), 363–389.

Part IV: **Institutionalization of Wealth and Business Families in Society**

Hanna Kuusela

19 Institutionalizing Family Legacy, Reproducing Dynasties

Abstract: The chapter discusses the contemporary and emerging socio-cultural mechanisms through which dynastic business families reproduce themselves as units of wealth accumulation in the midst of growing criticism against wealth concentration and hereditary privileges. It explores and theorizes contemporary and emerging mechanisms, narratives, and institutional practices of class-making through which the families legitimize and explain their dynastic wealth both for the public and the younger generations in the families.

Keywords: family legacy, dynastic wealth, wealth accumulation, hereditary privileges, class-making, legitimization

Introduction

The role of inherited or family wealth in sustaining, reproducing and even accelerating increasing wealth inequalities has been addressed in various studies in recent years (Carney & Nason, 2018; Hansen, 2014; Piketty, 2014; Toft & Friedman, 2021). This chapter describes and analyzes mechanisms behind this development by outlining a number of key practices that account for dynastic wealth accumulation among wealthy contemporary business families. The aim of the chapter is to guide the readers systematically through current and recent practices that have helped reproduce wealthy business families as units of dynastic accumulation. The chapter describes how growing wealth inequalities driven by the top groups (see, e.g., Piketty, 2014) coincide with increased professionalization, institutionalization, and transnationalization of dynasty-making since the end of the 1980s and the beginning of the 1990s.

Discussing the rise of educational programmes designed for family business successors, the use of family offices, the consolidation of family business lobbies, the boom in wealth management services, and the affective strategies peculiar to wealthy business families, the chapter thus describes and analyzes the classed and transnational nature of the processes through which wealthy families reproduce themselves in the globalized economy of the 21st century. In so doing, it also assesses the impact of such reproduction on cross-generational wealth accumulation and economic stratification. Analyzing both the practical and the more affective dimensions of different

Hanna Kuusela, Tampere University

https://doi.org/10.1515/9783110727968-019

reproduction strategies that have been on the rise since the 1980s, the chapter elaborates the role that dynastic wealth and business families play in today's inequality regimes, arguing that the institutionalization, formalization, and transnationalization of their dynasty-making gives these processes of reproduction a strong classed dimension. Contemporary wealthy families can be said to be involved in active class-making (Kuusela, 2018) in which larger family networks beyond the nuclear family and the social contexts are important (Beckert, 2022).

The wider context for the inquiry on contemporary dynasty-making is offered by the growing understanding that the economic growth of the past decades has been conservatizing. Those with the most capital perform economically better than others and accumulate wealth at a growing speed. Most notably, Piketty (2014, 2020; Piketty & Saez, 2014) together with his colleagues have shown that rather than being transformative, current economic growth is, in fact, reproducing and deepening existing economic hierarchies. As units that may transmit great wealth accumulated in the past to future generations in the same family, wealthy business families lie at the heart of these conservatizing tendencies. Whether desired or not, the casual aim of the members of such families to preserve and pass on the businesses and assets they have inherited is likely to contribute to growing wealth inequalities globally and, ultimately, to other forms of global and local inequalities if not addressed politically. Thus, this chapter is also an inquiry into the classed agency of contemporary wealthy families. The term "classed agency" here broadly refers to different ways of being and acting that are structured or steered by one's socio-economic status or socio-cultural background, which, in this case, is one's membership of a wealthy business family. While class and social class undoubtedly remain contested and ambiguous concepts (Lareau & Conley, 2008; Wright, 2005), the term social class is mainly used to refer to groups of people who more or less share similar and relatively stable socio-economic statuses, socio-cultural backgrounds and similar life chances. From such a perspective, wealthy business families and their members can be described as a social class.

In the following, I will outline in more detail the various class-making or reproduction strategies and practices used by wealthy business families. The use of the concepts of class and classed agency are, thus, also meant to direct attention to the active making (Bourdieu, 1987; Thompson, 1966) of family owners as a class and to different practices through which specific socio-economic interests of this particular group are taken care of and to those cultural processes that facilitate the formation of this class at the top. After introducing the research field in general, I will first describe practices aimed at keeping the families and their new generations mentally business- or wealth-oriented. I will then describe the legal and economic practices important for contemporary business families and the role of professional advisors in facilitating cross-generational accumulation. Finally, I will analyze the different institutions central for the legitimization of family wealth in societies at large, including the consolidation of lobbying infrastructures that serve wealthy families. In other words, the chapter will proceed from outlining the management of the internal dynamics of dynastic families, to the management of wealth and assets and, finally, to "the external management" of public opinion and public policies that concern dynastic wealth accumulation. Throughout the chapter, the focus is on wealthy business families, although similar dynamics may have proliferated to middle-sized or middle-class business families and are certainly available to them in the event their businesses grow and succeed.

Family Businesses and Wealth Accumulation

A growing number of scholars have recently emphasized the intertwined relationships between kinship, business, and wealth accumulation. Particularly, continental Europe is characterized by strong business families, so that a significant part of corporate ownership is concentrated in the hands of families and family dynasties (Faccio & Lang, 2002; LaPorta et al., 1999). Although most family businesses are small, many large and publicly listed companies can also be classified as such. Germany is a classic example of a country in which the business elite significantly consists of families that have passed on their businesses and assets over generations. In 2012, the accumulated wealth of the 100 richest families in Germany was estimated at over 320 billion euros, and they controlled revenues worth more than 400 billion euros. Dynastic tendencies are also strong, as approximately half of these business families are at least three generations old (Zellweger & Kammerlander, 2014).

However, even in countries often associated with self-made wealth, family dynasties have been found to play a substantial role at the top of wealth distribution. In their analysis of the super-rich in the US, Korom et al. (2017, p. 75) conclude that even though entrepreneurship increasingly matters in becoming super-rich, "it is first and foremost the ability of rich family dynasties to retain control over corporations and to access sophisticated financial advice that makes fortunes last". They reveal how heirs have a higher chance of remaining wealthy, as having other family members listed among the Forbes 400 – an indicator of the concentration of fortunes within families – significantly lessens the risk of dropping off the list. Moreover, Carney and Nason (2018) show how the wealthiest 1% households in the US typically derive their most significant portion of wealth from active ownership and management of unincorporated small- to medium-sized enterprises, generally considered to be "family firms". Demonstrating how business families constitute a significant part of the top 1%, they suggest that family businesses constitute a social class that serves their own dynastic interests through the use of distinct wealth accumulation mechanisms, which permit the transfer of wealth and social advantages to succeeding generations.

Similarly, Gilding's (1999, 2005, 2010) work in Australia shows that family relations are still key to the reproduction of elites in terms of not just succession but also the accumulation of wealth. In Finland, our studies show how a substantial part of the top 0.1% of earners are inheritors (Kuusela & Kantola, 2020), whereas other studies reveal the central role of inheritance in mature industrial societies more generally (Barone & Mocetti, 2016; Hansen, 2014; Piketty, 2014).

Reflecting on this intertwining of kinship, business and dynastic wealth accumulation, Yanagisako proclaims that family firms should be conceptualized not merely as profit-seeking enterprises but as kinship enterprises, where the demise of a particular family firm does not necessarily mean the demise of the kinship enterprise (Yanagisako, 2019, p. 5), as business families' economic interests and activities often endure beyond the life of the firm. An industrial business may be transformed several times in the course of generations and, finally, turn into a (purely) financial unit, the rationale of which is to further accumulate wealth (Kuusela, 2018). In such business families, economic decisions are shaped not only by business goals but also by intergenerational commitments to dynastic wealth-making.

While drawing attention to families as units of wealth accumulation, scholars have also described the increasing institutionalization and professionalization of the different processes that help to connect kinship sentiments with economic interests and dynastic reproduction. One can refer to a constantly growing social, legal, economic, and cultural infrastructure that has emerged to support wealthy business families in coping with their wealth, its protection, and its transfer to the next generations. The professionalization concerns both the legal and business activities as well as the more affective and intimate dimensions of dynasty-making. The management of dynastic advantages through legal vehicles such as trusts and family holding companies is combined with affective processes, family constitutions, and family councils aimed at keeping the family united.

Different tools and strategies are used to manage both the inner dynamics of wealthy families and their relationships with societies at large. These social processes and institutional structures that shape the quantitative patterns of wealth accumulation, as described by economists, have recently attracted new attention among scholars. Harrington (2016), Herlin-Giret (2018, 2020) and Higgins (2021), for example, have outlined the legal devices and strategies used by professional advisors to help clients manage dynastic wealth, whereas Glucksberg and Russell-Prywata (2020) have suggested how charitable giving is used to both educate the next generations of business families to manage finances and encourage them to invest in the family's dynastic success. From the perspective of the wealthy themselves, I myself have previously analyzed the social meanings as well as educational and emotional training attached to inherited wealth among wealthy inheritors in Finland (Kuusela, 2018), whereas Higgins (2021) has studied the pedagogical processes between wealth managers and wealthy families in North West England. The acceleration of such practices shows how wealthy families are increasingly looking for effective tools to help them navigate, on one hand, the legal and economic aspects, and on the other hand, the affective and cultural aspects of succession, as Sklair and Glucksberg (2021) note.

Managing the Family: Next Generation Programmes, Education, and Consultants

The cultural role and image of wealthy business families has been in flux in the new millennium. While family wealth seems to have endured and persisted, dynastic dynamics are not necessarily culturally in favour. As the outlook of elites has changed from a view that accepted inherited status as a legitimate source of wealth to one that stresses meritocratic achievement, hard work and entrepreneurship (see, e.g., Khan, 2011; Littler, 2017; Sherman, 2017), dynastic accumulation and privileges are not easily welcomed, and wealthy business families find themselves under new pressures. The rise of economic inequalities and the re-emergence of entrepreneurial discourses around self-made success (Kantola & Kuusela, 2019) seem to necessitate greater justification of dynastic wealth. Normatively, the intergenerational perpetuation of large fortunes seems to violate the principal of merit, which has been – and continues to be – a central normative justification for social inequality in liberal societies, as Beckert (2022) notes. Dynastically transferred wealth and privileges are hard to legitimate in such societies, partly because of resulting injustices and partly because of feared negative consequences for the economy and for democratic politics (Beckert, 2008).

Increasing wealth inequalities have also given rise to new demands for wealth taxes and more progressive taxation on capital income as well as on inheritances and gifts as ways to raise revenues and address wealth accumulation at the top. These global demands are primarily fuelled by civil societies, NGOs, and academics (Pogge & Mehta, 2016), but they seem to also attract increasing governmental attention particularly in the Global North. For example, the OECD (2018) reported in 2018 that "[n]et wealth taxes are far less widespread than they used to be in the OECD but there has recently been a renewed interest in wealth taxation", concluding that "there is a strong case for addressing wealth inequality through the tax system" (OECD, 2018, pp. 11, 98). Annual wealth taxes exist in a number of European countries, but many have also repealed them in the past few decades because of their alleged inefficiency or the observation that such taxes have frequently failed to meet their redistributive goals (OECD, 2018). However, new evidence on extreme wealth accumulation at the top together with popular movements such as Occupy Wall Street have fostered a new round of interest in wealth taxation and have led governments to reconsider their options. Such discussions are often coupled with demands for greater control of tax havens and offshore services, as contemporary wealth often escapes national jurisdictions.

Simultaneously with such popular demands, many countries – including those not regularly identified as tax havens – continue, however, to develop so-called exit options for wealth that enable evading or avoiding taxes and regulations. As the scrutiny and control of tax havens have improved (Ylönen & Finér, 2022, forthcoming), the financial industry, wealthy individuals and their businesses have sought refuge from states that are seemingly transparent and well-regulated, but which still offer loopholes that enable evading taxes in the name of tax competitiveness (see, e.g., Shaxson & Christensen, 2016) to attract (foreign) investments and investors. Contemporary wealthy business families need to navigate in the midst of such ambiguous forces, where, on the one hand, the popular critique against offshore services, tax avoidance, and tax evasion has been on the rise and has led to increased "tax shaming" (Bramall, 2018), while, on the other hand, many governments have been keen to offer exit options for those with great wealth, thereby proactively institutionalising ecosystems or wealth hubs for family businesses willing to avoid taxes. The environment for dynastic reproduction is, thus, rife with local and global ambiguities, within which wealthy business families try to justify their contribution to society while also perpetuating their family wealth.

Simultaneously, the decline of the traditional "one-family-one-business" model and the financialization of the global economy have created new challenges and needs for wealthy families. Maintaining family cohesion and keeping families business-oriented is becoming increasingly difficult, as many industrial families have sold their original businesses and transformed into investment houses. In contrast to founder-controlled firms, many later-generation family firms are controlled by multiple family owners, sometimes by several hundred family members (Zellweger & Kammerlander, 2015).

Family sociologists and advisors have provided accounts of the multiple interests behind seemingly united families and the need for family governance to align these interests (Kets De Vries, 1993). As Zellweger and Kammerlander (2015, p. 1282) note, the complexity arising from heterogeneous interests inside business families creates a demand for coordination among family members and, hence, mitigation of (what they label) family blockholder conflicts. Glucksberg and Burrows (2016) state how the problem for most contemporary wealthy business families is that traditional models – one factory, one family home, one set of children from married parents per generation, children who are physically close – are not often relevant anymore. With the growth of the family tree, "family members tend to develop looser ties among each other on average, pursue diverging career paths and interests, and vary in their involvement with and goals for the firm", as Zellweger and Kammerlander (2015, p. 12,823) write. This is also a challenge articulated by the Family Business Network (FBN), the central networking and lobbying organization of wealthy business families. It has recognized large families as a specific challenge, because as "business families grow beyond cousins' consortiums, they face specific issues related to family cohesion, affectio societatis, governance, professionalization, strategy and diversification" (FBN, 2021a).

Thus, preparing their children for the money, inherited privileges and ownership has become a key preoccupation for wealthy business families, as successful transmission of wealth and the family legacy requires work. A central observation of scholars is that business families are increasingly preoccupied with the affective dimensions of succession. Wealth needs to be protected from possible "family conflicts", as Harrington (2016, p. 209) writes. The management of family businesses and the more general pressures of cultural individualization and meritocracy have created a situation in which ensuring that offspring are interested in the family business and protecting the family's wealth is challenging. This means that along with the business, the families must also be managed (Glucksberg & Burrows, 2016). This growing awareness of, and interest in, the family dynamics has created an abundance of new practices and services that are tailor-made for dynastic families.

The use of short-term, exclusive, and commercial programmes, educational initiatives, and consultant services designed specifically for dynastic families has come up in research interviews with wealthy families (Kuusela, 2018), but their popularity can also be seen in the amount of such services among different service providers, whether fully commercial or academic. The educational next generation programmes aimed at "connecting influential families" (Citi, 2021), offered, for example, by the big four companies and smaller consulting firms, but also by banks and prestigious universities, promise above all to help new generations assume their roles in the family and family business. A key aspect of such programmes is, thus, their focus on affective and social dimensions. The promotional material of such programmes promises to develop the participants' skills to "promote trust", "authority", "governance and leadership mindset" and "confidence", while emphasizing the value of peer help and networking between different families (Kellogg, 2021). The focus is on cultural and social, rather than economic or juridical, skills and concepts. "You will also see how a common vision can unite family owners in a long-term commitment to continuity", as one of such programme promises (Kellogg, 2021).

Besides – or even instead of – the "hard skills" of business, young potential leaders in business families are, thus, taught what it takes to lead a family. The promotional material of the Institute for Management Development's (IMD) Global Family Business Centre, an institution offering services for "next generation family business leader[s]", suggests that understanding "family communications and one's own role in a team of family members helps to separate individual from team dynamics and enables the next-generation member to become a responsible family shareholder" (Kenyon-Rouvinez & Glemser, 2014, p. 3). According to the Centre's own testimony, the "demand for custom programs (tailor-made for your family business needs) has increased steadily and in 2004, after welcoming more than 400 families from over 40 countries, they [the Centre] celebrated the 1,000th Family Business participant milestone" (GFBC, 2021b).

Besides such programmes, researchers have also outlined how many affluent parents describe the need for specific parenting strategies to ensure their children learn to both appreciate their wealth and cope with the anxieties that wealth causes in times of meritocratic ideals and demands for greater economic justice, including tax justice. Particularly, Sherman (2017) described the concerns of affluent parents in New York to raise morally "good people" with a strong work ethic, prudent desires, and a reflexive awareness of their own privilege, whereas Schimpfössl (2018) charted the various strategies from schooling to philanthropy to support Russian inheritors' claims to inheritances. Similarly, our interviews in Finland revealed the active class-making inside Finnish business families (Kuusela, 2018): many members of dynastic families explained that their children were raised to value and understand the importance of continuity and what it takes to be an owner. Teaching such virtues can take very practical forms when children work as assistants in the family's investment company or are trained to make business decisions together, but training can also mean mental training to value dynastic fortunes against the pressures of meritocracy.

Such preparation of children may start early and is also being increasingly systemized. An interview study conducted by Deloitte's (2016) EMEA Family Business Centre found that more than a third of the respondents had "been preparing for succession to leadership since their childhood", and almost half of them started preparing before working life began.[1] Thus, even though today's wealthy heirs have different possible points of identification – be they professional, geographical, recreational, or individual values – they are taught early on to recognize themselves as owners and potential leaders, and speak and act in the name of such subjectivities, a feature that, for example, Bourdieu (1987) linked to the existence of a class.

Pointing in the same direction, Tait (2020, p. 984) has paid attention to family constitutions as one vehicle for upholding – what she calls – high-wealth exceptionalism. Modelled on national constitutions, a family constitution "sets forth the rules that family members must adhere to in order to protect the family fortune from various kinds of creditor claims, family feuds, and reckless investments". In the world of high-wealth exceptionalism and family constitutions, "every high-wealth family can and should create its own rules and regulations, its own value-system, and its own vision of rights and responsibilities" (Tait, 2020, p. 984). Consequently, such families have learned to think of themselves as islands apart from the larger polity, Tait (2020) suggests.

Different strategies aimed at reproducing family legacies and family wealth are, of course, not new phenomena. On the contrary, histories of aristocracies and monarchies are essentially histories of the cultural reproduction of family legacies and

---

1 The report was based on 92 in-depth, face-to-face interviews with next-generation representatives from family-owned companies in 19 countries across Europe, the Middle East, and Africa.

fortunes (for recent analysis, see Clancy, 2021). With the bourgeois revolutions, the rise of the merchant class, and the demise of old privileges based on status, these processes of reproduction took, however, new directions and are constantly doing so. What we are currently witnessing in the context of wealthy business families is increasing institutionalization, transnationalization, and professionalization of such processes, largely due to the simultaneous processes of financialization, globalization, and the rise of meritocratic ideals.

Contemporary reproduction processes often include private educational programmes and the use of a variety of consultants. Such new trends detach wealthy elites from traditional forms of elite education (Bourdieu, 1996) and move them towards professional services tailor-made for the wealthy or individual families. It is noteworthy that formal education or educational degrees do not necessarily appear important in the context of contemporary business families. Instead, the focus is more on exclusive and tailor-made services or on parenting strategies (see also Stamm, 2016), designed for those families with wealth in mind. A similar observation regarding business families was made as early as 1989 by Bourdieu, according to whom different groups differ significantly in their investment in and need for formal education. In contrast to clerical workers or primary schoolteachers, "who tend to concentrate all their investments in the academic market", according to Bourdieu (1996, p. 276), heads of family businesses, whose success does not depend to the same degree on academic success, invested less interest and work in their studies. The capital structure of wealthy business families is such that formal qualifications are not a central concern for them, but as recent developments indicate, the management of kinship dynamics and sentiments are. This differentiates such families from most other contemporary families, at least in the Global North, where the cultural importance of kinship ties has been on the decline and identities are rather constructed, for example, around professions, educational paths, lifestyles, or neighbourhoods.

Accumulating Wealth: Wealth Managers and Family Offices

In addition to the soft skills distributed and learned through next-generation programmes and parenting, another central practice that accounts for the reproduction of dynastic wealth in the contemporary milieu is the rise of wealth management services. Different studies have shown how wealth managers have gradually occupied an increasingly important role in facilitating wealth accumulation and its cross-generational transmission.

As a profession, wealth management has grown and become increasingly institutionalized over the past 30 to 40 years (Harrington, 2016; Herlin-Giret, 2018, 2020). During that period, wealth management practices expanded dramatically, and coordination among disparate industries offering products and services designed for the wealthy increased, including banks, law firms, accounting agencies and insurance providers as well as numerous boutique firms and individual practitioners (Harrington, 2016, p. 53). Consolidation of the profession is also seen in the expansion of the tasks of wealth managers, for example, in France in the early 1980s, wealth management simply meant asset management, but contemporary wealth managers handle a range of issues, from tax and succession planning to legal counselling. Most notably, Herlin-Giret (2018) has investigated the growing institutionalization of the wealth management industry in France, where practitioners have established their own associations, and boundary work between different service providers is on the rise.

As a result of this expansion, Harrington (2016), who has studied wealth managers across the globe, goes as far as to propose that it is exactly the increased use of wealth managers that accounts for the rise in wealth inequalities and that wealth managers are particularly important in reproducing dynastic wealth. In Harrington's (2016, p. 193) words, wealth managers "turn one generation's surplus into dynastic privilege", arresting the process in which family wealth (could) get destroyed. By "thwarting the usual processes through which assets get redistributed", wealth managers ultimately end up, as Harrington (2016, p. 193) suggests, "shoring up a larger system of inequality". According to her research, the key mechanisms through which family wealth is protected are the avoidance of taxes, debts, and penalties, access to exclusive investment opportunities with high growth and low risks and passing of wealth to subsequent generations with minimal transaction costs (Harrington, 2016, pp. 194–209). Harrington refers to "wealth protection" techniques and mechanisms that help create and grow dynastic wealth as relatively "undisturbed" and are essentially the know-how of wealth managers.

For those interested in the different infrastructures and institutions of private law that help protect dynastic wealth, Harrington's (2016, 2017), Pistor's (2019) and Beckert's (2008) work offer comprehensive accounts of the legal mechanisms and juridical institutions, such as trusts and foundations, that are crucially important for wealthy business families. In general, as Beckert (2022) notes, legal regulations in inheritance law, such as testamentary freedom, the rule against perpetuities in common law, trusts, family foundations, and primogeniture, are highly consequential for the long-term stability of wealth among the super-rich. Similarly, Tait (2020) has described how together with family constitutions and family offices, family trust companies and family foundations have led to a "high wealth exceptionalism", as these contemporary legal institutions allow for the long-term protection of wealth but can effectively only be used by those who have fortunes beyond 100 million dollars. Wealthy families escape from a number of regulations by taking advantage of tilts in the legal systems that exempt them from the rules constraining most families.

The juridical frameworks available for families, however, differ fundamentally according to national regimes, and differences in inheritance law as well as customs create different outcomes. Inside certain jurisdictions, family foundations, for example, allow wealthy families to protect their wealth through exemptions on various taxes while allowing them to still control their assets. The US and the United Kingdom (UK) systems allow, for example, the use of trusts, which can be registered in offshore jurisdictions to minimize tax obligations without effectively rendering control. Conversely, for example, continental Europe usually does not recognize trusts, but the proliferation of different legal tools that help minimise taxes at the time of inheritances, such as tax envelopes, are constantly being invented in different countries. Moreover, in some cases, differences in national jurisdictions concerning inheritance law have also led to high-profile emigration as rich families change their countries of residence in search of lower taxes and more favourable regulations.

In addition to legal counselling, wealth managers can also assist in the management of family sentiments, similar to other consultants and educational programmes described earlier. Writing of France, Herlin-Giret (2020) argues that instead of only managing their clients' fortunes, wealth managers actively engage in making their clients adopt "good" behaviour with regard to their wealth. This includes helping their clients give meaning to their wealth by inviting them to develop long-term strategies and by teaching them in practice to incorporate ethics of prudence and moderation. Similar to the next-generation programs, Herlin-Giret (2020, p. 203) refers to programmes and seminars organized by wealth managers to train younger generations and describes a case in which a wealth manager set up a tailor-made programme with business school teachers for the son of his client, who suddenly inherited a fortune.

Also, Higgins (2021), who has conducted research on first-generation ultra-wealthy owners in North West England, describes the pedagogical work done by wealth managers to "produce good clients". She maintains that both the wealthy and their wealth managers use family wealth as a pedagogical tool through which ideal subject positions are constructed. Like in Herlin-Giret's (2020) work, the ideal positions, or ideal clients as described by Higgins (2021), can balance between prudence, work- or business-orientation and accumulation.

The importance of balancing is recognized, and also produced, by consultants, as the report by Deloitte's Family Business Centre indicates. It states how "[f]amily firms need to maintain a balance between business goals (such as growth, innovation and recruiting talented staff) and family goals, such as maintaining family values and protecting the family wealth. They also need to arrange a smooth transition in leadership eventually, from one generation to the next" (Deloitte, 2016). Such balancing does not only help the members of the family to come along, but by placing the protection of family wealth at its centre, it also secures the reproduction of dynastic wealth (see also Kuusela, 2018) and, consequently, contributes to processes of inequality between those who inherit significant wealth and those who do not.

In the case of the wealthiest families, wealth management is often organized inside a family office. Dunn (1980) was one of the first researchers to explain the history and evolution of family offices, placing kinship bonds and shared economic interests at their core. According to Dunn, families utilized family offices to maintain a cohesive family unit through successive generations, to control their business, and to exercise political, cultural, and religious influence as a united force. For Dunn, family offices, which were relatively unknown at that time, facilitated class cohesion and corporate control.

The establishment of a family office is often caused by a triggering event, such as the death or retirement of the owners, the sale of the business, a new strategy to separate private wealth from business, or an opportunity in tax regulation, as Kenyon-Rouvinez and Park (2020) note. The need for such institutions of wealth preservation has no doubt increased – and continues to do so – with the financialization of the global economy and the internal growth of the wealthy business families. In general, industry experts agree that the family office industry is growing, and the number of family offices has been estimated at 10,000 globally, of which the US alone accounts for approximately half, although estimates show significant variances (Kenyon-Rouvinez & Park, 2020).

Economies of scale constitute one of the central reasons to set up a family office, making it a vehicle for wealthy families, in particular. By combining their buying power, the family members gain access to the best strategic advisors while keeping costs low (Kenyon-Rouvinez & Park, 2020). While wealth management is the key function expected of a family office, family offices aimed at also achieving non-financial goals is a growing trend, as discussed earlier. Notably, Kenyon-Rouvinez and Park (2020) found an increased focus on education programmes for next generations, involving outside educational institutions as well as internships inside the family business. Reflecting this spread of the family office model and their tasks, Glucksberg and Burrows (2016) have referred to them as the contemporary infrastructure of dynastic wealth.

Influencing Society: Lobbies, Networks, and Research Initiatives

Thus far, this chapter has described the increasingly institutionalized practices that dynastic business families use to keep their families together, prepare their offspring for the money and reproduce their wealth with the help of professional advisors. In addition to such internal reproduction practices, there are growing signs that wealthy business families are developing external strategies aimed at legitimizing the role of dynastic families for societies at large. The transnational activities between wealthy business families and their growing lobbying efforts in the past 30 years give reason to pay attention to the potential socio-political power of business families and to those cultural narratives and frames that may account for their dynasty-making and wealth accumulation.

In the past decade, sociologists working on economic inequalities and elites have shown interest in different forms of meaning-making and legitimization strategies to explain growing inequalities. With the assumption that different cultural "frames, narratives, and repertoires" (Lamont et al., 2014) help to reproduce existing inequalities, a number of scholars have examined how different elites, including the very wealthy, make sense and justify their position and advantages to themselves and others (Adamson & Johansson, 2020; Hecht, 2017; Kantola & Kuusela, 2019; Khan, 2011; Kuusela, 2018, 2020; Sherman, 2017). Thus far, the majority of this research has focused on business elites, such as managers and financial elites (Adamson & Johansson, 2020; Hecht, 2017) or on the affluent in general (Sherman, 2017), whereas the legitimization of dynastic tendencies has been only sparsely studied and mostly from the perspective of self-legitimization (Khan, 2011; Kuusela, 2018).

There are, however, signs that wealthy business families across the globe have become increasingly active in such processes of persuasion and legitimization, circulating strategies, narratives, and practices aimed at helping the cultural justification of family wealth. Such socio-cultural work is increasingly conducted through, or with the help of, lobbying organizations and networks specialising in family business and family wealth as well as consultants and educational institutions discussed earlier, but also through direct funding for research on family business.

Often mentioned in research (Gallo, 2004; Heck et al., 2008; Melin & Nordqvist, 2007; Pérez & Puig, 2009), the FBN, along with its local chapters, is one lobbying institution that constructs and disseminates a certain favourable image of family business and business families in the era of growing inequalities. Founded in 1989, it has quickly established itself as a notable proponent and representative of family business interests in a number of countries. According to its own information, FBN is a federation of more than 30 member associations spanning over 60 countries. The global network gathers 4,000 business families, encompassing 17,000 individuals of which 6,400 are next generation (FBN, 2021b). The 1990s saw the establishment of national chapters in countries such as Sweden, Spain, the US, France, the Netherlands, and Finland, while the latest round of expansion in countries such as Luxemburg, Canada, Norway, and Lebanon began to take place after 2015.

The goals of the network are explicitly tied to both societal impact and the needs of the (exclusive) member families. First, FBN (2021b) promises to help with the internal dynamics of the families, offering "business families a safe space to learn from, share with and inspire each other about how to guide the family involvement in the business, [and] facilitate relationships within the family", tasks described at length at the beginning of this chapter. However, its second promise is directly tied to the socio-political legitimization of family business and, consequently, family wealth, as the network vows to "raise the awareness and importance of family business models in society" (FBN, 2021b), which in the context of FBN refers above all to big business.[2]

It is worth recognizing and studying further how such organizations do not only promote cultural narratives favourable for dynastic families, but they can also be directly engaged in lobbying policymakers, for example, against wealth taxes and taxes on inheritance. While the political strength of FBN certainly varies depending on the location, and the predominance of Europe in the network is clear, for example, in Finland where the local chapter of FBN was established by a few dynastic families, the network has been extremely effective. It has directly been linked in research to several tax reforms advantageous to wealthy families (Blom, 2018), and the network has had close ties with political elites: one of its CEOs was the former prime minister of the country, whereas another CEO left her position by walking through a revolving door to a top position in the Ministry of Finance. Similarly, for example, the lobbying efforts and impact of the Spanish chapter, the Instituto de la Empresa Familiar (IEF), have also been well documented (Parada et al., 2010; Pérez & Puig, 2009).

The establishment and spread of the FBN(s) coincide with the expansion of other practices, such as the rise of wealth management and next-generation programmes, as described in other parts of this chapter. The end of the 1980s and the beginning of the 1990s can, thus, in many ways be identified as a key period in the global promotion and institutionalization of family business interests. Already a few years prior to the establishment of the FBN, professionals providing services for business families had founded their own networks, such as the Family Firm Institute (FFI), established in the US in 1986. It was founded as a global professional membership association for individuals and organizations that serve the family enterprise field. Since then, FFI has been "engaged in educating, connecting, and inspiring professionals who serve family enterprises" (FFI, 2021). With a legitimising tone, FFI presents itself as an organization that "understands family enterprise as a fundamental driver of global economic growth, prosperity, and stability" (FFI, 2021).

In addition, at the end of the 1980s, education and research on family business started to find their institutional forms. Next to the establishment of FBN, for example, the IMD, which heralds itself as the birthplace of family business education (GFBC, 2021a), launched in 1988 its Leading the Family Business (LFB) programme, which gradually grew into the Global Family Business Centre (GFBC). The Centre promises to "help you ensure the sustainable success of your business and family" by dedicating itself "to the real issues facing family businesses, family offices and family foundations" (GFBC, 2021a). The growth and spread of the legitimization narrative around wealthy business families can further be seen in different practices,

---

2 Its board of directors reflects well this focus on the very wealthy and often multi-generational business families.

such as the launch in 1996 of the IMD Global Family Business Award, the meaning of which is in "promoting the indispensable role family businesses play in the global economy" (GFBC, 2021b). Time and again, (multi-generational) family businesses are described as cornerstones of the global economy by these lobbying and educational organizations around business families.

Furthermore, the emergence and solidification of family business research as a distinct academic field coincides with other institutionalizing efforts around wealthy business families at the end of the 1980s. The research field has been actively engaged in the making, simultaneously with the rise of other transnational activities around family business interests. The expansion of the field can be seen, for example, in the number of research articles mapping the field in recent years (Debicki et al., 2009; Heck et al., 2008; Kellermanns & Hoy, 2017; Xi et al., 2015). The emergence of specific family business research can be largely attributed to the establishment of membership-based professional associations, consisting mainly of individuals, corporations, and organizations with family business constituents or clienteles, specifically, the FFI and the FBN (Heck et al., 2008, pp. 319–320). As Heck et al. (2008, p. 320) note, these "international organisations encouraged academic [sic] and practitioners to undertake research investigations for benchmark information and best practices that could be used to deliver emerging educational programs and to offer support service and consultancy to family enterprises". The research field has, thus, from early on been closely tied to the interests of the families and their service providers or lobbies, and many professorships in family business are sponsored by the wealthy families themselves.

For example, the *Family Business Review* journal was established in 1988 by the FFI, and in the mid-1990s, the FBN introduced the family business research forum (Heck et al., 2008, p. 320). Slightly later in 1998, *The Journal of Wealth Management* (originally named *The Journal of Private Portfolio Management*) was established specifically with the wealthy in mind, as "a surge in high net-worth individuals [had led] to an increase in private investment needs" (JWM, 2021). From the very beginning, the journal was explicitly designed to serve those (often families) who have benefitted most from growing wealth inequalities. Its first issue begins with a reference to the "explosive growth in high net-worth investable assets – fuelled by the ongoing intergenerational transfer of wealth, a record bull market and growing liquidity of assets by business owners" (Goyal, 1998). The original editors came from the wealth management industry, from J. P. Morgan, and investment consultancy to wealthy families, and the journal was planned to "contain practical ideas on issues of interest to wealthy families and their advisors (family office executives, portfolio and fund managers, private bankers, consultants, accountants, and others): defining investment objectives and risk parameter for individuals, determining the balance between growth and preservation of wealth, setting asset allocation in order to maximize after-tax returns" (Goyal, 1998).[3]

The institutionalization of the research field has continued ever since; for example, in 2001, the International Family Enterprise Research Academy (IFERA) was established to act as a global network of family business researchers, seeking to act as the bridge between the education practitioner (FFI) and the owner-managed family business community (FBN) (Heck et al., 2008, p. 320). As a consequence of the close ties between the industry and academic research, a substantial tranche of specialized industry publications currently exists, such as *Family Business Review, Trusts and Trustees, The Journal of Wealth Management,* and *Trusts and Estates,* all of which primarily serve the needs of wealthy business families or those striving for wealth. Focusing on questions such as (family business) management, agency issues, value of family business to the local economies, and successful wealth management practices, this industry literature rarely includes critical discussion on wealth accumulation and inequalities as part of (successful) business family dynamics, topics that have been left to elite scholars in sociology or political economy (Beckert, 2022; Glucksberg & Burrows, 2016; Harrington, 2016; Herlin-Giret, 2018, 2020; Kuusela, 2018).

Conclusions: Towards a (New) Class of Owner Families

The last few decades have witnessed an explosion of new sociocultural mechanisms and practices through which wealthy business families explain and legitimize their dynastic wealth both for the public and the younger generations in the families. Through lobbies, networks, consultants, and tailor-made educational programmes, different business families across the globe circulate strategies, narratives, and practices that help in the sociocultural reproduction of the wealthy families and, finally, in their dynastic survival as units of accumulation. These mechanisms have been developed and transnationalized in the midst of growing criticism against wealth concentration and hereditary privileges. Hence, they are supposed to meet the expectations and ethos of meritocratic societies while preserving the privileges and advantages of private or familial wealth accumulation.

Together with many other recent scholarly contributions, I have argued in this chapter that alongside the indispensable analysis of the mechanics of capital flows, research into the affective and narrative strategies supporting cross-generational

---

3 Similarly, for example, the editors of *Trusts and Trustees,* established in 1994, have usually been wealth management practitioners.

wealth accumulation is key to understanding the role of wealthy families in contemporary societies. The needs of contemporary business families are quite specific and do not always follow the needs or ethos of elites in general, not to mention societies at large. One reason is the central role of kinship often understood in the context of intimacy and affects in the reproduction of wealth. Several scholars have recently analysed the emotional governance of the family, which is partly done by wealth managers and other service providers (Herlin-Giret, 2020; Higgins, 2021), and partly by the family members themselves (Kuusela, 2018). Indeed, the successful transmission of wealth is not an easy process, and it involves substantial investments in affective labour (Yanagisako, 2002) by the older generations as well as by hired wealth managers and consultants. Even inheritance is not an automatic process but rather one that is laden with complex family dynamics (Yanagisako, 2015). However, the increasing professionalization, transnationalization, and institutionalization of such practices is making wealth transmission less difficult or risky, and it also gives these processes a strong classed dimension and one that is global in its dynamics. One may, thus, refer to the building of global class interests in the context of wealthy business families.

The active role that different families or their individual members have taken in institutionalizing and professionalizing their cross-generational wealth accumulation might imply a need to revisit some old fundamentals of elite research in ways that also seem pertinent to the contemporary situation. For example, in 1989, Bourdieu (English translation in 1996, p. 272) wrote "how a given capital structure tends to dictate a particular mode of reproduction, characterised by a set of reproduction strategies adapted to the particularities of the forms of capital to be reproduced". Writing in the early days of the institutionalization processes described in this chapter, Bourdieu, however, made a curious addition in which he downplayed the agency of elites, an observation that seems to diverge from contemporary dynamics. He noted that the strategies of reproduction "through which dominants manifest their tendency to maintain the status quo are [not necessarily] the result of rational calculation or even strategic intent" (Bourdieu 1996, p. 292). Bourdieu (1996, p. 272) proclaimed that the strategies that contribute to the reproduction of the capitals at hand are not always "explicitly designed and instituted with this end in mind", as these practices are founded in habitus.

Bourdieu's analysis may well have been insightful in his time when economic inequalities had been in decline for decades, but the more recent developments around business families hint towards a slightly different conclusion or at least towards a need to reconsider questions concerning the agency of wealthy families. A number of recent studies bear witness to a variety of highly institutionalized as well as conscious forms and strategies of reproduction; thus, it is exactly rational calculation and intentional strategies – rather than some more tentative expressions of habitus – that direct the practices of contemporary dynastic business families. Together, the practices and strategies discussed in this chapter seem to constitute a class-based culture aimed at responding to the pressures of meritocratic ideologies while securing the dynastic wealth accumulation and keeping the class position of the families intact.

Such a reading that emphasises the classed dimensions of wealth accumulation is partly intended to shed critical light on arguments that *exclusively* emphasise the role of professionals and intermediaries. Especially, scholars whose research focuses on the rise of wealth managers have occasionally suggested that the agency of dynastic wealth accumulation rests solely, or at least primarily, in the hands of professional intermediaries, rather than on the families themselves. According to such accounts, the power of professional and financial structures and strategies is such "that they can create dynastic wealth even when there is no intention to do so on the part of the clients", as, for example, Harrington (2016, p. 209) has suggested. Similarly, another study states that "[f]amilies can acquire a dynastic character in spite of explicit intentions, merely because of the *dynastic bias* built into the conventionalized process of giving structure" (Marcus & Hall, 1992, p. 55, cit. in Harrington, 2016, p. 210). While in many ways true, such claims also let the families, so to say, off the hook too easily. The institutionalization of business family interests and the transnational infrastructures supporting them are a relatively recent phenomenon, and temporarily, they coincide with the rise of global wealth inequalities. This development has not taken place by accident, and it appears to have also necessitated active contributions from the families. The possible roles that the members of wealthy families themselves play in such processes deserve further scrutiny, as the recent focus in research on the professionals has resulted in a situation where the agency of the wealthy has been empirically marginalized and, consequently, also untheorized.

There is considerable room in contemporary elite research for assessing the dimensions and strength of agency that the wealthy families themselves exercise both openly and behind the scenes. For example, the question to what extent do the socioeconomic privileges of wealthy business families result from actions that are expressions of articulated class consciousness, or to what extent do they reflect more organic and uncoordinated outcomes of decentralized alliances of interests, is also first and foremost an open one in need of empirical inquiry. Whether families are active agents, or more or less passive customers or targets of financial professionals and markets, is an empirical question, the answers to which may also differ, according to specific localities.

Equally, questions concerning the public and moral legitimation of family wealth and cross-generational privileges deserve further attention. In addition to the economic rationale of family business provided by researchers and the lobbies, the cultural narratives, and frames important for the endurance and justification of family wealth are often moral in nature. The moral economies around family businesses have been built, for example, on stories of how (concentrated) family ownership provides continuity and stability against the short-term approaches of the financial markets, how family businesses contribute to national economies and job growth much more than multi-national companies, and how business families carry their social responsibility, for example, through philanthropy. Such narratives often draw on old imaginaries of benevolent patriarchy and heritage, familiar, for example, from the context of monarchies (Clancy, 2021). Similar to monarchies, dynastic wealth accumulation is repeatedly moralized through ideas of philanthropy, social responsibility, history, and heritage, whereas corporate connections are idealized through representations of the families as custodians of the wealth. Such narratives that communicate an anti-individualistic, almost altruistic, ethos help to legitimize cross-generational wealth accumulation in times of meritocratic ideals and growing wealth inequalities. On a similar note, Sklair and Glucksberg (2021) highlight the importance of philanthropic activities in communicating an ethos of social responsibility of dynastic families.

Regarding the different narratives around wealthy business families, interesting and significant contradictions might also be at play: the internal narratives (as seen, e.g., in the promotional materials of next generation programmes) refer to the protection of family wealth, whereas the external narratives stress the distribution of wealth and benefits to the communities at large. While the internal narratives in the families focus on the continuity of family legacies, the preservation of wealth and the guarding of business interests, the external narratives often reach or refer to a common good. It is noteworthy that such moral narratives are also increasingly global or transnational.

Much more research is needed to study such ideological, and often internally contradictory, dimensions of family business and dynastic wealth. Thus far, research on the transnational dimensions of class-making and class structures has been scarce, and theories highlighting the transnational dimensions of class practices (Sklair, 2001) have focused on salaried managers, leaving the class-making of owners and dynastic families intact. Thus, the cultural categories of family business and business families call for assessments on the ideological dimensions of their institutionalization. Questions worth asking and contradictions worth analysing may include, for example, how the legitimacy of massive inheritances gets constructed in societies that are allegedly built on merit and ideas of social mobility; how ownership itself seems to have become a celebrated category in the 21st century and how this justifies extreme wealth; and how family-owned businesses may or may not benefit societies at large in times of record high dividends, increasingly outsourced production, and global wealth chains that seem to be leaking in favour of those who can opt out from local regulations and social contracts, such as taxation. The moral – as well as real – economies of family business are curious combinations of family continuity with the focus on succession and the successful transmission of wealth, and stories that emphasize the importance of family business for societies at large. The ideological as well as practical dimensions and social consequences of such economies should be of paramount interest for research, as large-scale wealth transfers of historical proportions are expected to be witnessed across the world in the coming decades.

References

Adamson, M., & Johansson, M. (2020). Writing class in and out: Constructions of class in elite businesswomen's autobiographies. *Sociology*, 55(3), 487–504.

Barone, G., & Mocetti, S. (2016). *Intergenerational Mobility in the Very Long Run: Florence 1427–2011*. Working Papers 1060. Banca D'Italia.

Beckert, J. (2008). *Inherited Wealth*. Princeton and Oxford: Princeton University Press.

Beckert, J. (2022). Durable wealth. Institutions, mechanisms, and practices of wealth perpetuation. *Annual Review of Sociology*, 48(1). https://doi.org/10.1146/annurev-soc-030320-115024

Blom, A. (2018). *Taloudelliset eturyhmät politiikan sisäpiirissä: Tutkimus liike-elämän poliittisesta vaikuttamisesta kolmikantaisessa Suomessa 1968–2011*. [Economic interest groups and political insiders. A research on the lobbying of Finnish business community in the tripartite system between 1986–2011.] PhD dissertation. University of Turku, Finland. Turku: Scripta Lingua Fennica Edita.

Bourdieu, P. (1987). What makes a social class? On the theoretical and practical existence of groups. *Berkeley Journal of Sociology*, 32, 1–17.

Bourdieu, P. (1996). *The State nobility. Elite Schools in the Field of Power*. Trans. L.C. Clough. Orig. in French 1989. Cambridge and Oxford: Polity Press.

Bramall, R. (2018). A 'powerful weapon'? Tax, avoidance, and the politics of celebrity shaming. *Celebrity Studies*, 9(1), 34–52. doi:10.1080/19392397.2017.1325762

Carney, M., & Nason, R. (2018). Family business and 1%. *Business & Society*, 57(6), 1191–1215.

Citi. (2021). *Next gen program*. Citi Private Bank. https://www.citigold.privateclient.citibank.com/home/next-gen.html (accessed August 13, 2021).

Clancy, L. (2021). *Running the Family Firm: How the Royal Family Manages its Image and Our Money*. Manchester, UK: Manchester University Press.

Debicki, B. J., Matherne, C., Kellermanns, F. Z., & Chrisman, J. J. (2009). Family business research in the new millennium: An overview of the who, the where, the what, and the why. *Family Business Review* [Online], 22(2), 151–166.

Deloitte. (2016). *Next-Generation Family Businesses. Evolution, Keeping Family Values Alive*. Deloitte. https://www2.deloitte.com/content/dam/Deloitte/at/Documents/familienunternehmen/nextgen-survey-2016.pdf (accessed August 13, 2021).

Dunn, M. G. (1980). The family office as a coordinating mechanism within the ruling class. *Insurgent Sociologist*, 9(2–3), 8–23.

Faccio, M., & Lang, L. H. (2002) The ultimate ownership of Western European corporations. *Journal of Financial Economics*, 65(3), 365–395.

FBN. (2021a). *Large families*. Family Business Network. https://www.fbn-i.org/communities/large-families-0 (accessed August 13, 2021).

FBN. (2021b). *About us*. Family Business Network. https://www.fbn-i.org/about-us (accessed August 13, 2021).

FFI. (2021). *About*. Family Firm Institute. https://www.ffi.org/about/ (accessed August 13, 2021).

Gallo, M. (2004). The family business and its social responsibilities. *Family Business Review*. [Online], 17(2),135–148.

GFBC. (2021a). *IMD Global Family Business Center*. https://www.imd.org/gfbc/family-business/ (accessed August 13, 2021).

GFBC. (2021b). *About*. Global Family Business Center, IMD. https://www.imd.org/gfbc/about/Mission-History/

Gilding, M. (1999). Superwealth in Australia: Entrepreneurs, accumulation and the capitalist class. *Journal of Sociology*, 35(2): 169–182. doi:10.1177/144078339903500203.

Gilding, M. (2005). Families and fortunes: Accumulation, management succession and inheritance in wealthy families. *Journal of Sociology*, 41(1), 29–45.

Gilding, M. (2010) Entrepreneurs, elites and the ruling class: The changing structure of power and wealth in Australian society. *Australian Journal of Political Science*, 39(1), 127–143.

Glucksberg, L., & Burrows, R. (2016). Family offices and the contemporary infrastructures of dynastic wealth. *Sociologica*, (2). doi:10.2383/85289.

Glucksberg, L., & Russell-Prywata, L. (2020). *Elites and Inequality: A Case Study of Plutocratic Philanthropy in the UK* (Occasional Paper 9). UNRISD. www.unrisd.org/unrisd/website/docu ment.nsf/(httpPublications)/3DEB03F541A5F100802585A7005CFC02?OpenDocument (accessed August 13, 2021).

Goyal, G. (1998). Publisher's letter. *The Journal of Private Portfolio Management*, 1(1).

Hansen, M. N. (2014). Self-made wealth or family wealth? Changes in intergenerational wealth mobility. *Social Forces*, 93, 457–481.

Harrington, B. (2016). *Capital Without Borders: Wealth Managers and the One Percent*. Cambridge and London: Harvard University Press.

Harrington, B. (2017). Trusts and financialisation. *Socio-Economic Review*, 15(1), 31–63.

Heck, R., Hoy, F., Poutziouris, P., & Steier, L. (2008). Emerging paths of family entrepreneurship research. *Journal of Small Business Management*, 46(3),317–330. https://doi.org/10.1111/j.1540-627X.2008.00246.x

Hecht, K. (2017). *A relational analysis of top incomes and wealth: Economic Evaluation, Relative (Dis)advantage and the Service to Capital*. III Working Papers. London School of Economics.

Herlin-Giret, C. (2018). Managing fortunes and privacy. Professional rhetoric and boundaries within wealth management. In V. Boussard (Ed.), *Finance at Work* (pp. 210–223). London and New York: Routledge.

Herlin-Giret, C. (2020). Wealth managers, guardians of enrichment. The case of wealth managers in France 1. In M. Benquet, & T. Bourgeron (Eds.), *Accumulating capital today. Contemporary Strategies of Profit and Dispossessive Policies*. London and New York: Routledge, 196–207.

Higgins, K. (2021). Dynasties in the making: Family wealth and inheritance for the first-generation ultra-wealthy and their wealth managers. *The Sociological Review*, 1–17. https://doi.org/10.1177/00380261211061931

Journal of Wealth Management. (2021). Journal information. *Journal of Wealth Management*. https://jwm.pm-research.com/page/aboutjwm (accessed August 13, 2021).

Kantola, A., & Kuusela, H. (2019). Wealth elite moralities: Wealthy entrepreneurs' moral boundaries. *Sociology*, 53(2): 368–384. doi:10.1177/0038038518768175.

Kellermanns, F., & Hoy, F. (2017). Long-term orientation: Reviewing the past and identifying future opportunities for family business research. In *The Routledge Companion to Family business* (pp. 100–119). Routledge. https://doi.org/10.4324/9781315688053-13

Kellogg. (2021). *Governing Family Enterprises. New Insights and Skills for All Involved in the Family Business*. An entry on the website for Kellogg executive education. https://www.kellogg.north western.edu/executive-education/individual-programs/executive-programs/family.aspx (accessed August 13, 2021).

Kenyon-Rouvinez, D. H., & Glemser, A-C. (2014). To be, or not to be, the next-generation family business leader Four questions younger family members should ask themselves. IMD. https://www.imd.org/contentassets/b5ee9fccec9c463cb0ab87ee15569d62/tc052-14.pdf

Kenyon-Rouvinez, D., & Park, J. E. (2020). Family office research review. *The Journal of Wealth Management*, 22, 4.

Kets De Vries, M. (1993). The dynamics of family controlled firms. The good news and the bad news. *Organizational Dynamics*, 21, 59–71.

Khan, S. (2011). *Privilege: The Making of an Adolescent Elite at St. Paul's School*. Princeton and Oxford: Princeton University Press.

Korom, P., Lutter, M., & Beckert, J. (2017). The enduring importance of family wealth: Evidence from the Forbes 400, 1982 to 2013. *Social Science Research*, 65, 75–95.

Kuusela, H. (2018). Learning to own: Cross-generational meanings of wealth and class-making in wealthy Finnish families. *The Sociological Review*, 66(6), 1161–1176.

Kuusela, H. (2020). The hyperopia of wealth: The cultural legitimation of economic inequalities by top earners. *Socio-Economic Review, OnlineFirst*. mwaa047, https://doi.org/10.1093/ser/mwaa047

Kuusela, H., & Kantola, A. (2020). Role of ownership in creating top incomes: Top 0.1% of earners in Finland. In M. Benquet & T. Bourgeron (Eds.), *Accumulating Capital Today. Contemporary Strategies of Profit and Dispossessive Policies*. London and New York: Routledge, 181–195.

Lamont, M., Beljean, S., & Clair, M. (2014). What is missing? Cultural processes and causal pathways to inequality. *Socio-Economic Review*, 12(3): 573–608.

LaPorta, R., Lopez-de-Silanes, F., & Shleifer, A. (1999). Corporate ownership around the world. *The Journal of Finance*, 54(2),471–517.

Lareau, A., & Conley, D. (2008). *Social Class: How Does It Work?* New York: Russell Sage Foundation.

Littler, J. (2017). *Against Meritocracy. Culture, Power and Myths of Meritocracy*. London and New York: Routledge.

Marcus, G., & Hall, P. (1992). *Lives in Trust: The Fortunes of Dynastic Families in Late Twentieth-Century America*. Boulder: Westview Press.

Melin, L., & Nordqvist, M. (2007). The reflexive dynamics of institutionalization: The case of the family business. *Strategic Organization* [Online], 5(3), 321–333.

OECD. (2018). *The Role and Design of Net Wealth Taxes in the OECD*. OECD Tax Policy Studies, No. 26, OECD Publishing, Paris.

Parada, M. J. et al. (2010). Institutionalizing the family business: The role of professional associations in fostering a change of values. *Family Business Review*, 23(4), 355–372.

Pérez, P. F., & Puig, N. (2009). Global lobbies for a global economy: The creation of the Spanish Institute of Family Firms in international perspective. *Business History*, 51(5), 712–733.

Piketty, T. (2014). *Capital in the Twenty-First Century*. Cambridge and London: Harvard University Press.

Piketty, T. (2020). *Capital and Ideology*. Trans. by A. Goldhammer. Cambridge and London: Harvard University Press.

Piketty, T., & Saez, E. (2014). Inequality in the long run. *Science*, 344, 838–843.

Pistor, K. (2019). *The Code of Capital. How the Law Creates Wealth and Inequality*. Princeton University Press.

Pogge, T., & Mehta, K. (Eds.). (2016). *Global Tax Fairness*. Oxford: Oxford University Press.

Schimpfössl, E. (2018). *Rich Russians*. Oxford: Oxford University Press.

Shaxson, N., & Christensen, J. (2016). Tax competitiveness – A dangerous obsession. In T. Pogge & K. Mehta (Eds.), *Global Tax Fairness*. Oxford: Oxford University Press, 265–297.

Sherman, R. (2017). *Uneasy Street. The Anxieties of Affluence*. Princeton and Oxford: Princeton University Press.

Sklair, L. (2001). *The Transnational Capitalist Class*. Oxford: Blackwell.

Sklair, J., & Glucksberg, L. (2021). Philanthrocapitalism as wealth management strategy: Philanthropy, inheritance and succession planning among the global elite. *The Sociological Review*, 69 (2), 314–329. doi:10.1177/0038026120963479.

Stamm, I. K. (2016). Coordination tasks and negotiation modes of linked lives in entrepreneurial families. *Journal of Marriage and Family*, 78(August 2016), 939–956.

Tait, A. A. (2020). The law of high-wealth exceptionalism. *Alabama Law Review*, 71, 983–1037.

Thompson, E. P. (1966). *The Making of the English Working Class*. Harmondsworth: Penguin.

Toft, M., & Friedman, S. (2021). Family wealth and the class ceiling: The propulsive power of the bank of mum and dad. *Sociology*, 55(1). https://doi.org/10.1177/0038038520922537

Wright, E. O. (2005). *Approaches to Class Analysis*. Cambridge: Cambridge University Press.

Xi, J., Kraus, S., Filser, M., & Kellermanns, F. (2015). Mapping the field of family business research: past trends and future directions. *International Entrepreneurship and Management Journal*, 11(1), 113–132. https://doi.org/10.1007/s11365-013-0286-z

Yanagisako, S. J. (2002). *Producing Culture and Capital: Family Firms in Italy*. Princeton and London: Princeton University Press.

Yanagisako, S. (2015). Kinship. Still at the core. *Hau: Journal of Ethnographic Theory*, 5(1): 489–494.

Yanagisako, S. (2019). *Family Firms as Kinship Enterprises*. Economics Discussion Papers, No. 2019–12, Kiel Institute for the World Economy. http://www.economics-ejournal.org/economics/discussionpapers/2019-12

Ylönen, M., & Finér, L. (2022, *forthcoming*). Global tax governance. In A. Garcia, C. Scherrer, & J. Wullweber (Eds.), *Handbook on Critical Political Economy and Public Policy*. Edward Elgar.

Zellweger, T., & Kammerlander, N. (2014). *Family business groups in Deutschland. Generationenübergreifendes Unternehmertum in grossen deutschen Unternehmerdynastie.* St. Gallen: Center for Family Business der Universität St. Gallen.

Zellweger, T., & Kammerlander, N. (2015). Family, Wealth, and Governance: An Agency Account. *Entrepreneurship Theory and Practice*, 39(6), 1281–1303.

Michael Carney and Robert S. Nason

20 The Varieties of Business Families: A Capitalist Class Perspective on Business Family Diversity

Abstract: We employ social class analysis to bring fresh insights into the development of business families. We derive a typology of three archetypal business families based on social class influences that engender cohesion or division. We describe how the basis of identity, network preferences, and intergenerational solidarity may interact to configure cohesive and focused business families, diversified family business groups, and rentier business families. With this framework, we open up theorizing to distinctive patterns of intergenerational development, accounting for both business family stability and growth. We urge family business scholars to go beyond firm-based definitions to examine business family behaviour in the context of social class segments.

Keywords: social class analysis, centrifugal, centripetal, kinship organization, rentier, business families

Introduction

There are competing ideas regarding patterns of family firm development over time in the extant literature. Much literature expects a downward course, citing high firm failure rates (Ward, 1987), family feuds (Gordon & Nicholson, 2010), the non-heritability of human capital (Becker & Tomes. 1994), and the dissolution of family wealth through generational fracturing and taxation (Beckert, 2004). Many scholars treat long-lived wealth as the exception rather than the norm. On the other hand, capitalist class literature asserts the persistence and growth of wealth over time (Piketty & Zucman, 2014). This literature focuses on the intergenerational transferability of financial wealth and physical and social assets (Keister 2005; Mazumber, 2005). In this view, business families transmit a package of educational, social, and cultural competencies to descendants (Clark, 2014; Hansen, 2014) in a manner that perpetuates their wealth and social class status.

Much family business literature essentializes its subjects, seeking to discover timeless and decontextualized "essences" through strict assumptions about family firm characteristics that distinguish them from non-family firms. For instance, socio-

Michael Carney, Concordia University
Robert S. Nason, McGill University

https://doi.org/10.1515/9783110727968-020

emotional wealth makes strong claims about family firms' idiosyncratic social and emotional endowments, especially their desire to maintain organizational control, and the resulting cognitive bias in strategic decision-making (Gomez-Mejia et al., 2011). We argue that the reality is more varied and requires a more nuanced understanding of business families and intergenerational development. A good theory of the family firm must go beyond distinguishing between family and non-family firms and "must also be able to explain variations among family firms" (Chua et al., 2012). Indeed, there is a rich variety of corporate constructions amongst family firms ranging from Europe's old money business families to new-money elites of Shanghai and Moscow; from Germany's *Mittelstand* to America's heartland family farms; from the House of Tata to the House of Saud. In varying degrees, kinship ties suffuse the firm's financial and management decisions in each of these examples.

Family business (FB) scholars have only recently addressed the question of family firm diversity, including by differentiating between a family business and business families (Steier, Chrisman, & Chua, 2015; Le Breton-Miller & Miller, 2017; Zellweger, Nason, & Nordqvist, 2012). For many decades, FB scholars have struggled to find a standard definition of the family firm. Recently, the search for a standard definition has moderated, and scholars have begun to recognize and accept their apparent heterogeneity (Chua, Chrisman, Steier, & Rau, 2012; Jaskiewicz & Dyer, 2017). This chapter addresses sources of heterogeneity in business families' development. We propose that heterogeneity arises from families' capacity to adapt the firms they own and control to family concerns and the opportunities and challenges they confront within specific cultural, institutional, and industrial contexts. Indeed, family firms' robust adaptability must, to some degree, explain their ubiquity as the world's most common organizational form (Schulze & Gedajlovic, 2010). Thus, a more encompassing theory of business families should account for the heterogeneity of relatively stable business family types. To do so, we identify a threefold typology of business family development

We suggest that social class analysis is ideal for understanding heterogeneity in business families because it is concerned with classifications, distinguishing among segments of families on objective criteria such as wealth, income, occupation, and regional or ethnic origin (Hill, 2012). Social class theorists are also concerned with the drivers and constraints on social mobility between class categories. The movement of individuals and families up and down multidimensional class strata can occur over an individual's lifetime (intragenerational mobility) and across generations (intergenerational mobility). Thus, social mobility analysis focuses on intra- and intergenerational development within the class structure. Social class analyses of business families are rare (for an exception see, Palmer & Barber, 2001).

We tap into the capitalist class body of literature, about the behaviour of wealthy business families and their capacity for wealth accumulation across generations (Dunn, 1980; Gilding 2005; Zeitlin, 1974) as well as literature on social mobility (De Nardi & Yang, 2016; Hansen, 2014; Quadrini, 1999). The capitalist class literature has recently enjoyed a renaissance focusing on the top 1% wealthiest households addressing concerns about growing income and wealth inequality (Piketty, 2014). Therefore, our capitalist class perspective enables us to contribute to a contemporary discourse that is typically beyond the domain of FB studies (Carney & Nason, 2018; Korom, Lutter, & Beckert, 2017).

We build upon social class theories of the family that identifies, across societies and families, factors that influence stability and change in family structure and business family capital accumulation. We frame these factors under the umbrella of centripetal and centrifugal social pressures, which influence business families as they develop over time. Centrifugal pressures expand the family beyond its original business boundaries and threaten to fracture family cohesion. On the other hand, centripetal pressures strengthen family integration and may also restrict potential business growth and development. Using this foundation, we identify the characteristics and development patterns for of three stable archetypes of business families arrayed along a single dimension from centripetal to centrifugal social influences that shape kinship organization (Farber, 1975). We characterize three business family archetypes: *rentiers* or financial families, *cohesive-focused* business families, *and diversified family business groups (FBGs)*.

We make two theoretical contributions to theories of business families. First, we incorporate social class theory as a powerful but underutilized theoretical base to shed new light on business families. As we demonstrate, a rich tradition of literature is very relevant to FB studies but has mostly remained adjacent to the field. Social class analysis overcomes limitations of undersocialized actors and incorporates a broader understanding of BFs social embeddedness (Biggart & Hamilton, 1992). Second, we provide a framework to identify and characterize family and business development within the structure of capitalist class segments. In doing so, we extend the literature on BF diversity by considering diverse types of business families and identifying pressures shaping the development. Our paper is structured as follows: We first review the capitalist class literature to identify and incorporate insights relevant to examining the family wealth and enterprise. Second, we illuminate centripetal and centrifugal pressures that influence business families' development. We use these to introduce and form the foundation of our business family typology. We close with consideration of the capitalist class literature and how family business scholars can apply our typology in future research.

The Capitalist Class in the Social Class Hierarchy

Gilbert (2008, p. 11) defined a social class as "groups of families more or less equal in rank and differentiated from other families above or below them with regards to characteristics such as occupation, income, wealth and prestige"" A significant theoretical benefit of social class analysis is the predictive power of class position on a wide range of social and economic outcomes. Sociologists continue to debate precisely how social classes should be divided, but there is substantial evidence that social class position is strongly linked to tangible and intangible outcomes (Savage, 2000). In the US context, there is some support for a three-class model that distinguishes between the elite upper class, the broad middle class, and the economically marginalized (Hill, 2012). In addition to holding substantial wealth, the upper class enjoys better access to healthcare, marrying people with higher social status, and has a lower probability of a first marriage terminating than those in the middle and lower classes. Gilbert (2008, p. 162) describes the social basis of the US national capitalist class as embeddedness in a "social world built on prestige and exclusive patterns of association". The upper classes attend more prestigious schools and universities and have greater political influence. Members of the upper class enjoy better positions in social networks that provide access to well-placed individuals who possess specialized knowledge. Social class position mediates access to social networks that confer advantages, reinforcing class disparities (Di Maggio & Grip, 2012).

The capitalist class is defined with ownership of the means of production but is also internally differentiated along both vertical and horizontal lines. Vertical differentiation is reflected in the variation of capital owned and the number of employees (Aldrich & Weiss, 1981). Horizontally, the capitalist class also segments along political, ethnic identity, and regional lines. Segmentation influences the ability of capitalist class factions (Farber, 1975) to cooperate on shared interests (Useem, 1982).

Business Families in the Capitalist Class

In the US context, the concept of a capitalist class originated between 1890 and 1920, described as an era of finance capitalism (Mizruchi, 2004). The formation of trusts, combinations of large firms under the control of entrepreneurs and families, such as J. P. Morgan, the Vanderbilts, Carnegie, and Rockefellers, witnessed the emergence of a capitalist class working through investments groups and commercial banks. These families dominated the business world and had substantial influence over politics. Interest in the capitalist class faded with the emergence of managerial capitalism (Chandler, 1977) and the separation of corporate ownership and control of public firms (Mizruchi, 2004). Sociologists and political scientists viewed this separation favourably as the decomposition of capital as the sidelining of the capitalist class (Dahrendorf, 1959), and some were proclaiming the "breakup of family capitalism" (Bell, 1961).

Whereas many accepted that the separation of ownership and control and the rise of managerialism had undermined the influence of the capitalist class, an exception to this consensus were scholars who argued that capital concentration remained in the hands of an "old money" class who continued to wield influence in business and politics. Zeitlin and his colleagues (Zeitlin, 1974; Zeitlin, Ewen & Ratcliffe, 1974, Soref & Zeitlin, 1987) challenged the prevailing consensus about the breakup of family capitalism, claiming the much-vaunted separation of ownership and control was a pseudo-fact. Zeitlin proposed that the capitalist class of wealthy families maintained a controlling position of US banks and leading industrial corporations: "prominent wealthy families . . . have identifiable principal ownership interests in some of the largest industrial corporations *and* leading commercial banks" (Soref & Zeitlin, 1987, p. 60). Wealthy families veiled their control using nominee accounts held by voting trusts, foundations, and holding companies that disguised the identity of beneficial owners. Research in recent decades diligently traced the ultimate beneficial ownership of publicly listed companies and confirms two the extensive ownership of public listed companies by business families (Anderson & Reeb, 2003; Villalonga & Amit, 2006).

Nevertheless, our argument recognizes differences in the capitalist class along economic, ideological, and political lines. Economic differentiation pertains to the quantity of capital owned and the capacity to exert influence over substantial pools of labor. In this chapter we show that, in addition to ownership of publicly listed companies, households in the upper wealth thresholds own considerable capital in the form of equity in unlisted, privately-held firms that family members actively manage.

Vertical and Horizontal Differentiation of the Capitalist Class

A neglected dimension of differentiation is the quantity of capital controlled by an owner (Aldrich & Weiss, 1981). The capitalist class category is extensive, including households with a few thousand dollars in assets and no employees, primarily self-employed, to individuals with millions and possibly billions of dollars in assets and thousands of employees. However, private business ownership is concentrated at the peak of the wealth hierarchy: among the wealthiest 1% of US households, 76% own and *actively manage* a private business, and 13% have a passive ownership stake in a private business, but these figures drop sharply in the lower wealth thresholds. Only about 50% of the next 9% wealthiest after the 1% own and actively manage a business and practically none of the lowest decile own and actively manage a business (Carney & Nason, 2018).

The household finance literature (Guiso & Sodini, 2013; Carroll, 2002) finds that the most striking feature of the 1% wealthiest households is the concentration of wealth in non-financial assets and especially the ownership of an actively managed private business. This is the most significant asset category for the wealthiest 1% in the US, comprising some 45% of total net worth on average, with mean and median firm value of $34 and $6 million, respectively (Federal Reserve, 2017). In other words, the majority segment in the highest wealth strata is the owner-manager of a small to medium-sized business that generates on average $13 million in revenues with some 30 employees. These business ownership patterns are not unique to the US. A European study of household asset portfolios finds that the rich differ from the rest of the population as they "hold a much higher proportion of their portfolios in risky investments with a particularly large concentration of net worth in their entrepreneurial ventures" (Carroll, 2002, p. 389).

The capitalist class is also heterogeneous via horizontal differentiation. Harvey (2005) notes that US capitalist class segments are based upon the distinct location in the social process of production (e.g., trading, finance, and manufacturing) as manifest in popular distinctions between Wall Street versus Main Street. Each segment develops an "intraclass consciousness" enabling common action towards other segments of the capitalist class. In the context of the US, a common regional distinction differentiates an old money Eastern establishment from "new money" families located in the American South and West (Marcus, 1992). Similarly, Palmer and Barber (2001) note that business families' various location in the regional social class structure influences their propensity to engage in hostile acquisitions. They find that old money capitalists (Eastern establishment) were less likely to make hostile tender offers compared with "outsiders" who are "disproportionately Jewish, from the South or the West" (Palmer & Barber, 2001: 90). Hence, we see that the horizontal segmentation of the capitalist class is differentiated on a variety of context-specific identities.

Wealth Mobility and Persistence in the Capitalist Class

Many family firm scholars expect that as a business family ages generationally, there is likely to be descending social mobility, a phenomenon captured in the adage "shirtsleeves to shirtsleeves in three generations". There are several proposed mechanisms for downward social mobility: a family fortune could dissipate through incompetence (Marcus, 1992), be taxed away by estate and inheritance taxes (Beckert, 2004), or be increasingly divided amongst numerous heirs as business families age generationally (Bertrand and Schoar, 2006). There is some support for the adage from Becker and Tomes (1986), who found a low correlation between a father and son's incomes. However, while income generation arising from human capital is not readily transferred across generations, but this is not the case for financial and physical assets. Wealth can be passed to descendants, limiting downward social mobility, such that business families may be able to transmit their social class position to succeeding generations (Hansen, 2014; Quadrini, 1999). Measuring wealth inequality is not an exact science since much wealth comprises non-financial assets such as real estate, factories, and art collections. The economic value of such assets is difficult to estimate subject to volatility.

Because financial and non-financial assets can pass to descendants, research finds intergenerational wealth much less elastic. Inherited wealth has a substantial direct effect on the wealth of the beneficiary. Apart from the principal residence, most households have relatively few assets to transmit to the following generation. Consequently, inheritances are concentrated in the upper registers of the wealth hierarchy. De Nardi & Yang (2016) find that family background is a potent source of wealth inequality, in no small measure due to bequest motives and inheritance across generations. This Moreover, Gale & Scholz (1994) employ a more comprehensive definition of inheritance to include inter-vivo transfers (i.e., gifts and transfers to adult children and grandchildren). They find that gifts are the source of another 20% of descendants' lifetime wealth. Hansen (2014) shows that there are practically no new entrants into the top 0.1% wealth group in egalitarian Norway over two decades. This suggests that there can be much social mobility in the broad middle classes with virtually no mobility at the highest echelons of wealth. Similar findings are reported for Sweden (Björklund, A., Roine, J., and Waldenström, 2012) and Finland (Kuusela, 2018). For instance, in a study of Finland's wealthiest 0.1% business families, Kuusela (2018) finds a self-reproducing capitalist class that avoids intergenerational wealth division by achieving very high returns on investment. A prominent norm in this group is that inheritances are simply loans that must be transmitted intact to the next generation.

Entrepreneurship can also play a pivotal role in generating and sustaining high wealth concentration (Quadrini, 1999). Entrepreneurs experience more significant upward mobility in that they have a greater probability of moving to higher wealth classes. Quadrini (1999) finds that wealth accumulation occurs in business families for three reasons: they receive high rates of employment and capital income, high saving rates, and they persist as business owners for extended periods, and there are low rates of exit from business ownership. Hence, entrepreneurship drives social mobility into the upper reaches of the wealth hierarchy.

The Wealthiest Capitalists

We find alternative sources of insight into the peak of the capitalist classes in rich lists, such as Forbes wealthiest 400 Americans. To qualify for the list of 400 wealthiest Americans in 2018 requires a minimum personal wealth of $2 billion. The exit and entry of individuals into these lists provide insight into capitalist class mobility at its highest level. However, the representation of inherited wealth on rich lists generates a continuing debate. Kaplan and Rauh (2013) argue that the number of Americans who have inherited their wealth has declined in the past three decades. They find that Forbes 400 individuals' share of "self-made" has risen from 40% in

1982 to 69% in 2011. Kaplan and Rauh offer a superstar explanation for this trend, suggesting that highly educated and skilled individuals have exploited information technology and finance opportunities. They claim that the superrich comprises "those who were able to access education while young and apply their skills to the most scalable industries: technology, finance, and mass retail" (Kaplan & Rauh, 2013: 36). This finding suggests that inherited family wealth is now less relevant in an increasingly economically mobile US society.

Nevertheless, Kaplan & Rauh's (2013) own study demonstrates the importance of growing up in a wealthy household. They find that 20% of the Forbes 400 wealthiest US individuals were raised grew up in a family with little to no wealth. In contrast, some 80% grew up in families with either some wealth or "wealthy". While there is growing mobility among the membership of rich lists, "the added mobility comes from those who would be considered upper-middle-class" (Kaplan & Rauh, 2013, p. 46). Thus, the ability to reach the top wealth echelons is still primarily determined by family background, and the observed wealth mobility is restricted mainly to the wealthiest classes.

Equally, the beneficiaries of inherited fortunes do not necessarily dissipate their wealth. Analysis of entry and exit to the Forbes wealth list find that wealth owners whose fortunes are older, founded in the 1940s have significantly higher survival chances than those created between 1975 and 1985 (Korom, Lutter, & Beckert, 2017). Large, diversified fortunes managed by wealth management professionals enable wealthier investors to earn higher rates of return (Piketty, 2014). The Forbes rich list underestimates the value of inherited fortunes because their valuation of wealth is made by assessing primarily visible assets such as the value of public stock prices. Inheritors' diversify their wealth among a range of assets whose value to estimate (Zeitlin, 1974). Wealthy families are typically reluctant to disclose their whole wealth, rendering rich lists unreliable (Kaplan & Rauh, 2013; Keister, 2005).

Together, the above insights suggest that societies can exhibit high levels of social mobility concerning income and intermediate levels of wealth. Simultaneously, they may exhibit low levels of social mobility at the very peaks of the wealth hierarchy. In other words, individual business families may experience different outcomes ranging from decline and dissipation, remaining relatively constant, or growth marked by the accumulation of wealth and social status. In this regard, the initial class position of an enterprise's founder is not necessarily determinative. What factors might propel business families on different developmental paths with divergent economic and social outcomes? We offer a preliminary attempt to uncover the social class and family level influences that illuminate these dynamics in the following section.

Patterns in Business Family Development

We propose that the development of business families is subject to both divisive (centrifugal) and cohesive (centripetal) pressures, and the balance of these pressures creates distinctive types of business families. The incidence of centrifugal pressures creates a separating trend where family members pursue their particular interests. The prevalence of centripetal pressures favours family cohesion, pulling family members together to pursue a shared interest. At the midpoint, where centrifugal and centripetal influences are approximately in balance, we observe a more complex dynamic of social influence.

We posit three broad types of social pressures which shape business family development patterns. Each of the three social pressures we describe below is grounded in particular branches of sociological theory, namely basis of social identity (Granovetter, 2005), social networks (Burt, Opper, & Zou, 2021), and intergenerational family solidarity (Silverstein & Bengston, 1997). We describe the first influence as the power and attraction of social segments arising from a business family's "axis of solidarity" (Granovetter, 2005), forming a basis for family identity. Weber's analysis of European capitalism centred on religious sectionalism (Farber, 1975), but Granovetter (2005) identifies other bases of identity, including ethnicity, regionalism, language, and political affiliation. A second tendency concerns the family's social network orientation. Families may display a preference for either homophilous (McPherson, Smith-Lovin, & Cook, 2001) or heterophilic (Lester & Cannella, 2006) networks. The former suggests families bond with similar others, creating relatively closed networks. The latter prefer to link with dissimilar others, providing the opportunity to build bridges across social groups (Burt, 2000). Third, drawing from family science, we consider the role of intergenerational solidarity. Intergenerational solidarity theory reveals social practices that govern the extent to which families are willing and able to provide financial and emotional resources across generations and family life cycles (Silverstein & Bengston, 1997).

Bases of Identity

Individuals are bonded together by common sources of identity. Granovetter (2005) describes how family-controlled business groups rely upon a shared social identity. For instance, family business groups may form ethnic and political identities (Carney, 2007; Birhanu & Wezel, 2020). While other bases of perceived commonality may be a foundation for shared identity, we consider capitalist class formation by considering religion as an exemplary basis of identity. Max Weber (1927) traced the origins of contemporary western capitalism to the 16th century and the emergence of Protestantism in Europe. In the *Protestant ethic and the spirit of capitalism*, Weber portrays religion as a motivator of human action. With the idea of predestination, Weber argued that the Protestant religion fostered an ethic of planning and material interests marked by frugality and saving. However, Weber believed that religion was also a basis for social identity. In this regard, Protestant sects, such as Calvinists, Lutherans, and Quakers, form the basis of social subgroups, which Farber (1975) describes as functions. Factionalism implants a competitive dynamic within society with groups vying for superiority in wealth, property, and power. This competitive dynamic serves as a segmenting mechanism in society since it implies the pulling inwards of influences to mobilize individuals for conflict and competition. Farber suggests that faction's inward pulling influences manifest within kinship organization as engaging the obligation and loyalty of members, which he describes as a centripetal form of kinship organization. Kinship organized along these lines will tend to "develop conduct appropriate to status maintenance" and support the accumulation of property that generates social class stratification (Farber 1975, p. 876).

Protestant sectarianism ran counter to the dominant European 16th-century religion, Roman Catholicism. The Roman Catholic Church espoused a universal and communal concept of the polity based on the common interests of a whole society (Farber, 1975). Communalism implies that subgroup interests, such as a clan or extended family, are subordinated to universal concerns. A fundamental tenet of Roman Catholic Orthodoxy held that a Universal good could prevail if the power of fictions and other extended kin groups were to be curtailed and an ethos that accentuated individual independence that disperse factional interests. Under the orthodoxy of Roman Catholic communalism, religious influence property-based familial ties to expel family members outward, which Farber describes as a centrifugal form of kinship organization. Roman Catholicism was organized along communal lines oriented towards redistributing property throughout society, minimizing kinship obligations.

Thus, in the earliest forms of European capitalism religious identity furnished a basis for the emergence of Protestant capitalist classes. The social class system perpetuates itself through the fusion of the family as an institution and prominent property relations, which in protestant sects favoured intragenerational capital accumulation, but less so in Catholic families. While religious identity has generally declined as an animating source of contemporary identity it remains strong in some segments of society. For example, Palmer and Barber (2001) describe Bostonian White Anglo-Saxon Protestants' disdain for leveraged acquisitions. More generally, despite centuries of secularization, religious affiliation impacts the family's social structure and property rights in complex and persistent ways (Reher, 1998).

Network Behaviour

Social networks tend to reflect homophilous preferences, meaning the tendency of individuals to form ties to others who are similar to themselves (Di Maggio & Garip, 2012). That upper-class families include homophilous groups sharing common values and opinions with fewer contacts with lower classes is well established (McPherson et al., 2001). Indeed, the upper classes may seek to avoid cross-class encounters, which can be a source of social embarrassment and anxiety (Gray & Kish-Gephart, 2013). More generally, affiliation with homophilous groups can endow members with high levels of social capital. Positive aspects of such endowed or bonding forms of social capital (Woolcock, 1998) include access to financial and material resources, information about opportunities, psychological support, and lowered risks of opportunism and transaction costs. Of course, not all homophilous groups are upper class. Ethnic enclaves that colonize a specific trade or neighbourhood, such as New York's Chinatown, Miami's Little Havana, or Los Angeles Koreatown, highlight the value of the mutual support in homophilous middle-class groups (Portes, & Shafer 2007).

However, having too much communal social capital can be harmful since an excess of embedded ties can become redundant (Uzzi, 1997). The negative aspects of this endowment can be evident in particularistic demands for loyalty and reciprocity and other restrictions on individual autonomy. Moreover, the same strong ties that bring benefits to group members may bar them from accessing sources of support beyond the group. Economic sociologists expect that affiliation with local segments may support basic forms of economic exchange, but not necessarily dynamism and growth. For families to achieve substantial capital accumulation, they must establish linkages beyond the social group to access resources and information in a broader network. Burt (2000) describes such links as bridging social ties cross-cultural providing non-redundant ties that provide opportunities for brokerage between social class segments. The combination of bonding and bridging social ties represents "social opportunity" (Woolcock, 1998). Regarding the language used in this paper Georg Simmel (2009), describing the relationship between group development and the growth of the autonomous individual:

> There arises a need in an inclination to reach out beyond the original spatial economic and mental boundaries of the group, and in connection with the increasing individualization, . . . supplement the original centripetal influences of the lone group with a centrifugal tendency that forms bridges with other groups. (p. 623)

In other words, entrepreneurial growth and development of a business family imply a partial decoupling process that entails moving away from one's initial social capital endowments to fashion new linkages, a network-building process across social class boundaries.

Intergenerational Solidarity

Much research in the family science literature is devoted to psychological and social influences that influence family cohesion. While Farber's (1975) typology of centrifugal and centripetal forms of kinship organization is intended to contribute to understanding cross-cultural kinship patterns, the concepts have entered the mainstream family science literature focusing on family stability and cohesion. Recent research suggests that insights from family science about family structure and its determinants could benefit FB scholarship (Jaskiewicz, Combs, Shanine, & Kacmar, 2017). We expect differences in family stability and cohesion are likely to be reflected in business family heterogeneity.

Of particular relevance for our purposes is intergenerational solidarity theory, which focuses on the extent to which parents and adult children provide mutual support to one another over the lifecycle. In particular, intergenerational solidarity governs the degree to which families are willing and able to provide financial and emotional resources in times of need. Silverstein & Benston (1997, p. 431) argue that contemporary North American society is subject to social and economic imperatives, such as high labor mobility, that can distance family members causing physical and psychological separation. However, they observe the tendency for some families to maintain cross-generational cohesion through modern communication and transportation technologies that allow contact "despite centrifugal social influences that distance family members" (Silverstein et al., 1997, p. 431).

Tightknit families and their adult children are engaged with their parents on many indicators of solidarity. However, they identify latent forms of solidarity such as affect, consensus, and practical assistance to make some families more cohesive than others. Based on their analysis, they identify a continuum of intergenerational relationships in contemporary American households. Specifically, on the centrifugal extreme are detached families in which adult children are not engaged with their parents based on any of the indicators of solidarity. This extreme progresses along increasing levels of cohesion, culminating with a tightknit archetype. Reviewing the family science literature, Jaskiewicz and his colleagues (2017) note that early intergenerational solidarity theory focused on family-based drivers of cohesion. Recent international research finds that structural factors can increase intergenerational solidarity, such as a weak welfare state or economic crises. The authors recommend that future research in this direction pay more attention to structural factors. In this regard, the intergenerational solidarity approach complements our social class analysis that identifies social class segments and differential patterns of social identity and network behaviour.

Accordingly, we can theorize at the centripetal end of the spectrum comprising the archetypal cohesive-focused business family, exhibiting a class identity based upon a religious, ethnic, linguistic, or regional basis of identity. At the other extreme, centrifugal families are more dispersed or fragmented. Individuals in this class segment are likely to reveal a more cosmopolitan identity. Cosmopolitan "citizens of the world" are likely to hold heterogeneous, loose-knit interpersonal ties. Hence, as one extends the lens to focus upon a range of non-western contexts, including transitional and emerging markets, one will likely encounter a wider variety of family capitalists ranging from highly cosmopolitan globalized business families to localized groups bounded by network homophily. The diversified family business group is at the midpoint where centrifugal and centripetal influences are temporarily in balance.

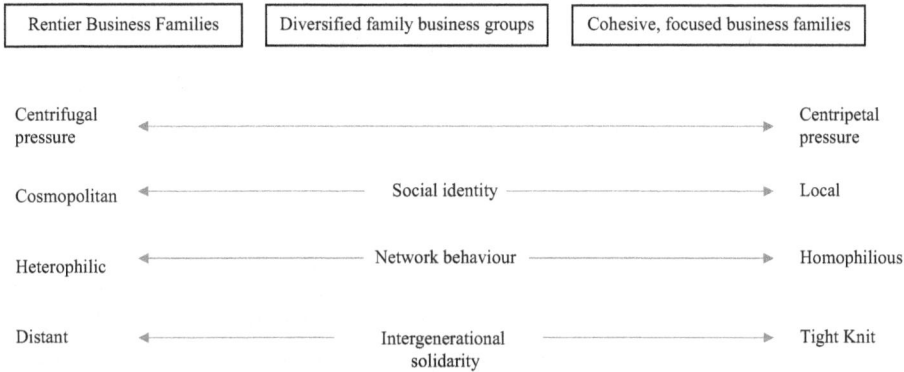

Rentier Business Families	Diversified family business groups	Cohesive, focused business families

Centrifugal pressure	←——————————————————————————→	Centripetal pressure
Cosmopolitan	←———————— Social identity ————————→	Local
Heterophilic	←———————— Network behaviour ————————→	Homophilious
Distant	←———— Intergenerational solidarity ————→	Tight Knit

Figure 20.1: Business family archetypes along a centrifugal-centripetal dimension.

Illustrating Business Family Archetypes

This section describes the pressures on each business family archetype and explains some of their primary characteristics. We reason rentier business families will be the dominant tendency in many societies as various contemporary social and economic influences generate centrifugal tendencies. Rentier business families can be defined as "those that have founded and continue to control at least one established and successful family business, plan to continue to have family members involved in business venturing, and regard the management of long-term family wealth rather than of any one business as the focal objective" (Le Breton-Miller & Miller, 2017, p. 2). However, we caution against holding this definition as conclusive since the governance infrastructure controlling wealth beyond the firm is likely to vary and be context specific. Comprising family offices, holding companies, trusts, and family councils and subject to jurisdictional legal codes, the quality of capital market institutions, and prevalent forms of kinship and family structures are relevant contextual factors (Harrington, 2016; Glucksberg & Burrows, 2016).

We define the cohesive, focused type as a long-lived multi-generational family-owned and controlled firm (Zellweger, 2017) that has been at the heart of the FB literature, emphasizing intra-family succession. However, we identify local class conditions that supply centripetal influences for its continued existence. At the midpoint, we suggest the diversified–family business group; can be characterized by "diversification across a wide range of businesses, partial financial interlocks among them, and, in many cases, familial control" (Ghemawat & Khanna, 1998, p. 34.) Family business groups will be comparatively rare, but their business scope will typically disproportionately impact their host economies. This archetype is found in advanced western economies (Colpan & Hikino, 2018). But attains the most significant prominence at the developmental stage of capitalism, and the form is expected to dissolve with the development of market-based institutions (Hoskisson et al., 2005). However, we note that the more powerful exemplars of the archetype can develop oligarchic tendencies and become entrenched within the ruling class (Fogel, 2006).

Rentier Business Families

Rentiers, or financial business families, are individuals or households whose income primarily derives from their self-made or inherited capital, either financial (e.g., equity in public listed companies) or non-financial assets, such as income from property or a private, unlisted business (Nason, Carney, Le Breton-Miller, & Miller, 2019). Rentiers exist across all income levels, from a retired widower living off the proceeds of a pension plan to someone like Bill Gates, who now retired from Microsoft, derives an immense income from the ownership stakes in the firm he co-founded. In advanced OECD countries, rentiers are heavily concentrated in the wealthiest 1% to 5% of households (Carrol, 2002). Due to the separation of ownership and control, rentier business families, typically have little control over businesses or because they gradually liquidate their ownership stakes (Franks et al., 2012). Rentier capital is often managed professionally by family offices and wealth management organizations (Harrington, 2016).

We suggest rentier business families will become a major class segment in institutionally mature societies resulting from the confluence of multiple centrifugal influences. These influences include social and economic demographics: the increasing value of intellectual property relative to physical assets as the basis of dramatic wealth creation (Hall & Marcus, 1998; Kaplan & Rauh, 2013). Other centrifugal pressures include the financialization of household assets (Fligstein & Goldstein, 2015) and the weakening of family attachments (Silverstein & Bengston, 1997).

Rentiers are less likely to hand down a particular business. Instead, they are likely to transmit financial wealth and privilege that enable adult children to pursue their autonomous career interests. In the US, Hall & Marcus (1998) propose that, historically, inheritance focused upon the transfer of physical assets and financial wealth. However, they suggest a fundamental shift has occurred in the contemporary ethos and practice of wealth transmission centred on the investment in skills and a change from testamentary to inter vivo transfers primarily to fund college and graduate education (Gale & Scholz, 1994). These effects are accentuated at the peak of the social class wealth hierarchy. This finding is consistent with Kaplan & Rauh's conclusion about the growing number of self-made billionaires in the Forbes richest 400 list, who are children of already wealthy families. The growth of financial investment in human capital by upper-class families exacerbates intergenerational educational attainment and represents a leading dynastic strategy for status reproduction (Kuusela, 2018).

We already noted the finding of all intergenerational solidarity that many US parent-adult children relationships have become more distant. With the weakening of intergenerational family ties structure, there is a growing preference for personal autonomy and individualism (Gilding, 2005). Wealthy families in mature capitalist countries have adopted the practice of equal inheritance among their adult children (Gilding, 2005). Along with intergenerational wealth transfer practices in developing human capital, these factors combine to diminish the likelihood of intra-family succession of a particular business. A new class of professional FB advisors and consultants has emerged that promotes the monetizing of businesses either by gradually liquidating share or outright sales of a long-held family business (Harrington, 2016). In a study of family offices, Rosplock (2012) found that the average age of a firm's establishing a family office was 56 years, but within five years of establishing the family office, 80% of family-founded firms were sold, thereby monetizing family firm assets. Monetizing a family business enables adult children to pursue their entrepreneurial and career interests.

Cohesive-focused Firms

The primary characteristic of cohesive, focused firms is a location within a well-defined faction of the capitalist class structure. Their social class embeddedness means that their network behaviour is characterized by homophily, for example, regarding their religious, ethnic, regional, linguistic, or political identity. Families tending towards the tightly knit end of the intergenerational solidarity dimension are more likely to demonstrate physical and emotional proximity with frequent contact with a high likelihood of providing or receiving assistance to one another and sharing similar opinions (Silverstein & Bengtson, 1997). The confluence of these centripetal pressures can inhibit exposure to opportunities and limiting economic mobility that is enabled by ties to heterophyllous networks. Consequently, cohesive, focused firms tend to remain relatively small in scale.

The epitome of the cohesive, focused family firm is Germany's *Mittelstand*, a term meaning"the middle rank" and signifying a "desirable social class, neither urban working poor nor wealthy landed estate owners living off rents but a person of solid and legitimate wealth" (Berghoff, 2006, p.264). Mittelstand families have mostly resisted market pressures to financialize family assets, preferring a patient capital strategy (Leher & Celo, 2016). Cohesive, focused firms rely upon self-generated funds (De Massis. et al., 2018) or credit from local banks. A typical business strategy focuses on a specific niche that enables them to become market leaders in a narrowly defined market segment (De Massis et al., 2018). The Mittelstand are typically located in rural and ethnically homogenous communities, which facilitates "shared understandings"

(Hall & Soskice, 2001) and a regional identity that promotes stakeholder collaboration (De Massis et al., 2018).

The phenomena of cohesive, focused firms segmented into homogenous localized communities are not limited to Germany. Italy's industrial districts centred in midsized cities and semi-rural areas in the Northeastern provinces share similarities to Mittelstand. Many are midsized, self-financing, family firms in craft industries steeped in tradition (De Massis et al., 2018), concentrating on high-quality production in relatively small market niches (Beccatini, 1991). Industrial districts thrive in socially homogeneous communities. For example, Trigillia (1991) notes a similar political class identification, distinguishing between red (left-leaning) and white (Roman Catholic leaning) among Italy's industrial districts. This model of segmented business family capitalism is now widely documented in contexts ranging from rural Denmark (Kristensen, 1992) to the populous prefecture of Wenzhou in coastal China (Christerson, & Lever-Tracy, 1997).

The reliance upon entrepreneurial legacy (Jaskiewicz et al., 2015) and localized tradition (De Massis et al., 2016) is much cited as a significant source of long-term vision and the longevity of the family firm. In their study of innovation from tradition, De Massis and his colleagues (2016) suggest that family firms' interiorizing knowledge from the territories past (raw materials and manufacturing processes) and reinterpreting these to enable new product functionalities.

Diversified Family Business Groups

Much is known about FBG structure, ownership, diversification, and performance (Masulis, Pham, & Zein, 2011). During the early to mid-20th-century, socialist regimes destroyed the nascent capitalist class in the Soviet Union, Eastern Europe, and China. Following the fall of the Soviet Union, many of these regimes sought to re-establish capitalist institutions. Similarly, after 1945 the dominant capitalist class in colonial societies, who would frequently be part of the colonial elite, began to repatriate their capital when post-colonial nationalist governments, often unfriendly to colonial-era capitalists, assumes power (Carney & Gedajlovic, 2002). Thus, a typical challenge for post-socialist and post-colonial regimes is to re-create and enable a capitalist class. It is impossible to generalize the various political and social conditions across such a broad range of countries, but the materialization of a domestic capitalist class (McVey, 1992) often entails cooperation between the state and a prominent capitalist class segment to lead an industrial capacity building project, described in the literature as late industrialization (Amsden, 2001). In most of these national cases, the emergent capitalist class comprises business families, for typical cases, see Mcvey (1992) and Strachan 1976).

The prominent historical view of these firms is that they represent a particular "stage" of capitalist development (Colli & Rose, 2008). Late industrialization is based on perceived needs to achieve rapid economic catch-up with mature capitalist economies in North America and Europe. In this context, we see the emergence of large, diversified family business groups in the past four decades. We characterize these FBGs as network-spanning capitalists that forged alliances with the state, military, bureaucracy, and in many cases, with foreign capital (as a source of technology and management expertise). Business groups (BGs) are multi-business entities defined as "a collection of firms bound together in some formal and informal ways" (Granovetter, 2005, p. 454). Though the entities are legally independent, they are "accustomed to taking coordinated action" (Khanna & Rivkin, 2001, p. 47).

The prevalent stage theory suggests that business groups arise in the absence of market-supporting institutions due to their capacity to fill these gaps through their internal capital markets supplying capital, managerial expertise, and property rights protection system. With the development of capitalism or market-supporting institutions, efficient capital markets business groups are expected to dismantle the group structure and refocus this (Hoskisson et al., 2005). However, business group dismantling is uncommon. The institutional voids theory of business group dismantling fails to adequately account for the adaptability of the family business as a social class and organizational form (Carney et al., 2018). FBGs remain competitive in advanced European countries (Colpan & Hikino, 2018).

We situate FBGs at the midpoint of Figure 20.1, where centrifugal and centripetal pressures balance. Family and other axes of identity provide a basis for centripetal cohesion, while institutional development can create centrifugal pressures that exert a divisive influence. These are found in business diversification as family members seek a sphere of influence within the business group (Bertrand et al., 2008; Tam, 1990). A fruitful research future awaits scholars who are willing to address the developments of FBGs in the evolving economic and political environments in former socialist and post-colonial societies.

Discussion

This paper identifies three business family archetypes arrayed along a continuum from centrifugal to centripetal with a balance between the two at the midpoint. The first archetype, *rentier* business families, liquidate their ownership interests in founding businesses. However, due to the persistence of wealth and status effects, they are highly likely to remain part of the upper class (Piketty, 2014; Keister, 2005). *Cohesive-focused* families are long-lived elements in the capitalist class but typically stay localized within a specific segment of the capitalist class structure. They are less socially mobile and relatively stable organizational form often attached by social and emotional ties to their local community. *Diversified-FBGs* typically break out from their social class segment into a broader domestic and international economy, chiefly by connecting to the ruling class through political and bureaucratic linkages. These families balance centrifugal and centripetal pressures that maintain coherence and business family longevity. These business families may become social and economic development instruments, yet they embody the potential to become oligarchic and entrenched.

With this approach, we have only begun to flesh out a framework that can advance understanding of business families' various behaviours in capitalist class structures worldwide. In particular, we do not consider our three centripetal/centrifugal pressures, (axis of identity, network preferences, and intergenerational solidarity) to be definitive. They the intended to be suggestive of complex social pressures upon business families that shape their development. Moreover, Figure 20.1 implies that the three types of centrifugal and centripetal pressures are correlated, and equally important. However, a particular pressure may become salient for any given family. For example, low levels of intergenerational solidarity may be a source of fragmentation, but a strong family social identity may be a salient basis for family cohesion.

Nevertheless, by theorizing different patterns of business family development, we contribute to the extant literature in significant ways. Notably, we incorporate and draw attention to social class theory as a powerful but underutilized theoretical lens for viewing the FB field. We apply insights from sociology to describe the characteristics of three business family archetypes and situate them to other capitalist class segments and the ruling political and upper classes. We have barely hinted at how these archetypes are likely to function in varied institutional settings such as Latin America, East, and South Asia. Additionally, we have suggested that our three typologies represent relatively stable forms of business family. However, in this section we discuss sources of discontinuity and the potential dissolution of particular business family types.

Our depiction of *cohesive, focused* archetypes is a business family at the core of FB research. Typically, long-lived and easily identified focused family firms have become a comfortable and familiar subject in FB research. However, if we restrict our attention to this archetype we address only a narrow population of firms. They depend upon innovation for their survival, but their internal cohesion and embeddedness in closed homophilous networks can deprive them of the linkages needed to access networks that hold the resources required to secure their future.

However, a localized geographic identity can be a source of myopia, rendering them vulnerable to the vicissitudes of global economic dynamics. A backward-looking focus on tradition can veil emerging issues delaying the family's response. For example, large but flexible MNEs hollowed out Italy's industrial districts consisting of cohesive, focused family firms (Harrison, 1997). Equally, Germany's family-controlled Mittelstand are subject to acquisition in a wave of mainland China foreign direct investment, raising concerns about 'China buying up Germany" (Bian and Emons, 2017, p. 156).

Similarly, the small privately-owned manufacturing firm that populated middle America and which John Ward (1987) described in such rich detail are comparable in this regard; Ward considered these family firms as a valued class of firms that formed the basis of middle America's prosperity. However, decades of offshoring production assured their mortality. Their vulnerability to the global pressures of free trade and investment is indicative of their relative powerlessness in the capitalist class structure. Thus, while the cohesive, focused business family is a stable archetype, whole populations of such business families are subject to competitive selection forces the challenges that their viability. While there remain many promising avenues for future research examining cohesive, focused business families, we seek to redirect scholars' attention to more elusive phenomena.

Diversified business families have become staple subjects in the International Business and Strategy literature, but their entrepreneurial behaviour and kinship-based leadership are infrequently put under the microscope by Entrepreneurship and FB scholars.

This business-family archetype emerged and attained prominence in economies in the early stages of capitalist development (Colli & Rose, 2008). Their capacities for relational contracting and filling market deficiencies provide an advantage over other types of firms, but these advantages are expected to erode with the development of capitalist institutions (Khanna & Rivkin, 2001). However, future research should examine this assumption more explicitly. While some business groups have failed and disappeared, FBGs as a category of corporate organization can persist even when market institutions become well-developed (Granovetter, 2005).

The continental model of family capitalism depicted by James (2009) provides a historical account of these business families as an early form of European industrial capitalism. In this account, modernizing industrial states carefully coordinate capital investment activity with elite families to develop strategic industries. However, these old-money families have become much larger, and family members are not prominently involved in these long-lived enterprises. What becomes of these long-lived business families remains somewhat mysterious and warrants further research, which draws on capitalist class perspectives.

One clue for dynastic family business groups' present location in the capitalist class structure is Hansen (2014) in her study of wealth mobility in Norway. Hansen (2014) finds that the very peak of the Norwegian wealth hierarchy (the top .1%) exhibits virtually no mobility and that entry into this class is highly restricted. The very top wealth category, in particular, appears to be a "rentier" class with a majority of their income from capital rather than earnings or entrepreneurship. Hansen describes a new Nordic class structure that "represent a type of society in which egalitarian tendencies in the general population coexist with thriving elites and capitalist dynasties" (2014, p. 478). In other words, the descendants of formerly eminent North European FBGs may have dissolved and become part of a rentier class.

These rentier families are practically invisible in the FB literature, yet we have argued that they represent a dominant business family segment.

Does the apparent transition to *rentier* status of formerly operational family firms mean that this class of business families no longer constitutes a subject worthy of FB scholars' attention? While their low visibility makes them challenging to study, we believe that if FB is to contribute to fields beyond its present scope, that we should use our comparative advantage in analyzing these phenomena. That is, if rentier families continue to use their power and heterogeneous networks to perpetuate their capacities for capital accumulation passed on to their descendants, then this rentier component of the capitalist class surely deserves greater scrutiny. We suggest that for this segment of the capitalist class owning and managing a business may not be an end in itself. Rather, it is a means to an end: a physical business is a disposable tool whose purpose is designed for other ends. Rentier business families may display social and emotional characteristics, for example, through philanthropy. Such sentiments can be interpreted as protecting social and emotional endowments, but we reason that SEW is not necessarily the highest priority for rentiers. Rather, consistent with a capitalist class theory, we submit a higher priority is further capital accumulation and status maintenance.

Nevertheless, rentier business families may be subject to wealth and status erosion. Countries that develop strong property rights of minority investors enable a market for corporate control between concentrated family owners and arms-length investors. For example, Zellweger and Kammerlander (2015) caution that the partial sales of a family business can empower and enable involvement by non-family block holders whose interests may not align with those of the family raising the possibility that

> [. . .] such conflicts create centrifugal influences within the family that poison family cohesiveness. In conjunction, if not addressed, these effects may undermine the continued influence of the family group as a powerful economic and social actor and ultimately herald its decline as a collective body.

Bertrand and colleagues (2006) document equally divisive phenomena in Thai business families. They find that business families with many sons experience greater conflict because of competition to appropriate their share of the family estate.

At the same time, other factors such as transnational migration may loosen family ties as individuals seek to transcend strong psychological and cultural pressures for family loyalty. For example, migration is associated with heterogeneous and loose-knit interpersonal ties that foster a cosmopolitan identity (Kwok Bun, 2013). Thus, in modernizing economies, where the grip of pre-capitalist values is weakening, engender centrifugal tendencies that begin to fragment rentier business families.

However, these arguments remain theoretically derived assertions that should be subjected to empirical scrutiny. Future research may also investigate whether rentier business families represent an end state for family business. Indeed, rentier families appear following the sale of a firm and allow for descendent generations to live off the fruits of a capital stock that will eventually deplete. However, few scholars have followed their eventual fate. Might descendants regenerate capital by starting their entrepreneurial ventures as suggested by rich lists?

Moreover, at the lower echelons of the wealthy business family class, Piketty (2014) notes the growth of smaller inheritances amongst the wealthiest 1%, valued at €1–€2 million. These inheritances are insufficient to finance the rentier lifestyle by living on returns from capital alone. Thus, these individuals are likely to pursue their careers beyond the family enjoying a combination of capital and employment income. For these reasons, we see that a rentier tendency is becoming a major class segment with benefactors of Inheritance and *intra vivos* wealth transfers, producing an emerging social class described as the working rich (Piketty & Zucman, 2014).

Investigating this question will require FB to bring a critical lens to their work. Many capitalist class scholars argue that BFs engage in barely legitimate wealth preservation strategies through aggressive tax avoidance and offshoring assets (Temouri, Nardella, Jones, & Brammer, 2022). These strategies diversity risk and allow wealthier households to exploit the scale advantages of contemporary portfolio capital management techniques, thereby earning superior returns. Harrington (2017, p. 25) argues that "rentier capitalists – use trusts to avoid their tax obligations . . . but also to shelter their wealth from the risks of the financial markets". The picture portrayed here suggests the appearance of a cosmopolitan and international capitalist class unhinged from local responsibilities such as philanthropy and providing local employment. Hence, the rentier perspective on wealth dynamics is focused on aggregate capital holdings held in diversified financial investments (Keister, 2014). This suggests that wealthy business-owning households utilize economic considerations as a driving force to create a diversified household asset portfolio.

Whether this represents an accurate picture surely calls for further analysis. However, preliminary research of the financial strategies of highest wealth echelons suggests that rentier characterizations of the 1% wealthiest American households may be off base. For instance, recent studies found that the wealthiest segments of society concentrate wealth in one or more businesses and may be better described as an *entrepreneurial* class who tend to take on more risks and debt than the rest of the population (Carney & Nason, 2016; Carroll, 2002). Hence, we advocate more fine-grained analysis of the financial and non-financial assets across the various segments of the wealth hierarchy.

Conclusion

Social class analysis suggests that business families vary in their class position and that such variance will influence the approach to entrepreneurship and the behaviour of the firms they own and control. In particular, it predicts their willingness to favour particular practices, such as the probability of engaging in philanthropy, favouring hostile takeovers, establishing a family office, or an offshore trust fund. Some business family practices may enjoy substantial public legitimacy, while others may not. Hence, the classification of business families and identifying some of their everyday practices may be controversial in these respects because social class analysis is necessarily a critical perspective. However, we hope to inspire further critical research since it facilitates a rewarding and engaged discourse with other academic disciplines.

References

Aldrich, H., & Weiss, J. (1981). Differentiation within the United States capitalist class: Workforce size and income differences. *American Sociological Review*, 46(3), 279–290.

Amsden, A. H. (2001). *The Rise of the "Rest": Challenges to the West from Late-Industrializing Economies*. New York, NY: Oxford University Press.

Anderson, R. C., & Reeb, D. M. (2003). Founding-family ownership and firm performance: evidence from the S&P 500. *The journal of finance*, 58(3), 1301–1328.

Becattini, G. (1991). Italian industrial districts: problems and perspectives. *International Studies of Management & Organization*, 21(1), 83–90.

Becker, G. S., & Tomes, N. (1986). Human capital and the rise and fall of families. *Journal of labor economics*, 4(3, Part 2), S1–S39.

Becker, G. S., & Tomes, N. (1994). Human capital and the rise and fall of families. In *Human Capital: A Theoretical and Empirical Analysis with Special Reference to Education (3rd ed.)* (pp. 257–298). Chicago, IL: The University of Chicago Press.

Beckert, J. (2004). *Inherited Wealth*, Princeton, NJ: Princeton University Press.

Bell, D. (1961). The breakup of family capitalism. *The End of Ideology*, 39–45.

Berghoff, H. (2006). The end of family business? The Mittlstand and German capitalism in transition, 1949–2000. *Business History Review*, 80(2), 263–295.

Bertrand, Marianne, and Antoinette Schoar. 2006. "The Role of Family in Family Firms". *Journal of Economic Perspectives*, 20(2): 73–96.

Bertrand, M., Johnson, S., Samphantharak, K., & Schoar, A. (2008). Mixing family with business: A study of Thai business groups and the families behind them. *Journal of Financial Economics*, 88(3), 466–498.

Bian, S., & Emons, O. (2017). Chinese investments in Germany: Increasing in line with Chinese industrial policy. *Chinese Investment in Europe: Corporate Strategies and Labour Relations, Brussels, ETUI*.

Biggart, N. W., & Hamilton, G. G. 1992. On the limits of a firm-based theory to explain business networks: The western bias of neoclassical economics'. In N. Nohria & R. G. Eccles (Eds.), *Networks and Organizations: Structure, Form and Action* (pp. 471–490). Boston: Harvard Business School Press.

Birhanu, AG., & Wezel, F. C. (2020). The competitive advantage of affiliation with business groups in the political environment: Evidence from the Arab Spring. *Strategic Organization*, 20(2), 389–411.

Björklund, A., Roine, J., & Waldenström, D. (2012). Intergenerational top income mobility in Sweden: Capitalist dynasties in the land of equal opportunity? *Journal of Public Economics*, 96(5–6), 474–484.

Burt, R. S. (2000). The network structure of social capital. *Research in Organizational Behavior*, 22, 345–423.

Burt, R. S., Opper, S., & Zou, N. (2021). Social network and family business: Uncovering hybrid family firms. *Social Networks*, 65, 141–156.

Carney, M. (2007). Minority family business in emerging markets: Organization forms and competitive advantage. *Family Business Review*, 20(4), 289–300.

Carney, M., Estrin, S., Van Essen, M., & Shapiro, D. (2018). Business Groups reconsidered: beyond paragons and parasites. *The Academy of Management Perspectives*, amp-2016.

Carney, M., & Nason, R. (2016). Family business and the 1%. *Business & Society*, published online (2016).

Carney, M., & Nason, R. S. (2018). Family business and the 1%. *Business & Society*, 57(6), 1191–1215.

Carney, M., & Gedajlovic, E. 2002. The co-evolution of institutional environments and organizational strategies: The rise of family business groups in the ASEAN region. *Organization Studies*, 23(1), 1–29.

Carroll, C. 2002. Portfolios of the Rich. In L. Guiso, M. Haliassos, & T. Jappepeli (Eds.), *Household Portfolios* (pp. 389–429). Cambridge, Massachusetts London, England: MIT Press.

Chandler, A. D. 1977. *The Visible Hand: The Managerial Revolution in American Business*. Cambridge, MA: Belknap Press.

Christerson, B., & Lever-Tracy, C. (1997). The third China? Emerging industrial districts in rural China. *International Journal of Urban and Regional Research*, 21(4), 569–588.

Chua, J. H., Chrisman, J. J., Steier, L. P., & Rau, S. B. (2012). Sources of heterogeneity in family firms: An introduction. *Entrepreneurship Theory and Practice*, 36(6), 1103–1113.

Clark, G. (2014). *The Son Also Rises. Surnames and the History of Social Mobility*. Princeton, NJ: Princeton University Press

Colli, A., & Rose, M. (2008). Family business. in *The Oxford Handbook of Business History*, Eds Jones, G., & Zeitlin, J. (195–217). Oxford University Press. Oxford, England.

Colpan, A. M., Hikino, T., & Lincoln, J. R. (Eds.). (2010). *The Oxford Handbook of Business Groups*. Oxford, England: Oxford University Press.

Colpan, A. M., & Hikino, T. (2018). *Business Groups in the West: Origins, Evolution Resilience* Oxford: Oxford University Press.

Dahrendorf, R. (1959). *Class and Class Conflict in Industrial Society*. Stanford, CA: Stanford University Press.

De Massis, A., Audretsch, D., Uhlaner, L., & Kammerlander, N. (2018). Innovation with limited resources: Management lessons from the German Mittelstand. *Journal of Product Innovation Management*, 35(1), 125–146.

De Massis, A., Frattini, F., Kotlar, J., Petruzzelli, A. M., & Wright, M. (2016). Innovation through tradition: lessons from innovative family businesses and directions for future research. *The Academy of Management Perspectives*, 30(1), 93–116.

De Nardi, M., & Yang, F. (2016). Wealth inequality, family background, and estate taxation. *Journal of Monetary Economics*, 77, 130–145.

DiMaggio, P., & Garip, F. 2012. Network effects and social inequality. *Annual Review of Sociology*, 38, 93–118.

Dunn, M. (1979). The Family Office as a Coordinating Mechanism within the Ruling Class. *Critical Sociology*, 9(2), 8–23

Dunn, M. G. (1980). The family office as a coordinating mechanism within the ruling class. *Insurgent Sociologist*, 9(2–3), 8–23.

Farber, B. (1975). Bilateral kinship: Centripetal and centrifugal types of organization. *Journal of Marriage and the Family*, 37(4), 871–888.

Federal Reserve (2017). Changes in US family finances from 2013 to 2016: Evidence from the Survey of Consumer Finances. *Federal Reserve Bulletin*, 103, 1.

Fligstein, N., & Goldstein, A. (2015). The emergence of a finance culture in American households, 1989–2007. *Socio-Economic Review*, 13(3), 575–601.

Fogel, K. (2006). Oligarchic family control, social economic outcomes, and the quality of government. *Journal of International Business Studies*, 37(5), 603–622.

Franks, J., Mayer, C., Volpin, P., & Wagner, H. F. 2012. The Life Cycle of Family Ownership: International Evidence. *Review of Financial Studies*, 25(6), 1675–1712.

Gale, W. G., & Scholz, J. K. 1994. Intergenerational transfers and the accumulation of wealth. *The Journal of Economic Perspectives*, 8(4), 145–160.

Ghemawat, P., & Khanna, T. (1998). The nature of diversified business groups: A research design and two case studies. *The Journal of Industrial Economics*, 46(1), 35–61.

Gilbert, D. L. 2008. *The American Class Structure in an Age of Growing Inequality*. Sage: Pine Forge Press.

Gilding, M. (2005). Families and fortunes: Accumulation, management succession and inheritance in wealthy families. *Journal of Sociology*, 41(1), 29–45.

Glucksberg, L., & Burrows, R. (2016). Family offices and the contemporary infrastructures of dynastic wealth. *Sociologica*, 10(2), 0–0.

Gomez-Mejia, L. R., Cruz, C., Berrone, P., & De Castro, J. (2011). The bind that ties: Socioemotional wealth preservation in family firms. *Academy of Management annals*, 5(1), 653–707.

Gordon, G., & Nicholson, N. (2010). *Family wars: Stories and insights from famous family business feuds*. Kogan Page Publishers.

Granovetter, M. 2005. Business groups and social organization. In N. J. Smelser, & R. Swedberg (Eds.). *The Handbook of Economic Sociology*, 2nd ed. (pp. 429–450). Princeton: Princeton University Press.

Gray, B., & Kish-Gephart, J. J. (2013). Encountering social class differences at work: How "class work" perpetuates inequality. *Academy of Management Review*, 38(4), 670–699.

Guiso, L., & Sodini, P. (2013). Household finance: An emerging field. In *Handbook of the Economics of Finance* (vol. 2, pp. 1397–1532). Elsevier.

Hall, P. D., & Marcus, G. E. (1998). Why should men leave great fortunes to their children? In *Inheritance and Wealth in America* (pp. 139–171). Boston: Springer.

Hall, P., & Soskice, D. 2001. *Varieties of Capitalism: The Institutional Foundations of Comparative Advantage*. Oxford: Oxford University Press.

Harrington, B. 2016. *Capital without Borders: Wealth Managers and the One Percent* Cambridge: Harvard University Press.

Harrington, B 2017 "Trusts and financialization." *Socio-Economic Review*, 15(1), 131–163.

Hansen, M. N. (2014). Self-made wealth or family wealth? Changes in intergenerational wealth mobility. *Social Pressures*, 93(2), 457–481.

Harrison, B. (1997). *Lean and Mean: The Changing Landscape of Corporate Power in the Age of Flexibility*. New York, NY: Guilford Press.

Harvey, D. (2005). From globalization to the new imperialism. In *Critical globalization studies* Eds Appelbaum, R. & Robinson, W. https://books.google.ca/books?hl=en&lr=&id=iR8-2p_Dw2MC&oi=fnd&pg=PA91&dq=harvey+2005+capitalist&ots=Kr7nwJPLoG&sig=38fqbM5jZwSYM2EHFdyyyJ6Odqw&redir_esc=y#v=onepage&q=harvey%202005%20capitalist&f=false

Harvey, D. (2007). *A Brief History of Neoliberalism*. Oxford, England: Oxford University Press.

Hill, S. A. (2012). *Families: A Social Class Perspective*. Los Angeles, CA: Pine Forge Press.

Hoskisson, R. E., Johnson, R. A., Tihanyi, L., & White, R. E. (2005). Diversified business groups and corporate refocusing in emerging economies. *Journal of Management*, 31(6), 941–965.

James, H. (2009). *Family Capitalism: Wendels, Haniels, Falcks, and the Continental European Model*. Cambridge, MA: Harvard University Press.

Jaskiewicz, P., Combs, J. G., & Rau, S. B. (2015). Entrepreneurial legacy: Toward a theory of how some family firms nurture transgenerational entrepreneurship. *Journal of business venturing*, 30(1), 29–49.

Jaskiewicz, P., Combs, J. G., Shanine, K. K., & Kacmar, K. M. (2017). Introducing the family: A review of family science with implications for management research. *Academy of Management Annals*, 11(1), 309–341.

Jaskiewicz, P., & Dyer, W. G. (2017). Addressing the elephant in the room: Disentangling family heterogeneity to advance family business research. *Family Business Review*, 30(2), 111–118.

Kaplan, S. N., & Rauh, J. D. 2013. Family, education, and sources of wealth among the richest Americans, 1982–2012. *The American Economic Review*, 103(3), 158–162.

Keister, L. A. (2005). *Getting rich: America's new rich and how they got that way*. Cambridge, England: Cambridge University Press.

Keister, L. A. (2014). The one percent. *Annual Review of Sociology*, 40, 347–367.

Khanna, T., & Rivkin, J. W. (2001). Estimating the performance effects of business groups in emerging markets. *Strategic Management Journal*, 22(1), 45–74.

Korom, P., Lutter, M., & Beckert, J. (2017). The enduring importance of family wealth: Evidence from the Forbes 400, 1982 to 2013. *Social Science Research*, 65, 75–95.

Kristensen, P. H. (1992). Industrial districts in West Jutland, Denmark. *Industrial Districts and Local Economic Regeneration. International Institute for Labour Studies, ILO, Geneva*.

Kuusela, H. (2018). Learning to own: Cross-generational meanings of wealth and class-making in wealthy Finnish families. *The Sociological Review*, 0038026118777698.

Kwok-Bun, C. (2013). A Family Affair: Migration, Dispersal and the Emergent Identity of the Chinese Cosmopolitan. In *International Handbook of Chinese Families* (pp. 23–35). New York: Springer.

Le Breton-Miller, I., & Miller, D. (2017). Beyond the firm: Business families as entrepreneurs. *Entrepreneurship Theory and Practice*, 42(4), 527–536.

Lehrer, M., & Celo, S. (2016). German family capitalism in the 21st century: patient capital between bifurcation and symbiosis. *Socio-Economic Review*, 14(4), 729–750.

Lester, R. H., & Cannella Jr, A. A. (2006). Interorganizational familiness: How family firms use interlocking directorates to build community–level social capital. *Entrepreneurship Theory and Practice*, 30(6), 755–775.

Marcus, G. E. 1992. *Lives in Trust: The Fortunes of Dynastic Families in Late 20th Century America*. Boulder, CO: Westview Press.

Masulis, R. W., Pham, P. K., & Zein, J. (2011). Family business groups around the world: Financing advantages, control motivations, and organizational choices. *The Review of Financial Studies*, 24(11), 3556–3600.

Mazumder, B. (2005). Fortunate sons: New estimates of intergenerational mobility in the United States using social security earnings data. *Review of Economics and Statistics*, 87(2), 235–255.

McPherson, M., Smith-Lovin, L., & Cook, J. M. (2001). Birds of a feather: Homophily in social networks. *Annual Review of Sociology*, 27(1), 415–444.

McVey, R. 1992. The materialization of the Southeast Asian entrepreneur. In R. McVey (Ed.), *Southeast Asian Capitalism*, 7–34. New York: Cornell University Southeast Asia program.

Mizruchi, M. S. (2004). Berle and Means revisited: The governance and power of large US corporations. *Theory and Society*, 33(5), 579–617.

Nason, R. S., Carney, M., Le Breton-Miller, I., & Miller, D. (2019). Who cares about socioemotional wealth? SEW and rentier perspectives on the one percent wealthiest business households. *Journal of Family Business Strategy*, 10(2), 144–158.

Palmer, D., & Barber, B. M. (2001). Challengers, elites, and owning families: A social class theory of corporate acquisitions in the 1980s. *Administrative Science Quarterly*, 46, 87–120.

Piketty, T. (2014). Capital in the 21st Century. Cambridge. MA: The Belknap Press.

Piketty, T., & Zucman, G. (2014). Capital is back: Wealth-income ratios in rich countries 1700–2010. *The Quarterly Journal of Economics*, 129(3), 1255–1310.

Portes, A., & Shafer, S. (2007). Revisiting the enclave hypothesis: Miami twenty-five years later. In *The Sociology of Entrepreneurship*. Emerald Group Publishing Limited.

Quadrini, V. 1999. The importance of entrepreneurship for wealth concentration and mobility. *Review of Income and Wealth*, 45(1), 1–19.

Reher, D. S. 1998. Family ties in Western Europe: persistent contrasts. *Population and Development Review* 24(2), 203–234.

Rosplock, K. (2012) 'Sustaining the Family Enterprise: The Intersection of the Family Business & the Family Office' Research Report, Gen Springs Family Offices.

Savage, M. (2000). *Class analysis and social transformation*. Buckingham, England: Open University Press.

Schulze, W., & Gedajlovic, E. 2010. Whither family business? *Journal of Management Studies*, 47(2), 191–204.

Silverstein, M., & Bengtson, V. L. (1997). Intergenerational solidarity and the structure of adult child-parent relationships in American families. *American journal of Sociology*, 103(2), 429–460.

Simmel, G. (2009). *Inquiries into the Construction of Social Forms, Volume 2* (translated by Anthony Blasi, Anton Jacobs, & Matthew Kanjirathinkal). Boston: Brill.

Soref, Michael, & Maurice Zeitlin. (1987). Finance capital and the internal structure of the capitalist class in the United States. *Intercorporate Relations: The Structural Analysis of Business*, Eds Mizruchi, M. and Schwartz, M. Cambridge University Press. Cambridge, England. 56–84.

Strachan, H. W. 1976. *Family and Other Business Groups in Economic Development: The Case of Nicaragua*. New York: Praeger.

Steier, L. P., Chrisman, J. J., & Chua, J. H. (2015). *Governance Challenges in Family Businesses and Business Families*, 1265–1280.

Tam, S. (1990). Centrifugal versus centripetal growth processes: Contrasting ideal types for conceptualizing the development patterns of Chinese and Japanese firms. *Capitalism in Contrasting Cultures*, Eds Clegg, Redding, S.G., Cartner, M. de Gruyter. Berlin. New York. 153–183.

Temouri, Y., Nardella, G., Jones, C., & Brammer, S. (2021). Haven-sent? Tax havens, corporate social irresponsibility and the dark side of family firm internationalization. *British Journal of Management*, 33(3), 1447–1467.

Trigilia, C. (1991). The paradox of the region: economic regulation and the representation of interests. *International Journal of Human Resource Management*, 20(3), 306–327.

Villalonga, B., & Amit, R. (2006). How do family ownership, control and management affect firm value? *Journal of Financial Economics*, 80(2), 385–417.

Useem, M. 1982. Classwide rationality in the politics of managers and directors of large corporations in the United States and Great Britain. *Administrative Science Quarterly*, 27(2), 199–226.

Uzzi, B. 1997. Social structure and competition in interfirm networks: The paradox of embeddedness. *Administrative Science Quarterly*, 42(1), 35–67.

Weber, M. (1927). 1981. *General Economic History*. Mineola, NY: Dover (Translated Frank Knight).

Ward, J. 1987. *Keeping the Family Business Healthy: How to Plan for Continuing Growth*. San Francisco: Jossey-Bass.

Wei, Y. D., Li, W., & Wang, C. (2007). Restructuring industrial districts, scaling up regional development: a study of the Wenzhou model, China. *Economic Geography*, 83(4), 421–444.

Woolcock, M. (1998). Social capital and economic development: Toward a theoretical synthesis and policy framework. *Theory and society*, 27(2), 151–208.

Zeitlin, M. 1974. Corporate ownership and control: The large corporation and the capitalist class. *American Journal of Sociology*, 79(5), 1073–1119.

Zeitlin, M., Ewen, L. A., & Ratcliff, R. E. (1974). "New Princes" for Old? The Large Corporation and the Capitalist Class in Chile. *American Journal of Sociology*, 80(1), 87–123.

Zellweger, T. (2017). *Managing the family business: Theory and practice*. Edward Elgar Publishing.

Zellweger, T., & Kammerlander, N. (2015). Family, wealth, and governance: An agency account. *Entrepreneurship Theory and Practice*, 39(6), 1281–1303.

Zellweger, T. M., Nason, R. S., & Nordqvist, M. (2012). From longevity of firms to transgenerational entrepreneurship of families: Introducing family entrepreneurial orientation. *Family Business Review*, 25(2), 136–155.

Elena Rivo-López and Mónica Villanueva-Villar

21 Philanthropy Through Family Offices

Abstract: In the last 10 years, the number of family offices and the volume of actively managed assets have experienced worldwide growth. As a result of this evolution, the ways in which business families carry out philanthropic activities have changed. A family office often is created when a business family decides to continue investing and carrying out various activities together, using their know-how to manage the family's assets and philanthropic projects. This chapter of the book focuses on the philanthropic activities of business families developed through family offices, by presenting examples of large family offices all over the world that are linked to business families.

Keywords: family office, philanthropy, wealth diversification, reputational capital, impact investment

Introduction

The family business is the most relevant business organizational structure worldwide, in terms of both numbers and its contribution to the economy and employment. Numerous studies published in the last 30 years have analyzed the family business from various perspectives, such as governance, succession, goals, private equity, and ethics (Benavides-Velasco et al., 2013; Dieleman & Koning, 2020; Schickinger et al., 2018; Qiu & Freel, 2020; Vázquez & Rocha, 2018). However, the current academic literature focuses on the family rather than on the business (Payne, 2020). The family decides the strategy of the business, and the family's values influence the activities it undertakes.

Families often separate themselves from their assets by creating new governance structures. Family offices (FOs) are organizational structures linked to business families. Specifically, "A single family office is a separate legal entity placed between the family and its assets that is solely devoted to managing the affairs of a single family" (Zellweger & Kammerlander, 2015, p. 1290). FOs are professional organizations created to manage the tangible and intangible assets of a business family, whose activities are strongly linked to the family's values and objectives. Among the activities performed, FOs support their clients in engaging in philanthropy and social entrepreneurship (Wessel et al., 2014). Business families are increasingly managing their philanthropic activity through FOs (Rivo-López et al., 2021a,b). Despite the current trend of generous giving by wealthy business families, the literature on FOs is not

Elena Rivo-López, Mónica Villanueva-Villar, University of Vigo

https://doi.org/10.1515/9783110727968-021

large, and studies on the links between FOs and philanthropy are much scarcer (Wessel et al., 2014).

FOs have existed for a long time and increasingly are becoming "a more widely known and an accepted wealth management solution for ultra-affluent families who are focused on multi-generational wealth management and building continuity across generations" (Wessel et al., 2014, p. 37). For this reason, we want to discuss FOs in this chapter, answering what, why, and what for, while focusing on their philanthropic activities. To this end, we will first discuss FOs from a theoretical perspective. We will then review the literature on philanthropy and business families. Then, we will analyze the philanthropy of business families through three examples of relevant FOs worldwide. We will end with the main conclusions of the chapter.

Family Offices: What, Why, and What For?

What is a Family Office?

FOs are family-owned and managed organizations whose assets are derived from either an ongoing family business or the cash from selling that business. Together, their main roles are to manage the family's wealth, preserve it for the next generation, and, if possible, increase it. An FO hands down a legacy that is both tangible and intangible (values, knowledge, etc.). At the centre of this structure is the business family, which will outline the FO based on the family's values and objectives.

Different types of FOs exist, depending on the assets under management (Rivo-López et al., 2017):
- **Single-family office (SFO):** An FO manages the assets of a single family, whereas an SFO guarantees uniqueness and full confidentiality of the family's business management.
- **Multi-family office (MFO):** administers the assets of several families, with each family knowing the families with which they share services. Because only one entity manages the assets of several families, the management costs are lower, which can be useful for families that do not have extensive resources.
- **Affiliated multi-family office:** administered either by banks or financial institutions.
- **Embedded FO:** an informal structure existing within a single business owned by an individual or a family. Private assets are considered part of their family business, so the family entrusts managing their private wealth to trustworthy employees of the family business. The chief financial officer (CFO) of the family business and their department's employees usually will be in charge of the FO tasks.

While perhaps not being the most efficient structure, an increasing number of entrepreneurial families seem to be separating their private wealth from that of their business and are considering taking the FO functions away from the family business, if only for reasons of privacy and tax compliance (Credit Suisse, 2017). We consider this to be the embryo or germ of a proper FO structure. SFOs are predominant in Europe, whereas MFOs are more prevalent in the US. The growth of FOs in Asia seems to be linked to SFOs, for cultural reasons, because families prefer confidentiality over sharing information with other families (Rivo-López et al., 2017).

The minimum level of net worth above which the creation of an EO is recommended also differs. An SFO in Europe requires equity of between €200,000,000 and €300,000,000, but for a MFO, 20,000,000 euro would be enough. Typical levels in the US are US$500,000,000 for an SFO and at least US$10,000,000 for a multi-family one. In addition, shareholder profiles vary by geographical are. In the US, shareholders tend to focus on financial assets, while European FOs prefer corporate and real estate activities (Rivo-López et al., 2017).

Why a Business Family Establishes a Family Office

Why does a business family set up an FO? This question can be answered by looking at a number of scenarios in which the entrepreneurial family may consider setting up an FO:
- **Managing a large family fortune:** Once a family business becomes large and profitable, it generates significant family wealth that must be managed. An FO structure allows the family's assets to be managed jointly while keeping the family together. If well managed, an FO can bring about greater family cohesion and improve harmony between the members of the next generations. Co-management of family wealth is also much more efficient.
- **Divestment from the family business:** The family business is sold, thus generating massive liquidity, which the family members decide to manage jointly.
- **Diversification of family wealth:** Family wealth is often focused solely on the family business, with all the risks that this situation entails. The FO can also finance business projects, both internal (raised by the new generations) and external (new business ventures from outside the family), thus stimulating entrepreneurial activity.

Confidentiality, personalized service, flexible structure, exclusivity, and discretion constitute the main reasons why wealthy business families choose to establish an FO over other wealth-management alternatives (Allen, 2007; Amit & Liechtenstein, 2012; Rivo-López et al., 2021b). Accordingly, both tangible (intergenerational wealth creation, taxation, asset management, etc.) and intangible reasons (family harmony, cohesion, generational continuity, philanthropy, etc.) exist for creating an

FO. An SFO manager states: "The most fundamental reason has to do with management challenge: no one will take your business as seriously as yourself" (Rivo-López et al., 2017).

What For?

An FO can carry out three types of activities (Amit, 2018; Rivo-López et al., 2017):
- **Administration-related activities:** for example, financial administration, information aggregating and client reporting, legal services, technology solutions and support, trust accounting, pooled and partnership accounting, and family real estate management.
- **Investment-related activities:** for example, asset allocation, manager selection and monitoring, investing, investment performance, measurement, and risk management.
- **Family-related activities:** for example, education of family members, philanthropy, insurance, custodial services, security, estate planning, and banking.

To the best of our knowledge, many business families owning an FO have channeled their philanthropic operations through their FO. Indeed, even when families had previously set up a foundation, their philanthropic operations are managed by the FO. The FO is also used to promote entrepreneurship, both externally (at times acting as a venture capital company) and internally (supporting new family projects).

Alternatively, an SFO has a key role to play in preserving the family's purpose and identity, and in facilitating the transition from one generation to the next. While managing the transgenerational heritage is the most important family objective for SFOs, educational programs can help families to plan their succession strategies, by enhancing family communication and harmonious relations between family members, thereby reducing their level of conflict (Rivo-López et al., 2017).

To this point, we have only discussed the positive aspects of FOs. However, this structure is also subject to criticism, especially from the fiscal perspective, and to objections about the disadvantages that could arise from the double agency costs generated. From the fiscal perspective, some critics believe that wealthy business families do not create FOs to manage wealth but to pay less taxes. In this sense, the need exists to study the role of legal and tax systems in shaping legal substitutes (Carney et al., 2014; Zellweger & Kammerlander, 2015).

On the other hand, evolving family structures may give rise to conflicts and agency problems, as a consequence of increasing heterogeneity in family goals as well as dispersion. In addition, double-agency problems may exist between a family CEO and external management or between a non-family CEO and family management (Carney & Child, 2013; Wessel et al., 2014; Zellweger & Kammerlander, 2015). In this regard, future research should study how the governance of such equity structures works in practice, including the resulting advantages and disadvantages in terms of related (agency) costs.

Philanthropy of Business Families

> Philanthropic innovation is not just about creating something new. It also means applying new thinking to old problems, processes, and systems.
>
> Laura Arrillaga-Andreessen

What is Philanthropy?

> Philanthropy is not about the money. It's about using whatever resources you have at your fingertips and applying them to improving the world.
>
> Melinda Gates

> No man becomes rich unless he enriches others.
>
> Andrew Carnegie

Little agreement exists regarding what actions are considered to be philanthropic in nature (Feliu & Botero, 2016). Indeed, numerous conceptual and empirical debates surround what is meant by philanthropy (Gautier & Pache, 2015; Liket & Simaens, 2015). The origins of these discussions lie in the changing definition of philanthropy over time and in individuals' interpretations of what constitutes a philanthropic act (Sulek, 2010). Until the 20th century, the terms "philanthropy" and "charity" were used interchangeably to refer to the voluntary act of donating funds to support hardship-stricken people (Schuyt, 2013). This traditional perspective focused on helping the needy and ensuring coverage for their basic needs (Schuyt, 2013). In the early 20th century, however, as affluent businessmen in the US increasingly made donations to a range to causes other than welfare and aid to the poor, the concept of philanthropy changed in at least three ways (Harvey et al., 2011; Rey-García & Puig-Raposo, 2013). To begin with, the nature of the causes supported by philanthropic efforts shifted, moving from focusing on basic physical and material needs such as food, clothing, and shelter towards a more wide-ranging array of concerns such as healthcare, the environment, education, and the arts (Schuyt, 2013). Secondly, philanthropic endeavors shifted from solely focusing on mitigating social problems, such as hunger or disease, towards finding solutions to the symptoms of these problems, such as education or skills shortages, or to the culture of poverty (Sulek, 2010). Finally, the driving motives behind philanthropy changed. In the early 1900s, companies were advised to take actions that the public perceived as good and beneficial to society, so that the companies would be viewed favourably (Gruning & Hunt, 1984). This shifted the motives for philanthropy from being purely altruistic (i.e., altruistic concern for the welfare of others) to a desire for "return on investment" through public recognition of philanthropic actions or through societal changes (Cutlip, 1994). Therefore, modern conceptualizations of philanthropy are moving beyond charitable giving to include a broader scope of activities (e.g., financial donations to social welfare, education, or the arts) and philanthropic acts (Aguilera et al., 2007; Barnett, 2007; Porter & Kramer, 1999).

Philanthropic activities in family-owned businesses have an impact on not only the donor company but also the owning family. From the company side, philanthropy is used as a means to demonstrate a company's commitment to long-term goals (Campopiano et al., 2014). It is also a tool to develop social and reputational capital (Cruz et al., 2014) and to improve the commitment and engagement of family and non-family employees with the company (Muller et al., 2014). On the family side, through philanthropy, the family stakeholders learn about family legacy matters, wealth (i.e., management and responsibilities) and the professional skills needed in the business world (Breeze, 2009; Eichenberger & Johnson, 2013; Ward, 2009). In addition, social capital can be transferred across generations as a result of philanthropy, by enabling different generations to work together towards a common goal (Breeze, 2009; Schwass & Lief, 2008).

Today, family business philanthropy activities constitute a way for business families to return part of the wealth to society they have generated through it. Family philanthropy may be undertaken by individual family members themselves, through the family business (corporate social responsibility), by means of a foundation, or through an FO.

> It is the person or entity that has the funding available to undertake projects which support society in its different spheres – Juan Entrecanales, honorary president, Acciona. (as cited in La Caixa, 2020, p. 16)

> Help people with a transformation idea in mind. Not just by giving money, but by making an impact and bringing about change in people's lives.
> Inés Entrecanales, vice president, Acciona (as cited in La Caixa, 2020, p. 16)

Why Philanthropy?

Throughout history, business families have exercised important patronage, which has had significant effects on their environment. (For example, Florence would be inconceivable without the patronage of the Medici family.) Of course, this role has not only been maintained but also has also grown and adapted to new political, economic, and social contexts throughout history, not only in terms of patronage but also philanthropy and, more recently, corporate social responsibility (CSR).

Family businesses like to give back some of what they receive from society. As a result of their long-term vision, they think about not only the short-term outcomes but also their legacy to future generations. Thus, through their CSR activities, companies and business families work with their immediate environment on many fronts, such as on economic, social, and health issues. This contribution to improve their community may be exemplified best by COVID-19, a contribution that has been most appreciated by citizens. Yet, one might say that a certain innovation has taken place: Philanthropy alone has not led to financial or material donations; rather, many companies' know-how and organizational capacity have been made available to different governments, as a way of contributing to managing and resolving this unprecedented crisis.

Philanthropic activities, either directly or through the CSR of their companies, stem from a wish to pass on a family's legacy to the next generation, their ties with the community in which they carry out their activities, their desire to maintain their social reputation, and, in short, to preserve and transmit their socioemotional wealth (Feliu & Botero, 2016; Rivo-López et al., 2021a). On the other hand, managing the family's philanthropic activities may contribute to successful family business succession. Philanthropic project development can provide alternative opportunities for personal growth and professional development opportunities for family members withdrawing from managing the family business, or for those who have never entered into management (Rey-García, 2013).

Along these lines, Rey-García (2013) mentioned a number of motivations for family members to engage in philanthropic activities. Among them are educating the family's children in pro-social values and even preventing them from being deprived of a sense of purpose in life due to inheriting excessive wealth. This approach was initiated in 1901 by Andrew Carnegie and was updated most recently in 2010 with the signing of the Giving Pledge. Andrew Carnegie retired in 1901 at the age of 66 as the richest man in the world and afterwards wished to become a philanthropist – a person who gives money towards good causes – after perhaps regretting how he made his fortune (including, among other ways, how he ended the Carnegie Steel Company strike, known as the Homestead Strike of 1892) or the inhumane conditions to which he subjected his workers. His belief in the "Gospel of Wealth" meant that the wealthy had a moral obligation to return their money to others in society. Before 1901, Carnegie had already made a number of charitable donations, but from then on, his new occupation became distributing his money. Thus, he founded the Carnegie Institution in 1902 to fund scientific research. In addition, he endowed a teachers' pension fund with $10,000,000. In Carnegie's view, the custom of leaving all money to heirs was shameful, and the wealthy instead should use their money to benefit society while they were still alive. He epitomized this philosophy perfectly, donating around 90% of his wealth during his lifetime.

One hundred years later, in August 2010, 40 of America's wealthiest people came together in a pledge to donate most of their wealth towards addressing some of society's most pressing problems (Giving Pledge, 2010). Created by Bill and Melinda Gates together with Warren Buffett, the Giving Pledge came to life following a series of conversations with philanthropists across the globe about collectively setting a new standard of generosity among the world's greatest fortunes by publicly pledging a significant amount of those fortunes to philanthropy. The Giving Pledge was conceived as a multi-generational effort with the aims, eventually, to contribute towards changing patronage social standards, inspire people to be more giving-minded, and structure the philanthropists' giving plans by anticipating and executing them more intelligently. The Giving Pledge now embraces more than 200 of the world's richest individuals, couples, and families between the ages of 30 and 90 years old from 25 countries. (Currently, there is nobody from Spain, although there is one from Portugal.)

For What Should Philanthropy be Developed?

Philanthropic activities conducted by business families may be involved in different areas, such as the following (La Caixa, 2020):
- **Culture:** initiatives intended to foster and promote culture, science, art, languages, or traditions.
- **Education:** philanthropic schemes promoting the transmission of new skills and knowledge across a wide range of groups to further those groups' personal development and social integration.
- **Health:** philanthropic initiatives supporting research and training related to health.
- **Social services:** philanthropic activities aimed at promoting welfare and integration of the vulnerable, through counseling, fostering, and education services.
- **Development support:** Philanthropic actions directed towards improving economic, social, and human conditions of the most vulnerable people and communities.
- **Environment:** philanthropic measures intended to preserve and protect their surroundings and environment.

Why use FOs as a Tool for Philanthropy?

Studies have cited foundations, individual donations, art patronage, impact investment (equity investments in companies and/or funds that generate social impact and a financial return for the investor), and FOs (La Caixa, 2020; Rey-García, 2013) as mechanisms for implementing philanthropic projects. On the other hand, research on family businesses shows little integration between professional and academically driven work (Gersick & Feliu, 2014). Thus, it is difficult to understand philanthropy because academically driven works focus almost exclusively on the business component, while professionals concentrate on the family component (Feliu & Botero, 2016; Michael-Tsabari et al., 2014). In this sense, the FO bridges the gap between the two, placing the business family at the centre.

An FO focuses on the business family, which, based on its values, decides on the objectives and, consequently, the activities to be carried out in all areas, including philanthropy. Joint philanthropic activities can unite a family around a common project and strengthen the family's connection with the community in which the family business operates, thus improving the family's reputational image. Cohesion, harmony, and joint activities among family members are all objectives pursued when creating an FO.

Philanthropy constitutes one of the most rewarding and distinctively different activities that can be undertaken by an FO. Just as in all FO activities, philanthropy must also be handled with professionalism and commitment. Challenges and rewards must also be recognized (Credit Suisse, 2015).

Recently, the growing levels of philanthropy by wealthy business families have come under some criticism. Obviously, several examples exist of philanthropy's benefits, including as a tool to develop social/reputational capital and to improve engagement with family and non-family employees. Engaging in high-profile philanthropic projects can contribute to the legitimacy of the core business. Philanthropy also represents an opportunity to appear in the "high society" of a city or country. Nevertheless, many critics suggest that philanthropy is a strategy for perpetuating family privilege, by providing family members with high-status jobs. Of course, business families may use philanthropy to deflect criticism about their business practices.

One prominent voice in this criticism is Anand Giridharadus (2019), who has attracted significant attention in North America. Giridharadus observed that business philanthropy is at an all-time high, suggesting growing levels of generosity. However, his core argument was that philanthropy often promotes social change but does so in narrow and self-interested ways. For example, philanthropy in education often takes the form of privatized commercial solutions to problems faced by particular social groups. He observed that endless do-good initiatives are also coinciding with exponentially growing levels of income inequality. He suggested that philanthropy appears to be a win-win strategy for families accumulating large fortunes, by producing outcomes that protect their ability to sustain the accumulation. This critical perspective has entered the political agenda, with many governments contemplating wealth taxes to ameliorate tendencies towards inequality.

Philanthropy Cases Through Family Offices: Historical Evolution

This section deals with examples of family businesses whose philanthropic activities have been developed by establishing FOs. In particular, we have selected the cases of the Ortega family, owners of the Inditex Group; the Kristiansen family, owners of the LEGO Group; and the Walton family, owner of Walmart Inc.

Illustrative Case 1: The Ortega Family (Inditex Group – Pontegadea SFO)

Where did the Ortega Family's Wealth Stem From?

Inditex is a family business presently owned by the first and second generations of the Ortega family. Amancio Ortega owns 59.294% of the company – 50.01% through his FO Pontegadea, and 9.284% through Partler Inversiones, SL. Sandra Ortega, Amancio's daughter from his first marriage, owns 5% through RospCorunna Participaciones Empresariales SL. As of 2021, Forbes estimated Amancio Ortega's wealth at $77,000,000,000, making him the 11th wealthiest man in the world and the wealthiest person in Europe.

Founded in 1963 in A Coruña, Spain, under the trade name of Confecciones GOA (Amancio Ortega's initials reverted), the company started its activity as a small manufacturing workshop for women's dressing gowns (Inditex, 2021). The first Zara shop opened in 1975 and began its expansion in Spain in 1985. During that same year, Inditex was founded as a holding company of the group. The group's international expansion began in 1988, and new brand names emerged within the group. In addition, new group brands were created within the group in 2001, and the company was floated on the stock exchange. The company has grown steadily over the last 20 years, as one of the most internationally recognized brands in the world. In 2011, Amancio Ortega handed over Inditex's management to Pablo Isla, a professional from outside the family, appointing him as chairman of the Board of Directors. That decision put an end to any uncertainty about his successor. The value of the company has tripled since then.

The Ortega Family

Amancio Ortega was brought up as the son of a railway employee in a very humble environment, and at the age of 14 he began working as an errand boy for a shirt manufacturer in his hometown of A Coruña, in Galicia, northern Spain. That was his first contact with textiles. He was known to be shy and would avoid any kind of press or media. The general public did not even know who the owner of the Inditex Group was until the 1990s, a fashion giant that came out of nowhere.

Amancio has three siblings: Antonio, Josefa, and Pilar. While the first two were involved in the beginnings of the company, Pilar, who lived abroad, was not. Antonio Ortega was the eldest of the siblings who owned more than a 1% a share in the family business. He died in 1987 at the age of 59. He was married to Primitiva Renedo. Their daughter, Dolores Ortega Renedo, currently holds a stake of almost 1% in Inditex and is actually one of the family members who has been in the news for making a large donation of health equipment in 2020, in the midst of the COVID-19 pandemic (15,000 plastic screens, 250,000 masks, 25,000 tests, and more than 200 monitors). Amancio Ortega's other sister, Josefa Ortega, was originally involved in the company's financial management. She has two children, María José and Miguel Jove Ortega. She currently holds 0.56% of the company's shares.

As for Amancio Ortega's immediate family, it consists of his three children: Sandra and Marcos, from his first marriage to Rosalía Mera, and Marta, from his second marriage to Flora Pérez. The eldest of his children, Sandra Mera Ortega, is currently the richest woman in Spain, after the death of her mother in 2013. She is the second largest shareholder of Inditex, with a 5% stake. His second son, Marcos, is affected by cerebral palsy (the Amancio Ortega Foundation carries out philanthropic projects linked to this disease) and is under his sister's guardianship. Finally, Marta Ortega Pérez, Ortega's most media daughter, has a 2.83% stake in the family business.

Does the Ortega Family have a Single FO?

The Ortega family manages its wealth through its single FO, Pontegadea SL. The family retains 50.01% of the Inditex business through the FO, thus guaranteeing continued control in succession. Amancio created Pontegadea in 2001, just as Inditex's IPO was taking place. Until then, Amancio Ortega owned nothing outside the company. Everything had been reinvested prior to the IPO, but the stock market flotation brought in €1,300,000,000, which needed to be managed. The company employs a workforce of 14 people. Amancio Ortega owns 97.16% of the company, and his daughter, Marta Ortega, owns 2.83% (Rivo-López et al., 2021b).

Philanthropic Activity

Pontegadea manages not only manages the family's real estate activities but also the Amancio Ortega Foundation, responsible for the philanthropic activities of the Ortega family. The Amancio Ortega Foundation (2021) is active in two main sectors: education and social welfare, many of which are carried out locally, in the hometown of the Ortega family (Galicia, Spain).

Some of the projects underway in Social Welfare include the following examples:
- **Nursery schools in Galicia**
- **Comprehensive care centres for the elderly:** specifically, seven public residential centres that generate over 800 direct jobs and provide innovative psychological and geriatric units specialized in treating Alzheimer's disease and other similar pathologies.

- **A special education and therapeutic care centre:** dedicated to people with cerebral palsy and related pathologies. This centre caters to users from 0 to 65 years of age, with a team of professionals made up of 51 people.
- **A health-support program for public oncology:** a supporting scheme for renewing technological equipment in public hospitals, more specifically for cancer diagnosis and radiotherapy treatment.
- **Health support program for the COVID-19 crisis in Spain:** The Amancio Ortega Foundation has launched a process for purchasing health equipment to combat COVID-19 for immediate donation to health centres throughout Spain. Equipment is acquired in accordance with the technical-sanitary guidelines established by the Spanish authorities and is being made available upon arrival in Spain.

In the educational area, the following list includes are some of the projects currently underway at the foundation:
- **Advanced talent training:** an educational program (in STEAM disciplines) designed by the foundation's technical team, in collaboration with the Massachusetts Institute of Technology (MIT) and the University of Cambridge, aimed at 600 fifth-year secondary education students.
- **Master's Degree in Journalism and Audiovisual Production:** aimed at providing both Spanish and international undergraduate students with access to high-quality training in communication and audiovisual production.
- **INSPIRATICS:** an educational platform specializing in the use of methodologies and technology for secondary schoolteachers.
- **Scholarship programs:** specifically for students in the fifth year of secondary school in Galicia (Spain) to study in the US.

Two main projects should be pointed out (Rivo-López et al., 2021a). First, the company gave the Spanish government logistical support for procuring and supplying essential medical equipment. It provided the Spanish health authorities with its logistical resources for procuring and transporting of medical supplies and provided the Spanish health sector with 35,000,000 units of personal protective equipment from China. In addition, it has avoided temporary layoffs, as a measure to support its employees and their communities' economies. This has shifted the focus back to the family that owns and controls the company, which has decided to be more concerned about the long-term and its employees rather than about its financial returns. On March 17, the Inditex Group temporarily closed 3,785 of its shops in 39 countries, yet it decided not to implement temporary layoffs of its workers and instead continued paying its employees their full salaries.

Illustrative Case 2: The Kristiansen Family (LEGO Group, KIRKBI FO)

Where does the Kristiansen Family's Wealth Stem From?

The LEGO Group is a Danish family-owned company, currently run by the third and fourth generations. It was founded in 1932 by Ole Kirk Kristiansen, a carpenter and cabinetmaker who originally produced wooden toys. The name comes from the combination of the two Danish words *leg godt*, meaning "play well" (LEGO Group, 2021). In 1949, Ole Kirk saw potential in plastic bricks. In 1957, Godtfred Kirk Kristiansen, his son, assumed day-to-day management. Soon after in 1958, the LEGO brick was patented. In the same year, Ole Kirk died of a heart attack and Godtfred took over managing the company. In 1968, the first Legoland park opened in Billund. In 1979, Kjeld Kirk Kristiansen, Godtfred's son, became CEO of the LEGO Group. In 2004, the firm faced a serious crisis and established a survival plan. Jørgen Vig Knudstorp succeeded Kjeld Kirk Kristiansen as president and CEO and revitalized the company. In 2007, Thomas Kirk Kristiansen, the fourth-generation heir, joined the board of directors. LEGO has opened factories in Hungary, Mexico, China, and elsewhere. In 2017, Niels B. Kristiansen took over as CEO.

The LEGO Group is now 75% owned by the FO, called KIRKBI, and 25% by the LEGO Foundation (LEGO Foundation, 2021). A smooth transition between the third and fourth generation is taking place. Kjeld Kirk Kristiansen is currently chairman of the KIRKBI Board of Directors. Thomas Kirk Kristiansen holds the position of chairman of the board for LEGO and the LEGO Foundation, and is a member of the KIRKBI board as well. Agnete Kirk Thinggaard, fourth-generation owner, is an observer on the KIRKBI board.

The Kristiansen Family

During its 87 years of existence and despite its growth, LEGO has always remained a family-owned company, oddly enough under single ownership. During the second generation (Ole Kirk Christiansen's children), Godtfred, the third of four boys (plus a sister), acquired the others' shares. This process was repeated in the third generation: Kjeld Kirk Kristiansen bought his sister Gunhild's shares, after which the family surname was spelled with a K rather than a Ch- (LEGO, 2021).

The new fourth generation Sofie (46), Thomas (40), and Agnete (36) have decided on shared ownership of LEGO, although Thomas runs the business. Thomas was brought up to succeed his father, Kjeld, who retired in 2016. He is the only one of the three siblings who works full-time at the company and makes most of the day-to-day decisions. It looks as though the fifth generation of the Kristiansen family will be six women: Thomas and his sisters have six girls ranging in age from 7 to 13.

Does the Kristiansen Family have a Single FO?

LEGO Group established an FO called KIRKBI in 2017 to protect, develop, and harness the LEGO brand's full potential while ensuring active and committed family ownership of LEGO brand entities from generation to generation. In addition to investment operations, KIRKBI is involved in training family members as owners while supporting their private interests, their businesses, and their philanthropic work. KIRKBI manages two foundations simultaneously: Ole Kirk's Fond and the QATO Foundation (KIRKBI, 2021).

Philanthropic Activity

Ole Kirk's Fond is a charity foundation that aims to improve living standards for children and their families. It supports cultural, religious, humanitarian, and educational purposes and has strong social concerns, identifying five target fields: (a) children of sick parents; (b) children from families facing substance abuse; (c) vulnerable households with infants and toddlers, (d) children and young people with developmental difficulties; and (e) children at risk of domestic violence (Ole Kirk's Fond, 2021).

Established in 2012 by Signe and Thomas Kirk Kristiansen, the QATO Foundation is an animal welfare charity. This foundation supports sustainable long-term solutions to ensure and promote animal welfare. Because it works internationally and deals with many different species of animals, the QATO Foundation supports various projects. These include studies targeted towards improved understanding of animal behaviour and health, animal welfare organization-led projects to help animals in acute distress, and educating children to create empathy for animals and to better understand their needs (QATO Foundation, 2021).

The Kristiansen family has its own charity, the LEGO Foundation, which was established by Edith and Godtfred Kirk Christiansen in 1986 as part of their philanthropic projects through the FO (LEGO Foundation, 2021). The LEGO Foundation and the LEGO Group share a common mission: inspiring and developing the LEGO builders of tomorrow.

The LEGO Foundation seeks a future where play-based learning will empower children to become lifelong creative, engaged learners. The foundation is dedicated to redefining what play should be and reimagining the learning process so that children gain the broad set of skills they need to succeed. Projects can be grouped into three themes:

- **Focal regions:** The LEGO Foundation operates in Denmark, Mexico, South Africa, and the Ukraine, all of which face challenges to achieving quality learning and academic outcomes.
- **Early childhood development:** The LEGO Foundation's early childhood programs work on anchoring and deepening learning through play across the environments where young children spend most of their time (home, early childhood centres, and their communities).
- **Education:** The aim of the education initiatives is to reach millions of children with play-based learning in different parts of the world.

Illustrative Case 3: The Walton Family (Walmart Inc., Walton Enterprises, LLC)

Where does the Waltons' Wealth Stem From?

Walmart is a family company. At the age of 32, an entrepreneur named Sam Walton opened a small business called Walton's 5 & 10 in the small town of Bentonville, Arkansas in 1950 (Walmart, 2021). His small shop was successful enough that years later, the first Walmart shop opened in 1962 in Rogers, Arkansas. Success lay in offering low-priced products and great customer service. The Walton family, now in its third generation, still owns 48% of the company. With a market capitalization of $241,397,000,000, it is considered the leading family-owned company in the US (Credit Suisse, 2015). As the world's largest retailer by revenue, Walmart has annual sales of $500 billion from its nearly 12,000 shops around the world (Walmart, 2021).

The Walton Family

The Waltons are the richest family in the US, and own 50% of Walmart's total shares. According to *Forbes* (2021), the Walton descendants have a combined wealth of $181.3 billion, which is more than Jeff Bezos, Bill Gates, and Warren Buffett, and almost $83 billion more than the Kochs, the second richest family in the US.

Sam Walton passed away in 1992. He and his wife Helen Robson had four children: Rob, John, Jim, and Alice. His first son, Samuel Robson Walton (Rob), was chairman of Walmart until 2015. According to *Forbes* (2021), Rob has a personal wealth of $59.5 billion.

Sam's second son, John Walton, died in a plane crash in 2005 at the age of 58. John was married to Christy Walton and had one son named Lukas. John left about 17% of his wealth to his wife, and the rest was given to charity and to his son (Walmart, 2021).

The youngest son is James Walton. He is worth an estimated $42.1 billion (Walmart, 2021). He is chairman of the board of directors of the family-owned Arvest Bank, which has assets of more than $18 billion. He also sat on the board of Walmart before being replaced by his son Stewart in 2016.

The youngest sister is Alice Walton. She has a personal wealth of $61.8 billion according to *Forbes* (2021), making her the richest woman worldwide. Twice divorced, she has no children. Although Alice has never played an active role in business management, she has become a patron of the arts. She has a massive private art collection including original works by Andy Warhol and Georgia O'Keefe. Alice donated 3,700,000 of her Walmart shares – valued at the time at about $225,000,000 – to the family's nonprofit, the Walton Family Foundation, in January 2016. That charity donated some $530,000,000 in 2017 (Walton Family Foundation, 2021).

Does the Walton Family have a Single FO?

Walton Enterprises, LLC was established as an FO to serve the personal and business requirements of Sam and Helen Walton's family. The SFO's primary mission is to enable every member of the Walton family to achieve their personal, philanthropic, and business goals. Among the services the foundation provides to the Walton family and its related entities are personal treasury, accounting, tax service, and administrative services. Furthermore, investment, legal, risk management/insurance, IT, human resources, and facilities management services are provided to clients of the family and their affiliated entities and businesses.

Philanthropic Activity

Walmart's philanthropic endeavors are conducted through the Walmart Foundation, which was established in 1982 as an independent entity. Its core areas of activity are diversity, equity, and inclusion through a range of programs (Walton Family Foundation, 2021). The Walton Enterprises FO manages the Walton Family Foundation, established in 1987. The foundation is active in three fields: improving K–12 education; environmental initiatives to protect rivers, oceans, and the communities they support; and investing in northwest Arkansas and the Arkansas–Mississippi Delta, home of the Walton family. The Walton Family Foundation works to eliminate racial and educational inequalities among the neediest families in three ways:
- **Increasing success and opportunity:** The foundation supports educational programs.
- **Driving diverse, enduring future coalitions:** The foundation aims to support political campaigns, create platforms, and implement tools to turn voice and vision into systemic solutions.

- **Boosting cutting-edge innovation:** The foundation funds entrepreneurs and innovators who will foster students' learning (Walton Family Foundation, 2021).

The Walton Family Foundation also undertakes environmental projects aimed at improving agricultural water quality and availability through climate-resilient methods, as well as water resource management and sustainable fisheries. Northwest Arkansas was Sam and Helen Walton's home. Therefore, the foundation invested funds in the region with several guiding principles: (a) enhance economic and cultural vibrancy; (b) build inclusive growth and a sense of belonging, (c) support community leadership and empowerment; and (d) release the delta's full potential (Walton Family Foundation, 2021).

However, despite their philanthropic activities, the family has come under fire. Some people believe that they resort to philanthropy to divert attention away from their low-wage corporate policies (Change Walmart, 2021). Moreover, they devote a very small percentage of their total personal wealth to this activity (only .04% net worth contribution in the case of the Walton family is dedicated to their foundation; Change Walmart, 2021).

Conclusion

Professionalizing business management is an ongoing challenge in a world as competitive and globalized as today's. Managing family wealth is part of this issue. Successful companies can jeopardize their futures if their corporate management overlooks family structures, intergenerational relationships, and the legitimate ambitions of each individual family member. For several years now, FOs have been a widespread practice in developed and emerging countries, given that their range of services and benefits often outweigh their implementation and operating costs (Credit Suisse, 2017).

This chapter discussed FOs, focusing on the perspective of philanthropic activities conducted by business families. We have talked about how philanthropy has evolved over time, transforming from traditional charitable giving into a certain professionalized paradigm. Today, entrepreneurial families want to get involved in managing their philanthropic activities and apply their businesses know-how when implementing entrepreneurial initiatives. In this regard, FOs are becoming one of the more widely used instruments for philanthropy, whether by directly managing family philanthropy or by running the family foundations responsible for these activities. As an organizational structure, an FO gives a family business a leading role in philanthropic activity while including entrepreneurial knowledge in its management.

Throughout history, business families have been involved in patronage activities linked to that society where their main business activity is carried out. Families' long-term goals and aspiration to build legacies that will last for generations stand out. There are different attitudes towards wealth, however. In the US, there has always been a strong distrust of a high concentration of wealth and of a society in which success depends on inheritance instead of individual merit. The abolition of the inheritance tax under the George W. Bush administration sparked a new discussion of this topic among the American public (Wessel et al., 2014). Kuusela (2018) considered the accumulation of wealth between generations one of the dynamics underpinning economic inequalities. Despite forces towards meritocratic managerialism, hyper-rational capital markets, and the rise of professional investors, family wealth has prevailed, and inheritors and families have retained control of business interests (Carney & Nason, 2018). The members of dynastic families learn to own and value cross-generational wealth accumulation through formalized practices that are shared between families. According to Kuusela (2018), these practices help form a class and reproduce its economic position and privileges. This situation generates a very controversial debate, a political discussion in societies that celebrate meritocracy but suffer from growing inequalities and wealth concentration.

As an organizational structure, an FO better ensures funds for philanthropic activities. FOs have sufficient resources to undertake activities determined by a family. Very often, an FO holds company shares and receives dividends that allow further activities, including those of a philanthropic nature.

An FO is a bridge between an entrepreneurial family and a family business. Family businesses can carry out CSR activities; however, it is the entrepreneurial families at their heads that decide which philanthropic projects to pursue in line with their values and the legacy they want to pass on. Business families are the true actors behind every aspect of FO creation and development. This alignment between family and business interests – as well as among family members from different generations, with different implications for the family business – makes an FO a very useful tool for entrepreneurial families, not least in philanthropy.

In this chapter, we analyzed the theoretical and practical perspectives of philanthropic ventures developed by business families by looking at three significant examples. Some conclusions can be drawn from this analysis. First, the projects in the cases we analyzed reflect the family values that drive them. Second, there is a strong link between the philanthropic activities developed by the three families and their places of origin (Galicia in Spain; Germany; and Arkansas in the US). This is yet another reflection of the importance of emotional attachment of families in philanthropic activity, as they attempt to give back part of what they have received to their immediate societies. The third point is that in all cases, the way philanthropy is carried out evolved, beginning with donations, followed by establishing foundations, then professionalizing philanthropic management by setting up FOs. Fourth, philanthropic projects are sometimes linked to the main activity developed by the entrepreneurial family, as is the case of the LEGO Group's owners, who sponsor educational projects linked to construction. Finally, SFOs manage family wealth as holders of the family business's shares. Dividends from these shares allow SFOs to benefit from a large amount of financial resources.

Currently, the term "impact investment" is used. Philanthropic activity developed by business families through FOs may be more focused on returns via prestige, reputation, and improving the environment surrounding the family business, not on economic returns. Younger generations seem to be shifting towards a new philanthropy in terms of social or human returns, advocating to disrupt the traditional philanthropic model and adopt a more entrepreneurial perspective. From this perspective, concepts such as social entrepreneurship and impact investment have much greater presence in philanthropy (La Caixa, 2020). Specifically, Rovner et al. (2013) revealed that, for 45% of baby boomers, monetary donations make a difference in terms of perceived impact; however, that figure drops to 25% for millennials. It remains to be seen whether these trends reach the philanthropic activities conducted by FOs.

Unlike traditional donations, business families channel financial and nonfinancial resources through FOs to boost an authorized process of social change. Philanthropists can professionalize their ventures' management and adopt a more collaborative approach, but also transform the way they assess their projects' success – that is, their impact on society. One future challenge is determining how to measure this impact.

References

Aguilera, R. V., Rupp, D. E., Williams, C. A., & Ganapathi, J. (2007). Putting the S back in corporate social responsibility: A multilevel theory of social change in organizations. *Academy of Management Review*, 32(3), 836–863.

Allen, C. (2007). The changing face of the family office. *Global Investor*, 200, 21–22.

Amit, R. (2018). *Wharton Global Family Alliance 2018 Family Office Benchmarking Report*. https://wgfa.wharton.upenn.edu/wp-content/uploads/2018/03/WGFA-2018-Benchmarking_EXEC-SUMMARY.pdf

Amit, R., & Liechtenstein, H. (2012). *Report Highlights for Benchmarking the Single-Family Office: Identifying the Performance Drivers* [Technical report]. University of Pennsylvania.

Barnett, M. L. (2007). Stakeholder influence capacity and the variability of financial returns to corporate social responsibility. *Academy of Management Review*, 32(3), 794–816.

Benavides-Velasco, C. A., Quintana-García, C., & Guzmán-Parra, V. F. (2013). Trends in family business research. *Small Business Economics*, 40(1), 41–57.

Breeze, A. (2009). *Natural Philanthropists: Findings of the Family Business Philanthropy and Social Responsibility Inquiry*. London, England: Institute for Family Business.

Campopiano, G., de Massis, A., & Chirico, F. (2014). Firm philanthropy in small-and medium-sized family firms: The effects of family involvement in ownership and management. *Family Business Review*, 27(3), 244–258.

Carney, M., Gedajlovic, E., & Strike, V. (2014). Dead money: Inheritance law and the longevity of family firms. *Entrepreneurship Theory and Practice*, 38(6), 1261–1283.

Carney, M., & Nason, R. S. (2018). Family business and the 1%. *Business & Society*, 57(6), 1191–1215.

Carney, R. W., & Child, T. B. (2013). Changes to the ownership and control of East Asian corporations between 1996 and 2008: The primacy of politics. *Journal of Financial Economics*, 107(2), 494–513.

Credit Suisse. (2017). *EY Family Office Guide: Pathway to Successful Family and Wealth Management*. Available at: https://coles.kennesaw.edu/familybusiness/docs/Family-Office-Guide-Pathway-to-successful-family-and-wealth-management.pdf [accessed 1 July 2022].

Credit Suisse. (2015). *Family Business Model*. Zurich, Switzerland: Credit Suisse Research Institute.

Cruz, C., Larraza-Kintana, M., Garcés-Galdeano, L., & Berrone, P. (2014). Are family firms really more socially responsible? *Entrepreneurship Theory and Practice*, 38(6), 1295–1316.

Cutlip, S. M. (1994). *The Unseen Power: Public Relations: A History*. New Jersey: Lawrence Erlbaum.

Dieleman, M., & Koning, J. (2020). Articulating values through identity work: Advancing family business ethics research. *Journal of Business Ethics*, 163(4), 675–687.

Eichenberger, E., & Johnson, J. (2013). Philanthropy: What it provides to families in business. *Tharawat Magazine*, 10, 327–330.

Feliu, N., & Botero, I. C. (2016). Philanthropy in family enterprises: A review of literature. *Family Business Review*, 29(1), 121–141.

Gautier, A., & Pache, A. C. (2015). Research on corporate philanthropy: A review and assessment. *Journal of Business Ethics*, 126(3), 343–369.

Gersick, K. E., & Feliu, N. (2014). Governing the family enterprise: Practices, performance, and research. In A. Editor & B. Editor (Eds.), *Sage Handbook of Family Business* (pp. 196–225).

Giridharadas, A. (2019). *Winners Take All: The Elite Charade of Changing the World*. London: Vintage.

Gruning, E. J., & Hunt, T. (1984). *Managing Public Relations* (6th ed.). New York: CBS College Publishing.

Harvey, C., Maclean, M., Gordon, J., & Shaw, E. (2011). Andrew Carnegie and the foundations of contemporary entrepreneurial philanthropy. *Business History*, 53(3), 425–450.

Kuusela, H. (2018). Learning to own: Cross-generational meanings of wealth and class-making in wealthy Finnish families. *Sociological Review*, 66(6), 1161–1176.

La Caixa (2020). Perfiles de filantropía personal en España https://www.caixabank.com/docs/co municacion/68433.pdf

Liket, K., & Simaens, A. (2015). Battling the devolution in the research on corporate philanthropy. *Journal of Business Ethics*, 126(2), 285–308.

Michael-Tsabari, N., Labaki, R., & Zachary, R. K. (2014). Toward the cluster model: The family firm's entrepreneurial behavior over generations. *Family Business Review*, 27(2), 161–185.

Muller, A. R., Pfarrer, M. D., & Little, L. M. (2014). A theory of collective empathy in corporate philanthropy decisions. *Academy of Management Review*, 39(1), 1–21.

Payne, G. T. (2020). Family Business Review in 2020: Focus on the family. *Family Business Review*, 33(1),6–9.

Porter, M. E., & Kramer, M. R. (1999). Philanthropy's new agenda: Creating value. *Harvard Business Review*, 77, 121–131.

Qiu, H., & Freel, M. (2020). Managing family-related conflicts in family businesses: A review and research agenda. *Family Business Review*, 33(1), 90–113.

Rey-García, M., & Puig-Raposo, N. (2013). Globalisation and the organization of family philanthropy: A case of isomorphism?. *Business History*, 55(6), 1019–1046.

Rivo-López, E., Villanueva-Villar, M., Michinel-Álvarez, M., & Reyes-Santías, F. (2021). Corporate social responsibility and family business in the time of COVID-19: Changing strategy? *Sustainability*, 13(4), 2041–2053.

Rivo-López, E., Villanueva-Villar, M., Suárez-Blázquez, G., & Reyes-Santías, F. (2021). How does a business family manage its wealth? A family office perspective. *Journal of Family Business Management*, 11(4), 496–511.

Rivo-López, E., Villanueva-Villar, M., Vaquero-García, A., & Lago-Peñas, S. (2017). Family offices: What, why and what for? *Organizational Dynamics*, 46(4), 262–270.

Rovner, M., Loeb, P., & Vogel, G. (2013). *The Next Generation of American Giving: The Charitable Habits of Generations Y, X, Baby Boomers, and Matures.* Charleston, SC: Blackbaud, Inc.

Schickinger, A., Leitterstorf, M. P., & Kammerlander, N. (2018). Private equity and family firms: A systematic review and categorization of the field. *Journal of Family Business Strategy*, 9(4), 268–292.

Schuyt, T. (2013). *Philanthropy and the philanthropy sector: An introduction.* Farnham, England: Ashgate.

Schwass, J., & Lief, C. (2008). About family, business and philanthropy. *Perspectives for managers*, (165), 1–4.

Sulek, M. (2010). On the modern meaning of philanthropy. *Nonprofit and Voluntary Sector Quarterly*, 39(2), 193–212.

Vazquez, P., & Rocha, H. (2018). On the goals of family firms: A review and integration. *Journal of Family Business Strategy*, 9(2), 94–106.

Ward, J. L. (2009). The ten hidden arts of successful business families. *Family Business*, 20(4), 49–52.

Wessel, S., Decker, C., Lange, K. S. G., & Hack, A. (2014). One size does not fit all: Entrepreneurial families' reliance on family offices. *European Management Journal*, 32(1),37–45. https://doi.org/10.1016/j.emj.2013.08.003

Zellweger, T., & Kammerlander, N. (2015). Family, Wealth, and Governance: An Agency Account. *Entrepreneurship Theory and Practice*, 39(6),1281–1303.

Change Walmart (2021). www.changewalmart.org Retrieved March 26, 2021.

Forbes (2021). www.forbes.com/billionaires/ Retrieved March 1, 2021.

Giving Pledge (2010). www.givingpledge.org Retrieved February 12, 2021.

Inditex (2021). www.inditex.com Retrieved January 18, 2021.

KIRBI (2021). www.kirkbi.com Retrieved January 25, 2021.

LEGO Foundation (2021). www.legofoundation.com Retrieved January 28, 2021.

LEGO Group (2021). www.lego.com Retrieved January 23, 2021.

Walmart (2021). https://walmart.org Retrieved March 3, 2021.

Walton Family Foundation (2021). www.waltonfamilyfoundation.org Retrieved March 12, 2021.

Roy Suddaby, Peter Jaskiewicz, Trevor Israelsen,
and Ravee Chittoor

22 Traditional Authority in Social Context: Explaining the Relation between Types of Family and Types of Family-Controlled Business Groups

Abstract: The existence of family-controlled business groups challenges assumptions of rational economic behaviour in a corporation. These organizations embrace unrelated diversification, appoint executives based on lineage rather than expertise, and engage in non-arms length transactions between firms in the family group that are often not based on market pricing. Despite contradicting well-established best practices of corporate behaviour, family-controlled business groups are successful and represent a growing proportion of global commerce. We lack an overarching theoretical explanation for the success of family-controlled business groups. This chapter offers a theoretical framework that explains the success and geographical variation of these unique organizational forms. Our core argument is that variations in the governance structure of FCBGs reflect variation in the manifestation of family authority globally. In the west, where FCBGs are quite rare, so too is the hierarchical authority structure of the traditional extended family. As a result, the success of FCBGs outside the US, Canada, and the UK occurs because of two factors: the legitimacy of the extended family and its prevailing governance structure premised on patriarchal authority, and the explosive growth in population in those countries that embrace the extended family.

Keywords: authority, family-controlled business groups, organizational forms, governance structure, patriarchal authority

Introduction

Management theorists have struggled to explain the paradoxical success of family-controlled business groups (FCBGs), an organizational form that is quite rare in the US, Canada, or the UK, but serves as the dominant organizational form in much of the rest of the world (Khanna & Yafeh, 2007; La Porta et al., 1999; Morck & Yeung, 2003; *The Economist*, 2015). FCBGs are a subset of business groups comprised of

Roy Suddaby, University of Victoria and Washington State University
Peter Jaskiewicz, University of Ottawa
Trevor Israelsen, Ravee Chittoor, University of Victoria

https://doi.org/10.1515/9783110727968-022

collections of firms that are legally independent from each other but are economically interdependent because of pre-existing social ties that, in the case of FCBGs, originate from formal familial connections (Barca & Becht, 2002; Claessens et al., 2000; Morck, 2009).

FCBGs defy many of the normal governance practices of Anglo-American corporations; they engage in unrelated diversification (Gopal, Manikandan, & Ramachandran, 2021), appoint executives because of lineage rather than expertise (Bellow, 2004; Chen, Chittoor, & Vissa, 2021), and engage in non-arms length transactions between firms in the family group that are often not based on market pricing (Fisman & Wang, 2010). Each of these practices challenges assumptions of rational economic behaviour in a corporation. If these practices were to occur in an Anglo-American publicly traded corporation, they would immediately trigger a reaction from shareholders, auditors and the board of directors as signals of failure of governance structures to manage agency relationships between the managers and the owners.

Yet despite contradicting the best practices of corporate strategy and governance in the US, Canada, and the UK, FCBGs are not only common, they are uncommonly successful, particularly in emerging markets (Khanna & Yafeh, 2007; Carney, 2005; Chittoor, Kale, & Puranam, 2015). As a result, the number of family-controlled businesses is growing rapidly, particularly in Asia (*The Economist,* 2015; Woolridge, 2015). Although the empirical evidence is complex and mixed, there is an emerging consensus that FCBGs outperform traditional corporations (Mazzi, 2011; Le Breton-Miller & Miller, 2006; Carney, 2005; Chittoor, Kale, & Puranam, 2015). While the consensus is not unanimous (Morck & Yeung, 2003), a variety of factors have been offered to explain why FCBGs succeed despite their failure to adopt Anglo-American practices of corporate governance. These factors include the high level of public trust in family-controlled businesses globally (Deephouse & Jaskiewicz, 2013); a more "strategic" approach to diversification (Carney & Gedajlovic, 2002; Gomez-Mejia, Marki, & Kintana, 2010; Gopal, Manikandan, & Ramachandran, 2021); an ability to adopt a longer time horizon (Sirmon & Hitt, 2003; Lumpkin, Brigham, & Moss, 2010); a unique capacity of the family to exert control over firm resources (Carney, 2005); and a capacity to balance tradition and change (Erdogan et al., 2020; Suddaby & Jaskiewicz, 2020).

While compelling, these factors offer somewhat ad hoc contingencies that explain the success of some FCBGs, but not all. More critically, they fail to account for the relatively consistent variation of types of FCBGs – for example, *grupos economicos* in Latin America, *chaebols* in Korea, or *guanxi qiye* in Taiwan – whose organizational characteristics vary across different country and cultural contexts. The uniqueness of FCBGs and the incredible variation in form is theoretically interesting because they represent a hybrid form of organizing somewhere between markets and hierarchies (Williamson, 1975). As such, their existence and growing popularity challenges western economic assumptions about the boundary between firms and markets. We lack an overarching theoretical narrative that can explain the ubiquity and heterogeneity of FCBGs that goes beyond assumptions that they are a "socially destructive" precursor to the publicly traded corporation (Morck & Yeung, 2003).

We propose an explanatory theoretical narrative in this chapter. Our core argument is that variations in the governance structure of FCBGs reflect variation in the manifestation of family authority globally. In the west, where FCBGs are quite rare, so too is the patriarchal authority structure of the traditional extended family. As a result, the success of FCBGs outside the US, Canada, and the UK is determined by two factors. The first is the legitimacy of patriarchal family authority in Asia, South America, and some parts of Europe where extended families predominate and family-controlled corporations and business groups are abundant. By contrast, the legitimacy of rational-legal authority is common in the US, Canada, UK, and parts of Western Europe where nuclear families and publicly controlled corporations predominate. The second factor is the dramatic difference in population growth in those parts of the world where patriarchal authority structures remain dominant and the reciprocal stagnation or decline in population growth in those parts of the world where more rational-legal authority structures are dominant. FCBG's, thus, thrive in contexts where patriarchal, extended families are the norm.

We adopt a configurational view that assesses the degree of fit between different types of authority in FCBGs and the prevailing value structure of the country from which a business group originated. We draw from German sociologist Max Weber's description of three types of legitimate authority: rational-legal, traditional, and charismatic. Most research on business groups implicitly assumes the primacy of rational-legal authority, which is the dominant form of authority in modern corporations. However, we observe that many FCBGs structure their governance practices on traditional or charismatic forms of authority (see, e.g., Carney, 2005), implying fundamentally different approaches to internal governance of FCBGs that call for more holistic theory development across countries.

One reason for the prevalence of different approaches to the internal governance of FCBGs across countries lies in cultural variation. Many scholars have rightfully criticized that management theories commonly used to study family businesses blatantly ignore the culture in which businesses are embedded. This omission is particularly precarious considering that families are shaped by the values of their culture and, as a result thereof, families and their businesses vary starkly across cultures (Hofstede, 2001; Jaskiewicz et al., 2021). To fill this pertinent void in our knowledge, we embed the type of legitimate authority in its particular cultural context by drawing from Inglehart's (2006) observation that global value systems map into two dimensions of cross-cultural variation; the traditional/secular dimension, and the survival/self expression dimension. Combining these two typologies, one of which captures the variation in internal governance practices while the other captures variation in cultural context, we create a configurational model that describes the relationship between cultural context, authority type, and organizational form, offering a framework to understand the prevalence and variation of different types of FCBGs worldwide.

We present our argument as follows: the next section describes the basic similarities and differences in FCBGs, why they are important, and how they cluster geographically. The subsequent section describes the three basic authority types and explains how each authority type maps onto different categories of FCBGs. Then, we describe two dimensions by which values cluster across different cultures. After describing the main family types in the subsequent section, we present our configurational model of FCBGs that shows how prevailing cultural assumptions of legitimate authority in different countries influences the prevalent type of family and FCBG most appropriate to that country. We then introduce four moderators that might help explain variation in the family type-FCBG type relationship within countries. In the next section on future trends, we briefly explore two effects that are likely to shape the prevalence and impact of particular types of FCBGs in the years to come. We conclude our chapter with a brief summary and a discussion of implications for the future study of FCBGs.

Family-Controlled Business Groups: Variations in Types

FCBGs have been prominent but relatively invisible component of the economies of developing countries for some time now. Recently, however, they have attracted attention in western media because of their growing capacity to compete with, and occasionally acquire large, publicly traded corporations in developed countries. The 2007 acquisition of the Dutch-UK steel manufacturer, Corus Group by Tata Steel, which is part of the highly successful Indian multi-national Tata Group, is one such example. Tata Group is a family-controlled business conglomerate consisting of 28 subsidiaries and over 80 operating businesses, all organized under the umbrella of its main holding company Tata Sons Limited, which itself is controlled by family trusts (Thomsen, 2011).

FCBGs are a subset of a larger category of business groups, loosely defined as "a collection of firms bound together in some formal and/or informal ways" (Granovetter, 1994, p. 454). A more precise definition of business groups is offered by Yiu, Bruton, and Lu (2005, p. 183) as "a collection of legally independent firms that are bound by economic (such as ownership, financial, and commercial) and social (such as family, kinship and friendship) ties". Our focus is on those firms that are economically integrated based on family or kinship ties. FCBGs are those in which "an individual or family are involved in the ownership, control, and management of the business group" in which "there is no separation of the roles" (Cuervo-Cazurra, 2006, p. 6).

There is considerable variation in how FCBGs are organized. In Korea, business groups are termed *chaebols* in which the family owns a majority interest in a parent company, and member firms, often led by family members, create a vertically linked network to transfer inputs and outputs between the member firms (Chang & Hong, 2000). Business houses in India tend to form as a densely structured network of cross-ownership by all family members (Khanna & Rivkin, 2001). There are related organizational and family relational differences that define *grupos economicos* in Latin America, *family holdings* in Turkey, and *guanxi qiye* in Taiwan. Perhaps unsurprisingly, scholars have struggled to organize them in one typology and, instead focused on rich descriptions of prominent FCBGs. Despite very valuable insights into the development of particular FCBGs, this approach has prevented efforts to develop theory on FCBGs *across* countries.

Fortunately, we do not need to start from scratch. Yiu and colleagues (2007) impose some conceptual order on the variations in corporate structure and social relations that define these business groups in a typology based on two dimensions – horizontal connectedness and vertical linkage. Horizontal connectedness focuses on the degree of interdependence between firms in strategic decision-making. Vertical control refers to the strength of control exercised by the parent firm or core owner elite and the affiliate firms in the business group. Based on these two dimensions, Yiu et al. (2005) identify four types of business groups: network form, club form, holding form, and multidivisional form.

While Yiu et al. (2007) do not explicitly theorize the role of family or kinship relations in each of these types, they do describe differences in the role of social relations between executives in each type. They also identify the country or cultural context in which each type is most likely to appear. Based on this, we can easily infer the dominant type of authority structure for each type when family ownership is the primary basis of the business group. We briefly elaborate each of the four types below and summarize their characteristics in Figure 22.1, which adapts the Yiu et al. (2007) typology to the context of FCBGs.

Network Form

This form is a linked group of firms that act as a horizontally integrated business group in which the parent firm concentrates in a single industry while the affiliate firms provide resources, intermediate products and related inputs to the parent firm. The network form operates as "a set of legally separate firms with stable relationships that operate in multiple strategically unrelated activities and under common ownership and control" (Cuervo-Cazurra, 2006, p. 420). The economic controls occur through fixed cost prices determined by the parent firm while legal integration arises through both board interlocks and cross ownership. Kinship relations between the executives and owners are the foundation of the network form and of the strategic alliances between affiliated firms. The *guanxi quiye* form of FCBGs common in Taiwan exemplifies the network form, although this form also appears

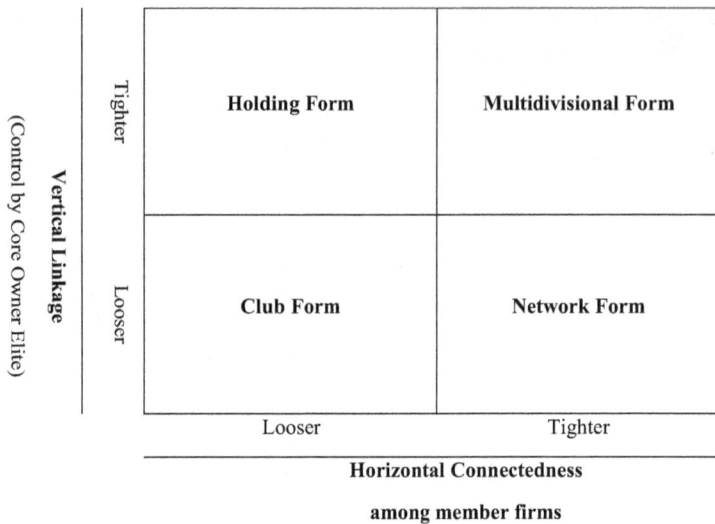

Figure 22.1: A typology of business group structural configurations.
Source: Based on Yiu, Lu, Burton, and Hoskisson (2007).

in discrete industries in the west, such as the fashion industry in Italy (Della Piana, Vecchi, & Cacia, 2012).

Club Form

The club form is a more densely connected network of firms in which each family member controls a cluster of firms comprised of both a parent and affiliate firms. The clusters are integrated horizontally into large conglomerate business groups that can share the costs of common activities, such as marketing, accounting, etc. The kinship ties and norms of seniority among kin ensure strong links and clear hierarchies across clusters. Because of their collective size, club form groups exert both market and political power. Japanese *zaibatsus* of the early 20th century, and their enduring legacy in contemporary family-controlled Japanese business groups (e.g., Nakamura, 2002), exemplify this form of organization.

Holding Form

Holding form business groups are typically composed of a parent holding company that has controlling shares in otherwise independent affiliate corporations. Family owners typically dominate the holding company but are removed from involvement in the operating companies. In so doing, the holding form fuels family control but prevents (ineffective) family leadership. The affiliates act like subsidiaries of the parent, but are less vertically and horizontally integrated with the core business of the parent firm. As a result, the Holding Form tends to be highly diversified, as exemplified by *business houses* such as the Tata Group or other pyramidal enterprises in India.

Multidivisional Form

Some FCBGs appear nearly identical to multidivisional corporations, but build connections between organizations through directors or executives that share a family connection. So, for example, FCBGs in the shipping industry tend to mimic most aspects of traditional multi-national corporations but, instead of cultivating board interlocks by having the same individual on multiple boards, they use board members who share a familial relationship (Andrikopoulos, Georgakopoulos, Merika, & Merikas, 2019). Like the multidivisional corporation, the multidivisional business group forms around a parent company that acts as the headquarters of several distinct business lines, which are populated by affiliate firms that, economically, are vertically integrated with the parent, and socially, cultivate board interlocks based on familial relations (Lester & Canella, 2006). Korean chaebols exemplify this business group form.

While the Yui et al. (2007) typology captures the essential differences between these configurations of business groups and accurately identifies their cultural and geographic variation, they do not explain why these configurations exist. That is, they do not elaborate how the differences in cultural context influence or determine the choice of business group form. *Our thesis is that the different configurations, identified in the* Yiu et al. (2007) *typology, are based on subtle but significant differences in how traditional authority is institutionalized within the family in different country and cultural contexts.*

In the balance of this paper, we theorize how the observed differences in FCBG types are based on differences in legitimate authority within each of these forms. Variation in authority, in turn, arises from prevailing values in the cultural contexts within which each of these forms predominantly occur. We elaborate our configurational model of family-controlled business groups in the next section.

Authority: Rational-legal versus Traditional

German sociologist Max Weber identified three types of legitimate authority in social entities – rational-legal, traditional, and charismatic.[1] Most organizational

---

1 Charismatic authority is a construct that operates more at the individual level and has been typically theorized as a form of individual leadership (Tucker, 1968). As such, it is less relevant for our

research has focused on rational-legal forms of authority, where an individual in an organization gains power, not from their personal attributes, as in charismatic authority, but, rather from a set of formal rules that define the role or office and establish its authority in the legal structure of the organization. Individuals gain access to these roles, not by virtue of their relationships to other high-ranking individuals, as in traditional authority, but instead by virtue of their merit or qualifications matched against formal criteria for the position.

Rational-legal authority is most closely associated with bureaucratic forms of organization, which Weber argued was a form of organizing superior to all others because of its machine-like efficiency. The assumed superiority of the bureaucracy, according to Weber, derives from the rigorous and scientific decision-making capacity of the rational-legal form of authority, which survives today in the governance structure of the modern corporation. So confident was Weber in the superiority of rational-legal modes of organizational governance that he predicted an inexorable shift, over time, from traditional or charismatic forms of authority to bureaucratic organizations and their more competitively efficient rational-legal governance.

The legitimate form of authority in families, Weber observed, is custom or tradition, as exemplified by the monarchy. The source of traditional authority arises from fealty to the patriarch or clan leader whose authority, in turn, will ultimately be transferred to one of the leaders' children according to long-standing customs of succession. Kinship relations, determined largely by genetic proximity to the monarch, provide the logic for the structure of authority within an organization. Subordinates show fealty to the new leader out of tradition. Historically, traditional authority has been the dominant form of political governance in society and in associated forms of social and economic organization (Beckert, 2018; Bellow, 2004).

The stubborn persistence of family businesses and the international proliferation of FCBGs offer a serious challenge to Weber's assumption that rational-legal authority and the corporate form of organization offer a superior model of economic governance and organization. There is, for example, considerable evidence of a decline in the influence of the publicly traded corporation (Kahle & Stulz, 2017; Davis, 2016; Martin, 2021). The number of publicly traded companies in the US declined by half between 1997 and 2012, the number of initial public offerings (IPOs) declined severely after 2000, and the number of workers employed by large US corporations has fallen dramatically in the last two decades (Davis, 2016). By contrast, recent estimates indicate that family businesses contribute 54% of the private GDP ($7.7 trillion) and employ 59% of the private workforce (83.3 million individuals) in the US (Pieper, Kellermanns, & Astrachan, 2021). Although representative numbers on the total number and impact of FCBGs in and beyond the US are missing, data on the most

---

conversation, which focuses on how different authority structures determine different modes of organizational governance.

prominent FCBGs in various countries provide important insights. For instance, in Europe, the Agnelli's family business group controls 10.4% of the Italian stock market, and the Wallenberg's family business group controls 43% of the Swedish stock market (Agnblad et al., 2001; Claessens, Djankov, & Lang, 2000; La Porta et al., 1999). In Asia, the most prominent 15 families in Hong Kong, Malaysia, Singapore, and the Philippines, respectively, hold in their business groups assets worth 84%, 76%, 47%, and 46% of GDP (Claessens et al., 2000; *The Economist*, 2015).[2]

Clearly, Weber's prediction of the inexorable domination of rational-legal authority is not accurate. How do we explain both the persistent strength and geographic variation of FCBGs? According to Guillen (2000), three main theories explain the success and persistence of FCBGs: they succeed where market imperfections occur; in vertical or patrimonial societies; or in highly autocratic states. The problem with each of these theories is that they implicitly assume the inherent superiority of US markets, as represented by multi-national corporations, and suggest that FCBGs only succeed in emerging or centrally planned economies. There is an implicit form of orientalism (Said, 1978) in prevailing assumptions that FCBGs are inferior to western models of organization.

Moreover, the recent success of FCBGs, such as Tata, in expanding their operations to developed economies raise serious questions about the accuracy of these assumptions. And Tata is not an exception. McKinsey estimates that 4,000 new family and founder businesses will reach annual sales of US$1 billion between 2015 and 2025. Many of these businesses will be FCBGs from Asia. Not surprisingly, the share of family businesses among the largest global companies is expected to rise from 15% to 40% over the next years (*The Economist,* 2015), providing another indication of the expected rise of family-controlled businesses groups. Although researchers have paid some attention to the rise of FCBGs in Asia, perhaps more egregiously, existing theoretical models overlook the success and persistence of FCBGs in established economies, such as France, Italy, and Scandinavia. Most critically, none of the existing theories can explain the broad variation in types of family-business groups.

We adopt a configurational perspective to offer a more nuanced explanation of the variation and persistence of FCBGs. To do this, we look to different combinations in *social values* across cultures and the degree of fit between given values and

---

2 The data support the continued relevance of family businesses and the decline of the public corporation. However, the data do not show that the public corporation is substituted by corporate structured based on traditional authority. Future research will need to determine whether fewer public corporations translate into a higher prevalence of family business structures (based on traditional authority) or more private equity and venture capital organizations (based on hyper legal-rational authority). Despite the decline of the public corporation, we do expect that the Weberian rationale of formal-legal authority will remain prevalent – possibly, though, in different forms than the public corporation (e.g., VCs).

different manifestations of traditional authority in families. Accordingly, we must describe our current understanding of global value systems that describe culture and its variation across countries.

Mapping Global Value Systems

As the first human institution (Castells, 1997; Bau & Fernandez, 2021), families are the primary societal unit through which societal values are shared and passed on to new generations. Although families differ in the values they transmit to offspring, sociologists observe that some values permeate particular historical-cultural context of most countries. Understanding families and their pertinent differences across countries therefore necessitate the mapping of stable societal values. In his comprehensive study of global values, Inglehart (2006) observes that national value systems are subject to two dominant historical shifts in social values. The first, triggered by the Industrial Revolution, is the shift from traditional values (religion, respect for authority, etc.) to secular-rational values (science, respect for expertise, etc.). The second, driven by intergenerational and geographical differences in prosperity following the Second World War, is the shift from achieving economic and physical security (i.e., concern with satisfying basic human needs) to the pursuit of self-expression, subjective wellbeing and quality of life (i.e., concern with satisfying higher order human needs).

Using data from longitudinal global survey research (i.e., the World Values Survey) beginning in 1981, Inglehart observes significant stability in the underlying values and beliefs of countries around the world. Factor analyses of this massive data set validated these two dimensions, which explain 71% of the cross-cultural variation in social value dispositions of respondents. When organized in a matrix, with the vertical dimension reflecting the traditional/secular dimension and the horizontal axis representing the survival self-expression dimension, the resultant two-by-two matrix describes four distinct clusters of countries based on differences in shared social values (see Figure 22.2). As Inglehart (2000, p. 123) observes the global map reflects both the social, religious, and cultural history of each country as distorted by economic development since the Second World War and the residual influence of each countries' political history (i.e., Communism, Socialism, Capitalism, Totalitarianism).

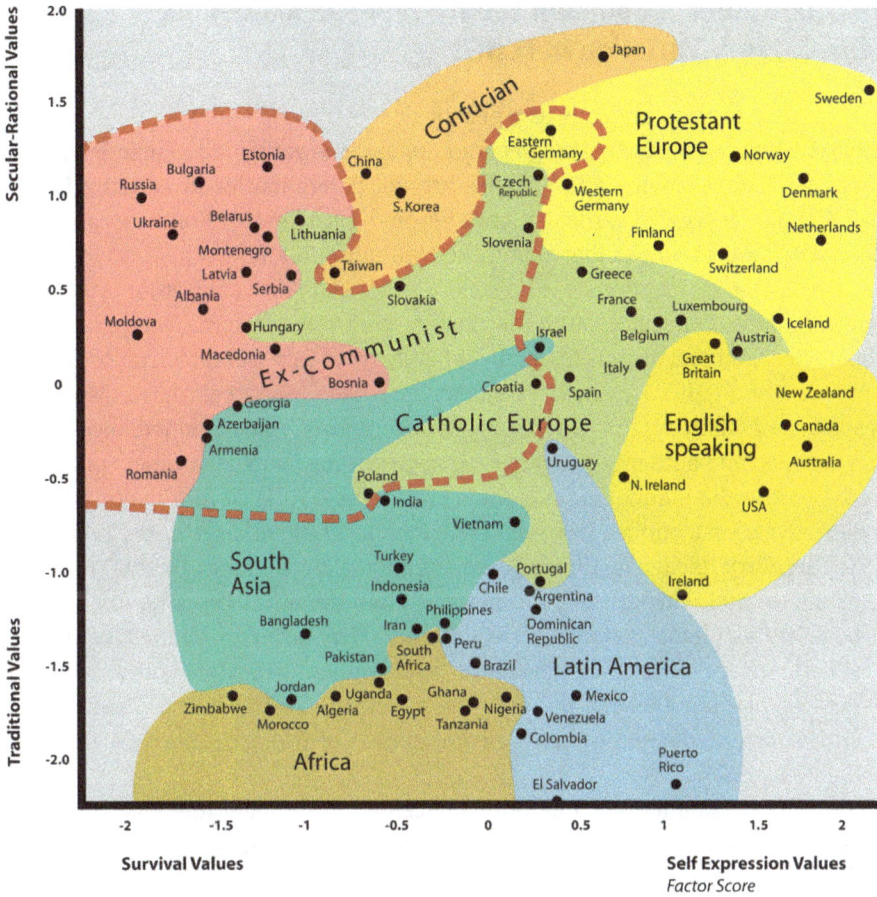

Figure 22.2: Cultural map of the world in 2000.
Source: Inglehart (2000, p. 122).

Global Values, Different Family Structures and FCBGs

In this section and the next one, we explain how different assumptions of authority, drawn from prevailing cultural values distinguish family types and help explain variation in FCBGs.

The Limitations of Common Family Types in Explaining Cross-Country Variation in FCBGs

While we tend to think of family as a genetically determined system of organization, sociologists and anthropologists agree that the extreme variation in family organization suggests that biology and genetics are not determinative in defining family types. Anthropologists, in particular, have devoted considerable effort to constructing typologies and taxonomies that capture the variation in family organization. Apart from some notable exceptions (see Boisot & Child, 1996; Fukayama, 2014; Jaskiewicz, Combs, Shanine, & Kacmar, 2016) few management scholars have incorporated anthropological and sociological research on family types into their theorization of family business and FCBGs. A variety of factors have been used to establish the critical dimensions of family types including the lineage system, rules of inheritance, living arrangements, and authority structures. Lineage systems draw on a variety of family-based factors, which might explain their prominence. At least four major types of families have been identified (Segalen, 1978; Parkin, 1997; Parkin & Stone, 2004)

1. **Segmentary** lineage families are descent groups divided into generational segments each of which, itself, is a descent group (Smith, 1956). The lineage can be patrilineal (most common) or matrilineal. They also vary by the type of possible marriage, that is, monogamous or polygamous (Levine, 2008). Segmentary lineage families can be relatively small or very large, encompassing an entire society, depending on the combination of marriage and descent rules (Sahlins, 1961).

2. **Clan** lineage families are a unilineal descent group, similar to segmentary lineage families, but one in which members do not necessarily trace their genealogy to a founding ancestor. Rather, the authority in the group is derived from a father or mother. Clans also identify lineage to mythical ancestors, including animals that occupy a sacred status with the group. They may be nested into larger clans, similar to segmentary families, in larger groupings termed the phratry, which is, itself, a type of clan.

3. **House societies** are family structures based primarily on living arrangements rather than descent lines. Claude Lévi-Strauss (1987) first identified house societies as a distinct category of family structure. He observed that, while some members may be related, genealogy is not a determinative factor. Rather, membership arises from a number of factors including marriage patterns, exchange relations, co-residence and shared labor. Because house societies display simultaneous patrimonial and matrimonial elements of lineage, Lévi-Strauss referred to this family structure as a form of "corporate" kinship (Gonzáles-Rubal, 2006).

4. **Grand Families** are forms of extended family structures that were first identified in China but also appear in parts of India where they are sometimes referred to as "joint families" (Lang, 1946). These are large, multi-generational

families living in a common household. They are typically patrilineal, but not necessarily so. Authority structures can be quite fluid, consistent with Confucian philosophy, where patriarchs and matriarchs cede authority as they age. Similarly, inheritance rules are particularly rigid and may be determined by need, expertise, or related contingencies. Grand-family structures are common in Mexico (Lomnitz, 2013), Korea and parts of China (Ebrey, 2003; Smith, 1992), and in several North American Indigenous communities (Cross & Day, 2008).

Although these types of family structures seem to be quite stable over time, the typology suffers from two important weaknesses. First, the critical dimensions or factors that define each type are not consistent across the four types. This issue arises, in part, because the factors are empirically rather than theoretically determined. For example, genealogy defines some but not all types. Second, there is substantial overlap between some types. For example, one can recognize elements of clan structure in each of the other family types. This issue is likely a consequence of the first concern – that is, that the types are empirically derived and thus lack the abstract precision of ideal types, which are informed by empirics but based on dimensions that are theoretically derived.

A Family Typology that Explains Cross-Country Variation in FCBGs

Fortunately, Emmanuel Todd (1985) has created a typology based on anthropological and sociological data that overcomes the limitations of prior typologies by using two theoretical dimensions that capture much of the prior empirical research on families. These dimensions draw from the two core social values of the French revolution: *liberté* and *égalité* (LePlay, 1895). Liberty refers to the degree of autonomy given by parents to children. If children continue to live under one roof with their parents, even after getting married, their liberty is constrained. Arranged marriages, marriages of strategic convenience or with economic ends in mind also indicate a lack of liberty in family structure. Equality is determined by the treatment of children by their parents. In the case of *primo geniture* (i.e., the eldest son becomes the designated successor at birth), the family is unequal. To provide another example, if all children in a family tend to receive equal distributions of parental wealth, the family structure is relatively equal. If, however, inheritance rules concentrate parental wealth in a single child, the family structure is not egalitarian.

When set in contrast to each other, liberty and equality describe a typology of four types of family (see Figure 22.3, adapted from Gutmann & Voigt, 2020): authoritarian family, absolute nuclear family, egalitarian nuclear family, and community family. Todd (1985), however, separated the community family type into two distinct categories based on whether they allow intermarriage within the family (endogamous) or prohibited the practice (exogamous). Todd (1985) also observed that these family types tend to occur in distinct geographic clusters, consistent with Inglehart's (1988, 1990) observation about the geographical stickiness of social value clusters. We briefly elaborate each of these family types and extend Todd's typology by describing how each one reflects a unique combination and emphasis of rational-legal and traditional modes of authority.

		Liberty	
		Low: *Married son stays with parents*	**High:** *Married son moves out*
Equality	*Low:* *Unequal treatment of brothers*	Authoritarian (e.g. Norway, Sweden, Germany, Ireland)	Absolute nuclear (e.g. UK, Canada, USA)
	High: *Equal Treatment of Brothers*	Endogamous community (e.g. India, Pakistan, Morocco)	Exogamous community (e.g. Russia, Mongolia, China)	Egalitarian nuclear (e.g. Spain, Italy, Poland)

Figure 22.3: Schematic representation of Todd's (1985) family types.
*Source: Based on:*Gutmann and Voigt (2022, p. 102).

Absolute Nuclear Family

The absolute nuclear family is a family group consisting of a man and a woman and their dependant children. The degree of liberty in the absolute nuclear family is high. Children have considerable autonomy and choice in whom they marry and, when they do, they do not cohabit with their parents. The degree of equality, however, is relatively low. Nuclear families divide property differentially depending on gender and/or birth order, typically. This type of family is the dominant social unit in the US, UK, Canada, and Australia.

It is unsurprising that countries in which the absolute nuclear family is most prevalent are also contexts in which the corporate form is the dominant institution for organizing economic activity among larger organizations. While these countries are highly supportive of progressive values of self-expression, their adoption of secular-rational values is moderated by a preference for more traditional assumptions of social hierarchy within the family that result in the unequal treatment of children with respect to the division of labour in the household across genders and division of property upon parents' death.

Egalitarian Nuclear Family

This type of family shares the attributes of liberty with the absolute nuclear family described above. However, they are more equitable in their treatment of children, particularly with respect to the division of property on death and the division of labor across genders. This type of family is the dominant social unit in Spain, Brazil, Poland, and parts of France. The egalitarian nuclear family is perhaps the ultimate expression of rational-legal authority combined with self-expression values. In combination, these dimensions describe organizational corporate form that is market-focused on logic, but communitarian in ethos, thus never quite achieves the hierarchical structure of the prototypical modern corporation.

Authoritarian Family

This family structure is low on the liberty dimension. Married heirs tend to cohabit with or next to parents, and parents may exercise considerable control in the selection of children's spouses. Authoritarian families are also low on the equality dimension. Family property is distributed unequally as are work responsibilities in the household and the business. This type of family structure is most common to Japan, Germany, South Korea, Norway, and Ireland. Importantly, although many of these countries now share more egalitarian and liberal values, the authoritarian family still prevails and trumps such societal values (Duranton, Rodríguez-Pose, & Sandall, 2009).

Endogamous Community Family

This family unit is characterized by high equality and low liberty. Married heirs tend to cohabit with parents and parents exercise high control over the selection of spouses for their children. Marriage within the family (i.e., between cousins) is acceptable. However, property is inherited equally, and family roles are shared based on expertise rather than family position. This family structure is most common in Pakistan, India, and Northern Africa (Rijpma, & Carmichael, 2016; Todd, 1985).

Exogamous Community Family

This family unit is high in equality but only moderate in terms of liberty. Married children will typically cohabit with parents, but marriage within the family is not appropriate. Property is distributed equitably, and work is based on capabilities rather than gender or birth order. The resultant family structure tends towards large, extended families. This structure is most common in China, Mongolia, and Russia (Duranton et al., 2009).

Family Types and FCBGs: Filling in the Missing Links

Our core thesis is that variation in the authority structure of the family is a major determinant of the prevailing form of FCBG in a society. The family types are defined by the authority structure of the family that, in turn, is founded on historically determined and deeply embedded beliefs and values of that culture that are taken-for-granted and extremely stable over time. Todd (1990) argues that, as an institution, family types are more stable than other institutional structures and suggests that while changes in economic institutions can occur within 50 years, changes in educational institutions take 500 years, and significant changes in family structures may take as much as 5,000 years.

Family types, thus, serve as a useful proxy for constellations of relatively permanent societal values. Because the family serves as the first experience individuals have with a social structure, they tend to serve as a template, or a micro-foundation of other, more complex social structures in society that become internalized in youth and reproduced in large social structures as adults. Considerable empirical research supports the argument that family types are an important determinant of other institutional structures in a society including political ideology (Reher, 1998), legal structure (Licht et al., 2007; Berggren & Bjørnskov, 2011; Gutmann & Voigt, 2018), and the character of civil society and social development (Guttman & Voigt, 2021). We extend this line of reasoning in this chapter to argue and demonstrate that family types also exhibit profound influence over the dominant form of organizing economic production in a given society. Our summary theoretical model is presented in Figure 22.4.

A cursory examination of Inglehart and Welzel's (2005) map of global values suggests that not only do the quadrants reflect distinct clusters of global social values, but they also offer *prima facie* evidence in support of our core thesis. First, the US, UK, and Canada tend to cluster quite closely together in the upper right corner of the lower right quadrant, which is defined as being high in self-expression, but on the border between low and high in terms of traditional and secular rational values. In line with this observation, the absolute nuclear family predominates (Duranton et al., 2009; Rijpma, & Carmichael, 2016). Because of the small size of this type of family coupled with the weak authority of parents over their adult children, families lack the size and transgenerational authority to control FCBGs. Moreover, there might be little need for developing FCBGs in the first place. Due to high trust in strangers and the efficacy of formal institutions (such as the legal system), family members do not need to rely on a limited number of kin (Jaskiewicz et al., 2021).

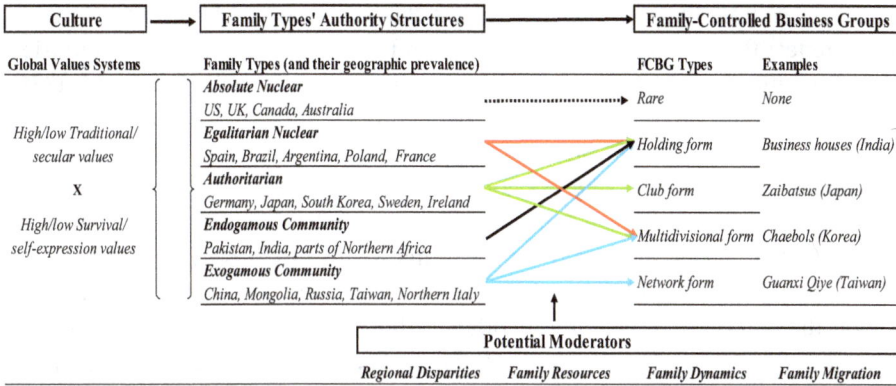

Figure 22.4: Comprehensive summary diagram.

Instead, they often sell their family business when approaching retirement, which helps to explain the prevalence of the widely held corporate form of organization in these countries.

More interesting, perhaps, is that each of the four family types tends to be prominent in the countries clustered in one of the four quadrants of Inglehart and Wetzel's two-by-two of global value systems. We theorize that the predominant family type helps explain the prevalence of particular FCBG types in countries. This is because family characteristics such as parental authority and family-based human capital, are manifest differently in different cultural settings. And parental authority over the next generation (Jaskiewicz et al., 2016) is, we suggest, often necessary to start, build, and control a large FCBG over time. Moreover, the size of the family and the scope of family-based human capital inherent in the family is essential to understand the predominance of particular types of FCBGs (Sirmon & Hitt, 2003). Thus, culturally situated family characteristics represent necessary (though not sufficient) conditions for the formation of successful FCBGs.

Russia, China, and Taiwan reflect the intersection of secular-rational values and survival values. In these countries, the exogamous community family type tends to predominate. Characterized by the equal treatment of sons (e.g., co-parcenary in China [Chau, 1991]) and parental authority over adult children (who stay in their parents' home after marriage), the exogamous community type offers the opportunity to integrate new human capital into the family (through marriage) and retain control of the growing family (Rijpma & Carmichael, 2016). The ability to grow and maintain control of family members helps explain why this family type is consistent with the empirical observations about where N-form FCBGs are most likely to thrive (Yui et al., 2007). The N-form requires trust and control among a significant group of family members; each leads another business within the FCBG. The exogamous community family type enables extended families coupled with traditional and transgenerational authority structures.

Next, we note that cultural regions like Pakistan, parts of India, and Northern Africa reflect the intersection of traditional and survival values. In these countries, the community family type predominates (Rijpma & Carmichael, 2016; Todd, 1985). This type combines the parental authority of adult children with equal treatment of male sons. However, these countries' high traditional values and inherent distrust in strangers help explain why the community family is endogamous. In endogamous families, it is accepted, and in some cases even encouraged, that cousins marry. These families can strengthen their inter-family ties through cousin marriage but fail to rejuvenate and grow with talented in-laws outside the family. Taken together, the endogamous community offers stable family size and transgenerational control of family members, which is consistent with empirical observations as to where H-form business groups are likely to prosper (Yui et al., 2007). The H-form commonly involves some family members in an umbrella holding company but does not require additional family members in the various affiliated operating companies. The limitations of the endogamous family in terms of their size might help explain why H-form FCBGs predominates.

The combination of secular-rational and self-expression values is common in Germany, Japan, Norway, and South Korea. In these countries, the authoritarian family type predominates (Duranton et al., 2009; Rijpma, & Carmichael, 2016; Todd, 1995). Characterized by the low equality of siblings as evidenced by the common preference of the eldest son (primogeniture) for the future leadership of the family and the inheritance of the business (Beckert, 2018), this family type results in small extended or core families. The limited family size results from parents encouraging the eldest sons' siblings to leave home as adults. In contrast, the eldest son has little choice but to stay in his parents' house, accepting to subordinate himself to parental authority and become the designated successor. Because this type of family comes with limited family size coupled with parental control of the designated successors, it is not surprising that the H-form FCBG is prevalent.

Finally, Spain, Brazil, Poland, and most of France tend to be at the intersection of modest traditional and modest self-expression values. In these countries, the equal treatment of children is coupled with adult children's ability to choose their level of engagement with the family predominates (Duranton et al., 2009; Rijpma, & Carmichael, 2016; Todd, 1985). Although children usually leave the parental household upon marriage, they often stay nearby and connected with them. Moreover, parents' equal treatment of children sets the foundation for stronger intra-generational ties. The outcome of this family type is the parents' ability to grow the family's size and influence their adult children and their families. In line with these family characteristics, the M-form FCBG is common (Yui et al., 2007). This form requires family members occupying interlocking board positions in vertically integrated companies within the FCBG. Because members of egalitarian nuclear families tend to live close to each other and the M-form has headquarters from which family members need to control all integrated companies, it appears logical that this family type is commonly associated with this type of FCBG.

Moderators of the Family Type-FCBG Type Relationship Within Countries

Although some family types (e.g., endogamous community) seem prototypical for a particular FCBG type (e.g., H-form), we note that other family types (e.g., egalitarian nuclear) can differ in their association with types of FCBGs (e.g., H- or M-form [Yui et al., 2007]). Fortunately, we are not the first to try to explain the ubiquity and variety in FCBGs around the globe. Randall Morck and his co-authors suggest that accidents of history, institutional changes, and the prevalence of institutional voids are key explanatory factors of variation in FCBGs within a country and over time (Dau, Morck, & Yeung, 2021; Morck, 2007). The historical accounts presented by these researchers, for instance, suggest that changes in the institutional environments, such as the decision to levy taxes on dividend payments to holding companies in the US, or the regulatory dismantling of family zaibatsu in Japan, explain shifts in FCBG prevalence or type (while culture remained constant) while also explaining oddities, such as the persistence of FCBGs in Sweden. Beyond these institutional characteristics (i.e., voids) and institutional shifts (i.e., legal changes [see also Carney & Gedajlovic, 2002]), we offer four complementary observations that might be particularly useful to help explain why in a given country, some families are associated with one type and others with a different kind of FCBG.

Regional Disparities

Regions within countries can vary enormously in their history, culture, religion, language and even their writing systems and prevailing laws. Not surprisingly, family types also differ across regions. Prominent examples include Italy or France. For instance, in Northern Italy, the community family is most common, whereas in Southern Italy, the egalitarian nuclear family historically predominates. The egalitarian nuclear family is also typical in large parts of France except for the Bretagne region. Due to this region's geographic proximity to the UK and past political rule by the English, the absolute nuclear family still prevails in that region of France (Duranton et al., 2009; Rijpma & Carmichael, 2016; Todd, 1995). Even in a predominantly patriarchal country such as India, large pockets of matriarchy exist (Jeffrey, 2016).

Family Resources

Families are embedded in the socio-cultural and historical context of their region and country, explaining their commonalities. However, families are equipped with differing bundles of financial and socioemotional resources that vary in terms of family and business development over time (Carney, 2005; Chua, Chrisman, Steier, & Rau, 2012; Habbershon & Williams, 1999; Sirmon & Hitt, 2003). Because of comparatively better education, social capital, and family leadership (Arregle et al., 2007; Carney, 2005; Zahra, 2010), for instance, some families will thrive across generations, and with their businesses, whereas others won't. Finally, families are not immune to disaster that often deplete available family resources quickly. Armed conflicts, tragic accidents, and debilitating health issues, among others, have brought many family and business legacies to an abrupt end (Bellow, 2004).

Family Dynamics

Finally, families have agency that appears most pertinent and relevant in terms of the interactions among adult family members and the upbringing of the next generation. Concerning the former, healthy interactions involve reciprocal behaviours reflecting generalized social exchanges, whereas asymmetrical altruism (i.e., unconditional support of members who do not return favours [Lubatkin, Schulze, Ling, & Dino, 2005; Schulze, Lubatkin, & Dino, 2002]) and entitlement stifling intrinsic motivation (e.g., Jaskiewicz et al., 2013; see also rotten kid syndrome, de Vries, 1993) are reflective of unhealthy interactions that can result in family businesses becoming unsustainable 'welfare hotels' for entitled members (Portes, 1998, p. 18). Concerning the upbringing of the next generation, demanding and emphatic parenting coupled with bi-directional communication are ingredients that, in the developed countries of the West, may help to imprint pertinent family values on the next generation and nurture functional and reciprocal transgenerational relationships over time (Jaskiewicz et al., 2016; Silverstein & Bengtson, 1997). However, in any country, families can suffer from unhealthy intra-generational (e.g., sibling rivalry, divorce) and intergenerational dynamics (e.g., parent-child conflicts) or both (e.g., abuse, disengagement), limiting the potential and sustainability of both families and their businesses. We believe that these three moderators – regional disparities, family resources, and family dynamics – can help explain variation in the family type-FCBG type relationship within countries. Moreover, we believe that two future trends will further enhance such variation.

Family Migration

Beyond micro-level differences among families due to their unique family dynamics, we note that structural differences among families persist in many societies due to migration. In many societies with traditional authority structures, the correspondence between the prevalent national family type and the business group organization may be neither exhaustive nor common due to inbound migration and the emergence of powerful diaspora communities whose business group organizations emulate the structures of FCBGs that they have become familiar with in their country of origins. We expect the effect of family migration to be particularly pervasive in traditional-authority societies that lack a functioning capitalist class and have historically relied upon "foreigners" to perform business functions. Examples of such powerful diaspora communities include Jewish families in Russia and Eastern Europe, the Chinese in Southeast Asia, European colonials in Africa, Gujarati Indians in East Africa, and Lebanese/Syrians in West Africa (see also Landa, 1994). In addition to setting up FCBGs that resemble those from their country of origin, minority groups sometimes also set up completely different FCBG structures to hide their wealth. Especially in postcolonial states, where politically dominant and majority indigenous communities have clashed with post-colonial minority entrepreneurs, the latter often responded by disguising their assets in low-profile business groups (e.g., McVey, 2018), providing another important rational for the heterogeneity of FCBGs within a country.

Family Types and Business Group Structures: Future Trends

While family types change very slowly, they do still change, largely in response to historically significant shifts in dominant value systems. Inglehart (1990) observes that the Industrial Revolution triggered a slow but clear shift from traditional to secular rational values that has influenced much of what we now term the industrialized west. A second significant shift, which continues to evolve in some parts of the world, is the shift from survival to self-expression values. While the family, as an institution, has proven to be very resistant to these changes, they are not immune, and we are beginning to observe growing and important changes in some parts of the world that hold powerful implications for the comparative prevalence of different family types and their FCBGs. Future trends that foster differential shifts around the world in the prevalence of family types include a declining propensity to marry, increasing divorce rates and changes in birth rates and overall population growth (Aldrich & Cliff, 2003; Jaskiewicz & Dyer, 2017; Jaskiewicz et al., 2021; OECD, 2011).

Unsurprisingly, such changes are occurring in qualitatively different ways and at different paces across the globe. So, for example, some parts of the world are experiencing massive population growth while other population sizes are rapidly decreasing. Based on such differential trends, we can make some rough predictions about the future prevalence of FCBGs across countries. We organize these predictions around two basic "effects": (1) The vanishing corporation and (2) The traditionalism effect. The former effect helps explain the expected rise in the prevalence of FCBGs outside of Anglo-American countries, whereas the latter effect suggests that existing types of FCBGs are not necessarily exhaustive and more intra-country variation in terms of FCBG types can be expected.

The Vanishing Corporation

Despite the prominent attention given to the publicly traded company by the business media, management education and popular culture, the publicly traded corporation is rapidly becoming an endangered species. The number of publicly traded American companies listed on the US stock exchange decreased by half between 1996 and 2012 (Davis, 2016). During that same period, the number of companies backed by private equity doubled (Stultz, 2020).

FCBGs, by contrast, are the dominant form of large-scale organization globally (Carney & Gedajlovic, 2002; Yui et al., 2007). As noted previously, FCBGs have a particularly significant and growing presence in Asia where, in some countries, 15 families control nearly two-thirds of the publicly traded corporations (Claessens et al., 2000; Mackie, 2018) and, if present growth trends continue, FCBGs will constitute 40% of the largest for-profit entities in the world. Perhaps the biggest indication of relative success of FCBGs over the traditional publicly traded corporation is the growing trend of acquisitions of the latter by the former (*The Economist*, 2015). We described the somewhat surprisingly aggressive acquisitions by the Tata family group in both the UK and the US, but there are other equally prominent indicia of the emerging exercise of financial muscularity by other FCBGs in the US, UK, and Canada. For instance, NewsCorp, controlled by Rupert Murdoch and two of his sons, has been on an M&A spree for the last two decades – acquiring numerous newspapers, TV stations, and media companies in the US, UK, Canada, and Australia – among others.

Based on the arguments presented in this chapter, the relative growth of FCBGs of the US, Canada, and the UK is not surprising. Rather, it is a reflection of two factors. First, the growth of FCGB power is the result of the configurational fit between the dominance of traditional authority in Asia, South America and much of Europe, as opposed to the configurational fit between rational-legal authority and the absolute nuclear family in the US, UK, and Canada. Second, and perhaps as importantly, the growth trend in FCBGs is fueled by the incredible population growth in those parts of the world where they originated and the reciprocal decline in population in the US, UK, and Canada (when excluding immigration). This trend, too, is underpinned by key differences in family types. Despite the variations in how traditional authority is expressed in different countries, the eminence of the family as the primary unit of social organization in those countries determines not only the primary organizational form, but also encourages the replication and growth of the family unit. That is, traditional authority encourages population growth. The rational-legal authority of the absolute nuclear family, however, does not.

Based on the statistics cited in this chapter and our core thesis that the family type determines the dominant organizational form of economic production in a society, we predict that FCBGs will continue to dominate much of the world and will eventually supplant the publicly traded corporation as the primary means of organizing in Europe, Asia, Latin America, and Northern Africa. We would expect that the holding type will predominate whenever core families, limited in size, prevail. Conversely, the club and multidivisional type of FCBGs will dominate where extended families prevail. Finally, the network type of FCBGs will predominate where family networks prevail. Our prediction thus not only highlights the expected growth of FCBGs globally but also distinguishes which type of FCBG is likely to dominate which part of the world – based on the unique combination of permanent social values, dominant authority structures and prevalent family types. Although it would appear that the widely held corporation remains the dominant form while business groups remain scarce in the US, UK, and Canada, there is one exception to this prediction, which we outline in the following section entitled the traditionalism effect.

The Traditionalism Effect

Within certain regions of the US and Canada, traditional forms of family authority still prevail. Consider, for example, the Hutterites in North America. Similar to the Amish and Mennonites, Hutterites are Anabaptists who escaped religious persecution in Europe in the latter part of the nineteenth century. In North America, the Hutterites settled primarily in the west and maintained their language and their religious traditions, most visibly their commitment to communal living. The three original colonies, first settled in 1874 in what was then called the Dakota Territory, by 2019 consisted of five hundred colonies spread over five states and four Canadian provinces.

Hutterite colonies consist of roughly fifteen to twenty families who live communally in multi-family houses and share all property. Once a colony grows to 150 people, the colony will split and half will leave to form a new colony, a process termed "hiving". This form of family organization, which most closely approximates a clan structure, is highly dependent upon traditions that reinforce traditional authority. Indeed, the colony structure likely exemplifies Weber's concept of traditional authority.

In contrast to the Amish, however, Hutterites embrace technology and their colony structure has transformed the community to become one of the most dominant sources of agricultural production in the states and provinces in which they operate. In Alberta, Hutterite colonies:

> own about 4 percent of Alberta's farmland but produce 80 percent of the province's eggs, 33 percent of its hogs, and more than 10 percent of its milk. This productivity is based on the Brethren's ability to deploy their relatively large labor force to carry out diversified mixed farming. Their willingness to embrace modern science and technology is matched by the links they have been able to establish with marketing chains in agribusiness. (Evans, 2019, p. 656)

In Montana, a neighbour state to Alberta, Hutterite communities produced approximately 18% of the state's poultry, over 30% of the state's dairy, over 90% of the hogs, and nearly 100% of the state's eggs (Haynes & Schumacher, 2019).

Hutterite colonies offer a somewhat unusual example of a FCBG. While the colonies are organized legally as corporations, which pay taxes, they organize work more as a family than a corporation and offer services (educational, health, etc.) that appear more like a religious society than a traditional corporation (Nordstrom & Jennings, 2018). Still, they are powerful economic actors in the regions that they occupy and, like their FCBG counterparts, are growing both in population and economic scope, much more rapidly than their local competitors.

Other segments of the US, Canada, and the UK also document a traditionalism effect that nurtures traditional authority in families and their businesses. So, for example, religiously-defined cultural regions such as the Evangelical Protestant American South or the Latter-day Saint American Mountain West point to the stability and resurgence of traditional authority in Anglo-American societies. It remains to be seen whether such traditionalist movements and the resilience of traditional and charismatic authority in modern societies will fuel the creation of a new type of FCBG characterized by the adaptive capacity to establish legitimacy within the prevailing hostile institutional conditions, and to what extent this type will be able to supplant other types of economic organization.

Conclusion

Max Weber assumed that the bureaucracy was an inherently superior form of organizing human productivity because of the efficiency derived from using rational-legal authority in decision-making. Western management scholarship, following Weber, have applied this logic to the modern manifestation of Weberian bureaucracy, the modern publicly traded corporation. A growing body of research, however, raises questions about the accuracy of this assumption. Business groups, most of which are founded on some form of family structure, have a stronger global presence than the publicly traded corporation, and are growing both in number and assets, while the publicly traded corporation is receding in frequency and diminishing in power.

In this chapter, we explain both the prevalence of family-controlled business groups based on the foundational idea that the bureaucratic form is not universally superior to other forms of organization. Rather, the corporation succeeds only when there is a degree of fit or congruence between its rational-legal form of authority and the prevailing value system of the country in which the corporation originates. The family is an equally powerful and stubbornly persistent institution that also offers an effective model for organizing human productivity. Our model is not premised on efficiency nor is it based on rational-legal assumptions of legitimate authority. Instead, it relies on traditional authority common to families in all societies.

Not all families are the same, however. Families vary by the degree to which they grant autonomy to their members and the degree to which they share wealth equally amongst their children (Beckert, 2018; Todd, 1985). We use this logic to construct a schema of family types that vary by the degree to which traditional authority is moderated by the integration of select aspects of rational-legal authority. We use the typology derived from these dimensions to explain the variation observed by researchers in FCBGs around the world. While family structures are surprisingly resilient, families do change, largely as a result of slow but inexorable changes in the value systems of the societies in which they exist. Moreover, families differ within their country due to regional differences, variation in family's stock of financial and socioemotional resources, and pertinent differences in family dynamics. We have drawn from sociological research to offer some projections on the future of FCBGs within and across countries, suggesting that the expected growth of various types of FCBGs will be inextricably tied to the prevalence of particular types of family as well as their pertinent differences within the socio-historical context in which they are embedded.

The underlying premise of our chapter – that is, that authority relations between parents and children provide a template for larger forms of social organization, including economic organizational structures – can explain other variation across FCBGs. For example, we know that business groups engage in unrelated diversification, a practice that is clearly inefficient for corporations (Yui et al., 2007). We also know that business groups vary in how they pursue diversification: organically through Greenfield investment; by portfolio, or acquisitions of existing unrelated companies; and by policy induction, or in response to incentives provided by government.

These variations in diversification, we believe can also be explained by the type of family behind the FCBG. Organic diversification is most consistent with the Authoritarian (clan) form of family, which is more distrustful of outside groups, particular those with coercive authority, and which values independence and autonomy more than other family structures. Portfolio forms of diversification are much more consistent with community (segmented) family structures that promote equality amongst siblings, but can use the inter-relations between corporate structures to mirror different forms of corporate control. Thus, we might expect the Endogamous Community Family, in which parents exert high degrees of control over children, to lean towards horizontal integration and the Exogamous Community Family, which prefers moderate forms of parental control, to adopt vertical integration in their corporate structure. Finally, policy induced forms of diversification, in which business groups and state governments collaborate to encourage domestic ownership of critical elements of the economy, seem to correspond to the values of the Absolute Nuclear Family, which is the family structure that most fully integrates traditional and rational-legal authority structures.

The growth, persistent success, and bewildering variation of FCBGs has taken many western management and finance scholars by surprise. Their existence seems irreconcilable with the superiority of rational-legal authority as reflected by the modern corporation and contemporary financial markets. As such, FCBGs represent an organizational form that defies both Weber's (2013) assumption of the superiority of the rational-legal bureaucracy and Williamson's (1975) assumption that hierarchies (organizations) emerge only to correct flaws in rationally efficient markets. Our paper offers an alternative explanation based on configurational fit. While the publicly traded corporation may well fit with North American cultural assumptions of legal-rational authority, FCBGs appear to be a good fit with non-North American cultural assumptions of traditional authority. Our chapter proposes that the family, as a social institution, can be an equally powerful and extremely resilient way of organizing economic activity. We clearly need much more empirical work to more accurately capture the nuanced variation in the relationship between different types of family authority structures and how they manifest in different organizational forms. In this context, we call for future research to study FCBGs in different parts of the world and delineate precisely how family members are involved in the ownership, leadership, and control of different types of FCBGs. Although our typology of FCBGs assumes family ownership and control, we have not considered possible interdependencies between family involvement in ownership, management, and board structures of FCBGs.

Another promising area for future research refers to studying the role of global management consultants. Traditional societies undergoing rapid capital accumulation in the hands of business families have attracted the attention of professional service firms in the West. These firms are increasingly targeted by family management consultants touting new management and financial practices through family offices, letterbox companies, and complex structures in tax havens to rationalize the continued allocation of resources in FCBGs. Arguably, these consultancies represent 'world society forces' that diffuse professional and technical rationality into the core of FCBGs. Sociologists (e.g., Zucker, 1986) argue that highly personalized authoritarian control relies on familiarity and proximity. To grow FCBGs that can scale into international markets, they must rely upon various structures and processes of formal-legal authority. Does reliance on international consultancies that disperse peculiar structures and processes lead to isomorphism among the largest FCBGs across diverse countries? While this is an empirical question that future research needs to answer, we believe that multi-national global FCBGs, such as Tata or Samsung, likely combine various elements of global rational-legal and national traditional authority.

We hope that this chapter offers a modest step towards explaining the rapid growth and success of FCBGs as well as their variation in form. Once the core relationship is elaborated empirically, we expect that western management and finance scholars may be less surprised by the persistence and ubiquity of this fascinating organizational form.

References

Agnblad, J., Berglöf, E., Högfeldt, P., & Svancar, H. (2001). Ownership and control in Sweden: Strong owners, weak minorities, and social control. In F. Barca & M. Becht (Eds.), *The Control of Corporate Europe* (pp. 228–258). New York: The European Corporate Governance Network and Oxford University Press.

Aldrich, H. E., & Cliff, J. E. (2003). The pervasive effects of family on entrepreneurship: Toward a family embeddedness perspective. *Journal of Business Venturing*, 18(5), 573–596.

Andrikopoulos, A., Georgakopoulos, A., Merika, A., & Merikas, A. (2019). Corporate governance in the shipping industry: board interlocks and agency conflicts. *Corporate Governance: The International Journal of Business in Society*, 19(4), 613–630.

Arregle, J. L., Hitt, M. A., Sirmon, D. G., & Very, P. (2007). The development of organizational social capital: Attributes of family firms. *Journal of Management Studies*, 44(1), 73–95.

Barca, F. & Becht, M. (2002). *The Control of Corporate Europe.* New York: Oxford University Press.

Bau, N. & Fernande, R. (2021). The family as a social institution. National Bureau of Economic Research, Working Paper 28918. Accessed on August 21, 2021 at http://www.nber.org/papers/w28918

Beckert, J. (2018). *Inherited Wealth.* Princeton, New Jersey: Princeton University Press.

Bellow, A. (2004). *In Praise of Nepotism: A History of Family Enterprise from King David to George W. Bush.* Anchor. New York.

Berggren, N., & Bjørnskov, C. (2011). Is the importance of religion in daily life related to social trust? Cross-country and cross-state comparisons. *Journal of Economic Behavior & Organization*, 80(3), 459–480.

Boisot, M., & Child, J. (1996). From fiefs to clans and network capitalism: Explaining China's emerging economic order. *Administrative Science Quarterly*, 41(4),600–628.

Carney, M. (2005). Corporate governance and competitive advantage in family-controlled firms. *Entrepreneurship Theory and Practice*, 29(3), 249–265.

Carney, M., & Gedajlovic, E. (2002). The co-evolution of institutional environments and organizational strategies: The rise of family business groups in the ASEAN region. *Organization Studies*, 23(1), 1–29.

Castells, M. (1997). *The Power of Identity.* Oxford, UK: Blackwell.

Chang, S. J., & Hong, J. (2000). Economic performance of group-affiliated companies in Korea: Intragroup resource sharing and internal business transactions. *Academy of Management Journal*, 43(3), 429–448.

Chau, T. T. (1991). Approaches to succession in East Asian business organizations. *Family Business Review*, 4(2), 161–179.

Chen, G., Chittoor, R., & Vissa, B. (2021). Does nepotism run in the family? CEO pay and pay-performance sensitivity in Indian family firms. *Strategic Management Journal*, 42(7), 1326–1343.

Chittoor, R., Kale, P., & Puranam, P. (2015). Business groups in developing capital markets: Towards a complementarity perspective. *Strategic Management Journal*, 36(9), 1277–1296.

Chua, J. H., Chrisman, J. J., Steier, L. P., & Rau, S. B. (2012). Sources of heterogeneity in family firms: An introduction. *Entrepreneurship Theory and Practice*, 36(6), 1103–1113.

Claessens, Stijn, Djankov, S., & Lang, H. P. (2000). The separation of ownership and control in East Asian corporations. *Journal of Financial Economics*, 58, 81–112.

Cross, S. L., & Day, A. G. (2008). American Indian grand families: Eight adolescent and grandparent dyads share perceptions on various aspects of the kinship care relationship. *Journal of Ethnic & Cultural Diversity in Social Work*, 17(1), 82–100.

Cuervo-Cazurra, A. (2006). Business groups and their types. *Asia Pacific Journal of Management*, 23, 419–437.

Dau, L. A., Morck, R., & Yeung, B.Y. (2021). Business groups and the study of international business: A Coasean synthesis and extension. *Journal of International Business Studies*, 52, 161–211.

Davis, G. F. (2016). *The Vanishing American Corporation: Navigating the Hazards of a New Economy* (Vol. 16). Oakland, California: Berrett-Koehler Publishers.

de Vries, M. F. K. (1993). The dynamics of family controlled firms: The good and the bad news. *Organizational Dynamics*, 21(3), 59–71.

Deephouse, D. L., & Jaskiewicz, P. (2013). Do family firms have better reputations than non-family firms? An integration of socioemotional wealth and social identity theories. *Journal of Management Studies*, 50(3), 337–360.

Della Piana, B., Vecchi, A., & Cacia, C. (2012). Towards a better understanding of Family Business Groups and their key dimensions. *Journal of Family Business Strategy*, 3(3), 174–192.

Duranton, G., Rodríguez-Pose, A., & Sandall, R. (2009). Family types and the persistence of regional disparities in Europe. *Economic Geography*, 85(1), 23–47.

Ebrey, P. (2003). *Women and the Family in Chinese History*. New York: Routledge.

The Economist. (2015). Special Report. April, 18th, 2015. Accessed online on August 22, 2021 at https://www.economist.com/special-report/2015/04/16/to-have-and-to-hold.

Erdogan, I., Rondi, E., & De Massis, A. (2020). Managing the tradition and innovation paradox in family firms: A family imprinting perspective. *Entrepreneurship Theory and Practice*, 44(1), 20–54.

Evans, S. M. (2019). Hutterite agriculture in Alberta: The contribution of an ethnic isolate. *Agricultural History*, 93(4), 656–681.

Fisman, R., & Wang, Y. (2010). Trading favors within Chinese business groups. *American Economic Review*, 100(2), 429–433.

Fukuyama, F. (2014). *Political Order and Political Decay: From the Industrial Revolution to the Globalization of Democracy*. New York: Macmillan.

Gomez-Mejia, L. R., Makri, M., & Kintana, M. L. (2010). Diversification decisions in family-controlled firms. *Journal of Management Studies*, 47(2), 223–252.

Gonzáles-Rubal, A. (2006). House societies vs. kinship-based societies: An archaeological case from Iron Age Europe. *Journal of Anthropological Archaeology*, 25(1), 144–173.

Gopal, S., Manikandan, K. S., & Ramachandran, J. (2021). Are there limits to diversification in emerging economies? Distinguishing between firm-level and business group strategies. *Journal of Management Studies*, 58(6), 1532–1568.

Granovetter, M. (1994). Business groups. In N. J. Smelser & R. Swedberg (Eds.), *Handbook of Economic Sociology* (pp. 453–475). Princeton, NJ: Princeton University Press.

Guillen, M. F. (2000). Business groups in emerging economies: A resource-based view. *Academy of Management Journal*, 43(3), 362–380.

Gutmann, J. & Voigt, S. (2018). The rule of law: Measurement and deep roots. *European Journal of Political Economy*, 54, 68–82.

Gutmann, J., & Voigt, S. (2020). *Family Types and Political Development*. Available at SSRN 3602226. Accessed online on October 8, 2021 at: https://www.econstor.eu/bitstream/10419/216096/1/ile-wp-2020-34.pdf

Habbershon, T. G., & Williams, M. L. (1999). A resource-based framework for assessing the strategic advantages of family firms. *Family Business Review*, 12(1), 1–25.

Haynes, G., & Schumacher, J. (2019). *The Economic Contributions of Hutterite Communities in Montana*. Helena, MT: Bureau of Business and Economic Research.

Hofstede, G. (2001). *Culture's Consequences: Comparing Values, Behaviors, Institutions, and Organizations Across Nations*, 2nd ed. Beverly Hills: Sage.

Inglehart, R. (2000). Culture and democracy. In L.E. Harrison and S. P. Huntington (Eds.). *Culture Matters: How Values Shape Human Progress* (pp. 80–97). New York: Basic Books.

Inglehart, R., & Welzel, C. (2005). *Modernization, Cultural Change, and Democracy: The Human Development Sequence*. Cambridge: Cambridge University Press.

Inglehart, R. (1988). The renaissance of political culture. *American Political Science Review*, 82, 1203–1230.

Inglehart, R. (1990). *Culture Shift in Advanced Industrial Society*. Princeton: Princeton University Press.

Inglehart, R. (2006). Mapping global values. *Comparative Sociology*, 5(2–3), 115–136.

Jaskiewicz, P., & Dyer, W. G. (2017). Addressing the elephant in the room: Disentangling family heterogeneity to advance family business research. *Family Business Review*, 30(2), 111–118.

Jaskiewicz, P., Block, J., Wagner, D., Carney, M., & Hansen, C. (2021). How do cross-country differences in institutional trust and trust in family explain the mixed performance effects of family management? A meta-analysis. *Journal of World Business*, 56(5), 101196.

Jaskiewicz, P., Combs, J. G., Shanine, K. K., & Kacmar, K. M. (2016). Introducing the family: A review of family science with implications for management research. *Academy of Management Annals*, 11(1), 309–341.

Jaskiewicz, P., Uhlenbruck, K., Balkin, D. B., & Reay, T. (2013). Is nepotism good or bad? Types of nepotism and implications for knowledge management. *Family Business Review*, 26(2), 121–139.

Jeffrey, R. (2016). *Politics, Women and Well-Being: How Kerala Became 'a Model'*. New York: Springer.

Kahle, K. M., & Stulz, R. M. (2017). Is the US public corporation in trouble? *Journal of Economic Perspectives*, 31(3), 67–88.

Khanna, T., & Rivkin, J. W. (2001). Estimating the performance effects of business groups in emerging markets. *Strategic Management Journal*, 22(1), 45–74.

Khanna, T., & Yafeh, Y. (2007). Business groups in emerging markets: Paragons or parasites? *Journal of Economic Literature*, 45(2), 331–372.

La Porta, R., Lopez-de-Silanes, F., & Shleifer, A. (1999). Corporate ownership around the world. *Journal of Finance*, 54(2), 471–517.

Landa, J. T. (1994). *Trust, Ethnicity, and Identity: Beyond the New Institutional Economics of Ethnic Trading Networks, Contract Law, and Gift-Exchange*. Ann Arbor, Michigan: University of Michigan Press.

Lang, O. (1946). *Chinese Family and Society*. New Haven: Yale University Press.

Le Breton-Miller, I., & Miller, D. (2006). Why do some family businesses out-compete? Governance, long-term orientations, and sustainable capability. *Entrepreneurship Theory and Practice*, 30(6), 731–746.

Le Play, F. (1895), *L'organisation de la famille selon le vrai modèle signalé par l'histoire de toutes les races et de tous les temps*. Paris: Mame Publishers.

Lester, R. H., & Cannella Jr, A. A. (2006). Interorganizational familiness: How family firms use interlocking directorates to build community-level social capital. *Entrepreneurship Theory and Practice*, 30(6), 755–775.

Levine, N. E. (2008). Alternative kinship, marriage, and reproduction. *Annual Review of Anthropology*, 37, 375–389.

Lévi-Strauss, C. (1987). *Anthropology and Myth: Lectures 1951–1982*. Oxford, UK: Blackwell.

Licht, A. N., Goldschmidt, C., & Schwartz, S. H. (2007). Culture rules: The foundations of the rule of law and other norms of governance. *Journal of Comparative Economics*, 35(4), 659–688.

Lomnitz, L. A. (2013). Family, networks, and survival on the threshold of the 21st century in urban México. In *The Family on the Threshold of the 21st Century* (pp. 125–138). London, England: Psychology Press.

Lubatkin, M. H., Schulze, W. S., Ling, Y., & Dino, R. N. (2005). The effects of parental altruism on the governance of family-managed firms. *Journal of Organizational Behavior: The International Journal of Industrial, Occupational and Organizational Psychology and Behavior*, 26(3), 313–330.

Lumpkin, G. T., Brigham, K. H., & Moss, T. W. (2010). Long-term orientation: Implications for the entrepreneurial orientation and performance of family businesses. *Entrepreneurship & Regional Development*, 22(3–4), 241–264.

Mackie, J. (2018). Changing patterns of Chinese big business in Southeast Asia. In McVey, R. T. (Ed.), *Southeast Asian Capitalists* (pp. 161–190). Ithaca, NY: Cornell University Press.

Martin, R. L. (2021). It's time to replace the public corporation. *Harvard Business Review*, 99(1), 34–42.

Mazzi, C. (2011). Family business and financial performance: Current state of knowledge and future research challenges. *Journal of Family Business Strategy*, 2(3), 166–181.

McVey, R. T. (2018). *Southeast Asian Capitalists*. Ithaca, NY: Cornell University Press.

Morck, R. (Ed.) (2007). *A History of Corporate Governance around the World: Family Business Groups to Professional Managers*. Chicago: Chicago University Press.

Morck, R. (2009). The riddle of the great pyramids (No. w14858). National Bureau of Economic Research Working Paper 14858, DOI 10.3386/w14858. Accessed online on October 8, 2021 at: https://www.nber.org/papers/w14858

Morck, R., & Yeung, B. (2003). Agency problems in large family business groups. *Entrepreneurship Theory and Practice*, 27(4), 367–382.

Nakamura, N. (2002). The present state of research on Zaibatsu: The case of Mitsubishi. *Social Science Japan Journal*, 5(2), 233–242.

Nordstrom, O., & Jennings, J. E. (2018). Looking in the other direction: An ethnographic analysis of how family businesses can be operated to enhance familial well-being. *Entrepreneurship Theory and Practice*, 42(2), 317–339.

OECD. (2011). Family Business Database. Accessed online on October 8, 2021 at https://www.oecd.org/els/family/database.htm.

Parkin, D., & Stone, L. (2004). *Kinship and Family: An Anthropological Reader*. New York: Wiley.

Parkin, D. (1997). *Kinship: An Introduction to the Basic Concepts*. New York, Wiley.

Pieper, T. M., Kellermanns, F. W., & Astrachan, J. H. (2021). *Update 2021: Family Businesses' Contribution to the US Economy*. Washington, DC: Family Enterprise USA.

Portes, A. (1998). Social capital: Its origins and applications in modern sociology. *Annual Review of Sociology*, 24(1), 1–24.

Reher, D. S. (1998). Family ties in Western Europe: persistent contrasts. *Population and Development Review*, 24(2), 203–234.

Rijpma, A., & Carmichael, S. G. (2016). Testing Todd and matching Murdock: Global data on historical family characteristics. *Economic History of Developing Regions*, 31(1), 10–46.

Sahlins, M. D. (1961). The segmentary lineage: An organization of predatory expansion. *American Anthropologist*, 63(2), 322–345.

Said, E. (1978). *Orientalism*. New York: Vintage.

Schulze, W. S., Lubatkin, M. H., & Dino, R. N. (2002). Altruism, agency, and the competitiveness of family firms. *Managerial and Decision Economics*, 23, 247–259.

Segalen, M. (1978). *Historical Anthropology of the Family* (translated by J.C. Whitehouse & S. Mattews). Cambridge, UK: Cambridge University Press.

Silverstein, M., & Bengtson, V. L. (1997). Intergenerational solidarity and the structure of adult child-parent relationships in American families. *American Journal of Sociology*, 103(2), 429–460.

Sirmon, D. G., & Hitt, M. A. (2003). Managing resources: Linking unique resources, management, and wealth creation in family firms. *Entrepreneurship Theory and Practice*, 27(4), 339–358.

Smith, D. C. (1992). The Chinese Family in Transition: Implications for Education and Society in Modern Taiwan. Paper presented at the Comparative Education Association/World Bank Seminar, Spring, 1992, Annapolis Maryland. Accessed online at https://files.eric.ed.gov/full text/ED352295.pdf on September 12, 2021.

Smith, M. G. (1956). On segmentary lineage systems. *The Journal of the Royal Anthropological Institute of Great Britain and Ireland*, 86(2), 39–80.

Stulz, R. M. (2020). Public versus private equity. *Oxford Review of Economic Policy*, 36(2), 275–290.

Suddaby, R., & Jaskiewicz, P. (2020). Managing traditions: A critical capability for family business success. *Family Business Review*, 33(3), 234–243.

Thomsen, S. (2011). Trust ownership of the Tata Group. Available at SSRN 1976958. Accessed online on October 8, 2021 https://papers.ssrn.com/sol3/papers.cfm?abstract_id=1976958

Todd, E. (1985). *The Explanation of Ideology: Family Structures and Social Systems*. Oxford [Oxfordshire]; New York, NY, USA: B. Blackwell.

Tucker, R. C. (1968). The theory of charismatic leadership. *Daedalus*, Philosophers and Kings. Studies in Leadership, 97(3).

Weber, M. (2013). *Economy and Society* (Volume 1). Berkeley, CA: University of California Press.

Williamson, O. E. (1975). *Markets and Hierarchies: Analysis and Antitrust Implications*. New York: Free Press.

Woolridge, A. (2015). Family Companies – To have and to hold. *The Economist*, Special Report. April 18th, 2015. Accessed online on August 22, 2021 at https://www.economist.com/special-report/2015/04/16/to-have-and-to-hold

Yiu, D., Bruton, G. D., & Lu, Y. (2005). Understanding business group performance in an emerging economy: Acquiring resources and capabilities in order to prosper. *Journal of Management Studies*, 42, 183–206.

Yiu, D. W., Lu, Y., Bruton, G. D., & Hoskisson, R. E. (2007). Business groups: An integrated model to focus future research. *Journal of Management Studies*, 44(8), 1551–1579.

Zahra, S. A. (2010). Harvesting family firms' organizational social capital: A relational perspective. *Journal of Management Studies*, 47(2), 345–366.

Zucker, L. G. (1986). Production of trust: Institutional sources of economic structure, 1840–1920. *Research in Organizational Behavior*, 8, 53–111.

Allan Discua Cruz and Leonardo Centeno-Caffarena

23 Migrant Business Families in Central America

Abstract: This study deals with migrant business families. The main argument of this chapter is that migrant business families, as a category, underscores a capacity to adapt to new and changing environments. While some recent studies have suggested the prevalence of migrant business families around the world, we still know little about the challenges they face to create and develop their firms, particularly in underexplored contexts. Using a historical approach, we advance understanding by concentrating on Arab and German migrant business families in two Central American developing countries, Honduras and Nicaragua, respectively. We find that initial and subsequent contextual changes in host countries may support and/ or disadvantage some migrant families over others over time. Yet a reliance on ethnic and transnational networks may allow migrant business families to adapt and thrive. In contrast to prior work, migrant business family members in developing economies contextually adapt through a cultivating an ethnic family culture, enhancing ethnic networks and strengthening transnational business links. Our chapter argues that the ability of business families to adapt and prosper in a wide range of environments explains their prevalence around the world.

Keywords: migrant business families, honduras, nicaragua, ethnic networks, transnational networks, developing economies, business history

Introduction

This chapter is motivated by the need to understand migrant business families in developing economies. The emergence and development of businesses by migrants or their descendants has not gone unnoticed in the developed world (Fearnow, 2019; Moules, 2014; Spielmann et al., 2021) yet there is little understanding about how migrant business families emerged and adapted in developing countries. In this study, a migrant business family relates to members of a family of migrants, or descendants of migrants, that engage in the foundation, management and continuity of one or several family business ventures over time (Centeno-Caffarena, & Discua Cruz, 2021; Elo et al., 2018). Studying migrant business families is important as recent studies suggest shifting our attention from the firm to the family level of analysis (Discua Cruz & Basco,

Allan Discua Cruz, Lancaster University
Leonardo Centeno-Caffarena, Keiser University

https://doi.org/10.1515/9783110727968-023

2018; Hamilton et al., 2017). Such shift can help our understanding about how family firms, established and run by migrant business families, achieve long-term competitiveness in challenging environments (Discua Cruz et al., 2019). As strategies to develop firms started by migrant families may be only understandable within the context in which they operate (Roscoe et al., 2013; Wright et al., 2014) attention to how migrant business families emerged and survive is needed (James et al., 2020).

The migrant business family concept associates to interrelated theoretical discussions around context, ethnicity, networks, skills and transnationalism. The importance of context relates to the conditions that inhibit or support the development of a firm by any business family (Wright et al., 2014). Much of the migrant or immigrant entrepreneurship literature concerns the experience of communities from less developed economies migrating to richer economies in Europe and North America (Centeno-Caffarena, 2016). Yet, ethnicity for business families relates to how people from similar background share information (Larson & Lewis, 2017). Ethnic networks, that is, networks of social relationships connected by ethnicity have been found to be relevant for business (Brzozowski et al., 2014). Such networks become instrumental through transnationalism, that is, the processes by which migrants create and preserve multiple economic, cultural, and social relationships that link them to their origin and host societies (Vertovec, 2001). Transnational networks relate to multiple social relationships (e.g., familial, economic, social, organizational, religious, and political) that span borders, linking members of migrant business families to others across borders to provide information, resources to trade or identify international markets (Mustafa & Chen, 2010). Around the world families rely on such ethnic resources to start and develop their firms (Vershinina et al., 2019).

Migrant business families have been found to emerge and thrive in developing economies, such as countries in the Central American region (Bull et al., 2014), characterized by weak institutions, social unrest, economic volatility, and political turmoil, prevalent in most countries in Latin America (Nordqvist et al., 2011). While Central America represents an interesting milieu to explore how migrant business families have developed over time, most work has been conducted in larger Latin American countries, with smaller countries remaining underexplored, and with little attention as to what has allowed their adaptation in new environment (Gupta et al., 2008). Thus, this study aims to answer the following question: *how have migrant business families emerged and adapted in Central America?*

To answer this research question this study relies on a historical approach (Carney & Gedajlovic, 2003) to understand the emergence, development, and adaptation of migrant business families in Nicaragua and Honduras. Central America represents a context where some migrant business families have thrived, often amidst adverse contextual conditions (Müller et al., 2019). This study depicts a contrast between these two countries and migrant communities. Both contexts share some historical similarities such as state intervention fuelling the arrival of migrant families (Amaya, 2000; Von Houwald, 1975). Yet historical accounts also hint that several crises and contextual issues influenced the way migrant business families adapted and endured (Barahona, 2005; Kühl, 2014). Exploring the approach and rationale of migrant business families in both contexts is relevant as some families, when facing diverse contextual pressures may either adapt or abandon such environments (Fernández Pérez & Lluch, 2016). This chapter is relevant as it depicts families within communities from old Middle Eastern and European countries migrating to a new and developing world, which is seeking to accelerate its own economic and political development.

Our approach extends understanding on migrant business families in three ways. First, we find that migrant business families in uncertain contexts may adapt by cultivating shared values associated to their ethnic heritage. Findings suggest divergent experiences of a less welcome Palestinian/Arabic groups in Honduras compared with the generally favourable but somewhat ambiguous Protestant Germans reception in Nicaragua. When setbacks have occurred, shared understandings between family members are critical to adapt and ensure business survival. Second, we find a deliberate approach to nurture and cultivate local ethnic networks to explore new business opportunities and business expansion. Finally, migrant business families gradually adapt to their host environments by developing multicultural understandings to advance business purposes, without neglecting their ethnic heritage. Moreover, we find that distant third parties, (e.g., US), may have a lasting influence during war or conflict periods over the process and outcomes particularly in the Nicaraguan context. Taken together, the findings extend understanding in the literature of migrant business families in developing countries.

The chapter continues as follows: First, it describes briefly the conceptual background and initial argument on migrant business families. Then, it shows how migrant family businesses have emerged adapted in two contexts. It continues by focusing on findings and discussion. Finally, it suggests limitations and opportunities for further research.

Migrant Business Families

Migration is not a new phenomenon. Migrant families that have established their firms in host countries around the world are widespread (Elo et al., 2018). Migration policies, the pursuit of business opportunities or the need for a safer place (Elo & Minto-Coy, 2019) may encourage the arrival of migrants to developing economies, often resulting in the establishment of family enterprises (Fernández Pérez & Lluch, 2016). Upon arrival, many migrant families often settle, based on government incentives or policies, in urban or peripheral areas of a host country, with diverse access to business and resource frameworks influencing the pace and breadth of entrepreneurial activities (Elo et al., 2019).

We depart from the argument that migrant families settled in developing economies adapt through support from strong relationships in family and ethnic networks and changing relationships in business and transnational networks (Evansluong et al., 2019; Jack et al., 2010). The nature of strong and weak ties suggests a focus on the relevance of relationships in both networks and the importance of social capital. As social capital resides in the relationships between individuals in networks, which facilitates business activities (Anderson et al., 2007) it provides a theoretical perspective that has traction in studies of family businesses (Anderson and Miller, 2003; Arregle et al., 2007; Uzzi, 1997). We acknowledge that many migrant families may arrive to host countries with limited relational resources, and therefore they may initially rely on family members and those with whom they share some background characteristics yet must develop relationships within the host country if they want to adapt to its environment (Elo et al., 2018; Evansluong et al., 2019)

Yet, while previous literature suggests that ethnic networks are relevant in the emergence of a firm created by migrants, such networks appear to become less significant for subsequent generations as descendants become more embedded in their host countries (Deakins, Ishaq, Smallbone, Whittam, & Wyper, 2007).

Our study is in line with recent views about a phenomenon where ethnic minority dominance of the economy can be observed (Davis et al., 2001). Such phenomenon can be observed where deficiencies in formal institutions exist and will continue to be observed in developing countries under free market conditions. Davis et al. (2001) introduced the term "economic dominance" and discusses the factors that cause a group to become economically dominant in terms of levels of entrepreneurship (e.g., levels of ownership and control of commercial enterprises). While prior studies have suggested how this phenomenon can be observed in Asia with minorities, they also suggest that migrant communities may be dominant in terms of entrepreneurship they may also have relatively low levels of income and include large numbers of members who have not engaged in business sectors, and may be underrepresented in diverse sectors of the economy.

Recent studies suggest that in adverse or uncertain environments the features of social ethnic networks could be relevant for migrant families in business over time (Centeno-Caffarena & Discua Cruz, 2021) yet do not expand as to how such features emerge or influence their adaptation over time. We argue that further exploration of the historical and contextual influences may provide some explanations (Carney & Gedajlovic, 2003; Colli et al., 2003; Wright et al., 2014)

A historical approach is important to understand business families In previously unexplored contexts (Carney & Gedajlovic, 2003). In this study we focus on two Central American countries for two reasons. First, since their independence from Spain, Nicaragua, and Honduras have tried to develop the productive capacity of its various regions. Scholars have documented how such approach was guided through promoting immigration from Europe (Becerra, 2011; Kühl, 2019). Prior historical studies suggest that that not all migrant families were treated the same upon arrival. Second, in both countries diverse contextual crisis emerged over time thus changing the business environment for business families. Such changes may have resulted in some migrant business families experiencing either a favourable or a hostile treatment compared to others. A historical approach may reveal how (whether) migrant business families have endured and the role played by ethnic features to contextually adapt to changing conditions. We now focus on Honduras and Nicaragua, respectively.

Honduras and Arab-Palestine Migrant Business Families

Honduras is a developing Central American country with a population of around 9.2 million and a GDP of about US$22.9 billion (World Bank, 2018). The Honduran economy has been strongly dependent on agricultural exports with some diversifications of transformed goods in the last decades (Becerra, 2011). Honduras is interesting for this study for the following reasons. First, in the past, state intervention aimed to increase foreign direct investment and the number of immigrants from specific countries to settle in the country, which influenced the emergence of migrant business families (Discua Cruz et al., 2016). Second, immigration was seen as a way to facilitate foreign direct investment, technology transfer, the development of an enterprising culture, the creation of manufacturing activities to develop productive areas in the country not all immigrant families were treated fairly (Amaya, 2011, p. 30). Finally, of all the different migrant families that arrived in the country, the Arab-Palestinian ethnic group showcased a unique adaptability and development in business (Euraque, 2009; Illescas, 2009) and thus relevant to understand the adaptability of segregated migrant business families.

The Segregated Welcome of Arab-Palestinian Migrant Business Families in Honduras

For Honduras, it was between 1883 and 1899 when immigration was most stimulated. In 1895, a new Immigration Law was introduced giving equal civil rights to Hondurans and immigrants (Lemus & Bourgeois, 1897). Foreign investment security, generous legal and commercial advantages were offered (Lombard, 1887). After the introduction of this law, Honduras began receiving the highest levels of foreign immigration from North American, British, German, French, Italian, and later Arabs and Chinese (Amaya, 2011, p. 35). New immigrants settled mostly around the productive and coastal northern areas of the country (Euraque, 1997). In the early 20th century, Honduras was still promoted as the country of greatest natural wealth in Central America with clear advantages over neighbours, such as low labour costs, diversity in agriculture, trade, and mining in the northern and central regions of the country (Scott, 1909).

In 1906, a new immigration reform was introduced, fuelling immigration during the first three decades of the 20th century. Immigration from the US and Europe reached significant levels in industry and trade (Euraque, 2001). This law aimed to support a new productive process: banana production on the northern coast of Honduras. By 1911, the participation of European families (mainly from Germany, Italy, and France) is significant in the lists of trading, manufacturing and distribution companies, particularly in the northern area of the country (Fletes, 1911). Imports came directly from the countries of origin of European immigrants (Koebel, 1917) and the country increased their exports of banana, coffee, wood, gold, and silver based on state interventions to promote immigration in specific geographical areas to improve agricultural production (Alonso, 2007). Yet, such immigration laws were devised to favour migrants from Europe in providing them with land and incentives for production compared to those who came from the Middle Eastern regions.

In the beginning of the 20th century, agricultural production was considered mainly a sector for first class citizens (Barahona, 2005). Compared to concessions provided to Germans or British immigrants to develop the agricultural capability of the country, the role for Arab-Palestinian migrant families was ascribed to internal commerce, occupation that was considered for lower class members of the new migrant society (Indiano, 2014, p. 130). Despite such constraints, by 1918, the greatest percentage of immigrants was of Arab-Palestinian origin, with some coming from Syria and Lebanon (Amaya, 2000) who settled near the location of transnational and export companies (Discua Cruz et al., 2016).

The Changing Adaptation Strategies of Arab-Palestinian Migrant Families

From their arrival, the Arab-Palestinian community adhered to a patriarchal style, dominated by the first wave of migrants, who concentrated information, influence, and resources among people of the same ethnic group and ensured solidarity among their members (Amaya, 2000). These migrants used what has been described by Indiano (2014) as an adaptation of a cultural symbol, the "olive tree" strategy, which is based on a traditional custom by which an olive tree is planted for every child born to benefit them in the future (Rohan, 2010). Yet in the Honduran variant, as they did not have access to land, they decided to "plant" a business for every child born. The patriarchs of these migrant community oversaw the gradual development of family businesses based on key principles. The olive tree strategy was characterized, suggests Indiano (2014) by three aspects: first, austerity; second, family first, then family and ultimately family. Such approach meant a focus on relentless working hours alongside family members, focus on developing family skills and the preservation of ethnic heritage (Indiano, 2014). These rules, representing a survival and defence mechanism, were not written yet visible for anyone who dealt with them.

The Arab-Palestinian families did not actively seek to settle in the country, not only because they did not see their residency in the region as permanent but also because the immigration laws were not geared to make them feel welcomed (Indiano, 2014). The initial migrant families arrived speaking Arab, yet they adapted with some ease to prevalent norms as they were Coptic Christians, whose norms were mostly aligned with the major religious culture of the country at the time (Catholic faith). They adapted by learning the language and started importing and trading unique products from their countries of origin (items related to religious practices close to the Holy Land), which was welcomed by working class citizens. The initial approach of Arab-Palestinian migrant families related to selling their products door to door without any fixed address, allowing customers to pay in instalments over time. Gradually they started to import other products from their countries which could be affordable to the majority of the population. They leased large houses to establish retail businesses, which were never intended for the next generation to continue. As they were segregated from social and business circles, they cultivated a strong family culture avoiding social interaction with natives. Such commercial instruments and strategies continued over the next generation. In doing so, the first and second generation stoically endured their classification as "second hand" citizens and contextually adapted to a hostile environment.

Yet, as Arab-Palestinian family businesses developed, the local perception of immigration to the country was increasingly characterized by animosity (Euraque, 2009). Local business families linked to the government pressured the government to enact a new immigration law in 1929, which, in contrast to previous ones, was characterized by xenophobia and racism. These laws limited the arrival of "Arabs" and demanded greater contribution of capital for trade activities further encouraging the immigration of "white" Europeans and North Americans.

To counteract the effects of the new immigration laws, the Arab immigrant families adapted by applying their increased know-how of the local culture and turned to ethnical support practices. As a result of restrictions, the initial families became more reliant in their ethnic networks. As they were not considered worthy of being accepted in social circles, they made businesses their sole purpose (Indiano, 2014, p. 136). Moreover, to create a close ethnic circle the initial migrant families endeavoured to bring to Honduras extended family members from their countries of origin or motivated sons born in Honduras to return to Palestine, marry and bring their wives back (Amaya, 2000). As soon as relatives arrived, they were supported financially to locate themselves in diverse cities in the country and create a rudimentary commercial supply and financial network. They kept their ethnic circles strong, and were discouraged to interact with locals, prompting a preference for ethnic-based marriages. To preserve their ethnic heritage, they created their own educational circles and promoted social encounters to preserve the distinctive features of their community.

Between 1933–1948, the Arab-Palestinian immigrant community began to settle supported by protection from a new president who became a friend of the initial patriarchs. By granting them citizenship status, the new generations engaged into business diversification, redirecting investments to other sectors of the economy supported by the state such as tobacco, light manufacturing, textiles, and sugar. All these industries prospered in the years after the Great Depression and before and during the Second World War. Between 1949–1979, descendants of Arab-Palestinian migrant business expanded operations and took economic advantage of stated-led fiscal and economic policies, investing in the industrial, trade, financial and agricultural sectors (Amaya, 2000). Moreover, at the end of the 1950s new migrant business businesses of Arab-Palestinian descent emerged spurred by another process of immigration: the Cuban crisis of 1959. According to Romero (2008, p. 73), a "small but decisive migration of Arab families arrived from Cuba as part of the exile provoked by the 1959 revolution, among them the Lamas and Atala families, who became prominent in financial activity".

In this period the third generation of descendants of Arab-Palestinian families, sent their offspring to study overseas (e.g., US or Europe) so they could return and take over growing businesses, supported by strong ethnic networks, knowledge of local and ethnic culture, new acquired skills and a strong interest to continue preserving their ethnic heritage. An exemplar of such development is Corporacion Dinant, led by Miguel Facussé Barjum, who graduated in the US and established his business in the 1960s, expanding operations gradually in the whole Central American region, eventually controlling more than 60% the regional market for household cleaning products (Illescas, 2009). Moreover, the Atala family, descendants from the Cuban exile, went on to create the Grupo Financiera Comercial Hondureña (FICOHSA) in 1974 supported by the gradual training of their succeeding generations in US universities.

Since the 1980s, the Arab-Palestinian migrant business families strategy has concentrated on business diversification and a focus on preparing upcoming generations to adapt a local, ethnic and international culture to do business (Discua Cruz et al., 2016). Such approach allowed the gradual development of family business groups compared to the approach of local business families, who lost the opportunity to develop existing capabilities or diversify (Leyva, 2000). Interestingly, in spite of several intermarriages with elite local families, the Arab-Palestinian migrant business families always remained a somewhat separate and reserved group (Euraque, 2009) who, since their initial segregation, may have decided to instil in upcoming generations a strong reliance on ethnic networks to create and expand their businesses.

The previous depictions suggest that despite their prejudicial reception in Honduras it appears that the Arab Palestinians have maintained the unity of their ethnic solidarity while successfully accommodating local communities and political interests. As a result, this ethnic group has emerged as the dominant capitalist class in the country to which politicians and authorities must take into account in their governance (Indiano, 2014). In other words, although, Arab Palestinians experienced a difficult start they have more successfully overcome obstacles to cement their prominent economic and social role in their adopted Honduran society.

Nicaragua and German Migrant Business Families

Nicaragua is a developing country located in Central America with a population of about 6.2 million and a GDP of about US$13.8 billion (World Bank, 2017). The Nicaraguan economy is strongly associated to agricultural production, which plays a vital role in employment generation, entrepreneurship, food security, poverty alleviation, biodiversity conservation, culture tradition, and financial investments (Salcedo & Guzman, 2014). Nicaragua is particularly interesting in this study for several reasons: First, Nicaragua was one of the first Latin American contexts that highlighted the dominance of family businesses in the region (Strachan, 1976) and where migration waves, mainly from European countries, helped initial economic development (Leogrande, 1996). Second, similar to Honduras, migration from Europe was enticed to promote production and improve the local economy; resulting in migrant families dominating business trade and export) yet historical records suggest that contextual crisis (e.g., wars and governmental changes) affected migrant business families in business in Nicaragua (Duarte, 2009). Finally, of all the migrant families that developed businesses in Nicaragua, the presence and relevance of the German community has been well documented (Kühl, 2014; Von Houwald, 1975) and thus relevant to explore what characterises their adaptability.

The Welcomed Genesis of German Migrant Business Families in Nicaragua

The first European migrants arrived in Nicaragua in 1800s when the Nicaraguan government, following similar policies from other Latin American countries, enticed migration from Europe by facilitating land to promote the production of coffee and improve the local economy. Historical records place migration from Germany since the 1840s, fueled by an interest to explore and colonize regions of the Central American isthmus and dreams of establishing a new German protectorate in prior Spanish colonies (Von Houwald, 1975).

Early German migrants settled primarily near the Atlantic coast and in the northern areas of Nicaragua. Earlier records reveal that many arrived without having any idea about the country or the local people, and they came without knowledge of the language or defined goals – they were interested in testing their fortune and so many German migrants who stayed in Nicaragua, did it by pure chance. The first migrant waves perceived significant cultural distance between German migrants and Nicaraguan natives (Kühl, 2014). Some had planned to spend only a short time outside their home country and explore the tropical regions and then return to Germany.

Yet, as many German migrants were single males upon arrival, marriage with local women occurred, which created an opportunity to develop new businesses led by a German-Nicaraguan business family that cater for products of interest in both Nicaragua and Germany (Kühl, 2011b). Some of the principles that characterized the first Germans arriving in Nicaragua and their families related to punctuality, solidarity among countrymen, hard work, honesty, businesses diversification, frugality and zeal towards excessive expenses, which contrasted to more relaxed attitude of locals (Kühl, 2014). These features characterized the business culture of the first German migrant families in the country.

Yet, the need to develop strong ethnic ties to conduct business activities, both in Nicaragua with the German community became necessary. Many German migrant business families created firms with the German market as the prime target for export, developing diverse industries in the country, and strengthening the commercial and ethnic links between families in the two countries (Centeno-Caffarena & Discua Cruz, 2021). From 1852 to 1858 the German government appointed consuls in the most important Nicaraguan cities linked to a growth in trade between the two countries fueled by German migrant business families. By the turn of the century, Germany was already a respectable customer from Nicaragua, a good buyer of coffee, cotton, wood, colorants, and other tropical products and also a preferred supplier of quality articles "Made in Germany" (Von Houwald, 1975).

At the beginning of the 20th century German migrants accounted for the largest value of Nicaraguan exports, mainly to Germany, with several corporations, managers, and workers, migrating and settling in the country (Von Houwald, 1975, p. 41). In this period, contrary to German migrants who stayed in the country by chance, a second wave arrived seeking fortune based on their professions as traders, technicians, physicians, and farmers. Several accounts of intermarriages within the already established German community and also with locals suggest that the German migrant business families created a diverse community who could leverage their ethnic ties over time (Kühl, 2017).

In some cases, those who had already arrived sent for their brothers, relatives, or friends to settle in the country creating a greater influx and the development of new German migrant business families. Moreover, many German trading houses began to send their own employees to Nicaragua, reinforcing the ethnic circles in the country. The riches of the country were already known, and new German migrants wanted to trade, invest, and settle (Kühl, 2012). The arrival of German migrants was well regarded in Nicaragua (Kühl, 2014). Moreover, German migrants were proud of their homeland and many, who since their arrival did not care much about their nationality, tried to keep their ethnic heritage alive in business and within their ethnic or mixed families (Von Houwald, 1975, p. 60). This is exemplified, in the practices of trading or commercial houses founded by German migrants where the German flag would be shown outside their firms or to play German music such as the "Gemütlichkeit" in their premises (Von Houwald, 1975).

Notwithstanding, whilst German migrants in Nicaragua were a close-knit community, the tendency to isolate did not characterise them (Kühl, 2011b, 2012, 2014). On the contrary, the German colony in Nicaragua was always open to embrace the culture of their host country, evidenced by the many marriages with locals found in the national registry. Moreover, they were keen to establish cultural institutions where locals could also learn about their culture (Von Houwald, 1975). In places where large numbers of Germans lived, such as in the capital city Germany's diplomatic representatives and consular officers, concerned about their compatriots, supported the creation of German cultural, educational, leisure, and social associations.

Yet, it is in this period where cultural tensions were first encountered by German migrants. When marriages with locals occurred, the Catholic Church did not approve their marriage, as Germans were predominantly Lutherans. Conversion to Catholicism was demanded, which most of the Germans did not accept (Von Houwald, 1975). Hence, conversion to Lutheranism or Protestantism by Nicaraguan partners occurred, influencing in the family culture, which impacted in the way business was done.

The Arrested Development of German Business Families in Nicaragua

Despite enjoying a privileged position as migrants in the last century, German migrant families would be affected by changing local governments and two worldwide events in the 20th century. Whilst prior immigration laws favoured land ownership and settlement support for German migrants, a new government in 1911 started to introduce laws that restricted privileges to migrants and started to evade responsibilities in state-supported financial instruments were Germans had invested substantial capital (Von Houwald, 1975, p. 142).

Moreover, during the First World War (1914 to 1918) the German colony endured severe business penalties as the Nicaraguan government sided with the US in declaring war to Germany and thus German families were seen with suspicion. The trading routes between Germany and Nicaragua, which were the backbone of German migrant families were severed. Following World War I, and the restoration of diplomatic relationships, German migrant families were affected by years of political instability in Nicaragua (Von Houwald, 1975). Despite the growing adversities during the interwar period and to address the setbacks of World War I, German families created diverse associations such as a German club (1932) and a German school (1934) (von Houwald, 1975), which aimed to nurture and strengthen ethnics ties.

Yet, it was during the Second World War (1939) the Nicaraguan government, like most Central American countries honoring pacts with the US, declared war on

Nazi Germany and its allies. In 1939, the German community accounted for 330 residents, not including descendants. Government officials confiscated all property and assets (commercial property, farms, machinery, vehicles, etc.) from any person of German origin, including those born in Nicaragua; all men, including the elderly, were detained and taken to detention centres, commercial houses were dismantled and business leaders incarcerated (Von Houwald, 1975, p. 150). This approach saw the abrupt interruption of ethnic and commercial connections with the country of origin, bankrupting many German migrant business families.

Following World War II, several German families continued in the country. German migrant families decided to continue strengthening their ethnic circles to the creation of cultural centres. The German ethnic community in Nicaragua aimed to preserve over time specific values, skills and cultural features which have endured through diverse crisis. Many descendants developed new businesses in new areas, such as construction and engineering in the 1960s and 1970s (Kühl, 2011a). Yet compared to previous decades, in the 1970s the German community only accounted for 300 Germans living in the country (von Houwald, 1975, pp. 44–45).

Yet again, in the 1980s, German families in business suffered the confiscation of assets due to communist policies enforced during the Sandinista government (Leogrande, 1996; Tyroler, 1991). Several companies founded by German migrant families did not survive the Sandinista Era. Many German business leaders exiled to neighboring Central American countries (e.g., Honduras and Costa Rica) or fled to the US with family successors, whilst some others remained in the country looking after any remaining property, amidst tense diplomatic relationships between Sandinista Nicaragua and Germany (Helm, 2014; Roche, 2006). In many cases, employees defended the property and prevented the destruction of business premises from revolution fighters honoring the good relationships between German business families and Nicaraguan employees (Centeno-Caffarena & Discua Cruz, 2021).

Following such adverse events, and with the return of democratic governments to Nicaragua in the 1990s the descendants of German migrants, shaped their family and business strategies to reinforce the relevance of ethnic ties. Upon their return from exile, German migrant business families prompted the reactivation of ties in transnational ethnic networks, to procure trustworthy information, knowledge and skills that would benefit their firm's internationalization process. In addition, many incorporated the lessons learned from experiences about the expropriation of family assets and mistreatment in World War I, World War II, and the Sandinista era in Nicaragua. The narratives around such adverse circumstances became part of a collective family memory, fueling diversification, strengthening of transnational business links and preserving a German ethos in business (Centeno-Caffarena & Discua Cruz, 2021). Such shared understandings by German business families also generated a distrustful attitude towards government officials and reinforced the relevance of strengthening relationships within the German community. This approach shifted the previously open approach of German business families towards a more reserved culture.

Thus, it is not surprising to find that following such adverse circumstances, the composition and strategies of German migrant business families has varied from previous centuries. Many Germans who arrived following the interwar periods have lived for decades in the country and made Nicaragua their second homeland, yet keep their German nationality and ensure that their descendants have a dual nationality option (Von Houwald, 1975). There are numerous "sons of Germans", who were born in the country and that represent the fourth or fifth generation of the immigrants who arrived early in the last century (Kühl, 2014). Many of them still speak the German language and proudly cultivate the memory of their origin, maintaining connections with relatives in their country of origin. For these families, successor training, and business relationships in diverse networks are linked to external markets (Centeno-Caffarena & Discua Cruz, 2021). Successors are sent to Germany to study and sometimes return with a German spouse. Despite adverse circumstances, the remaining German business families in Nicaragua represent a bridge of friendship and understanding between the two nations.

Our study suggests that despite a favourable start, German Protestants in Nicaragua, may have capitalized on their cultural traits and individual differences from locals (Davis et al., 2001) yet as contextual challenges increase their expected dominance as a minority group was curtailed. For instance, this is represented in the perception that Germans were economically dominant, based in large part upon their business leadership in areas of the economy (e.g., exports) and for their network organization, nevertheless they were gradually uninterested to involve in other sectors of the economy, including retailing and public services, due to several contextual events (e.g., World War I, World War II, Sandinista era) limiting over time the development of their family businesses, and moving to sectors where they could capitalize on their individual preferences and cultural approach to business.

Discussion

At the outset of this chapter, we were concerned with understanding how have migrant business families developed and adapted in Central America. We uncovered that there are different varieties of migrant business families that may be affected by contextual factors (Carney et al., 2009; Wright et al., 2014). By exploring the emergence and adaptability of migrant business families in Honduras and Nicaragua, we can appreciate how many migrant families devise ways of doing things into a host country because their cultural background, training and mind-set are different from local counterparts (Elo et al., 2018). Many migrant business family members arrived often with limited resources yet had already access to relationships that could procure access to trade networks and could support ethnic solidarity (Amaya, 2000; 2011).

In terms of social relationships, we support the view that migrant business families have an advantage in terms of a transnational link when they arrive but also can create a close-knit network (Anderson et al., 2005). A key aspect of developing a close-knit network, is the supportive nature of relationships where you share some features, such as ethnicity. Such features provided a strong bond between members that allowed them to endure diverse challenges, either from their arrival (e.g., Arab-Palestinian families) or over time (German families). This study reveals that migrant business families focus on developing strong family relationships where an ethnic element is developed as a family feature to ensure solidarity and to shape and preserve a way of conducting business that would differentiate migrant from local families. Such features are exemplified in the business and family values observed in both countries. As these migrant families established themselves in industry and commerce, such values influenced the way diverse resources (human, social, financial) were gradually managed (Sirmon & Hitt, 2003) to take advantage of opportunities or to restart affected businesses.

In terms of contextual aspects, it is clear that contextual changes are influential in the way migrant business families develop (Wright et al., 2014). This study reveals that state intervention, in terms of sponsoring migration waves and creating welcoming conditions, whether intended to boost the productivity of a country or shape its cultural development, is a determinant factor for the emergence and development of migrant business families in developing economies. Further state intervention however, when it creates discrimination for migrant families (e.g., alliances to deal with world conflicts) may curtail their development (Davis et al., 2001) and force families to rely strongly on their family and ethnic ties to survive. State intervention (or lack of it) may support reforms intended to minimize or arrest the development of migrant business families as some of these contexts may not have the institutional framework to capitalize on migrant families. In doing so, state intervention may foster, probably inadvertently, the rapid development of some migrant business families, while limiting the growth or causing the demise of others, only to revert such process as world events occur. We contribute further to our understanding of context influencing business families by revealing that whilst some contexts may be unwelcoming to migrants and create hardships in their initial development (e.g., Arab-Palestinian migrant business families) they may ease their approach over time whilst other contexts may initially display welcoming conditions yet turn hostile over time (German migrant business families in Nicaragua) to be in-sync with world events.

An interesting finding in this chapter relates to adaptability. Regardless of the origin of the migrant business families, this chapter shows that despite adverse conditions, only families that capitalized on resources provided by kinship and ethnic fabric, diversified and prepared their successors professionally, were able to react to, participate in, and even influence their environment (Evansluong & Ramírez-Pasillas, 2018). Families in both countries developed an initial culture, based on ethnic elements, that cemented the way they would work for future generations. Future generations, compared to prior studies, can reinforce their ethnic heritage, speak fluently several languages and navigate ethnic and host country cultures efficiently. Thus, subsequent generations not only have the advantages of knowing both the unique migrant family cultures but also and in most cases are able to either incorporate a new way of doing things by studying overseas in either a new (Arab successors in the US) or somewhat familiar culture (German successors in Germany). In doing so, they can reinforce their transnational links when they return to their countries and manage multiple cultures, facilitating their adaptability over time.

This study suggests that state intervention may have an influence in the reliance of family and ethnic ties as a resource for business families. Davis et al. (2001) suggests that discrimination might tend, to increase a group's endowment of "social capital" and if a group faces discrimination, then they will find it advantageous to participate in business activities in which they face less adverse conditions (i.e., Honduran state-sponsored discrimination against Arab-Palestinians reduced the opportunity costs of engaging in certain types of activities for initial migrants). Yet despite their prejudicial reception in Honduras, it appears that the Arab Palestinians have maintained the unity of their ethnic solidarity while successfully accommodating local communities and political interests. Recent studies suggest that this ethnic group has emerged as the dominant capitalist class in Honduras, to which politicians and authorities must take into account in their governance, as they control the largest businesses and are providers of essential services to the country (e.g., electricity). In other words, although, Arab Palestinians despite their most difficult start they have more successfully overcome obstacles to cement their prominent economic and social role in their adopted societies (Amaya, 2000; Indiano, 2014).

On the other hand, the German Protestants in Nicaragua with the more favourable welcome and seemingly better integrated into the local community have experienced a difficult development. Despite evident adaptability and commercial success upon their arrival, they have not fared well. Recent accounts suggest that their openness to blend with the local culture has meant that whilst Nicaraguans with German ethnicity have increased whereas close to one percent (1%) of the population has German roots (Kuhl, 2021) their business dominance has waned. This can be attributed to experiencing an initial softer challenge to meet in order to integrate and whilst their efforts fail to adequately maintain solidarity was evident (e.g., creation of ethnic institutions) the effect of the third parties, namely US interference in the region during World War I and World War II and the asset confiscation under the Sandinistas affected deeply their development. Moreover, our study also suggests that the strength of the German ethnic community was also influenced by their assimilation of Nicaraguan culture through marriage with locals and the lack of interest of subsequent generations in strengthening the relevance of a German ethnic heritage in business.

Given the long timeframe of our study there is an opportunity to suggest the effectiveness of collective solidarity by migrant business families – that is the degree to which ethnic and family solidarity is successful in allowing their development and

Table 23.1: Migrant Business Family Ties and Context.

		Ties	
		Family	**Ethnic**
Context			
	Adverse	Family dynamics aimed to remain private	Increased reliance on building cohesiveness within group Close and private ethnic interactions
		Essential for business emergence in terms of labour and skills	Important for business setup and survival as transaction costs are reduced
		Provider of emotional support Transnational family link strengthened	Provider of business relevant information, societal connections, goods, and services
		Business activity supported by around family skills in restricted industries	Business activity expansion around collective ethnic skills and resources
			Reliance on ethnically-based trading network to minimize opportunistic behaviour
	Favourable	Family ties aimed to blend with society	Creation of ethnic social institutions to enhance embeddedness within host societies
		Relevant for business emergence and development	Provider of information and resources for business diversification
		Provider of emotional support and societal connection	Replicator of business reputation
		Business activity around family preferences and preferred sector	Business activity in association with resourceful locals
			Shared linguistic and cultural aspects minimize misunderstandings in business activities

adaptability in adverse or favourable contexts based on family and ethnic ties. Such effectiveness will vary in different communities and under different circumstances. Table 23.1 shows that such effectiveness may be understood in terms of the context, the level of family openness and the type of business activities that different generations engage over time. The effectiveness of collective solidarity can be understood when family and ethnic ties can be seen as a resource, depending on the nature of the context.

This study suggests that the intertwining between family and ethnic ties cannot be underestimated to understand the way migrant business families adapt in their societies. Table 23.1 suggests that family ties become essential as the main provider of key resources for businesses to emerge and survive. In adverse contextual conditions, family dynamics become close and safeguarded. Family marriages may be preferred within the local ethnic community only or arranged through family networks in countries of origin. Business activity may then be only influenced by the skills provided by family members. Conversely, in favourable conditions, family ties may become less attached to ethnic networks as incoming members may be welcomed by society and mixed marriages allows further embeddedness within the local context. Favourable conditions may allow family members to explore diverse business opportunities and exploit the local connections, cementing their gradual integration in society and their participation in diverse business activities over generations.

Table 23.1 also shows that ethnic ties serve as a key resource for migrant business families in adverse and favourable contextual settings. Based on Davis et al. (2001) we suggest that ethnic ties may encourage collective solidarity by reducing the contract/transaction costs within an ethnic group. Such enhancement occurs by providing relevant information about other migrants or locals thus allowing the screening of potential trading partners. Moreover, sharing similar cultural and linguistic factors may make it relatively easy for members of the same ethnic group to assess each other trustworthiness and to agree on mutual business understandings. Table 23.1 suggests that in adverse settings ethnic communities may help support a transnational link which may turn into the lifeline of existing businesses. Conversely, in favourable settings migrant families may be encouraged to formalize their social interactions and culture and share it with the host society through the creation of cultural institutions (e.g., schools, social clubs). Association to such institutions and to minority ethnic groups may serve as a replicator of business reputation for emergent and existing businesses. Yet dense ethnic networks can also produce ethnic gatekeepers (e.g., Arab-Palestinian patriarchs in Honduras (Indiano, 2014) which may both safeguard or encourage social interaction outside ethnic groups depending on how favourable the contextual setting becomes. In both adverse of favourable conditions ethnic group solidarity may allow screening of members of the same ethnic group or members outside the groups to create and develop businesses.

Our study brings forward the notion that migrant business families, due to often dynamic contextual conditions (e.g., going from adverse to favourable contexts and vice versa) may be in favour of developing diverse business ventures and engage in the development of business groups (Carney & Gedajlovic, 2003). Such portrayal differs from the family business as a nuclear family with a single business, which is something that is more common in western settings, but less applicable to the merchant communities described in this chapter. As the dynamics of contextual conditions may change, migrant business families may create and de-velop diverse businesses based on family skills, preferences, and resources alone or in conjunctions with trusted locals (Rosa, Howorth, & Discua Cruz, 2014), thus in-cluding other forms of kinship based on their lived experiences. Therefore, our study challenges researchers to critically examine traditional notions of the nuclear family with a single business to understand the historical dynamics of business families not only in Central America but in diverse contexts where contextual con-ditions may change such as emerging or transitional economies and affect business families (e.g., Cuba, Venezuela, Tibet, Afghanistan, communist-based governments transitioning to more democratic and capitalist-based societies).

Finally, in both contexts explored, ethnic culture reinforcement occurs through influx of new migrants or through the going back and forth from their family home country. We find that such reinforcement is important, as migrant business families may develop a unique culture based on ethnic heritage. Thus, the opportunity to see cultural relevance in host contexts may only be reinforced and amplified through new migration waves. When such waves reoccur, migrant business families may reinforce share understandings and ways of doing things in business with others, highlighting the relevance of ethnicity and family for business (Vershinina et al., 2019). Taken to-gether, our findings support the relevance of a historical approach (Carney & Gedaj-lovic, 2003) to understand that migrant business families can develop a capability over time to overcome diverse obstacles by adapting to changing circumstances and capitalising on family and ethnic relationships.

Conclusion

This chapter suggests that some contexts may be often unkind to migrant business families yet their adaptability emerges through features related to nurturing ethnic and family relationships, creating spaces that support their ethnic heritage and learning from adverse situations. Some migrant business families may become ex-tremely successful whilst others may fade away and disappear. The possibility that discrimination against a group might contribute to its economic success has impor-tant implications for business family researchers and policymakers. The findings in this chapter present a challenge to business family researchers to carry out more in-depth investigations into the impact of contextual challenges and historical processes to understand how migrant and local business families operate. Yet their audacity in exploring new frontiers and adaptability amidst adverse circum-stances suggest that their approach and responses must not be underestimated in our understanding of business families around the world.

References

Alonso, B. S. (2007). The Other Europeans: Immigration into Latin America and the International Labour Market (1870–1930). *Revista de Historia Económica (Second Series)*, 25(03), 395–426. https://doi.org/10.1017/S0212610900000185

Amaya, J. (2000). *Los Arabes y Palestinos en Honduras (1900–1950)*. Tegucigalpa, Honduras: Editorial Guaymuras.

Amaya, J. (2011). *Los Judíos en Honduras* (2d ed.). Tegucigalpa, Honduras: Editorial Guaymuras.

Anderson, A., Park, J., & Jack, S. L. (2007). Entrepreneurial Social Capital: Conceptualizing Social Capital in New High-tech Firms. *International Small Business Journal*, 25(3), 245–272. https://doi.org/10.1177/0266242607076526

Anderson, A. R., Jack, S. L., & Drakopoulou Dodd, S. (2005). The Role of Family Members In Entrepreneurial Networks: Beyond the Boundaries of the Family Firm. *Family Business Review*, 18(2), 135–154. https://doi.org/10.1111/j.1741-6248.2005.00037.x

Anderson, A. R., & Miller, C. J. (2003). "Class matters": Human and social capital in the entrepreneurial process. *The Journal of Socio-Economics*, 32(1), 17–36. https://doi.org/10.1016/S1053-5357(03)00009-X

Arregle, J.-L., Hitt, M. A., Sirmon, D. G., & Very, P. (2007). The Development of Organizational Social Capital: Attributes of Family Firms. *Journal of Management Studies*, 44(1), 73–95.

Barahona, M. (2005). *Honduras en el Siglo XX: Una Sintesis Historica*. Tegucigalpa, Honduras: Editorial Guaymuras.

Becerra, L. (2011). *Evolucion Historica de Honduras* (21ava ed.). Baktun Editorial, Litografia Lopez.

Brzozowski, J., Cucculelli, M., & Surdej, A. (2014). Transnational ties and performance of immigrant entrepreneurs: The role of home-country conditions. *Entrepreneurship and Regional Development*, 26(7–8), 546–573. https://doi.org/10.1080/08985626.2014.959068

Bull, B., Castellacci, F., & Kasahara, Y. (2014). *Business Groups and Transnational Capitalism in Central America: Economic and Political Strategies*. Basingstoke, UK: Palgrave Macmillan.

Carney, M., & Gedajlovic, E. (2003). Strategic innovation and the administrative heritage of East Asian family business groups. *Asia Pacific Journal of Management*, 20, 5–26.

Carney, M., Gedajlovic, E., & Yang, X. (2009). Varieties of Asian capitalism: Toward an institutional theory of Asian enterprise. *Asia Pacific Journal of Management*, 26(3), 361–380. https://doi.org/10.1007/s10490-009-9139-2

Centeno-Caffarena, L. (2016): Entrepreneurship and family business phenomenon: corresponding, antagonist or indifferent from each other?, In J. M. Saiz-Alvarez (Ed.), *Handbook of Research on Social Entrepreneurship and Solidarity Economic*. (pp. 298–328). IGI Global.

Centeno-Caffarena, L., & Discua Cruz, A. (2021). Internationalization of a migrant family firm and contextual uncertainty: The role of ethnic social networks. In T. Leppäaho & S. L. Jack (Eds.), *The Palgrave Handbook of Family Firm Internationalization* (pp. 431–460). Cham, Switzerland: Palgrave Macmillan.

Colli, A., Fernandez, P., & Rose, M. (2003). National Determinants of Family Firm Development? Family Firms in Britain, Spain and Italy in the Nineteenth and Twentieth Centuries. *Enterprise and Society*, 4(1), 28–64.

Davis, K., Trebilock, M. J., & Heys, B. (2001). Ethnically homogeneous commercial elites in developing countries. *Law & Policy in International Business*, 32, 330–361.

Deakins, D., Ishaq, M., Smallbone, D., Whittam, G., & Wyper, J. (2007). Ethnic minority businesses in Scotland and the role of social capital. *International Small Business Journal*, 25(3), 307–326.

Discua Cruz, A., & Basco, R. (2018). Family Perspective on Entrepreneurship. In R. V. Turcan and N. M. Fraser (Eds.), *The Palgrave Handbook of Multidisciplinary Perspectives on*

Entrepreneurship (pp. 147–175). Springer International Publishing. https://doi.org/10.1007/ 978-3-319-91611-8_8

Discua Cruz, A., Basco, R., Parada, M. J., Malfense Fierro, A. C., & Alvarado Alvarez, C. (2019). Resilience and family business groups in unstable economies. In M. Rautianinen, P. Rosa, T. Pihkala, M. J. Parada, & A. Discua Cruz. *The Family Business Group Phenomenon – Emergence and Complexities* (pp. 315–352). Cham, Switzerland: Palgrave MacMillan.

Discua Cruz, A., Ramos Rodas, C., Raudales, C., & Fortin, L. (2016). Large family businesses in Honduras: The influence of state intervention and immigration in the twentieth century. In *Evolution of Family Businesses: Continuity and Change in Latin America and Spain*. Edward Elgar Publishing.

Duarte, L. E. (2009). Los Nazis y Nicaragua Magazine, La Prensa. *La Prensa*, www.laprensa.com.ni/ magazine/reportaje/los-nazis-y-nicaragua.

Elo, M., & Minto-Coy, I. (Eds.). (2019). *Diaspora Networks in International Business: Perspectives for Understanding and Managing Diaspora Business and Resources*. Springer International Publishing. //www.springer.com/us/book/9783319910949

Elo, M., Sandberg, S., Servais, P., Basco, R., Discua Cruz, A., Riddle, L., & Täube, F. (2018). Advancing the views on migrant and diaspora entrepreneurs in international entrepreneurship. *Journal of International Entrepreneurship*, 16(2),119–133. https://doi.org/ 10.1007/s10843-018-0231-x

Elo, M., Servais, P., Sandberg, S., Discua Cruz, A., & Basco, R. (2019). Entrepreneurship, Migration, and Family in Peripheral Contexts – Avenues for Growth and Internationalisation. *International Journal of Entrepreneurship and Small Business*, 36(1/2), 1–15. https://doi.org/10.1504/ IJESB.2019.096973

Euraque, D. A. (1997). The Arab-Jewish Economic Presence in San Pedro Sula, the Industrial Capital of Honduras: Formative Years, 1880s-1930s. *Immigrants and Minorities*, 16(1 y 2), 94–124.

Euraque, D. A. (2001). *El Capitalismo de San Pedro Sula y la Historia Política Hondureña (1870– 1972)* (2d ed.). Tegucigalpa, Honduras: Editorial Guaymuras.

Euraque, D. A. (2009). Los árabes de Honduras: Entre la inmigración, la acumulación y la política. In *Contribuciones Arabes a las Identidades Iberoamericanas* (pp. 233–284). ROTOSA. http://www.pensamientocritico.org/primera-epoca/casara0511.pdf#page=234

Evansluong, Q., Ramirez Pasillas, M., & Nguyen Bergström, H. (2019). From breaking-ice to breaking-out: Integration as an opportunity creation process. *International Journal of Entrepreneurial Behavior and Research*, 25(5), 880–899. https://doi.org/10.1108/IJEBR-02- 2018-0105

Evansluong, Q., & Ramírez-Pasillas, M. (2018). The role of family social capital in immigrants' entrepreneurial opportunity creation processes. *International Journal of Entrepreneurship and Small Business*, 36(1–2), 164–188. https://doi.org/10.1504/IJESB.2019.096973

Fearnow, B. (2019, July 22). *Nearly half of all Fortune 500 companies were founded by immigrants or their children, study finds*. Newsweek. https://www.newsweek.com/immigrant-founded- fortune-500-companies-us-gdp-1450498

Fernández Pérez, P., & Lluch, A. (2016). *Evolution of Family Business: Continuity and Change in Latin America and Spain*. Cheltenham, UK: Edward Elgar Publishing.

Fletes, E. (1911). *Commercial Directory of Honduras, 1911*. Hamburg: Schröder and Jeve.

Gupta, V., Levenburg, N., Moore, L., Motwani, J., & Schwarz, T. (Eds.). (2008). *Culturally Sensitive Models of Family Businesses in Latin America* (Vol. 1–10). ICFAI University Press.

Hamilton, E., Discua Cruz, A., and Jack, S. (2017). Re-framing the status of narrative in family business research: Towards an understanding of families in business. *Journal of Family Business Strategy*, 8(1), 3–12. https://doi.org/10.1016/j.jfbs.2016.11.001

Helm, C. (2014). Booming solidarity: Sandinista Nicaragua and the West German Solidarity movement in the 1980s. *European Review of History: Revue Européenne d'histoire*, 21(4), 597–615. https://doi.org/10.1080/13507486.2014.933179

Illescas, J. (2009). *Los Grupos de Poder y los Sectores Industrial y Agrícola. Honduras: Poderes facticos y sistema político* (Tercera reimpresión 2009). CEDOH.

Indiano, C. (2014). *Los Oligarcas: ¿De Donde Salieron los Ricos?* Zafra.

Jack, S., Moult, S., Anderson, A. R., & Dodd, S. (2010). An entrepreneurial network evolving: Patterns of change. *International Small Business Journal*, 28(4), 315–337. https://doi.org/10.1177/0266242610363525

James, A., Hadjielias, E., Guerrero, M., Discua Cruz, A., & Basco, R. (2020). Entrepreneurial families in business across generations, contexts and cultures. *Journal of Family Business Management* (ahead of print). https://doi.org/10.1108/JFBM-01-2020-0003

Koebel, W. H. (1917). *CENTRAL AMERICA: Guatemala, Nicaragua, Costa Rica, Honduras, Panama and Salvador. London:* T. Fisher Unwin Publishers.

Kühl, E. (2011b). Jinotega y su Café por Eddy Kuhl. *Revista de Temas Nicaraguenses*, 44, 158–167.

Kühl, E. (2012). La Primera despulpadora de café en Matagalpa. *Revista de Temas Nicaraguenses*, 49, 4–5.

Kühl, E. (2014). Primeros Inmigrantes a Nicaragua por Origen. *Revista de Temas Nicaraguenses*, 77, 228–258.

Kühl, E. (2017). Algunos Inmigrantes Alemanes a Nicaragua y sus Obras. *Revista de Temas Nicaraguenses*, 112, 281–293.

Kühl, Eddy. (2011a). Construcción y Constructores: El Boom de la Construcción en Nicaragua, Décadas de los 60s y 70s. *Revista de Temas Nicaraguenses*, 38, 70–86.

Kühl, Eddy. (2019). *Los Buenos y los Malos en la Historia de Nicaragua.* Managua, Nicaragua: PAVSA.

Kühl, Eddy. (2021). Interview to Mr. Eddy Kuhl on August 11.

Larson, J. M., & Lewis, J. I. (2017). Ethnic Networks. *American Journal of Political Science*, 61(2),350–364. https://doi.org/10.1111/ajps.12282

Lemus, M., & Bourgeois, H. G. (1897). *Breve Noticia sobre Honduras: Datos Geográficos, Estadísticos e Informaciones Prácticas.* Tipografia Nacional.

Leogrande, W. M. (1996). Making the economy scream: Us economic sanctions against Sandinista Nicaragua. *Third World Quarterly*, 17(2), 329–348. https://doi.org/10.1080/01436599650035716

Leyva, H. M. (2000). *Hacia una Dinamica Cultural del Desarrollo en Honduras.* Programa de las naciones unidas para el desarrollo, PNUD.

Lombard, T. R. (1887). *The New Honduras: Its Situation, Resources, Opportunities and Prospects, Concisely Stated from Recent Personal Observations (1887).* Brentano Publishers.

Müller, C., Botero, I. C., Discua Cruz, A., & Subramanian, R. (2019). *Family Firms in Latin America.* New York, USA and London, UK: Routledge.

Mustafa, M., & Chen, S. (2010). The strength of family networks in transnational immigrant entrepreneurship. *Thunderbird International Business Review*, 52(2), 97–106. https://doi.org/10.1002/tie.20317

Moules, J. (2014, 04). Migrants set up one in seven UK companies, study reveals. *Financial Times.* http://www.ft.com/content/dc7f9f0e-a3ae-11e3-88b0-00144feab7de

Nordqvist, M., Marzano, G., Brenes, E. R., Jimenez, G., & Fonseca-Paredes, M. (2011). Understanding entrepreneurial family businesses in uncertain environments: The case of Latin America. In M. Nordqvist, G. Marzano, E. R. Brenes, G. Jimenez, & M. Fonseca-Paredes (Eds.), *Understanding Entrepreneurial Family Businesses in Uncertain Environments: Opportunities and Resources in Latin America* (pp. 1–29). Cheltenham: Edward Elgar.

Roche, M. (2006). Competing Claims: The Struggle for Title in Nicaragua Note. *Vanderbilt Journal of Transnational Law*, 39(2), 577–606.

Rohan, D. (2010). *El sueño del olivar*. Suma de Letras.

Romero, R. (2008). Los grupos financieros y el poder político. In L. S. Víctor Meza Ramón Romero, Manuel Torres y Jorge Illescas (Ed.), *HONDURAS: Poderes Fácticos y Sistema Político*. CEDOH.

Rosa, P., Howorth, C., & Discua Cruz, A. (2014). Habitual and portfolio entrepreneurship and the family in business. In L. Melin, M. Nordqvist, & P. Sharma (Eds.), *The SAGE Handbook of Family Business* (pp. 364–382). London: Sage.

Roscoe, P., Discua Cruz, A., & Howorth, C. (2013). How does an old firm learn new tricks? A material account of entrepreneurial opportunity. *Business History*, 55(1), 53–72. https://doi.org/10.1080/00076791.2012.687540

Salcedo, S., & Guzman, L. (2014). El concepto de agricultura familiar en América Latina y el Caribe, FAO, Chile. In S. Salcedo and L. Guzman (Eds.), *Agricultura Familiar en América Latina y el Caribe: Recomendaciones de Política*. FAO.

Scott, L. S. (1909). *Honduras: The New Eldorado*. J. G. Hauser.

Sirmon, D. G., & Hitt, M. A. (2003). Managing Resources: Linking Unique Resources, Management, and Wealth Creation in Family Firms. *Entrepreneurship Theory and Practice*, 27(4), 339–358. https://doi.org/10.1111/1540-8520.t01-1-00013

Spielmann, N., Discua Cruz, A., Tyler, B. B., & Beukel, K. (2021). Place as a nexus for corporate heritage identity: An international study of family-owned wineries. *Journal of Business Research*, 129, 826–837. https://doi.org/10.1016/j.jbusres.2019.05.024

Strachan, H. (1976). *Family and Other Business Groups in Economic Development: The Case of Nicaragua*. Praeger.

Tyroler, D. (1991). Nicaragua: Recent Debate Surrounding Property Confiscated by Sandinista Government. https://Digitalrepository.Unm.Edu/Noticen/5557, 1–2.

Uzzi, B. (1997). Social structure and competition in inter-firm networks: The paradox of embeddedness. *Administrative Science Quarterly*, 42, 35–67.

Vershinina, N., Rodgers, P., Mcadam, M., & Clinton, E. (2019). Transnational migrant entrepreneurship, gender and family business. *Global Networks*, 19(2), 238–260. https://doi.org/10.1111/glob.12225

Vertovec, S. (2001). Transnationalism and identity. *Journal of Ethnic and Migration Studies*, 27(4), 573–582. https://doi.org/10.1080/13691830120090386

Von Houwald, G. (1975). *Los Alemanes en Nicaragua, Vol. Colección Cultural*. Banco de América. Nicaragua.

World Bank (2017) The World Bank In Nicaragua. https://www.worldbank.org/en/country/nicaragua

World Bank. (2018). *Doing Business in Honduras and Nicaragua – World Bank Group*. http://www.doingbusiness.org/

Wright, M., Chrisman, J. J., Chua, J. H., & Steier, L. P. (2014). Family Enterprise and Context. *Entrepreneurship Theory and Practice*, 38(6), 1247–1260. https://doi.org/10.1111/etap.12122

Rodrigo Basco and Arpita Vyas

24 Succession Process and the Model of Change in a Transgenerational Family Business

Abstract: Drawing on the micro-foundation of institutional logics, this chapter aims to explore how successors address the demand to introduce changes in their family firms. When a successor takes over a family firm, market and family pressures challenge the existing family business model; however, these pressures do not necessarily result in changes. Relying on a single case study, we discovered that successors respond to these pressures based on the level of successor status quo in terms of the family and business logics. To generalize our results, this chapter presents a model of change during the succession process.

Keywords: transgenerational family business, micro-foundations, succession, family logics, business logics

Introduction

Management succession has received significant attention from researchers in the field of family business studies (Cisneros, Ibanescu, Keen, Lobato-Calleros, & Niebla-Zatarain, 2018), demonstrating the importance of the succession as an event/process that affects the evolutionary pattern of family firms (Handler, 1994). Management succession introduces renewal and strategic changes (Cucculelli, Le Breton-Miller, & Miller, 2016), which is characterized by the family life cycle imposing a leadership shift from one family generation to the next. The existing literature indicates towards a common pattern of evolution that family firms experience during succession. This is manifested in ownership and governance methods of an organization across generations (Parada, Gimeno, Samara, & Saris, 2020). However, because all family firms do not evolve in a similar way, we investigate the reason for changes in ownership, governance, and management levels to occur during the succession process. To address this research gap, we use a model of the micro-foundation of succession changes to explain how changes occur in family businesses across generations.

Applying the micro-foundation perspective of institutional logics (Thornton, Ocasio, & Lounsbury, 2012) to succession, we argue that family firms are formed by two systems (the family and the firm) with different sets of logic – the market logic (the firm system) and family logic (Micelotta & Fairclough, 2013), exercising different

Rodrigo Basco, Arpita Vyas, American University of Sharjah

https://doi.org/10.1515/9783110727968-024

kinds of pressure (market and family pressures) for achieving stability and change. Ignoring these pressures can lead to a mismatch between the firm and its context, thereby jeopardizing the continuity of the family firm. However, the market and family pressures perceived by successors before, during, and after the leadership shift are not necessarily correlated with changes. While some successors decide to introduce radical changes, others introduce marginal or no changes, as part of their deliberate decision-making processes. In this sense, our research attempts to answer the following question: How do successors react towards the market and family pressures during the management shift from one generation to another?

To address our research question, we use a qualitative methodology by focusing on a holistic and single case study to analyze a business family across two different generational shifts in the United Arab Emirates (UAE). The UAE is an emerging economy in which development is based on the exploitation of natural resources, with the unique evolution of formal and informal institutional context (Krueger, Bogers, Labaki, & Basco, 2021) and important cultural changes across generations (Schvaneveldt, Kerpelman, & Schvaneveldt, 2005), through which family businesses navigate their succession (Basco, Omari, & Abouchkaier, 2020). Firm ownership structures in the UAE are highly concentrated and mostly controlled by families (Martinez Garcia, Boubakri, Gomez-Anson, & Basco, 2022). The family owners/controlling generation tends to exacerbate their risks due to the family portfolio investment, which forces the firm to pursue conservative strategies and address its goal asymmetries due to prioritization of family-oriented goals. The successor generation has to base his/her reactions on different market and family pressures, in accordance with the status quo of the firm and the controlling generation (Martínez-García, Basco, & Gómez-Ansón, 2021), considering the high power distance and low levels of individualism as part of informal institutional contexts prevalent in the UAE. In this sense, our study addresses the call for further research in emerging, developing, and transitional economies to better understand the nuances of family firms (Basco, 2018).

The results of our study show that both market and/or family pressures could result in business, organizational, or strategic changes. When successors experience pressures and receive signals that the well-being of the family firm could be jeopardized, the implementation of changes relies on the successor's willingness to introduce and implement changes. In other words, a successor's willingness to introduce and implement changes is related to the current affairs or level of status quo regarding the firm and the family, as well as the risk evaluation of the consequences of implementing a change as a response to the pressures. The evaluation of risk is influenced by the institutional logic in which the successor is embedded; this defines the successors' schemas. Moreover, all succession processes face similar or common pressures of change; however, the firm renewal strategy from one generation to another depends on the successor schemas to understand the extent of the threat imposed on the family firm by the market and family pressures. We summarize our results by proposing a model of change during management succession.

This chapter contributes to theory and practice in several ways. First, by addressing the call to investigate the micro-foundation of institutional logics (Thornton et al., 2012), we explore how successors respond to the pressures of institutional logics to explain governance, organizational, and strategic changes during succession. In line with the institutional logic prediction, we thus observe that successors use their schemas and patterns of thoughts to organize categories of information according to their level of status quo, interpreting market and family pressures and eventually implementing governance, organizational, and/or strategic changes. Moreover, the status quo level may differ among the family and firm system because each follows its specific logic. Second, our chapter also contributes to a better understanding of succession in family firms through a successor's perspective. By challenging the principle that succession is a mechanism to rejuvenate the company (Hoy & Sharma, 2009), and there are common patterns of governance evolution (Parada et al., 2020), we explain why successors possibly respond to market and family pressures by introducing governance, organizational, and/or strategic changes in their family firms.

Finally, we propose a practical model of change during succession to interpret the pressures of the family and firm, the successor's level of status quo, and the type and nature of changes. This model could help business families, successors, and practitioners reflect on the changes associated with a management succession shift to overcome the fear of introducing strategic changes.

Succession and Change from an Institutional Logics Perspective

The institutional logics perspective is a useful approach for studying the relationship between individuals, organizations, and institutions. The concept of institutional logics is defined as "the socially constructed, historical patterns of material practices, assumptions, values, beliefs, and rules by which individuals produce and reproduce their material subsistence, organize time and space, and provide meaning to their social reality" (Thornton & Ocasio, 1999, p. 804). While the macro perspective of institutional logics proposes that institutions shape actors' cognition and behaviour, the micro-foundations attempt to explain the heterogeneity of behaviours among these actors.

In the case of family firms, the importance and dominance of family and business logic define their strategic behaviour. Family firm strategy is based on two domains: market and non-market. While the market domain refers to the way a family firm competes in its industry/sector, the non-market domain refers to a firm's pattern of actions to improve its performance and survival by managing its social, cultural, political, and legal contexts (Baron, 1995; Mellahi, Frynas, Sun, & Siegel, 2016). Although the political non-market domain dominates the debate in strategic literature, we are interested in the family as a specific dimension of the non-market domain (Basco, Rodriguez Escudero, Martin-Cruz, & Barros-Contreras, 2021). Each of these domains has its logic and both can co-exist, affecting how family members perceive reality and how to behave to legitimize their existence (Basco, 2019). However, the dynamics of the market and non-market domains are not static and are constantly changing, shaping actors' decision-making by prioritizing one or another logic (Thornton et al., 2012).

When family members are involved in the top management team, and there is an intention to pursue intra-family succession, succession in family firms is subject to the family's incumbent lifecycle. In the context of family firms, the controlling generation serves for a long time and is thus short-sighted to warn of the pressures of change (Hambrick & Mason, 1984). Family firms may have misaligned strategies in terms of their market and non-market domains during management succession. Therefore, intra-family management succession would imply changes related to re-aligning the family business strategy to the market and non-market domains (Zhao, Carney, Zhang, & Zhu, 2020). During management succession, the dynamics of market and non-market pressures become more evident for the upcoming generation.

Market pressures in family firms, as in any other type of firm, arise from firms' competitive environment. Family firms must position themselves with a competitive strategy. From the perspective of Porter (1980), family firms must define their strategies by crafting a profitable and sustainable position within the industry. To this end, the forces of competition, potential new entrants, power of suppliers, power of customers, and threat of substitute products define the intensity, attractiveness, and profitability of an industry or market. Within this context, institutional logic of market defines priorities, goals, and expectations shaping a family firm's decision-making process and thus its behaviour.

However, the context in which family firms compete is not static and is subject to change. In other words, firms must adapt their strategies to survive in a competitive environment (Reeves & Deimler, 2011). Since succession implies a retrospective analysis of the firm's strategic position as an adaptive event (Quigley & Hambrick, 2012), a new generation of family leaders may bring fresh ideas to re-align the family firm with its competitive environment. In this sense, the managerial discretion of the new family leaders to interpret and reinterpret the logic of the five forces will result in strategic changes in the firm. Family firms initiating the succession process are more likely to increase their level of strategic change (Zhao et al., 2020).

Conversely, non-market pressures emerge, which are specifically related to the family – that is, a group of people related to each other by consanguinity or affinity with specific collective identities. Family pressures emerge because of the evolution of the family over time in terms of their structural, psychosocial, and transactional dimensions (Wamboldt & Reiss, 1989). The structural dimension refers to the structure of the family in terms of the number of members constituting the group, such as parents and children. Based on the number of family members and their types of relationships, different types of families can be defined, such as families of procreation, nuclear families, joint families, and extended families, among others. The psychosocial dimension refers to the task and roles that family members collaboratively perform towards mutual need fulfillment, nurturance, and development (Fitzpatrick & Ritchie, 1993). Finally, the transactional dimension refers to family members' actions/processes that develop a sense of belonging, family identity, strong bonds of loyalty and emotion, creating a common history and projection of the future through communication patterns (Fitzpatrick & Wamboldt, 1990).

Since these dimensions are not constant and change across the family lifecycle (Stangej & Basco, 2017), the family – as an institution – transforms itself based on old and new collective identities formed by cognitive, normative, structural, and emotional connections. In most families, the changesin the structural dimension are a natural corollary of the passage of time when new family members are added to the family through marriage, adoption, or birth. The family genogram becomes more complex, with additional layers displaying more interpersonal relationships. Because of structural changes in the family, psychosocial and transactional dimensions are affected. The psychosocial dimension becomes more complex because of an increase in overlapping family roles. For instance, overlapping roles emerge because family members must play different roles within the boundaries of the family system (for instance, a person simultaneously plays the roles of both grandfather and father). Finally, the changes experienced by the structural and psychosocial dimensions of the family are manifested in the interpersonal relationships building the family identity and sense of belonging. Therefore, the number, frequency, and quality of interpersonal relationships are more complex over time because of the number of members involved and the roles played by each member in the family business systems.

Consequently, the transformation of the three dimensions of a family over time defines the uniqueness of the business family, in line with the interaction of the family with its business. In this sense, the lifecycle of the family imposes changes on the family business, which requires constant family-business fit adjustments. The explicit consequences of the family-business lifecycle include the intra-family management succession changes. However, the constant evolution of the structural, psychosocial, and transactional dimensions represents the family pressure experienced by management successors to adjust their non-market strategy in terms of the family-business relationship.

If the market and family domains evolve, and the institutional pressures are more visible during the transition period, why do some family management successors introduce changes to family firms, while others do not.

Method

To explore the market and family pressures and how successors respond to them, this research uses the qualitative method of a case study because it helps examine complex phenomena (Yin, 2009). In this sense, the purpose of this case study is to engage in analytical generalization (Eisenhardt, 1989) by exploring the phenomenon being studied. A single case study may provide nuanced and rich empirical evidence from a holistic perspective (Discua Cruz, 2020), relying on the narrative of participants for the phenomenological description (Hamilton et al., 2017). In line with the study of Leppäaho, Plakoyiannaki, and Dimitratos (2015), we use a case study because it could be revelatory of the market and family pressures and how successors react to them by introducing changes to family firms. Additionally, a single case study could allow us to perform context-sensitive analyses (Patton, 2002), which is relevant for the family business field of research (Gomez-Mejia, Basco, Müller, & Gonzalez, 2020; Krueger et al., 2021).

Selection of the Case

The firm selected for this case study is a private third-generation Emirati family firm. The company was established in the late seventies by the grandfather of the current supervising generation. The family firm initiated its activities in the construction and real estate sectors and benefited from the rapid growth experienced by the UAE due to the favourable international context associated with its natural resource-based economic model. Beyond the two original economic activities, the family firm has a third stream of revenue dedicated to national and international investments, acting as a wealth management division in the firm to diversify the family's wealth.

There were three reasons for choosing this case. First, the case could be representative of an Emirati firm, despite having cultural characteristics to maintain privacy. This Emirati firm cooperated with us by providing access to valuable information to conduct our research. In general, it is difficult to collect personal, family, and business data from Emirati firms, as they are less likely to share private information to keep their family and social life separate. Second, the preliminary evidence revealed that family involvement in the firm (family participation) is high, and there is an intention to maintain intra-family succession across generations. The last two CEOs were family members, and all shares of the company were owned by the family. Finally, during this research, the selected family firm finalized the second succession transition (from the second to the third generation), which represented an interesting moment to understand the market and family pressure to change, along with the changes introduced to the family firm.

Data Sources

Similar to most qualitative studies, this study relied on multiple sources of information. The data collection process and data analysis began in 2017 and lasted until 2019. The most important source of information was the two interviews conducted with the second and third generations of successors and one interview with a non-family manager who worked in the company and was a witness of the two intra-family successions. In addition to these interviews, we collected reports and family and business documents, such as family constitution and financial information. Finally, one of the authors of this chapter participated in several family meetings involving discussions related to the family firm, all the notes from these meetings were used in this research. The interviews with key family members and non-family employees were taped and transcribed and were aimed to gain an in-depth understanding of the two succession transitions that took place in the family firm; from the first to the second generation and from the second to the third generation. It is important to highlight the successful transition from the second to the third generation was in its final stage during the data collection. Therefore, while the first succession transition was analyzed based on a retrospective perspective in which informants provided their experiences and analysis of the process, the second succession transition was partially occurred during data collection.

Each interview had a guide template with a set of questions to ensure that the basic and important information for our research was collected. Despite having an interview guide, the interviews were like an open conversation, allowing the participants to comment and transmit their emotions and understand the processes and circumstances of the succession.

Data Analysis

The analysis of interview transcripts followed an interactive process initiated by reading the transcripts to gain an overview of the data collected. This reading was triangulated with the documents collected from the family and the firm, along with the research notes from the family and ownership meetings. Thus, data analysis was inductive, as the study focused on understanding the perceptions and experiences of the participants. The coding process commenced with reading the interviews and additional material to identify emerging themes following the theoretical framework and other themes emerging from our interpretation to link the market and non-market pressures with family business changes.

Our theoretical framework to interpret the pressures of the market and family domains on the successors' decision to introduce changes was used as the first step of the coding process, which was developed by one of the authors of this study. This was analyzed and discussed with the second author to obtain a consensus. Furthermore, this coding methodology was used for the first and second succession transitions in the given family business case. The second step in the process of analyzing the data included the interpretation of changes introduced by incumbents and successors based on the pressure observed or experienced by them during the transition.

The Context of United Arab Emirates

Because family firms are embedded in multiple contexts shaping and constraining their existence (Basco, 2017), to understand the market and family pressures, our study of intra-family succession was contextualized in the broader institutional and cultural environment of the UAE where the selected family and firm exist. The UAE emerged as a federation of seven emirates (Abu Dhabi, Dubai, Sharjah, Ras al-Khaimah, Ajman, Umm-al-Qaiwain, and Fujairah) at the beginning of the 1970s. The new country had its cultural, institutional, and economic roots in Islam, the tribal nature of Gulf society, and the pearl fishing and trade economy. This would have a significant implication for the family as an institution whose individuals develop strong family oriented relations (Lalonde, 2013) and thus the intention to pursue intra-familial succession within the boundaries of the firm. However, the family's intention to pursue intra-familial succession is dominated by cultural patterns such as patriarchal family structures and religious principles, including the application of Sharia law by introducing rights and restrictions in terms of inheritance, which limits the development of family ownership and management across generations.

However, the cultural roots have been affected by the UAE's economic transformation, growth, and development based on a natural resource-based economy (oil reserves), accompanied by government leadership to finance development projects and education and health programs. For instance, Schvaneveldt, Kerpelman, and Schvaneveldt (2005) have unveiled the generational and cultural changes in family life between mothers and daughters in the UAE by highlighting differences in terms of marriage, family life, childcare practices, and gender role attitudes, demonstrating the acceptance of new ideas by the next generation through their reinterpretation of old traditions, norms, and beliefs.

Therefore, in the context of a "centralized tribe" institutional system (Fainshmidt, Judge, Aguilera, & Smith, 2018), the next generation of family members – who are supposed to assume the leadership role in the business families and family businesses across the UAE – are confronting their intra-family succession experience in the context of economic and social changes characterized by government's effort to diversify the economy. This implies shifting the market domain rules from a natural resource-based economy to a knowledge-based economy and the opening of the society due to the economic development and educational levels, thereby eroding the traditional cultural parameters of the family (e.g., primogeniture, gender roles, female/male ownership and management participation, education, etc.).

Results

We explain our results by following the previously mentioned data analysis. First, we focus on the different pressures described and explained by the successors (second and third generations) during the interview. This information was complemented with notes taken during family meetings. Second, we analyze the interpretation of successors and non-family employees regarding the market and family pressure of deciding whether to introduce changes in the firm. Finally, we interpret why successors introduced changes to their family firms.

Family Domain Pressures

Table 24.1 illustrates the information extracted from the data collection and the results of the coding process. The first group of family pressures comes from the structural dimensions of the family. Our interviewees highlighted the family transformation from the first to the second generation and from the second to the third generation. For instance, the current successor anticipated upcoming pressure, since the fourth generation of family members has been growing exponentially. The second group of family pressures arise from the psychosocial dimensions of the family. Participants mentioned the changing and overlapping roles experienced by them while the family was expanding. Additionally, there were new family roles assumed by the in-laws, even when they did not work or participate in any meeting related to the business. The final group of family pressures are imposed by the transactional dimension of the family, and participants mentioned anecdotes that made them feel a part of the family. The shared actions of their family boosted their commitments; however, they also recognized the deteriorating level of family interactions while the family moved from one generation to another.

Market Domain Pressures

Table 24.2 illustrates the information extracted from our data collection and the results of the coding process for market domain pressures. We have identified four first-order concepts to capture and summarize market pressures: demographic issues, informal institutional issues, economic issues, and competitive issues.

The Strategic Changes

During the second phase of our data analysis, the association between pressures and changes implemented by successors, or the new generation of family members,

Table 24.1: Coding of Family Pressures.

Information Extracted (quotes)	First-Order Concepts
"In the beginning, it was just my father and my mother working to make things happen. When my father got sick his seven children had something to say about the family and the firm" (second-generation successor)	Structural pressures
"My father has more than 25 grandchildren . . . We are not a bank for the family" (second-generation successor)	
"One founder and 9 shareholders, now you have the potential of having up to 30+ family shareholders . . . " (second-generation successor)	
" . . . we are more than 30 cousins and half of them have children. So, you can imagine the number of family members in the fourth generation . . . " (third generation successor)	
"The possibility of continuing . . . if my nephew is able to play a very neutral role between all his uncles and aunts and cousins" (second generation successor)	Psychosocial pressures
"Some of my brothers are passive shareholders, but others are more involved in the firm . . . [one of them] . . . . Is semi-retired, but his role is very important in the family and in the business, he is the eldest brother . . . he brings opportunities . . . " (second-generation successor)	
" . . . I stepped in [the firm] . . . because I was outside of the country, I was neutral and did not have tension with my brothers and sisters . . . " (second-generation successor)	
"[other roles than managing the firm] . . . I also mange relationships between family members, between the family and the company, and inside the company" (second-generation successor)	
"My mother's presence in the family meetings calms everybody down" (second-generation successor)	
"[regarding the successor] . . . His role is that of a conflict manager . . . to manage family relationships" (second-generation successor)	
"My uncle, who is the same age as me, is interested in the firm since I joined it. I have a higher position in the firm but a lower position in the family" (third-generation successor)	
"I have the highest rank between my siblings and my cousins because I am the oldest of the oldest" (third-generation successor)	
"Some family members play a significant role inside the family in order to have some kind of vision and to convince the rest of the family members to continue . . . " (non-family employee)	

Table 24.1 (continued)

Information Extracted (quotes)	First-Order Concepts
"[talking about the successor from the third generation] . . . he will be able to maintain the family together because he is not conflicting . . . He is patient, knowledgeable, educated, and has worked outside, he was involved in the company absorbing knowledge" (non-family employee)	
" . . . we are still siblings, still brothers and sisters, but the next generation will not be the same with cousins . . . they do not have the same close [ties]" (second-generation successor)	Transactional pressures
" . . . I came back. I wasn't interested in the company, I was interested in sustaining my father's vision" (second-generation successor)	
" . . . what I learned in the university was theoretical, everything I leaned from my father was much more practical, I saw who is buying, who is not buying, who is a crook . . . who has a reputation . . . " (second-generation successor)	
"My father used to make me read the newspaper to him . . . I still do so . . . It was an emotional aspect . . . On a personal level those were the best years of my life" (second-generation successor)	
"I told the shareholders bring their sons and daughters who are over 18 because if they die their children are going to assume as shareholders . . . " (second-generation successor)	
"We are moving into a new building because this is old . . . We will move my father's office, as it is standing today and the same way he left, and shift it in the new building, as he is still there . . . " (second-generation successor)	
"My siblings always talk about our father to their kids." (second-generation successor)	
"For my father the company was his income and his social status . . . For us siblings, because I assume, most of us like each other, it was a source of income and a way to stay together . . . For the third generation, some of them are friends some not . . . it will only be a source of income . . . " (second-generation successor)	
"Our aim is to be one family, and to be one firm" (third-generation successor)	
"we try to hold the family together and my grandmother is the central part of our life" (third-generation successor)	
"I joined the company because my family really needed me there" (third-generation successor)	
"The current managing director [second generation] is mentoring the third successor from the third generation" (non-family employee)	

Table 24.2: Coding of Market Pressures.

Information from Data	First-Order Concepts
"Before 2003 there were no stock market, my father's generation used their social network to invest. In the 60's the entire country was 100,000 people. Now it's 10 million." (second-generation successor)	Demographic issues
"The people in the UAE have changed. The UAE has half a million new people coming every year so imagine . . . " (second-generation successor)	
" . . . [during my father's time] . . . everything was about reputation to run a business . . . Everything was conducted on the basis of trust . . . " (second-generation successor)	Informal institutional issues
" . . . I do not have my father's network to run a business anymore . . . but we have a good reputation and the industry recognizes it" (second-generation successor)	
"During my grandfather's leadership, there was an economic boom in our country, everything was growing so fast . . . during my father and uncle's leadership the pace of growth continued . . . today the market has changed, the country is not the same . . . ." (third-generation successor)	Economic issues
"The only major threat is if we borrow too much . . . it will make us aggressive" (non-family employee)	Competitive issues

emerged. However, the existence of market and family pressures does not imply governance, organizational, or strategic changes in the family firm. Each successor evaluated the risk of pressure by comparing the consequences of acting to over-come the challenge and not taking any actions. Risk evaluation follows a bounded rationality cognitive process influenced by the institutional logic in which the successor is embedded. In other words, institutional logic defines successors' schemas, which determine the level of the successor's status quo. In this case, the schema concerns risk and the extent to which a change can be implemented.

Table 24.3 presents the results of the analysis. We observed a clear differentiation of schemas – that is, the level of status quo – when interviewees talked about market and family pressures and the previously implemented changes or those in the pipeline. There are two status quos associated with the successor: one related to the market logic, and the other to the family logic. This was followed by the occurrence of changes to overcome the threat associated with one or more pressures (Table 24.4).

Table 24.3: Governance, Organizational, or Strategic Changes During the First Succession Transition.

Quotes	Type of Change	Researcher Interpretation
"We are entrepreneurial in the investment side not in the idea of the company. The idea of the company is to be risk averse" (second-generation successor)	Business changes	The meaning of business changes is related to the diversification strategy of the family wealth investment. The business model does not suffer significant changes.
"There are lot of differences and similarities between my father's firm and the second-generation firm. While my father invested in companies only in our county and in the gulf area, we move into a geographical diversification strategy" (second-generation successor)		The second generation was risk averse. The leaders of this generation prefer to maintain the status quo by introducing marginal changes to follow a harvest posture.
"I accelerate the process of investment concentration, selling assets that we do not know about or with little or negative return" (second-generation successor)		The market signal was positive in terms of the well-performing UAE resource-based economy because of the international price of commodities, the real estate opportunities in the market, and the low power of customers
"When my father passed away we accelerated the reorganization of our investments. We needed to change to adjust our strategy to the new internet era" (second generation successor)		The only problem they visualize was the risk of having their investment concentrated in the local/regional firms. Interpreting this as a risk, they decided to introduce changes into their business model by diversifying their investments across the world.
"We had a portfolio . . . 99% east and 1% west now our portfolio is 67% gulf and 33% west" (second-generation successor)		
"The second generation went very conservative after introducing changes in the way in terms of diversification (to diversify risk), not leverage, and the way they pay dividends" (non-family employee)		
" . . . major dramatic changes we haven't done, maybe a little bit here and there [referring to the business side during the transition from the first to the second generation]" (non-family employees)		

Table 24.3 (continued)

Quotes	Type of Change	Researcher Interpretation
"I manage relationships between family members, the family and the company, and inside the company" (second-generation successor) " . . . family firms have to have some kind of unity within the family, what brings them together should be grandfather, or grandmother . . . " "It is a source of income, but it is also a way for us to stay together . . . most of us like each other"	Family changes	The second generation successor was a family leader to maintain the unity of the family after the founder passed away. During that time, several strategic changes were introduced from the family side to stabilize the family-business relationship. For instance, the ownership meeting was institutionalized. The ownership meeting was also a family meeting. This helped family members start constructive communication and debate around the family and the business. Additionally, family members signed a short constitution to preserve their father's legacy. Explicit commitment to assume their owner responsibility. Finally, all brothers and sisters assumed the compromise to restore to the firm the assets received from their father before passing away.

Table 24.4: Governance, Organizational, or Strategic Changes During the Second Succession Transition.

Quotes	Type of Change	Researcher Interpretation
"without a change the firm will be stagnant" "There has to be a change between now and then. Like my uncle changed a lot from my grandfather" (third-generation successor) "For me, now the market is a bit different from my uncle's period" (third-generation successor) "Now if you do not take risk you do not make money" (third-generation successor)	No business changes	The third generation recognized the market pressures and visualized that the market has changed. Thus, a new business model is needed. However, the third generation have not introduced any single change. The level of status quo is high because the successor leadership co-exists with the second generation (a conservative-oriented generation).

Table 24.4 (continued)

Quotes	Type of Change	Researcher Interpretation
"Maybe we need to adjust the business model we inherited from the second generation, we have to adjust or balance the source of income" (third-generation successor) ". . . . . . the successor of the third generation is coming, he is very patient also. So hopefully if he continues the same way the company will continue the same way" (non-family employee)		As the third generation observed, the economy has changed since the 2008 crisis and the flourishing that the UAE's economy experienced based on natural resources has resented. The third-generation successor is trapped in a family/family business culture where there is no room for risk. In this case, the institutional logic of the family defines the behaviour of the successor.
". . . for the third generation there is no need to stay together, they have no such strong relationships. The cousins, some of them are friends . . . some not . . . I told him (third generation successor) you will have a problem and we have to re-structure the ownership and governance of the firm" (second-generation successor) ". . . . . .you will have a problem and I want to get him ready for it . . . . . . In the short term the shareholding structure guarantees some stabilities if their generation attempts to introduce changes that are not aligned with our tradition . . . . But I do not know what will happen next . . . . . . a new ownership and governance structure will be needed" (second-generation successor)	Family changes	The third generation is implementing a new ownership structure to limit the conflicts coming from the different family branches. The proposal is that each family branch should create its own company owned by the family members of each family branch. Then, each family branch company owns the mother company (maintaining the proportions that each sibling of the second generation has). With this change it is possible to maintain the legacy and tradition of the family firm, reduce the number of family members participating in the ownership meeting (since one representative for each family branch will join), and reduce the family conflicts that can jeopardize the whole family.

Discussion

The aim of our research was to explore the micro-foundation of successors' reactions to market and family pressures to introduce governance, organizational, or strategic changes in their family firms. Drawing from the institutional logics approach, and by using the literature from strategic management and the family field, we assume that the market and family institutional logics evolve across time, generating pressures for successors to introduce changes in their firm and adjust the firm-environment fit. However, all successors do not react to the market and family pressures in a similar way. Thus, successors' schemas that are related to the level of status quo regarding the firm or the family are used to interpret the pressures and introduce governance, organizational, or strategic changes.

Our chapter contributes to theory by addressing the call to further investigate and understand the micro-foundation of institutional logics (Thornton et al., 2012). To achieve this, we focused our research efforts on the individual level of analysis and explored how successors respond to the pressures of institutional logics. Institutional logics sustain availability and accessibility to institutional forces directing the attention of individuals; in this case, the market and family pressures, signaling threats, problems, and potential issues, can affect the well-being of the family firm. However, as the micro-foundation of institutional logics predicts, individual social identity, goals, and schemas define the final intention and behaviour. From our data, we observe how successors use their schemas and patterns of thought to organize categories of information, interpret market and family pressures, and implement governance, organizational, or strategic changes.

Second, our chapter also contributes to a better understanding of succession in family firms through a micro-foundation perspective. Traditionally, succession was perceived as a mechanism to rejuvenate the company (Hoy & Sharma, 2009), and it is believed that family firms follow common patterns of evolution (Parada et al., 2020). Even when the pressures of changes are similar or common in all succession processes, the firm's renewal strategy depends on successor schemas to understand the threat of pressures over the family firm. We related the successor schema to their level of status quo framing their bounded rationality.

Finally, Figure 24.1 can be used to generalize our results as a conceptual framework. The market and family domains in which successors are embedded are constantly changing, signaling potential threats to the well-being of the family firm. Family pressures occur through changes produced in the family system at structural, psychosocial, and transactional levels, including explicit signals, such as the number of shareholders or individual behaviours, and silent signals, such as mental states perceived in the interpersonal relationships of participants. Conversely, market pressures occur because of demographic, cultural, economic, and competitive changes. The successor perceives and interprets market and family pressures.

Based on the pre-existing successor schemas defined by the institutional logics of the family and the firm, successors evaluate pressures in terms of the risk. These schemas are related to the successor's status quo as a specific cognitive bias used by the successor to judge the pressures. The status quo represents their intention to maintain or change the structure and values of the current system and defines the magnitude of the changes. However, the levels of the successors' status quo are not similar, when evaluating family pressures and market pressures, as their willingness to change may be different. The level of the successor's status quo differs because the market and the family are different institutions with their unique states of affairs. This distinction is important because, for a change to occur, decision-making is framed with the logic of each institution and, to a certain extent, both are separate

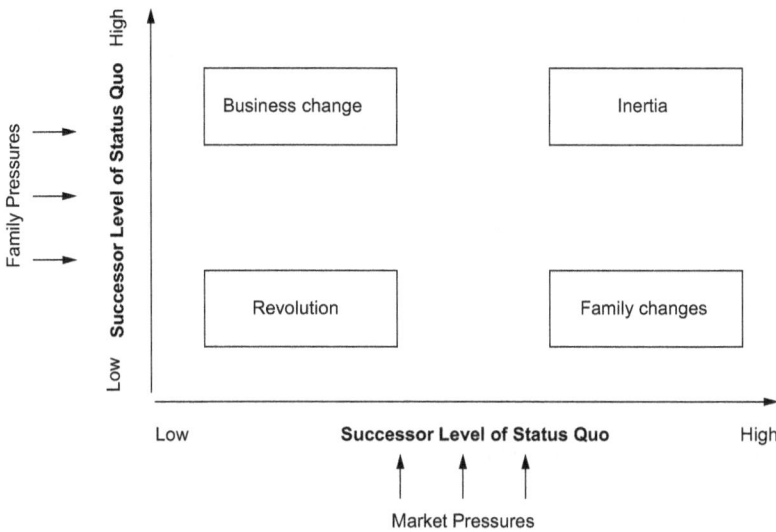

Figure 24.1: The model of change in transgenerational family businesses.

from each other. Therefore, governance, organizational, or strategic changes forced by family and firm pressures do not necessarily follow the same patterns. Thus, when the level of status quo in the family (or the firm) is high, changes are unlikely to occur or are marginal in the family (or in the firm). Conversely, when the level of status quo is low, changes tend to occur or are more radical.

Limitations and Future Research

Our study has a few caveats, and our findings must be interpreted with caution.

First, we rely on a simple in-depth case study, and despite providing a comprehensive understanding of successors' reactions to market and non-market pressures, it limits the generalization of the results. Future research should use a wider sample of family firms to have a larger spectrum of pressures, successor schemas, and changes from the families and businesses. This will further develop the proposed model of change during the succession process.

Second, the case study is taken from a specific country, which constrains the market and non-market domains because of cultural, historical, and institutional context (James, Hadjielias, Guerrero, Discua Cruz, & Basco, 2021). Future research should extend our study using different and diverse contexts. This is important to advance family business science through context theorizing (Krueger et al., 2021). For instance, multiple case studies in contrasting regions may help explore the diversity of succession reactions to market and non-market pressures and discover other elements beyond schemas for interpreting market and non-market pressures.

Finally, this research could be expanded by applying the micro-foundations of the institutional model developed by Thornton et al. (2012) to better understand how social identity, individual goals, and schemas work to interpret the macro logic in which successors are embedded. Thus, the successor's reaction is not a direct reaction to institutional logics. In fact, logics are filtered in accordance with the successor's cognition.

References

Baron, D. P. (1995). Integrated strategy: Market and nonmarket components. *California Management Review*, 37(2), 47–65.

Basco, R. (2017). Epilogue: The multiple embeddedness of family Firms in the Arab world. In S. Basly (Ed.), *Family Businesses in the Arab World: Governance, Strategy, and Financing* (pp. 247–256). Springer, Cham.

Basco, R. (2018). Family business in emerging economies. In R. Grosse & K. Meyer (Eds.), *Oxford Hansbook on Management in Emerging Markets* (pp. 527–546). Oxford University Press, Oxford, UK.

Basco, R. (2019). What kind of firm do you owner-manage? An institutional logics perspective of individuals' reasons for becoming an entrepreneur. *Journal of Family Business Management*, 9(3), 297–318.

Basco, R., Omari, Y., & Abouchkaier, L. (2020). *Family Business Ecosystem in United Arab Emirates*. Retrieved from https://familyfirmblog.files.wordpress.com/2020/02/family-business-ecosystem-in-uae.pdf

Basco, R., Rodriguez Escudero, A. I., Martin-Cruz, N., & Barros-Contreras, I. (2021). The combinations of market and non-market strategies that facilitates family firm survival. *Entrepreneurship Research Journal*, 11(3), 245–286.

Cisneros, L., Ibanescu, M., Keen, C., Lobato-Calleros, O., & Niebla-Zatarain, J. (2018). Bibliometric study of family business succession between 1939 and 2017: Mapping and analyzing authors' networks. *Scientometrics*, 117(2), 919–951.

Cucculelli, M., Le Breton-Miller, I., & Miller, D. (2016). Product innovation, firm renewal and family governance. *Journal of Family Business Strategy*, 7(2), 90–104.

Discua Cruz, A. (2020). There is no need to shout to be heard! The paradoxical nature of corporate social responsibility (CSR) reporting in a Latin American family small and medium-sized enterprise (SME). *International Small Business Journal*, 38(3), 243–267.

Eisenhardt, K. M. (1989). Building theories from case study research. *The Academy of Management Review*, 14(4), 532–550.

Fainshmidt, S., Judge, W. Q., Aguilera, R. V, & Smith, A. (2018). Varieties of institutional systems: A contextual taxonomy of understudied countries. *Journal of World Business*, 53(3), 307–322.

Fitzpatrick, M. A., & Ritchie, L. D. (1993). *Communication Theory and the Family BT – Sourcebook of Family Theories and Methods: A Contextual Approach* (P. Boss, W. J. Doherty, R. LaRossa, W. R. Schumm, & S. K. Steinmetz, eds.). https://doi.org/10.1007/978-0-387-85764-0_22

Fitzpatrick, M., & Wamboldt, F. (1990). Where is all said and done toward an integration of intrapersonal and interpersonal models of marital and family communication. *Communication Research*, 17, 421–430.

Gomez-Mejia, L. R., Basco, R., Müller, C., & Gonzalez, A. C. (2020). Family business and local development in Iberoamerica. *Cross-Cultural Management Journal*, 21(1), 51–56.

Hambrick, D., & Mason, P. (1984). Upper echelons: The organization as a reflection of its top management. *Academy of Management Review*, 9, 193–206.

Hamilton, E., Discua Cruz, A., & Jack, S. (2017). Re-framing the status of narrative in family business research: Towards an understanding of families in business. *Journal of Family Business Strategy*, 8(1), 3–12.

Handler, W. C. (1994). Succession in family business: A review of the research. *Family Business Review*, 7(2), 133–157.

Hoy, F., & Sharma, P. (2009). *Entrepreneurial Family Firms*. Upper Saddle River: Prentice Hall.

James, A. E., Hadjielias, E., Guerrero, M., Discua Cruz, A., & Basco, R. (2021). Entrepreneurial families in business across generations, context, and cultures. *Journal of Family Business Management* 11(4), 355–367.

Krueger, N., Bogers, M., Labaki, R., & Basco, R. (2021). Advancing Family Business Science through Context Theorizing: The Case of the Arab World. *Journal of Family Business Strategy*, 12 (1), [100377].

Lalonde, J. (2013). Cultural determinants of Arab entrepreneurship: An ethnographic perspective. *Journal of Enterprising Communities: People and Places in the Global Economy*, 7(3), 213–232.

Leppäaho, T., Plakoyiannaki, E., & Dimitratos, P. (2015). The case study in family business: An analysis of current research practices and recommendations. *Family Business Review*, 29(2), 159–173.

Martínez-García, I., Basco, R., & Gómez-Ansón, S. (2021). Dancing with giants: Contextualizing state and family ownership effects on firm performance in the Gulf Cooperation Council. *Journal of Family Business Strategy*, 12(4), 100373.

Martinez Garcia, I., Boubakri, N., Gomez-Anson, S., & Basco, R. (2022). Ownership concentration in the Gulf cooperation council. *International Journal of Emerging Markets*, 17(1), 219–252.

Mellahi, K., Frynas, J. G., Sun, P., & Siegel, D. (2016). A Review of the nonmarket strategy literature. *Journal of Management*, 42(1), 143–173.

Micelotta, E. R., & Fairclough, S. (2013). Beyond the family firm: Reasserting the influence of the family institutional logic across organizations. In *Research in the Sociology of Organizations: Vol. 39 Part B. Institutional Logics in Action, Part B* (pp. 63–98). https://doi.org/doi:10.1108/S0733-558X(2013)0039AB016

Parada, M. J., Gimeno, A., Samara, G., & Saris, W. (2020). The adoption of governance mechanisms in family businesses: An institutional lens. *Journal of Family Business Management*. https://doi.org/10.1108/JFBM-07-2019-0054.

Patton, M. (2002). *Qualitative Research and Evolution Methods* (3rd ed.). Thousand Oaks, CA: SAGE.

Porter, M. E. (1980). *Competitive Startegy. Techniques for Analizing Industies and Competitors*. New York: The Free Press.

Quigley, T. J., & Hambrick, D. C. (2012). When the former ceo stays on as board chair: effects on successor discretion, strategic change, and performance. *Strategic Management Journal*, 33(7), 834–859.

Reeves, M., & Deimler, M. (2011). Adaptability: The new competitive advantage. *Harvard Business Review*, 89(7/8), 134–141.

Schvaneveldt, P. L., Kerpelman, J. L., & Schvaneveldt, J. D. (2005). Generational and Cultural Changes in Family Life in the United Arab Emirates: A Comparison of Mothers and Daughters.

Journal of Comparative Family Studies, 36(1),77–91. Retrieved from http://www.jstor.org/stable/41603981

Stangej, O., & Basco, R. (2017). The entrepreneurial role of families in transitional economies: The case of Lithuania. In A. Sauka & A. Chepurenko (Eds.), *Entrepreneurship in Transition Economies: Diversity, Trends, and Perspectives* (pp. 345–365). Cham: Springer International Publishing.

Thornton, P. H., & Ocasio, W. (1999). Institutional logics and the historical contingency of power in organizations: Executive succession in the higher education publishing industry, 1958-1990. *American Journal of Sociology*, *105*(3), 801–843.

Thornton, P. H., Ocasio, W., & Lounsbury, M. (2012). *The Institutional Logics Perspective: A New Approach to Culture, Structure, and Process*. Oxford: OUP.

Wamboldt, F., & Reiss, D. (1989). Task performance and the social construction of meaning: Juxtaposing normality with contemporary family research. In D. Offer & M. Sabshin (Eds.), *Normality: Context and theory* (pp. 2–40). New York: Basic Books.

Yin, R. K. (2009). *Case Study Research: Design and Methods*. UK: Sage Publications.

Zhao, J., Carney, M., Zhang, S., & Zhu, L. (2020). How does an intra-family succession effect strategic change and performance in China's family firms? *Asia Pacific Journal of Management*, *37*(2), 363–389.

Part V: **The Future of Business Families Research**

Michael Carney and Marleen Dieleman

25 Business Families: Promising Future Research Directions

Abstract: We revisit the emerging construct of business families as it is being used by four different strands of family business scholarship: the family behind the firm, the entrepreneurial family with a portfolio of activities, the governance of business families, and the role of business families in society. For each of these streams we suggest future research directions that can help to clarify heterogeneity among family businesses as well as lead to theorizing through connections with other disciplines. We suggest that the thriving area of scholarly attention around business families holds the potential to open a new research direction among family business scholars.

Keywords: business families, kinship, portfolio, extended family, family governance, family wealth, dynastic families, capitalist class

Introduction

This handbook has advocated that the construct of business families merits further scrutiny and that a focus on business families (rather than family business) has the potential of advancing the family business field. We defined business families earlier in this handbook as: *extended families connected by kinship who jointly manage commonly held assets and activities, institutionalized through family governance strategies, and whose collective wealth exerts a significant impact on society.* A range of chapters by prominent scholars explored this phenomenon, grouped into four overlapping categories: the family behind the firm, the entrepreneurial family with a portfolio of activities, the governance of business families, and the role of business families in society. In this concluding chapter, we summarize the suggestions for future research that emerge from the scholarly work collected in this handbook. We review each of the categories separately and attempt to synthesize this into an overarching research program that, we suggest, has the potential to lead to new theorizing.

Michael Carney, Concordia University
Marleen Dieleman, National University of Singapore

https://doi.org/10.1515/9783110727968-025

Family Behind the Firm

We argue that a razor focus on the dynamics of families and family members can open new avenues for theorizing on business families. Recent scholarly work has focused on nuclear families. It draws from family sciences to theorize on the types of functional and dysfunctional relationships among family members (e.g., Comb et al., 2020). Other work draws on network theory to map out the relationships between individual family members in a granular manner, suggesting that the transposition of these family relationships from one domain to another affects the dynamics among family members, for instance, when a successor joins the business. These insights, drawing on network theory, have already led to new theories of family influence on succession and the roles of hidden family members (Li & Piezunka, 2020). Others looked at parenting styles for antecedents of family member behaviour and entrepreneurial skills, while yet others consider mechanisms needed to bind larger entrepreneurial families. We suggest a holistic focus on the family can lead to further theorizing in two key areas: the family dynamics in extended families and leveraging the variety of families in different cultural contexts.

From Nuclear to Extended Family Dynamics

Scholarly work on family dynamics still focuses mostly on nuclear families, but could be applied to extended families too, including older business families with hundreds of members whose relationships differ from those of small nuclear families. Thus, family science models could be applied to extended families. Moreover, network theorists may map out the extended family networks while further theorizing on the open/closed nature of these networks and the transpositions and resource exchanges that occur in different domains, depending on the positioning of the family member in a more varied set of kinship relations. In Chapter 3 in this handbook, Kleve and colleagues show that business families spanning hundreds of years are characterized by tenuous family bonds between the descendants of the founder. Open questions include whether the horizontal binding of descendants connected through vertical kinship bonds is useful or necessary. If so, how does such binding among larger kinship groups affect family business features such as performance or longevity?

From Western-centric to Context-sensitive Theorizing

Another promising area is the notion that family-formation displays variety across countries, thus inviting both a comparative perspective as well as a focus on deeper insights into the local context of business families. Several chapters in this book have made advances in this area. For instance, in Chapter 22, Suddaby and his colleagues as well as Nason and Carney (see Chapter 20) explore typologies of families and the organizations they typically construct across the world. Moreover, Koning and Verver take an anthropological approach in Chapter 6 in this handbook and advocate for studying the "lived experiences" of actors. They further suggest that the boundaries of the family could be extended to broader groupings that experience kinship, including ethnic groupings, clans or extended families that experience mutual moral obligations due to their ties. The moral obligations are culture-specific and merit further investigation. These insights apply to all business families, but we believe they can be especially important when families coordinate their resources resulting in multiple businesses. Indeed, people connected by kinship ties may be active in multiple entrepreneurial ventures that draw on common family resources such as relationships, without those businesses being under a single holding company. Moreover, some families coordinate their resources and skills to generate income without the presence of a company, as Chapter 18 on show business families by Gorji and Simarasl in this handbook suggests. Thus, by taking the business family as the unit of analysis, future research can also transcend the focus on the single business that characterizes the majority of the family business research today. While the predominant model in European countries and the US has been to focus on a single business, the typical experience in emerging markets has been one of business groups. A focus on business families can reorient the literature away from a Western-centric viewpoint to encompass a wider variety of business family patterns.

Business Families with a Portfolio of Assets and Activities

While many families have just one business, several others combine multiple activities under common coordination, ranging from for-profit to non-profit. Multi-generational families have often moved beyond the original business, perhaps creating new businesses, a foundation or investing through family offices. Other business families, including many in emerging markets, build diversified business groups from their founding days. Hence, there is ample reason to move beyond the single business focus into the realm of the family activity portfolio. Several chapters in this book investigated the nature of venture creation (Chapter 7, Bhatnagar & Ramachandran; Chapter 10, Fathallah & Samara), the relative emotional importance of different portfolio firms (Michael-Tsabari), the timing of portfolio changes (Chapter 12, Colli; Chapter 11, Rosa & Bika) as well as the benefits across portfolio firms (Chapter 9, Bacq & Nason). We see three areas that could be especially suitable for future research: portfolio variety, portfolio trajectories and not-for-profit activities.

Explaining Portfolio Variety Across Families

While there is a body of literature discussing the nature of family business groups, it primarily takes an institutional perspective, explaining the scope of business groups drawing on external factors including the strength of institutions in a country or the scarcity of inputs leading to vertical integration decisions (e.g., Morck, 2005). Family business scholars, including the contributors to this handbook, suggest that internal family dynamics matter too for decisions about exit, new venture creation, or portfolio re-alignment. For instance, the number of next generation members joining may have an influence on the number of new ventures created, suggesting that family characteristics matter. Empirical studies using new variables on the nature of the business family, such as the number of generations, the number of owners in the next generation, or the place of residence of family members could add new insights to the body of literature on corporate diversification. Beyond simple family characteristics, several questions that delve deeper into the motivations of business families remain open for exploration. In particular, how does family reputation and legacy play a role in portfolio decisions? Do business families invest merely to gain profits and reduce risk, or do they leverage their investments for other purposes, including learning, social impact, or reputation gain? What are the linkages between portfolio activities in terms of sharing of resources and why are certain portfolio components more or less integrated with other activities? There is much scope to leverage family business theories such as socio-emotional wealth to explore such relationships, while a business families focus can also offer a more nuanced view of commonly used management theories and constructs, such as hold-up problems (see Chapter 9, Bacq and Nason in this handbook).

Explaining Portfolio Transitions Over Time

How family dynamics and external factors interact to shape the nature of the portfolio of a business family is still largely unchartered territory covered mostly by business historians and development economists. There is a need to explain the evolution of business families through history and to elicit patterns that point to different types of trajectories, as Colli has done in Chapter 11 in this handbook. Building on transgenerational family histories embedded in historical and national contexts, family business scholars can leverage evolutionary theory to contribute to broader debates on the role of business families in economic history as well as the nature of adaptive behaviours by families in the face of environmental changes. For instance, as Fathallah and Samara suggest in Chapter 10 in this volume, business families from emerging markets may leverage their knowledge of weak institutions to diversify, but once successful they become motivated to access the security that less volatile developed markets offer. There is still scant attention to the sequential portfolio decisions prevalent in business families, which could be a fertile area to explore with longitudinal studies.

Beyond for-profit

As work in this handbook shows, many business families have activities that reach beyond for-profit businesses. For instance, families may create a museum dedicated to their family history, they may set up a foundation to contribute to social impact or they may invest in the development of certain technologies or inventions through donations with the objective to use such technologies for future business activities. How such non-profit activities relate to business activities, however, has not yet been fully investigated within the field of family business. Meanwhile, observers have called attention to the trend of philanthrocapitalism (Bishop, 2006) leading to academic work in the area. While there is work on corporate social responsibility in family firms (e.g., Campopiano & De Massis, 2014) this primarily takes the firm as the unit of analysis, rather than the business family. By moving the focus to the business family, future research can investigate the inter-relationships between different portfolio components ranging from for-profit, for-impact and for-long term survival.

Governing the Business Family

The primary focus of corporate governance as applied to family businesses concerns family involvement in management and the governing board's role, independence, and composition (Villalonga, Amit, Trujillo, & Guzmán, 2015). However, an analytical shift towards governing business families suggests the family also requires good governance. We refer to this as business family governance. In response to these needs, a range of new professions is emerging and multiplying to provide governance advice to business families (Gersick, 2015). Much of this advice concerns wealth management. The rapid emergence, growth and global scope of a wealth management ecology are well documented (Beaverstock, Hall, & Wainwright, 2013; Harrington & Seabrooke, 2020).

Business families are prone to intergenerational tensions about wealth, autonomy, and authority (Gilding, 2005). The ensuing conflict often arises from "the insurgencies of dependent descendants and extended family members" (Marcus, 2005, p. 619), and effective business family governance may require assistance from lawyers and relational professionals who act as mediating agents seeking to mitigate emotional and legal conflicts (Meyer, 2010). Moreover, professionals provide advice on responsible ownership to adolescents and young adults (Kuusela, 2018). We propose two distinct lines of future research around these emergent phenomena. The first line concerns the efficacy and efficiency of proliferating governance advisors and their solutions. The second question concerns diffusion, who will avail themselves of the governance solutions and where?

Efficacy and Efficiency

The question of effective corporate governance practices in family business is a well-established field, with a comprehensive quantitative analysis of the performance of publicly listed family firms using particular governance choices. While research into the relative efficiency of business family governance choice is amenable to a similar analysis, there are still hurdles for this field to progress further. Business families are private entities that are not currently obliged to provide ample publicly available financial disclosures. Indeed, business families are likely to be concerned about confidentiality and secrecy about the origins and allocation of wealth (Harrington; 2021; Decker & Lange, 2013). This is a concern recognized by Song in Chapter 15 on family offices. She asks how one should conduct critical-based research mitigating the methodological limitations with family offices arising from privacy and non-transparency. Accordingly, scholars investigating issues of efficacy and the efficiency of business family governance will need to bring innovative research designs. There are also exciting opportunities to leverage and revisit existing theories when applied to business family governance practices. For instance, in her review of the family office research, Song identifies a series of questions concerning the kind of investment logic family offices apply when making entrepreneurial investments.

Kammarlander and Bertschi-Michel, in Chapter 16 on family wealth advisors, raise a raft of questions about the accreditation and education of trusted wealth advisors and the kinds of skills and practices required to identify practical advice. Thus, the current challenge is to identify the types of standards and desirable criteria needed to evaluate the performance of this diverse range of business family advisories. Howorth and colleagues suggest in Chapter 14 that because family business governance codes treat every firm as a separate entity, this practice overlooks the issue that multi-business families are likely to be made at the group level and raises concern about expropriation risks for minority shareholders. The governance of business family groupings is still underdeveloped, providing room for further research and opportunities to pose questions regarding whether the current corporate and business family governance standards are adequate.

The International Diffusion of Business Family Governance Practices

In performing their professional roles, advisors serve as surrogates for the family as fiduciaries, with legally defined obligations to protect family interests (Harrington & Strike, 2018). If they are to function effectively, fiduciaries must be regulated by formal institutions comprising solid principal-agent relationships and the protection of property rights. The globalization of advisory networks such as STEP (Society of Trust and Estate Practitioners) coordinated by financial institutions and other global organizations such as the Family Business Network and the Family Firm Institute seeks to establish family governance practices globally, including in emerging markets. However, in some contexts, the quality of property rights protection and institutions supporting fiduciary relationships is poor. In the absence of strong institutions, business families may be unwilling to rely upon professional advisors and find other solutions to protect family wealth and interests. Indeed, scholars familiar with institutional theory would expect low trust levels in the rule of law and institutions protecting property rights to encourage business families to rely on informal solutions, such as personal connections and opaque governance structures, to safeguard against political uncertainty and weak principal-agent relationships. Accordingly, whether business family advisories will take root in these jurisdictions remains an open question that researchers could explore.

Family business researchers are preoccupied with the internationalization of family firms (Arregle, Chirico, & Kano, 2021; Kano, Ciravegna & Rattalino, 2020), usually assuming greater internationalization of family businesses is a positive development. However, business families also internationalize, an area of research currently underexplored. Business family scholars might consider how business families and their advisors use internationalization to address business family governance matters such as wealth management, conflict management and taxes through jurisdiction shopping to mitigate uncertainty related to fiduciary rights, duties, and competencies. This question also relates to how business families contribute to their host societies. An emerging research theme concerns the "hypermobility" of business families (Harrington, 2021), which refers to the international diversification of family wealth through tax-flight (Temouri, Nardella, Jones, & Brammer, 2021). Hypermobility is also associated with business family members owning multiple residences, holding golden passports, and acquiring citizenships through investment (Surak, 2020). Multi-national enterprises have come under scrutiny for their arbitrage of different national tax regimes (e.g., Cuervo-Cazurra et al., 2021). We believe future research could address similar questions on business families and their hypermobile governance practices.

Institutionalizing Wealth and Business Families in Society

The last section of this handbook offered a macro perspective on the relationship between business families and society, and is concerned with a broad range of business families. In this perspective, we see the importance of the socio-economic context is related to the prevalence and prosperity of certain types of firms. At the same time, politics, and socio-economic development can threaten the very existence of business families. We suggest that analysis of the intersection of business families and society is a fertile field for future research. To inform future research, we propose two interrelated themes. The first theme concerns the extent of business family agency in shaping their destinies and environments. The second theme concerns how business families positively or negatively impact social and economic outcomes.

Business Family Agency

Some of the earliest empirical work on wealthy business families concerned the ownership and governance of a nation's largest firms. Early work in this tradition identified "kin-econ" ownership groups, a capitalist class of extended kinship relations among major business groups (Zeitlin, Ewan, & Ratlcliff, 1974). Zeitlin and his colleagues inspired a stream of capitalist class research by organization theorists about the wealthy US and European families that formed an "inner circle" linked through interlocking directorships and coordinated political engagement (e.g., Palmer & Barber, 2001; Useem, 1982). This perspective suggests business families engage in informal collective action, indicating high levels of agency. However, with the embrace of microeconomic theories of the firm, such as transactions costs and agency theories, interest in the capitalist class largely "fizzled out" (Gilding, 2005). Nevertheless, since Piketty's (2014) treatise on growing income inequality, there is a renewed interest in shifting the unit of analysis from firms to owners and investigating business families' wealth perpetuation strategies designed to guard against environmental forces that may disperse wealth and power (Hansen & Toft, 2021; Storti & Dagnes, 2021)

This handbook has called attention to business family governance strategies such as establishing family offices for wealth management. We suggest that these strategies aim to increase the agency of business families in determining their transgenerational futures, including influencing their environments to achieve this goal. Sociologists have already observed that these wealth preservation strategies go beyond wealth management and relate to proactive legitimation of durable wealth reproduction across generations, including influencing institutions such as inheritance law and tax treatments of charitable foundations (Beckert, 2022). In Chapter 19 in this handbook, Kuusela suggests "the possible roles of members of wealthy families themselves play in our such processes deserve further scrutiny as a recent focus in research on the professionals has resulted in a situation where the agency of the wealthy has been empirically marginalized and also untheorized". It seems evident that the wealthiest business families have sufficient resources to exercise agency, although the extent to which it is coordinated is an open question. Campaign contributions and lobbying are two well-known mechanisms for exerting political influence. In the US, a member of a prominent business family achieved the highest political office.

However, while the capitalist class has fallen out of view as a community of shared interests, individual business families or local networks may exert sufficient coordination to attain favourable political outcomes. Family business scholars, who typically focus on firms as their unit of analysis, have paid little attention to the significant agency of business families in their academic studies. To the extent that family business scholars fail to critically question the accumulation of family wealth and its connection to the ability to influence society, their work on optimal governance mechanisms may inadvertently legitimize extreme income inequality. Kuusela, in this volume, calls attention to the role of professional family business organizations, such as the global Family Business Network and the Family Firm Institute sponsorship of family business research as a broader ecosystem of wealth accumulation. Thus, family business scholars can build on sociologists' work by taking family groupings as a unit of analysis to examine the extent and nature of agency in wealthy families and their ecosystem of advisors and networks.

Conversely, another research stream that is more prominent in management that views business families primarily as passive victims of institutional forces that may marginalize them and eradicate the results of their entrepreneurial efforts. Research on migrant or ethnic minority families (e.g., Shelton, 2010) suggests the opposite of proactive agency, while pointing instead to the risks of oppression and precarity in their host societies. Discua Cruz and Centeno-Caffarena's depiction of immigrant business families in Central America in Chapter 23 in this handbook suggests diverging trajectories of oppression. While one Middle Eastern group of migrants successfully struggled to overcome discrimination and political marginalization, another group of migrant entrepreneurs failed to do so as they articulated their German identity, which could not withstand the political circumstances of the 20th century. These authors call for a better understanding of the historical dynamics of business families in diverse contexts where contextual conditions may the negative effects on business families. In line with Chapter 12 by Colli in this handbook and other longitudinal work on business families (e.g., Dieleman & Sachs, 2008), there is much scope for studies that assess how agency on the part of business families evolves over time while outlining factors that increase or decrease it.

Business Families' Positive or Negative Impact on Socio-economic Outcomes

US family business research finds that family firms have a tremendous and positive impact on the overall US economy in terms of tax returns, percentage of the workforce employed, and contribution to GDP (Astrachan & Shanker, 2003; Pieper, Kellermanns & Astrachan, 2021). However, there is considerable ambiguity about business families' effect upon socio-economic outcomes. In this handbook, there is much emphasis on the positive entrepreneurial contributions of business families. However, research on wealthy business families themselves is more ambiguous. One stream of research concerned with the power of business families in emerging markets depicts them as having a parasitic effect on economic and social development (Fogel, 2006; Khanna & Yafeh, 2007) with practices that are opportunistic, extractive, and oligarchic. In this handbook, Carney & Nason identify a class of business families who are rentiers whose income derives primarily from their self-made or inherited capital, suggesting their contribution to society is relatively limited. Moreover, the increase in rentiers raises concerns about meritocracy and the re-emergence of a generation of wealthy individuals who live well on their inherited wealth alone.

The proverbial saying "shirtsleeves to shirtsleeves in three generations" is a well-known trope in the family business literature. However, sociological and economic literature suggests great wealth is durable (Beckert, 2022; Tilly, 1998). Since recent revelations about the extent of wealth concentration in the upper reaches of the wealth hierarchy (Keister, 2005; Piketty, 2014; Wolfe, 2017; Zucman, 2015), there is a growing body of work that is critical of families' capacity to accumulate further wealth (Hansen, 2014; Marcus & Hall 1992). Much empirical research on wealthy business families has accumulated based upon two distinct sampling strategies. The first approach identifies individuals situated at the long tail end of the wealth distribution in rich lists, such as the Forbes 400. In recent years, this sample has identified billionaires. A focal concern in this research is the distinction between self-made and inherited wealth. While the former is associated with entrepreneurship and merit, many self-made billionaires are "born on third base" (Moriarty, 2012), who come from already wealthy backgrounds (Kaplan & Ruah, 2013) and privileged families (Toft & Freidman, 2021). Naturally, this literature contradicts much of the entrepreneurial, multi-business, and multi-generational business families celebrated in Section 2 of this handbook. The prevailing arguments in this critical literature to suggest access to entrepreneurship as a structural feature of the wealth hierarchy. We believe that a shift away from the family business to the business family as a unit of analysis will stimulate family business researchers to investigate the processes and implications of wealth accumulation over time and its effects on society.

Another approach pioneered in economics and sociology relies on household finance surveys, such as the Federal Reserve's Survey of Consumer Finance (SCFs). The surveys employ random sampling across the wealth distribution and collect detailed anonymized data on household income, debt, and financial and non-financial assets ownership. For example, the 2019 SCF shows that the top 1% of households have a mean net worth of approximately $20 million. The wealthiest 1% of this population are multimillionaires. In the US, the 1% wealthiest comprises 1.26 million households, of which 74% own and actively manage a sole proprietorship, limited partnership, or other types of private business that are not publicly traded. In an analysis of the SCF asset composition of business-owning households in the 1% wealthiest US households, Carney & Nason (2018) found that 45% of 1 percenters net worth consisted of business equity in actively managed businesses. These businesses had a median asset value of $6 million, generating an average revenue of $13 million with an average of 30 employees. Similar patterns are found in household finance data drawn in Europe (Carroll, 2002). While critical sociology scholars portray the 1% as super-rich self-made entrepreneurs and rentier capitalists, a substantial proportion of the 1% own and manage a small to medium-sized business, corresponding to a worthy entrepreneurial middle class of solid and legitimate wealth (Berghoff, 2006, p. 206). As such Berghoff's *Mittelstand* are neither wealthy rentiers nor self-made billionaires. Whether or not the owner-manager SMEs that populate the upper echelons of the wealth hierarchy constitute a comparable *Mittelstand* class remains an open and not unfanciful question. We suggest that research on business families' impact on society needs to consider the varied nature of business families and their activities, ranging from owner-entrepreneurs to rentiers.

Conclusion

We suggest that this handbook gives rise to an exciting new research program with business families as the unit of analysis. In moving beyond the single-business focus that characterizes much the family business research, we propose a variety of new themes to explore. The first set of themes revolves around families, and includes the micro-dynamics of extended families and the cultural variety in families worldwide. Here, we suggest drawing on family science and anthropology to explore new ideas on kinship ties that drive entrepreneurial behaviour. The second set of themes results from the varied nature of business family activities, resulting in various portfolios that evolve and are not limited to commercial activities. We suggest drawing on economics and family business theories to explain the composition of business family activities and their integration or separation. The third set of themes revolves around the governance of business families, where we suggest looking at the efficiency and efficacy of the advisor ecosystem and the global diffusion of governance practices. Here we recommend novel empirical research strategies to mitigate the lack of data availability and ask critical questions about the nature of business family governance standards and their effectiveness across geographies, especially those characterized by weak property rights regimes. The professionalization of family governance has generated a global industry with hypermobile wealthy families at the centre – a new phenomenon we suggest is worthy of further scholarly attention. The final set of themes concerns the effects of business families on society, including their extent of agency and the beneficial or adverse effects of entrepreneurship and extreme wealth accumulation. While the beneficial effects of family entrepreneurship are covered extensively in the family business literature, the downsides of transgenerational wealth have not attracted much attention among family business scholars. Here we suggest drawing on critical sociology and capitalist class literature to assess the likelihood that business families' rapidly developing wealth preservation strategies may lead to a global wealthy class that utilizes entrepreneurship as a vehicle for further advancement, possibly at the expense of meritocratic principles in society. In summary, we believe that a focus on business families has the potential to reorient the family business literature by offering a new lens that allows scholars to ask novel questions, building on adjacent disciplines in the social sciences.

References

Arregle, JL., Chirico, F., & Kano, L. (2021). Family firm internationalization: Past research and an agenda for the future. *Journal of International Business Studies*, 52, 1159–1198.

Astrachan, J., & Shanker, M. (2003). Family businesses' contribution to the US economy: A closer look. *Family Business Review*, 16(3), 211–219.

Beaverstock, J. V., Hall, S., & Wainwright, T. (2013). Servicing the super-rich: New financial elites and the rise of the private wealth management retail ecology. *Regional Studies*, 47(6), 834–849.

Beckert, J. (2022). Durable Wealth: Institutions, Mechanisms, and Practices of Wealth Perpetuation. *Annual Review of Sociology*, 48, 233–255.

Berghoff, H. (2006). The end of family business? The Mittelstand and German capitalism in transition, 1949–2000. *Business History Review*, 80(2), 263–295.

Bishop, M. (2006). The birth of philanthrocapitalism: The leading new philanthropists see themselves as social investors. *The Economist*. https://www.economist.com/node/5517656

Campopiano, G., & De Massis, A. (2014). Corporate social responsibility reporting: A content analysis in family and non-family firms. *Journal of Business Ethics*, 129(3), 1–24.

Carney, M., & Nason, R. S. (2018). Family Business and the 1%. *Business & Society*, 57(6), 1191–1215.

Carney, M., Van Essen, M., Estrin, S., & Shapiro, D. (2018). Business groups reconsidered: beyond paragons and parasites. *Academy of Management Perspectives*, 32(4), 493–516.

Carroll, C. D. (2002). Portfolios of the Rich in (Eds.) L. Guiso, M. Haliassos, and T. Jappelli, *Household Portfolios* (pp. 389–429). Cambridge, MA: MIT Press.

Combs, J. G., Shanine, K. K., Burrows, S., Allen, J. S., & Pounds, T. W. (2020). What do we know about business families? Setting the stage for leveraging family science theories. *Family Business Review*, 33(1), 38–63. https://doi.org/10.1177/0894486519863508.

Cuervo-Cazurra, A., Dieleman, M., Hirsch, P., Rodrigues, S.B., & Zyglidopoulos, S. (2021). Multinationals' misbehavior, *Journal of World Business*, 56(5), 101244.

Dieleman, M. & Sachs, W.M. (2008). Coevolution of Institutions and Corporations in Emerging Economies: How the Salim Group Morphed into an Institution of Suharto's Crony Regime. *Journal of Management Studies*, 45(7), 1274–1300.

Decker, C., & Lange, K. S. (2013). Exploring a secretive organization: What can we learn about family offices from the public sphere. *Organizational Dynamics*, 42(4), 298–306.

Fogel, K. (2006). Oligarchic family control, social economic outcomes, and the quality of government. *Journal of International Business Studies*, 37(5), 603–622.

Gersick, K. E. (2015). Essay on Practice: Advising Family Enterprise in the Fourth Decade. *Entrepreneurship Theory and Practice*, 39(6), 1433–1450.

Gilding, M. (2005). Families and fortunes: Accumulation, management succession and inheritance in wealthy families. *Journal of Sociology*, 41(1), 29–45.

Hansen M.N. (2014). Self-made wealth or family wealth? Changes in intergenerational wealth mobility. *Social Forces*, 93, 457–481.

Hansen, M. N., & Toft, M. (2021). Wealth accumulation and opportunity hoarding: class-origin wealth gaps over a quarter of a century in a Scandinavian country. *American Sociological Review*, 86(4), 603–638.

Harrington, B. (2021). Secrecy, Simmel and the new sociology of wealth. *Sociologica*, 15(2), 143–152.

Harrington, B., & Seabrooke, L. (2020). Transnational professionals. *Annual Review of Sociology*, 46, 399–417.

Harrington, B., & Strike, V. M. (2018). Between kinship and commerce: Fiduciaries and the institutional logics of family firms. *Family Business Review*, 31(4), 417–440.

Kano, L., Ciravegna, L. & Rattalino, F. (2020). The family as a platform for FSA development: Enriching new internalization theory with insights from family firm research. *Journal of International Business Studies*, 52, 148–160.

Kaplan, S. N., & Rauh, J. D. (2013). Family, education, and sources of wealth among the richest Americans, 1982–2012. *American Economic Review*, 103, 158–162.

Keister L. (2005). *Getting Rich: America's New Rich and How They Got That Way*. Cambridge, UK: Cambridge University Press.

Khanna, T., & Yafeh, Y. (2007). Business groups in emerging markets: Paragons or parasites? *Journal of Economic Literature*, 45(2), 331–372.

Kuusela, H. (2018). Learning to own: Cross-generational meanings of wealth and class-making in wealthy Finnish families. *Sociological Review*. http://dx.doi.org/10.1177/0038026118777698.

Li, J.B., & Piezunka, H. (2020). The uniplex third: Enabling single-domain role transitions in multiplex relationships. *Administrative Science Quarterly*, 65(2), 314–358. https://doi.org/10.1177%2F0001839219845875.

Marcus, G. E. (2005). Family firms amidst the creative destruction of capitalism. *American Ethnologist*, 32(4), 618–622.

Marcus, G., & Hall, P. (1992). *Lives in Trust: The Fortunes of Dynastic Families in Late Twentieth Century America*. Boulder: Westview Press.

Meyer, J. W. (2010). World society, institutional theories, and the actor. *Annual Review of Sociology*, 36, 1–20.

Morck, R. (Ed.) (2005). *A History of Corporate Governance Around the World: Family Business Groups to Professional Managers*. Chicago: University of Chicago Press.

Moriarty, S. (Ed.). (2012). Born on third base: What the Forbes 400 really says about economic equality and opportunity in America. Retrieved from http://www.FairEconomy.org/BornOnThirdBase2012

Palmer, D., & Barber, B. M. (2001). Challengers, elites, and owning families: A social class theory of corporate acquisitions in the 1960s. *Administrative Science Quarterly*, 46(1),87–120.

Pieper, Torsten M., Franz W. Kellermanns, and Joseph H. Astrachan. (2021). *Update 2021: Family Businesses' Contribution to the US Economy*. Washington, DC: Family Enterprise USA.

Piketty T. (2014). *Capital in the Twenty-First Century*. Cambridge, MA: Harvard Univ. Press.

Shelton, L. M. (2010). Fighting an uphill battle expansion barriers, intra–industry social stratification, and minority firm growth. *Entrepreneurship Theory and Practice*, 34(2), 379–398.

Storti, L., & Dagnes, J. (2021). The super-rich: origin, reproduction, and social acceptance. *Sociologica*, 15(2), 5–23.

Surak, K. (2020): Who wants to buy a visa? Comparing the uptake of residence by investment programs in the European Union. *Journal of Contemporary European Studies*, DOI: 10.1080/14782804.2020.1839742

Temouri, Y., Nardella, G., Jones, C., & Brammer, S. (2021). Haven-sent? tax havens, corporate social irresponsibility and the dark side of family firm internationalization. *British Journal of Management*, https://doi.org/10.1111/1467-8551.12559

Tilly C. (1998). Durable Inequality. Berkeley: University of California Press.

Toft, M., & Friedman, S. (2021). Family wealth and the class ceiling: the propulsive power of the bank of Mum and Dad. *Sociology*, 55(1), 90–109.

Useem, M. 1982. Classwide rationality in the politics of managers and directors of large corporations in the United States and Great Britain. *Administrative Science Quarterly*, 27(2), 199–226.

Villalonga, B., Amit, R., Trujillo, M. A., & Guzmán, A. (2015). Governance of family firms. *Annual Review of Financial Economics*, 7, 635–654.

Wolff, E. (2017). *A Century of Wealth in America*. Cambridge, MA: Belknap.

Zeitlin, M., Ewen, L.A. & Ratcliff, R.E. (1974). "New princes" for old? The large corporation and the capitalist class in Chile. *American Journal of Sociology*, 80(1), 87–123.

Zucman G. (2015). *The Hidden Wealth of Nations: The Scourge of Tax Havens*. Chicago: University Chicago Press.

List of Figures

https://doi.org/10.1515/9783110727968-026

List of Tables

https://doi.org/10.1515/9783110727968-027

Index

https://doi.org/10.1515/9783110727968-028

www.ingramcontent.com/pod-product-compliance
Lightning Source LLC
Chambersburg PA
CBHW081213220326
41598CB00037B/6767